South Methodist Episcopal Church, L. C Everett

The Wesleyan hymn and tune book

Comprising the entire collection of hymns in the hymn book of the Methodist Episcopal Church, South, with appropriate music adapted to each hymn

South Methodist Episcopal Church, L. C Everett

The Wesleyan hymn and tune book
Comprising the entire collection of hymns in the hymn book of the Methodist Episcopal Church, South, with appropriate music adapted to each hymn

ISBN/EAN: 9783337649302

Printed in Europe, USA, Canada, Australia, Japan

Cover: Foto ©ninafisch / pixelio.de

More available books at **www.hansebooks.com**

THE

WESLEYAN

HYMN AND TUNE BOOK:

COMPRISING

THE ENTIRE COLLECTION OF HYMNS

IN THE HYMN BOOK OF THE

METHODIST EPISCOPAL CHURCH, SOUTH,

WITH

APPROPRIATE MUSIC ADAPTED TO EACH HYMN.

BY

L. C. EVERETT.

Sing praises to God, sing praises.—*Psalm*, xlvii, 6.
There are no songs comparable to the Songs of Zion.—*Milton*.

Nashville, Tenn.:
SOUTHERN METHODIST PUBLISHING HOUSE.
1860.

Notice.—A large majority of the Tunes contained in this work, are copy-right property, and publishers are, therefore, cautioned against using them without permission.

To the Members and Friends of the
Methodist Episcopal Church, South.

At the last session of the General Conference of the Methodist Episcopal Church, South, the propriety of publishing a "Tune-Hymn Book," was discussed, and an opinion favorable to the measure was generally expressed. The Conference finally left the matter in the hands of the Book Agent and Editor, to be disposed of at their discretion. After due deliberation, they determined upon the issue of such a work.

Meanwhile, a book comprising tunes adapted to all the hymns in the hymn book, the latter being printed in connection with the former, having been prepared by Mr. L. C. Everett, of Virginia, a gentleman well-known through the South and South-west, as an author and teacher of sacred vocal music, and being considered in every way answerable to the demands of the connection at large, the Book Agent made an arrangement with the compiler for the exclusive publication of the work. The tunes, both original and selected, it is believed, are admirably suited to the hymns to which they are set, as well as to the wants of our wide-spread community.

As it is impossible to publish a book which shall contain every tune that every one may desire, some of our friends may regret, as I do, the absence of certain favorite pieces; but it is hoped that tastes and preferences of this sort will not interfere with the circulation of the book. Its introduction into every church and every family is greatly to be desired. The grand design had in view in its publication, is the promotion of congregational singing, according to the spirit and letter of our Book of Discipline:

"In *all* our congregations let the *people learn to sing. Recommend our tune book. Exhort every person in the congregation to sing; not one in ten only.*"

THOS. O. SUMMERS.

Nashville, Tenn., *May 20th*, 1859.

valuable suggestions in regard to a few important changes which have been made, greatly to the advantage of the work, his acknowledgments are particularly due to his venerable and esteemed friend, D'Arcy Paul, Esq., of Petersburg, Va.

L. C. EVERETT.

RICHMOND, Va., *July 14th*, 1859.

NOTICE TO THE CLERGY

It is respectfully suggested that the use of more than one hymn from any one folio, during the same day, if the minister can suit his subject otherwise, might, with profit, be avoided, at least, until the congregation shall have practiced and learned both tunes presented on each opening; and even then, there should not be more than one hymn for each tune used during the same day.

The object of this, is to avoid the alternative of singing a hymn to a tune located in a different part of the work, which would be inconvenient; or the monotony of *repeating* the same tune during the same day, which would be offensive to some, and, indeed, to many of our most pious and devoted Christians; for such have been frequently known to express their disapprobation of occurrences of that sort. Variety is an agreeable and necessary element in every employment of life, and in order to inspire and maintain a proper degree of interest in the congregation, it is no less needful in the various branches of divine worship, and especially in the service of song, than it is in any other exercise, whether physical or mental, in which we may engage.

It is farther suggested that the *number* of the hymn, when read from the regular hymn book, be always *distinctly* announced, so as to enable those using the tune book to find it readily by referring to the Numerical Index.

It would also be well for every minister, in whose church a congregational singing class may be formed, to supply the leader of the music, previous to each weekly rehearsal, with the hymns to be used on the following Sabbath, that they may be well practiced in connection with the tunes with which they are associated in the tune book. This delightful part of the worship, thereby, would be greatly improved, and thus rendered more imposing and effective.

As the success of the work will depend in a great measure upon the proper observance of the above regulations, it is hoped that the clergy, everywhere, will duly regard them.

THE AUTHOR.

MR. L. C. EVERETT,

DEAR SIR:

I have examined, in the proof sheets, "The Wesleyan Hymn and Tune Book" which has been prepared by you for the use of the Methodist Episcopal Church South. In this work, which attests your practical information and energy, you have brought together, from available sources, a great variety of selected and original tunes, which, generally, in my judgment, are excellent, and well adapted to the metres and sentiments contained in the principal hymn book of the Church.

Hoping that the music and arrangement may prove to be generally acceptable to our very numerous and widely-spread congregations, I remain,

Very truly yours,

D'ARCY PAUL.

PETERSBURG, Va., *July 8th*, 1859.

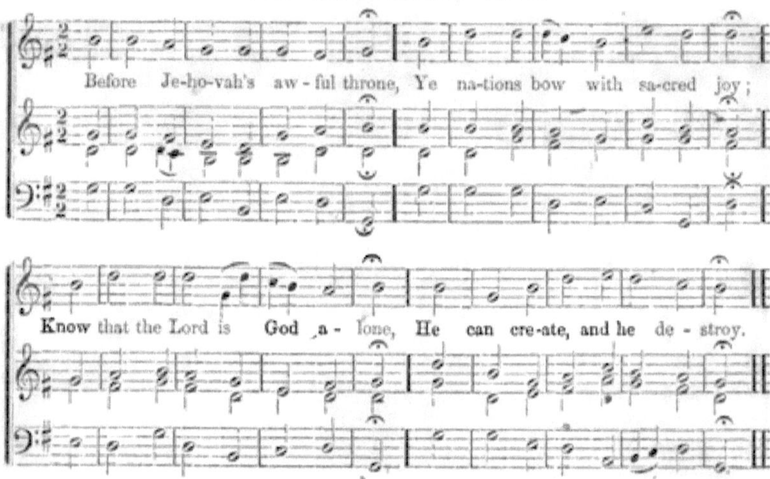

59. *Psalm c.*

BEFORE Jehovah's awful throne,
Ye nations bow with sacred joy;
Know that the Lord is God alone,
He can create, and he destroy.

2 His sovereign power, without our aid,
Made us of clay, and form'd us men;
And when like wand'ring sheep we stray'd,
He brought us to his fold again.

3 We'll crowd thy gates with thankful songs,
High as the heavens our voices raise;
And earth, with her ten thousand tongues,
Shall fill thy courts with sounding praise.

4 Wide as the world is thy command,
Vast as eternity thy love;
Firm as a rock thy truth must stand,
When rolling years shall cease to move.

242. *The primitive Church.*

JESUS, from whom all blessings flow,
Great Builder of thy church below,
If now thy Spirit move my breast,
Hear, and fulfill thine own request.

2 The few that truly call thee Lord,
And wait thy sanctifying word,
And thee their utmost Saviour own,—
Unite, and perfect them in one.

3 O let them all thy mind express!
Stand forth thy chosen witnesses;
Thy power unto salvation show,
And perfect holiness below.

4 In them let all mankind behold
How Christians lived in days of old;
Mighty their envious foes to move,
A proverb of reproach—and love.

5 Call them into thy wondrous light,
Worthy to walk with thee in white!
Make up thy jewels, Lord, and show
Thy glorious, spotless church below.

6 From every sinful wrinkle free,
Redeem'd from all iniquity,
The fellowship of saints make known,
And O, my God, may I be one!

324. *The eternal Sabbath.*

THINE earthly sabbaths, Lord, we love;
But there's a nobler rest above;
To that our lab'ring souls aspire,
With ardent pangs of strong desire.

2 No more fatigue, no more distress;
Nor sin nor hell shall reach the place;
No sighs shall mingle with the songs
Which warble from immortal tongues.

3 No rude alarms of raging foes;
No cares to break the long repose;
No midnight shade, no clouded sun,
But sacred, high, eternal noon.

4 O long-expected day, begin;
Dawn on these realms of woe and sin;
Fain would we leave this weary road,
And sleep in death to rest with God.

67. *Psalm cxvi. 8, 9.*

MY soul, through my Redeemer's care,
Saved from the second death, I feel;
Mine eyes from tears of dark despair,
My feet from falling into hell.

2 Wherefore to him my feet shall run;
Mine eyes on his perfections gaze;
My soul shall live for God alone;
And all within me shout his praise

1054. *Doxology.*

PRAISE God, from whom all blessings flow
Praise him all creatures here below;
Praise him above, ye heavenly host;
Praise Father, Son, and Holy Ghost.

6. *The Trinity.*

BLESS'D be the Father, and his love,
  To whose celestial source we owe
Rivers of endless joy above,
  And rills of comfort here below.

2 Glory to thee, great Son of God!
  From whose dear wounded body rolls
A precious stream of vital blood,
  Pardon and life for dying souls.

3 We give thee, sacred Spirit, praise,
  Who, in our hearts of sin and woe,
Mak'st living springs of grace arise,
  And into boundless glory flow.

4 Thus God the Father, God the Son,
  And God the Spirit, we adore;
That sea of life and love unknown,
  Without a bottom or a shore.

38. *The Father of Mercies.*

GOD of my life, whose gracious power
  Through various deaths my soul hath led,
Or turned aside the fatal hour,
  Or lifted up my sinking head.

2 In all my ways thy hand I own,
  Thy ruling providence I see:
Assist me still my course to run,
  And still direct my paths to thee.

3 Whither, O whither should I fly!
  But to my loving Saviour's breast;
Secure within thine arms to lie,
  And safe beneath thy wings to rest.

4 I have no skill the snare to shun,
  But thou, O Christ, my wisdom art;
I ever into ruin run,
  But thou art greater than my heart.

5 Foolish, and impotent, and blind,
  Lead me a way I have not known;
Bring me where I my heaven may find,
  The heaven of loving thee alone.

27. *"Glorious in holiness."*

OUR God ascends his lofty throne,
  Arrayed in majesty unknown;
His lustre all the temple fills,
  And spreads o'er all th' ethereal hills.

2 The holy, holy, holy Lord,
  Is by the seraphim adored;
And, while they stand beneath his seat,
  They veil their faces and their feet.

3 And can a sinful worm endure
  The presence of a God so pure?
Or these polluted lips proclaim
  The honors of so grand a name?

4 O for thine altar's glowing coal
  To touch my lips, to fire my soul,
To purge the sordid dross away,
  And into crystal turn my clay!

231. *Psalm lxv. 1-5.*

THE praise of Zion waits for thee,
  My God; and praise becomes thy house:
There shall thy saints thy glory see,
  And there perform their public vows.

2 O thou, whose mercy bends the skies,
  To save when humble sinners pray,
All lands to thee shall lift their eyes,
  And grateful isles of every sea.

3 Blessed is the man whom thou shalt choose,
  And give him kind access to thee,—
Give him a place within thy house,
  To taste thy love divinely free.

4 Soon shall the flocking nations run
  To Zion's hill, and own their Lord;
The rising and the setting sun
  Shall see the Saviour's name adored.

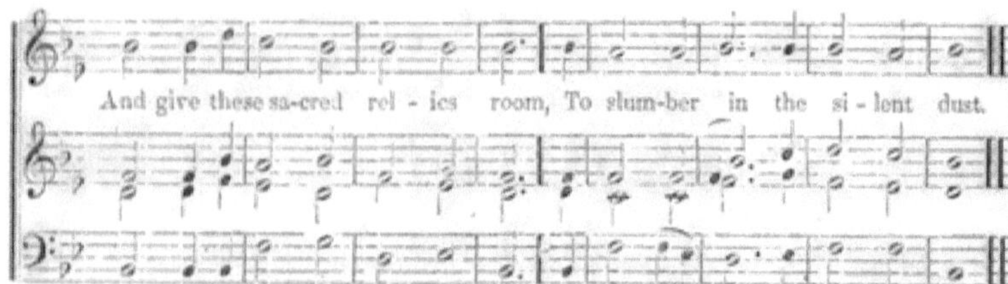

728 *Funeral of a Christian.*

UNVEIL thy bosom, faithful tomb;
Take this new treasure to thy trust,
And give these sacred relics room,
To slumber in the silent dust.

2 Nor pain, nor grief, nor anxious fear,
Invades thy bounds; no mortal woes
Can reach the peaceful sleeper here,
While angels watch the soft repose.

3 So Jesus slept: God's dying Son
Pass'd through the grave, and bless'd the bed,
Rest here, bless'd saint, till from his throne
The morning break, and pierce the shade.

4 Break from his throne, illustrious morn!
Attend, O earth, his sovereign word!
Restore thy trust; a glorious form
Shall then arise to meet the Lord.

741 *Psalm lxxii.*

JESUS shall reign where'er the sun
Does his successive journeys run;
His kingdom stretch from shore to shore,
Till moons shall wax and wane no more.

2 From north to south the princes meet
To pay their homage at his feet;
While western empires own their Lord,
And savage tribes attend his word.

3 For him shall endless prayer be made,
And endless praises crown his head;
His name, like sweet perfume, shall rise
With every morning sacrifice.

4 People and realms, of every tongue,
Dwell on his love with sweetest song,
And infant voices shall proclaim
Their early blessings on his name.

5 Blessings abound where'er he reigns,
The pris'ner leaps to lose his chains,
The weary find eternal rest,
And all the sons of want are blest.

6 Where he displays his healing power,
Death and the curse are known no more;
In him the tribes of Adam boast
More blessings than their father lost.

7 Let every creature rise and bring
Peculiar honours to our King;
Angels descend with songs again,
And earth repeat the long Amen!

351 *"Return unto me."*

RETURN, O wanderer, return!
And seek an injured Father's face;
Those warm desires that in thee burn
Were kindled by reclaiming grace.

2 Return, O wanderer, return,
And seek a Father's melting heart;
His pitying eyes thy grief discern,
His hand shall heal thine inward smart.

3 Return, O wanderer, return,
Thy Saviour bids thy spirit live;
Go to his bleeding feet, and learn
How freely Jesus can forgive.

4 Return, O wanderer, return,
And wipe away the falling tear;
'Tis God who says, "No longer mourn;"
'Tis mercy's voice invites thee near.

1655 *Doxology.*

TO Father, Son, and Holy Ghost,
The God whom earth and heaven adore,
Be glory, as it was of old,
Is now, and shall be evermore.

FOGARTY. L. M.

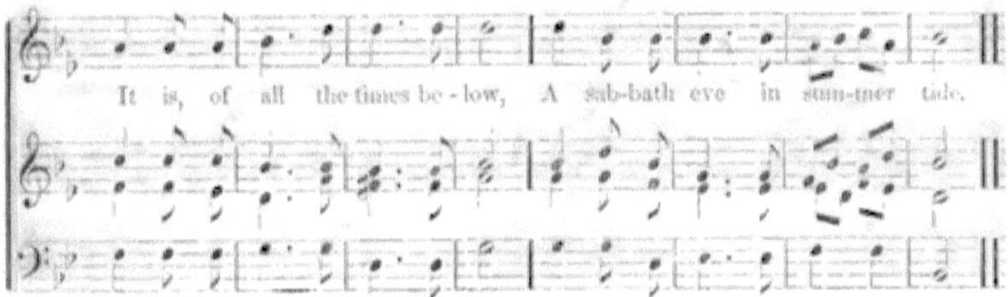

1002 *A Sabbath evening meditation.*

IS there a time when moments flow
  More lovelily than all beside?
It is, of all the times below,
  A sabbath eve in summer tide.

2 O then the setting sun smiles fair,
  And all below, and all above,
The diff'rent forms of nature wear
  One universal garb of love.

3 And then the peace that Jesus beams,—
  The life of grace, the death of sin,
With nature's placid woods and streams,—
  Is peace without, and peace within.

4 Delightful scene!—a world at rest—
  A God all love—no grief nor fear—
A heavenly hope—a peaceful breast—
  A smile unsullied by a tear!

5 Delightful hour! how soon will night
  Spread her dark mantle o'er thy reign,
And morrow's quick-returning light
  Must call us to the world again.

6 Yet will there dawn at last a day,
  A sun that never sets shall rise;
Night will not veil his ceaseless ray!
  The heavenly sabbath never dies!

291 *The table prepared.*

MY God, and is thy table spread?
  And does thy cup with love o'erflow?
Thither be all thy children led,
  And let them all its sweetness know!

2 Hail, sacred feast, which Jesus makes!
  Rich banquet of his flesh and blood!
Thrice happy he who here partakes
  That sacred stream, that heavenly food!

3 Why are its bounties all in vain
  Before unwilling hearts display'd?
Was not for you the Victim slain?
  Are you forbid the children's bread?

4 O let thy table honour'd be,
  And furnish'd well with joyful guests!
And may each soul salvation see,
  That here its sacred pledges tastes!

5 Let crowds approach with hearts prepared,
  With hearts inflamed let all attend;
Nor, when we leave our Father's board,
  The pleasure or the profit end.

777 *Spread of the Scriptures.*

THE law and prophets all foretold
  That Christ should die, and leave the grave,
Gather the world into his fold,
  The church of Jews and Gentiles save.

2 Yet by the prince of darkness bound,
  The nations still are wrapp'd in night;
They never heard the joyful sound,
  They never saw the gospel light.

3 Light of the world, again appear
  In mildest majesty of grace,
And bring the great salvation near,
  And claim our whole apostate race.

86 *The Lord's Prayer. Sixth petition.*

GIVER and Lord of life, whose power
  And guardian care for all are free,
To thee, in fierce temptation's hour,
  From sin and Satan let us flee.

2 Thine, Lord, we are, and ours thou art:
  In us be all thy goodness show'd;
Renew, enlarge, and fill our heart
  With peace, and joy, and heaven, and God.

EVENING HYMN. L. M.

659 *Discipline.*

MY hope, my all, my Saviour thou,
To thee, lo, now my soul I bow;
I feel the bliss thy wounds impart,
I find thee, Saviour, in my heart.

2 Be thou my strength, be thou my way,
Protect me through my life's short day:
In all my acts may wisdom guide,
And keep me, Saviour, near thy side.

3 Correct, reprove, and comfort me;
As I have need, my Saviour be:
And if I would from thee depart,
Then clasp me, Saviour, to thy heart.

4 In fierce temptation's darkest hour,
Save me from sin and Satan's power;
Tear every idol from thy throne,
And reign, my Saviour, reign alone.

5 My suff'ring time shall soon be o'er,
Then shall I sigh and weep no more;
My ransomed soul shall soar away,
To sing thy praise in endless day.

863 *Calm in the storm.*

GLORY to Thee, whose powerful word,
Bids the tempest'ous winds arise!
Glory to thee, the sovereign Lord
Of air, and earth, and sea, and skies!

2 Let air, and earth, and skies obey,
And seas thine awful will perform:
From them we learn to own thy sway,
And shout to meet the gath'ring storm.

3 What though the floods lift up their voice,
Thou hearest, Lord, our louder cry;
They cannot damp thy children's joys,
Or shake the soul when God is nigh.

4 Headlong we cleave the yawning deep,
And back to highest heaven are borne,
Unmoved, though rapid whirlwinds sweep,
And all the wat'ry world upturn.

5 Roar on, ye waves! our souls defy
Your roaring to disturb our rest;
In vain t' impair the calm ye try,
The calm in a believer's breast.

6 Rage, while our faith the Saviour tries,
Thou sea, the servant of his will;
Rise, while our God permits thee rise,
But fall when he shall say, *Be still!*

681 *Death of the righteous.*

HOW bless'd the righteous when he dies,
When sinks a weary soul to rest,
How mildly beam the closing eyes!
How gently heaves th' expiring breast!

2 So fades a summer cloud away;
So sinks the gale when storms are o'er
So gently shuts the eye of day;
So dies a wave along the shore.

3 Life's duty done, as sinks the clay,
Light from its load the spirit flies;
While heaven and earth combine to say,
"How bless'd the righteous when he dies."

82 *The Lord's Prayer. Second petition.*

SON of thy Sire's eternal love,
Take to thyself thy mighty power,
Let all earth's sons thy mercy prove,
Let all thy wondrous grace adore:

2 The triumphs of thy love display;
In every heart reign thou alone,
Till all thy foes confess thy sway,
And glory end what grace begun.

1055 *Doxology*

TO Father, Son, and Holy Ghost,
The God whom earth and heaven adore,
Be glory, as it was of old,
Is now, and shall be evermore.

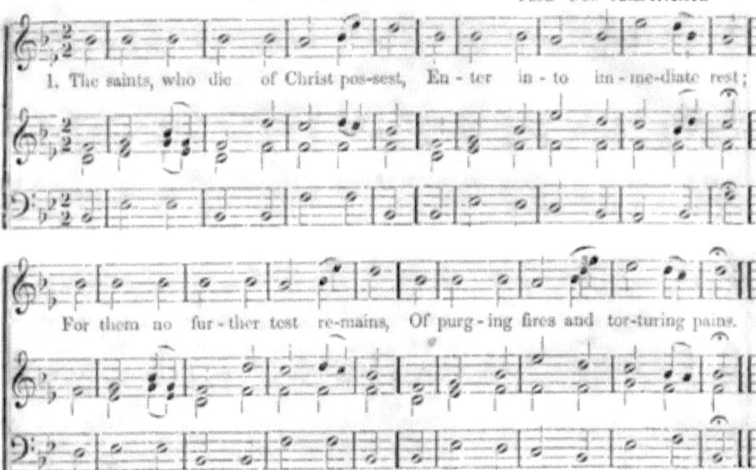

684 *Disembodied Saints.*

THE saints, who die of Christ possest
  Enter into immediate rest;
For them no further test remains
Of purging fires and torturing pains.

2 Who trusting in their Lord depart,
Cleansed from all sin and pure in heart,
The bliss unmix'd, the glorious prize,
They find with Christ in paradise.

3 Close follow'd by their works they go,
Their Master's purchased joy to know.
Their works enhance the bliss prepared,
And each hath its distinct reward.

4 Yet glorified by grace alone,
They cast their crowns before the throne;
And fill the echoing courts above
With praises of redeeming love.

943 *Revelation, iii. 14-19.*

GOD of unspotted purity,
  Us and our works canst thou behold?
Justly we are abhorr'd by thee,
  For we are neither hot nor cold.

2 A lifeless form we still retain;
  Of this we make our empty boast,
Nor know the name we take in vain;
  The power of godliness is lost.

3 Better that we had never known
  The way to heaven through saving grace,
Than basely in our lives disown,
  And slight and mock thee to thy face.

4 O let us our own works forsake,
  Ourselves and all we have deny,—
Thy condescending counsel take,
  And come to thee, pure gold to buy!

5 O may we through thy grace attain
  The faith thou never wilt reprove,—
  The faith that purges every stain,
  The faith that always works by love!

789 *Psalm xciii.*

WITH glory clad, with strength array'd,
  The Lord that o'er all nature reigns,
The world's foundations strongly laid,
  And the vast fabric still sustains.

2 How sure establish'd is thy throne,
  Which shall no change or period see!
For thou, O Lord, and thou alone,
  Art King from all eternity.

3 The floods, O Lord, lift up their voice,
  And toss their troubled waves on high;
But God above can still their noise,
  And make the angry sea comply.

4 Thy promise, Lord, is ever sure:
  And they that in thy house would dwell,
That happy station to secure,
  Must still in holiness excel.

316 *Opening morning service.*

ANOTHER six days' work is done;
  Another sabbath is begun:
Return, my soul, enjoy thy rest;
Improve the day thy God hath blest.

2 O that our thoughts and thanks may rise,
As grateful incense, to the skies;
And draw from Christ that sweet repose
Which none but he that feels it knows.

3 This heavenly calm within the breast
Is the dear pledge of glorious rest,
Which for the church of God remains,
The end of cares, the end of pains.

4 In holy duties let the day,
In holy comforts, pass away;
How sweet, a sabbath thus to spend,
In hope of one that ne'er shall end!

STONEFIELD. L. M.

526 *The act of consecration.*

COME, Saviour, Jesus, from above!
Assist me with thy heavenly grace;
Empty my heart of earthly love,
And for thyself prepare the place.

2 O let thy sacred presence fill,
And set my longing spirit free,
Which pants to have no other will,
But day and night to feast on thee.

3 While in this region here below,
No other good will I pursue:
I'll bid this world of noise and show,
With all its glittering snares, adieu!

4 That path with humble speed I'll seek
In which my Saviour's footsteps shine,
Nor will I hear, nor will I speak,
Of any other love but thine.

5 Henceforth may no profane delight
Divide this consecrated soul;
Possess it, thou, who hast the right,
As Lord and Master of the whole.

570 *Zeal implored.*

O THOU who all things canst control,
Chase this dread slumber from my soul;
With joy and fear, with love and awe,
Give me to keep thy perfect law.

2 O may one beam of thy bless'd light
Pierce through, dispel, the shade of night,
Touch my cold breast with heavenly fire,
With holy, conqu'ring zeal inspire.

4 With outstretch'd hands and streaming eyes,
Oft I begin to grasp the prize;
I groan, I strive, I watch, I pray;
But ah! how soon it dies away!

5 The deadly slumber soon I feel
Afresh upon my spirit steal;
Rise, Lord, stir up thy quick'ning power,
And wake me, that I sleep no more.

613 *Not ashamed of Jesus.*

JESUS! and shall it ever be
A mortal man ashamed of thee?
Ashamed of thee, whom angels praise,
Whose glories shine through endless days?

2 Ashamed of Jesus! sooner far
Let evening blush to own a star:
He sheds the beams of light divine
O'er this benighted soul of mine.

3 Ashamed of Jesus! just as soon
Let midnight be ashamed of noon:
'Tis midnight with my soul, till he,
Bright Morning Star, bid darkness flee!

4 Ashamed of Jesus! that dear Friend
On whom my hopes of heaven depend!
No: when I blush, be this my shame,
That I no more revere his name.

850 *Deliverance from sickness.* *Psalm cvii. 19-22.*

WE to Jehovah raised our cry,
Who heard us in our agony,
He sent his word, our souls to save,
His word redeems us from the grave.

2 O praise Jehovah for his grace,
His wonders to our guilty race!
Your off'rings pay with grateful voice,
Recount his mercies and rejoice.

846 *The patriot's prayer.* *Psalm cxliv. 12-15.*

LORD, let our vig'rous sons be seen
Like plants in youthful verdure green:—
Our daughters virtuous, graceful, fair
As columns deck'd with sculptured care.

2 Let the rich harvest, from the field,
To the full floor abundance yield;
Our garners fill'd with varied store,
The hope and refuge of the poor.

3 Our teeming ewes, by thousands told,
Add their ten thousands to the fold:
The lab'ring oxen, strong for toil,
Graze o'er the mead, or work the soil.

4 Then shall no foes irruptive break,
No tribes their native shores forsake,
Nor murm'rings through the land resound,
But sweet content spread all around.

5 Happy the people thus at rest,
With laws, and peace, and commerce blest;
Then happier we—no good denied,
Who claim the Lord *our* God beside!

448 *The backslider's confession.*

SAVIOUR, I now with shame confess
My thirst for creature happiness;
By base desires I wrong'd thy love,
And forced thy mercy to remove.

2 Yet would I not regard thy stroke;
But, when thou didst thy grace revoke,
And when thou didst thy face conceal,
Thy absence I refused to feel.

3 I knew not that the Lord was gone;
In my own froward will went on;
I lived to the desires of men,
And thou hast all my wand'rings seen.

4 Yet, O the riches of thy grace!
Thou, who hast seen my evil ways,
Wilt freely my backslidings heal,
And pardon on my conscience seal.

5 For this I at thy footstool wait,
Till thou my peace again create—
Fruit of thy gracious lips—restore
My peace, and bid me sin no more!

853 *Psalm cvii. 33–38.*

WHEN guilt lies heavy on the land,
God's works obey his just command,
His scorching heat consumes the ground,
And spreads a wilderness around.

2 The channel of the copious stream
Stands dry—nor midst the sultry gleam
Flows the sweet spring; all nature dies,
And earth a dreary desert lies.

3 But when again, his judgments known,
His penitents surround his throne,
With *showers* of blessings from on high,
His streams the parched grounds supply.

4 Over the now productive soil
The husbandman renews his toil;
He sows, he plants, and o'er the field
His vines their fruit and fragrance yield.

5 'Tis God! *his* blessing he commands,
And spreads abundance o'er the lands;
The flocks and herds his hand confess,
And crowd the fields with vast increase.

859 *Ember day.*

LORD of the wide, extensive main,
Whose power the wind, the sea, controls,
Whose hand doth earth and heaven sustain,
Whose Spirit leads believing souls:

2 'Tis here thy unknown paths we trace,
Which dark to human eyes appear;
While through the mighty waves we pass,
Faith only sees that God is here.

3 Throughout the deep thy footsteps shine,
We own thy way is in the sea,
O'erawed by majesty divine,
And lost in thine immensity.

4 Thy wisdom here we learn t' adore,
Thine everlasting truth we prove;
Amazing heights of boundless power,
Unfathomable depths of love.

225 *His universal effusion.*

O SPIRIT of the living God!
In all the fulness of thy grace,
Where'er the foot of man hath trod,
Descend on our apostate race.

2 Give tongues of fire and hearts of love
To preach the reconciling word:
Give power and unction from above,
Whene'er the joyful sound is heard.

3 Be darkness, at thy coming, light;
Confusion, order, in thy path;
Souls without strength, inspire with might;
Bid mercy triumph over wrath!

4 Baptize the nations! far and nigh
The triumphs of the cross record;
The name of Jesus glorify,
Till every kindred call him Lord.

5 God from eternity hath will'd
All flesh shall his salvation see:
So be the Father's love fulfill'd,
The Saviour's suff'rings crown'd through thee!

510 *The believer's rest.*

COME, O thou greater than our heart,
And make thy faithful mercies known;
The mind which was in thee impart;
Thy constant mind in us be shown.

2 O let us by thy cross abide,
Thee, only thee, resolved to know,—
The Lamb for sinners crucified,
A world to save from endless wo.

3 Take us into thy people's rest,
And we from our own works shall cease;
With thy meek spirit arm our breast,
And keep our minds in perfect peace.

4 Jesus, for this we calmly wait,
O let our eyes behold thee near!
Hasten to make our heaven complete,
Appear, our glorious God, appear!

964. *Evening.*

THUS far the Lord hath led me on,
 Thus far his power prolongs my days,
And every evening shall make known
 Some fresh memorial of his grace.

2 Much of my time has run to waste,
 And I perhaps am near my home:
But he forgives my follies past,
 And gives me strength for days to come.

3 I lay my body down to sleep,
 Peace is the pillow for my head;
While well-appointed angels keep
 Their watchful stations round my bed.

4 Thus when the night of death shall come,
 My flesh shall rest beneath the ground,
And wait thy voice to rouse my tomb,
 With sweet salvation in the sound.

1011. *Eucharistic vow.*

O HAPPY day, that fixed my choice
 On thee, my Saviour and my God!
Well may this glowing heart rejoice,
 And tell its raptures all abroad.

2 O happy bond, that seals my vows
 To Him who merits all my love!
Let cheerful anthems fill his house,
 While to that sacred shrine I move.

3 'Tis done; the great transaction 's done!
 I am my Lord's, and he is mine;
He drew me, and I follow'd on,
 Charm'd to confess the voice divine.

4 Now rest, my long-divided heart;
 Fixed on this blissful centre, rest;
With ashes who would grudge to part,
 When call'd on angels' bread to feast.

5 High Heaven, that heard the solemn vow,
 That vow renew'd shall daily hear,
Till in life's latest hour I bow,
 And bless in death a bond so dear.

207. *Pentecost.*

FATHER, if justly still we claim,
 To us and ours the promise made,
To us be graciously the same,
 And crown with living fire our head.

2 Our claim admit, and from above
 Of holiness the Spirit shower,
Of wise discernment, humble love,
 And zeal, and unity, and power.

3 The Spirit of convincing speech,
 Of power demonstrative, impart;
Such as may every conscience reach,
 And sound the unbelieving heart.

4 The Spirit of refining fire,
 Searching the inmost of the mind,
To purge all fierce and foul desire,
 And kindle life more pure and kind.

5 The Spirit breathe of inward life,
 Which in our hearts thy laws may write;
Then grief expires, and pain, and strife;
 'T is nature all,—and all delight.

85. *The Lord's Prayer—Fifth petition.*

ETERNAL, spotless Lamb of God,
 Before the world's foundation slain!
Sprinkle us ever with thy blood:
 O cleanse and keep us ever clean!

2 To every soul, (all praise to thee!)
 Our bowels of compassion move;
And all mankind by this may see,
 God is in us; for God is love.

1054. *Doxology.*

PRAISE God from whom all blessings flow,
 Praise him, all creatures here below;
Praise him above, ye heavenly host;
Praise Father, Son, and Holy Ghost.

198. *"Over all, God blessed for ever."*

THE day of Christ, the day of God,
We humbly hope with joy to see,
Wash'd in the sanctifying blood
Of an expiring Deity—

2 Who did for us his life resign:
There is no other God but one;
For all the plenitude divine
Resides in the Eternal Son.

3 Spotless, sincere, without offence,
O may we to his day remain!
Who trust the blood of Christ to cleanse
Our souls from every sinful stain.

4 Lord, we believe the promise sure!
The purchased Comforter impart!
Apply thy blood to make us pure—
To keep us pure in life and heart!

5 Then let us see that day supreme,
When none thy Godhead shall deny!
Thy sovereign majesty blaspheme,
Or count thee less than the Most High!

6 When all who on their God believe,
Who here thy last appearing love,
Shall thy consummate joy receive,
And see thy glorious face above.

772. *Excellency of God's word.*

LET everlasting glories crown,
Thy head, my Saviour, and my Lord,
Thy hands have brought salvation down,
And writ the blessings in thy word.

2 In vain the trembling conscience seeks
Some solid ground to rest upon;
With long despair the spirit breaks,
Till we apply to Christ alone.

3 How well thy blessed truths agree!
How wise and holy thy commands!
Thy promises—how firm they be!
How firm our hope, our comfort, stands.

4 Should all the forms that men devise,
Assault my faith with treach'rous art,
I'd call them vanity and lies,
And bind the gospel to my heart.

280. *Baptism.—Adult.*

COME, Father, Son, and Holy Ghost,
Honour the means ordain'd by thee;
Make good our apostolic boast,
And own thy glorious ministry.

2 We now thy promised presence claim,
Sent to disciple all mankind—
Sent to baptize into thy name—
We now thy promised presence find.

3 Father, in these reveal thy Son—
In these, for whom we seek thy face,
The hidden mystery make known,
The inward, pure, baptizing grace.

4 Jesus, with us thou always art;
Effectuate now the sacred sign,
The gift unspeakable impart,
And bless the ordinance divine.

5 Eternal Spirit, come from high,
Baptizer of our spirits thou!
The sacramental seal apply,
And witness with the water now.

87. *Lord's Prayer.—The Doxology.*

BLESSING and honour, praise and love,
Co-equal, co-eternal Three,
In earth below, in heaven above,
By all thy works, be paid to thee!

2 Thrice Holy! thine the kingdom is;
The power omnipotent is thine;
And when created nature dies,
Thy never-ceasing glories shine.

380 *Psalm li. 1—4.*

SHOW pity, Lord, O Lord, forgive,
Let a repenting rebel live:
Are not thy mercies large and free?
May not a sinner trust in thee?

2 My crimes are great, but don't surpass
The power and glory of thy grace;
Great God, thy nature hath no bound,
So let thy pard'ning love be found.

3 O wash my soul from every sin!
And make my guilty conscience clean!
Here on my heart the burden lies,
And past offences pain mine eyes.

4 My lips with shame my sins confess,
Against thy law, against thy grace;
Lord, should thy judgments grow severe,
I am condemn'd, but thou art clear.

5 Should sudden vengeance seize my breath,
I must pronounce thee just in death;
And if my soul were sent to hell,
Thy righteous law approves it well.

6 Yet save a trembling sinner, Lord,
Whose hope, still hov'ring round thy word,
Would light on some sweet promise there,
Some sure support against despair.

121 *The Crucifixion.*

EXTENDED on a cursed tree,
Besmear'd with dust, and sweat, and blood,
See there, the King of glory, see!
Sinks, and expires, the Son of God!

2 Who, who, my Saviour, this hath done?
Who could thy sacred body wound?
No guilt thy spotless heart hath known,
No guile hath in thy lips been found.

3 I,—I alone have done the deed,
'Tis I thy sacred flesh have torn;
My sins have caused thee, Lord, to bleed,
Pointed the nail, and fix'd the thorn.

4 For me, the burden, to sustain
Too great, on thee, my Lord, was laid
To heal me, thou hast borne the pain;
To bless me, thou a curse wast made.

5 In the devouring lion's teeth,
Torn, and forsook of all, I lay;
Thou sprang'st into the jaws of death,
From death to save the helpless prey.

6 My Saviour, how shall I proclaim,
How pay the mighty debt I owe?
Let all I have, and all I am,
Ceaseless to all thy glory show.

7 Too much to thee I cannot give;
Too much I cannot do for thee:
Let all thy love, and all thy grief,
Grav'n on my heart forever be!

8 The meek, the still, the lowly mind,
O may I learn from thee, my God,
And love, with softest pity join'd,
For those that trample on thy blood!

9 Still let thy tears, thy groans, thy sighs,
O'erflow my eyes, and heave my breast;
Till loose from flesh and earth I rise,
And ever in thy bosom rest.

1054 *Doxology.*

PRAISE God, from whom all blessings flow,
Praise him, all creatures here below;
Praise him above, ye heavenly host;
Praise Father, Son, and Holy Ghost.

538 *Seeking perfect rest in Christ.*

O THAT my load of sin were gone!
O that I could at last submit
At Jesus' feet to lay it down!
To lay my soul at Jesus' feet!

2 Rest for my soul I long to find:
Saviour of all, if mine thou art,
Give me thy meek and lowly mind,
And stamp thine image on my heart.

3 Break off the yoke of inbred sin,
And fully set my spirit free;
I cannot rest till pure within,
Till I am wholly lost in thee.

4 Fain would I learn of thee, my God,
Thy light and easy burden prove,
The cross, all stained with hallow'd blood,
The labour of thy dying love.—

5 I would, but thou must give the power,
My heart from every sin release;
Bring near, bring near the joyful hour,
And fill me with thy perfect peace.

6 Come, Lord, the drooping sinner cheer,
Nor let thy chariot wheels delay:
Appear, in my poor heart appear!
My God, my Saviour, come away!

830 *Public fast. Ezek. ix. 4—6.*

O RIGHTEOUS God, thou Judge supreme,
We tremble at thy dreadful name!
And all our crying guilt we own,
In dust and tears, before thy throne.

2 Justly might this polluted land
Prove all the vengeance of thy hand;
And, bathed in heaven, thy sword might come
To drink our blood, and seal our doom.

3 Yet hast thou not a remnant here,
Whose souls are filled with pious fear?
O bring thy wonted mercy nigh,
While prostrate at thy feet they lie!

4 Behold their tears, attend their moan,
Nor turn away their secret groan:
With these we join our humble prayer;
Our nation shield, our country spare.

414 *"Heal my soul."*

O THOU, whom once they flock'd to hear,
Thy words to hear, thy power to feel;
Suffer the sinners to draw near,
And graciously receive us still.

2 They that be whole, thyself hast said,
No need of a physician have;
But I am sick, and want thine aid,
And ask thine utmost power to save.

3 Thy power, and truth, and love divine,
The same from age to age endure:
A word, a gracious word of thine,
The most invet'rate plague can cure.

4 Helpless, howe'er, my spirit lies,
And long hath languish'd at the pool,
A word of thine shall make it rise,
Shall speak me in a moment whole.

84 *The Lord's Prayer. Fourth petition.*

FATHER, 'tis thine each day to yield
Thy children's wants a fresh supply;
Thou cloth'st the lilies of the field,
And hearest the young ravens cry:

2 On thee we cast our care; we live
Through thee, who know'st our every need;
O feed us with thy grace, and give
Our souls this day the living bread!

81 *The Lord's Prayer. Preface, and first petition.*

FATHER of all, whose powerful voice
Call'd forth this universal frame!
Whose mercies over all rejoice,
Through endless ages still the same;

2 Thou by thy word upholdest all;
Thy bounteous love to all is show'd;
Thou hear'st thy every creature's call;
And fillest every mouth with good.

3 In heaven thou reign'st enthroned in light,
Nature's expanse before thee spread;
Earth, air, and sea, before thy sight,
And hell's deep gloom, are open laid!

4 Wisdom, and might, and love, are thine;
Prostrate before thy face we fall,
Confess thine attributes divine,
And hail thee sovereign Lord of all.

5 Thee, sovereign Lord, let all confess,
That move in earth, or air, or sky;
Revere thy power, thy goodness bless,
Tremble before thy piercing eye.

6 All ye who owe to him your birth,
In praise your every hour employ:
Jehovah reigns; be glad, O earth,
And shout, ye morning stars, for joy!

144 *Col. iii. 1-4.*

YE faithful souls, who Jesus know,
If risen indeed with him ye are,
Superior to the joys below,
His resurrection's power declare.

2 Your faith by holy tempers prove,
By actions show your sins forgiven!
And seek the glorious things above,
And follow Christ, your Head, to heaven.

3 There your exalted Saviour see,
Seated at God's right hand again,
In all his Father's majesty,
In everlasting pomp, to reign.

4 To him continually aspire,
Contending for your native place,
And emulate the angel-choir,
And only live to love and praise.

5 For who by faith your Lord receive,
Ye nothing seek or want beside;
Dead to the world and sin ye live;
Your creature-love is crucified.

6 Your real life, with Christ conceal'd,
Deep in the Father's bosom lies;
And, glorious as your Head reveal'd,
Ye soon shall meet him in the skies.

83 *The Lord's Prayer. Third petition.*

SPIRIT of grace, and health, and power,
Fountain of light and love below;
Abroad thy healing influence shower,
O'er all the nations let it flow.

2 Inflame our hearts with perfect love,
In us the work of faith fulfil;
So not heaven's host shall swifter move,
Than we on earth, to do thy will.

208 *Pentecost.*

ON all the earth thy spirit shower,
The earth in righteousness renew:
Thy kingdom come, and hell's o'erpower,
And to thy sceptre all subdue.

2 Like mighty winds or torrents fierce,
Let it opposers all o'errun;
And every law of sin reverse,
That faith and love may make all one.

3 Yea, let it, Lord, in every place
Its richest energy declare;

While lovely tempers, fruits of grace,
The kingdom of thy Christ prepare.

4 Grant this, O holy God and true!
The ancient seers thou didst inspire!
To us perform the promise due;
Descend, and crown us now with fire!

252 *The Great Commission.*

"GO preach my Gospel," saith the Lord;
"Bid the whole earth my grace receive;
He shall be saved who trusts my word;
He shall be damn'd, who won't believe.

2 "I'll make your great commission known;
And ye shall prove my gospel true,
By all the works that I have done,
By all the wonders ye shall do.

3 "Teach all the nations my commands;
I'm with you till the world shall end:
All power is trusted in my hands;
I can destroy, and I defend."

4 He spake—and light shone round his head,
On a bright cloud to heaven he rode;
They to the furthest nations spread
The grace of their ascended God.

126 *Gal. vi. 14.*

WHEN I survey the wondrous cross
On which the Prince of glory died,
My richest gain I count but loss,
And pour contempt on all my pride.

2 Forbid it, Lord, that I should boast,
Save in the death of Christ, my God;
All the vain things that charm me most,
I sacrifice them to his blood.

3 See, from his head, his hands, his feet,
Sorrow and love flow mingled down!
Did e'er such love and sorrow meet?
Or thorns compose so rich a crown?

4 Were the whole realm of nature mine,
That were a present far too small;
Love, so amazing, so divine,
Demands my soul, my life, my all.

189 *Love which passeth knowledge.*

OF Him who did salvation bring
I could for ever think and sing;
Arise, ye needy, he'll relieve;
Arise, ye guilty, he'll forgive.

2 Ask but his grace, and lo, 'tis given!
Ask, and he turns your hell to heaven:
Though sin and sorrow wound my soul,
Jesus, thy balm will make it whole.

3 To shame our sins he blush'd in blood,
He closed his eyes to show us God;
Let all the world fall down and know
That none but God such love can show.

4 'Tis thee I love, for thee alone
I shed my tears and make my moan!
Where'er I am, where'er I move,
I meet the object of my love.

5 Insatiate to this spring I fly;
I drink, and yet am ever dry;
Ah! who against thy charms is proof?
Ah! who that loves can love enough?

130 *Micah vi. 6-8.*

JESUS, the Lamb of God, hath bled;
He bore our sins upon the tree;
Beneath our curse he bow'd his head;
'Tis finish'd! he hath died for me!

2 See where before the throne he stands,
And pours the all-prevailing prayer!
Points to his side, and lifts his hands,
And shows that I am graven there!

3 He ever lives for me to pray;
He prays that I with him may reign;
Amen, to what my Lord doth say!
Jesus, thou canst not pray in vain.

101 *The great Teacher.*

HOW sweetly flow'd the gospel sound
From lips of gentleness and grace,
When list'ning thousands gather'd round,
And joy and gladness fill'd the place!

2 From heaven he came, of heaven he spoke,
To heaven he led his followers' way;
Dark clouds of gloomy night he broke,
Unveiling an immortal day.

3 "Come, wand'rers, to my Father's home;
Come, all ye weary ones, and rest:"
Yes, sacred Teacher, we will come,
Obey thee, love thee, and be blest.

16 *The Glory of God.*

THY parent hand, thy forming skill,
Firm fix'd this universal chain:
Else empty, barren darkness still
Had held his unmolested reign.

2 Whate'er in earth, or sea, or sky,
Or shuns or meets the wand'ring thoughts,
Escapes or strikes the searching eye,
By thee was to perfection brought!

3 High is thy power above all height;
Whate'er thy will decrees, is done:
Thy wisdom, equal to thy might,
Only to thee, O God, is known!

4 Heaven's glory is thy awful throne,
Yet earth partakes thy gracious sway:
Vain man! thy wisdom, folly own,
Lost is thy reason's feeble ray.

5 What our dim eye could never see
Is plain and naked to thy sight;
What thickest darkness veils, to thee
Shines clearly as the morning light.

6 In light thou dwell'st; light, that no shade,
No variation, ever knew;
Heaven, earth, and hell, stand all display'd,
And open to thy piercing view.

195 *The grace of Christ.*

NOW to the Lord a noble song!
Awake, my soul; awake, my tongue;
Hosanna to th' Eternal Name,
And all his boundless love proclaim.

2 See, where it shines in Jesus' face,
The brightest image of his grace;
God, in the person of his Son,
Has all his mightiest works outdone.

3 The spacious earth and spreading flood,
Proclaim the wise, the powerful God;
And thy rich glories, from afar,
Sparkle in every rolling star.

4 But in his looks a glory stands,
The noblest labour of thy hands:
The pleasing lustre of his eyes
Outshines the wonders of the skies.

5 Grace!—'tis a sweet, a charming theme;
My thoughts rejoice at Jesus' name!
Ye angels, dwell upon the sound;
Ye heav'ns, reflect it to the ground!

6 O may I reach the happy place,
Where he unveils his lovely face!
Where all his beauties you behold,
And sing his name to harps of gold.

73 *Psalm cxlvii. 1-11.*

PRAISE ye the Lord! 'tis good to raise
Your hearts and voices in his praise:
His nature and his works invite
To make this duty our delight.

2 He form'd the stars, those heavenly flames,
He counts their numbers, calls their names;
His wisdom's vast, and knows no bound:
A deep where all our thoughts are drown'd.

3 Sing to the Lord, exalt him high,
Who spreads his clouds along the sky;
There he prepares the fruitful rain,
Nor lets the drops descend in vain.

4 He makes the grass the hills adorn;
He clothes the smiling fields with corn:
The beasts with food his hands supply,
And the young ravens when they cry.

5 What is the creature's skill or force?
The sprightly man, or warlike horse?
The piercing wit, the active limb?
All are too mean delights for him.

6 But saints are lovely in his sight,
He views his children with delight;
He sees their hope, he knows their fear,
He looks, and loves his image there.

527 *The act of consecration.*

WEALTH, honour, pleasure, and what else
This short-enduring world can give,
Tempt as ye will, my soul repels,
To Christ alone resolved to live.

2 Thee I can love, and thee alone,
With pure delight and inward bliss:
To know thou tak'st me for thine own,
O what a happiness is this!

3 Nothing on earth do I desire
But thy pure love within my breast
This, only this, will I require,
And freely give up all the rest.

1054 *Doxology.*

PRAISE God, from whom all blessings flow
Praise him, all creatures here below;
Praise him above, ye heavenly host;
Praise Father, Son, and Holy Ghost.

328 *The hearty welcome.*

COME, sinners, to the gospel feast;
Let every soul be Jesus' guest;
Ye need not one be left behind,
For God hath bidden all mankind.

2 Sent by my Lord, on you I call;
The invitation is to all:
Come, all the world! come, sinner, thou!
All things in Christ are ready now.

3 Come, all ye souls by sin opprest,
Ye restless wand'rers after rest,
Ye poor, and maim'd, and halt, and blind,
In Christ a hearty welcome find.

4 My message as from God receive:
Ye all may come to Christ and live:
O let his love your hearts constrain,
Nor suffer him to die in vain!

5 See him set forth before your eyes,
That precious, bleeding sacrifice!
His offered benefits embrace,
And freely now be saved by grace!

92 *"The Word was made flesh."*

SING, all in heaven, at Jesus' birth,
Glory to God, and peace on earth:
Incarnate love in Christ is seen,
Pure mercy and good-will to men.

2 Praise him, extoll'd above all height,
Who doth in worthless worms delight;
God reconciled in Christ confess,
Your present and eternal peace.

3 From Jesus, manifest below,
Rivers of pure salvation flow;
And pour on man's distinguish'd race
Their everlasting streams of grace.

4 Sing, every soul of Adam's line,
The favourite attribute divine;
Ascribing, with the hosts above,
All glory to the God of love.

331 *Isaiah lv. 1-3.*

HO! every one that thirsts, draw nigh;
'Tis God invites the fallen race:
Mercy and free salvation buy;
Buy wine, and milk, and gospel grace.

2 Come to the living waters, come!
Sinners, obey your Maker's call;
Return, ye weary wand'rers, home,
And find my grace is free for all.

3 See from the Rock a fountain rise,
For you in healing streams it rolls;
Money ye need not bring, nor price,
Ye lab'ring, burden'd, sin-sick souls.

4 Nothing ye in exchange shall give,
Leave all you have, and are, behind,
Frankly the gift of God receive,
Pardon and peace in Jesus find.

181 *Rev. i. 5, 6.*

NOW to the Lord, who makes us know
The wonders of his dying love,
Be humble honours paid below,
And strains of nobler praise above.

2 'Twas he who cleansed our foulest sins,
And wash'd us in his richest blood:
'Tis he who makes us priests and kings,
And brings us rebels near to God.

3 To Jesus, our atoning Priest,
To Jesus, our superior King,
Be everlasting power confest—
Let ev'ry tongue his glory sing.

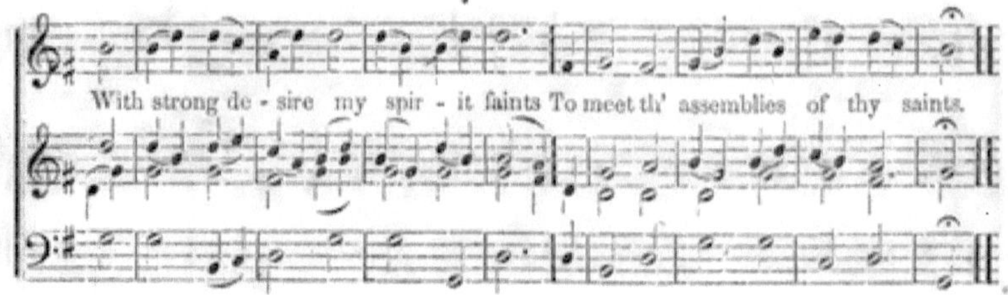

233 *Psalm* lxxxiv. 1—7.

HOW pleasant, how divinely fair,
O Lord of hosts, thy dwellings are!
With strong desire my spirit faints
To meet th' assemblies of thy saints.

2 Bless'd are the saints that sit on high,
Around thy throne of majesty;
Thy brightest glories shine above,
And all their works is praise and love.

3 Bless'd are the souls that find a place
Within the temple of thy grace:
Here they behold thy gentler rays,
And seek thy face, and learn thy praise.

4 Bless'd are the men whose hearts are set
To find the way to Zion's gate;
God is their strength, and through the road
They lean upon their helper, God.

5 Cheerful they walk with growing strength,
Till all shall meet in heaven at length,
Till all before thy face appear,
And join in nobler worship there.

320 *Psalm* xcii.

SWEET is the work, my God, my King,
To praise thy name, give thanks, and sing,
To show thy love by morning light,
And talk of all thy truth by night.

2 Sweet is the day of sacred rest,
No mortal cares shall seize my breast;
O may my heart in tune be found,
Like David's harp of solemn sound!

3 My heart shall triumph in my Lord,
And bless his works, and bless his word;
Thy works of grace, how bright they shine!
How deep thy counsels! how divine!

4 Then I shall share a glorious part
When grace hath well refined my heart,
And fresh supplies of joy are shed,
Like holy oil, to cheer my head.

5 Then shall I see, and hear, and know,
All I desired or wish'd below:
And every power find sweet employ
In that eternal world of joy.

349 *Revelation* iii. 20.

BEHOLD a stranger at the door!
He gently knocks, has knock'd before:
Has waited long—is waiting still;
You treat no other friend so ill.

2 O lovely attitude! He stands
With melting heart and bleeding hands:
O matchless kindness! and he shows
This matchless kindness to his foes!

3 But will he prove a Friend indeed?
He will; the very Friend you need:
The Friend of sinners—yes, 'tis He,
With garments dyed on Calvary.

4 Rise, touch'd with gratitude divine,
Turn out his enemy and thine,
That soul-destroying monster, sin,
And let the heavenly Stranger in.

5 Admit him, ere his anger burn;
His feet departed, ne'er return;
Admit him, or the hour's at hand,
You'll at his door rejected stand.

1055 *Doxology.*

TO Father, Son, and Holy Ghost,
The God whom earth and heaven adore,
Be glory, as it was of old,
Is now, and shall be evermore.

323 *In the sanctuary.*

FAR from my thoughts, vain world, begone!
Let my religious hours alone:
Fain would my eyes my Saviour see;
I wait a visit, Lord, from thee.

2 My heart grows warm with holy fire,
And kindles with a pure desire:
Come, my dear Jesus, from above,
And feed my soul with heavenly love.

3 Bless'd Jesus, what delicious fare!
How sweet thine entertainments are!
Never did angels taste above
Redeeming grace and dying love.

240 *The primitive church.*

HAPPY the souls that first believed,
To Jesus and each other cleaved;
Join'd, by the unction from above,
In mystic fellowship of love.

2 Meek, simple followers of the Lamb,
They lived, and spake, and thought the same,
Thy joyfully conspired to raise
Their ceaseless sacrifice of praise.

3 With grace abundantly endued,
A pure, believing, multitude!
They all were of one heart and soul,
And only love inspired the whole.

4 O what an age of golden days!
O what a choice, peculiar race!
Wash'd in the Lamb's all-cleansing blood,
Anointed kings and priests to God!

5 Where shall I wander now to find
Their true successors left behind?
The faithful, whom I seek in vain,
Are 'minish'd from the sons of men.

19 *The glory of God.*

GOD is a name my soul adores,
Th' almighty Three, th' eternal One;
Nature and grace, with all their powers,
Confess the Infinite unknown.

2 Thy voice produced the sea and spheres,
Bade the waves roar, the planets shine:
But nothing like thyself appears
Through all these spacious works of thine.

3 Still restless nature dies and grows,
From change to change the creatures run:
Thy being no succession knows,
And all thy vast designs are one.

4 A glance of thine runs through the globe,
Rules the bright worlds and moves their frame;
Of light thou form'st thy dazzling robe,
Thy ministers are living flame.

5 How shall polluted mortals dare
To sing thy glory or thy grace?
Beneath thy feet we lie afar,
And see but shadows of thy face.

6 Who can behold the blazing light?
Who can approach consuming flame?
None but thy wisdom knows thy might,
None but thy word can speak thy name.

1024 *Beginning work.*

FORTH in thy name, O Lord, I go,
My daily labor to pursue;
Thee, only thee, resolved to know
In all I think, or speak, or do.

2 Thee may I set at my right hand,
Whose eyes my inmost substance see;
And labour on at thy command,
And offer all my works to thee.

PILESGROVE. L. M.

65 *Psalm cvi.*

O RENDER thanks to God above,
The fountain of eternal love,
Whose mercy firm through ages past
Hath stood, and shall for ever last.

2 Who can his mighty deeds express,
Not only vast, but numberless?
What mortal eloquence can raise
His tribute of immortal praise?

3 Extend to me that favour, Lord,
Thou to thy chosen dost afford;
When thou return'st to set them free,
Let thy salvation visit me.

4 O may I worthy prove to see
Thy saints in full prosperity;
That I the joyful choir may join,
And count thy people's triumph mine.

5 Let Israel's God be ever bless'd,
His name eternally confess'd;
Let all his saints, with full accord,
In solemn hymns proclaim their Lord.

103 *The credentials of Jesus.*

BEHOLD the blind their sight receive!
Behold the dead awake and live!
The dumb speak wonders! and the lame
Leap like the hart, and bless his name!

2 Thus does th' eternal Spirit own,
And seal the mission of the Son;
The Father vindicates his cause,
While he hangs bleeding on the cross.

3 He dies!—the heavens in mourning stood!
He rises—and appears a God!
Behold the Lord ascending high,
No more to bleed, no more to die.

4 Hence, and for ever from my heart
I bid my doubts and fears depart;
And to those hands my soul resign,
Which bear credentials so divine.

105 *His exemplary life.*

MY dear Redeemer, and my Lord,
I read my duty in thy word;
But in thy life the law appears,
Drawn out in living characters.

2 Such was thy truth, and such thy zeal,
Such def'rence to thy Father's will,
Such love and meekness so divine,
I would transcribe, and make them mine.

3 Cold mountains, and the midnight air,
Witness'd the fervour of thy prayer;
The desert thy temptations knew,
Thy conflict, and thy vict'ry too.

4 Be thou my pattern; make me bear
More of thy gracious image here;
Then God, the Judge, shall own my name,
Among the followers of the Lamb.

235 *Psalm lxxxvii.*

GOD, in his earthly temple, lays
Foundations for his heavenly praise;
He likes the tents of Jacob well;
But still in Zion loves to dwell.

2 His mercy visits every house
That pay their night and morning vows;
But makes a more delightful stay
Where churches meet to praise and pray.

3 When God makes up his last account
Of natives in his holy mount,
'Twill be an honour to appear,
As one new-born or nourish'd there.

17 *The glory of God.*

THOU, true and only God, lead'st forth
Th' immortal armies of the sky:
Thou laugh'st to scorn the gods of earth;
Thou thund'rest, and amazed they fly!

2 With downcast eye th' angelic choir
Appear before thy awful face;
Trembling, they strike the golden lyre,
And thro' heaven's vault resound thy praise.

3 In earth, in heaven, in all, thou art:
The conscious creature feels thy nod;
Thy forming hand on every part
Impress'd the image of its God.

4 Thine, Lord, is wisdom, thine alone!
Justice and truth before thee stand:
Yet nearer to thy sacred throne
Mercy withholds thy lifted hand.

5 Each evening shows thy tender love,
Each rising morn thy plenteous grace;
Thy waken'd wrath doth slowly move,
Thy willing mercy flies apace!

6 To thy benign, indulgent care,
Father, this light, this breath, we owe;
And all we have, and all we are,
From thee, great Source of being, flow.

18 *The glory of God.*

PARENT of good! thy bounteous hand
Incessant benefits distils;
And all in air, or sea, or land,
With plenteous food and gladness fills.

2 All things in thee live, move, and are,
Thy power infused doth all sustain:
E'en those thy daily favors share
Who, thankless, spurn thy easy reign.

3 Thy sun thou bidd'st his genial ray
Alike on all impartial pour;
On all who hate or bless thy sway
Thou bidd'st descend the fruitful shower.

4 Yet while, at length, who scorn'd thy might,
Shall feel thee a consuming fire,
How sweet the joys, the crown how bright,
Of those who to thy love aspire!

5 All creatures praise th' eternal Name:
Ye hosts that to his court belong,
Cherubic choirs, seraphic flames,
Awake the everlasting song!

6 Thrice holy! thine the kingdom is,
The power omnipotent is thine;
And when created nature dies,
Thy never-ceasing glories shine.

109 *The Transfiguration.*

WHEN at this distance, Lord, we trace
The various glories of thy face,
What transport pours o'er all our breast,
And charms our cares and woes to rest!

2 With thee, in the obscurest cell,
On some bleak mountain would I dwell,
Rather than pompous courts behold,
And share their grandeur and their gold.

3 Away, ye dreams of mortal joy;
Raptures divine my thoughts employ:
I see the King of glory shine;
And feel his love, and call him mine.

4 On Tabor thus his servants view'd
His lustre, when transform'd he stood;
And, bidding earthly scenes farewell,
Cried, "Lord, 'tis pleasant here to dwell."

5 Yet still our elevated eyes
To nobler visions long to rise;
That grand assembly would we join,
Where all thy saints around thee shine.

6 That mount, how bright! those forms, how fair!
'T is good to dwell for ever there!
Come death, dear envoy of my God,
And bear me to that blest abode!

679 *The peaceful death.*

WHY should we start and fear to die?
What tim'rous worms we mortals are!
Death is the gate to endless joy,
And yet we dread to enter there.

2 The pains, the groans, the dying strife,
Fright our approaching souls away;
And we shrink back again to life,
Fond of our prison and our clay.

3 O if my Lord would come and meet,
My soul would stretch her wings in haste,
Fly fearless through death's iron gate,
Nor feel the terrors as she past!

4 Jesus can make a dying bed
Feel soft as downy pillows are,
While on his breast I lean my head,
And breathe my life out sweetly there.

597 *Titus ii. 10-13.*

SO let our lips and lives express
The holy gospel we profess;
So let our works and virtues shine,
To prove the doctrine all divine.

2 Thus shall we best proclaim abroad
The honours of our Saviour God,
When the salvation reigns within,
And grace subdues the power of sin.

3 Our flesh and sense must be denied,—
Passion and envy, lust and pride;
While justice, temp'rance, truth, and love,
Our inward piety approve.

4 Religion bears our spirits up,
While we expect that blessed hope,—
The bright appearance of the Lord;—
And faith stands leaning on his word.

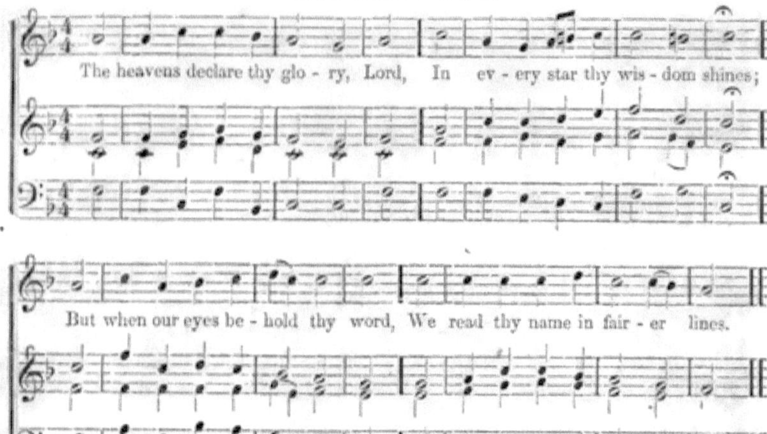

770 *Psalm* xix.

THE heavens declare thy glory, Lord,
In every star thy wisdom shines;
But when our eyes behold thy word,
We read thy name in fairer lines.

2 The rolling sun, the changing light,
And night and day thy power confess;
But the bless'd volume thou hast writ
Reveals thy justice and thy grace.

3 Sun, moon, and stars, convey thy praise
Round the whole earth, and never stand;
So when thy truth began its race,
It touch'd and glanced on every land.

4 Nor shall thy spreading gospel rest,
Till through the world thy truth has run;
Till Christ has all the nations blest,
That see the light, or feel the sun.

5 Great Sun of righteousness, arise!
Bless the dark world with heavenly light.
Thy gospel makes the simple wise;
Thy laws are pure, thy judgments right.

648 *The cloudy and fiery pillar.*

WHEN Israel, of the Lord beloved,
Out from the land of bondage came,
Their father's God before them moved,
An awful guide in smoke and flame.

2 By day, along th' astonish'd lands
The cloudy pillar glided slow;
By night, Arabia's crimson'd sands
Return'd the fiery column's glow.

3 Thus present still, though now unseen,
When brightly shines the prosp'rous day,
Be thoughts of thee a cloudy screen,
To temper the deceitful ray!

4 And O, when gathers on our path,
In shade and storm the frequent night,
Be thou, long-suffering, slow to wrath,
A burning and a shining light!

605 *At charitable collections.*

WHEN Jesus dwelt in mortal clay,
What were his works from day to day
But miracles of power and grace,
That spread salvation through our race?

2 Teach us, O Lord, to keep in view
Thy pattern, and thy steps pursue;
Let alms bestow'd, let kindness done,
Be witness'd by each rolling sun.

3 That man may *last*, but never *lives*,
Who much receives, but nothing gives,
Whom none can love, whom none can thank,
Creation's blot, creation's blank:

4 But he who marks, from day to day,
In generous acts his radiant way;
Treads the same path the Saviour trod,
The path to glory and to God.

601 *Apostacy deprecated.*

AH! Lord, with trembling I confess,
A gracious soul may fall from grace;
The salt may lose its seas'ning power,
And never, never find it more!

2 Lest that my fearful case should be,
Each moment knit my soul to thee
And lead me to the mount above,
Through the low vale of humble love.

932 *Heb.* iv. 14-16.

WHERE high the heavenly temple stands,
The house of God not made with hands,
A great High Priest our nature wears,
The guardian of mankind appears.

2 He, who for men their surety stood,
And poured on earth his precious blood,
Pursues in heaven his mighty plan,
The Saviour and the Friend of man.

3 In every pang that rends the heart,
The Man of sorrows had a part;

He sympathizes in our grief,
And to the suff'rer sends relief.

4 With boldness, therefore, at the throne,
Let us make all our sorrows known;
And ask the aids of heavenly power,
To help us in the evil hour!

629 *Adversity.*

O THOU, to whose all-searching sight
The darkness shineth as the light,
Search, prove my heart, it pants for thee,
O burst these bonds, and set it free!

2 Wash out its stains, refine its dross,
Nail my affections to the cross;
Hallow each thought, let all within
Be clean, as thou, my Lord, art clean.

3 If in this darksome wild I stray,
Be thou my light, be thou my way;
No foes, no violence I fear,
No fraud, while thou, my God, art near.

4 When rising floods my soul o'erflow,
When sinks my heart in waves of wo,
Jesus, thy timely aid impart,
And raise my head, and cheer my heart.

5 Saviour, where'er thy steps I see,
Dauntless, untired, I follow thee:
O let thy hand support me still,
And lead me to thy holy hill!

6 If rough and thorny be the way,
My strength proportion to my day;
Till toil, and grief, and pain, shall cease,
Where all is calm, and joy, and peace.

21 *Divine Majesty.*

ETERNAL Power, whose high abode
Becomes the grandeur of a God;
Infinite lengths, beyond the bounds
Where stars revolve their little rounds.

2 Thee while the first archangel sings,
He hides his face behind his wings:
And ranks of shining thrones around
Fall worshipping, and spread the ground.

3 Lord, what shall earth and ashes do?
We would adore our Maker too!
From sin and dust to thee we cry,
The great, the holy, and the high!

4 Earth from afar hath heard thy fame,
And worms have learn'd to lisp thy name;
But O! the glories of thy mind
Leave all our soaring thoughts behind!

5 God is in heaven, and men below:
Be short our tunes; our words be few!
A solemn rev'rence checks our songs,
And praise sits silent on our tongues.

15 *The glory of God.*

O GOD, thou bottomless abyss!
Thee to perfection who can know?
O height immense! What words suffice
Thy countless attributes to show?

2 Unfathomable depths thou art!
O plunge me in thy mercy's sea!
Void of true wisdom is my heart;
With love embrace and cover me!

3 While thee, all infinite, I set,
By faith, before my ravish'd eye,
My weakness bends beneath the weight;
O'erpowered I sink, I faint, I die.

4 Eternity thy fountain was,
Which, like thee, no beginning knew;
Thou wast ere time began his race,
Ere glow'd with stars th' ethereal blue.

5 Greatness unspeakable is thine,
Greatness, whose undiminish'd ray,
When short-lived worlds are lost, shall shine,
When earth and heaven are fled away.

6 Unchangeable, all perfect Lord,
Essential life's unbounded sea,
What lives, and moves, lives by thy word,
It lives, and moves, and is from thee!

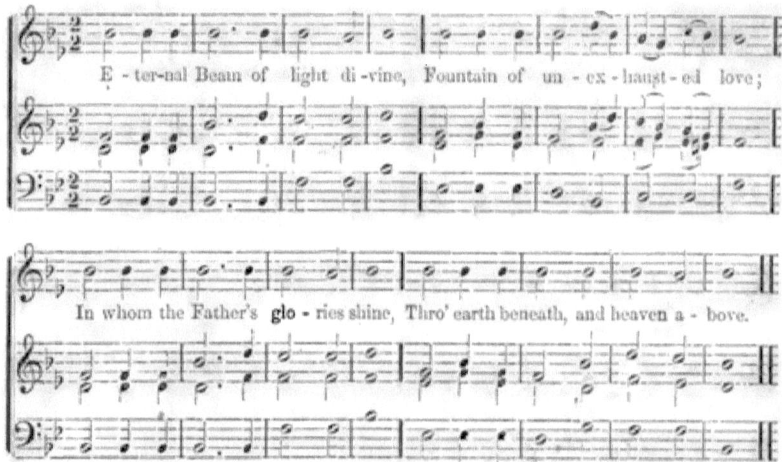

1034 *Submission to the will of God.*

ETERNAL Beam of light divine,
Fountain of unexhausted love;
In whom the Father's glories shine,
Thro' earth beneath, and heaven above.

2 Jesus, the weary wand'rer's rest,
Give me thy easy yoke to bear;
With steadfast patience arm my breast,
With spotless love and lowly fear.

3 Thankful I take the cup from thee,
Prepared and mingled by thy skill,
Though bitter to the taste it be,
Powerful the wounded soul to heal.

4 Be thou, O Rock of ages, nigh!
So shall each murm'ring thought be gone
And grief, and fear, and care, shall fly
As clouds before the mid-day sun.

5 Speak to my warring passions, "Peace;"
Say to my trembling heart, "Be still;"
Thy power my strength and fortress is,
For all things serve thy sovereign will.

6 O death! where is thy sting? Where now
Thy boasted victory, O grave?
Who shall contend with God? or who
Can hurt whom God delights to save?

1015 *Recovery from sickness.*

AND live I yet, by power divine?
And have I still my course to run?
Again brought back, in its decline,
The shadow of my parting sun?

2 Wond'ring I ask—Is this the breast
Struggling so late, and torn with pain?
The eyes that upward look'd for rest,
And dropp'd their weary lids again?

3 The recent horrors still appear:
O may they never cease to awe!
Still be the king of terrors near,
Whom late in all his pomp I saw.

4 Jesus to my deliv'rance flew,
Where, sunk in mortal pangs, I lay;
Pale death his ancient Conqu'ror knew,
And trembled, and ungrasp'd his prey.

5 God of my life, what just return
Can sinful dust and ashes give?
I only live my sin to mourn;
To love my God I only live.

6 To thee, benign and saving Power,
I consecrate my lengthen'd days
While, mark'd with blessings, every hour
Shall speak thy co-extended praise.

1010 *Self-dedication.*

LORD, I am thine, entirely thine,
Purchased and saved by blood divine;
With full consent thine would I be,
And own thy sovereign right in me.

2 Grant one poor sinner more a place
Among the children of thy grace;
A wretched sinner, lost to God,
But ransom'd by Immanuel's blood.

3 Thine would I live, thine would I die,
Be thine through all eternity;
The vow is past beyond repeal,
Now will I set the solemn seal.

4 Here at that cross where flows the blood
That bought my guilty soul for God;
Thee, my new Master, now I call,
And consecrate to thee my all.

5 Do thou assist a feeble worm
The great engagement to perform;
Thy grace can full assistance lend,
And on that grace I dare depend.

959 *Evening.*

ALL praise to thee, my God, this night,
For all the blessings of the light:
Keep me, O keep me, King of kings,
Under thine own Almighty wings.

2 Forgive me, Lord, for thy dear Son,
The ills that I this day have done;
That with the world, myself, and thee,
I, ere I sleep, at peace may be.

3 Teach me to live, that I may dread
The grave as little as my bed;
Teach me to die, that so I may
Rise glorious at the awful day.

4 O may my soul on thee repose,
And with sweet sleep mine eyelids close,—
Sleep, that may me more vig'rous make,
To serve my God, when I awake.

5 Praise God, from whom all blessings flow;
Praise him, all creatures here below;
Praise him above, ye heavenly host;
Praise Father, Son, and Holy Ghost.

1013 *Gratitude.*

GOD of my life, through all my days,
My grateful powers shall sound thy praise;
The song shall wake with opening light,
And warble to the silent night.

2 When anxious cares would break my rest,
And griefs would tear my throbbing breast,
Thy tuneful praises raised on high
Shall check the murmur and the sigh.

3 When death o'er nature shall prevail,
And all the powers of language fail,
Joys thro' my swimming eyes shall break,
And mean the thanks I cannot speak.

4 But O, when that last conflict 's o'er,
And I am chain'd to flesh no more,
With what glad accents shall I rise
To join the music of the skies!

5 Soon shall I learn the exalted strains
Which echo through the heavenly plains;
And emulate, with joy unknown,
The glowing seraphs round the throne.

6 The cheerful tribute will I give,
Long as a deathless soul shall live:
A work so sweet, a theme so high,
Demands, and crowns eternity.

22 *Absolute perfection.*

HOLY as thou, O Lord, is none,
Thy holiness is all thy own;
A drop of that unbounded sea
Is ours, a drop derived from thee.

2 And when thy purity we share,
Thy only glory we declare;
And humbled into nothing, own
Holy and pure is God alone.

3 Sole, self-existing God and Lord,
By all thy heavenly hosts adored;
Let all on earth bow down to thee,
And own thy peerless majesty:

4 Thy power unparallel'd confess,
Establish'd on the rock of peace;
The rock that never shall remove,
The rock of pure, almighty love.

818 *"We all do fade as a leaf."*

WELL doth a summer leaf explain
The transient state of feeble man:
We flourish fair in youthful bloom,
Till age and pallid autumn come.

2 He comes with sickness at his side—
He withers all our verdant pride,
And, shaken by the stormy gust,
We drop, and crumble into dust.

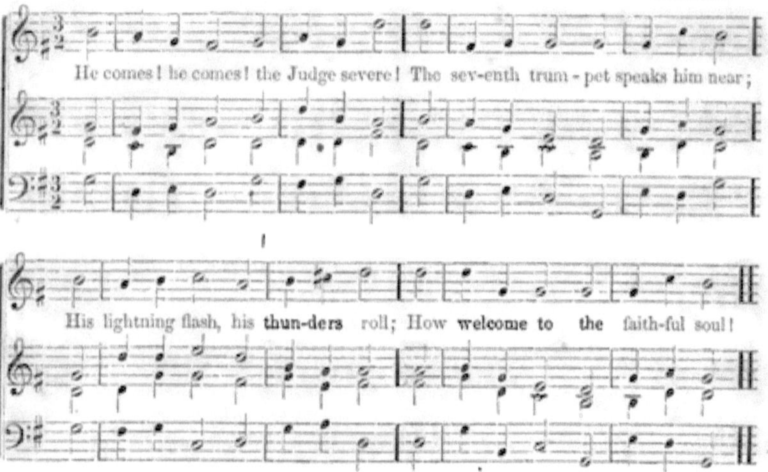

168 *Rev.* xi. 15.

HE comes! he comes! the Judge severe!
The seventh trumpet speaks him near;
His lightnings flash, his thunders roll;
How welcome to the faithful soul!

2 From heaven angelic voices sound;
See the almighty Jesus crown'd!
Girt with omnipotence and grace,
And glory decks the Saviour's face.

3 Descending on his azure throne,
He claims the kingdoms for his own;
The kingdoms all obey his word,
And hail him their triumphant Lord!

4 Shout, all the people of the sky,
And all the saints of the Most High,
Our Lord, who now his right obtains,
For ever and for ever reigns.

175 1 *Cor.* i. 30, 31.

WHEN gloomy shades my soul o'erspread,
"Let there be light," th' Almighty said;
And Christ, my Sun, his beams displays,
And scatters round celestial rays.

2 Condemn'd, a criminal I stood,
And awful justice asked my blood;
That welcome Saviour from thy throne
Brought righteousness and pardon down.

3 My soul was all o'erspread with sin,
And lo, his grace hath made me clean;
He rescues from th' infernal foe,
And full redemption will bestow.

4 Ye saints, assist my grateful tongue:
Ye angels, warble back my song:
For love like this demands the praise
Of heavenly harps and endless days.

184 *Rev.* v. 12-14.

WHAT equal honours shall we bring
To thee, O Lord our God, the Lamb,
When all the notes that angels sing
Are far inferior to thy name!

2 Worthy is He that once was slain,
The Prince of life, that groan'd and died;
Worthy to rise, and live, and reign
At his almighty Father's side.

3 Pow'r and dominion are His due,
Who stood condemn'd at Pilate's bar;
Wisdom belongs to Jesus too,
Though he was charged with madness here.

4 All riches are his native right,
Yet he sustain'd amazing loss;
To him ascribe eternal might,
Who left his weakness on the cross.

5 Honour immortal must be paid,
Instead of scandal and of scorn;
While glory shines around his head,
And a bright crown without a thorn.

6 Blessings for ever on the Lamb,
Who bore our sin, and curse, and pain;
Let angels sound his sacred name,
And ev'ry creature say, Amen!

973 *Morning & evening.*

MY God, how endless is thy love!
Thy gifts are every evening new;
And morning mercies from above,
Gently distil like early dew.

2 Thou spread'st the curtains of the night,
Great Guardian of my sleeping hours;
Thy sovereign word restores the light,
And quickens all my drowsy powers.

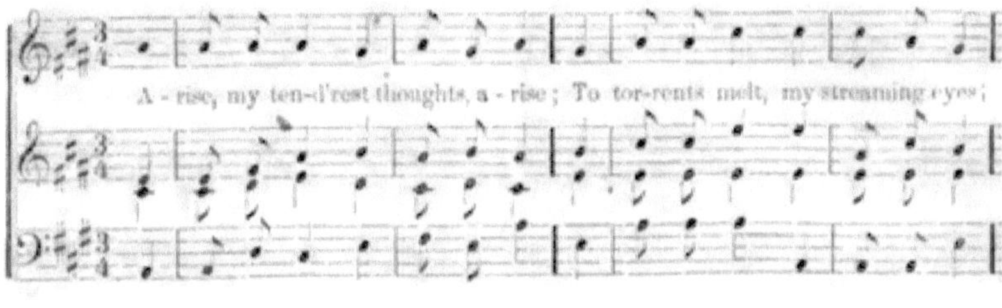

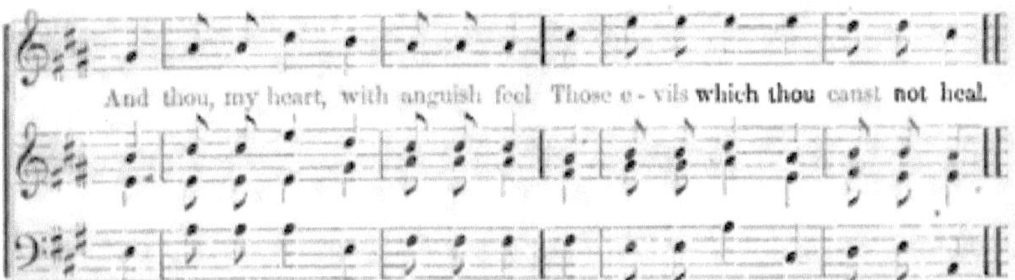

3 I yield myself to thy command,
To thee devote my nights and days:
Perpetual blessings from thy hand
Demand perpetual songs of praise.

362 *Grieving for the transgressors.*

ARISE, my tend'rest thoughts, arise;
To torrents melt, my streaming eyes;
And thou, my heart, with anguish feel
Those evils which thou canst not heal.

2 See human nature sunk in shame;
See scandals pour'd on Jesus' name;
The Father wounded through the Son;
The world abused, the soul undone.

3 See the short course of vain delight
Closing in everlasting night—
In flames, that no abatement know,
Though briny tears for ever flow.

4 My God, I feel the mournful scene;
My bowels yearn o'er dying men;
And fain my pity would reclaim,
And snatch the firebrands from the flame.

5 But feeble my compassion proves,
And can but weep where most it loves;
Thy own all-saving arm employ,
And turn these drops of grief to joy.

354 *"Now is the accepted time."*

WHILE life prolongs its precious light,
Mercy is found, and peace is given;
But soon, ah soon, approaching night
Shall blot out every hope of heaven.

2 While God invites, how bless'd the day!
How sweet the gospel's charming sound;
Come, sinners, haste, O haste away,
While yet a pard'ning God is found.

3 Soon, borne on time's most rapid wing,
Shall death command you to the grave,
Before his bar your spirits bring,
And none be found to hear or save.

4 In that lone land of deep despair
No Sabbath's heavenly light shall rise,
No God regard your bitter prayer,
No Saviour call you to the skies.

275 *Before receiving Appointments.*

JESUS, the truth and power divine,
Send forth these messengers of thine;
Their hands confirm, their hearts inspire,
And touch their lips with hallow'd fire.

2 Be thou their mouth and wisdom, Lord;
Thou, by the hammer of thy word,
The rocky hearts in pieces break,
And bid the sons of thunder speak.

3 To those who would their Lord embrace,
Give them to preach the word of grace,—
Sweetly their yielding bosoms move,
And melt them with the fire of love.

4 Let all with thankful hearts confess
Thy welcome messengers of peace,
Thy power in their report be found,
And let thy feet behind them sound.

793 *"Young men—exhort to be sober-minded."*

YOUNG men exhort, th' apostle said,
To cherish soberness of mind;
So when the bloom of life is fled,
Substantial fruit shall stay behind.

2 If God's eternal word of truth
Affect your hearts, your thoughts engage,
Its guardian power shall shield your youth,
Its consolations cheer your age.

3 Come, then, and choose religion's ways,
In life's sweet fragrancy and prime:
So peace shall crown your foll'wing days—
Peace, indestructible by time.

550 *Rejoicing in entire sanctification.*

QUICKEN'D with our immortal Head,
 Who daily, Lord, ascend with thee,
Redeem'd from sin, and free indeed,
 We taste our glorious liberty.

2 Saved from the fear of hell and death,
 With joy we seek the things above;
And all thy saints the spirit breathe
 Of power, sobriety, and love.

3 Power o'er the world, the fiend, and sin,
 We through thy gracious Spirit feel:
Full power the victory to win,
 And answer all thy righteous will.

4 Pure love to God thy members find,
 Pure love to every soul of man;
And in thy sober, spotless mind,
 Saviour, our heaven on earth we gain.

250 *Isaah. lii. 1—12.*

AWAKE, Jerusalem, awake!
 No longer in thy sins lie down;
The garment of salvation take,
 Thy beauty and thy strength put on.

2 Shake off the dust that blinds thy sight,
 And hides the promise from thine eyes;
Arise, and struggle into light,
 The great Deliverer calls, Arise!

3 Shake off the bands of sad despair,
 Sion, assert thy liberty;
Look up, thy broken heart prepare,
 And God shall set the captive free.

4 Vessels of mercy, sons of grace,
 Be purged from every sinful stain,
Be like your Lord, his word embrace,
 Nor bear his hallowed name in vain.

5 The Lord shall in your front appear,
 And lead the pompous triumph on;
His glory shall bring up the rear,
 And perfect what his grace begun.

253 *The Divine Institution.*

THE Saviour, when to heaven he rose,
 In splendid triumph o'er his foes,
Scatter'd his gifts on men below,
 And wide his royal bounties flow.

2 Hence sprang the *apostles'* honor'd name,
 Sacred beyond heroic fame;
Hence dictates the *prophetic* sage,
 And hence the *evangelic* page.

3 In lowlier forms, to bless our eyes,
 Pastors from hence and *teachers* rise;
Who, though with feebler rays they shine
 Still gild a long-extended line.

4 From Christ their varied gifts derive,
 And, fed by Christ, their graces live:
While guarded by his potent hand,
 'Midst all the rage of hell they stand.

5 So shall the bright succession run
 Through the last courses of the sun:
While unborn churches by their care
 Shall rise and flourish large and fair

6 Jesus our Lord, their hearts shall know,
 The spring whence all these blessings flow;
Pastors and people shout his praise,
 Through the long round of endless days.

259 *Angels of the church.*

DRAW near, O Son of God, draw near!
 Us with thy flaming eye behold;
Still in thy church vouchsafe t' appear,
 And let our candlestick be gold.

2 Still hold the stars in thy right hand,
And let them in thy lustre glow,
The lights of a benighted land,
The angels of thy church below.

3 Make good their apostolic boast,
Their high commission let them prove,
Be temples of the Holy Ghost,
And fill'd with faith, and hope, and love.

4 Their hearts from things of earth remove,
Sprinkle, them, Lord, from sin and fear;
Fix their affections all above,
And lay up all their treasures there.

5 Give them an ear to hear thy word;
Thou speakest to the churches now;
And let all tongues confess their Lord,
Let every knee to Jesus bow.

260 *Shepherds of the flock.*

SHEPHERD of Israel, thou dost keep,
With constant care, thy humble sheep;
By thee inferior pastors rise,
To feed our souls and bless our eyes.

2 To all thy churches such impart,
Modell'd by thy own gracious heart,
Whose courage, watchfulness, and love,
Men may attest and God approve.

3 Fed by their active, tender care,
Healthful may all thy sheep appear,
And, by their fair example led,
The way to Zion's pasture tread!

332 *Isaiah* lv. 1—3.

WHY seek ye that which is not bread,
Nor can your hungry souls sustain?
On ashes, husks, and air ye feed;
Ye spend your little all in vain.

2 In search of empty joys below,
Ye toil with unavailing strife:
Whither, ah! whither would ye go?
I have the words of endless life.

3 Hearken to me with earnest care,
And freely eat substantial food;
The sweetness of my mercy share,
And taste that I alone am good.

4 I bid you all my goodness prove:
My promises for all are free:
Come, taste the manna of my love,
And let your souls delight in me.

5 Your willing ear and heart incline,
My words believingly receive;
Quicken'd your souls by faith divine,
An everlasting life shall live.

625 *Doing all to the glory of God.*

O THOU, who camest from above,
The pure celestial fire t' impart,
Kindle a flame of sacred love,
On the mean altar of my heart.

2 There let it for thy glory burn,
With inextinguishable blaze,
And trembling to its source return,
In humble love, and fervent praise.

3 Jesus, confirm my heart's desire,
To work, and speak, and think, for thee;
Still let me guard the holy fire,
And still stir up thy gift in me.

4 Ready for all thy perfect will,
My acts of faith and love repeat,
Till death thy endless mercy seal,
And make the sacrifice complete.

651 *Patience.*

THOU Lamb of God, thou Prince of peace!
For thee my thirsty soul doth pine;
My longing heart implores thy grace,
O make me in thy likeness shine!

2 With fraudless, even, humble mind,
Thy will in all things may I see;
In love be every wish resign'd,
And hallow'd my whole heart to thee.

3 When pain o'er my weak flesh prevails,
With lamb-like patience arm my breast;
When grief my wounded soul assails,
In lowly meekness may I rest.

4 Close by thy side still may I keep,
Howe'er life's various current flow;
With steadfast eye mark every step,
And follow thee where'er thou go.

5 Thou, Lord, the dreadful fight hast won,
Alone thou hast the wine-press trod:
In me thy strength'ning grace be shown;
O may I conquer through thy blood!

6 So, when on Sion thou shalt stand,
And all heaven's host adore their King,
Shall I be found at thy right hand,
And, free from pain, thy glories sing.

43 *The rainbow round about the throne.*

LORD, round thy throne the rainbow shines,
Fair emblem of thy kind designs:
Bright pledge, that speaks thy cov'nant sure,
Long as thy kingdom shall endure.

2 No more shall deluges of wo
Thy new-created world o'erflow;
Jesus, our Sun, his beams displays,
And gilds the clouds with beauteous rays.

3 No gems so bright, no forms so fair;
Mercy and truth still triumph there:
Thy saints shall bless the peaceful sign,
When stars and suns forget to shine.

1055 *Doxology.*

TO Father, Son, and Holy Ghost,
The God whom earth and heaven adore,
Be glory, as it was of old,
Is now, and shall be evermore.

687 *Desiring to depart.*

WHILE on the verge of life I stand,
And view the scene on either hand,
My spirit struggles with my clay,
And longs to wing its flight away.

2 Where Jesus dwells my soul would be;
It faints my much-loved Lord to see:
Earth twine no more about my heart,
For 'tis far better to depart.

3 Come, ye angelic envoys, come,
And lead the willing pilgrim home;
Ye know the way to Jesus' throne,
Source of my joys and of your own.—

4 Lord, with these prospects full in sight,
I'll wait thy signal for my flight;
For, while thy service I pursue,
I find my heaven begun below.

39 *The God of all grace.*

ETERNAL depth of love divine,
In Jesus, God with us, display'd,
How bright thy beaming glories shine!
How wide thy healing streams are spread!

2 With whom dost thou delight to dwell?
Sinners, a vile and thankless race;
O God! what tongue aright can tell
How vast thy love, how great thy grace?

3 The dictates of thy sovereign will
With joy our grateful hearts receive;
All thy delight in us fulfil,
Lo! all we are to thee we give.

4 To thy sure love, thy tender care
Our flesh, soul, spirit, we resign;
O fix thy sacred presence there,
And seal th' abode for ever thine.

5 O King of glory, thy rich grace
Our feeble thought surpasses far;
Yea, e'en our crimes, though numberless,
Less numerous than thy mercies are.

6 Still, Lord, thy saving health display,
And arm our souls with heavenly zeal;
So fearless shall we urge our way
Through all the powers of earth and hell.

45 *Opening worship.*

O THOU, whom all thy saints adore,
We now with all thy saints agree,
And bow our inmost souls before
Thy glorious, awful majesty.

2 The King of nations we proclaim;
Who would not our great Sovereign fear?
We long t' experience all thy name,
And now we come to meet thee here.

3 We come, great God, to seek thy face,
And for thy loving-kindness wait;
And O, how dreadful is this place!
'Tis God's own house, 'tis heaven's gate!

4 Tremble our hearts to find thee nigh,
To thee our trembling hearts aspire;
And lo! we see descend from high
The pillar and the flame of fire.

5 Still let it on th' assembly stay,
And all the house with glory fill:
To Canaan's bounds point out the way,
And lead us to thy holy hill.

6 There let us all with Jesus stand,
And join the general church above;
And take our seats at thy right hand,
And sing thine everlasting love.

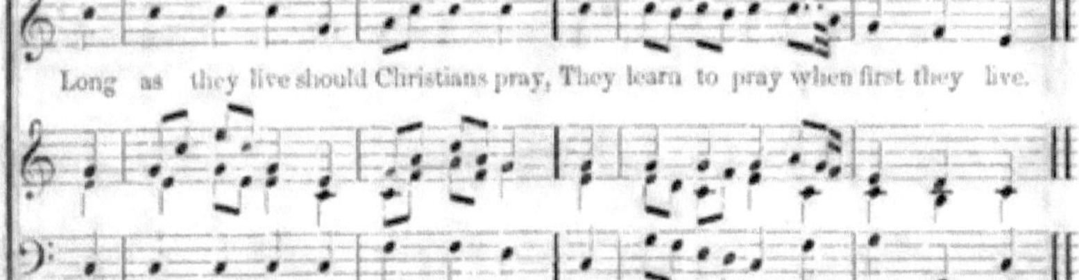

589 *Prayer.*

PRAYER is appointed to convey
The blessings God designs to give:
Long as they live should Christians pray,
They learn to pray when first they live.

2 If pain afflict, or wrongs oppress;
If cares distract, or fears dismay;
If guilt deject; if sin distress;—
In every case, still watch and pray.

3 'Tis prayer supports the soul that's weak:
Though thought be broken, language lame,
Pray if thou canst, or canst not speak:
But pray with faith in Jesus' name.

4 Depend on him; thou canst not fail:
Make all thy wants and wishes known;
Fear not; his merits must prevail:
Ask but in faith it shall be done.

724 *Funeral of a youth.* 1 *Peter* i. 24, 25.

THE morning flowers display their sweets,
And gay their silken leaves unfold,
As careless of the noontide heats,
As fearless of the evening cold.

2 Nipp'd by the wind's untimely blast,
Parch'd by the sun's directer ray,
The momentary glories waste,
The short-lived beauties die away.

3 So blooms the human face divine,
When youth its pride of beauty shows;
Fairer than spring the colours shine,
And sweeter than the virgin rose.

4 Or worn by slowly-rolling years,
Or broke by sickness in a day,
The fading glory disappears,
The short-lived beauties die away.

5 Yet these, new rising from the tomb,
With lustre brighter far shall shine,
Revive with ever-during bloom,
Safe from diseases and decline.

6 Let sickness blast, let death devour,
If heaven must recompense our pains.
Perish the grass, and fade the flower,
If firm the word of God remains.

758 *"Come, Lord Jesus."*

HEAD of thy church, whose Spirit fills,
And flows through every faithful soul,
Unites in mystic love, and seals
Them one, and sanctifies the whole.

2 "Come, Lord," thy glorious Spirit cries,
And souls beneath the altar groan;
"Come, Lord," the bride on earth replies,
"And perfect all our souls in one."

3 Pour out the promised gift on all,
Answer the universal "Come!"
The fulness of the Gentiles call,
And take thine ancient people home.

4 To thee let all the nations flow,
Let all obey the gospel word;
Let all their bleeding Saviour know,
Fill'd with the glory of the Lord.

744 *Psalm* cxvii.

FROM all that dwell below the skies,
Let the Creator's praise arise,—
Let the Redeemer's name be sung
Through every land, by every tongue.

2 Eternal are thy mercies, Lord,
Eternal truth attends thy word;
Thy praise shall sound from shore to shore,
Till suns shall rise and set no more.

228 *Psalm* xlvi. 6-11.

LET Zion in her King rejoice,
Though Satan rage, and kingdoms rise,
He utters his almighty voice,
The nations melt, the tumult dies.

2 The Lord of old for Jacob fought;
And Jacob's God is still our aid:
Behold the works his hand hath wrought!
What desolations he hath made!

3 From sea to sea, through all their shores,
He makes the noise of battle cease;
When from on high his thunder roars,
He awes the trembling world to peace.

4 He breaks the bow, he cuts the spear;
Chariots he burns with heavenly flame;
Keep silence, all the earth, and hear
The sound and glory of his name:

5 "Be still, and learn that I am God,
Exalted over all the lands;
I will be known and fear'd abroad;
For still my throne in Zion stands."

6 O Lord of hosts, almighty King!
While we so near thy presence dwell,
Our faith shall rest secure, and sing
Defiance to the gates of hell.

234 *Psalm* lxxxiv. 8-12.

GREAT God, attend while Zion sings
The joy that from thy presence springs;
To spend one day with thee on earth
Exceeds a thousand days of mirth.

2 Might I enjoy the meanest place
Within thy house, O God of grace,
Not tents of ease, nor thrones of power,
Should tempt my feet to leave thy door.

3 God is our sun, he makes our day:
God is our shield, he guards our way
From all th' assaults of hell and sin—
From foes without, and foes within.

4 All needful grace will God bestow,
And crown that grace with glory too;
He gives us all things, and withholds
No real good from upright souls.

5 O God our King, whose sovereign sway
The glorious hosts of heaven obey,
And devils at thy presence flee,
Bless'd is the man that trusts in thee.

262 *The minister's welcome.*

WE bid thee welcome in the name
Of Jesus, our exalted Head;—
Come as a servant,—so *He* came,
And we receive thee in his stead.

2 Come as a shepherd;—guard and keep
This fold from hell, and earth, and sin,
Nourish the lambs, and feed the sheep,
The wounded heal, the lost bring in.

3 Come as a watchman;—take thy stand
Upon the tower amidst the sky,
And when the sword comes on the land,
Call us to fight, or warn to fly

4 Come as an angel,—hence to guide
A band of pilgrims on their way,
That, safely walking at thy side,
We fail not, faint not, turn nor stray.

5 Come as a teacher,—sent from God,
Charged his whole counsel to declare;
Lift o'er our ranks the prophet's rod,
While we uphold thy hands with prayer.

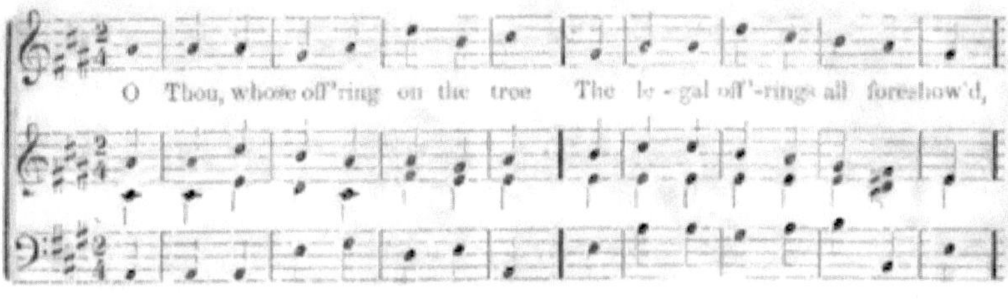

138 *The great Antitype.*

O THOU whose offering on the tree
The legal offerings all foreshow'd,
Borrow'd their whole effect from thee,
And drew their virtue from thy blood:

2 The blood of goats and bullocks slain
Could never for one sin atone;
To purge the guilty off'rer's stain,
Thine was the work, and thine alone.

3 Vain in themselves their duties were,
Their services could never please,
Till join'd with thine, and made to share
The merits of thy righteousness.

4 Forward they cast a faithful look
On thy approaching sacrifice;
And thence their pleasing savour took,
And rose accepted in the skies.

5 Those feeble types and shadows old
Are all in thee, the Truth, fulfill'd:
We in thy sacrifice behold
The substance of those rights reveal'd.

6 Thy meritorious suff'rings past,
We see by faith to us brought back,
And on thy grand oblation cast,
Its saving benefits partake.

201 *The promised Comforter.*

JESUS, we on the words depend,
Spoken by thee while present here,
"The Father in my name shall send
The Holy Ghost, the Comforter."

2 That promise made to Adam's race,
Now, Lord, in us, e'en us, fulfil;
And give the Spirit of thy grace,
To teach us all thy perfect will.

3 That heavenly Teacher of mankind,
That Guide infallible, impart,
To bring thy sayings to our mind,
And write them on our faithful heart.

4 That peace of God, that peace of thine,
O might he now to us bring in,
And fill our souls with power divine,
And make an end of fear and sin!

5 The length and breadth of love reveal,
The height and depth of Deity;
And all the sons of glory seal,
And change, and make us all like thee.

54 *Psalm xxiv. 1—6.*

THE earth, with all her fulness, owns
Jehovah for her sovereign Lord;
The countless myriads of her sons
Rose into being at his word.

2 His word did out of nothing call
The world, and founded all that is;
Launch'd on the floods this solid ball,
And fix'd it in the floating seas.

3 But who shall quit this low abode,
Who shall ascend the heavenly place,
And stand upon the mount of God,
And see his Maker face to face?

4 The man whose hands and heart are clean
That blessed portion shall receive;
Whoe'er by grace is saved from sin,
Hereafter shall in glory live.

5 He shall obtain the starry crown;
And, number'd with the saints above,
The God of his salvation own,
The God of his salvation love.

RETREAT. L. M.

HASTINGS.

Retard.

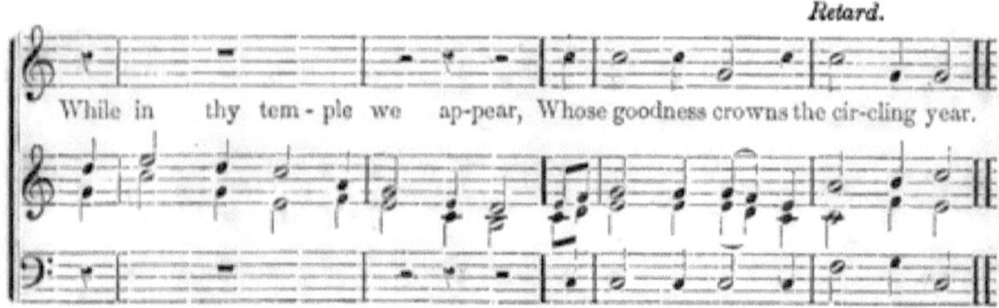

809 *"Thou crownest the year with thy goodness."*

ETERNAL Source of every joy,
Well may thy praise our lips employ,
While in thy temple we appear,
Whose goodness crowns the circling year.

2 The flowery spring, at thy command,
Embalms the air, and paints the land;
The summer rays with vigour shine,
To raise the corn and cheer the vine.

3 Thy hand in autumn richly pours,
Through all our coasts, redundant stores;
And winters, soften'd by thy care,
No more a face of horror wear.

4 Seasons, and months, and weeks, and days,
Demand successive songs of praise;
Still be the cheerful homage paid
With op'ning light, and ev'ning shade.

5 Here in thy house shall incense rise,
As circling sabbaths bless our eyes;
Still we will make thy mercies known
Around thy board, and round our own.

6 O may our more harmonious tongue
In worlds unknown pursue the song;
And in those brighter courts adore,
Where days and years revolve no more!

791 *For a College Commencement. Psalm lxxviii. 1—7.*

HEAR ye my law, my people, hear;
Lend to my words the list'ning ear;
My mouth shall lofty lore unfold,—
My lips dark sentences of old.

2 Such truths to us our sires have shown,
Our ears have heard, our hearts have known,
Nor shall our lips forbear to trace
The image for our future race:

3 But times remote,—the latter days,—
The story of Jehovah's praise
Shall hear; and ponder with delight
His wondrous deeds, his arm of might.

4 His law to Jacob he reveal'd,
His covenant with Israel seal'd,
And gave our sires the charge divine,
In trust for their succeeding line;

5 That year to year, and age to age,
Might safe convey the sacred page,
And still his truth perpetual run,
Transmitted down from sire to son:

6 That on the arm of power divine
Sons yet unborn might still recline;
Nor e'er forget the works of God,
Nor e'er forsake his guiding rod.

697 *Heaven. Psalm xvii. 15.*

WHAT sinners value, I resign;
Lord, 'tis enough that thou art mine;
I shall behold thy blissful face,
And stand complete in righteousness.

2 This life 's a dream, an empty show;
But the bright world to which I go
Hath joys substantial and sincere:
When shall I wake and find me there?

3 O glorious hour! O bless'd abode!
I shall be near, and like my God;
And flesh and sin no more control
The sacred pleasures of the soul.

4 My flesh shall slumber in the ground,
Till the last trumpet's joyful sound;
Then burst the chains with sweet surprise,
And in my Saviour's image rise.

839 *Psalm lx. 9—12.*

WHO shall our troops to vict'ry lead?
What arm our cause triumphant plead?
Through the strong fortress bid them break,
And all their ancient courage wake?

2 Will not our God his arm display,
Though long beneath thy wrath we lay?
Will not the Lord our help prepare,
Though long denied thy guardian care?

3 Rise, rise, Jehovah, God of hosts!
Vain is the strength the nation boasts;
Vain are our fleets, our armies vain,
Without thy favour to sustain.

4 Bold in our God we'll onward go,
Assured of vict'ry o'er the foe:
His word our conquest can complete,
And lay the foe beneath our feet.

856 *General Thanksgiving.*

WE thank thee, Lord of heaven and earth,
Who hast preserved us from our birth;
Redeem'd us oft from death and dread,
And with thy gifts our table spread.

2 We thank thee for thy still small voice,
Which oft has check'd our wayward choice;
For life preserved, for senses clear,
And for our friendships, doubly dear.

3 Thy providence has been our stay,
When other helps were far away;
Our constant guide through every stage
From infancy to riper age.

4 How shall we half our task fulfil?
We thank thee for thy mind and will,
For present joys, for blessings past,
And for the hope of heaven at last.

860 *Embarking.*

INFINITE God! thy greatness spann'd
These heavens, and meted out the skies;
Lo! in the hollow of thy hand
The measured waters sink and rise!

2 Thee to perfection who can tell!
Earth and her sons beneath thee lie,
Lighter than dust within thy scale,
And less than nothing in thine eye.

3 Yet, in thy Son, divinely great,
We claim thy providential care;
Boldly we stand before thy seat—
Our Advocate hath placed us there.

4 With him we are gone up on high,
Since he is ours, and we are his;
With him we reign above the sky,
We walk upon our subject seas.

867 *Psalm cvii. 23—32.*

WHO to the sea in ships descend,
And mid the waves their business tend,
There see Jehovah's works abound,
His wonders in the vast profound.

2 He speaks. The tempest's breath is stirr'd;
The swelling billows hear his word:
They climb to heaven; they sink to hell;
Danger and wo their spirit quell.

3 They stagger, and, like drunkards, reel,
Baffled the seaman's art they feel:
They to Jehovah raise their cry,
He saves them from their agony.

4 The stormy deep he deigns to soothe,
The agitated wave is smooth,
They hail the end of all their woes,
And in the destined port repose.

5 O praise Jehovah for his grace,
His wonders to our wretched race!
His mercies to his church proclaim,
And mid the elders praise his name!

759 *Missionary meeting.*

ASSEMBLED at thy great command,
Before thy face, dread King, we stand;
The voice that marshall'd every star
Has call'd thy people from afar.

2 We meet through distant lands to spread
The truth for which the martyrs bled;
Along the line—to either pole—
The anthem of thy praise to roll.

3 Our prayers assist; accept our praise;
Our hopes revive; our courage raise;
Our counsels aid; to each impart
The single eye, the faithful heart.

4 Forth with thy chosen heralds come;
Recall the wand'ring spirits home:
From Zion's mount send forth the sound,
To spread the spacious earth around.

861 *The seaman's Friend.*

O THOU whose wisdom gives a path
To man upon the trackless sea,
Whose power controls the ocean's wrath,
We raise our fervent prayers to thee:—
To thee whom once in human form
A bark of Galilee convey'd;
Whose voice assuaged the raging storm
When sinking seamen sought thine aid.

2 O, when the sailor leaves the home
A wife or mother's love hath blest,
And spreads his sail through climes to roam
Where storms draw life from ocean's breast;
Be near his bark in danger's hour,
To hear the prayer that shall ascend:
And guard him from the tempest's power,
And be, as erst, the SEAMAN'S FRIEND.

3 But more, when passion's gust would harm,
Or pleasure's smooth, deceitful flood,
Be near to break the syren's charm;
And be the tempted sailor's God.
Teach him to steer by Bethleh'm's Star
That brightest star of Heaven's host,
That shines and guides from danger far,
Though every other light be lost.

MENDON. L. M.

458 *Opening worship.*

JESUS, thou everlasting King
Accept the tribute which we bring;
Accept thy well-deserved renown,
And wear our praises as thy crown.

2 Let every act of worship be
Like our espousals, Lord, to thee—
Like the bless'd hour, when from above
We first received the pledge of love.

3 The gladness of that happy day,
O may it ever, ever stay!
Nor let our faith forsake its hold,
Nor hope decline, nor love grow cold!

4 Each foll'wing minute as it flies,
Increase thy praise, improve our joys,
Till we are raised to sing thy name
At the great supper of the Lamb.

488 *"Our rejoicing is this"—*

LORD, how secure and bless'd are they
Who feel the joys of pardon'd sin!
Should storms of wrath shake earth and sea,
Their minds have heaven and peace within.

2 The day glides sweetly o'er their heads,
Made up of innocence and love;
And soft and silent as the shades
Their nightly minutes gently move.

3 Quick as their thoughts their joys come on
But fly not half so fast away;
Their souls are ever bright as noon,
And calm as summer evenings be.

4 How oft they look to th' heavenly hills,
Where groves of living pleasures grow!
And longing hopes and cheerful smiles
Sit undisturbed upon their brow.

5 They scorn to seek our golden toys,
But spend the day and share the night
In numbering o'er the richer joys
That heaven prepares for their delight.

489 *Luke xv. 10.*

WHO can describe the joys that rise
Through all the courts of paradise,
To see a prodigal return,
To see an heir of glory born!

2 With joy the Father doth approve
The fruit of his eternal love;
The Son with joy looks down and sees
The purchase of his agonies.

3 The Spirit takes delight to view
The holy soul he form'd anew;
And saints and angels join to sing
The growing empire of their King.

205 *Pentecost.*

LORD, we believe to us and ours
The apostolic promise given;
We wait the pentecostal powers,
The Holy Ghost sent down from heaven.

2 Ah! leave us not to mourn below,
Or long for thy return to pine;
Now, Lord, the Comforter bestow,
And fix in us the Guest divine.

3 Assembled here with one accord,
Calmly we wait the promised grace,
The purchase of our dying Lord
Come, Holy Ghost, and fill the place.

1054 *Doxology.*

PRAISE God, from whom all blessings flow;
Praise him, all creatures here below;
Praise him above, ye heavenly host;
Praise Father, Son, and Holy Ghost.

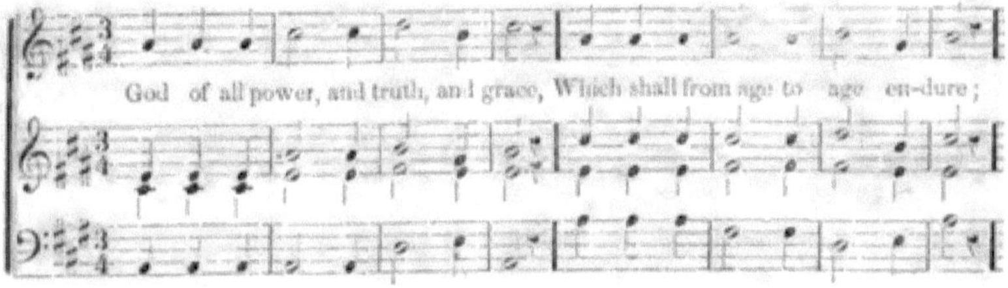

518 *Ezekiel* xxxvi. 23—25.

GOD of all power, and truth, and grace,
  Which shall from age to age endure;
Whose word, when heaven and earth shall pass,
  Remains, and stands for ever sure:

2 Calmly to thee my soul looks up,
  And waits thy promises to prove,
The object of my steadfast hope,
  The seal of thy eternal love.

3 That I thy mercy may proclaim,
  That all mankind thy truth may see,
Hallow thy great and glorious name,
  And perfect holiness in me.

4 Thy sanctifying Spirit pour,
  To quench my thirst, and make me clean:
Now, Father, let the gracious shower
  Descend, and make me pure from sin.

5 The Lord shall clear his way through all;
  Whate'er obstructs, obstructs in vain;
The vale shall rise, the mountain fall,
  Crooked be straight, and rugged plain.

6 The glory of the Lord display'd
  Shall all mankind together view,
And what his mouth in truth hath said,
  His own almighty hand shall do.

254 *Isaiah* xl. 1—5.

COMFORT, ye ministers of grace,
  Comfort the people of your Lord,
O lift ye up the fallen race,
  And cheer them by the gospel word.

2 Go into every nation, go,
  Speak to their trembling hearts, and cry
Glad tidings unto all we show:
  Jerusalem, thy God is nigh.

3 Hark! in the wilderness a cry,
  A voice that loudly calls, Prepare;
Prepare your hearts, for God is nigh,
  And means to make his entrance there!

4 The Lord your God shall quickly come;
  Sinners, repent, the call obey;
Open your hearts to make him room;
  Ye desert souls, prepare his way.

461 *The work of faith.*

AUTHOR of faith, eternal Word,
  Whose Spirit breathes the active flame,
Faith, like its finisher and Lord,
  To-day, as yesterday, the same:

2 To thee our humble hearts aspire,
  And ask the gift unspeakable;
Increase in us the kindled fire,
  In us the work of faith fulfil.

3 By faith we know thee strong to save:
  (Save us, a present Saviour thou!)
Whate'er we hope, by faith we have;
  Future and past subsisting now.

4 To him that in thy name believes,
  Eternal life with thee is given;
Into himself he all receives,—
  Pardon, and holiness, and heaven.

5 The things unknown to feeble sense,
  Unseen by reason's glimm'ring ray,
With strong, commanding evidence,
  Their heavenly origin display.

6 Faith lends its realizing light,
  The clouds disperse, the shadows fly;
Th' Invisible appears in sight,
  And God is seen by mortal eye.

CEPHAS. L. M. Double.

49 *Psalm xix. 1—6.*

THE spacious firmament on high,
With all the blue ethereal sky,
And spangled heavens, (a shining frame,)
Their great Original proclaim:
Th' unwearied sun from day to day
Doth his Creator's power display,
And publishes to every land
The work of an almighty hand.

2 Soon as the evening shades prevail,
The moon takes up the wondrous tale,
And nightly to the list'ning earth
Repeats the story of her birth:
While all the stars that round her burn,
And all the planets in their turn,
Confirm the tidings as they roll,
And spread the truth from pole to pole.

3 What though in solemn silence, all
Move round the dark terrestrial ball;
What though no real voice nor sound
Amid the radiant orbs be found;
In reason's ear they all rejoice,
And utter forth a glorious voice,
For ever singing as they shine,
"The hand that made us is divine."

1023 *For a Servant.* 1 Tim. vi. 1, 2.

WITH a believing master bless'd,
His equal in the Saviour's eyes,
His brother in the Lord confess'd,
Shall I neglect him, or despise—
Forget the diff'rence of estate,
And scorn at his commands to bow;
As high and low, as small and great,
Were all upon a level now?

2 Rather I would, with warmer zeal,
My just fidelity approve;
Gladly perform his utmost will,
And love whom God is pleased to love;—
Worthy of double honor deem
The heir of joys that never end;
And serve and cordially esteem,
Whom Jesus deigns to call his friend.

862 *Star of Bethlehem.*

WHEN marshall'd on the nightly plain,
The glitt'ring host bestud the sky,
One star alone of all the train
Can fix the sinner's wand'ring eye.
Hark! hark! to God the chorus breaks
From every host, from every gem;
But one alone the Saviour speaks,
It is the Star of Bethlehem.

2 Once on the raging seas I rode,
The storm was loud, the night was dark,
The ocean yawn'd, and rudely blow'd
The wind that toss'd my found'ring bark.
Deep horror then my vitals froze;
Death-struck, I ceased the tide to stem:
When suddenly a star arose,
It was the Star of Bethlehem.

3 It was my guide, my light, my all;
It bade my dark foreboding cease;
And, through the storm and danger's thrall
It led me to the port of peace.
Now, safely moor'd, my perils o'er,
I'll sing, first in night's diadem,
For ever, and for evermore,
The Star!—the Star of Bethlehem!

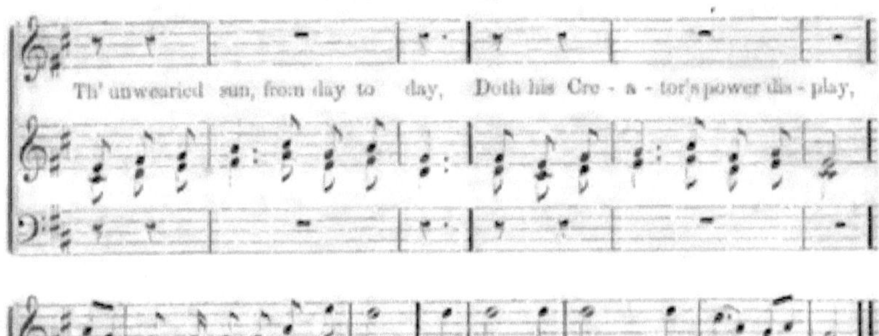
Th' unwearied sun, from day to day, Doth his Cre - a - tor's power dis - play,

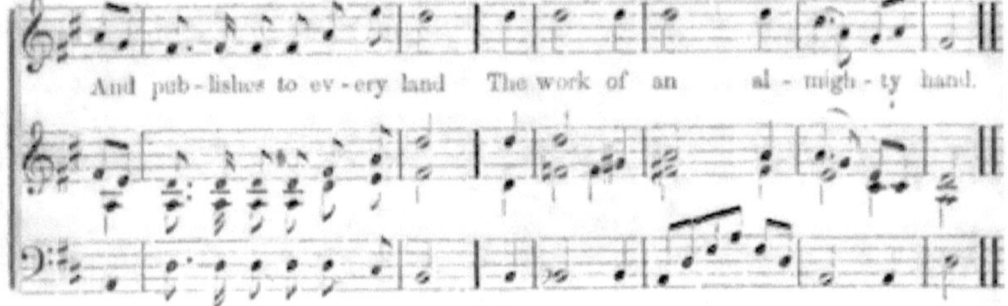
And pub - lishes to ev - ery land The work of an al - migh - ty hand.

411 *Self-despair.*

LORD, I despair myself to heal;
I see my sin, but cannot feel,—
I cannot, till thy Spirit blow,
And bid th' obedient waters flow.

2 'Tis thine a heart of flesh to give;
Thy gifts I only can receive;
Here, then, to thee I all resign,
To draw, redeem, and seal—are thine.

3 With simple faith on thee I call;
My light, my life, my Lord, my all:
I wait the moving of the pool;
I wait the word that speaks me whole.

4 Speak, gracious Lord, my sickness cure,
Make my infected nature pure:
Peace, righteousness, and joy, impart,
And pour thyself into my heart!

1021 *For a Master.*

MASTER supreme! I look to thee
For grace and wisdom from above;
Vested with thy authority,
Endue me with thy patient love.
That, taught according to thy will,
To rule my family aright,
I may th' appointed charge fulfil,
With all my heart, and all my might.

2 Inferiors, as a sacred trust,
I from the sovereign Lord receive,
That what is suitable and just,
Impartial I to all may give;—
O'erlook them with a guardian eye;
From vice and wickedness restrain;
Mistakes and lesser faults pass by,
And govern with a looser rein.

3 The servant faithful and discreet,
Gentle to him, and good, and mild,
Him I would tenderly entreat,
And scarce distinguish from a child.
Yet let me not my place forsake,
Th' occasion of his stumbling prove,
The servant to my bosom take,
Or mar him by familiar love.

4 Order, if some invert, confound,
Their Lord's authority betray,—
I hearken to the gospel sound,
And trace the providential way.
As far from abjectness as pride,
With condescending dignity,
Jesus, I make thy word my guide,
And keep the post assign'd by thee.

5 O could I emulate the zeal
Thou dost to thy poor servants bear!
The troubles, griefs, and burden feel,
Of souls entrusted to my care!—
In daily prayer to God commend
The souls whom Christ expired to save,
And think how soon my sway may end,
And all be equal in the grave!

1049 *Doxology.*

THE peace which God alone reveals,
And by his word of grace imparts,
Which only the believer feels,
Direct, and keep, and cheer our hearts;
And may the holy Three in One,
The Father, Word, and Comforter,
Pour an abundant blessing down
On every soul assembled here.

149 *Psalm lxviii. 17, 18.*

LORD, when thou didst ascend on high,
Ten thousand angels fill'd the sky;
Those heavenly guards around thee wait,
Like chariots that attend thy state.

2 Not Sinai's mountain could appear
More glorious, when the Lord was there;
While he pronounced his dreadful law,
And struck the chosen tribes with awe.

3 How bright the triumph none can tell,
When the rebellious powers of hell,
That thousand souls had captive made,
Were all in chains—like captives—led.

4 Raised by his Father to the throne,
He sent the promised Spirit down,
With gifts and grace for rebel men,
That God might dwell on earth again.

193 *Wonders of the Cross.*

NATURE with open volume stands
To speak her Maker's praise abroad;
And every labour of his hands
Shows something worthy of a God.

2 But in the grace that rescued man
His brightest form of glory shines;
Here, on the cross, 'tis fairest drawn
In precious blood and crimson lines.

3 O! the sweet wonders of that cross,
Where God, the Saviour, loved and died!
Her noblest life my spirit draws
From his dear wounds and bleeding side.

4 I would for ever speak his name,
In sounds to mortal ears unknown;
With angels join to praise the Lamb,
And worship at his Father's throne.

257 *Ambassadors for Christ.*

GOD, the offended God most high,
Ambassadors to rebels sends;
His messengers his place supply,
And Jesus begs us to be friends.

2 Us, in the stead of Christ, they pray,
Us, in the stead of God, entreat,
To cast our arms, our sins away,
And find forgiveness at his feet.

3 Our God in Christ! thine embassy,
And proffer'd mercy, we embrace;
And gladly reconciled to thee,
Thy condescending mercy praise.

4 Poor debtors, by our Lord's request,
A full acquittance we receive!
And criminals, with pardon blest,
We, at our Judge's instance, live!

521 *Ezekiel, xxxvi. 31, 32.*

HOLY, and true, and righteous Lord,
I wait to prove thy perfect will.
Be mindful of thy gracious word,
And stamp me with thy Spirit's seal.

2 Open my faith's interior eye;
Display thy glory from above;
And all I am shall sink and die,
Lost in astonishment and love!

3 Confound, o'erpower me by thy grace;
I would be by myself abhorr'd
All might, all majesty, all praise,
All glory, be to Christ my Lord!

4 Now let me gain perfection's height,
Now let me into nothing fall!
As less than nothing in thy sight;
And feel that Christ is *all* in *all!*

STETTINIUS. L. M.

L. C. EVERETT.

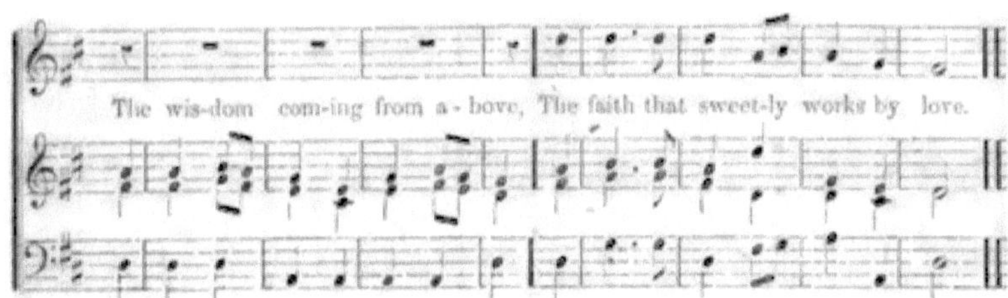

480 *Proverbs iii. 13-18.*

HAPPY the man that finds the grace,
  The blessing of God's chosen race,
The wisdom coming from above,
The faith that sweetly works by love.

2 Happy; beyond description, he
Who knows "the Saviour died for me!"
The gift unspeakable obtains,
And heavenly understanding gains.

3 Wisdom divine! who tells the price
Of wisdom's costly merchandise?
Wisdom to silver we prefer,
And gold is dross compared to her.

4 Her hands are fill'd with length of days,
True riches, and immortal praise—
Riches of Christ on all bestow'd,
And honour that descends from God.

5 To purest joys she all invites,
Chaste, holy, spiritual delights;
Her ways are ways of pleasantness,
And all her flowery paths are peace.

6 Happy the man who wisdom gains,
Thrice happy who his guest retains:
He owns, and shall for ever own,
Wisdom, and Christ, and heaven, are one.

509 *The promised land of perfect love.*

IF, Lord, I have acceptance found
  With thee, or favour in thy sight,
Still with thy grace and truth surround,
  And arm me with thy Spirit's might.

2 O may I hear thy warning voice,
  And timely fly from danger near,
With rev'rence unto thee rejoice,
  And love thee with a filial fear.

3 Still hold my soul in second life,
  And suffer not my feet to slide:
Support me in the glorious strife,
  And comfort me on every side.

4 O give me faith, and faith's increase;
  Finish the work begun in me,
Preserve my soul in perfect peace,
  And let me always rest on thee!

5 O let thy gracious Spirit guide
  And bring me to the promised land,
Where righteousness and peace reside,
  And all submit to love's command.

6 A land where milk and honey flow,
  And springs of pure delights arise,
Delights which I shall shortly know,
  When I regain my paradise.

507 *"This is the will of God—"*

HE wills that I should holy be:
  That holiness I long to feel;
That full divine conformity
  To all my Saviour's righteous will.

2 See, Lord, the travail of thy soul,
  Accomplish'd in the change of mine;
And plunge me, every whit made whole,
  In all the depths of love divine!

519 *Ezekiel xxxvi. 26-28.*

GIVE me a new, a perfect heart,
  From doubt, and fear, and sorrow free
The mind which was in Christ impart,
  And let my spirit cleave to thee.

2 O take this heart of stone away!
  Thy sway it doth not, cannot own:
In me no longer let it stay;
  O take away this heart of stone!

3 O that I now, from sin releast,
  Thy word may to the utmost prove
Enter into the promised rest,
  The Canaan of thy perfect love.

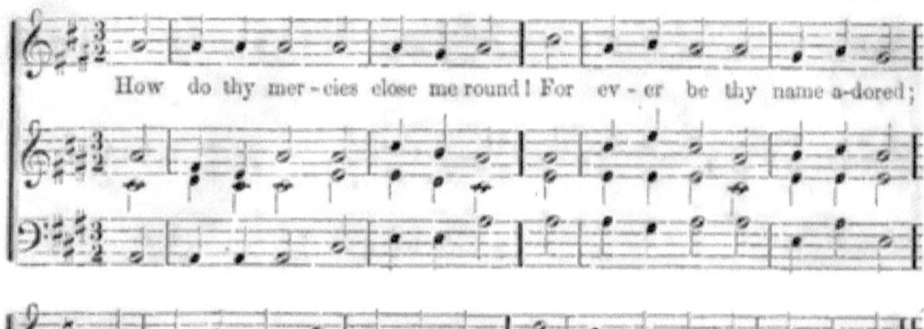

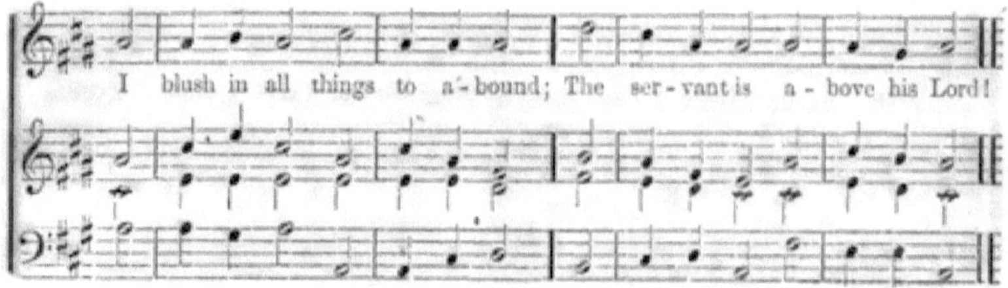

968 *Evening.*

HOW do thy mercies close me round!
For ever be thy name adored;
I blush in all things to abound;
The servant is above his Lord!

2 Inured to poverty and pain,
A suff'ring life my Master led;
The Son of God, the Son of man,
He had not where to lay his head.

3 But, lo! a place he hath prepared
For me, whom watchful angels keep;
Yea, he himself becomes my guard;
He smooths my bed, and gives me sleep.

4 Jesus protects; my fears, begone!
What can the Rock of ages move!
Safe in thy arms I lay me down,
Thy everlasting arms of love!

972 *Sabbath evening.*

THE holy song hath died away,
But still it vibrates through our hearts:
And we return, though fain to stay;
Each to his family departs.

2 Now for the household sacrifice;
The evening rite as incense spread,
And let our blameless hands arise,
Doubting and wrath for ever fled.

3 O 'tis an hour of holy calm!
Our tabernacle is in peace;
To thee shall swell the cheerful psalm,
Teach us thy word, our faith increase.

4 Good, though not best, 'tis to be here,
Soon no such diff'rence shall there be,
"True sanctu'ry," within thy sphere
Shall worship "the whole family."

982 *Birth of a child.*

FATHER of all, by whom we are,
For whom was made whatever is;
Who hast entrusted to our care
A candidate for glorious bliss:

2 Poor worms of earth, to thee we cry,
For grace to guide what grace has given,
We ask for wisdom from on high,
To train our infant up for heaven.

3 Him let us tend severely kind,
As guardians of his giddy youth;
As set to form his tender mind,
By principles of virtuous truth;—

4 To fit his soul for heavenly grace;
Discharge the Christian parent's part;
And keep him, till thy love takes place,
And Jesus rises in his heart.

996 *Household consecration.*

FATHER of men, thy care we bless,
Which crowns our families with peace;
From thee they spring; and by thy hand
They are, and shall be still, sustained.

2 To God, most worthy to be praised,
Be our domestic altars raised;
Who, Lord of heaven, yet deigns to come,
And sanctify our humblest home.

3 To thee may each united house
Morning and night present its vows:
Our servants there, and rising race,
Be taught thy precepts, and thy grace.

4 So may each future age proclaim
The honours of thy glorious name;
And each succeeding race remove
To join the family above.

267 *Ministerial fidelity.*

SHALL I, for fear of feeble man,
The Spirit's course in me restrain?
Or, undismay'd in deed and word,
Be a true witness for my Lord?

2 Awed by a mortal's frown, shall I
Conceal the word of God most high?
How then before thee shall I dare
To stand, or how thine anger bear?

3 Shall I, to soothe th' unholy throng,
Soften thy truth, and smooth my tongue
To gain earth's gilded toys, or flee
The cross endured, my Lord, by thee?

4 What then is he whose scorn I dread,
Whose wrath or hate makes me afraid?
A man! an heir of death! a slave
To sin! a bubble on the wave!

5 Yea, let men rage; since thou wilt spread
Thy shad'wing wings around my head:
Since in all pain thy tender love
Will still my sure refreshment prove.

1000 *Noon.*

FULL speed along the world's highway
By crowds of eager trav'lers trod,
My soul, my soul, a moment stay,
To hold communion here with God.

2 He spake with Abrah'm at the oak,
He call'd Elisha from the plough,
David he from the sheepfolds took,—
Thy day, thine hour of grace, is now.

3 Earth, with thy vanities, depart!
My God, I stand alone with thee;
Thine eye is looking on my heart;—
O what a noon is risen on me!

1003 *Midnight.*

MY God, I now from sleep awake,
The sole possession of me take;
From midnight terrors me secure,
And guard my heart from thoughts impure.

2 Bless'd angels, while we silent lie,
You hallelujahs sing on high;
You, joyful, hymn the Ever-blest,
Before the throne, and never rest.

3 I with your choir celestial join,
In off'ring up a hymn divine;
With you in heaven I hope to dwell,
And bid the night and world farewell.

4 Lord, lest the tempter me surprise,
Watch over thine own sacrifice;
All loose, all idle thoughts cast out,
And make my very dreams devout.

5 Praise God, from whom all blessings flow,
Praise him, all creatures here below;
Praise him above, ye heavenly host;
Praise Father, Son, and Holy Ghost!

1001 *Psalm lxiii.*

O GOD, my God, my all thou art!
Ere shines the dawn of rising day,
Thy sovereign light within my heart,
Thy all-enlivening power display.

2 For thee my thirsty soul doth pant,
While in this desert land I live;
And hungry as I am, and faint,
Thy love alone can comfort give.

3 In a dry land, behold I place
My whole desire on thee, my Lord,
And more I joy to gain thy grace,
Than all earth's treasures can afford.

4 More dear than life itself, thy love
My heart and tongue shall still employ,
And to declare thy praise will prove
My peace, my glory, and my joy.

5 In blessing thee with grateful songs,
My happy life shall glide away;
The praise that to thy name belongs,
Hourly with lifted hands I'll pay.

6 Abundant sweetness while I sing
Thy love, my ravish'd heart o'erflows;
Secure in thee, my God and King,
Of glory that no period knows.

7 Thy name, O God, upon my bed,
Dwells on my lips, and fires my thought:
With trembling awe, in midnight shade,
I muse on all thy hands have wrought.

8 In all I do I feel thine aid;
Therefore thy greatness will I sing,
O God, who bidd'st my heart be glad,
Beneath the shadow of thy wing!

9 My soul draws nigh and cleaves to thee
Then let or earth or hell assail,
Thy mighty hand shall set me free;
For whom thou sav'st, he ne'er shall fail.

957 *Morning. Psalm iii. 5—8.*

TIRED with the burdens of the day,
To God I raised an evening cry;
He heard when I began to pray,
And his almighty help was nigh.

2 Supported by his heavenly aid,
I laid me down, and slept secure;
Not death should make my heart afraid,
Though I should wake and rise no more

3 But God sustain'd me all the night:
Salvation doth to God belong:
He raised my head to see the light,
And make his praise my morning song.

1055 *Doxology.*

TO Father, Son, and Holy Ghost,
The God whom earth and heaven ado
Be glory, as it was of old,
Is now, and shall be evermore.

890 *For the mourners in Zion.*

O LET the pris'ners' mournful cries
As incense in thy sight appear!
Their humble wailings pierce the skies,
If haply they may feel thee near.

2 The captive exiles make their moans,
From sin impatient to be free:
Call home, call home thy banish'd ones!
Lead captive their captivity!

3 Show them the blood that bought their peace,
The anchor of their steadfast hope,
And bid their guilty terrors cease,
And bring the ransom'd pris'ners up.

4 Out of the deep regard their cries,
The fallen raise, the mourners cheer;
O Sun of righteousness, arise,
And scatter all their doubt and fear!

5 Pity the day of feeble things;
O gather every halting soul!
And drop salvation from thy wings,
And make the contrite sinner whole.

243 *The primitive Church.*

O MIGHT my lot be cast with these;
The least of Jesus' witnesses:
O that my Lord would count me meet
To wash his dear disciples' feet.

2 This only thing do I require:
Thou know'st 'tis all my heart's desire,
Freely what I receive to give,
The servant of thy church to live;—

3 After my lowly Lord to go,
And wait upon thy saints below;
Enjoy the grace to angels given,
And serve the royal heirs of heaven.

4 Lord, if I now thy drawings feel,
And ask according to thy will,
Confirm the prayer, the seal impart,
And speak the answer to my heart.

5 Tell me, or thou shalt never go,
"Thy prayer is heard; it shall be so:"
The word hath pass'd thy lips, and I
Shall with thy people live and die.

881 *Admission into the church.*

BRETHREN in Christ, and well beloved,
To Jesus and his servants dear,
Enter, and show yourselves approved;
Enter, and find that God is here.

2 Welcome from earth: lo, the right hand
Of fellowship to you we give!
With open hearts and hands we stand,
And you in Jesus' name receive.

3 Say, are your hearts resolved as ours?
Then let them burn with sacred love,
Then let them taste the heavenly powers,
Partakers of the joys above.

4 Jesus, attend; thyself reveal!
Are we not met in thy great name?
Thee in the midst we wait to feel,
We wait to catch the spreading flame.

5 Truly our fellowship below,
With thee and with the Father is;
In thee eternal life we know,
And heaven's unutterable bliss.

1054 *Doxology.*

PRAISE God, from whom all blessings flow;
Praise him all creatures here below;
Praise him above, ye heavenly host;
Praise Father, Son, and Holy Ghost.

FARMER. L. M.

From "New Thes. Musicus."

896 *"In the bond of peace."*

GIVER of peace and unity,
  Send down thy mild, pacific Dove;
We all shall then in one agree,
  And breathe the spirit of thy love.

2 We all shall think and speak the same
  Delightful lesson of thy grace,
One undivided Christ proclaim,
  And jointly glory in thy praise.

3 O let us take a softer mould,
  Blended and gather'd into thee;
Under one shepherd make one fold,
  Where all is love and harmony.

4 Regard thine own eternal prayer,
  And send a peaceful answer down,
To us thy Father's name declare;
  Unite and perfect us in one!

5 So shall the world believe and know
  That God hath sent thee from above,
When thou art seen in us below
  And every soul displays thy love.

906 *At the expulsion of a member.*

LOVE is a pure and heavenly flame,
  And much regards a brother's name;
  It hopeth all things and believes,
  Nor easily a charge receives.

2 Yet if it could of sin allow,
  And not a brother disavow,
  Who has the Christian name disgraced,—
  Affection then would be misplaced.

3 Yet it will strive, and hope, and wait,
  Th' offender still to reinstate;
  And when a broken heart it views,
  Its former friendship it renews.

4 Thus, Lord, would we the grace possess,
  And thus fulfil all righteousness;
  And while we now a friend disown,
  Do thou the painful duty crown.

5 Lead him to mourn his follies past,
  Afresh may he thy mercy taste,
  And should thy grace his soul restore,
  We'll own and love him as before.

914 *Opening the exercises.*

WHAT various hind'rances we meet,
  In coming to a mercy seat!
  Yet who that knows the worth of prayer,
  But wishes to be often there?

2 Prayer makes the darken'd cloud withdraw,
  Prayer climbs the ladder Jacob saw;
  Gives exercise to faith and love;
  Brings every blessing from above.

3 Restraining prayer, we cease to fight:
  Prayer makes the Christian's armour bright;
  And Satan trembles when he sees
  The weakest saint upon his knees.

4 Have you no words? Ah! think again:
  Words flow apace when you complain,
  And fill your fellow-creature's ear
  With the sad tale of all your care.—

5 Were half the breath thus vainly spent,
  To Heaven in supplication sent,
  Your cheerful song would oft'ner be,
  "Hear what the Lord has done for me.

1055 *Doxology.*

TO Father, Son, and Holy Ghost,
  The God whom earth and heaven adore,
Be glory, as it was of old,
  Is now, and shall be evermore.

SAXONY. L. M.

ANCIENT GERMAN CHORAL.

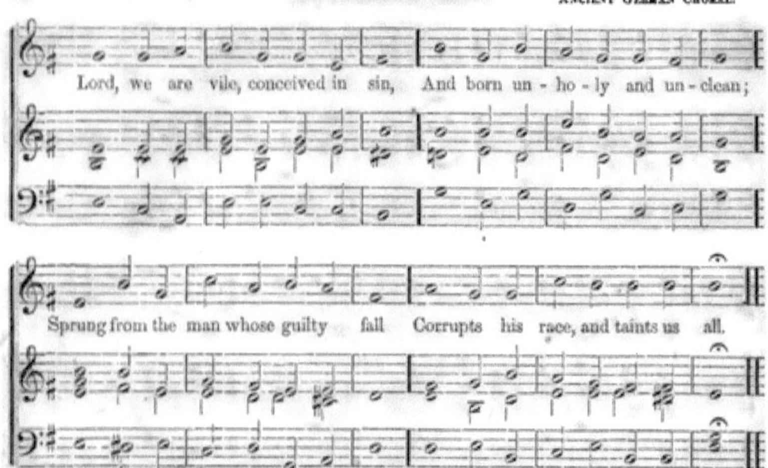

381 *Psalm li. 5—8.*

LORD, we are vile, conceived in sin,
And born unholy and unclean;
Sprung from the man whose guilty fall
Corrupts his race, and taints us all.

2 Soon as we draw our infant breath,
The seeds of sin grow up for death;
Thy law demands a perfect heart,
But we're defiled in every part.

3 Great God, create my heart anew,
And form my spirit pure and true;
O make me wise betimes to see
My danger and my remedy!

4 Behold, I fall before thy face;
My only refuge is thy grace:
No outward forms can make me clean;
The leprosy lies deep within.

5 No bleeding bird, nor bleeding beast,
Nor hyssop branch, nor sprinkling priest,
Nor running brook, nor flood, nor sea,
Can wash the dismal stain away.

6 Jesus, my God, thy blood alone
Hath power sufficient to atone;
Thy blood can make me white as snow;
No Jewish types could cleanse me so.

7 While guilt disturbs and breaks my peace,
Nor flesh nor soul hath rest or ease;
Lord, let me hear thy pard'ning voice,
And make my broken heart rejoice.

401 *Pathetic pleadings.*

MY suff'rings all to thee are known,
Tempted in every point like me!
Regard my grief, regard thy own;
Jesus, remember Calvary!

2 O call to mind thy earnest prayers!
Thy agony and sweat of blood!
Thy strong and bitter cries and tears!
Thy mortal groan, "My God! my God!"

3 For whom didst thou the cross endure?
Who nail'd thy body to the tree?
Did not thy death my life procure?
O let thy bowels answer me!

4 Art thou not touch'd with human wo?
Hath pity left the Son of man?
Dost thou not all my sorrows know,
And claim a share in all my pain?

5 Thou wilt not break a bruised reed,
Or quench the smallest spark of grace,
Till through the soul thy power is spread,
Thy all-victorious righteousness.

6 The day of small and feeble things
I know thou never wilt despise;
I know, with healing in his wings,
The Sun of righteousness shall rise.

682 *Death of the sinner.*

WHAT scenes of horror and of dread
Await the sinner's dying bed!
Death's terrors all appear in sight,
Presages of eternal night.

2 His sins, in dreadful order, rise,
And fill his soul with sad surprise;
Mount Sinai's thunders stun his ears,
And not one ray of hope appears.

3 Tormenting pangs distract his breast;
Where'er he turns he finds no rest:
Death strikes the blow—he groans and cries,
And in despair and horror—dies

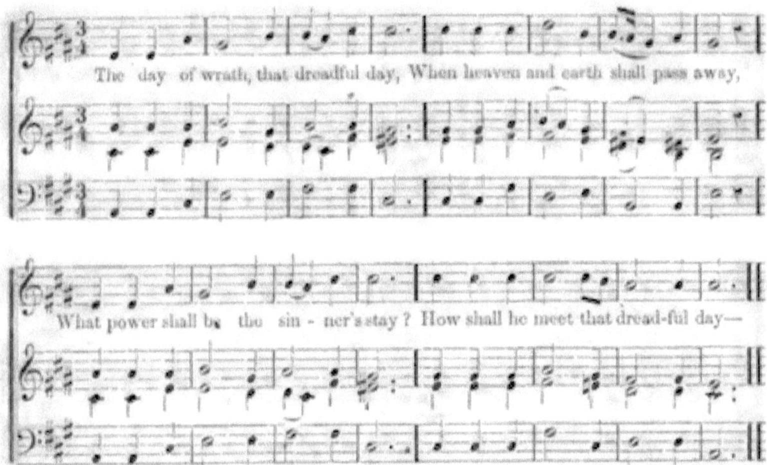

693 *Dies Iræ.*

THE day of wrath, that dreadful day,
 When heaven and earth shall pass away,
 What power shall be the sinner's stay?
 How shall he meet that dreadful day—

2 When, shriv'ling like a parched scroll,
 The flaming heavens together roll;
 And, louder yet, and yet more dread,
 Swells the high trump that wakes the dead!

3 O on that day, that wrathful day,
 When man to judgment wakes from clay,
 Be thou, O Christ, the sinner's stay,
 Though heaven and earth shall pass away!

1029 *For condemned malefactors.*

O THOU that hangedst on the tree,
 Our curse and suff'rings to remove,
Pity the souls that look to thee,
 And save us by thy dying love.

2 We have no outward righteousness,
 No merits, or good works, to plead:
We only can be saved by grace:
 Thy grace will here be free indeed.

3 Save us by grace, through faith alone,
 A faith thou must thyself impart;
A faith that would by works be shown,
 A faith that purifies the heart;—

4 A faith that doth the mountains move,
 A faith that shows our sins forgiven,
A faith that sweetly works by love,
 And ascertains our claim to heaven;—

5 This is the faith we humbly seek,
 The faith in thy all-cleansing blood;
That faith which doth for sinners speak,
 O let it speak us up to God.

102 *Awful distress.*

THOU man of griefs, remember me,
 Who never canst thyself forget,
Thy last mysterious agony,
 Thy fainting pangs and bloody sweat!

2 When wrestling in the strength of prayer
 Thy spirit sunk beneath its load;
Thy feeble flesh abhorr'd to bear
 The wrath of an almighty God.

3 Father, if I may call thee so,
 Regard my fearful heart's desire;
Remove this load of guilty wo,
 Nor let me in my sins expire!

4 I tremble, lest the wrath divine,
 Which bruises now my wretched soul,
Should bruise this wretched soul of mine
 Long as eternal ages roll.

5 To thee my last distress I bring;
 The heighten'd fear of death I find;
The tyrant, brandishing his sting,
 Appears, and hell is close behind.

6 I deprecate that death alone,
 That endless banishment from thee;
O save, and give me to thy Son,
 Who trembled, wept, and bled for me!

677 *The solemn question.*

PASS a few swiftly fleeting years,
 And all that now in bodies live
Shall quit, like me, the vale of tears,
 Their righteous sentence to receive.

2 But all, before they hence remove,
 May mansions for themselves prepare
In that eternal house above:
 And, O my God, shall I be there?

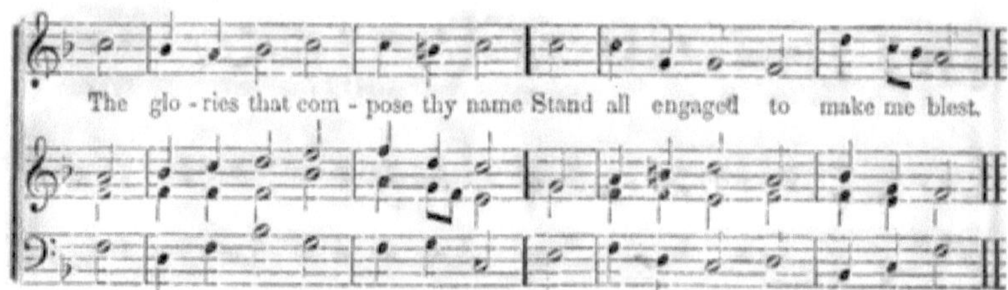

919 *Psalm* lxiii. 1—4.

GREAT God, indulge my humble claim;
Be thou my hope, my joy, my rest;
The glories that compose thy name
Stand all engaged to make me blest.

2 Thou great and good, thou just and wise,
Thou art my Father, and my God!
And I am thine by sacred ties,
Thy son, thy servant bought with blood.

3 With heart, and eyes, and lifted hands,
For thee I long, to thee I look,
As travellers in thirsty lands
Pant for the cooling water brook.

4 E'en life itself, without thy love,
No lasting pleasure can afford;
Yea, 'twould a tiresome burden prove,
If I were banish'd from thee, Lord!

5 I'll lift my hands, I'll raise my voice,
While I have breath to pray or praise;
This work shall make my heart rejoice,
And spend the remnant of my days.

396 *Feeling after Christ.*

WHEN, gracious Lord, when shall it be
That I shall find my all in thee?
The fulness of thy promise prove,
The seal of thine eternal love.

2 A poor blind child I wander here,
If haply I may feel thee near.
O dark! dark! dark! I still must say,
Amidst the blaze of gospel day.

3 Thee, only thee, I fain would find,
And cast the world and flesh behind:
Thou, only thou, to me be given,
Of all thou hast in earth or heaven.

4 When from the arm of flesh set free,
Jesus, my soul shall fly to thee:
Jesus, when I have lost my all,
I shall upon thy bosom fall.

55 *Psalm* xxxvi. 5—9.

HIGH in the heavens, eternal God,
Thy goodness in full glory shines;
Thy truth shall break through every cloud
That veils and darkens thy designs.

2 For ever firm thy justice stands,
As mountains their foundations keep;
Wise are the wonders of thy hands;
Thy judgments are a mighty deep.

3 Thy providence is kind and large,
Both man and beast thy bounty share;
The whole creation is thy charge,
But saints are thy peculiar care.

4 My God! how excellent thy grace!
Whence all our hope and comfort springs,
The sons of Adam in distress
Fly to the shadow of thy wings.

5 Life, like a fountain, rich and free,
Springs from the presence of the Lord;
And in thy light our souls shall see
The glories promised in thy word.

617 *Jer.* ix. 23, 24.

LET not the wise their wisdom boast;
The mighty glory in their might!
The rich in flatt'ring riches trust,
Which take their everlasting flight.

2 The rush of num'rous years bears down
The most gigantic strength of man;
And where is all his wisdom gone,
When dust he turns to dust again?

3 One only gift can justify
The boasting soul that knows his God;
When Jesus doth his blood apply,
I glory in his sprinkled blood.

4 The Lord, my righteousness I praise,
I triumph in the love divine,
The wisdom, wealth, and strength of grace,
In Christ to endless ages mine.

691 *"Come, Lord Jesus."*

JESUS, thy saints unite their cries,
And pray, and wait the general doom;
Come thou, the soul of all our joys;
Thou, the Desire of nations, come.

2 Now let our cheerful eyes survey
The blazing earth and melting hills;
And smile to see the lightnings play,
And flash along before thy wheels.

3 Hark! what a shout of gushing joys
Joins with the mighty trumpet's sound.
The angel herald shakes the skies,
Awakes the graves, and tears the ground.

4 Ye slumb'ring saints, a heavenly host
Stands waiting at your gaping tombs;
Now shall your sacred, sleeping dust
Leap into life; for Jesus comes.

5 Jesus, the God of might and love,
New-moulds our limbs of cumbrous clay;
Quick as seraphic flames we move,
To reign with him in endless day.

710 *"Ever with the Lord."*

JESUS! what ecstasy unknown
Fills the wide circle round thy throne,
Where every rapturous hour appears
Nobler than millions of our years!

2 Millions by millions multiplied,
Shall ne'er thy saints from thee divide;
But the bright legions live and praise
Through all thy own immortal days.

3 O happy dead, in thee that sleep,
While o'er their mould'ring dust we weep;
O faithful Saviour, who shalt come
That dust to ransom from the tomb!

4 While thy unerring word imparts
So rich a cordial to our hearts,
Through tears our triumphs shall be shown,
Though round their graves, and near our own.

717 *The contrast.*

IN what confusion earth appears—
God's dearest children bathed in tears!
While they who heaven itself deride
Riot in luxury and pride.

2 But patient let my soul attend,
And, ere I censure, view the end;
That end how diff'rent!—who can tell
The wide extremes of heaven and hell?

3 See the red flames around him twine
Who did in gold and purple shine:
Nor can his tongue one drop obtain
T' allay the scorching of his pain.

4 While round the saint, so poor below,
Full rivers of salvation flow;
On Abrah'm's breast he leans his head,
And banquets on celestial bread.

5 Jesus, my Saviour, let me share
The meanest of thy servants' fare;
May I at last approach to taste
The blessings of thy marriage feast.

766 *"The morning cometh."*

GLORY to God, whose sovereign grace
Hath animated senseless stones;
Call'd us to stand before his face,
And raised us into Abrah'm's sons.

2 The people that in darkness lay,
In sin and error's deadly shade,
Have seen a glorious gospel-day,
In Jesus' lovely face display'd.

3 Thou only, Lord, the work hast done,
And bared thine arm in all our sight:
Hast made the reprobates thine own,
And claimed the outcasts as thy right.

4 Thy single arm, almighty Lord,
To us the great salvation brought:
Thy Word, thy all-creating Word,
That spake at first the world from naught.

5 For this the saints lift up their voice,
And ceaseless praise to thee is given;
For this the hosts above rejoice:—
We raise the happiness of heaven.

6 For this, (no longer sons of night,)
To thee our thankful hearts we give;
To thee, who call'dst us into light:
To thee we die, to thee we live.

219 *Isaiah* li. 9—11.

ARM of the Lord, awake, awake!
Thine own immortal strength put on!
With terror clothed, hell's kingdom shake,
And cast thy foes with fury down.

3 As in the ancient days, appear!
The sacred annals speak thy fame;
Be now omnipotently near,
To endless ages still the same.

3 By death and hell pursued in vain,
To thee the ransom'd seed shall come;
Shouting, their heavenly Sion gain,
And pass through death triumphant home.

4 The pain of life shall then be o'er,
The anguish and distracting care;
There sighing grief shall weep no more,
And sin shall never enter there.

5 Where pure, essential joy is found,
The Lord's redeem'd their heads shall raise,
With everlasting gladness crown'd,
And fill'd with love, and lost in praise.

BEAUFORT. L. M. Double.

L. C. EVERETT.

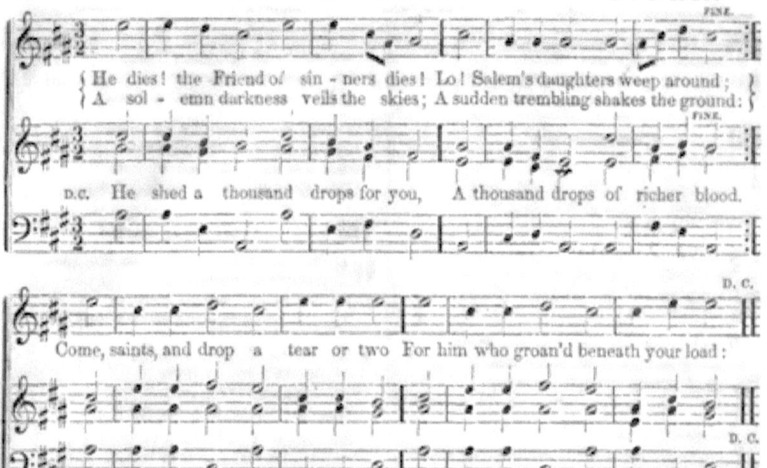

145 *Dying, rising, reigning.*

HE dies! the Friend of sinners dies!
Lo! Salem's daughters weep around;
A solemn darkness veils the skies;
A sudden trembling shakes the ground:
Come, saints, and drop a tear or two
For Him who groan'd beneath your load:
He shed a thousand drops for you,
A thousand drops of richer blood.

2 Here 's love and grief beyond degree,
The Lord of glory dies for man!
But lo! what sudden joys we see!
Jesus, the dead, revives again!
The rising God forsakes the tomb;
Up to his Father's courts he flies;
Cherubic legions guard him home,
And shout him welcome to the skies!

3 Break off your tears, ye saints, and tell
How high your great Deliv'rer reigns;
Sing how he spoil'd the hosts of hell,
And led the monster death in chains!
Say, "Live for ever, wondrous King!
Born to redeem, and strong to save!"
Then ask the monster, "Where's thy sting?"
And, "Where's thy vict'ry, boasting grave?"

147 *Psalm xxiv. 7—10.*

OUR Lord is risen from the dead;
Our Jesus is gone up on high!
The powers of hell are captive led,
Dragg'd to the portals of the sky.
There his triumphal chariot waits,
And angels chant the solemn lay:
Lift up your heads, ye heavenly gates;
Ye everlasting doors, give way.

2 Loose all your bars of massy light,
And wide unfold th' ethereal scene;
He claims these mansions as his right—
Receive the King of glory in.
Who is the King of glory? Who?
The Lord that all our foes o'ercame,
The world, sin, death, and hell, o'erthrew;—
And Jesus is the conqu'ror's name.

3 Lo! his triumphal chariot waits,
And angels chant the solemn lay;
Lift up your heads, ye heavenly gates;
Ye everlasting doors, give way.
Who is the King of glory? Who?
The Lord, of glorious power possess'd;
The King of saints and angels too,
God over all, for ever bless'd.

639 *Hab. iii. 17, 18.*

AWAY, my unbelieving fear!
Fear shall in me no more have place;
My Saviour doth not yet appear,
He hides the brightness of his face:
But shall I therefore let him go,
And basely to the tempter yield?
No, in the strength of Jesus, no,
I never will give up my shield.

2 Although the vine its fruit deny,
Although the olive yield no oil,
The with'ring fig-tree droop and die,
The fields elude the tiller's toil,
The empty stall no herd afford,
And perish all the bleating race,—
Yet will I triumph in the Lord,
The God of my salvation praise.

373 *Praying for repentance.*

JESUS, my Advocate above,
My Friend before the throne of love,
If now for me prevails thy prayer,
If now I find thee pleading there,
If thou the secret wish convey,
And sweetly prompt my heart to pray;
Hear, and my weak petitions join,
Almighty Advocate, to thine.

2 Fain would I know my utmost ill,
And groan my nature's weight to feel!
To feel the clouds that round me roll,
The night that hangs upon my soul,
The darkness of my carnal mind,
My will perverse, my passions blind,
Scatter'd o'er all the earth abroad,
Immeasurably far from God.

3 O sovereign Love, to thee I cry!
Give me thyself, or else I die!
Save me from death; from hell set free!
Death, hell, are but the want of thee.
Quicken'd by thy imparted flame;
Saved, when possess'd of thee, I am:
My life, my only heaven thou art;
O might I feel thee in my heart!

382 *Psalm li. 9—12.*

O THOU, who hear'st when sinners cry,
Though all my crimes before thee lie,
Behold them not with angry look,
But blot their mem'ry from thy book.

2 Create my nature pure within,
And form my soul averse from sin;
Let thy good Spirit ne'er depart,
Nor hide thy presence from my heart.

3 I cannot live without thy light,
Cast out and banish'd from thy sight!
Thy holy joys, my God, restore,
And guard me that I fall no more.

4 Though I have grieved thy Spirit, Lord,
Thy help and comfort still afford;
And let a wretch come near thy throne,
To plead the merits of thy Son.

413 *The good Physician.*

JESUS, thy far-extended fame
My drooping soul exults to hear;
Thy name, thy all-restoring name,
Is music in a sinner's ear.

2 Sinners of old thou didst receive,
With comfortable words, and kind,
Their sorrows cheer, their wants relieve,
Heal the diseased, and cure the blind.

3 And art thou not the Saviour still,
In every place and age the same?
Hast thou forgot thy gracious skill,
Or lost the virtue of thy name?

4 Faith in thy changeless name I have:
The good, the kind Physician, thou
Art able now our souls to save,
Art willing to restore them now.

5 Wouldst thou the body's health restore,
And not regard the sin-sick soul?
The sin-sick soul thou lov'st much more,
And surely thou wilt make it whole.

6 All my disease, my every sin,
To thee, O Jesus, I confess:
In pardon, Lord, my cure begin,
And perfect it in holiness.

1031 *Praying for recovery.*

ANGEL of covenanted grace,
Come, and thy healing power infuse;
Descend in thy own time, and bless,
And give the means their hallow'd use.

2 Obedient to thy will alone,
To thee in means I calmly fly;
My life, I know, is not my own,
To God I live, to God I die.

3 Thy holy will be ever mine:
If thou on earth detain me still,
I bow, and bless the grace divine,—
I suffer all thy holy will.

4 I come, if thou my strength restore,
To serve thee with my strength renew'd;
Grant me but this, I ask no more—
To spend and to be spent for God.

397 *Feeling after Christ.*

WHOM man forsakes thou wilt not leave,
Ready the outcasts to receive:
Though all my simpleness I own,
And all my faults to thee are known.

2 Ah! wherefore did I ever doubt?
Thou wilt in no wise cast me out,—
A helpless soul that comes to thee,
With only sin and misery.

3 Lord, I am sick,—my sickness cure:
I want,—do thou enrich the poor:
Under thy mighty hand I stoop,
O lift the abject sinner up!

4 Lord, I am blind,—be thou my sight:
Lord, I am weak,—be thou my might:
A helper of the helpless be,
And let me find my all in thee!

1049 *Phil. iv. 7.*

THE peace which God alone reveals,
And by his word of grace imparts,
Which only the believer feels,
Direct, and keep, and cheer our hearts;
And may the holy Three in One,
The Father, Word, and Comforter,
Pour an abundant blessing down
On every soul assembled here.

FEDERAL STREET. L. M.

H. K. OLIVER.

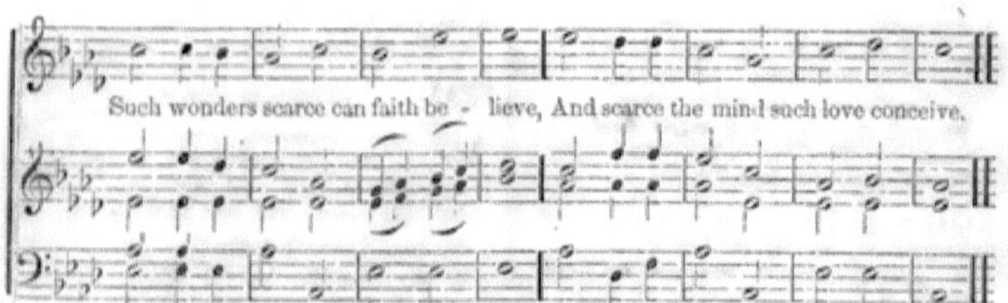

115 *Agony in the garden.*

TO whom is our report made known
  Of mercies which the Lord hath shown?
Such wonders scarce can faith believe,
And scarce the mind such love conceive.

2 The Son of God, for sinful man
In purpose slain, since time began,
His body now in deed supplies
As our atoning sacrifice.

3 But wherefore, Saviour, dost thou lie
In such a mournful agony?
And why those bloody drops that show
Thy soul's deep anguish as they flow?

4 Doth the dread cup deter thy soul?
But O! unless thou drink the whole,
For us poor sinners it must flow,
A draught of never ending wo.

5 But heavenly love is ne'er dismay'd,
And God may not be disobey'd;
And lo! he yields him to the hour
Of darkness, and to hell's dark power.

6 The Father, who the victim gave,
The Son, who died mankind to save,
The Holy Ghost, we all adore,
One God, both now and evermore.

117 *The Passion.*

O THOU dear suffering Son of God,
  How doth thy heart to sinners move!
Help me to catch thy precious blood!
  Help me to taste thy dying love!

2 The earth could to her centre quake,
  Convulsed while her Creator died:
O let my inmost nature shake,
  And die with Jesus crucified!

3 At thy last gasp the graves display'd
  Their horrors to the upper skies:
O that my soul might burst the shade,
  And, quicken'd by thy death, arise!

4 The rocks could feel thy powerful death,
  And tremble, and asunder part:
O rend with thine expiring breath
  The harder marble of my heart!

119 *The Cross.*

WHILE in the agonies of death,
  The Saviour yields his latest breath,
We, too, will mount on Calv'ry's height,
And contemplate the wondrous sight!

2 O Lamb of God, by faith we see
How all our hopes are fix'd on thee:
Thy cross we see ordain'd by Heaven,
For man to look, and be forgiven.

3 By this thy saints to glory come;
By this they brave the martyr's doom;
In this the surest proof we find
Of God's vast love to lost mankind.

4 On this, O Lord, enthroned on high,
With more than royal majesty,
Thou spreadest forth thine arms abroad,
And callest all mankind to God.

5 O grant us then to find a place
Around the footstool of thy grace,
And there in humble faith to stay,
Till all our sins are wash'd away!

6 O, banner of the cross, unfurl'd
To shine with glory through the world,
O may we ever cleave to thee,
And thou shalt our salvation be!

FEORTSCH. L. M.

From "New Thes. Musicus."

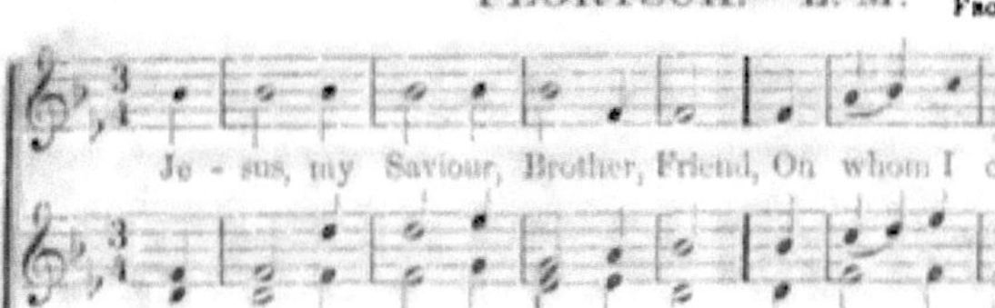

583 *A watchful spirit.*

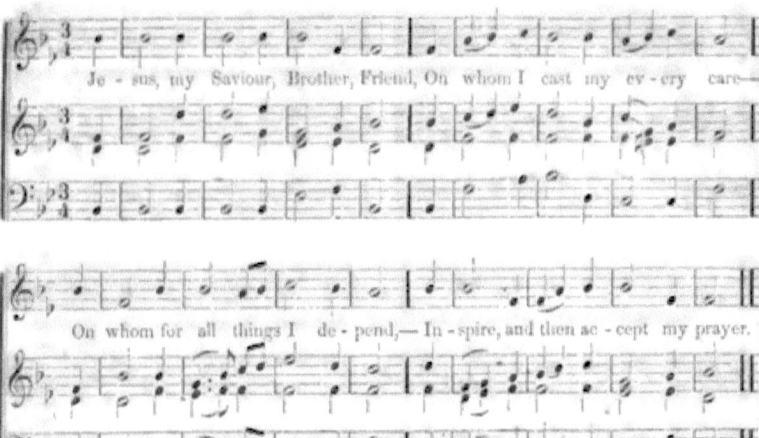

JESUS, my Saviour, Brother, Friend,
On whom I cast my every care,—
On whom for all things I depend,—
Inspire, and then accept my prayer.

2 If I have tasted of thy grace,
The grace that sure salvation brings;
If with me now thy Spirit stays,
And hov'ring, hides me in his wings.

3 Still let him with my weakness stay,
Nor for a moment's space depart;
Evil and danger turn away,
And keep till he renews my heart.

4 When to the right or left I stray,
His voice behind me may I hear,
"Return, and walk in Christ, thy way;
Fly back to Christ, for sin is near!"

5 Jesus, I fain would walk in thee,
From nature's every path retreat:
Thou art my way; my leader be,
And set upon the rock my feet.

628 *The choice of Mary.*

BESET with snares on every hand,
In life's uncertain path I stand:
Saviour divine! diffuse thy light
To guide my doubtful footsteps right.

2 Engage this roving, treach'rous heart
To fix on Mary's better part,
To scorn the trifles of a day,
For joys that none can take away.

3 Then let the wildest storms arise;
Let tempests mingle earth and skies;
No fatal shipwreck shall I fear,
But all my treasures with me bear.

If thou, my Jesus, still be nigh,
Cheerful I live, and joyful die;
Secure, when mortal comforts flee,
To find ten thousand worlds in thee.

653 *Submission.*

WAIT, O my soul, thy Maker's will!
Tumultuous passions, all be still!
Nor let a murmuring thought arise;
His ways are just, his counsels wise.

2 He in the thickest darkness dwells,
Performs his work, the cause conceals;
But though his methods are unknown,
Judgment and truth support his throne.

3 Wait, then, my soul, submissive wait,
Prostrate before his awful seat:
And, midst the terrors of his rod,
Trust in a wise and gracious God.

412 *Fleeing to the sinner's Friend.*

JESUS, the sinner's Friend, to thee,
Lost and undone, for aid I flee;
Weary of earth, myself, and sin;
Open thine arms and take me in.

2 Pity and heal my sin-sick soul;
'Tis thou alone canst make me whole,
Fall'n, till in me thine image shine,
And lost I am till thou art mine.

3 Awake, the woman's conqu'ring seed,
Awake, and bruise the serpent's head!
Tread down thy foes, with power control
The beast and devil in my soul.

4 What shall I say thy grace to move?
Lord, I am sin,—but thou art love:
I give up every plea beside,
"Lord, I am lost—but thou hast died."

STERLING. L. M.

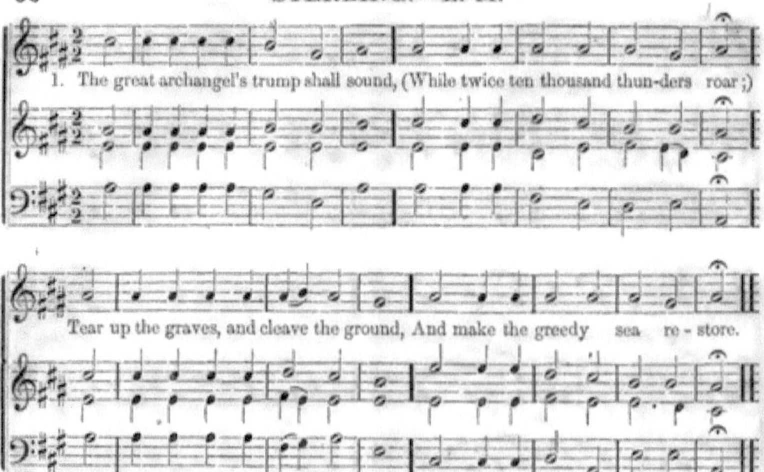

690 *The last day.*

THE great archangel's trump shall sound,
 (While twice ten thousand thunders roar,)
Tear up the graves, and cleave the ground,
 And make the greedy sea restore.

2 The greedy sea shall yield her dead,
 The earth no more her slain conceal;
Sinners shall lift their guilty head,
 And shrink to see a yawning hell.

3 But we, who now our Lord confess,
 And faithful to the end endure,
Shall stand in Jesus' righteousness,—
 Stand, as the Rock of ages, sure.

4 We, while the stars from heaven shall fall,
 And mountains are on mountains hurl'd,
Shall stand unmoved amidst them all,
 And smile to see a burning world.

5 The earth, and all the works therein,
 Dissolve, by raging flames destroy'd;
While we survey the awful scene,
 And mount above the fiery void.

6 By faith we now transcend the skies,
 And on that ruin'd world look down:
By love above all height we rise,
 And share the everlasting throne.

940 *For enlargement and guidance.*

O THOU, our Husband, Brother, Friend,
 Behold a cloud of incense rise!
The prayers of saints to heaven ascend,
 Grateful, accepted sacrifice!

2 Regard our prayers for Sion's peace:
 Shed in our hearts thy love abroad:
Thy gifts abundantly increase:
 Enlarge and fill us all with God!

3 Before thy sheep, great Shepherd, go,
 And guide into thy perfect will;
Cause us thy hallow'd name to know,
 The work of faith in us fulfil.

4 Help us to make our calling sure;
 O let us all be saints indeed!
And pure, as thou thyself art pure;
 Conform'd in all things to our Head.

951 *Morning.*

AWAKE, my soul, and with the sun
 Thy daily stage of duty run;
 Shake off dull sloth, and early rise
 To pay thy morning sacrifice.

2 Wake, and lift up thyself, my heart,
 And with the angels bear thy part;
 Who all night long unwearied sing,
 High praise to the eternal King.

3 Glory to Thee, who safe hast kept,
 And hast refresh'd me while I slept:
 Grant, Lord, when I from death shall wake,
 I may of endless life partake.

4 Direct, control, suggest this day,
 All I design, or do, or say,
 That all my powers, with all their might,
 In thy sole glory may unite.

5 Praise God, from whom all blessings flow,
 Praise him, all creatures here below,
 Praise him above, ye heavenly host,
 Praise Father, Son, and Holy Ghost.

1055 *Doxology.*

TO Father, Son, and Holy Ghost,
 The God whom earth and heaven adore,
Be glory, as it was of old,
 Is now, and shall be evermore.

520 *Ezekiel xxxvi. 29, 30.*

FATHER, supply my every need;
  Sustain the life thyself hast given;
O grant the never-failing bread,
  The manna that comes down from heaven!

2 The gracious fruits of righteousness,
  Thy blessings' unexhausted store,
In me abundantly increase,
  Nor ever let me hunger more!

3 Let me no more, in deep complaint,
  "My leanness, O my leanness!" cry;
Alone consumed with pining want,
  Of all my Father's children, I.

4 The painful thirst, the fond desire,
  Thy joyous presence shall remove!
But my full soul shall still require
  A whole eternity of love.

786 *Dedication.*

AND will the great, eternal God,
  On earth establish his abode?
And will he, from his radiant throne,
  Avow our temple for his own?

2 We bring the tribute of our praise;
  And sing that condescending grace,
Which to our notes will lend an ear,
  And call us sinful mortals near.

3 These walls we to thy honour raise,
  Long may they echo to thy praise;
And thou, descending, fill the place
  With choicest tokens of thy grace.

4 And in the great, decisive day,
  When God the nations shall survey,
May it before the world appear
  That crowds were born to glory here

780 *Laying the foundation.*

WHEN to the exiled seer was given
  A rapt'rous foregaze into heaven,
All glorious though the visions were,
  Yet he beheld no temple there.

2 The New Jerusalem on high
  Hath one pervading sanctity;
No sin to mourn, no grief to mar,—
  God and the Lamb its temple are.

3 But we, frail sojourners below,
  The pilgrim-heirs of guilt and wo,
Must seek a tabernacle, where
  Our scatter'd souls may blend in prayer.

4 O Thou! who o'er the cherubim
  Didst shine in glories veil'd and dim,
With purer light our temple cheer,
  And dwell in unveil'd glory here.

840 *Thanksgiving for peace.*

WHEN angry nations rush to arms,
  And rage, and noise, and tumult reign,
And war resounds its dire alarms,
  And slaughter spreads the hostile plain;

2 Thine eye, O God, looks calmly down,
  And marks their course, and bounds their power;
Thy word the angry nations own,
  And noise and war are heard no more.

3 Then peace returns with balmy wing,
  (Sweet peace, with her what blessings fled!)
Glad plenty laughs, the valleys sing,
  Reviving commerce lifts her head.

4 To thee we pay our grateful songs,
  Thy kind protection still implore:
O may our hearts, and lives, and tongues,
  Confess thy goodness and adore!

429 *Micah vi. 6—8.*

WHEREWITH, O Lord, shall I draw near,
And bow myself before thy face?
How in thy purer eyes appear?
What shall I bring to gain thy grace?

2 Will gifts delight the Lord most high?
Will multiplied oblations please?
Thousands of rams his favour buy?
Or slaughter'd hecatombs appease?

3 Can these avert the wrath of God?
Can these wash out my guilty stain?
Rivers of oil, and seas of blood,
Alas! they all must flow in vain.

4 Whoe'er to thee themselves approve,
Must take the path thyself hast show'd;
Justice pursue, and mercy love,
And humbly walk by faith with God.

5 But though my life henceforth be thine,
Present for past can ne'er atone:
Though I to thee the whole resign,
I only give thee back thine own.

6 What have I then wherein to trust;
I nothing have, I nothing am;
Excluded is my every boast;
My glory swallow'd up in shame.

7 Guilty I stand before thy face;
On me I feel thy wrath abide;
'Tis just the sentence should take place,
'Tis just,—but O, thy Son hath died!

460 *Receiving the Atonement.*

JESUS, thy blood and righteousness
My beauty are, my glorious dress:
'Midst flaming worlds, in these array'd,
With joy shall I lift up my head.

2 Bold shall I stand in thy great day,
For who aught to my charge shall lay?
Fully absolved through these I am,
From sin and fear, from guilt and shame.

3 The holy, meek, unspotted Lamb,
Who from the Father's bosom came,
Who died for me, e'en me, t' atone,
Now for my Lord and God I own.

4 Lord, I believe thy precious blood,
Which, at the mercy-seat of God,
For ever doth for sinners plead,
For *me*, e'en for *my* soul was shed.

5 Lord, I believe were sinners more
Than sands upon the ocean shore,
Thou hast for ALL a ransom paid,
For ALL a full atonement made.

477 *Love and joy.*

I THIRST, thou wounded Lamb of God,
To wash me in thy cleansing blood;
To dwell within thy wounds: then pain
Is sweet, and life or death is gain.

2 Take my poor heart, and let it be
For ever closed to all but thee!
Seal thou my breast, and let me wear
That pledge of love for ever there.

3 How bless'd are they who still abide
Close shelter'd in thy bleeding side!
Who life and strength from thence derive,
And by thee move, and in thee live.

4 What are our works but sin and death,
Till thou thy quick'ning Spirit breathe?
Thou giv'st the power thy grace to move,
O wondrous grace! O boundless love!

784 *Dedication.*

BEHOLD thy temple, God of grace,
The house that we have rear'd for thee,
Regard it as thy resting place,
And fill it with thy majesty.

2 When from its altar shall arise
Joint supplication to thy name,
Deign to accept the sacrifice,
Thyself our answering God proclaim.

3 And when from hence the voice of praise
Shall lift its triumphs to thy throne,
Show thy acceptance of our lays,
By making all thy glory known.

4 When here thy ministers shall stand,
To speak what thou shalt bid them say,
Maintain thy cause with thy own hand,
And give thy truth a winning way.

5 Now, therefore, O our God, arise!
In this thy resting place appear;
And let thy people's longing eyes
Behold thee fix thy dwelling here.

478 *Love and joy.*

HOW can it be, thou heavenly King,
That thou shouldst us to glory bring?
Make slaves the partners of thy throne,
Decked with a never-fading crown!

2 Hence our hearts melt, our eyes o'erflow,
Our words are lost, nor will we know—
Nor will we think of aught beside,
"My Lord, my Love is crucified."

3 Ah! Lord, enlarge our scanty thought,
To know the wonders thou hast wrought;
Unloose our stamm'ring tongues to tell
Thy love immense, unsearchable!

4 First-born of many brethren thou,
To thee, lo, all our souls we bow:
To thee our hearts and hands we give,
Thine may we die, thine may we live.

891 *For the lambs of the flock.*

AUTHOR of faith, we seek thy face,
For all who feel thy work begun:
Confirm, and strengthen them in grace,
And bring thy feeblest children on.

2 Thou seest their wants, thou know'st their names,
Be mindful of thy youngest care;
Be tender of the new-born lambs,
And gently in thy bosom bear.

3 The lion roaring for his prey,
With rav'ning wolves on every side,
Watch over them to tear and slay,
If found one moment from their Guide.

4 In safety lead thy little flock!
From hell, the world, and sin secure;
And set their feet upon the rock,
And make in thee their goings sure.

279 *The Commission.—For adult's baptism.*

'TWAS the commission of our Lord,
"Go, teach the nations, and baptize;"
The nations have received the word
Since he ascended to the skies.

2 "Repent, and be baptized," he saith,
"For the remission of your sins;"
And thus our sense assists our faith,
And shows us what his gospel means.

3 Our souls he washes in his blood,
As water makes the body clean;
And the good Spirit from our God
Descends like purifying rain.

4 Thus we engage ourselves to thee,
And seal our cov'nant with the Lord;
O may the great Eternal Three
In heaven our solemn vows record!

579 *Reverence and godly fear.*

THE voice that speaks Jehovah near,
The still, small voice, I long to hear;
O may it now my Lord proclaim,
And fill my soul with holy shame!

2 Ashamed I must for ever be,
Afraid the God of love to see,
If saints and prophets hide their face,
And angels tremble while they gaze!

517 *Ezekiel xvi. 62, 63.*

O GOD, most merciful and true,
Thy nature to my soul impart;
Stablish with me the cov'nant new,
And stamp thine image on my heart.

2 To real holiness restored,
O let me gain my Saviour's mind,
And in the knowledge of my Lord,
Fulness of life eternal find.

3 Remember, Lord, my sins no more,
That them I may no more forget;
But, sunk in guiltless shame, adore
With speechless wonder, at thy feet.

4 O'erwhelm'd with thy stupendous grace,
I shall not in thy presence move;
But breathe unutterable praise,
And rapt'rous awe, and silent love.

5 Then every murm'ring thought, and vain,
Expires, in sweet communion lost:
I cannot of my cross complain,—
I cannot of my goodness boast.

6 Pardon'd for all that I have done,
My mouth as in the dust I hide;
And glory give to God alone,
My God for ever pacified!

MIGDOL. L. M.

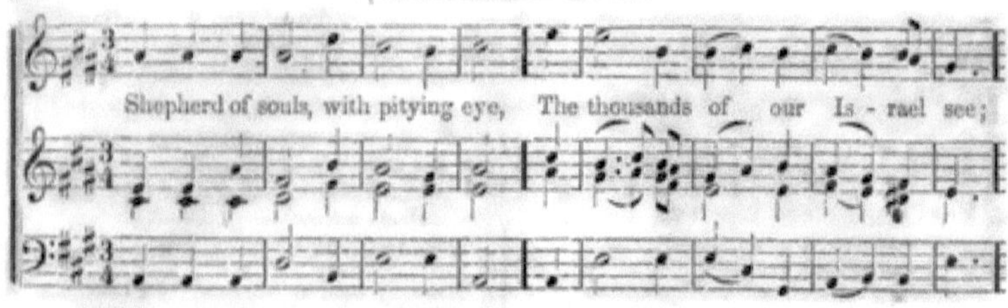

369 *Before an inviting sermon.*

SHEPHERD of souls, with pitying eye,
  The thousands of our Israel see;
To thee in their behalf we cry,
  Ourselves but newly found in thee.

2 See where o'er desert wastes they err,
  And neither food nor feeder have;
Nor fold nor place of refuge near;
  For no man cares their souls to save.

3 Thy people, Lord, are sold for naught;
  Nor know they their Redeemer nigh:
They perish whom thyself hast bought;
  Their souls for lack of knowledge die.

4 Why should the foe thy purchase seize?
  Remember, Lord, thy dying groans:
The meed of all thy suff'rings these;
  O claim them for thy ransom'd ones!

5 Still let the publicans draw near:
  Open the door of faith and heaven;
And grant their hearts thy word to hear,
  And witness all their sins forgiven.

393 *Hardness of heart lamented.*

O FOR a glance of heavenly day,
  To take this stubborn heart away,
And thaw with beams of love divine,
  This heart, this frozen heart of mine!

2 The rocks can rend; the earth can quake;
  The seas can roar; the mountains shake:
Of feeling, all things show some sign,
  But this unfeeling heart of mine.

3 To hear the sorrows thou hast felt,
  O Lord, an adamant would melt!
But I can read each moving line,
  And nothing moves this heart of mine.

4 Thy judgments, too, unmoved I hear,
  (Amazing thought!) which devils fear;
Goodness and wrath in vain combine
  To stir this stupid heart of mine.

5 But something yet can do the deed;
  And that bless'd something much I need:
Thy spirit can from dross refine,
  And melt and change this heart of mine.

405 *"Beginning at Jerusalem."*

"GO," saith the Lord, "proclaim my grace
  To all the sons of Adam's race;
Pardon for every crimson sin,
  And at Jerusalem begin.

2 "There, where my blood, not fully dry,
  Stands warm upon Mount Calvary,
That blood shall purge away their guilt,
  By whom so lately it was spilt.

3 "Now let the daring rebels turn,
  And o'er their bleeding Sovereign mourn;
Their bleeding Sovereign shall forgive,
  And bid the rebels look and live."

4 Is this thy voice, all-gracious Lord?
  And did the rebels hear thy word?
And did they fall beneath thy feet,
  And on their knees forgiveness meet?

5 Then may I hope for mercy too:
  Such love can my hard heart subdue,
And give this guilty soul a place
  Among these captives of thy grace.

1055 *Doxology.*

TO Father, Son, and Holy Ghost,
  The God whom earth and heaven adore,
Be glory, as it was of old,
  Is now, and shall be evermore.

873 *Opening the exercises.*

SAVIOUR of all, to thee we bow,
And own thee faithful to thy word:
We hear thy voice, and open now
Our hearts to entertain our Lord.

2 Come in, come in, thou heavenly Guest,
Delight in what thyself hast given;
On thy own gifts and graces feast,
And make the contrite heart thy heaven.

3 Smell the sweet odour of our prayers,
Our sacrifice of praise approve;
And treasure up our gracious tears,
And rest in thy redeeming love.

4 O let us on thy fulness feed!
And eat thy flesh, and drink thy blood!
Jesus, thy blood is drink indeed,
Jesus, thy flesh is angels' food!

293 *The sign and seal.*

AUTHOR of our salvation, thee,
With lowly, thankful hearts, we praise,
Author of this great mystery,
Figure and means of saving grace.

2 The sacred, true, effectual sign,
Thy body and thy blood it shows;
The glorious instrument divine
Thy mercy and thy strength bestows.

3 We see the blood that seals our peace,
Thy pard'ning mercy we receive;
The bread doth visibly express
The strength through which our spirits live.

4 Our spirits drink a fresh supply,
And eat the bread so freely given,
Till borne on eagles' wings we fly,
And banquet with our Lord in heaven.

303 *The penitent at the table.*

HOW long, thou faithful God, shall I
Here in thy ways forgotten lie?
When shall the means of healing be
The channels of thy grace to me?

2 Sinners, on every side, step in,
And wash away their pain and sin,
But I, a helpless, sin-sick soul,
Still lie expiring at the pool.

3 In vain I take the broken bread,
I cannot on thy mercy feed;
In vain I drink the hallow'd wine,
I cannot taste the love divine.

4 Thou seest me lying at the pool,
I would, thou know'st, I would be whole;
O let the troubled waters move,
And minister thy healing love.

5 Surely if thou the symbols bless,
The cov'nant blood shall seal my peace,
Thy flesh, e'en now, shall be my food,
And all my soul be fill'd with God.

1005 *Self-examination.*

O THOU great God, whose piercing eye
Distinctly marks each deep recess,
In these sequester'd hours draw nigh,
And with thy presence fill the place.

2 Through all the mazes of my heart,
My search let heavenly wisdom guide,
And still its radiant beams impart,
Till all be search'd and purified.

3 Then with the visits of thy love,
Vouchsafe my inmost soul to cheer;
'Till every grace shall join to prove
That God has fix'd his dwelling there.

128 *"It is finished."*

'TIS finish'd! The Messiah dies,
Cut off for sins, but not his own!
Accomplish'd is the sacrifice,
The great redeeming work is done.

2 'Tis finish'd! All the debt is paid;
Justice divine is satisfied;
The grand and full atonement made;
God for a guilty world hath died.

3 The veil is rent in Christ alone;
The living way to heaven is seen;
The middle wall is broken down,
And all mankind may enter in.

4 The types and figures are fulfill'd,
Exacted is the legal pain;
The precious promises are seal'd;
The spotless Lamb of God is slain.

5 Saved from the legal curse I am,
My Saviour hangs on yonder tree,
See there the meek, expiring Lamb!
'Tis finish'd!. He expires for me.

6 Death, hell, and sin, are now subdued;
All grace is now to sinners given;
And, lo! I plead th' atoning blood,
And in thy right I claim thy heaven.

110 *Christ weeping over Jerusalem.*

WHAT venerable sight appears!
The Son of God, dissolved in tears!
Trace, O my soul, with sad surprise,
The sorrows of a Saviour's eyes!

2 For whom, bless'd Jesus, we would know,
Doth such a sacred torrent flow?
What brother, or what friend of thine,
Is graced and mourn'd with drops divine?

3 Nor brother there, nor friend I see—
But sons of pride and cruelty;
Who, like rapacious tigers, stood,
Insatiate, panting for thy blood.

4 Dear Lord, and did thy gushing eyes
Thus stream o'er dying enemies?
And can thy tenderness forget
The sinner, humbled at thy feet?

5 With deep remorse our bowels move,—
That we have wrong'd such matchless love;
Thy gentle pity, Lord, display,
And smile these trembling fears away.

116 *The Passion.*

YE that pass by, behold the man!
The man of griefs, condemn'd for you
The Lamb of God, for sinners slain,
Weeping to Calvary pursue!

2 See! how his back the scourges tear,
While to the bloody pillar bound!
The ploughers make long furrows there,
Till all his body is one wound.

3 Nor can he thus their hate assuage;
His innocence to death pursued,
Must fully glut their utmost rage;
Hark! how they clamour for his blood!

4 "To us our own Barabbas give,
Away with him," (they loudly cry,)
"Away with him, not fit to live,
The vile seducer crucify!"

5 His sacred limbs they stretch, they tear,
With nails they fasten to the wood!
His sacred limbs, exposed and bare,
Or only cover'd with his blood.

6 See there, his temples crown'd with thorn!
His bleeding hands extended wide!
His streaming feet transfix'd and torn!
The fountain gushing from his side!

7 Where is the King of glory now?
The everlasting Son of God?
Th' Immortal hangs his languid brow;
Th' Almighty faints beneath his load!

8 Beneath *my* load he faints and dies:
I fill'd his soul with pangs unknown:
I caused those mortal groans and cries—
I kill'd the Father's only Son!

133 *The fountain.*

BY faith I to the fountain fly,
Open'd for all mankind and me,
To purge my sins of deepest dye,
My life and heart's impurity.

2 From Christ, the smitten rock, it flows,
The purple and the crystal stream
Pardon and holiness bestows;
And both I gain through faith in him.

224 *His departure earnestly deprecated.*

STAY, thou insulted Spirit! stay!
Though I have done thee such despite,
Nor cast the sinner quite away,
Nor take thine everlasting flight.

2 Though I have steel'd my stubborn heart,
And still shook off my guilty fears;
And vex'd, and urged thee to depart,
For many long rebellious years:—

3 Though I have most unfaithful been,
Of all who e'er thy grace received;
Ten thousand times thy goodness seen,
Ten thousand times thy goodness grieved—

4 Yet O! the chief of sinners spare,
In honour of my great High Priest;
Nor in thy righteous anger swear
T' exclude me from thy people's rest.

5 This only wo I deprecate;
This only plague I pray remove;
Nor leave me in my lost estate;
Nor curse me with this want of love.

6 Now, Lord, my weary soul release,
Upraise me with thy gracious hand,
And guide me into perfect peace,
And bring me to the promised land.

237 *Psalm xcii. 12—15.*

LORD, 'tis a pleasant thing to stand
In gardens planted by thy hand;
Let me within thy courts be seen,
Like a young cedar, fresh and green.

2 There grow thy saints in faith and love,
Bless'd with thine influence from above;
Not Lebanon, with all its trees,
Yields such a comel- sight as these.

3 Laden with fruits of age they show
The Lord is holy, just, and true;
None that attend his gates shall find
A God unfaithful or unkind.

241 *The primitive church.*

YE diff'rent sects, who all declare,
"Lo, here is Christ!" or, "Christ is there!"
Your stronger proofs divinely give,
And show me where the Christians live.

2 Your claim, alas! ye cannot prove;
Ye want the genuine mark of love:
Thou only, Lord, thine own canst show;
For sure thou hast a church below.

3 The gates of hell shall not prevail;
The church on earth can never fail:
Ah! join me to thy secret ones!
Ah! gather all thy living stones!

4 Scatter'd o'er all the earth they lie,
Till thou collect them with thine eye;
Draw by the music of thy name,
And charm into a beauteous frame.

5 For this the pleading Spirit groans,
And cries in all thy banish'd ones,
Greatest of gifts, thy love impart,
And make us of one mind and heart.

6 Join every soul that looks to thee
In bonds of perfect charity;
Now, Lord, the glorious fulness give,
And *all in all* for ever live!

835 *In time of war.*

WHILE o'er our guilty land, O Lord,
We view the terrors of thy sword;
O! whither shall the helpless fly?
To whom but thee direct their cry?

2 The helpless sinner's cries and tears
Are grown familiar to thine ears;
Oft has thy mercy sent relief,
When all was fear and hopeless grief.

3 See, we repent, we weep, we mourn,
To our forsaken God we turn;
O spare our guilty country, spare
The church which thou hast planted there.

4 We plead thy grace, indulgent God;
We plead thy Son's atoning blood;
We plead thy gracious promises—
And are they unavailing pleas?

5 These pleas, presented at thy throne,
Have brought ten thousand blessings down
On guilty lands in helpless wo;
Let them prevail to save us too.

1054 *Doxology.*

PRAISE God, from whom all blessings flow;
Praise him, all creatures here below;
Praise him above, ye heavenly host;
Praise Father, Son, and Holy Ghost.

THE PENITENT. L. M.

383 *Psalm li. 13—19.*

A BROKEN heart, my God, my King,
To thee a sacrifice I bring;
The God of grace will ne'er despise
A broken heart for sacrifice.

2 My soul lies humbled in the dust,
And owns thy dreadful sentence just;
Look down, O Lord, with pitying eye,
And save the soul condemned to die.

3 Then will I teach the world thy ways,
Sinners shall learn thy sovereign grace;
I'll lead them to my Saviour's blood,
And they shall praise a pard'ning God.

4 O may thy love inspire my tongue!
Salvation shall be all my song;
And all my powers shall join to bless
The Lord, my strength and righteousness.

428 *"I am the way."*

JESUS, my all, to heaven is gone,
He whom I fix my hopes upon;
His track I see, and I'll pursue
The narrow way till him I view.

2 The way the holy prophets went,
The road that leads from banishment,
The King's highway of holiness,
I'll go, for all his paths are peace.

3 This is the way I long have sought,
And mourn'd because I found it not;
My grief a burden long has been,
Because I was not saved from sin.

4 The more I strove against its power,
I felt its weight and guilt the more;
Till late I heard my Saviour say,
"Come hither, soul, I AM THE WAY."

5 Lo! glad I come, and thou, bless'd Lamb,
Shalt take me to thee as I am;
Nothing but sin have I to give,
Nothing but love shall I receive.

6 Then will I tell to sinners round,
What a dear Saviour I have found;
I'll point to thy redeeming blood,
And say, "Behold the way to God!"

508 *"That the body of sin might be destroyed."*

THOU God that answerest by fire,
On thee in Jesus' name we call;
Fulfil our faithful hearts' desire,
And let on us thy Spirit fall.

2 Bound on the altar of thy cross,
Our old offending nature lies;
Now, for the honour of thy cause,
Come, and consume the sacrifice!

3 Consume our lusts as rotten wood;
Consume our stony hearts within;
Consume the dust, the serpent's food,
And dry up all the streams of sin.

4 Its body totally destroy!
Thyself the Lord, the God approve!
And fill our hearts with holy joy,
And fervent zeal, and perfect love.

5 O that the fire from heaven might fall!
Our sins its ready victims find,—
Seize on our sins, and burn up all,
Nor leave the least remains behind.

6 Then shall our prostrate souls adore;
The Lord, he is the God, confess;
He is the God of saving power!
He is the God of hall'wing grace.

1055 *Doxology.*

TO Father, Son, and Holy Ghost,
The God whom earth and heaven adore,
Be glory, as it was of old,
Is now, and shall be evermore.

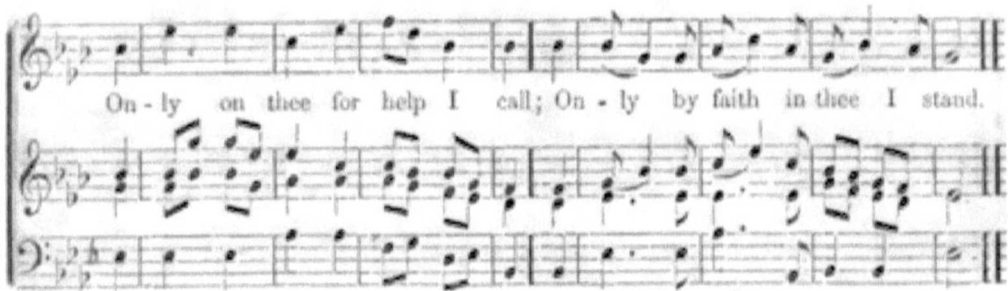

584 *A watchful spirit.*

UPHOLD me, Saviour, or I fall;
O reach me out thy gracious hand!
Only on thee for help I call;
Only by faith in thee I stand.

2 Pierce, fill me with an humble fear;
My utter helplessness reveal!
Satan and sin are always near,
Thee may I always nearer feel.

3 O that to thee my constant mind
Might with an even flame aspire!
Pride in its earliest motions find,
And mark the risings of desire!

4 O that my tender soul might fly
The first abhorr'd approach of ill;
Quick, as the apple of an eye,
The slightest touch of sin to feel!

5 Till thou anew my soul create,
Still may I strive, and watch, and pray,—
Humbly and confidently wait,
And long to see the perfect day.

635 *The trial of Abraham.*

ABRAHAM, when severely tried,
His faith by his obedience show'd;
He with the harsh command complied,
And gave his Isaac back to God.

2 His son the father offer'd up,
Son of his age, his only son,
Object of all his joy and hope,
And less beloved than God alone.

3 O for a faith like his, that we
The bright example may pursue!
May gladly give up all to thee,
To whom our more than all is due.

4 Is there a thing than life more dear?
A thing from which we cannot part?
We can; we now rejoice to tear
The idol from our bleeding heart.

5 For what to thee, O Lord, we give,
A hundred-fold we here obtain;
And soon with thee shall all receive,
And loss shall be eternal gain.

678 *Death welcome to the Christian.*

SHRINKING from the cold hand of death,
I soon shall gather up my feet;
Shall soon resign this fleeting breath,
And die,—my father's God to meet.

2 Number'd among thy people, I
Expect with joy thy face to see:—
Because thou didst for sinners die,
Jesus, in death remember me!

3 O that without a ling'ring groan
I may the welcome word receive!
My body with my charge lay down,
And cease at once to work and live!

4 Walk with me through the dreadful shade,
And, certified that thou art mine,
My spirit, calm and undismayed,
I shall into thy hands resign.

5 No anxious doubt, no guilty gloom,
Shall damp whom Jesus' presence cheers:
My light, my life, my God is come,
And glory in his face appears!

543 *Praying for perfection.*

WHAT! never speak one evil word,
Or rash, or idle, or unkind?
O how shall I, most gracious Lord,
This mark of true perfection find?

2 Thy sinless mind in me reveal;
Thy Spirit's plenitude impart;
And all my spotless life shall tell
Th' abundance of a loving heart.

MISSIONARY CHANT. L. M.

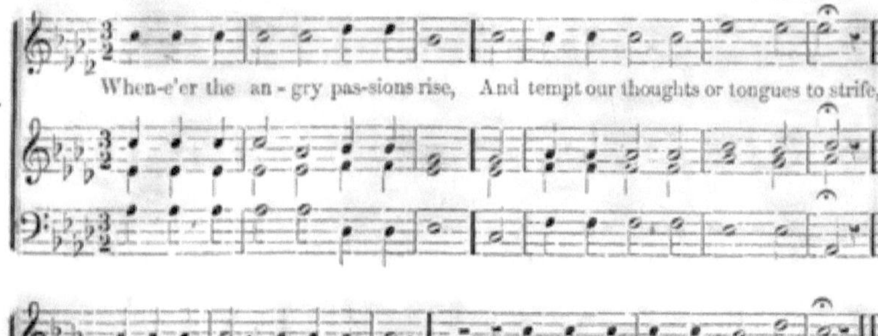

107 *"Leaving us an example."*

WHENE'ER the angry passions rise,
And tempt our thoughts or tongues to strife,
On Jesus let us fix our eyes,
Bright pattern of the Christian life.

2 O how benevolent and kind!
How mild! how ready to forgive!
Be this the temper of our mind,
And these the rules by which we live.

3 To do his heavenly Father's will
Was his employment and delight:
Humility and holy zeal
Shone through his life divinely bright.

4 Dispensing good where'er he came,
The labours of his life were love:
If then we love the Saviour's name,
Let his divine example move!

227 *Psalm* xlvi. 1—5.

GOD is the refuge of his saints,
When storms of sharp distress invade;
Ere we can offer our complaints,
Behold him present with his aid.

2 Let mountains from their seats be hurl'd
Down to the deep and buried there—
Convulsions shake the solid world—
Our faith shall never yield to fear.

3 Loud may the troubled ocean roar—
In sacred peace our souls abide;
While every nation, every shore,
Trembles and dreads the swelling tide.

4 There is a stream, whose gentle flow
Supplies the city of our God,
Life, love, and joy, still gliding through
And wat'ring our divine abode.

5 That sacred stream, thy holy word,
Our grief allays, our fear controls;
Sweet peace thy promises afford,
And give new strength to fainting souls.

6 Zion enjoys her Monarch's love,
Secure against a threatening hour;
Nor can her firm foundations move,
Built on his truth, and arm'd with power.

270 *For an efficient ministry.*

JESUS, thy wand'ring sheep behold!
See, Lord, with yearning bowels, see,
Poor souls that cannot find the fold,
Till sought and gather'd in by thee.

2 Lost are they now, and scatter'd wide,
In pain, and weariness, and want:
With no kind shepherd near, to guide
The sick, and spiritless, and faint.

3 Thou, only thou, the kind and good,
And sheep-redeeming Shepherd art;
Collect thy flock, and give them food,
And pastors after thine own heart.

4 Give the pure word of gen'ral grace,
And great shall be the preachers' crowd;
Preachers who all the sinful race
Point to the all-atoning blood.

5 Open their mouth, and utt'rance give;
Give them a trumpet-voice to call
A world, who all may turn and live,
Through faith in Him who died for all.

6 In every messenger reveal
The grace they preach divinely free;
That each may by thy Spirit tell,
"He died for all, who died for me."

136 *Isaiah xlii. 6, 7.*

ADAM, descended from above,
Saviour and Head of all mankind,
The cov'nant of redeeming love
In thee let every sinner find.

2 Thee, the paternal grace divine,
A universal blessing gave;
A light in every heart to shine;
A Saviour,—every soul to save.

3 Light of the Gentile world, appear,
Command the blind thy rays to see:
Our darkness chase, our sorrows cheer,
And set the plaintive prisoner free.

4 Me, me, who still in darkness sit,
Shut up in sin and unbelief,
Deliver from this gloomy pit,
This dungeon of despairing grief.

5 Open mine eyes the Lamb to know
Who bears the gen'ral sin away;
And to my ransom'd spirit show
The glories of eternal day.

310 *At the close of the Lord's supper.*

STARS, that did herald in, or mark
The night when Jesus was betray'd,—
This feast ends not till ye are dark,
And all your glorious courses stay'd.

2 For from that night, successive bands
Have kept this banquet of the cross,
Saint, pilgrim, martyr of all lands,
And counted earthly portions loss.

3 And here we still forget our woes,
Midst what long ages saw bequeath'd;
The bread is life, the cup o'erflows,
As when the blessing first was breathed.

4 When we rise up and leave our seat,
Millions shall press and fill our place;
Still shall the poor and needy eat,
And sing, like us, the Founder's grace

326 *The gospel supper.*

SINNERS, obey the gospel word!
Haste to the supper of my Lord.
Be wise to know your gracious day;
All things are ready; come away!

2 Ready the Father is to own,
And kiss his late-returning son;
Ready your loving Saviour stands,
And spreads for you his bleeding hands.

3 Ready the Spirit of his love
Just now your hardness to remove;
T' apply and witness with the blood,
And wash and seal the sons of God.

4 Ready for you the angels wait,
To triumph in your bless'd estate:
Tuning their harps, they long to praise
The wonders of redeeming grace.

5 The Father, Son, and Holy Ghost,
Are ready with their shining host:
All heaven is ready to resound,
"The dead's alive! the lost is found!"

327 *Concluded.*

COME, O ye sinners, to your Lord,
In Christ to paradise restored;
His proffer'd benefits embrace,
The plenitude of gospel grace:

2 A pardon written with his blood,
The favour and the peace of God;
The seeing eye, the feeling sense,
The mystic joys of penitence:

3 The godly fear, the pleasing smart,
The meltings of a broken heart;
The tears that tell your sins forgiven;
The sighs that waft your souls to heaven.

4 The guiltless shame, the sweet distress,
Th' unutterable tenderness;
The genuine, meek humility;
The wonder, "Why such love to me!"

5 Th' o'erwhelming power of saving grace,
The sight that veils the seraph's face;
The speechless awe that dares not move,
And all the silent heaven of love.

268 *Ministerial fidelity.*

SAVIOUR of men, thy searching eye
Doth all my inmost thoughts descry:
Doth aught on earth my wishes raise,
Or the world's pleasures, or its praise?

2 The love of Christ doth me constrain
To seek the wand'ring souls of men;
With cries, entreaties, tears to save,
To snatch them from the gaping grave.

3 For this let men revile my name,
No cross I shun, I fear no shame;
All hail reproach, and welcome pain;
Only thy terrors, Lord, restrain.

4 My life, my blood, I here present,
If for thy truth they may be spent;
Fulfil thy sovereign counsel, Lord!
Thy will be done, thy name adored!

5 Give me thy strength, O God of power,
Then let winds blow, or thunders roar,
Thy faithful witness will I be:
'Tis fix'd; I can do all through thee.

1055 *Doxology.*

TO Father, Son, and Holy Ghost,
The God whom earth and heaven adore,
Be glory, as it was of old,
Is now, and shall be evermore.

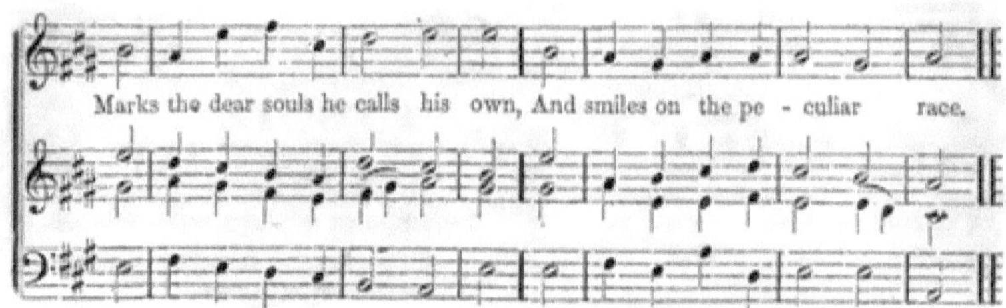

261 *Labourers.*

HIGH on his everlasting throne,
The King of saints his work surveys,
Marks the dear souls he calls his own,
And smiles on the peculiar race.

2 He rests well pleased their toils to see;
Beneath his easy yoke they move;
With all their heart and strength agree
In the sweet labour of his love.

3 See, where the servants of their God,
A busy multitude, appear:
For Jesus day and night employ'd,
His heritage they toil to clear.

4 The love of Christ their hearts constrains,
And strengthens their unwearied hands;
They spend their sweat, and blood, and pains,
To cultivate Immanuel's lands.

5 O multiply thy sowers' seed,
And fruit we every hour shall bear:
Throughout the world thy gospel spread,
Thine everlasting truth declare!

848 *For magistrates. Psalm ci.*

MERCY and judgment are my song;
And, since they both to thee belong,
My gracious God, my righteous King,
To thee my songs and vows I bring.

2 If I am raised to bear the sword
I'll take my counsels from thy word;
Thy justice and thy heavenly grace
Shall be the pattern of my ways.

3 Let wisdom all my actions guide,
And let my God with me reside;
No wicked thing shall dwell with me,
Which may provoke thy jealousy.

4 No sons of slander, rage, and strife,
Shall be companions of my life;
The haughty look, the heart of pride,
Within my doors shall ne'er abide.

5 I'll search the land, and raise the just
To posts of honour, wealth, and trust;
The men who work thy holy will,
Shall be my friends and fav'rites still.

6 In vain shall sinners hope to rise,
By flatt'ring or malicious lies;
And while the innocent I guard,
The bold offender shan't be spared.

7 The impious crew, that factious band,
Shall hide their heads, or quit the land;
And all who break the public rest,
Where I have power, shall be suppress.

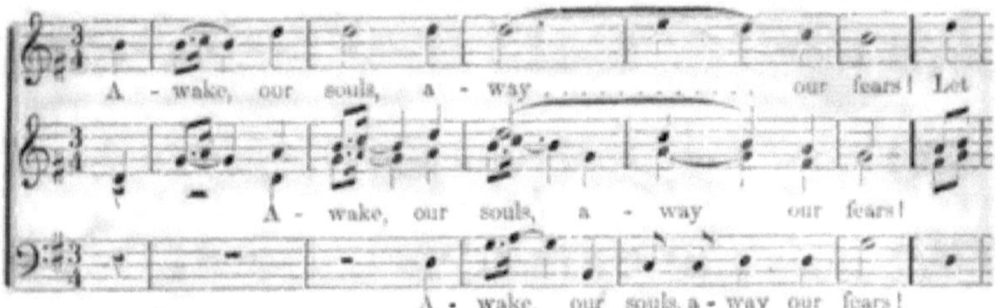

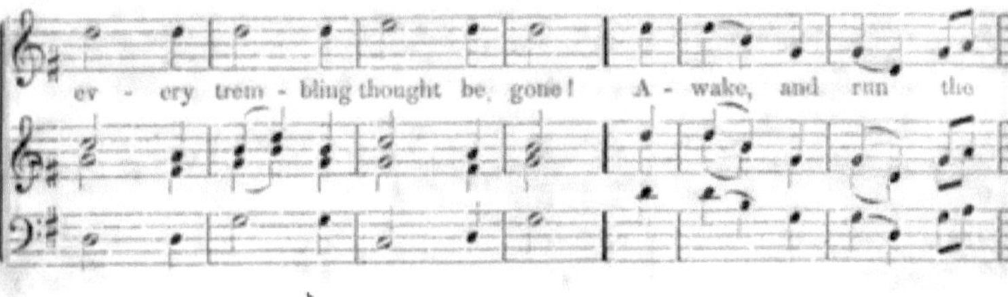

566 *The Christian race.*

AWAKE, our souls! away, our fears!
 Let every trembling thought be gone!
Awake, and run the heavenly race,
 And put a cheerful courage on.

2 True, 'tis a strait and thorny road,
 And mortal spirits tire and faint;
But they forget the mighty God
 That feeds the strength of every saint.

3 From Him, the overflowing spring,
 Our souls shall drink a fresh supply;
While such as trust their native strength,
 Shall melt away, and droop, and die.

4 Swift as the eagle cuts the air,
 We'll mount aloft to his abode;
On wings of love our souls shall fly,
 Nor tire amidst the heavenly road.

96 *"Unto us a Son is given."*

TO us a child, of royal birth,
 Heir of the promises, is given;
Th' Invisible appears on earth,
 The Son of man, the God of heaven.

2 A Saviour born, in love supreme
 He comes, our fallen souls to raise;
He comes, his people to redeem,
 With all his plenitude of grace.

3 The Christ, by raptured seers foretold,
 Fill'd with th' eternal Spirit's power;
Prophet, and Priest, and King, behold,
 And Lord of all the worlds adore.

4 The Lord of hosts, the God most high,
 Who quits his throne, on earth to live,
With joy we welcome from the sky,
 With faith into our hearts receive.

942 *Psalm lxxx. 8—19.*

HAST thou not planted, with thy hand,
 A lovely vine in this our land?
Did not thy power defend it round,
 And heavenly dews enrich the ground?

2 How did the spreading branches shoot,
 And bless the nation with the fruit!
But now, O Lord, look down and see
 Thy mourning vine, that lovely tree.

3 Why is its beauty thus defaced?
 Why hast thou laid its fences waste?
Strangers and foes against it join,
 And every beast devours the vine.

4 Return, almighty God, return;
 Nor let thy bleeding vineyard mourn:
Turn us to thee, thy love restore;
 We shall be saved, and sigh no more.

CORONATION. C. M.

O. HOLDEN.

155 *Coronation of Christ.*

ALL hail the power of Jesus' name,
  Let angels prostrate fall;
Bring forth the royal diadem,
  And crown him Lord of all.

2 Ye chosen seed of Israel's race,—
  A remnant weak and small,—
Hail him, who saves you by his grace,
  And crown him Lord of all.

3 Ye Gentile sinners, ne'er forget
  The wormwood and the gall;
Go, spread your trophies at his feet,
  And crown him Lord of all.

4 Let every kindred, every tribe,
  On this terrestrial ball,
To him all majesty ascribe,
  And crown him Lord of all.

5 O that, with yonder sacred throng,
  We at his feet may fall!
We'll join the everlasting song,
  And crown him Lord of all.

94 *Luke* ii. 8—14.

WHILE shepherds watched their flocks by night,
  All seated on the ground,
The angel of the Lord came down,
  And glory shone around.

2 "Fear not," said he, (for mighty dread
  Had seized their troubled mind,)
"Glad tidings of great joy I bring
  To you and all mankind.

3 "To you, in David's town, this day,
  Is born of David's line,
The Saviour, who is Christ the Lord;
  And this shall be the sign:

4 "The heavenly babe you there shall find
  To human view display'd
All meanly wrapp'd in swathing bands,
  And in a manger laid."

5 Thus spake the seraph, and forthwith
  Appear'd a shining throng
Of angels praising God, on high,
  And thus address'd their song:

6 "All glory be to God on high,
  And to the earth be peace;
Good will henceforth, from heaven to men,
  Begin and never cease."

749 *Spiritual restoration of the Jews.*

BUT who shall see the glorious day,
  When, throned on Zion's brow,
The Lord shall rend that veil away
  Which blinds the nations now?

2 When earth no more beneath the fear
  Of his rebuke shall lie,—
When pain shall cease, and every tear
  Be wiped from every eye,—

3 Then, Judah, thou no more shalt mourn
  Beneath the heathen's chain;
Thy days of splendour shall return,
  And all be new again.

4 The fount of life shall then be quaff'd
  In peace by all who come,
And every wind that blows shall waft
  Some long-lost exile home.

813 *Thanksgiving for rain. Psalm* lxv. 9—13.

GOOD is the Lord, the heavenly King
  Who makes the earth his care:
Visits the pastures every spring,
  And bids the grass appear.

2 The clouds, like rivers raised on high,
Pour out at his command
Their watery blessings from the sky,
To cheer the thirsty land.

3 The soften'd ridges of the field
Permit the corn to spring;
The valleys rich provision yield,
And the poor lab'rers sing.

4 The little hills on every side
Rejoice at falling showers;
The meadows, dress'd in all their pride,
Perfume the air with flowers.

5 The various months thy goodness crowns,
How bounteous are thy ways!
The bleating flocks spread o'er the downs,
And shepherds shout thy praise.

140 *Resurrection.*

THE Sun of righteousness appears,
To set in blood no more;
Adore the Scatterer of your fears,
Your rising Sun adore.

2 The saints, when he resign'd his breath,
Unclosed their sleeping eyes;
He breaks again the bands of death,
Again the dead arise.

3 Alone the dreadful race he ran,
Alone the wine-press trod;
He dies and suffers as a man,
He rises as a God.

4 In vain the stone, the watch, the seal,
Forbid an early rise
To Him who breaks the gates of hell,
And opens paradise.

11 *Divine excellence.*

HAIL, Father, Son, and Holy Ghost,
One God in persons three;
Of thee we make our joyful boast,
Our songs we make of thee!

2 Thou neither canst be felt nor seen;
Thou art a spirit pure;
Thou from eternity hast been,
And always shalt endure.

3 Present alike in every place,
Thy Godhead we adore:
Beyond the bound of time and space
Thou dwell'st for evermore.

4 In wisdom infinite thou art,
Thine eye doth all things see;
And every thought of every heart
Is fully known to thee.

5 Whate'er thou wilt, in earth below,
Thou dost in heaven above;
But chiefly we rejoice to know
Th' almighty God of love.

6 Thou lov'st whate'er thy hands have made,
Thy goodness we rehearse,
In shining characters display'd
Throughout our universe.

7 Mercy, with love and endless grace,
O'er all thy works doth reign:
But mostly thou delight'st to bless
Thy favourite creature man.

8 Wherefore let every creature give
To thee the praise design'd;
But chiefly, Lord, the thanks receive,
The hearts, of all mankind.

101 *The holy child Jesus.*

ABASH'D be all the boast of age,
Be hoary learning dumb!
Expounder of the mystic page,
Behold an infant come!

2 O Wisdom! whose unfading power
Beside the Eternal stood,
To frame, in nature's earliest hour,
The land, the sky, the flood.

3 Yet didst not thou disdain awhile
An infant form to wear;
To bless thy mother with a smile,
And lisp thy falter'd prayer.

4 But in thy Father's own abode,
With Israel's elders round,
Conversing high with Israel's God,
Thy chiefest joy was found.

5 So may our youth adore thy name!
And, Saviour, deign to bless,
With fostering grace, the timid flame
Of early holiness.

41 *Exodus xxxiv. 6, 7.*

THY ceaseless, unexhausted love,
Unmerited and free,
Delights our evil to remove,
And help our misery.

2 Thou waitest to be gracious still,
Thou dost with sinners bear,
That saved, we may thy goodness feel,
And all thy grace declare.

3 Thy goodness and thy truth to me,
To every soul, abound;
A vast, unfathomable sea,
Where all our thoughts are drown'd.

4 Its streams the whole creation reach,
So plenteous is the store;
Enough for all, enough for each,
Enough for evermore.

5 Faithful, O Lord, thy mercies are!
A rock that cannot move:
A thousand promises declare
Thy constancy of love.

6 Throughout the universe it reigns,
Unalterably sure;
And while the truth of God remains,
His goodness must endure.

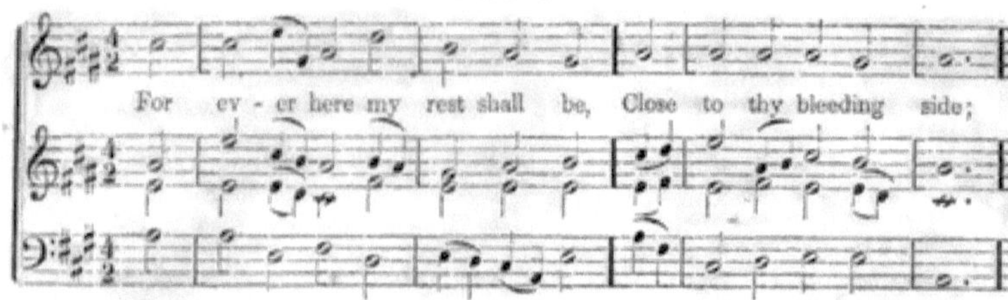

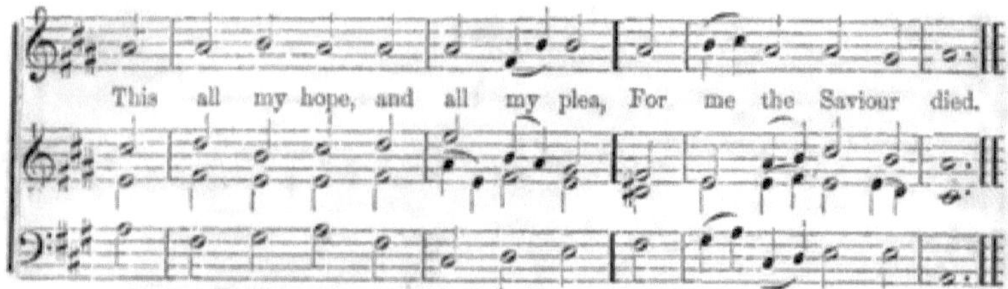

494 *Perfect purification.*

FOR ever here my rest shall be,
Close to thy bleeding side,
This all my hope, and all my plea,
For me the Saviour died.

2 My dying Saviour, and my God,
Fountain for guilt and sin,
Sprinkle me ever with thy blood,
And cleanse and keep me clean.

3 Wash me, and make me thus thine own;
Wash me, and mine thou art;
Wash me, but not my feet alone,
My hands, my head, my heart.

4 Th' atonement of thy blood apply,
Till faith to sight improve,
Till hope in full fruition die,
And all my soul be love.

13 *To God the Holy Ghost.*

HAIL, Holy Ghost, Jehovah, third
In order of the three;
Sprung from the Father and the Word,
From all eternity!

2 Thy Godhead, brooding o'er th' abyss
Of formless waters, lay;
Spoke into order all that is,
And darkness into day.

3 In deepest hell, or heaven's height,
Thy presence who can flee?
Known is the Father to thy sight,
Th' abyss of Deity.

4 Thy power through Jesus' life display'd,
Quite from the virgin's womb,
Dying, his soul an off'ring made,
And raised him from the tomb.

5 God's image, which our sins destroy,
Thy grace restores below;
And truth, and holiness, and joy,
From thee, their Fountain, flow.

6 Hail, Holy Ghost, Jehovah, third
In order of the three;
Sprung from the Father and the Word
From all eternity!

403 *The earnest suit.*

O THAT I could my Lord receive,
Who did the world redeem;
Who gave his life that I might live
A life conceal'd in him!

2 O that I could the blessing prove,
My heart's extreme desire!
Live happy in my Saviour's love,
And in his arms expire!

3 In answer to ten thousand prayers,
Thou pard'ning God, descend:
Number me with salvation's heirs,
My sins and troubles end.

4 Nothing I ask or want beside,
Of all in earth or heaven,
But let me feel thy blood applied,
And live and die forgiven.

138 *Waiting for the blessing.*

FATHER, I wait before thy throne;
Call me a child of thine;
Send down the Spirit of thy Son,
To form my heart divine.

2 There shed thy promised love abroad,
And make my comfort strong;
Then shall I say, "My Father, God!"
With an unwav'ring tongue.

619 *Surrendering all for Christ.*

HOW vain are all things here below!
How false, and yet how fair!
Each pleasure hath its poison too,
And every sweet a snare.

2 The brightest things below the sky
Give but a flatt'ring light;
We should suspect some danger nigh
Where we possess delight.

3 Our dearest joys and nearest friends,
The partners of our blood,
How they divide our wav'ring minds,
And leave but half for God!

4 The fondness of a creature's love,
How strong it strikes the sense!
Thither the warm affections move,
Nor can we call them thence.

5 Dear Saviour, let thy beauties be
My soul's eternal food?
And grace command my heart away
From all created good.

71 *Psalm cxlv.*

LET every tongue thy goodness speak,
Thou sovereign Lord of all,
Thy strength'ning hands uphold the weak,
And raise the poor that fall.

2 When sorrows bow the spirit down,
When virtue lies distrest,
Beneath the proud oppressor's frown,
Thou giv'st the mourner rest.

3 Thou know'st the pains thy servants feel,
Thou hear'st thy children's cry,
And their best wishes to fulfil,
Thy grace is ever nigh.

4 Thy mercy never shall remove
From men of heart sincere:
Thou sav'st the souls whose humble love
Is join'd with holy fear.

5 My lips shall dwell upon thy praise,
And spread thy fame abroad;
Let all the sons of Adam raise
The honours of their God.

364 *Before preaching to the young.*

YE hearts with youthful vigour warm,
In smiling crowds draw near,
And turn from every mortal charm,
A Saviour's voice to hear.

2 He, Lord of all the worlds on high,
Stoops to converse with you;
And lays his radiant glories by,
Your friendship to pursue.

3 "The soul that longs to see my face,
Is sure my love to gain;
And those that early seek my grace,
Shall never seek in vain."

4 What object, Lord, my soul should move
If once compared with thee?
What beauty should command my love
Like what in Christ I see?

5 Away, ye false, delusive toys,
Vain tempters of the mind!
'Tis here I fix my lasting choice,
And here true bliss I find.

1053 *Doxology.*

NOW let the Father, and the Son,
And Spirit be adored;
Where there are works to make him known,
Or saints to love the Lord.

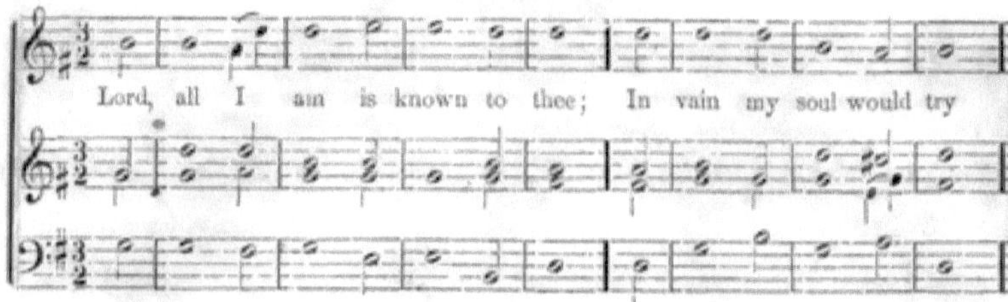

69 *Psalm cxxxix. 1—6.*

LORD, all I am is known to thee;
  In vain my soul would try
To shun thy presence, or to flee
  The notice of thine eye.

2 Thy all-surrounding sight surveys
  My rising and my rest,
My public walks, my private ways,
  The secrets of my breast.

3 My thoughts lie open to thee, Lord,
  Before they're form'd within,
And ere my lips pronounce the word
  Thou know'st the sense I mean.

4 O wond'rous knowledge! deep and high!
  Where can a creature hide?
Within thy circling arms I lie,
  Beset on every side.

5 So let thy grace surround me still,
  And like a bulwark prove,
To guard my soul from every ill,
  Secured by sovereign love.

37 *Too wise to err—too good to be unkind.*

SINCE all the varying scenes of time
  God's watchful eye surveys,
O, who so wise to choose our lot,
  Or to appoint our ways!

2 Good when he gives—supremely good—
  Nor less when he denies;
E'en crosses, from his sovereign hand,
  Are blessings in disguise.

3 Why should we doubt a Father's love,
  So constant and so kind?
To his unerring, gracious will,
  Be every wish resign'd.

36 *"Excellent in working."*

GOD, in the high and holy place,
  Looks down upon the spheres;
Yet, in his providence and grace,
  To every eye appears.

2 The forests in his strength rejoice;
  Hark! on the evening breeze,
As once of old, the Lord God's voice
  Is heard among the trees.

3 Here, on the hills, he feeds his herds,
  His flocks on yonder plains;
His praise is warbled by the birds;
  O could we catch their strains!

4 In every stream his bounty flows,
  Diffusing joy and wealth;
In every breeze his Spirit blows
  The breath of life and health.

5 His blessings fall in plenteous showers
  Upon the lap of earth,
That teems with foliage, fruits, and flowers,
  And rings with infant mirth.

6 If God hath made this world so fair,
  Where sin and death abound,
How beautiful, beyond compare,
  Will paradise be found!

48 *Psalm xviii. 9, 10.*

THE Lord descended from above,
  And bow'd the heavens most high;
And underneath his feet he cast
  The darkness of the sky.

2 On cherub and on cherubim
  Full royally he rode,
And on the wings of mighty winds
  Came flying all abroad.

HENSEL. C. M.

E. G. EVERETT

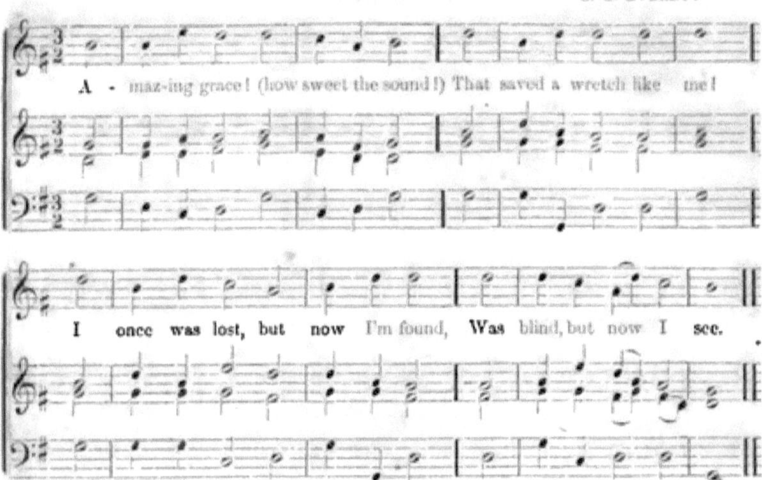

654 *Gratitude and hope.*

AMAZING grace! (how sweet the sound!)
 That saved a wretch like me!
I once was lost, but now am found,
 Was blind, but now I see.

2 'Twas grace that taught my heart to fear,
 And grace my fears relieved;
How precious did that grace appear,
 The hour I first believed!

3 Through many dangers, toils, and snares,
 I have already come;
'Tis grace has brought me safe thus far,
 And grace will lead me home.

4 The Lord has promised good to me,
 His word my hope secures;
He will my shield and portion be
 As long as life endures.

5 Yea, when this flesh and heart shall fail,
 And mortal life shall cease,
I shall possess, within the veil,
 A life of joy and peace.

34 *1 Chron. xxix. 10—13.*

BLESS'D be our everlasting Lord,
 Our Father, God, and King!
Thy sovereign goodness we record,
 Thy glorious power sing.

2 By thee the victory is given:
 The majesty divine,
And strength, and might, and earth, and heaven,
 And all therein, are thine.

3 The kingdom, Lord, is thine alone,
 Who dost thy right maintain;
And, high on thy eternal throne,
 O'er men and angels reign.

4 Riches, as seemeth good to thee,
 Thou dost, and honour, give;
And kings their power and dignity
 Out of thy hand receive.

5 Thou hast on us the grace bestow'd,
 Thy greatness to proclaim;
And therefore now we thank our God,
 And praise thy glorious name.

6 Thy glorious name, and nature's powers,
 Thou dost to us make known;
And all the Deity is ours,
 Through thy incarnate Son.

667 *Psalm xxxix.*

TEACH me the measure of my days,
 Thou Maker of my frame;
I would survey life's narrow space,
 And learn how frail I am.

2 A span is all that we can boast,
 An inch or two of time;
Man is but vanity and dust,
 In all his flower and prime.

3 What should I wish, or wait for, then,
 From creatures, earth, and dust?
They make our expectations vain,
 And disappoint our trust.

4 Now I forbid my carnal hope,
 My fond desires recall;
I give my mortal interest up,
 And make my God my all.

1053 *Doxology.*

NOW let the Father, and the Son,
 And Spirit, be adored;
Where there are works to make him known,
 Or saints to love the Lord.

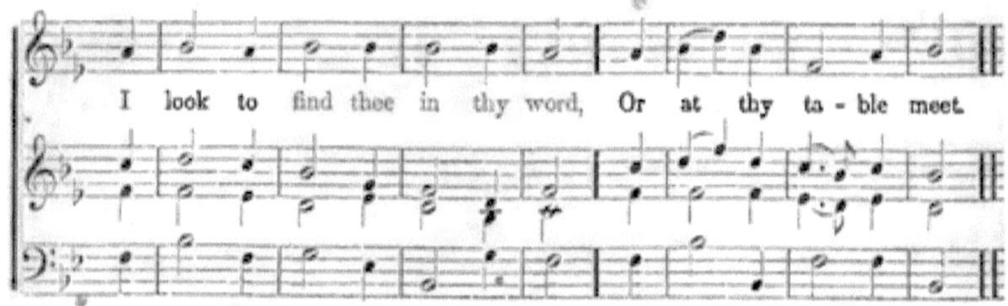

388 *Seeking the power.*

STILL, for thy loving kindness, Lord,
I in thy temple wait:
I look to find thee in thy word,
Or at thy table meet.

2 Here in thine own appointed ways,
I wait to learn thy will:
Silent I stand before thy face,
And hear thee say, "Be still!

3 "Be still! and know that I am God!"—
'Tis all I live to know;
To feel the virtue of thy blood,
And spread its praise below!

4 I wait my vigour to renew,
Thine image to retrieve!
The veil of outward things pass through,
And gasp in thee to live.

5 I work; and own the labour vain,
And thus from works I cease:
I strive; and see my fruitless pain,
Till God create my peace.

6 Fruitless, till thou thyself impart,
Must all my efforts prove;
They cannot change a sinful heart,
They cannot purchase love.

7 I do the things thy laws enjoin,
And then the strife give o'er;
To thee I then the whole resign,
I trust in means no more.

8 I trust in Him who stands between
The Father's wrath and me;
Jesus, thou great eternal Mean,
I look for all from thee!

418 *Urgent pleadings.*

JESUS! Redeemer, Saviour, Lord,
The weary sinner's Friend;
Come to my help, pronounce the word,
And bid my troubles end.

2 Deliv'rance to my soul proclaim,
And life and liberty;
Shed forth the virtue of thy name,
And *Jesus* prove to me!

3 Faith to be heal'd thou know'st I have,
For thou that faith hast given;
Thou canst, thou wilt, the sinner save,
And make me meet for heaven.

4 Thou canst o'ercome this heart of mine;
Thou wilt victorious prove:
For everlasting strength is thine,
And everlasting love.

5 Thy powerful Spirit shall subdue
Unconquerable sin,
Cleanse this foul heart, and make it new,
And write thy law within.

6 Bound down with twice ten thousand ties,
Yet let me hear thy call,
My soul in confidence shall rise,
Shall rise and break through all.

7 Speak, and the deaf shall hear thy voice,
The blind his sight receive;
The dumb in songs of praise rejoice;
The heart of stone believe.

8 The Ethiop then shall change his skin:
The dead shall feel thy power:
The loathsome leper shall be clean,
And I shall sin no more.

421 *"Help thou my unbelief."*

HOW sad our state by nature is!
Our sin how deep it stains!
And Satan binds our captive souls
Fast in his slavish chains.

2 But there's a voice of sovereign grace
Sounds from the sacred word:
Ho! ye despairing sinners, come,
And trust a faithful Lord.

3 My soul obeys the gracious call,
And runs to this relief;
I would believe thy promise, Lord,
O help my unbelief!

4 To the bless'd fountain of thy blood,
Incarnate God, I fly;
Here let me wash my spotted soul
From crimes of deepest dye.

5 A guilty, weak, and helpless worm,
Into thy arms I fall,
Be thou my strength and righteousness,
My Jesus and my all.

454 *The backslider's recovery.*

O WHY did I my Saviour leave,
So soon unfaithful prove!
How could I thy good Spirit grieve,
And sin against thy love.

2 But O! how soon thy wrath is o'er,
And pard'ning love takes place!
Assist me, Saviour, to adore
The riches of thy grace.

3 O could I lose myself in thee,
Thy depth of mercy prove,
Thou vast, unfathomable sea
Of unexhausted love!

4 My humbled soul, when thou art near,
In dust and ashes lies:
How shall a sinful worm appear,
Or meet thy purer eyes?

5 I loathe myself when God I see,
And into nothing fall;
Content if thou exalted be,
And Christ be ALL IN ALL.

668 *Psalm xc.*

O GOD, our help in ages past,
Our hope for years to come,
Our shelter from the stormy blast,
And our eternal home:

2 Under the shadow of thy throne,
Still may we dwell secure;
Sufficient is thine arm alone,
And our defence is sure.

3 Before the hills in order stood,
Or earth received her frame,
From everlasting thou art God,
To endless years the same.

4 A thousand ages, in thy sight,
Are like an evening gone;
Short as the watch that ends the night
Before the rising sun.

5 The busy tribes of flesh and blood,
With all their cares and fears,
Are carried downward by the flood,
And lost in following years.

6 Time, like an ever-rolling stream,
Bears all its sons away;
They fly, forgotten, as a dream
Dies at the op'ning day.

7 O God, our help in ages past,
Our hope for years to come;
Be thou our guard while life shall last,
And our perpetual home!

42 *Exodus xxxiv. 7.*

RESERVES of unexhausted grace
Are treasured up in thee,
For myriads of the fallen race;
For all mankind and me.

2 The flowing stream continues full,
Till time its course hath run;
And while eternal ages roll
Thy mercy shall flow on.

3 Merciful God, long-suffering, kind,
To me thy name is show'd;
But sinners must exult to find
Thou art a pard'ning God.

4 Our sins in deed, and word, and thought,
Thou freely dost forgive;
For us thou by thy blood hast bought,
And died that I might live.

5 Yet wilt thou not the guilty clear,
If we to sin return:
Thy wrath, vindictively severe,
From age to age shall burn.

6 Unless our sinful misery
We, self-condemn'd, bemoan,
And find an Advocate in thee,
Before thy Father's throne.

283 *Infant baptism.*

HOW large the promise, how divine,
To Abr'am and his seed!
"I am a God to thee and thine,
Supplying all their need."

2 The words of his extensive love
From age to age endure:
The angel of the cov'nant proves,
And seals the blessing sure.

3 Jesus the ancient faith confirms,
To our great father given;
He takes our children to his arms,
And calls them heirs of heaven.

4 O God, how faithful are thy ways
Thy love endures the same;
Nor from the promise of thy grace
Blots out our children's name.

11 *To God the Father.*

HAIL, Father, whose creating call
Unnumber'd worlds attend;
Jehovah, comprehending all,
Whom none can comprehend!

2 In light unsearchable enthroned,
Whom angels dimly see;
The fountain of the Godhead own'd,
And foremost of the three!

3 From thee, through an eternal now,
The Son, thine offspring, flow'd;
An everlasting Father, thou,
An everlasting God.

4 Nor quite display'd to worlds above,
Nor quite on earth conceal'd;
By wondrous unexhausted love
To mortal man reveal'd.

5 Supreme and all-sufficient God,
When nature shall expire,
And worlds created by thy nod
Shall perish by thy fire,—

6 Thy name, Jehovah, be adored
By creatures without end;
Whom none but thy essential Word
And Spirit comprehend.

333 *Isaiah lv. 1—3.*

LET every mortal ear attend,
And every heart rejoice;
The trumpet of the gospel sounds
With an inviting voice.

2 Ho! all ye hungry, starving souls,
That feed upon the wind,
And vainly strive with earthly toys
To fill an empty mind

3 Eternal Wisdom hath prepared
A soul-reviving feast,
And bids your longing appetites
The rich provision taste.

4 Ho! ye that pant for living streams,
And pine away and die,
Here you may quench your raging thirst
With springs that never dry.

5 Rivers of love and mercy here,
In a rich ocean, join
Salvation, in abundance, flows
Like floods of milk and wine.

6 The happy gates of gospel grace
Stand open night and day:
Lord, we are come to seek supplies,
And drive our wants away.

265 *The minister's theme.*

JESUS, the name high over all
In hell, or earth, or sky!
Angels and men before it fall,
And devils fear and fly.

2 Jesus, the name to sinners dear,
The name to sinners given!
It scatters all their guilty fear;
It turns their hell to heaven.

3 Jesus the pris'ner's fetters breaks,
And bruises Satan's head;
Power into strengthless souls it speaks,
And life into the dead.

4 O that the world might taste and see
The riches of his grace!
The arms of love that compass me,
Would all mankind embrace!

5 His only righteousness I show,
His saving truth proclaim
'Tis all my business here below
To cry, "Behold the Lamb!"

6 Happy, if with my latest breath
I may but gasp his name;
Preach him to all, and cry in death,
"Behold, behold the Lamb!"

238 *Psalm cxxii.*

HOW did my heart rejoice to hear
  My friends devoutly say,
"In Zion let us all appear
  And keep the solemn day!"

2 I love her gates, I love the road!
  The church, adorn'd with grace,
Stands like a palace built for God
  To show his milder face.

3 Up to her courts, with joys unknown,
  The holy tribes repair;
The Son of David holds his throne,
  And sits in judgment there.

4 He hears our praises and complaints;
  And, while his awful voice
Divides the sinners from the saints,
  We tremble, and rejoice.

5 Peace be within this sacred place,
  And joy a constant guest!
With holy gifts and heavenly grace
  Be her attendants blest.

6 My soul shall pray for Zion still,
  While life or breath remains;
There my best friends, my kindred dwell,
  There God, my Saviour, reigns.

457 *Opening Worship.*

LOOK unto Him, ye nations; own
  Your God, ye fallen race;
Look, and be saved through faith alone,
  Be justified by grace.

2 See all your sins on Jesus laid:
  The Lamb of God was slain;
His soul was once an off'ring made
  For every soul of man.

3 Awake from guilty nature's sleep,
  And Christ shall give you light;
Cast all your sins into the deep,
  And wash the Ethiop white.

4 With me, your chief, ye then shall know
  Shall feel, your sins forgiven;
Anticipate your heaven below,
  And own that love is heaven.

236 *Psalm lxxxix. 15–18.*

BLESS'D are the souls who hear and know
  The gospel's joyful sound;
Peace shall attend the paths they go,
  And light their steps surround.

2 Their joy shall bear their spirits up,
  Through their Redeemer's name;
His righteousness exalts their hope;
  Nor Satan dares condemn.

3 The Lord, our glory and defence,
  Strength and salvation gives;
Israel, thy King for ever reigns,
  Thy God for ever lives.

792 *For a Commencement.*

WHILE we with fear and hope survey
  This youthful, blooming throng,
And little know th' eventful way
  Their steps may pass along;—

2 One day is as a thousand years,
  Eternal God, to thee,
And present to thine eye appears
  Their whole futurity.

3 Thou seest temptation's subtle thread,
  Or torture's fiery test:—
Mid scenes of pleasure, or of dread,
  Screen thou th' unguarded breast.

4 Saviour! through each portentous change,
  And dangers yet untrod,
Where'er they rest, where'er they range,
  Be thou their present God!

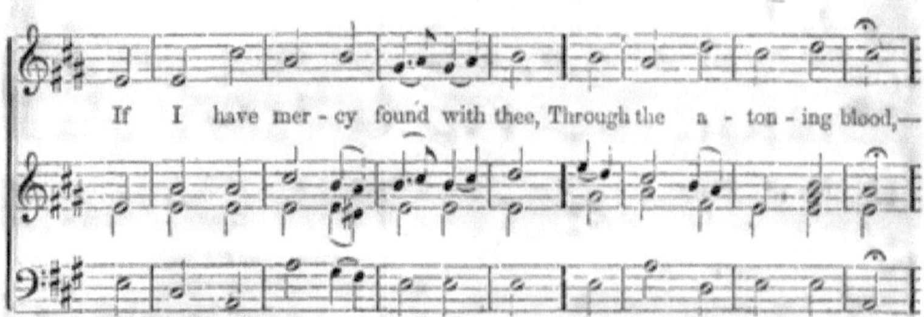

578 *Filial fear.*

GOD of all grace and majesty,
  Supremely great and good,
If I have mercy found with thee,
  Through the atoning blood,—
The guard of all thy mercies give,
  And to my pardon join
A fear lest I should ever grieve
  The Comforter divine.

2 Still may I walk as in thy sight,
  My strict Observer see;
And thou, by rev'rent love, unite
  My childlike heart to thee:
Still let me, till my days are past,
  At Jesus' feet abide;
So shall he lift me up at last,
  And seat me by his side.

582 *A tender conscience.*

I WANT a principle within,
  Of jealous, godly fear,—
A sensibility of sin,
  A pain to feel it near;
I want the first approach to feel
  Of pride, or fond desire,—
To catch the wand'ring of my will,
  And quench the kindling fire.

2 From thee that I no more may part
  No more thy goodness grieve,
The filial awe, the fleshly heart,
  The tender conscience, give.
Quick as the apple of an eye,
  O God, my conscience make!
Awake my soul when sin is nigh,
  And keep it still awake.

3 If to the right or left I stray,
  That moment, Lord, reprove;
And let me weep my life away
  For having grieved thy love.
O may the least omission pain
  My well-instructed soul!
And drive me to the blood again
  Which makes the wounded whole.

593 *Waiting in the sanctuary.*

FATHER, behold with gracious eyes
  The souls before thy throne,
Who now present their sacrifice,
  And seek thee in thy Son.
Well pleased in him thyself declare,
  Thy pard'ning love reveal,
The peaceful answer of our prayer
  To every conscience seal.

2 Meanest of all thy servants, I
  Those happier spirits meet,
And mix with theirs my feeble cry,
  And worship at thy feet.
On me, on all, some gift bestow,
  Some blessing now impart;
The seed of life eternal sow
  In every mournful heart.

3 Thy loving, powerful Spirit shed,
  And speak our sins forgiven,
Or haste throughout the lump to spread
  The sanctifying leaven.
Refresh us with a ceaseless shower
  Of graces from above,
Till all receive the perfect power
  Of everlasting love.

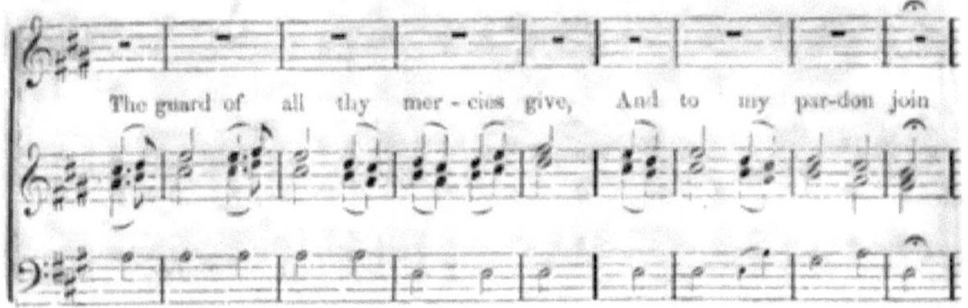
The guard of all thy mer - cies give, And to my par-don join

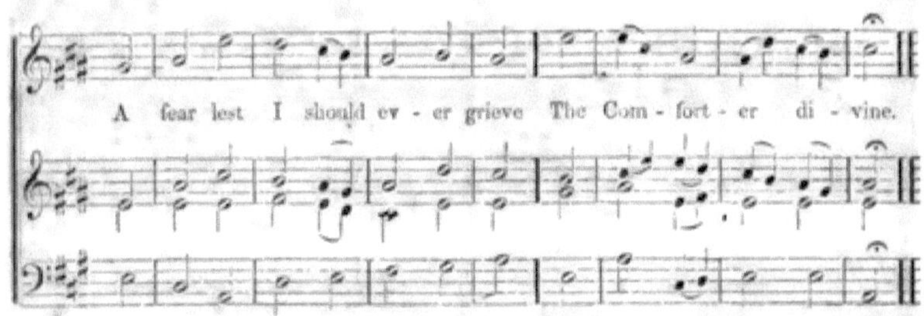
A fear lest I should ev - er grieve The Com - fort - er di - vine.

711 *Visions of heaven.*

AND let this feeble body fail,
 And let it droop or die;
My soul shall quit the mournful vale,
 And soar to worlds on high,—
Shall join the disembodied saints,
 And find its long-sought rest,
That only bliss for which it pants,
 In my Redeemer's breast.

2 In hope of that immortal crown,
 I now the cross sustain,
And gladly wander up and down,
 And smile at toil and pain:
I suffer out my threescore years,
 Till my Deliv'rer come,
And wipe away his servant's tears,
 And take his exile home.

3 Surely he will not long delay;
 I hear his Spirit cry,
"Arise, my love, make haste away!
 Go, get thee up and die.
O'er death, who now has lost his sting,
 I give thee victory,
And with me my reward I bring,
 I bring my heaven for thee."

4 Lord, I the welcome word receive,
 Thee on the mount adore,
For thy dear sake content to live
 Some painful moments more:
I live in holy grief and joy,
 On Pisgah's top I stand,
And life's important point employ,
 To view the promised land.

712 *Visions of heaven.*

O WHAT hath Jesus bought for me
 Before my ravish'd eyes
Rivers of life divine I see,
 And trees of paradise!
They flourish in perpetual bloom,
 Fruit every month they give;
And to the healing leaves who come
 Eternally shall live.

2 I see a world of spirits bright,
 Who reap the pleasures there!
They all are robed in spotless white,
 And conqu'ring palms they bear:
Adorn'd by their Redeemer's grace,
 They close pursue the Lamb,
And every shining front displays
 Th' unutterable name.

3 They drink the vivifying stream,
 They pluck th' ambrosial fruit,
And each records the praise of Him
 Who tuned his golden lute:
At once they strike th' harmonious wire,
 And hymn the great Three-One;
He hears; he smiles; and all the choir
 Fall down before his throne.

4 O what are all my suff'rings here,
 If, Lord, thou count me meet
With that enraptured host t' appear,
 And worship at thy feet!
Give joy or grief, give ease or pain:
 Take life or friends away,
I come to find them all again
 In that eternal day.

40 *Exodus* xxxiv. 5, 6.

GREAT God! to me the sight afford
  To him of old allow'd;
And let my faith behold its Lord,
  Descending in a cloud!

2 In that revealing Spirit come down,
  Thine attributes proclaim,
And to my inmost soul make known
  The glories of thy name.

3 Jehovah, Christ, I thee adore,
  Who gav'st my soul to be!
Fountain of being, and of power,
  And great in majesty.

4 The Lord, the mighty God, thou art,
  But let me rather prove
That name inspoken to my heart,
  That fav'rite name of Love.

5 Merciful God, thyself proclaim
  In this polluted breast;
Mercy is thy distinguish'd name,
  And suits the sinner best.

6 Our misery doth for pity call,
  Our sin implores thy grace;
And thou art merciful to all
  Our lost, apostate race.

139 *Resurrection of Christ.*

THE Lord of sabbath let us praise,
  In concert with the blest,
Who, joyful, in harmonious lays,
  Employ an endless rest.

2 Thus, Lord, while we remember thee,
  We bless'd and pious grow;
By hymns of praise we learn to be
  Triumphant here below.

3 On this glad day a brighter scene
  Of glory was display'd,
By God, th' eternal Word, than when
  This universe was made.

4 He rises, who mankind has bought
  With grief and pain extreme:
'Twas great to speak the world from naught,
  'Twas greater to redeem.

192 *"He conquered when he fell."*

I SING my Saviour's wondrous death,
  He conquer'd when he fell;
'*Tis finish'd!* said his dying breath,
  And shook the gates of hell.

2 '*Tis finish'd!* our Immanuel cries,
  The dreadful work is done!
Hence shall his sovereign throne arise:
  His kingdom is begun.

3 His cross a sure foundation laid
  For glory and renown,
When through the regions of the dead
  He pass'd, to reach the crown.

4 Exalted at his Father's side,
  Sits our victorious Lord;
To heaven and hell his hands divide
  The vengeance or reward.

5 The saints from his propitious eye
  Await their several crowns:
And all the sons of darkness fly
  The terror of his frowns.

1053 *Doxology.*

NOW let the Father, and the Son,
  And Spirit, be adored;
Where there are works to make Him known,
  Or saints to love the Lord.

196 *The Name of Jesus.*

HOW sweet the name of Jesus sounds
In a believer's ear!
It soothes his sorrows, heals his wounds,
And drives away his fear.

2 It makes the wounded spirit whole,
And calms the troubled breast;
'Tis manna to the hungry soul,
And to the weary, rest.

3 Dear Name, the rock on which I build,
My shield and hiding place;
My never-failing treasury, fill'd
With boundless stores of grace.

4 Jesus, my Shepherd, Husband, Friend,
My Prophet, Priest, and King!
My Lord, my Life, my Way, my End,
Accept the praise I bring.

5 Weak is the effort of my heart,
And cold my warmest thought;
But when I see thee as thou art,
I'll praise thee as I ought.

6 Till then I would thy love proclaim
With every fleeting breath;
And may the music of thy name
Refresh my soul in death.

296 *Penitent sinners welcome to the Lord's table.*

THIS is the feast of heavenly wine,
And God invites to sup;
The juices of the living vine
Were press'd to fill the cup.

2 O! bless the Saviour, ye who eat,
With royal dainties fed;
Not heaven affords a costlier treat,
For Jesus is the bread!

3 The vile, the lost—he calls to them;
"Ye trembling souls, appear!
The righteous in their own esteem
Have no acceptance here.

4 "Approach, ye poor, nor dare refuse
The banquet spread for you;"
Dear Saviour, this is welcome news!
Then I may venture too.

348 *Worth of the soul.*

WHAT is the thing of greatest price,
The whole creation round!
That which was lost in Paradise,
That which in Christ is found:

2 The soul of man—Jehovah's breath—
That keeps two worlds at strife;
Hell moves beneath to work its death,
Heaven stoops to give it life.

3 God, to reclaim it, did not spare
His well-beloved Son;
Jesus, to save it, deign'd to bear
The sins of all in one.

4 The Holy Spirit seal'd the plan,
And pledged the blood divine,
To ransom every soul of man;—
That price was paid for mine.

5 And is this treasure borne below,
In earthen vessels frail?
Can none its utmost value know,
Till flesh and spirit fail?

6 Then let us gather round the cross,
That knowledge to obtain;
Not by the soul's eternal loss,
But everlasting gain.

671 *A voice from the tombs.*

HARK! from the tombs a doleful sound,
My ears attend the cry:
"Ye living men, come view the ground
Where you must shortly lie.

2 "Princes, this clay must be your bed,
In spite of all your towers;
The tall, the wise, the reverend head,
Must lie as low as ours."

3 Great God! is this our certain doom!
And are we still secure!
Still walking downward to the tomb,
And yet prepared no more!

4 Grant us the power of quick'ning grace,
To fit our souls to fly,
Then, when we drop this dying flesh,
We'll rise above the sky.

719 *Eternal death.*

THAT awful day will surely come,
Th' appointed hour makes haste,
When I must stand before my Judge,
And pass the solemn test.

2 Jesus, thou source of all my joys,
Thou ruler of my heart,
How could I bear to hear thy voice,
Pronounce the sound, "Depart!"

3 The thunder of that awful word
Would so torment my ear,
'Twould tear my soul asunder, Lord,
With most tormenting fear.

4 What, to be banish'd from my Lord,
And yet forbid to die!
To linger in eternal pain,
And death for ever fly!

5 O wretched state of deep despair,
To see my God remove,
And fix my doleful station where
I must not taste his love!

670 *Dwelling among the tombs.*

BENEATH our feet and o'er our head
Is equal warning given:
Beneath us lie the countless dead,
Above us is the heaven!

2 Their names are graven on the stone,
Their bones are in the clay
And ere another day is gone
Ourselves may be as they.

3 Death rides on every passing breeze,
And lurks in every flower;
Each season has its own disease,
Its peril every hour!

4 Our eyes have seen the rosy light
Of youth's soft cheek decay,
And fate descend in sudden night
On manhood's middle day.

5 Our eyes have seen the steps of age
Halt feebly to the tomb;
And yet shall earth our hearts engage,
And dreams of days to come?

6 Turn, mortal, turn! thy danger know:
Where'er thy foot can tread,
The earth rings hollow from below,
And warns thee of her dead!

7 Turn, Christian, turn! thy soul apply
To truths divinely given:
The forms which underneath thee lie,
Shall live for hell or heaven.

118 *The Passion.*

FROM whence these dire portents around
Which heaven and earth amaze?
Wherefore do earthquakes cleave the ground?
Why hides the sun his rays?

2 Not thus did Sinai's trembling head
With sacred horror nod,
Beneath the dark pavilion spread,
Of legislative God.

3 Thou earth, thy lowest centre shake,
With Jesus sympathize!
Thou sun, as hell's deep gloom, be black,
'Tis thy Creator dies.

4 See, streaming from th' accursed tree,
His all-atoning blood;
Is this the Infinite? 'tis he,
My Saviour and my God.

5 For me these pangs his soul assail;
For me this death is borne;
My sins gave sharpness to the nail,
And pointed every thorn.

6 Let sin no more my soul enslave;
Break, Lord, the tyrant's chain;
O save me, whom thou cam'st to save,
Nor bleed, nor die in vain.

683 *The sinner's end.*

MY thoughts on awful subjects roll,—
Damnation and the dead;
What horrors seize the guilty soul
Upon a dying bed!

2 Ling'ring about these mortal shores,
She makes a long delay;
Till, like a flood with rapid force,
Death sweeps the wretch away.

3 Then, swift and dreadful, she descends
Down to the fiery coast,
Among abominable fiends,
Herself a frighted ghost.

4 There endless crowds of sinners lie,
And darkness makes their chains:
Tortured with keen despair, they cry;
Yet wait for fiercer pains.

5 Not all their anguish and their blood,
For their old guilt atones;
Nor the compassion of a God
Shall hearken to their groans.

649 *Contentment.*

MY span of life will soon be done,
The passing moments say;
As length'ning shadows o'er the mead
Proclaim the close of day.

2 O that my heart might dwell aloof
From all created things,
And learn that wisdom from above
Whence true contentment springs!

3 Courage, my soul, thy bitter cross,
In every trial here,
Shall bear thee to thy heaven above,
But shall not enter there.

4 The sighing ones that humbly seek
In sorrowing paths below,
Shall in eternity rejoice,
Where endless comforts flow.

5 Soon will the toilsome strife be o'er
Of sublunary care,
And life's dull vanities no more
This anxious breast ensnare.

6 Courage, my soul, on God rely,
Deliv'rance soon will come;
A thousand ways has Providence
To bring believers home.

357 *Acts xvii. 30, 31.*

REPENT, the voice celestial cries,
No longer dare delay;
The wretch that scorns the mandate dies,—
And meets a fiery day.

2 The summons goes through all the earth,
Let earth attend and fear;
Listen, ye men of royal birth,
And let your vassals hear.

3 Together in his presence bow,
And all your guilt confess;
Accept the offer'd Saviour now,
Nor trifle with the grace.

4 Bow, ere the awful trumpet sound,
And call you to his bar;
For mercy knows th' appointed bound,
And turns to vengeance there.

358 *Romans ii. 4, 5.*

UNGRATEFUL sinners, whence this scorn
Of long-extended grace?
And whence this madness, that insults
Th' Almighty to his face?

2 Is it because his patience waits,
And pitying bowels move,
You multiply audacious crimes,
And spurn his richest love?

3 Is all the treasured wrath so small,
You labour still for more,
Though not eternal rolling years
Can e'er exhaust the store?

4 Swift doth the day of vengeance come,
Which must your sentence seal;
And righteous judgment, now unknown,
In all its pomp reveal.

5 Alarm'd and melted at thy voice,
Our conquer'd hearts would bow;
And to escape the Thunderer then,
Embrace the Saviour now.

COWPER. C. M.

Dr. L. MASON, 1830.

131 *The fountain.*

THERE is a fountain fill'd with blood,
Drawn from Immanuel's veins;
And sinners, plunged beneath that flood,
Lose all their guilty stains.

2 The dying thief rejoiced to see
That fountain in his day;
And there may I, though vile as he,
Wash all my sins away.

3 Dear dying Lamb, thy precious blood
Shall never lose its power,
Till all the ransom'd church of God
Be saved to sin no more.

4 E'er since, by faith, I saw the stream
Thy flowing wounds supply,
Redeeming love has been my theme,
And shall be till I die.

5 Then, in a nobler, sweeter song,
I'll sing thy power to save,
When this poor lisping, stammering tongue
Lies silent in the grave.

904 *Mutual aid.*

TRY us, O God, and search the ground
Of every sinful heart:
Whate'er of sin in us is found,
O bid it all depart!

2 When to the right or left we stray,
Leave us not comfortless;
But guide our feet into the way
Of everlasting peace.

3 Help us to help each other, Lord,
Each other's cross to bear:
Let each his friendly aid afford,
And feel his brother's care.

4 Help us to build each other up,
Our little stock improve;
Increase our faith, confirm our hope,
And perfect us in love.

5 Up into thee, our living Head,
Let us in all things grow;
Till thou hast made us free indeed,
And spotless here below.

6 Then, when the mighty work is wrought,
Receive thy ready bride:
Give us in heaven a happy lot
With all the sanctified.

264 *The treasure in earthen vessels.*

HOW rich thy bounty, King of kings!
Thy favours, how divine!
The blessings which thy gospel brings,
How splendidly they shine!

2 Gold is but dross, and gems but toys,
Should gold and gems compare;
How mean, when set against those joys
Thy poorest servants share!

3 Yet all these treasures of thy grace
Are lodged in urns of clay;
And the weak sons of mortal race
Th' immortal gifts convey.

4 Feebly they lisp thy glories forth,
Yet grace the vict'ry gives;
Quickly they moulder back to earth—
Yet still thy gospel lives.

5 Such wonders power divine effects;
Such trophies God can raise;
His hand, from crumbling dust, erects
His monuments of praise.

1001 *Evening.*

I LOVE to steal awhile away
From every cumb'ring care;
And spend the hours of setting day,
In humble, grateful prayer.

2 I love in solitude to shed
The penitential tear;
And all his promises to plead,
Where none but God can hear.

3 I love to think on mercies past,
And future good implore;
And all my cares and sorrows cast
On Him whom I adore.

4 I love by faith to take a view
Of brighter scenes in heaven.
The prospect does my strength renew,
While here by tempests driven.

5 Thus, when life's toilsome day is o'er,
May its departing ray
Be calm as this impressive hour,
And lead to endless day.

291 *Remembering Christ.*

ACCORDING to thy gracious word,
In meek humility,
This will I do, my dying Lord,
I will remember thee.

2 Thy body, broken for my sake,
My bread from heaven shall be;
Thy testamental cup I take,
And thus remember thee.

3 Gethsemane can I forget?
Or there thy conflict see,
Thine agony and bloody sweat,
And not remember thee?

4 When to the cross I turn mine eyes,
And rest on Calvary,
O Lamb of God, my Sacrifice,
I must remember thee!

5 Remember thee and all thy pains,
And all thy love to me;
Yea, while a breath, a pulse remains,
Will I remember thee.

6 And when these failing lips grow dumb,
And mind and memory flee,
When thou shalt in thy kingdom come,
Jesus, remember me.

1019 *The aged minister's prayer.*

LORD, I believe thy every word,
Thy every promise, true;
And lo! I wait on thee, my Lord,
Till I my strength renew.

2 If in this feeble flesh I may
Awhile show forth thy praise,
Jesus, support the tott'ring clay,
And lengthen out my days.

3 If such a worm as I can spread
The common Saviour's name,
Let him who raised thee from the dead
Quicken my mortal frame.

4 Still let me live thy blood to show,
Which purges every stain;
And gladly linger out below
A few more years in pain.

1053 *Doxology.*

NOW let the Father, and the Son,
And Spirit, be adored;
Where there are works to make Him known,
Or saints to love the Lord.

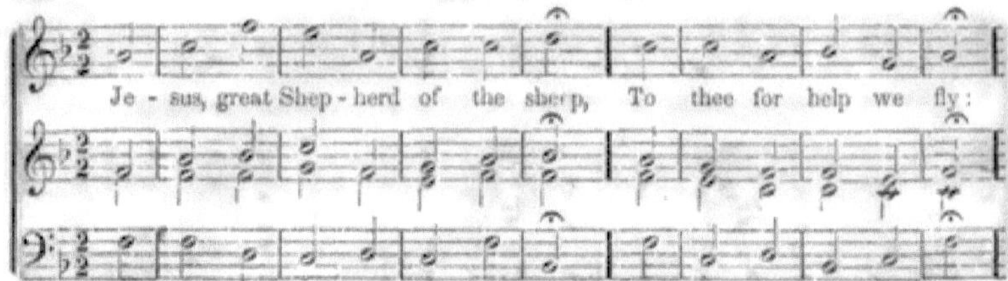

892 *Safety in union.*

JESUS, great Shepherd of the sheep,
  To thee for help we fly:
Thy little flock in safety keep!
  For O, the wolf is nigh!

2 He comes, of hellish malice full,
  To scatter, tear, and slay:
He seizes every straggling soul
  As his own lawful prey.

3 Us into thy protection take,
  And gather with thy arm:
Unless the fold we first forsake,
  The wolf can never harm.

4 We laugh to scorn his cruel power,
  While by our Shepherd's side:
The sheep he never can devour,
  Unless he first divide.

5 O do not suffer him to part
  The souls that here agree:
But make us of one mind and heart,
  And keep us one in thee!

6 Together let us sweetly live,
  Together let us die;
And each a starry crown receive,
  And reign above the sky.

33 *Dominion.*

THE Lord our God is clothed with might,
  The winds obey his will;
He speaks—and in his heavenly height
  The rolling sun stands still.

2 Rebel, ye waves, and o'er the land
  With threatening aspect roar!
The Lord uplifts his awful hand,
  And chains you to the shore.

3 Howl, winds of night! your force combine
  Without his high behest,
Ye shall not, in the mountain pine,
  Disturb the sparrow's nest.

4 His voice sublime is heard afar,
  In distant peals it dies;
He yokes the whirlwind to his car,
  And sweeps the howling skies.

5 Ye nations, bend—in rev'rence bend;
  Ye monarchs, wait his nod,
And bid the choral song ascend
  To celebrate our God.

123 *The Crucifixion.*

BEHOLD the Saviour of mankind
  Nail'd to the shameful tree!
How vast the love that him inclined
  To bleed and die for thee!

2 Hark, how he groans! while nature shakes,
  And earth's strong pillars bend!
The temple's veil in sunder breaks,
  The solid marbles rend.

3 'Tis done! the precious ransom's paid!
  "Receive my soul!" he cries:
See where he bows his sacred head!
  He bows his head, and dies!

4 But soon he'll break death's envious chain,
  And in full glory shine:
O Lamb of God, was ever pain,
  Was ever love, like thine?

1053 *Doxology*

NOW let the Father, and the Son,
  And Spirit be adored;
Where there are works to make Him known,
  Or saints to love the Lord.

314 *Opening morning service.*

COME, let us join with one accord
In hymns around the throne!
This is the day our rising Lord
Hath made and call'd his own.

2 This is the day which God hath blest,
The brightest of the seven,
Type of that everlasting rest
The saints enjoy in heaven.

3 Then let us in his name sing on,
And hasten to that day
When our Redeemer shall come down,
And shadows pass away.

4 Not one, but all our days below,
Let us in hymns employ;
And in our Lord rejoicing, go
To his eternal joy.

182 *Rev. v. 6—10.*

BEHOLD the glories of the Lamb
Amidst his Father's throne!
Prepare new honours for his name,
And songs, before unknown.

2 Let elders worship at his feet,
The church adore around;
With vials full of odours sweet,
And harps of sweetest sound.

3 Those are the prayers of all the saints,
And these the hymns they raise;
Jesus is kind to our complaints,
He loves to hear our praise.

4 Now to the Lamb that once was slain
Be endless blessings paid;
Salvation, glory, joy, remain,
For ever, on thy head.

5 Thou hast redeem'd our souls with blood,
Hast set the pris'ners free;
Hast made us kings and priests to God;
And we shall reign with thee!

102 *The Inauguration.*

SEE, from on high, a light divine
On Jesus' head descend;
And hear the sacred voice from heaven,
That bids us all attend:—

2 "This is my well-beloved Son,"
Proclaim'd the voice divine;
"Hear him," his heavenly Father said,
"For all his words are mine."

3 His mission thus confirm'd from heaven,
The great Messiah came,
And heavenly wisdom taught to man,
In God the Father's name.

4 The path of heavenly peace he show'd,
That leads to bliss on high,
Where all his faithful foll'wers here
Shall live no more to die.

5 O may we then, who own him Lord,
And his loved name profess,
By all our words and actions prove
That we his mind possess!

322 *Rev. i. 10.*

MAY I throughout this day of thine
Be in thy Spirit, Lord;
Spirit of humble fear divine,
That trembles at thy word;—

2 Spirit of faith, my heart to raise,
And fix on things above;
Spirit of sacrifice and praise,
Of holiness and love.

ARLINGTON. C. M.

DR. ARNE.

321 *Psalm cxviii. 24.*

THIS is the day the Lord hath made,
He calls the hours his own;
Let heaven rejoice, let earth be glad,
And praise surround the throne.

2 To-day he rose and left the dead,
And Satan's empire fell;
To-day the saints his triumph spread,
And all his wonders tell.

3 Hosanna to th' anointed King,
To David's holy Son:
Help us, O Lord, descend, and bring
Salvation from thy throne!

1018 *For a minister after preaching.*

JESUS, my strength and righteousness,
My Saviour, and my King,
Triumphantly thy name I bless,
Thy conqu'ring name I sing.

2 Thou, Lord, hast magnified thy name,
Thou hast maintain'd thy cause,
And I enjoy the glorious shame,
The scandal of thy cross.

3 Thou gavest me to speak thy word
In the appointed hour:
I have proclaim'd my dying Lord,
And felt thy Spirit's power.

4 Superior to my foes I stood,
Above their smile or frown:
On all the strangers to thy blood
With pitying love look'd down.

5 O let me have thy presence still;
Set as a flint my face,
To show the counsel of thy will,
Which saves a world by grace!

6 O never let me blush to own
The glorious gospel word,
Which saves a world through faith alone,
Faith in a dying Lord!

616 *"The Lord is my portion."*

MY God, my portion, and my love,
My everlasting all,
I've none but thee in heaven above,
Or on this earthly ball.

2 What empty things are all the skies,
And this inferior clod!
There's nothing here deserves my joys,
There's nothing like my God.

3 How vain a toy is glitt'ring wealth,
If once compared to thee:
Or what's my safety, or my health,
Or all my friends, to me?

4 Were I possessor of the earth,
And call'd the stars my own,
Without thy graces and thyself,
I were a wretch undone.

5 Let others stretch their arms like seas,
And grasp in all the shore:
Grant me the visits of thy face,
And I desire no more.

680 *The happy death.*

JESUS, the vision of thy face
Hath overpowering charms!
Scarce shall I feel death's cold embrace,
If Christ be in my arms.

2 Then, while ye hear my heart-strings break,
How sweet my minutes roll!
A mortal paleness on my cheek,
And glory in my soul.

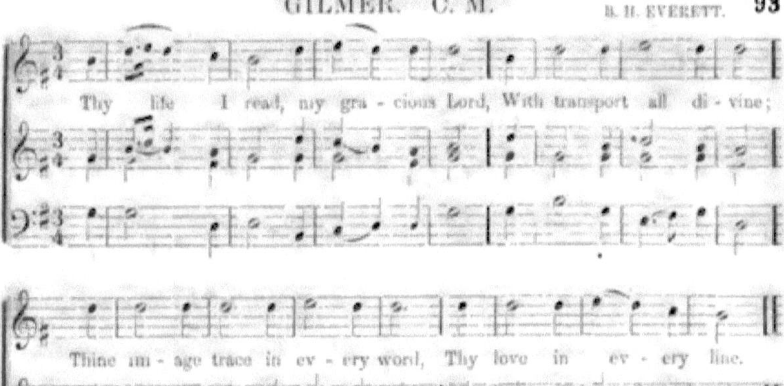

720 *Funeral of a child.*

THY life I read, my gracious Lord,
With transport all divine;
Thine image trace in every word,
Thy love in every line.

2 Methinks I see a thousand charms
Spread o'er thy lovely face,
While infants in thy tender arms
Receive the smiling grace.

3 "I take these little lambs," said he,
"And lay them in my breast;
Protection they shall find in me,
In me be ever blest.

4 "Death may the bands of life unloose,
But can't dissolve my love;
Millions of infant souls compose
The family above.

5 "Their feeble frames my power shall raise,
And mould with heavenly skill;
I'll give them tongues to sing my praise,
And hands to do my will."

6 His words the happy parents hear,
And shout with joy divine;
O Saviour, all we have and are
Shall be for ever thine.

500 *The rapture of love.*

I KNOW that my Redeemer lives,
And ever prays for me:
A token of his love he gives,
A pledge of liberty.

2 I find him lifting up my head,
He brings salvation near;
His presence makes me free indeed,
And he will soon appear.

3 He wills that I should holy be!
What can withstand his will?
The counsel of his grace in me
He surely shall fulfil.

4 Jesus, I hang upon thy word;
I steadfastly believe
Thou wilt return, and claim me, Lord,
And to thyself receive.

5 Joyful in hope, my spirit soars
To meet thee from above:
Thy goodness thankfully adores:
And sure I taste thy love.

6 Thy love I soon expect to find,
In all its depth and height:
To comprehend th' Eternal Mind,
And grasp the Infinite.

989 *Evening.*

DREAD Sovereign, let my evening song
Like holy incense rise;
Assist the off'rings of my tongue,
To reach the lofty skies.

2 Through all the dangers of the day
Thy hand was still my guard;
And still, to drive my wants away,
Thy mercy stood prepared.

3 Sprinkled afresh with pard'ning blood,
I lay me down to rest;
As in the embraces of my God,
Or on my Saviour's breast.

1053 *Doxology.*

NOW let the Father, and the Son,
And Spirit, be adored;
Where there are works to make Him known,
Or saints to love the Lord.

926 *"Lighten mine eyes."*

O SUN of righteousness, arise
With healing in thy wing!
To my diseased, my fainting soul,
Life and salvation bring.

2 These clouds of pride and sin dispel,
By thine all-piercing beam;
Lighten mine eyes with faith, my heart
With holy hope inflame.

3 My mind, by thy all-quick'ning power
From low desires set free;
Unite my scatter'd thoughts, and fix
My love entire on thee.

4 Father, thy long-lost son receive;
Saviour, thy purchase own;
Bless'd Comforter, with peace and joy
Thy new-made creature crown.

5 Eternal, undivided Lord,
Co-equal One and Three,
On thee all faith, all hope be placed,
All love be paid to thee.

292 *The legacy sealed.*

THE promise of my Father's love
Shall stand for ever good:
He said, and gave his soul to death,
And seal'd the grace with blood.

2 To this dear cov'nant of thy word
I set my worthless name;
I seal the engagement to my Lord,
And make my humble claim.

3 Thy light, and strength, and pard'ning grace,
And glory, shall be mine;
My life and soul, my heart and flesh,
And all my powers, are thine.

4 I call that legacy my own
Which Jesus did bequeath,
'Twas purchased with a dying groan,
And ratified in death.

5 Sweet is the mem'ry of his name,
Who bless'd us in his will,
And to his testament of love
Made his own blood the seal.

424 *Praying for faith.*

FATHER, I stretch my hands to thee,
No other help I know;
If thou withdraw thyself from me,
Ah! whither shall I go?

2 What did thine only Son endure,
Before I drew my breath!
What pain, what labour, to secure
My soul from endless death!

3 O Jesus, could I this believe,
I now should feel thy power!
Now my poor soul thou wouldst retrieve,
Nor let me wait one hour.

4 Author of faith, to thee I lift
My weary, longing eyes:
O let me now receive that gift,
My soul without it dies.

5 Surely thou canst not let me die;
O speak, and I shall live;
And here I will unwearied lie,
Till thou thy Spirit give.

6 The worst of sinners would rejoice,
Could they but see thy face:
O let me hear thy quick'ning voice,
And taste thy pard'ning grace!

997 *Retirement.*

FAR from the world, O Lord, I flee,
From strife and tumult far;
From scenes where Satan wages still
His most successful war.

2 The calm retreat, the silent shade,
With prayer and praise agree;
And seem by thy sweet bounty made
For those who follow thee.

3 There, if thy Spirit touch the soul,
And grace her mean abode,
O with what peace, and joy, and love,
She communes with her God!

4 There, like the nightingale, she pours
Her solitary lays;
Nor asks a witness of her song,
Nor thirsts for human praise.

5 O let me wing my hallow'd flight
From earth-born wo and care,
And soar above these clouds of night,
My Saviour's bliss to share!

637 *Hope in trouble.*

WHEN musing sorrow weeps the past,
And mourns the present pain,
'Tis sweet to think of peace at last,
And feel that death is gain.

2 'Tis not that murm'ring thoughts arise,
And dread a Father's will;
'Tis not that meek submission flies,
And would not suffer still:—

3 It is that heav'n-born faith surveys
The path that leads to light,
And longs her eagle plumes to raise,
And lose herself in sight.—

4 It is that hope with ardour glows,
To see Him face to face,
Whose dying love no language knows
Sufficient art to trace.

638 *Psalm xxxiv. 1—3.*

THROUGH all the changing scenes of life,
In trouble and in joy,
The praises of my God shall still
My heart and tongue employ

2 Of this deliv'rance I will boast,
Till all that are distrest
From my example comfort take,
And charm their griefs to rest.

3 O magnify the Lord with me,
With me exalt his name:
When in distress to him I call'd,
He to my rescue came.

4 The angel of the Lord encamps
Around the good and just;
Deliv'rance he affords to all
Who on his succour trust.

5 O make but trial of his love,
Experience will decide
How bless'd they are, and only they,
Who in his truth confide.

6 Fear him, ye saints; and you will then
Have nothing else to fear:
Make you his service your delight;
Your wants shall be his care.

1053 *Doxology.*

NOW let the Father, and the Son,
And Spirit, be adored;
Where there are works to make Him known,
Or saints to love the Lord.

CHRISTMAS. C. M.

From HANDEL.

93 *The song of the angels.*

"SHEPHERDS, rejoice, lift up your eyes,
And send your fears away,
News from the regions of the skies—
A Saviour's born to-day.

2 "Jesus, the God whom angels fear,
Comes down to dwell with you;
To-day he makes his entrance here,
But not as monarchs do.

3 "No gold, nor purple swaddling bands,
Nor royal shining things;
A manger for his cradle stands,
And holds the King of kings.

4 "Go, shepherds, where the infant lies,
And see his humble throne;
With tears of joy in all your eyes,
Go, shepherds, kiss the Son."

5 Thus Gabriel sang, and straight around
The heavenly armies throng;
They tune their harps to lofty sound,
And thus conclude the song

6 "Glory to God that reigns above,
Let peace surround the earth;
Mortals shall know their Maker's love,
At their Redeemer's birth."

7 Lord! and shall angels have their songs,
And men no tunes to raise?
O may we lose these useless tongues
When we forget to praise!

562 *Psalm lxxi. 15.*

MY Saviour, my almighty Friend,
When I begin thy praise,
Where will the growing numbers end,
The numbers of thy grace?

2 Thou art my everlasting trust;
Thy goodness I adore:
Send down thy grace, O blessed Lord,
That I may love thee more.

3 My feet shall travel all the length
Of the celestial road:
And march with courage in thy strength
To see the Lord my God.

4 Awake! awake! my tuneful powers:
With this delightful song,
I'll entertain the darkest hours,
Nor think the season long.

567 *The Christian race.*

AWAKE, my soul! stretch every nerve,
And press with vigour on:
A heavenly race demands thy zeal,
And an immortal crown.

2 A cloud of witnesses around
Hold thee in full survey,
Forget the steps already trod,
And onward urge thy way.

3 'Tis God's all-animating voice
That calls thee from on high;
'Tis his own hand presents the prize
To thine aspiring eye.

4 That prize, with peerless glories bright,
Which shall new lustre boast,
When victors' wreaths and monarchs' gems
Shall blend in common dust.

5 Bless'd Saviour! introduced by thee,
Have I my race begun;
And, crown'd with vict'ry, at thy feet
I'll lay my honours down.

666 *Heb.* xiii. 20, 21.

NOW may the God of peace and love,
Who from th' impris'ning grave
Restored the Shepherd of the sheep,
Omnipotent to save ;—

2 Through the rich merits of that blood,
Which he on Calv'ry spilt,
To make th' eternal cov'nant sure,
On which our hopes are built ;—

3 Perfect our souls in every grace,
T' accomplish all his will ;
And all that's pleasing in his sight
Inspire us to fulfil !

4 For the great Mediator's sake
We every blessing pray ;
With glory let his name be crown'd,
Through heaven's eternal day.

718 *Hell.*

SING to the Lord, ye heavenly hosts,
And thou, O earth, adore ;
Let death and hell through all their coasts
Stand trembling at his power.

2 His sounding chariot shakes the sky,
He makes the clouds his throne,
There all his stores of lightning lie,
Till vengeance darts them down.

3 Think, O my soul, the dreadful day
When this incensed God
Shall rend the sky, and burn the sea,
And fling his wrath abroad.

4 What shall the wretch, the sinner do ?
He once defied the Lord :
But he shall dread the Thund'rer now,
And sink beneath his word.

5 Tempests of angry fire shall roll,
To blast the rebel-worm,
And beat upon his naked soul
In one eternal storm.

827 *Watch-night.*

JOIN all ye ransom'd sons of grace,
The holy joy prolong,
And shout to the Redeemer's praise
A solemn midnight song.

2 Blessing, and thanks, and love, and might,
Be to our Jesus given,
Who turns our darkness into light,—
Who turns our hell to heaven.

3 Thither our faithful souls he leads,—
Thither he bids us rise,
With crowns of joy upon our heads,
To meet him in the skies.

953 *Morning.*

ONCE more, my soul, the rising day
Salutes thy waking eyes ;
Once more, my voice, thy tribute pay
To Him that rules the skies.

2 Night unto night his name repeats,
The day renews the sound ;
Wide as the heavens on which he sits,
To turn the seasons round.

3 'Tis he supports my mortal frame ;
My tongue shall speak his praise ;
My sins might rouse his wrath to flame,
But yet his wrath delays.

4 O God, let all my hours be thine,
While I enjoy the light !
Then shall my sun in smiles decline,
And bring a pleasant night.

956 *Morning.*

AWAKE, my soul, to meet the day,
Unfold thy drowsy eyes,
And burst the pond'rous chain that loads
Thine active faculties.

2 God's guardian shield was round me spread,
In my defenceless sleep :
Let him have all my waking hours
Who doth my slumbers keep.

3 Pardon, O God, my former sloth,
And arm my soul with grace ;
As rising now, I seal my vows
To prosecute thy ways.

4 Bright Sun of righteousness, arise,
Thy radiant beams display ;
And guide my dark, bewilder'd soul,
To everlasting day.

745 *Isaiah* ii. 1—5.

BEHOLD, the mountain of the Lord,
In latter days shall rise
Above the mountains and the hills,
And draw the wond'ring eyes.

2 To this the joyful nations round,
All tribes and tongues, shall flow ;
" Up to the hill of God," they say,
" And to his house, we'll go."

3 The beam that shines on Zion's hill
Shall lighten every land :
The King who reigns in Zion's towers
Shall all the world command.

4 Among the nations he shall judge ;
His judgments truth shall guide ;
His sceptre shall protect the just,
And quell the sinner's pride.

5 No strife shall rage, nor hostile feuds
Disturb those peaceful years ;
To ploughshares men shall beat their swords,
To pruning-hooks their spears.

6 No longer hosts encount'ring hosts,
Shall crowds of slain deplore ;
They hang the trumpet in the hall,
And study war no more.

7 Come then, O house of Jacob ! come
To worship at his shrine ;
And, walking in the light of God,
With holy beauties shine.

DEVIZES. C. M.

J. TUCKER.

29 *"Doing wonders."*

FATHER, how wide thy glory shines!
  How high thy wonders rise!
Known through the earth by thousand signs,
  By thousands through the skies.

2 Those mighty orbs proclaim thy power;
  Their motions speak thy skill:
And on the wings of every hour
  We read thy patience still.

3 Part of thy name divinely stands,
  On all thy creatures writ:
They show the labour of thy hands,
  Or impress of thy feet:

4 But when we view thy strange design,
  To save rebellious worms,
Where vengeance and compassion join
  In their divinest forms:

5 Our thoughts are lost in reverent awe;
  We love and we adore;
The first archangel never saw
  So much of God before.

6 Here the whole Deity is known,
  Nor dares a creature guess
Which of the glories brighter shone,
  The justice or the grace.

7 Now the full glories of the Lamb
  Adorn the heavenly plains:
Bright seraphs learn Immanuel's name,
  And try their choicest strains.

8 O may I bear some humble part
  In that immortal song!
Wonder and joy shall tune my heart,
  And love command my tongue.

888 *"Ye are come unto Mount Sion."*

HAPPY the souls to Jesus join'd,
  And saved by grace alone;
Walking in all his ways, they find
  Their heaven on earth begun.

2 The church triumphant in thy love,
  Their mighty joys we know:
They sing the Lamb in hymns above,
  And we in hymns below.

3 Thee, in thy glorious realm, they praise,
  And bow before thy throne;
We, in the kingdom of thy grace:
  The kingdoms are but one.

4 The holy to the holiest leads;
  From thence our spirits rise;
And he that in thy statutes treads,
  Shall meet thee in the skies.

183 *Rev. v. 11—13.*

COME, let us join our cheerful songs
  With angels round the throne;
Ten thousand thousand are their tongues,
  But all their joys are one.

2 Worthy the Lamb that died, they cry,
  To be exalted thus:
Worthy the Lamb, our hearts reply,
  For he was slain for us.

3 Jesus is worthy to receive
  Honour and power divine,
And blessings more than we can give
  Be, Lord, for ever thine.

4 The whole creation join in one,
  To bless the sacred name
Of Him that sits upon the throne,
  And to adore the Lamb.

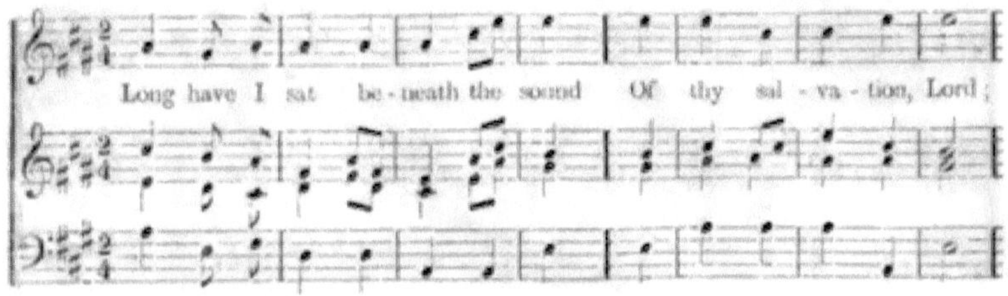

599 *Before or after sermon.*

LONG have I sat beneath the sound
  Of thy salvation, Lord;
But still how weak my faith is found,
  And knowledge of thy word!

2 How cold and feeble is my love!
  How negligent my fear!
How low my hopes of joys above!
  How few affections there!

3 Great God, thy sovereign aid impart
  To give thy word success;
Write thy salvation on my heart,
  And make me learn thy grace.

4 Show my forgetful feet the way
  That leads to joys on high,
Where knowledge grows without decay,
  And love shall never die.

391 *Contrition.*

WHEN, rising from the bed of death,
  O'erwhelm'd with guilt and fear,
I view my Maker face to face,
  O how shall I appear!

2 If yet, while pardon may be found,
  And mercy may be sought,
My soul with inward horror shrinks,
  And trembles at the thought:

3 When thou, O Lord, shalt stand disclosed
  In majesty severe,
And sit in judgment on my soul,
  O how shall I appear!

4 O may my broken, contrite heart,
  Timely my sins lament,
And early with repentant tears,
  Eternal wo prevent.

5 Behold the sorrows of my heart,
  Ere yet it be too late;
And hear my Saviour's dying groan,
  To give those sorrows weight!

6 For never shall my soul despair
  Her pardon to secure,
Who knows thine only Son hath died
  To make that pardon sure.

197 *"He is precious."*

JESUS, I love thy charming name,
  'Tis music to my ear;
Fain would I sound it out so loud,
  That earth and heaven should hear.

2 Yes, thou art precious to my soul,
  My transport and my trust;
Jewels, to thee, are gaudy toys,
  And gold is sordid dust.

3 All my capacious powers can wish,
  In thee doth richly meet;
Nor to mine eyes is light so dear,
  Nor friendship half so sweet.

4 Thy grace still dwells upon my heart,
  And sheds its fragrance there;
The noblest balm of all its wounds,
  The cordial of its care.

5 I'll speak the honours of thy name
  With my last, lab'ring breath;
Then speechless clasp thee in mine arms,
  The antidote of death.

1053 *Doxology.*

NOW let the Father, and the Son,
  And Spirit be adored;
Where there are works to make him known,
  Or saints to love the Lord.

90 *The Incarnation.*

MORTALS, awake, with angels join,
And chant the solemn lay;
Joy, love, and gratitude, combine
To hail th' auspicious day.

2 In heaven the rapturous song began,
And sweet seraphic fire
Through all the shining legions ran,
And strung and tuned the lyre.

3 Swift through the vast expanse it flew,
And loud the echo roll'd;
The theme, the song, the joy, was new,
'Twas more than heaven could hold.

4 Down through the portals of the sky
The impetuous torrent ran;
And angels flew with eager joy
To bear the news to man.

5 With joy the chorus we'll repeat,
"Glory to God on high!
Good will and peace are now complete;
Jesus was born to die."

6 Hail, Prince of life, for ever hail!
Redeemer, brother, friend!
Though earth, and time, and life, shall fail,
Thy praise shall never end.

456 *Opening worship.*

O FOR a thousand tongues to sing
My great Redeemer's praise!
The glories of my God and King,
The triumphs of his grace!

2 My gracious Master and my God,
Assist me to proclaim,—
To spread through all the earth abroad
The honours of thy Name.

3 Jesus! the Name that charms our fears,
That bids our sorrows cease;
'Tis music in the sinner's ears,
'Tis life, and health, and peace.

4 He breaks the power of cancell'd sin,
He sets the pris'ner free;
His blood can make the foulest clean;
His blood avail'd for me.

5 He speaks—and, listening to his voice,
New life the dead receive;
The mournful, broken hearts rejoice;
The humble poor believe.

6 Hear him, ye deaf; his praise, ye dumb,
Your loosen'd tongues employ;
Ye blind, behold your Saviour come;
And leap, ye lame, for joy.

88 *The Advent.*

HARK! the glad sound! the Saviour comes!
The Saviour promised long!
Let every heart prepare a throne—
And every voice a song.

2 He comes—the pris'ners to release,
In Satan's bondage held;
The gates of brass before him burst—
The iron fetters yield!

3 He comes—from thickest films of vice
To clear the mental ray;
And on the eye-balls of the blind
To pour celestial day.

4 He comes—the broken heart to bind—
The bleeding soul to cure;
And, with the treasures of his grace,
T' enrich the humble poor.

5 Our glad hosannas, Prince of peace,
Thy welcome shall proclaim;
And heaven's eternal arches ring
With thy beloved name.

481 *God the source of joy.*

MY God, the spring of all my joy,
The life of my delights,
The glory of my brightest days,
And comfort of my nights!—

2 In darkest shades if thou appear,
My dawning is begun;
Thou art my soul's bright morning star,
And thou my rising sun.

3 The opening heavens around me shine
With beams of sacred bliss,
If Jesus show his mercy mine,
And whisper I am his.

4 My soul would leave this heavy clay,
At that transporting word,
Run up with joy the shining way,
To see and praise my Lord.

5 Fearless of hell and ghastly death,
I'd break through every foe;
The wings of love and arms of faith
Would bear me conqu'ror through.

843 *For American Independence.*

THY mighty arm, O God, was nigh
When we our foes assail'd;
'Tis thou hast raised our honours high,
And o'er their hosts prevail'd.

2 The thund'ring horse, the martial band,
Without thine aid were vain,
And vict'ry flies at thy command
To crown the bright campaign.

3 Their mounds, their camps, their lofty towers
Into our hands are given;
Not from desert or strength of ours,
But through the grace of heaven.

4 The faithful tablet of our heart
These mercies shall record,
And never thence shall they depart,
Nor we forget the Lord.

5 To our young race will we proclaim
The mercies God has shown;
That they may learn to bless his name,
And choose him for their own.

6 Thus, while we sleep in silent dust,
When threat'ning dangers come,
Their fathers' God shall be their trust,
Their refuge, and their home.

907 *Closing the exercises.*

LIFT up your hearts to things above,
Ye foll'wers of the Lamb,
And join with us to praise his love,
And glorify his name.

2 To Jesus' name give thanks and sing,
Whose mercies never end:
Rejoice! rejoice! the Lord is King!
The King is now our Friend!

3 We for his sake count all things loss,
On earthly good look down:
And joyfully sustain the cross,
Till we receive the crown.

4 O let us stir each other up,
Our faith by works t' approve,
By holy, purifying hope,
And the sweet task of love.

5 Love us, though far in flesh disjoin'd,
Ye lovers of the Lamb;
And ever bear us on your mind,
Who think and speak the same:

6 You on our minds we ever bear,
Whoe'er to Jesus bow;
Stretch out the arms of faith and prayer,
And, lo! we reach you now.

7 The blessings all on you be shed,
Which God in Christ imparts;
We pray the Spirit of our Head
Into your faithful hearts.

8 Mercy and peace your portion be,
To carnal minds unknown;
The hidden manna, and the tree
Of life, and the white stone.

9 Let all who for the promise wait
The Holy Ghost receive;
And, raised to our unsinning state,
With God in Eden live!

10 Live till the Lord in glory come,
And wait his heaven to share!
He now is fitting up your home:
Go on;—we'll meet you there!

Ye wretched, hungry, starving poor, Behold a royal feast! Where mercy spreads her bounteous store

CODA.
For every humble guest, Halle - lu - jah! halle - lu - jah! halle - lu - jah!

329 *And yet there is room.*

YE wretched, hungry, starving poor,
Behold a royal feast!
Where mercy spreads her bounteous store
For every humble guest.

2 See, Jesus stands with open arms;
He calls, he bids you come:
O stay not back, though fear alarms!
For yet there still is room.

3 O come, and with his children taste
The blessings of his love;
While hope attends the sweet repast
Of nobler joys above!

4 There, with united heart and voice,
Before th' eternal throne,
Ten thousand thousand souls rejoice,
In ecstasies unknown.

5 And yet ten thousand thousand more
Are welcome still to come:
Ye happy souls, the grace adore;
Approach, there yet is room.

341 *The free invitation.*

JESUS, thy blessings are not few,
Nor is thy gospel weak:
Thy grace can melt the stubborn Jew,
And bow th' aspiring Greek.

2 Wide as the reach of Satan's rage
Doth thy salvation flow;
'Tis not confined to sex or age,
The lofty or the low.

3 While grace is offer'd to the prince,
The poor may take their share;
No mortal has a just pretence
To perish in despair.

4 Come, all ye vilest sinners, come;
He'll form your souls anew:
His gospel and his heart have room
For rebels such as you.

790 *Psalm cxxxii. 8, 15.*

ARISE, O King of grace, arise,
And enter to thy rest!
Lo! thy church waits, with longing eyes,
Thus to be own'd and blest.

2 Enter, with all thy glorious train,
Thy Spirit and thy word;
All that the ark did once contain,
Could no such grace afford.

3 Here, mighty God, accept our vows;
Here let thy praise be spread;
Bless the provisions of thy house,
And fill thy poor with bread.

800 *For an orphan asylum.*

FATHER of mercies, hear our prayers
For those that do us good,
Whose love for us a place prepares,
And gives the orphans food.

2 Their alms in blessings on their head
A thousand fold restore;
O feed their souls with living bread,
And let their cup run o'er!

3 For ever in thy Christ built up
Thy bounty let them prove;
Steadfast in faith, joyful through hope,
And rooted deep in love.

4 For those who kindly founded this,
A better house prepare;
Remove them to thy heavenly bliss,
And let us meet them there.

221 *His quickenings implored.*

COME, Holy Spirit, heavenly Dove,
With all thy quick'ning powers,
Kindle a flame of sacred love
In these cold hearts of ours.

2 Look how we grovel here below,
Fond of these earthly toys;
Our souls, how heavily they go,
To reach eternal joys!

3 In vain we tune our formal songs,
In vain we strive to rise;
Hosannas languish on our tongues,
And our devotion dies.

4 And shall we then for ever live
At this poor dying rate?
Our love so faint, so cold to thee,
And thine to us so great?

5 Come, Holy Spirit, heavenly Dove,
With all thy quick'ning powers;
Come, shed abroad a Saviour's love,
And that shall kindle ours.

305 *The Passion realised.*

COME, Holy Ghost, set to thy seal,
Thine inward witness give,
To all our waiting souls reveal
The death by which we live.

2 Spectators of the pangs divine
O that we now may be,
Discerning in the sacred sign
His passion on the tree!

3 Give us to hear the dreadful sound
Which told his mortal pain,
Tore up the graves, and shook the ground,
And rent the rocks in twain.

4 Repeat the Saviour's dying cry
In every heart so loud,
That every heart may now reply,
"This was the Son of God!"

188 *Stupendous love.*

PLUNGED in a gulf of dark despair,
We wretched sinners lay,
Without one cheering beam of hope,
Or spark of glimm'ring day.

2 With pitying eyes the Prince of grace
Beheld our helpless grief;
He saw, and (O amazing love!)
He ran to our relief.

3 Down from the shining seats above
With joyful haste he fled,
Enter'd the grave in mortal flesh,
And dwelt among the dead.

4 O for this love let rocks and hills
Their lasting silence break!
And all harmonious human tongues
The Saviour's praises speak.

5 Angels, assist our mighty joys,
Strike all your harps of gold;
But when you raise your highest notes,
His love can ne'er be told!

285 *Infant baptism.—Mark x. 13—16.*

SEE Israel's gentle Shepherd stand
With all-engaging charms:
Hark how he calls the tender lambs,
And folds them in his arms!

2 "Permit them to approach," he cries,
"Nor scorn their humble name:
For 'twas to bless such souls as these
The Lord of angels came."

3 We bring them, Lord, in thankful hands,
And yield them up to thee,
Joyful that we ourselves are thine,
Thine let our offspring be.

WARWICK. C. M.

STANLEY.

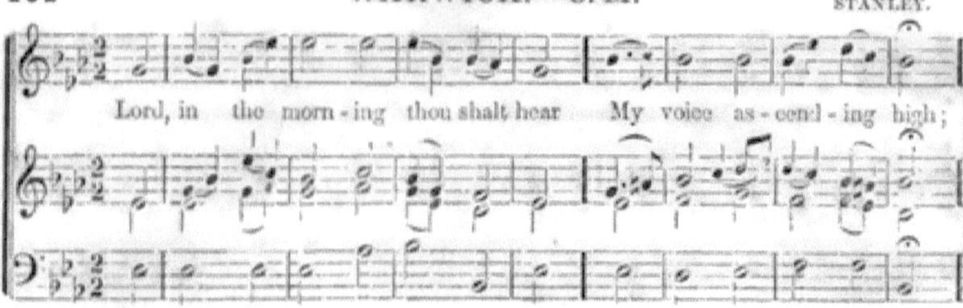

958 *Sabbath morning. Psalm v. 1—8.*

LORD, in the morning thou shalt hear
My voice ascending high;
To thee will I direct my prayer,
To thee lift up mine eye.

2 Up to the hills where Christ is gone,
To plead for all his saints,
Presenting at his Father's throne
Our songs and our complaints.

3 Thou art a God, before whose sight
The wicked shall not stand;
Sinners shall ne'er be thy delight,
Nor dwell at thy right hand.

4 But to thy house will I resort,
To taste thy mercies there;
I will frequent thy holy court,
And worship in thy fear.

5 O may thy Spirit guide my feet,
In ways of righteousness,
Make every path of duty straight,
And plain before my face.

828 *Renewing the covenant.*

COME, let us use the grace divine,
And all, with one accord,
In a perpetual cov'nant join
Ourselves to Christ the Lord;—

2 Give up ourselves, through Jesus' power,
His name to glorify;
And promise, in this sacred hour,
For God to live and die.

3 The cov'nant we this moment make,
Be ever kept in mind:
We will no more our God forsake,
Or cast his words behind.

4 We never will throw off his fear,
Who hears our solemn vow;
And if thou art well pleased to hear,
Come down, and meet us now!

5 Thee, Father, Son, and Holy Ghost,
Let all our hearts receive;
Present with the celestial host,
The peaceful answer give.

6 To each the cov'nant blood apply
Which takes our sins away;
And register our names on high,
And keep us to that day

210 *Interpreter. After sermon.*

THE Spirit breathes upon the word,
And brings the truth to sight;
Precepts and promises afford
A sanctifying light.

2 A glory gilds the sacred page,
Majestic like the sun;
It gives a light to every age,
It gives—but borrows none.

3 The Hand that gave it still supplies
The gracious light and heat;
His truths upon the nations rise,—
They rise, but never set.

4 Let everlasting thanks be thine
For such a bright display,
As makes a world of darkness shine
With beams of heavenly day

1053 *Doxology.*

NOW let the Father, and the Son,
And Spirit be adored;
Where there are works to make Him known,
Or saints to love the Lord.

222 *Invoked.*

CELESTIAL Dove, Come from above,
And guide me in thy ways;
My heart prepare, For solemn prayer,
And tune my lips to praise.

2 Open mine eyes, And make me wise,
My interest to discern;
From every sin, Without, within,
Incline my heart to turn.

3 Fly to my aid, When I'm afraid,
Or plunged in deep distress;
My foes subdue, And bring me through
This howling wilderness.

277 *Closing Conference.*

BLESS'D be the dear uniting love
That will not let us part;
Our bodies may far off remove,—
We still are one in heart.

2 Join'd in one spirit to our Head,
Where he appoints we go;
And still in Jesus' footsteps tread
And show his praise below.

3 O may we ever walk in him,
And nothing know beside,
Nothing desire, nothing esteem,
But Jesus crucified!

4 Closer and closer let us cleave
To his beloved embrace;
Expect his fulness to receive,
And grace to answer grace.

5 Partakers of the Saviour's grace,
The same in mind and heart,
Nor joy, nor grief, nor time, nor place,
Nor life, nor death, can part.

6 But let us hasten to the day
Which shall our flesh restore,
When death shall all be done away,
And bodies part no more.

187 *Indebtedness to Christ.*

MAJESTIC sweetness sits enthroned
Upon the Saviour's brow;
His head with radiant glories crown'd,
His lips with grace o'erflow.

2 He saw me plunged in deep distress,
And flew to my relief;
For me he bore the shameful cross,
And carried all my grief.

3 To heaven, the place of his abode,
He brings my weary feet,
Shows me the glories of my God,
And makes my joys complete.

4 Since from his bounty I receive
Such proofs of love divine,
Had I a thousand hearts to give,
Lord, they should all be thine.

935 *"Come quickly."*

COME quickly, gracious Lord, and take
Possession of thine own;
My longing heart vouchsafe to make
Thy everlasting throne.

2 Assert thy claim, maintain thy right,
Come quickly from above;
And sink me to perfection's height,
The depth of humble love.

WOODSTOCK. C. M.

D. DUTTON, Jr.

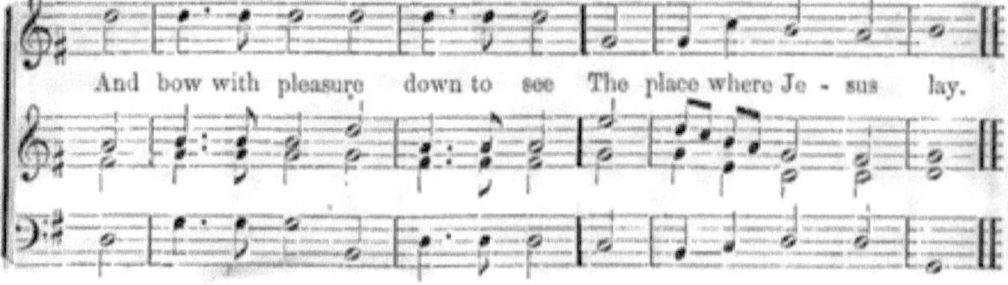

143 *He is risen.*

YE humble souls, that seek the Lord,
Chase all your fears away;
And bow with pleasure down to see
The place where Jesus lay.

2 Thus low the Lord of life was brought,
Such wonders love can do:
Thus cold in death that bosom lay,
Which throbb'd and bled for you.

3 But raise your eyes, and tune your songs,
The Saviour lives again;
Not all the bolts and bars of death
The Conqu'ror could detain.

4 High o'er th' angelic bands he rears
His once dishonour'd head;
And through unnumber'd years he reigns,
Who dwelt among the dead.

5 With joy like his shall every saint
His empty tomb survey;
Then rise with his ascending Lord,
Through all his shining way.

427 *The effort.*

APPROACH, my soul, the mercy-seat
Where Jesus answers prayers;
There humbly fall before his feet,
For none can perish there.

2 Thy promise is my only plea,
With this I venture nigh;
Thou call'st the burden'd soul to thee,
And such, O Lord, am I.

3 Bow'd down beneath a load of sin,
By Satan sorely prest,
By wars without, and fears within,
I come to thee for rest.

4 Be thou my shield and hiding-place,
That, shelter'd near thy side,
I may my fierce accuser face,
And tell him thou hast died.

5 O, wondrous love! to bleed and die,
To bear the cross and shame,
That guilty sinners, such as I,
Might plead his gracious name.

6 "Poor tempest-tossed soul, be still,
My promised grace receive;"—
'Tis Jesus speaks—I must, I will,
I can, I do believe.

761 *Responding to the appeal.*

THE nations call! from sea to sea
Extends the thrilling cry,
"Come over, Christians, if there be,
And help us, ere we die."

2 Our hearts, O Lord, the summons feel;
Let hand with heart combine,
And answer to the world's appeal
By giving "that is thine."

3 Say to thy gifted servants, "Speed!
Behold the world your field;"
Say to the gold, "The Lord hath need,"
Till hoarded treasures yield.

4 Say to the slumb'ring soul, "Awake!
Ere wanes thy noon away;
Lo! soon I come th' account to take,
Ye stewards of a day."

5 Saviour, forgive; ashamed we lie,
Thy gracious will we know:
Behold, while we delay, they die!
Bid, bid us send, or go.

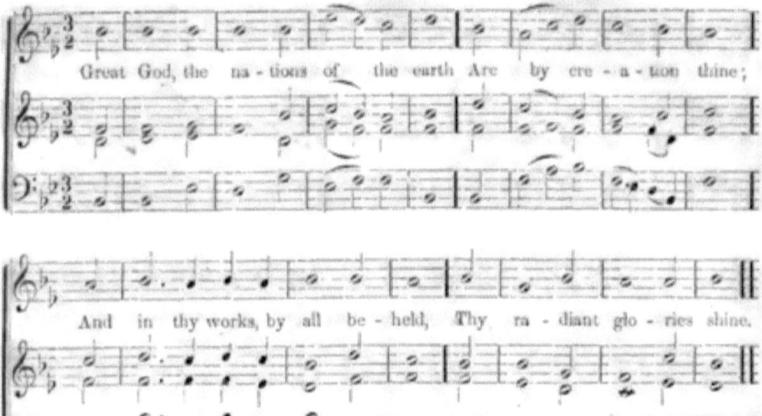

779 *Spreading over all the earth.*

GREAT God, the nations of the earth
 Are by creation thine;
And in thy works, by all beheld,
 Thy radiant glories shine.

2 But, Lord, thy greater love has sent
 Thy gospel to mankind,
Unveiling what rich stores of grace
 Are treasured in thy mind.

3 O when shall these glad tidings spread
 The spacious earth around,
Till every tribe and every soul
 Shall hear the joyful sound?

4 Smile, Lord, on each divine attempt
 To spread the gospel's rays,
And build on sin's demolish'd throne,
 The temples of thy praise.

626 *"Our good is all divine."*

FATHER, to thee my soul I lift;
 My soul on thee depends,
Convinced that every perfect gift
 From thee alone descends.

2 Mercy and grace are thine alone,
 And power and wisdom too:
Without the Spirit of thy Son
 We nothing good can do.

3 We cannot speak one useful word,
 One holy thought conceive,
Unless, in answer to our Lord,
 Thyself the blessing give.

4 His blood demands the purchased grace;
 His blood's availing plea
Obtain'd the help for all our race,
 And sends it down to me.

5 Thou all our works in us hast wrought;
 Our good is all divine
The praise of every virtuous thought,
 And righteous word, is thine.

6 From thee, through Jesus, we receive
 The power on thee to call;
In whom we are, and move, and live,
 Our God is ALL IN ALL.

627 *The choice of Moses.*

MY soul, with all thy waken'd powers,
 Survey the heavenly prize;
Nor let these glitt'ring toys of earth
 Allure thy wand'ring eyes.

2 The splendid crown which Moses sought
 Still beams around his brow;
Though soon great Pharaoh's sceptred pride
 Was taught by death to bow.

3 The joys and treasures of a day
 I cheerfully resign;
Rich in that large immortal store,
 Secured by grace divine.

4 Let fools my wiser choice deride,
 Angels and God approve;
Nor scorn of men, nor rage of hell,
 My steadfast soul shall move.

5 With ardent eye, that bright reward
 I daily will survey;
And in the blooming prospect lose
 The sorrows of the way.

1053 *Doxology.*

NOW let the Father, and the Son,
 And Spirit be adored;
Where there are works to make him known,
 Or saints to love the Lord.

AVON. C.M.

384 *The resolve.*

SHALL I, amidst a ghastly band,
  Dragg'd to the judgment seat,
Far on the left with horror stand,
  My fearful doom to meet?—

2 Dissolved are nature's closest ties,
  And bosom-friends forgot,
When God, the just avenger, cries,
  Depart, I know you not!—

3 But must I from his glorious face,
  From all his saints retire?
But must I go to my own place
  In everlasting fire?—

4 Ah! no;—I still may turn and live,
  For still his wrath delays;
He now vouchsafes a kind reprieve,
  And offers me his grace.

5 I will accept his offers now:
  From every sin depart;
Perform my oft-repeated vow,
  And render him my heart.

6 I will improve what I receive,
  The grace through Jesus given;
Sure, if with God on earth I live,
  To live with God in heaven.

298 *Approaching the table.*

JESUS, at whose supreme command
  We now approach to God,
Before us in thy vesture stand,
  Thy vesture dipp'd in blood.

2 The tokens of thy dying love
  O let us all receive,
And feel the quick'ning Spirit move,
  And sensibly believe!

3 The living bread sent down from heaven
  In us vouchsafe to be;
Thy flesh for all the world is given,
  And all may live by thee.

4 Now, Lord, on us thy flesh bestow,
  And let us drink thy blood,
Till all our souls are fill'd below
  With all the life of God.

106 *"I have given you an example."*

BEHOLD where in a mortal form
  Appears each grace divine!
The virtues, all in Jesus met,
  With mildest radiance shine.

2 To spread the rays of heavenly light,
  To give the mourner joy,
To preach glad tidings to the poor,
  Was his divine employ.

3 Lowly in heart, to all his friends
  A friend and servant found;
He wash'd their feet, he wiped their tears,
  And heal'd each bleeding wound.

4 Midst keen reproach and cruel scorn,
  Patient and meek he stood:
His foes, ungrateful, sought his life:
  He labour'd for their good.

5 In the last hours of deep distress,
  Before his Father's throne,
With soul resign'd, he bow'd, and said,
  "Thy will, not mine, be done!"

6 Be Christ our pattern and our guide!
  His image may we bear!
O may we tread his holy steps,
  His joy and glory share!

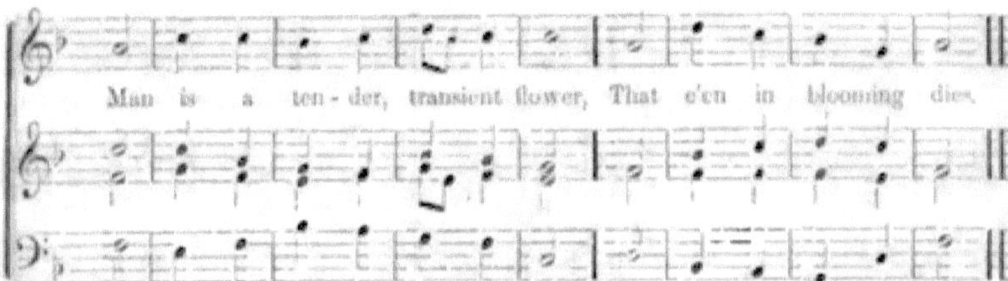

721 *Funeral of a child.*

LIFE is a span, a fleeting hour,—
 How soon the vapour flies!
Man is a tender, transient flower,
 That e'en in blooming dies.

2 Death spreads his with'ring, wintry arms,
 And beauty smiles no more;
Ah! where are now those rising charms
 Which pleased our eyes before?

3 That once loved form, now cold and dead,
 Each mournful thought employs:
We weep our earthly comforts fled,
 And wither'd all our joys.

4 Hope looks beyond the bounds of time,
 When what we now deplore,
Shall rise in full, immortal prime,
 And bloom to fade no more.

443 *The backslider. His retrospect.*

O THAT I were as heretofore!
 When, warm in my first love,
I only lived my God t' adore,
 And seek the things above!

2 Upon my head his candle shone,
 And, lavish of his grace,
With cords of love he drew me on,
 And half unveil'd his face.

3 Far, far above all earthly things,
 Triumphantly I rode;
I soar'd to heaven on eagles' wings,
 And found and talk'd with God.

4 Where am I now? from what a height
 Of happiness cast down!
The glory swallow'd up in night,
 And faded is the crown.

5 Through the wide world of sin and wo,
 A banish'd man, I roam;
But cannot find my rest below,
 But cannot wander home.

6 O God, thou art my home, my rest,
 For which I sigh in pain!
How shall I 'scape into thy breast,
 My Eden how regain?

771 *Psalm cxix.*

HOW shall the young secure their hearts,
 And guard their lives from sin?
Thy word the choicest rule imparts,
 To keep the conscience clean.

2 When once it enters to the mind,
 It spreads such light abroad,
The meanest souls instruction find,
 And raise their thoughts to God.

3 'Tis like the sun, a heavenly light,
 That guides us all the day;
And, through the dangers of the night,
 A lamp to lead our way.

4 Thy word is everlasting truth;
 How pure is every page!
That holy book shall guide our youth,
 And well support our age.

974 *Morning or evening.*

HOSANNA, with a cheerful sound,
 To God's upholding hand!
Ten thousand snares attend us round,
 And yet secure we stand.

2 God is our sun, whose daily light
 Our joy and safety brings;
Our feeble flesh lies safe at night
 Beneath his shady wings.

ORTONVILLE. C. M.

HASTINGS.

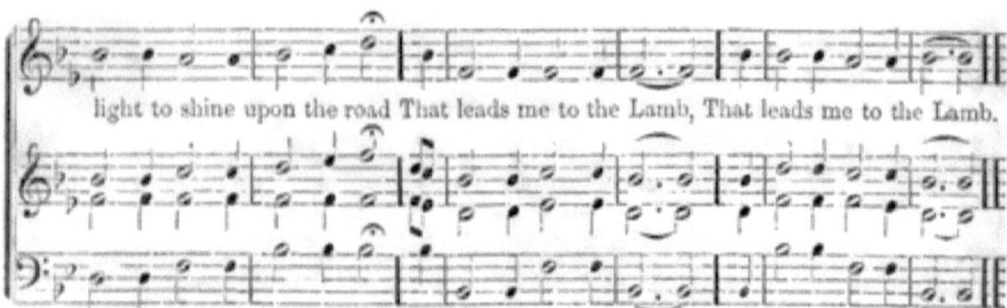

449 *The backslider's prayer.*

O FOR a closer walk with God,
  A calm and heavenly frame;
A light to shine upon the road
  That leads me to the Lamb.

2 Where is the blessedness I knew
  When first I saw the Lord?
Where is the soul-refreshing view
  Of Jesus and his word?

3 What peaceful hours I once enjoy'd!
  How sweet their mem'ry still!
But they have left an aching void
  The world can never fill.

4 Return, O holy Dove, return,
  Sweet messenger of rest!
I hate the sins that made thee mourn,
  And drove thee from my breast.

5 The dearest idol I have known,
  Whate'er that idol be,
Help me to tear it from thy throne,
  And worship only thee.

6 So shall my walk be close with God,
  Calm and serene my frame;
So purer light shall mark the road
  That leads me to the Lamb.

726 *Funeral of a Christian. Rev. xiv. 13.*

HEAR what the voice from heaven proclaims,
  For all the pious dead!
Sweet is the savour of their names,
  And soft their sleeping bed.

2 They die in Jesus, and are bless'd,
  How kind their slumbers are!
From suff'rings, and from sins, released,
  And freed from every snare.

3 Far from this world of toil and strife,
  They're present with the Lord;
The labours of their mortal life
  End in a large reward.

802 *Pleading for the Orphan.*

O HOW can they look up to heaven,
  And ask for mercy there,
Who never sooth'd the poor man's pang,
  Nor dried the orphan's tear!

2 The dread omnipotence of Heaven
  We every hour provoke;
Yet still the mercy of our God
  Withholds th' avenging stroke:

3 And Christ was still the healing friend
  Of poverty and pain;
And never did imploring wretch
  His garment touch in vain.

4 May we with humble effort take
  Example from above;
And thence the active lesson learn
  Of charity and love!

5 But chiefly be the labour ours
  To shade the early plant;
To guard from ignorance and guilt
  The infancy of want;

6 To graft the virtues, ere the bud
  The canker-worm has gnaw'd,
And teach the rescued child to lisp
  Its gratitude to God.

548 *The heart dissolving in love.*

JESUS hath died that I might live,
  Might live to God alone;
In him eternal life receive,
  And be in spirit one.

2 Saviour, I thank thee for the grace,
The gift unspeakable;
And wait with arms of faith t' embrace,
And all thy love to feel.

3 My soul breaks out in strong desire
The perfect bliss to prove;
My longing heart is all on fire
To be dissolved in love.

4 Give me thyself; from every boast,
From every wish set free:
Let all I am in thee be lost;
But give thyself to me.

5 Thy gifts, alas! cannot suffice,
Unless thyself be given;
Thy presence makes my paradise,
And where thou art is heaven.

435 *Subdued by the Cross.*

IN evil long I took delight,
Unawed by shame or fear;
Till a new object struck my sight,
And stopp'd my wild career.

2 I saw one hanging on a tree,
In agonies and blood,
Who fix'd his languid eyes on me,
As near his cross I stood.

3 Sure, never to my latest breath
Can I forget that look;
It seem'd to charge me with his death,
Though not a word he spoke.

4 My conscience felt, and own'd the guilt,
And plunged me in despair;
I saw my sins his blood had spilt,
And help'd to nail him there.

5 A second look he gave, which said
"I freely all forgive;
This blood is for thy ransom paid;
I die, that thou may'st live."

6 Thus, while his death my sin displays
In all its blackest hue;
Such is the mystery of grace,
It seals my pardon too.

387 *Having the form of godliness.*

LONG have I seem'd to serve thee, Lord,
With unavailing pain:
Fasted, and pray'd, and read thy word,
And heard it preach'd in vain.

2 Oft did I with th' assembly join,
And near thy altar drew;
A form of godliness was mine,
The power I never knew.

3 I rested in the outward law,
Nor knew its deep design:
The length and breadth I never saw,
And height, of love divine.

4 To please thee thus at length I see,
Vainly I hoped and strove:
For what are outward things to thee,
Unless they spring from love?

5 I see the perfect law requires
Truth in the inward parts;
Our full consent, our whole desires,
Our undivided hearts.

6 But I of means have made my boast,
Of means an idol made:
The spirit in the letter lost,
The substance in the shade.

7 Where am I now?—what is my hope?
What can my weakness do?
Jesus, to thee my soul looks up:
'Tis thou must make it new.

213 *Witness and Seal.*

WHY should the children of a King
Go mourning all their days?
Great Comforter, descend and bring
The tokens of thy grace.

2 Dost thou not dwell in all thy saints,
And seal the heirs of heaven?
When wilt thou banish my complaints,
And show my sins forgiven?

3 Assure my conscience of her part
In the Redeemer's blood:
And bear thy witness with my heart,
That I am born of God.

4 Thou art the earnest of his love,
The pledge of joys to come;
May thy bless'd wings, celestial Dove,
Safely convey me home!

444 *The backslider's misery.*

WRETCH that I am! from God I've stray'd,
Have most rebellious been,—
Of faith a dreadful shipwreck made,
And added sin to sin.

2 Vilest of all th' apostate race,
I have his love withstood;
And sinn'd against his pard'ning grace,
And trampled on his blood.

3 More desp'rate is my damn'd estate,
And more enslaved I am,
Than when I by the flesh-pots sat,
And wallow'd in my shame.

4 What shall I do? by guilt oppress,
Shall I in Egypt dwell?
Alas! in sinning to seek rest,
Is to seek rest in hell.

5 The grace I have abused, alone
Can help and comfort give:
O Jesus, hear my dying groan,
And bid the sinner live!

CAMBRIDGE. C. M.

DR. RANDALL.

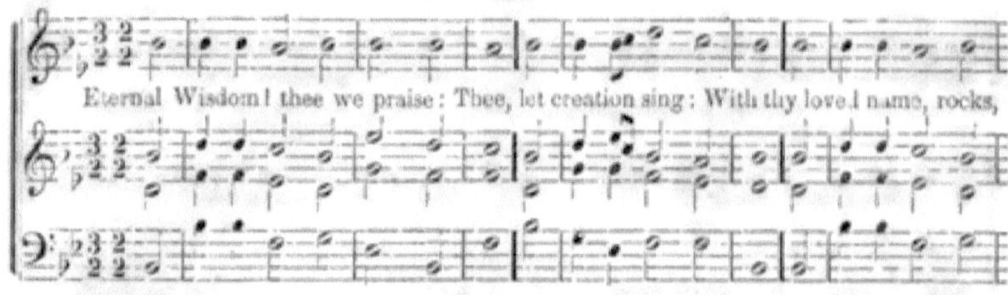

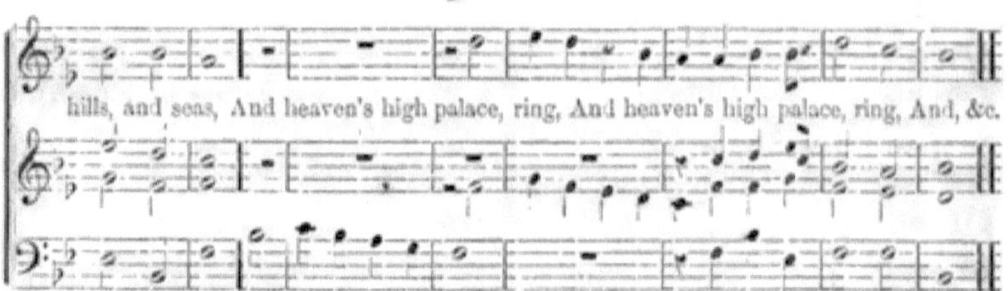

30 *"All thy works praise thee."*

ETERNAL Wisdom! thee we praise:
  Thee, let creation sing:
With thy loved name, rocks, hills, and seas,
  And heaven's high palace, ring.

2 Thy hand, how wide it spreads the sky,
  How glorious to behold!
Tinged with a blue of heavenly dye,
  And starr'd with sparkling gold.

3 There thou hast bid the globes of light
  Their endless circles run:
There the pale planet rules the night:
  The day obeys the sun.

4 If down I turn my wond'ring eyes
  On clouds and storms below;
Those under regions of the skies
  Thy numerous glories show.

5 The noisy winds stand ready there,
  Thy orders to obey;
With sounding wings they sweep the air,
  To make thy chariot way.

6 There, like a trumpet loud and strong,
  Thy thunder shakes our coast;
While the red lightnings wave along,
  The banners of thy host.

7 On the thin air, without a prop,
  Hang fruitful showers around;
At thy command they sink and drop
  Their fatness on the ground.

10 *The Trinity.*

HAIL, holy, holy, holy Lord!
  Whom one in three we know:
By all thy heavenly host adored,
  By all thy church below.

2 One undivided Trinity
  With triumph we proclaim;
Thy universe is full of thee,
  And speaks thy glorious name.

3 Thee, holy Father, we confess;
  Thee, holy Son, adore;
Spirit of truth and holiness,
  We praise thee evermore.

4 The incommunicable right,
  Almighty God, receive!
Which angel-choirs, and saints in light,
  And saints embodied, give.

5 Three persons, equally divine,
  We magnify and love:
And both the choirs ere long shall join
  To sing thy praise above.

6 Hail, holy, holy, holy Lord,
  (Our heavenly song shall be,)
Supreme, essential One, adored
  In co-eternal Three!

838 *Psalm lx. 1–5.*

GOD, thou hast scatter'd us and driven,
  Forget thy wrath once more!
Thy land is by thy fury riven,
  O heal its trembling sore.

2 With grief thy people thou hast fed,
  And drench'd with deadly wine,
Yet o'er thy saints thy banner spread,
  Inscribed with truth divine!

3 O be thou still in wo our light!
  In vain to man we sue;
God yet will nerve our arm in fight,
  And all our foes subdue.

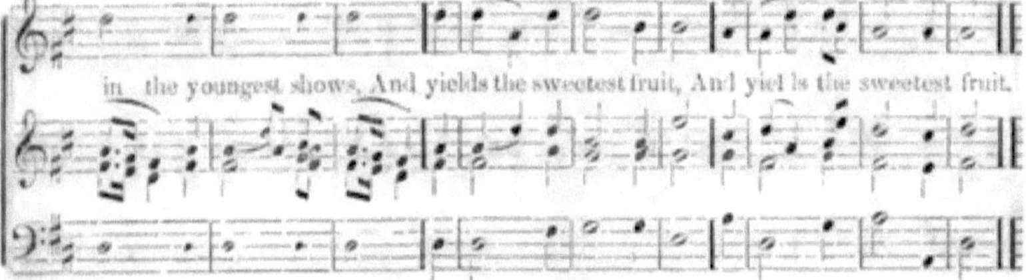

363 *Before preaching to the young.*

GRACE is a plant, where'er it grows,
  Of pure and heavenly root:
But fairest in the youngest shows,
  And yields the sweetest fruit.

2 Ye careless ones, O hear betimes
  The voice of sovereign love!
Your youth is stain'd with many crimes,
  But mercy reigns above.

3 True, you are young, but there's a stone
  Within the youngest breast,
Or half the crimes which you have done
  Would rob you of your rest.

4 For you the public prayer is made,
  O join the public prayer!
For you the secret tear is shed,
  O shed yourselves a tear!

5 We pray that you may early prove
  The Spirit's power to teach;
You cannot be too young to love
  That Jesus whom we preach.

474 *The transports of love.*

O 'TIS delight, without alloy,
  Jesus, to hear thy name;
My spirit leaps with inward joy,
  I feel the sacred flame.

2 My passions hold a pleasing reign,
  When love inspires my breast,
Love, the divinest of the train,
  The sovereign of the rest.

3 This is the grace must live and sing
  When faith and hope shall cease,
Must sound from every joyful string
  Through the sweet groves of bliss.

4 Let life immortal seize my clay;
  Let love refine my blood;
Her flames can bear my soul away,
  Can bring me near my God.

5 Swift I ascend the heavenly place,
  And hasten to my home;
I leap to meet thy kind embrace,
  I come, O Lord, I come!

6 Sink down, ye separating hills,
  Let sin and death remove;
'Tis love that drives my chariot wheels,
  And death must yield to love.

476 *"The fruit of the Spirit is—joy."*

JOY is a fruit that will not grow
  In nature's barren soil;
All we can boast, till Christ we know,
  Is vanity and toil.

2 But where the Lord has planted grace,
  And made his glories known,
There fruits of heavenly joy and peace
  Are found—and there alone.

3 A bleeding Saviour seen by faith—
  A sense of pard'ning love—
A hope that triumphs over death—
  Give joys like those above.

4 To take a glimpse within the veil—
  To know that God is mine—
Are springs of joy that never fail,
  Unspeakable, divine!

5 These are the joys which satisfy,
  And sanctify the mind;
Which make the spirit mount on high,
  And leave the world behind.

WOODLAND. C. M.

GOULD.

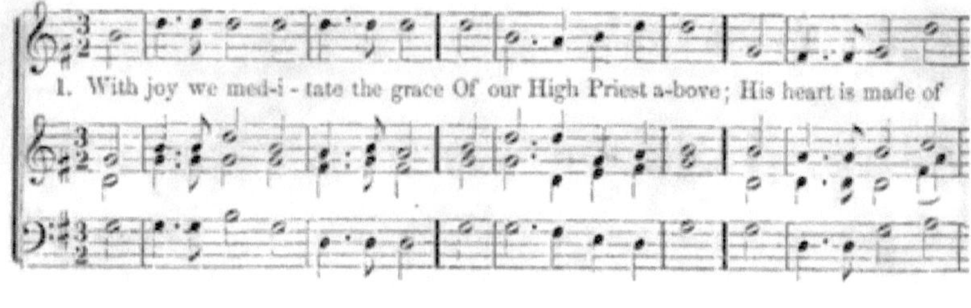

153 *Heb. iv. 14—16.*

WITH joy we meditate the grace
  Of our High Priest above;
His heart is made of tenderness,
  His bowels melt with love.

2 Touch'd with a sympathy within,
  He knows our feeble frame;
He knows what sore temptations mean,
  For he hath felt the same.

3 He in the days of feeble flesh
  Pour'd out strong cries and tears,
And in his measure feels afresh
  What every member bears.

4 He'll never quench the smoking flax,
  But raise it to a flame;
The bruised reed he never breaks,
  Nor scorns the meanest name.

5 Then let our humble faith address
  His mercy and his power;
We shall obtain deliv'ring grace
  In the distressing hour.

970 *Evening. Psalm iv.*

LORD, thou wilt hear me when I pray,
  I am for ever thine:
I fear before thee all the day,
  Nor would I dare to sin.

2 And while I rest my weary head,
  From cares and business free,
'Tis sweet conversing on my bed
  With my own heart and thee.

3 I pay this evening sacrifice;
  And when my work is done,
Great God, my faith, my hope, relies
  Upon thy grace alone.

4 Thus, with my thoughts composed to peace,
  I'll give mine eyes to sleep;
Thy hand in safety keeps my days,
  And will my slumbers keep.

917 *What is prayer?*

PRAYER is the soul's sincere desire,
  Utter'd, or unexpress'd;
The motion of a hidden fire
  That trembles in the breast.

2 Prayer is the burden of a sigh,
  The falling of a tear;
The upward glancing of an eye,
  When none but God is near.

3 Prayer is the simplest form of speech
  That infant lips can try;
Prayer, the sublimest strains that reach
  The Majesty on high.

4 Prayer is the Christian's vital breath,
  The Christian's native air;
His watchword at the gates of death;
  He enters heaven with prayer.

5 Prayer is the contrite sinner's voice,
  Returning from his ways,
While angels in their songs rejoice,
  And cry, "Behold, he prays!"

6 O Thou, by whom we come to God,
  The Life, the Truth, the Way!
The path of prayer thyself hast trod:
  Lord, teach us how to pray.

1053 *Doxology.*

NOW let the Father, and the Son,
  And Spirit be adored;
Where there are works to make Him known,
  Or saints to love the Lord.

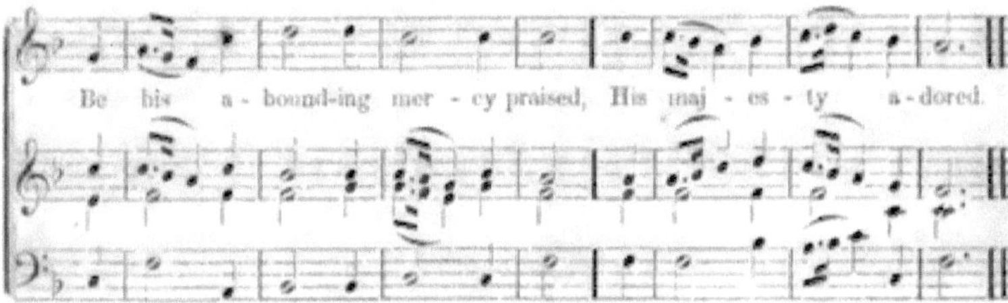

700 *1 Peter i. 3—5.*

BLESS'D be the everlasting God,
The Father of our Lord;
Be his abounding mercy praised,
His majesty adored.

2 When from the dead he raised his Son,
And call'd him to the sky,
He gave our souls a lively hope,
That they should never die.

3 There's an inheritance divine,
Reserved against that day;
'Tis uncorrupted, undefiled,
And cannot waste away.

4 Saints by the power of God are kept,
Till the salvation come:
We walk by faith, as strangers here,
Till Christ shall call us home.

816 *Harvest.*

TO praise the ever-bounteous Lord,
My soul, wake all thy powers!
He calls, and at his voice come forth
The smiling harvest hours.

2 His cov'nant with the earth he keeps;
My tongue his goodness sing;
Summer and winter know their time,
His harvest crowns the spring.

3 Well pleased the toiling swains behold
The waving yellow crop:
With joy they bear the sheaves away,
And sow again in hope.

4 Thus teach me, gracious God, to sow
The seeds of righteousness:
Smile on my soul, and with thy beams
The ripening harvest bless.

5 Then, in the last great harvest, I
Shall reap a glorious crop:
The harvest shall by far exceed
What I have sown in hope.

954 *Morning.*

GIVER and guardian of my sleep,
To praise thy name I wake:
Still, Lord, thy helpless servant keep,
For thine own mercy's sake.

2 The blessing of another day
I thankfully receive:
O may I only thee obey,
And to thy glory live!

3 Upon me lay thy mighty hand,
My words and thoughts restrain:
Bow my whole soul to thy command,
Nor let my faith be vain.

4 Pris'ner of hope, I wait the hour
Which shall salvation bring;
When all I am shall own thy power,
And call my Jesus King.

811 *Seed-time.*

ETERNAL God! we humbly bow
Before thy sacred throne,
From thee our varied comforts flow,
From thee, and thee alone.

2 We plead the promise in thy word,
That seed-time shall be given;
Now verify thy promise, Lord,
And send us help from heaven.

3 Then we will give thee lasting praise
For all thy love and care;
Unite in fervent, grateful lays,
For prospects bright and fair.

782 *Psalm cxviii. 22, 23.*

BEHOLD the sure Foundation-stone
  Which God in Zion lays,
To build our heavenly hopes upon,
  And his eternal praise.

2 Chosen of God, to sinners dear,
  We now adore thy name;
We trust our whole salvation here,
  Nor can we suffer shame.

3 The foolish builders, scribe and priest,
  Reject it with disdain:
Yet on this Rock the church shall rest,
  And envy rage in vain.

4 What though the gates of hell withstood,
  Yet must this building rise:
'Tis thine own work, almighty God,
  And wondrous in our eyes.

611 *Judges v. 31.*

JESUS, let all thy lovers shine,
  Illustrious as the sun;
And, bright with borrow'd rays divine,
  Their glorious circuit run.

2 Beyond the reach of mortals, spread
  Their light where'er they go;
And heavenly influences shed
  On all the world below.

3 As giants may they run their race,
  Exulting in their might;
As burning luminaries, chase
  The gloom of hellish night.

4 As the bright Sun of righteousness,
  Their healing wings display;
And let their lustre still increase
  Unto the perfect day.

5 Such honour all thy saints receive,
  Who thee sincerely love:
Dispensers of thy gifts we live,
  And general blessings prove;—

6 And when our useful course is run,
  Enjoy the kingdom given,
Bright as the uncreated sun,
  In the eternal heaven.

603 *Relieving Christ in his members.*

JESUS, my Lord, how rich thy grace!
  Thy bounties, how complete!
How shall I count the matchless sum?
  How pay the mighty debt?

2 High on a throne of radiant light
  Dost thou exalted shine;
What can my poverty bestow,
  When all the worlds are thine?

3 But thou hast brethren here below,
  The partners of thy grace,
And wilt confess their humble names
  Before thy Father's face.

4 In them thou may'st be clothed and fed,
  And visited and cheer'd,
And in their accents of distress
  My Saviour's voice is heard.

5 Thy face with rev'rence and with love,
  I, in thy poor would see;
O rather let me beg my bread,
  Than hold it back from thee!

1053 *Doxology.*

NOW let the Father, and the Son,
  And Spirit, be adored;
Where there are works to make Him known,
  Or saints to love the Lord.

606 *"Bags that wax not old."*

THESE mortal joys, how soon they fade!
How swift they pass away!
The dying flower reclines its head,
The beauty of a day.

2 The bags are rent, the treasure's lost,
We fondly call'd our own:
Scarce could we the possession boast,
When, lo! we found it gone.

3 But there are joys that cannot die,
With God laid up in store;
Treasure, beyond the changing sky,
Brighter than golden ore.

4 To that my rising heart aspires,
Secure to find its rest,
And glories in such wide desires,
Of all its wish possest.

5 The seeds which piety and love
Have scatter'd here below,
In the fair fertile fields above,
To ample harvests grow.

6 The mite my willing hands can give,
At Jesus' feet I lay;
Grace shall the humble gift receive,
And heaven at large repay.

601 *The good Samaritan.*

FATHER of mercies, send thy grace,
All-powerful, from above,
To form in our obedient souls
The image of thy love.

2 O may our sympathising breasts
That generous pleasure know;
Kindly to share in others' joy,
And weep for others' wo!

3 When the most helpless sons of grief
In low distress are laid,
Soft be our hearts their pains to feel,
And swift our hands to aid.

4 So Jesus look'd on dying men,
When throned above the skies;
And 'midst th' embraces of thy love,
He felt compassion rise.

5 On wings of love the Saviour flew,
To raise us from the ground;
And gave the richest of his blood,
A balm for every wound.

386 *Feeling after God.*

GOD is in this and every place!
But O, how dark and void!
To me 'tis one great wilderness,
This earth without my God.

2 Empty of Him who all things fills,
Till he his light impart,
Till he his glorious self reveals,
The veil is on my heart.

3 O thou who seest and know'st my grief,
Thyself unseen, unknown;
Pity my helpless unbelief,
And break my heart of stone.

4 Regard me with a gracious eye,
The long-sought blessing give;
And bid me, at the point to die,
Behold thy face and live.

5 Now, Jesus, now the Father's love
Shed in my heart abroad;
The middle wall of sin remove,
And let me into God.

669 *Brevity of life.*

THEE we adore, eternal Name!
And humbly own to thee
How feeble is our mortal frame,
What dying worms we be!

2 The year rolls round, and steals away
The breath that first it gave:
Whate'er we do, where'er we be,
We're trav'ling to the grave.

3 Dangers stand thick through all the ground,
To push us to the tomb;
And fierce diseases wait around
To hurry mortals home.

4 Great God! on what a slender thread
Hang everlasting things!
Th' eternal states of all the dead
Upon life's feeble strings.

5 Infinite joy, or endless wo,
Attends on every breath;
And yet how unconcern'd we go
Upon the brink of death!

6 Waken, O Lord, our drowsy sense,
To walk this dangerous road,
And if our souls be hurried hence,
May they be found with God!

112 *Gethsemane.*

DARK was the night, and cold the ground,
On which the Lord was laid;
His sweat, like drops of blood, ran down;
In agony he pray'd,—

2 "Father, remove this bitter cup,
If such thy sacred will,
If not, content to drink it up,
Thy pleasure I fulfil."

3 Go to the garden, sinner, see
Those precious drops that flow;
The heavy load he bore for thee;
For thee he lies so low.

689 *The day of judgment.*

AND must I be to judgment brought,
And answer in that day
For every vain and idle thought,
And every word I say?

2 Yes, every secret of my heart
Shall shortly be made known,
And I receive my just desert
For all that I have done.

3 How careful, then, ought I to live!
With what religious fear!
Who such a strict account must give
For my behaviour here!

4 Thou awful Judge of quick and dead,
The watchful power bestow;
So shall I to my ways take heed,
To all I speak or do.

5 If now thou standest at the door,
O let me feel thee near!
And make my peace with God, before
I at thy bar appear.

288 *The Institution.*

THAT doleful night before his death,
The Lamb for sinners slain,
Did, almost with his dying breath,
This solemn feast ordain.

2 To keep the feast, Lord, we have met,
And to remember thee:
Help each poor trembler to repeat,
"For me, he died for me!"

3 Thy suff'rings, Lord, each sacred sign
To our remembrance brings;
We eat the bread, and drink the wine,
But think on nobler things.

4 O tune our tongues, and set in frame
Each heart that pants for thee,
To sing, "Hosanna to the Lamb!"
The Lamb that died for me!

998 *"Enter into thy closet."*

ENT'RING into my closet, I
The busy world exclude;
In secret prayer for mercy cry,
And groan to be renew'd.

2 Far from the paths of men to Thee
I solemnly retire;
See Thou, who dost in secret see,
And grant my heart's desire.

3 Fain would I all thy goodness feel,
And know my sins forgiven;
And do on earth thy perfect will,
As angels do in heaven.

4 O Father, glorify thy Son,
And grant what I require;
For Jesus' sake the gift send down,
And answer me by fire.

5 Kindle the flame of love within,
Which may to heaven ascend:
And now the work of grace begin,
Which shall in glory end.

371 *Before an inciting sermon.*

JESUS, thou all-redeeming Lord,
Thy blessing we implore,
Open the door to preach thy word,
The great effectual door.

2 Gather the outcasts in, and save
From sin and Satan's power;
And let them now acceptance have,
And know their gracious hour.

3 Lover of souls! thou know'st to prize
What thou hast bought so dear:
Come, then, and in thy people's eyes,
With all thy wounds appear!

4 Appear, as when of old confest,
The suff'ring Son of God;
And let them see thee in thy vest,
But newly dipp'd in blood.

5 The hardness from their hearts remove,
Thou who for all hast died;
Show them the tokens of thy love,
Thy feet, thy hands, thy side.

6 Thy feet were nail'd to yonder tree,
To trample down their sin;
Thy hands stretch'd out, they all may see,
To take thy murd'rers in.

7 Thy side an open fountain is,
Where all may freely go,
And drink the living streams of bliss,
And wash them white as snow.

8 Ready thou art the blood t' apply,
And prove the record true:
And all thy wounds to sinners cry,
"I suffer'd this for you!"

415 *Miracles of grace.*

JESUS, if still thou art to-day,
As yesterday, the same,
Present to heal, in me display
The virtue of thy name!

2 If still thou go'st about to do
Thy needy creatures good,
On me, that I thy praise may show,
Be all thy wonders show'd.

3 Now, Lord, to whom for help I call,
Thy miracles repeat;
With pitying eyes behold me fall
A leper at thy feet.

4 Loathsome, and vile, and self-abhorr'd,
I sink beneath my sin;
But, if thou wilt, a gracious word
Of thine can make me clean.

5 Thou seest me deaf to thy command,
Open, O Lord, my ear:
Bid me stretch out my wither'd hand,
And lift it up in prayer.

6 Silent, (alas! thou know'st how long,)
My voice I cannot raise;
But O! when thou shalt loose my tongue,
The dumb shall sing thy praise.

7 Lame at the pool I still am found:
Give, and my strength employ;
Light as a hart I then shall bound;
The lame shall leap for joy.

8 Blind from my birth to guilt and thee,
And dark I am within:
The love of God I cannot see,
The sinfulness of sin:—

9 But thou, they say, art passing by:
O let me find thee near!
Jesus, in mercy hear my cry,
Thou Son of David, hear!—

10 Behold me waiting in the way
For thee, the heavenly Light:
Command me to be brought, and say,
"Sinner, receive thy sight!"

1053 *Doxology.*

NOW let the Father, and the Son,
And Spirit, be adored;
Where there are works to make Him known,
Or saints to love the Lord.

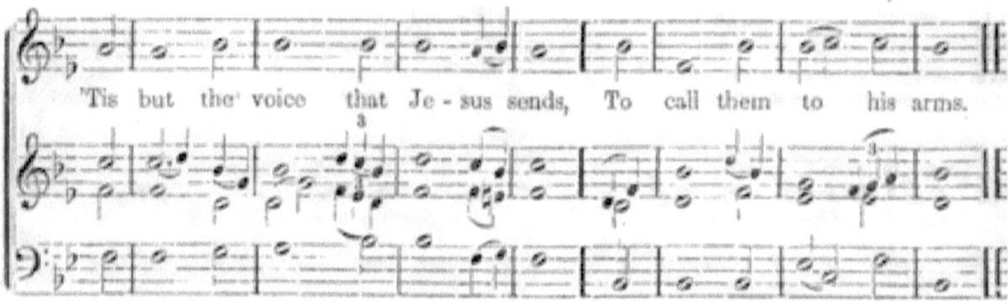

729 *Funeral of a Christian.*

WHY do we mourn departing friends,
Or shake at death's alarms?
'Tis but the voice that Jesus sends,
To call them to his arms.

2 Are we not tending upward too,
As fast as time can move?
Nor should we wish the hours more slow
To keep us from our Love.

3 Why should we tremble to convey
Their bodies to the tomb?
There once the flesh of Jesus lay,
And left a long perfume.

4 The graves of all his saints he blest,
And soften'd every bed:
Where should the dying members rest,
But with their dying Head?

5 Thence he arose, ascending high,
And show'd our feet the way:
Up to the Lord our flesh shall fly,
At the great rising day.

6 Then let the last loud trumpet sound,
And bid our kindred rise:
Awake, ye nations under ground;
Ye saints, ascend the skies!

694 *"Prepare to meet thy God."*

WO to the men on earth who dwell,
Nor dread th' Almighty's frown;
When God doth all his wrath reveal,
And shower his judgments down!

2 Sinners, expect those heaviest showers:
To meet your God prepare!
For lo! the seventh angel pours
His phial on the air.

3 Lo! from their seats the mountains leap;
The mountains are not found;
Transported far into the deep,
And in the ocean drown'd.

4 Who then shall live and face the throne,
And face the Judge severe?
When heaven and earth are fled and gone,
O where shall I appear?

5 Now, only now, against that hour,
We may a place provide;
Beyond the grave, beyond the power
Of hell, our spirits hide:

6 Firm in the all-destroying shock,
May view the final scene;
For lo! the everlasting Rock
Is cleft to take us in.

652 *Waiting patiently for death.*

WHY thus impatient to be gone?
Such wishes breathe no more;
Let Him who lock'd thy spirit in,
When meet, unbolt the door.

2 Why wouldst thou snatch the victor's palm
Before the conquest 's won?
Or wish to seize th' immortal prize,
Ere yet the race is run?

3 Inglorious wish, to haste away,
And leave thy work undone!—
To serve thy Lord will please no less
Than praising round the throne.

4 While thou art standing in the field,
For bliss thou'lt riper grow;—
Then wait thy Lord's appointed time,
Till he shall bid thee go.

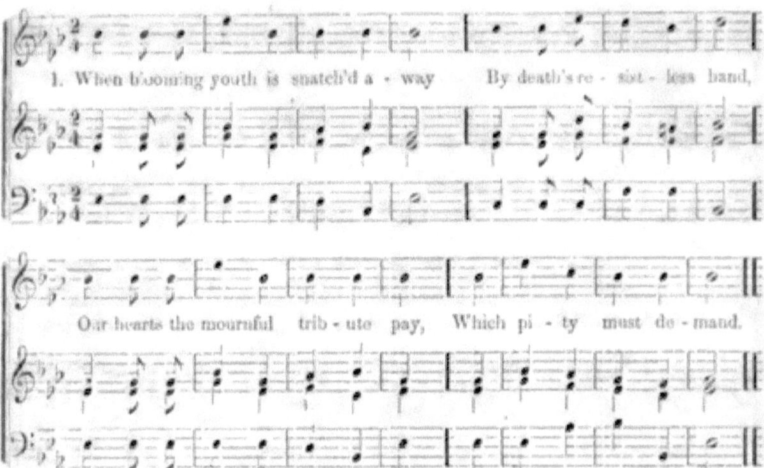

723 *Funeral of a young person.*

WHEN blooming youth is snatch'd away
By death's resistless hand,
Our hearts the mournful tribute pay
Which pity must demand.

2 While pity prompts the rising sigh,
O may this truth, imprest
With awful power—I too must die—
Sink deep in every breast!

3 Let this vain world delude no more;
Behold the gaping tomb!
It bids us seize the present hour,
To-morrow death may come.

4 The voice of this alarming scene,
Let every heart obey;
Nor be the heavenly warning vain,
Which calls to watch and pray.

722 *Funeral of a child.*

YE mourning saints, whose streaming tears
Flow o'er your children dead,
Say not in transports of despair,
That all your hopes are fled.

2 Though, your young branches torn away,
Like wither'd trunks ye stand,
With fairer verdure shall ye bloom,
Touch'd by th' Almighty's hand.

3 "I'll give the mourner," saith the Lord,
"In my own house a place;
No names of daughters and of sons
Could yield so high a grace.

4 "Transient and vain is every hope
A rising race can give;
In endless honour and delight
My children all shall live."

5 We welcome, Lord, those rising tears,
Through which thy face we see,
And bless those wounds which thro' our hearts
Prepare a way for thee.

636 *Solace in woe.*

O THOU who driest the mourner's tear,
How dark this world would be,
If, when deceived and wounded here,
We could not fly to thee!

2 The friends, who in our sunshine live,
When winter comes are flown;
And he who has but tears to give,
Must weep those tears alone.

3 But thou wilt heal that broken heart,
Which, like the plants that throw
Their fragrance from the wounded part,
Breathes sweetness out of wo.

4 When joy no longer soothes or cheers,
And e'en the hope that threw
A moment's sparkle o'er our tears,
Is dimm'd and vanish'd too,—

5 O who could bear life's stormy doom,
Did not thy wing of love
Come brightly wafting through the gloom,
Our peace-branch from above!

6 Then sorrow, touch'd by thee, grows bright
With more than rapture's ray,
As darkness shows us worlds of light,
We never saw by day.

1053 *Doxology.*

NOW let the Father, and the Son,
And Spirit, be adored;
Where there are works to make Him known,
Or saints to love the Lord.

GENEVA. C. M.

JOHN COLE.

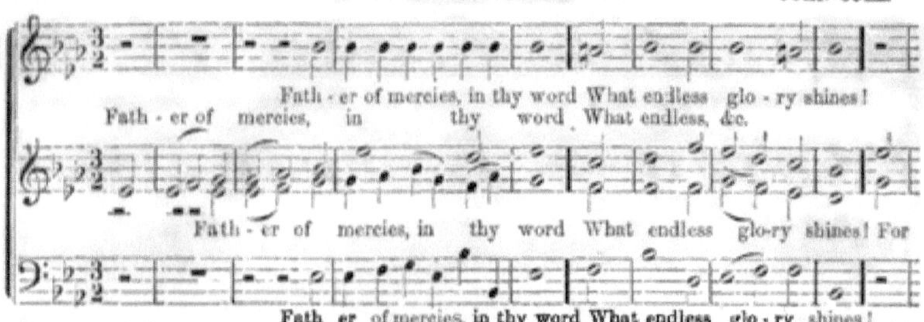

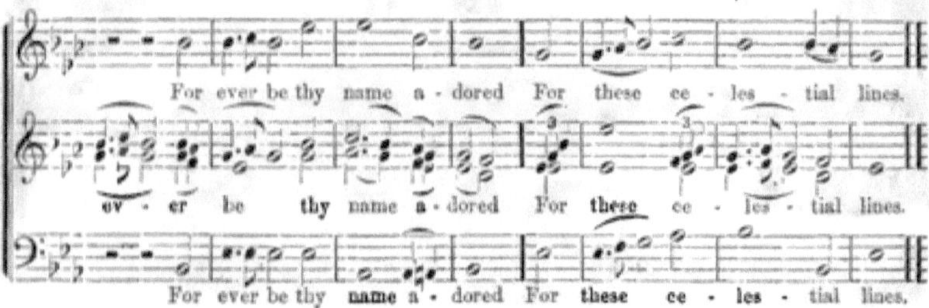

775 *Delighting in the word.*

FATHER of mercies, in thy word
What endless glory shines!
For ever be thy name adored
For these celestial lines.

2 Here may the wretched sons of want
Exhaustless riches find,
Riches above what earth can grant,
And lasting as the mind.

3 Here the fair tree of knowledge grows,
And yields a free repast,
Sublimer sweets than nature knows
Invite the longing taste.

4 Here the Redeemer's welcome voice
Spreads heavenly peace around;
And life, and everlasting joys,
Attend the blissful sound.

5 O may these heavenly pages be
My ever dear delight;
And still new beauties may I see,
And still increasing light!

6 Divine Instructer, gracious Lord,
Be thou for ever near;
Teach me to love thy sacred word,
And view my Saviour there.

541 *Longing to be established in love.*

O THAT in me the sacred fire
Might now begin to glow!
Burn up the dross of base desire,
And make the mountains flow!

2 O that it now from heaven might fall
And all my sins consume!
Come, Holy Ghost, for thee I call,
Spirit of burning, come.

3 Refining fire, go through my heart,
Illuminate my soul!
Scatter thy life through every part,
And sanctify the whole.

4 No longer then my heart shall mourn,
While, purified by grace,
I only for his glory burn,
And always see his face.

12 *To God the Son.*

HAIL, God the Son, in glory crown'd,
Ere time began to be;
Throned with thy Sire, through half the round
Of vast eternity!

2 Let heaven and earth's stupendous frame
Display their Author's power;
And each exalted seraph-flame,
Creator, thee adore.

3 Thy wondrous love the Godhead show'd
Contracted to a span—
The co-eternal Son of God,
The mortal Son of man.

4 To save us from our lost estate,
Behold his life-blood stream:
Hail, Lord, almighty to create,
Almighty to redeem!

5 The Mediator's God-like sway
His church below sustains;
Till nature shall her Judge survey,
The King Messiah reigns.

6 Hail, with essential glory crown'd,
When time shall cease to be;
Throned with thy Father, through the round
Of whole eternity.

1014 *Gratitude.*

WHEN all thy mercies, O my God,
My rising soul surveys,
Transported with the view, I'm lost
In wonder, love, and praise!

2 O how can words with equal warmth
The gratitude declare
That glows within my ravish'd heart?
But thou canst read it there!

3 Thy providence my life sustain'd,
And all my wants redress'd,
While in the silent womb I lay,
And hung upon the breast.

4 To all my weak complaints and cries
Thy mercy lent an ear,
Ere yet my feeble thoughts had learn'd
To form themselves in prayer.

5 Unnumber'd comforts on my soul
Thy tender care bestow'd,
Before my infant heart conceived
From whom those comforts flow'd.

6 When in the slipp'ry paths of youth
With heedless steps I ran,
Thine arm, unseen, convey'd me safe,
And led me up to man.

7 Through hidden dangers, toils, and deaths,
It gently clear'd my way;
And through the pleasing snares of vice,—
More to be fear'd than they.

8 When worn with sickness, oft hast thou
With health renew'd my face;
And, when in sins and sorrows sunk,
Revived my soul with grace.

9 Thy bounteous hand with worthy bliss
Has made my cup run o'er;
And in a kind and faithful friend
Hast doubled all my store.

10 Ten thousand thousand precious gifts
My daily thanks employ.
Nor is the least a cheerful heart,
That tastes those gifts with joy.

11 Through every period of my life
Thy goodness I'll pursue;
And after death, in distant worlds,
The pleasing theme renew.

12 When nature fails, and day and night
Divide thy works no more,
My ever grateful heart, O Lord,
Thy mercies shall adore.

13 Through all eternity to thee
A grateful song I'll raise;
But O! eternity 's too short
To utter all thy praise.

565 *"And Enoch walked with God."*

CHEER'D with thy converse, Lord, I trace
The desert with delight;
Through all the gloom, one smile of thine
Can dissipate the night.

2 Nor shall I through eternal days
A restless pilgrim roam;
Thy hand, that now directs my course,
Shall soon convey me home.

3 I ask not Enoch's rapt'rous flight
To realms of heavenly day;
Nor seek Elijah's fiery steeds,
To bear this flesh away.

4 Joyful my spirit will consent
To drop this mortal load;
And hail the sharpest pangs of death,
That break its way to God.

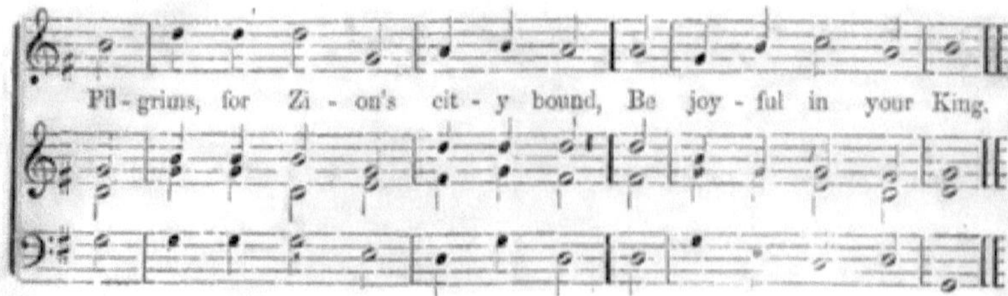

563 *Isaiah xxxv. 10.*

SING, O ye ransom'd of the Lord,
Your great Deliv'rer sing;
Pilgrims, for Zion's city bound,
Be joyful in your King.

2 A hand divine shall lead you on,
Through all the blissful road,
Till to the sacred mount you rise,
And see your smiling God.

3 There garlands of immortal joy
Shall bloom on every head;
While sorrow, sighing, and distress,
Like shadows all are fled.

4 March on in your Redeemer's strength;
Pursue his footsteps still;
And let the prospect cheer your eye,
While lab'ring up the hill.

549 *The cleansing act.*

COME, O my God, the promise seal,
This mountain, sin, remove!
Now in my waiting soul reveal
The virtue of thy love.

2 I want thy life, thy purity,
Thy righteousness, brought in:
I ask, desire, and trust in thee
To be redeem'd from sin.

3 For this, as taught by thee, I pray,
And can no longer doubt!
Remove from hence! to sin I say;
Be cast this moment out!

4 Anger and sloth, desire and pride,
This moment be subdued!
Be cast into the crimson tide
Of my Redeemer's blood.

5 Saviour, to thee my soul looks up,
My present Saviour thou!
In all the confidence of hope
I claim the blessing now!

6 'Tis done; thou dost this moment save,
With full salvation bless;
Redemption through thy blood I have,
And spotless love and peace.

475 *Love and praise.*

INFINITE, unexhausted Love!—
Jesus and Love are one—
If still to me thy bowels move,
They are restrain'd to none.

2 What shall I do my God to love,
My loving God to praise,
The length, and breadth, and height to prove,
And depth of sovereign grace?

3 Thy sovereign grace to all extends,
Immense and unconfined;
From age to age it never ends,
It reaches all mankind.

4 Throughout the world its breadth is known,
Wide as infinity,—
So wide, it never pass'd by one,
Or it had pass'd by me.

5 My trespass was grown up to heaven;
But far above the skies,
Through Christ abundantly forgiven,
I see thy mercies rise.

6 The depth of all-redeeming love,
What angel tongues can tell?
O may I to the utmost prove
The gift unspeakable!

564 *Walking with God.*

TALK with us, Lord, thyself reveal,
While here o'er earth we rove;
Speak to our hearts, and let us feel
The kindlings of thy love.

2 With thee conversing, we forget
All time, and toil, and care:
Labour is rest, and pain is sweet,
If thou, my God, art here.

3 Here then, my God, vouchsafe to stay,
And bid my heart rejoice;
My bounding heart shall own thy sway,
And echo to thy voice.

4 Thou callest me to seek thy face,
'Tis all I wish to seek;
T' attend the whispers of thy grace,
And hear thee inly speak.

5 Let this my every hour employ,
Till I thy glory see,
Enter into my Master's joy,
And find my heaven in thee!

547 *Sanctifying faith implored.*

GOD of eternal truth and grace,
Thy faithful promise seal!
Thy word, thy oath, to Abrah'm's race,
In us, e'en us, fulfil.

2 Let us, to perfect love restored,
Thy image here retrieve,
And in the presence of our Lord,
The life of angels live.

3 That mighty faith on me bestow
Which cannot ask in vain;
Which holds, and will not let thee go,
Till I my suit obtain,—

4 Till thou into my soul inspire
The perfect love unknown,
And tell my infinite desire,
"Whate'er thou wilt, be done."

5 But is it possible that I
Should live and sin no more?
Lord, if on thee I dare rely,
The faith shall bring the power.

6 On me the faith divine bestow,
Which doth the mountain move;
And all my spotless life shall show
Th' omnipotence of love.

450 *The backslider's wail.*

JESUS, the all-restoring Word,
My fallen spirit's hope,
After thy lovely likeness, Lord,
Ah! when shall I wake up!

2 Thou, O my God, thou only art
The Life, the Truth, the Way;
Quicken my soul, instruct my heart,
My sinking footsteps stay.

3 Of all thou hast in earth below,
In heaven above, to give,
Give me thy only love to know,
In thee to walk and live.

4 Fill me with all the life of love;
In mystic union join
Me to thyself, and let me prove
The fellowship divine.

5 Open the intercourse between
My longing soul and thee,
Never to be broke off again
To all eternity.

214 *Witness of Adoption.*

SOVEREIGN of all the worlds on high,
Allow my humble claim;
Nor, while a worm would raise its head,
Disdain a Father's name.

2 "My Father, God!" how sweet the sound!
How tender and how dear!
Not all the melody of heaven
Could so delight the ear.

3 Come, sacred Spirit, seal the name
On my expanding heart;
And show that in Jehovah's grace
I share a filial part.

4 Cheer'd by a signal so divine,
Unwav'ring I believe;
Thou know'st I "Abba, Father," cry;
Nor can the sign deceive.

35 *"Wonderful in counsel."*

GOD moves in a mysterious way,
His wonders to perform;
He plants his footsteps in the sea,
And rides upon the storm.

2 Deep in unfathomable mines
Of never-failing skill,
He treasures up his bright designs,
And works his sovereign will.

3 Ye fearful saints, fresh courage take;
The clouds ye so much dread
Are big with mercy, and shall break
In blessings on your head.

4 Judge not the Lord by feeble sense,
But trust him for his grace;
Behind a frowning providence
He hides a smiling face.

5 His purposes will ripen fast,
Unfolding every hour:
The bud may have a bitter taste,
But sweet will be the flower.

6 Blind unbelief is sure to err,
And scan his work in vain;
God is his own interpreter,
And he will make it plain.

NORTHFIELD. C. M.

J. INGALLS.

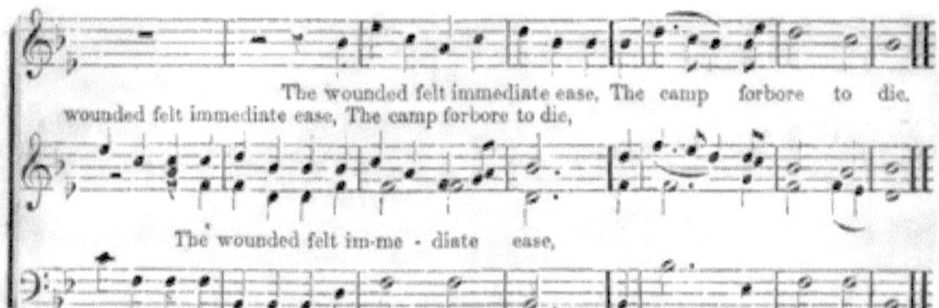

mediate ease, The wounded felt im-me - diate ease, The camp for - bore to die.

174 *John iii. 14, 15.*

SO did the Hebrew prophet raise
The brazen serpent high;
The wounded felt immediate ease,
The camp forbore to die.

2 "Look upward in the dying hour,
And live!" the prophet cries!
But Christ performs a nobler cure,
When faith lifts up her eyes.

3 High on the cross the Saviour hung!
High in the heavens he reigns!
Here sinners, by th' old serpent stung,
Look, and forget their pains.

4 When God's own Son is lifted up,
A dying world revives;
The Jew beholds a glorious hope;
Th' expiring Gentile lives.

335 *The chief of sinners invited.*

LOVERS of pleasure more than God,
For you he suffer'd pain;
Swearers, for you he spilt his blood;
And shall he bleed in vain?

2 Misers, his life for you he paid,
Your basest crimes he bore;
Drunkards, your sins on him were laid,
That you might sin no more.

3 The God of love, to earth he came,
That you might come to heaven:
Believe, believe in Jesus' name,
And all your sin 's forgiven.

4 Believe in Him who died for thee,
And sure as he hath died,
Thy debt is paid, thy soul is free,
And thou art justified.

407 *The prisoner of hope.*

LET the redeem'd give thanks and praise
To a forgiving God!
My feeble voice I cannot raise,
Till wash'd in Jesus' blood:

2 Till at thy coming from above,
My mountain-sin depart,
And fear gives place to filial love,
And peace o'erflows my heart.

3 Pris'ner of hope, I still attend
Th' appearance of my Lord,
These endless doubts and fears to end,
And speak my soul restored:

4 Restored by reconciling grace;
With present pardon blest;
And fitted by true holiness
For my eternal rest.

5 The peace which man can ne'er conceive,
The love and joy unknown,
Now, Father, to thy servant give,
And claim me for thine own.

6 My God, through Jesus pacified,
My God, thyself declare;
And draw me to his open side,
And plunge the sinner there!

837 *Psalm xx. 7—9.*

SOME trust their chariots' wedged array,
And some their warlike steeds;
The Lord's great name is all our stay,
And God our vict'ry leads.

2 Chariot and steed!—o'erthrown they fall:
We stand, and upward rise:
Save, Lord, and hear us when we call,
King of the earth and skies!

160 *"Let all the angels of God worship him."*

HOW great the wisdom, power, and grace,
Which in redemption shine!
The heavenly host with joy confess
The work is all divine.

2 Before his feet they cast their crowns,—
Those crowns which Jesus gave,—
And, with ten thousand thousand tongues,
Proclaim his power to save.

3 They tell the triumphs of his cross,
The suff'rings which he bore,—
How low he stoop'd, how high he rose,
And rose to stoop no more.

4 O let them still their voices raise,
And still their songs renew;
Salvation well deserves the praise
Of men and angels too!

528 *The act of consecration.*

LET Him to whom we now belong
His sovereign right assert!
And take up every thankful song,
And every loving heart.

2 He justly claims us for his own,
Who bought us with a price
The Christian lives to Christ alone,
To Christ alone he dies.

3 Jesus, thine own at last receive,
Fulfil our hearts' desire;
And let us to thy glory live,
And in thy cause expire!

4 Our souls and bodies we resign;
With joy we render thee
Our all, no longer ours, but thine
To all eternity.

533 *Praying for a holy heart.*

O FOR a heart to praise my God,
A heart from sin set free!
A heart that always feels thy blood
So freely spilt for me!—

2 A heart resign'd, submissive, meek,
My great Redeemer's throne,—
Where only Christ is heard to speak,
Where Jesus reigns alone.

3 O for a lowly, contrite heart,
Believing, true, and clean!
Which neither life nor death can part
From him that dwells within:

4 A heart in every thought renew'd,
And full of love divine;
Perfect, and right, and pure, and good,—
A copy, Lord, of thine.

591 *Opening worship.*

ONCE more we come before our God;
Once more his blessings ask:
O may not duty seem a load,
Nor worship prove a task!

2 Father, thy quick'ning Spirit send
From heaven, in Jesus' name,
To make our waiting minds attend,
And put our souls in frame.

3 May we receive the word we hear,
Each in an honest heart;
And keep the precious treasure there,
And never with it part.

4 To seek thee all our hearts dispose,
To each thy blessings suit,
And let the seed thy servant sows,
Produce abundant fruit.

SILOAM. C. M.

I. B. WOODBURY.

498 *The rest of faith.*

I WOULD be thine, thou know'st I would,
And have thee all my own;
Thee,—O my all-sufficient Good!
I want,—and thee alone.

2 Thy name to me, thy nature grant!
This, only this, be given:
Nothing besides my God I want;
Nothing in earth or heaven.

3 Come, O my Saviour, come away!
Into my soul descend!
No longer from thy creature stay,
My Author and my End!

4 Come, Father, Son, and Holy Ghost,
And seal me thine abode!
Let all I am in thee be lost;
Let all be lost in God!

353 *Urgent appeal.*

SINNERS, the voice of God regard,
'Tis mercy speaks to-day;
He calls you by his sacred word
From sin's destructive way.

2 Like the rough sea that cannot rest,
You live devoid of peace;
A thousand stings within your breast
Deprive your souls of ease.

3 Your way is dark, and leads to hell;
Why will you persevere?
Can you in endless torments dwell,
Shut up in black despair?

4 Why will you in the crooked ways
Of sin and folly go?
In pain you travel all your days,
To reap eternal wo.

5 But he that turns to God shall live
Through his abounding grace:
His mercy will the guilt forgive
Of those that seek his face.

6 Bow to the sceptre of his word,
Renouncing every sin,
Submit to him, your sovereign Lord,
And learn his will divine.

419 *Vehement desires.*

I ASK the gift of righteousness,
The sin-subduing power,—
Power to believe, and go in peace,
And never grieve thee more.

2 I ask the blood-bought pardon seal'd,
The liberty from sin,
The grace infused, the love reveal'd,
The kingdom fix'd within.

3 Thou hear'st me for salvation pray;
Thou seest my heart's desire;
Made ready in thy powerful day,
Thy fulness I require.

4 My v'hement soul cries out, opprest,
Impatient to be freed!
Nor can I, Lord, nor will I rest,
Till I am saved indeed.

5 Art thou not able to convert?
Art thou not willing too?
To change this old rebellious heart,
To conquer and renew?

6 Thou canst, thou wilt, I dare believe,
So arm me with thy power,
That I to sin may never cleave,
May never feel it more.

290 *"This do in remembrance of me."*

IF human kindness meets return,
And owns the grateful tie;
If tender thoughts within us burn
To feel a friend is nigh;—

2 O shall not warmer accents tell
The gratitude we owe
To Him who died, our fears to quell,
Our more than orphan's wo!

3 While yet his anguish'd soul survey'd
Those pangs he would not flee;
What love his latest words display'd,—
"Meet and remember me!"

4 Remember thee! thy death, thy shame,
Our sinful hearts to share!
O mem'ry, leave no other name
But his recorded there!

366 *Before evening sermon.*

THOU Son of God, whose flaming eyes
Our inmost thoughts perceive,
Accept the evening sacrifice
Which now to thee we give.

2 We bow before thy gracious throne,
And think ourselves sincere:
But show us, Lord, in every one,
Thy real worshipper?

3 Is here a soul that knows thee not,
Nor feels his want of thee;
A stranger to the blood which bought
His pardon on the tree?

4 Convince him now of unbelief,
His desp'rate state explain;
And fill his heart with sacred grief,
And penitential pain.

5 Speak with that voice that wakes the dead,
And bid the sleeper rise;
And bid his guilty conscience dread
The death that never dies.

6 Extort the cry, "What must be done
To save a wretch like me?
How shall a trembling sinner shun
That endless misery?

7 "I must this instant now begin
Out of my sleep to wake,
And turn to God, and every sin
Continually forsake:

8 "I must for faith incessant cry,
And wrestle, Lord, with thee,
I must be born again, or die
To all eternity!"

367 *Before preaching to formalists.*

THE men who slight thy faithful word,
In their own lies confide,
These are the temple of the Lord,
And heathens all beside!

2 The temple of the Lord are these,
The only church and true,
Who live in pomp, and wealth, and ease,
And Jesus never knew!

3 O wouldst thou, Lord, reveal their sins,
And turn their joy to grief;
The world, the Christian world, convince
Of damning unbelief!

4 The formalists confound, convert,
And to thy people join;
And break, and fill the broken heart
With confidence divine!

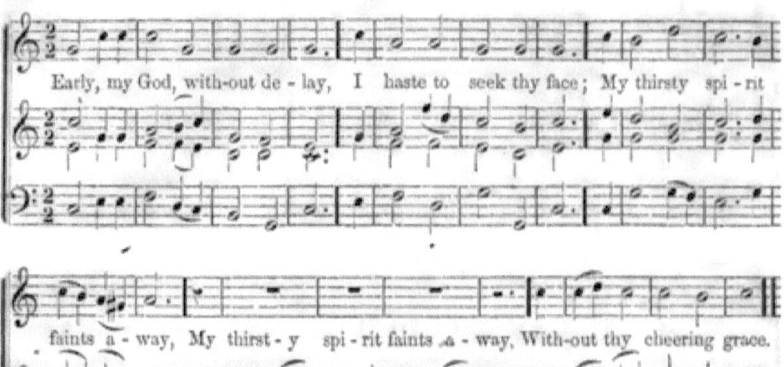

56 *Psalm* lxiii. *Opening morning service.*

EARLY, my God, without delay,
I haste to seek thy face;
My thirsty spirit faints away,
Without thy cheering grace.

2 So pilgrims, on the scorching sand,
Beneath a burning sky,
Long for a cooling stream at hand;
And they must drink or die.

3 I've seen thy glory and thy power
Through all thy temple shine;
My God, repeat that heavenly hour,
That vision so divine.

4 Not all the blessings of a feast
Can please my soul so well,
As when thy richer grace I taste,
And in thy presence dwell.

5 Not life itself, with all its joys,
Can my best passions move;
Or raise so high my cheerful voice,
As thy forgiving love.

6 Thus, till my last expiring day,
I'll bless my God and King;
Thus will I lift my hands to pray,
And tune my lips to sing.

258 *Zion's Watchmen.*

LET Zion's watchmen all awake,
And take th' alarm they give;
Now let them from the mouth of God
Their awful charge receive.

2 'Tis not a cause of small import
The pastor's care demands;
But what might fill an angel's heart,
And fill'd a Saviour's hands.

3 They watch for souls, for which the Lord
Did heavenly bliss forego:
For souls which must for ever live
In raptures, or in wo.

4 May they that Jesus whom they preach,
Their own Redeemer see,
And watch thou daily o'er their souls,
That they may watch for thee.

31 *"All thy works praise thee."*

HOW doth thy wondrous skill array
The earth in cheerful green!
A thousand herbs thy art display,
A thousand flowers between.

2 The rolling mountains of the deep
Obey thy strong command:
Thy breath can raise the billows steep,
Or sink them to the sand.

3 Thy glories blaze all nature round,
And strike the wond'ring sight,
Through skies, and seas, and solid ground,
With terror and delight.

4 Infinite strength, and equal skill,
Shine through thy works abroad·
Our souls with vast amazement fill,
And speak the builder God!

5 But the mild glories of thy grace
Our softer passions move:
Pity divine in Jesus' face,
We see, adore, and love.

1 *The Trinity.*

A THOUSAND oracles divine
Their common beams unite,
That sinners may with angels join
To worship God aright:

2 To praise a Trinity adored
By all the hosts above;
And one thrice holy God and Lord
Through endless ages love.

3 Triumphant host! they never cease
To laud and magnify
The Triune God of holiness,
Whose glory fills the sky:

4 Whose glory to this earth extends,
When God himself imparts,
And the whole Trinity descends
Into our faithful hearts.

5 By faith the upper choir we meet,
And challenge them to sing
Jehovah, on his shining seat,
Our Maker and our King.

6 But God made flesh is wholly ours,
And asks our nobler strain;
The Father of celestial powers,
The Friend of earth-born man.

7 Ye seraphs, nearest to the throne,
With rapturous amaze
On us, poor ransom'd worms, look down,
For Heaven's superior praise!

8 The King, whose glorious face ye see,
For us his crown resign'd;
That Fulness of the Deity,
He died for all mankind!

660 *Ministering spirits.*

ANGELS, where'er we go, attend
Our steps, whate'er betide,
With watchful care their charge defend
And evil turn aside.

2 A sudden thought t' escape the blow,
A ready help we find,
And to their secret presence owe
The presence of our mind.

3 Their instrumental aid, unknown
They day and night supply;
And, free from fear, we lay us down,
Though Satan's host be nigh.

4 Our lives the holy angels keep
From every hostile power,
And, unconcern'd, we sweetly sleep,
As Adam in his bower.

695 *"Prepare to meet thy God."*

BY faith we find the place above,
The Rock that rent in twain,
Beneath the shade of dying love,
And in the cleft remain.

2 Jesus, to thy dear wounds we flee,
We sink into thy side:
Assured that all who trust in thee
Shall evermore abide.

3 Then let the thund'ring trumpet sound,
The latest lightnings glare;
The mountains melt; the solid ground
Dissolve as liquid air;

4 The huge celestial bodies roll
Amidst the general fire:
And shrivel as a parchment scroll,
And all in smoke expire!—

5 Yet still the Lord, the Saviour reigns,
When nature is destroy'd,
And no created thing remains
Throughout the flaming void.

6 Sublime upon his azure throne,
He speaks th' almighty word:
His *fiat* is obey'd! 'tis done;
And paradise restored.

7 So be it! let this system end!
This ru'nous earth and skies!
The New Jerusalem descend!
The new creation rise!

8 Thy power omnipotent assume!
Thy brightest majesty!
And when thou dost in glory come,
My Lord, remember me!

872 *Opening the exercises.*

ALL praise to our redeeming Lord,
Who joins us by his grace,
And bids us, each to each restored,
Together seek his face.

2 He bids us build each other up;
And, gather'd into one,
To our high calling's glorious hope,
We hand in hand go on.

3 The gift which he on one bestows,
We all delight to prove,
The grace through every vessel flows,
In purest streams of love.

4 E'en now we think and speak the same,
And cordially agree,
United all through Jesus' name
In perfect harmony.

5 We all partake the joy of one,
The common peace we feel,—
A peace to sensual minds unknown,
A joy unspeakable.

6 And if our fellowship below
In Jesus be so sweet,
What height of rapture shall we know
When round his throne we meet!

1053 *Doxology.*

NOW let the Father, and the Son,
And Spirit, be adored;
Where there are works to make Him known,
Or saints to love the Lord.

ANTIOCH. C. M.

From HANDEL.

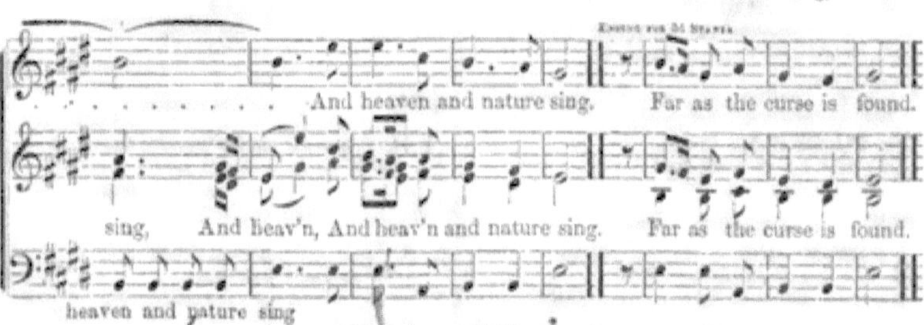

99 *Psalm xcviii.*

JOY to the world—the Lord is come!
  Let earth receive her King;
Let every heart prepare him room,
  And heaven and nature sing.

2 Joy to the earth—the Saviour reigns!
  Let men their songs employ;
While fields and floods, rocks, hills, and plains,
  Repeat the sounding joy.

3 No more let sins and sorrows grow,
  Nor thorns infest the ground;
He comes to make his blessings flow,
  Far as the curse is found.

4 He rules the world with truth and grace,
  And makes the nations prove
The glories of his righteousness,
  And wonders of his love.

491 *The benediction.—Numbers vi. 24—27.*

JEHOVAH, God the Father, bless,
  And thy own work defend!
With mercy's outstretch'd arms embrace,
  And keep us to the end.

Preserve the creatures of thy love
  By providential care,
Conducted to the realms above,
  To sing thy goodness there!

2 Jehovah, God the Son, reveal
  The brightness of thy face,
And all thy pardon'd people fill
  With plenitude of grace!

Shine forth with all the Deity,
  Which dwells in thee alone;
And lift us up, thy face to see,
  On thy eternal throne.

3 Jehovah, God the Spirit, shine,
  Father and Son to show!
With bliss ineffable, divine,
  Our ravish'd hearts o'erflow!

Sure earnest of that happiness
  Which human hope transcends,
Be thou our everlasting peace,
  When grace in glory ends!

226 *Psalm xxvii.*

THE Lord of glory is my light,
And my salvation too;
God is my strength; nor will I fear
What all my foes can do.

2 One privilege my heart desires—
O grant me an abode
Among the churches of thy saints,
The temples of my God!

3 There shall I offer my requests,
And see thy beauty still;
Shall hear thy messages of love,
And there inquire thy will.

4 When troubles rise, and storms appear,
There may his children hide:
God has a strong pavilion, where
He makes my soul abide.

5 Now shall my head be lifted high,
Above my foes around;
And songs of joy and victory
Within thy temple sound.

159 *His regal state.*

REJOICE and sing, The Lord is King,
And make a cheerful noise;
To God your ceaseless praises bring,
Again, I say, Rejoice!

2 The great I AM!—From heaven he came,
To make that heaven our own:
Bow every knee to Jesus' name,
And kiss th' incarnate Son.

3 The Son of God Pour'd out his blood
And soul in sacrifice:
Plunge all in that mysterious flood,
That bears you to the skies.

4 The Victim slain Arose again,
Returning from the dead:
Ye saints, essay your choicest strain,
And shout your living Head.

5 His glorious reign He shall maintain;—
Your crowns from him receive;
And live, redeem'd from death and pain,
As long as God shall live.

925 *"Thy kingdom come."*

FATHER of me, and all mankind,
And all the hosts above,
Let every understanding mind
Unite to praise thy love;—

2 To know thy nature and thy name,
One God in persons three,
And glorify the great I AM
Through all eternity.

3 Thy kingdom come, with power and grace,
To every heart of man:
Thy peace, and joy, and righteousness,
In all our bosoms reign.

4 Thy righteousness our sins keep down,
Thy peace our passions bind;
And let us, in thy joy unknown,
The first dominion find.

5 The righteousness that never ends,
But makes an end of sin,
The joy that human thought transcends,
Into our souls bring in:

6 The kingdom of establish'd peace,
Which can no more remove;
The perfect power of godliness,
Th' omnipotence of love.

774 *"Search the Scriptures."*

THE counsels of redeeming grace
 The sacred leaves unfold:
And here the Saviour's lovely face
 Our raptured eyes behold.

2 Here light descending from above
 Directs our doubtful feet;
Here promises of heavenly love
 Our ardent wishes meet.

3 Our num'rous griefs are here redress'd,
 And all our wants supplied:
Naught we can ask to make us bless'd,
 Is in this book denied.

4 For these inestimable gains,
 That so enrich the mind,
O may we search with eager pains,
 Assured that we shall find!

152 *Priesthood of Christ.*

NOW let our cheerful eyes survey
 Our great High Priest above:
And celebrate his constant care,
 And sympathetic love.

2 Though raised to a superior throne,
 When angels bow around,
And high o'er all the shining train,
 With matchless honours crown'd,—

3 The names of all his saints he bears,
 Deep graven on his heart;
Nor shall the meanest Christian say,
 That he hath lost his part.

4 Those characters shall fair abide,
 Our everlasting trust,
When gems, and monuments, and crowns
 Are moulder'd down to dust.

743 *Psalm lxxii. 16—19.*

THE seed, in scanty handfuls sown,
 Upon the mountain-tops,—
Nourish'd by heaven's enliv'ning beams,
 By heaven's enriching drops,—

2 Shall in an ample harvest rise,
 Shall overspread the ground,
Shall shake like Lebanon with woods
 Of tow'ring cedar crown'd.

3 The cities, through the world dispersed,
 By crowds of men possess'd,
Shall flourish like the blooming meads
 In spring's embroid'ry dress'd.

4 Long as the sun shall rule the day,
 Mankind shall sound his fame;
In him all nations shall be bless'd,
 And all shall bless his name.

5 Immortal and unbounded praise
 Let Israel's God receive;
These miracles of power and grace
 He only could achieve.

6 Now let our Lord, as summer-suns,
 Make haste the world to gild,
Shine all abroad till all our globe
 Is with his glories fill'd!

7 *Amen*, with joy divine, let earth's
 Unnumber'd myriads cry;
Amen, with joy divine, let heaven's
 Unnumber'd choirs reply!

1053 *Doxology.*

NOW let the Father, and the Son,
 And Spirit be adored;
Where there are works to make Him known,
 Or saints to love the Lord.

612 *"Thou knowest that I love thee."*

DO not I love thee, O my Lord?
Behold my heart, and see;
And turn each cursed idol out,
That dares to rival thee.

2 Do not I love thee from my soul?
Then let me nothing love;
Dead be my heart to every joy,
When Jesus cannot move.

3 Is not thy name melodious still
To mine attentive ear?
Doth not each pulse with pleasure bound
My Saviour's voice to hear?

4 Hast thou a lamb in all thy flock
I would disdain to feed?
Hast thou a foe, before whose face
I fear thy cause to plead?

5 Would not mine ardent spirit vie
With angels round the throne,
To execute thy sacred will,
And make thy glory known?

6 Would not my heart pour forth its blood
In honour of thy name?
And challenge the cold hand of death
To damp th' immortal flame?

7 Thou know'st I love thee, dearest Lord;
But O! I long to soar
Far from the sphere of mortal joys,
And learn to love thee more.

524 *Rom. iv. 16—25.*

FATHER of Jesus Christ, my Lord,
My Saviour and my Head,
I trust in thee, whose powerful word
Hath raised him from the dead.

2 Thou know'st for my offence he died,
And rose again for me;
Fully and freely justified,
That I might live to thee.

3 Eternal life to all mankind
Thou hast in Jesus given:
And all who seek, in him shall find
The happiness of heaven.

4 All nations of the earth are blest
In him, who would restore,
And take them all into his rest,
And bid them sin no more.

5 O God, thy record I believe,
In Abrah'm's footsteps tread;
And wait, expecting to receive
The Christ, the promised Seed!

497 *The rest of faith.*

LORD, I believe a rest remains,
To all thy people known;
A rest where pure enjoyment reigns,
And thou art loved alone.

2 A rest, where all our soul's desire
Is fix'd on things above;
Where fear, and sin, and grief expire,
Cast out by perfect love.

3 O that I now the rest might know,
Believe, and enter in!
Now, Saviour, now the power bestow,
And let me cease from sin!

4 Remove this hardness from my heart,
This unbelief remove:
To me the rest of faith impart,
The sabbath of thy love.

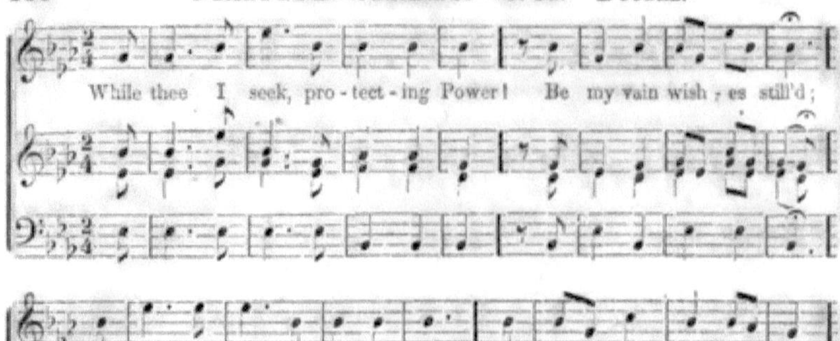

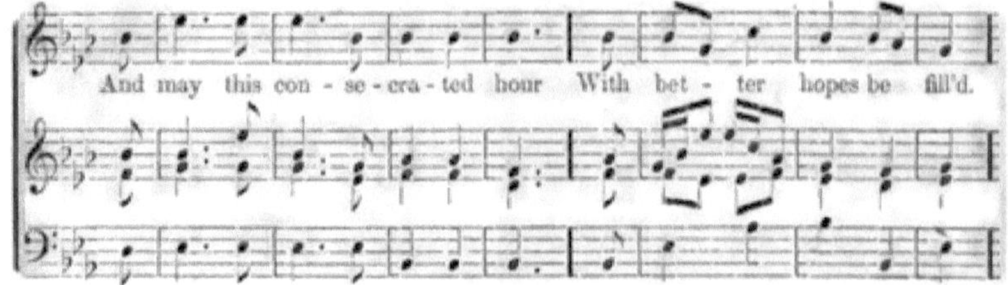

1009 *"My meditation of him shall be sweet."*

WHILE thee I seek, protecting Power!
 Be my vain wishes still'd;
And may this consecrated hour
 With better hopes be fill'd.

2 Thy love the power of thought bestow'd,
 To thee my thoughts would soar:
Thy mercy o'er my life has flow'd,
 That mercy I adore.

3 In each event of life, how clear
 Thy ruling hand I see,
Each blessing to my soul most dear,
 Because conferr'd by thee.

4 In every joy that crowns my days,
 In every pain I bear,
My heart shall find delight in praise,
 Or seek relief in prayer.

5 When gladness wings the favour'd hour,
 Thy love my thoughts shall fill;
Resign'd, when storms of sorrow lower,
 My soul shall meet thy will.

6 My lifted eye, without a tear,
 The gath'ring storm shall see;
My steadfast heart shall know no fear—
 That heart will rest on thee.

911 *Opening the exercises.*

SHEPHERD Divine, our wants relieve,
 In this our evil day:
To all thy tempted foll'wers give
 The power to watch and pray.

2 Long as our fiery trials last,
 Long as the cross we bear,
O let our souls on thee be cast
 In never-ceasing prayer!

3 The Spirit of interceding grace,
 Give us in faith to claim;
To wrestle till we see thy face,
 And know thy hidden name.

4 Till thou thy perfect love impart,
 Till thou thyself bestow,
Be this the cry of every heart—
 I will not let thee go:—

5 I will not let thee go, unless
 Thou tell thy name to me,
With all thy great salvation bless,
 And make me all like thee.

6 Then let me, on the mountain top,
 Behold thy open face;
Where faith in sight is swallow'd up,
 And prayer in endless praise.

365 *Eccles. xii. 1.*

IN the soft season of thy youth,
 In nature's smiling bloom,
Ere age arrives, and trembling waits
 Its summons to the tomb,—
Remember thy Creator now;
 For him thy powers employ;
Make him thy fear, thy love, thy hope,
 Thy confidence, and joy.

2 He shall defend and guide thy youth
 Through life's uncertain sea,
Till thou art landed on the coast
 Of bless'd eternity.
Then seek the Lord betimes, and choose
 The path of heavenly truth;
This earth affords no lovelier sight
 Than a religious youth.

416 *Miracles of grace.*

WHILE dead in trespasses I lie,
Thy quick'ning Spirit give;
Call me, thou Son of God, that I
May hear thy voice and live.

2 While full of anguish and disease,
My weak, distemper'd soul
Thy love compassionately sees,
O let it make me whole!

3 Cast out thy foes, and let them still
To Jesus' name submit:
Clothe with thy righteousness, and heal,
And place me at thy feet.

4 To Jesus' name, if all things now
A trembling homage pay,
O let my stubborn spirit bow,
My stiff-neck'd will obey!

5 Impotent, dumb, and deaf, and blind,
And sick, and poor, I am:
But sure a remedy to find
For all in Jesus' name.

6 I know in thee all fulness dwells,
And all for wretched man:
Fill every want my spirit feels,
And break off every chain.

7 If thou impart thyself to me,
No other good I need:
If thou, the Son, shalt make me free,
I shall be free indeed.

8 I cannot rest, till in thy blood
I full redemption have:
But thou, through whom I come to God,
Canst to the utmost save.

9 From sin, the guilt, the power, the pain,
Thou wilt redeem my soul:
Lord, I believe, and not in vain:
My faith shall make me whole.

10 I too, with thee, shall walk in white,
With all thy saints shall prove
What is the length, and breadth, and height,
And depth, of perfect love.

501 *The rapture of love.*

WHEN Christ doth in my heart appear,
And love erects its throne,
I then enjoy salvation here,
And heaven on earth begun.

2 When God is mine, and I am his,
Of paradise possest,
I taste unutterable bliss,
And everlasting rest.

3 The bliss of those that fully dwell,
Fully in thee believe,
'Tis more than angel-tongues can tell,
Or angel-minds conceive.

4 Thou only know'st who didst obtain,
And die to make it known:
The great salvation now explain,
And perfect us in one.

5 May I, may all who humbly wait,
The glorious joy receive;
Joy above all conception great,
Worthy of God to give.

6 Lord, I believe, and rest secure
In confidence divine;
Thy promise stands for ever sure,
And all thou art is mine.

MEDFIELD. C. M.

W. MATHER.

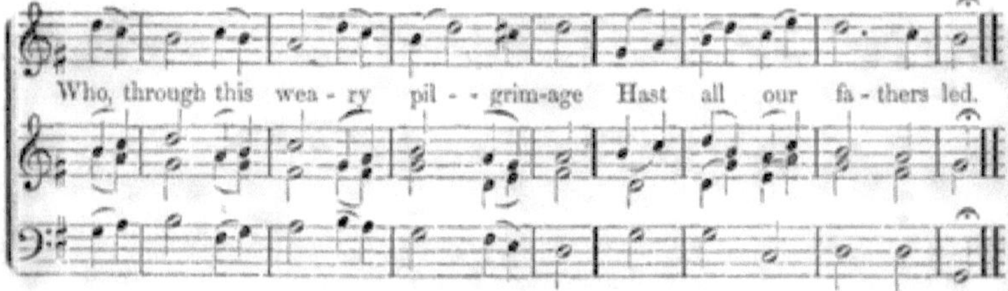

646 *Jacob's Vow.* Gen. xxviii. 20—22.

O GOD of Jacob, by whose hand
Thine Israel still is fed,
Who, through this weary pilgrimage
Hast all our fathers led;—

2 To thee our humble vows we raise,
To thee address our prayer,
And in thy kind and faithful breast
Deposit all our care.

3 If thou, through each perplexing path
Wilt be our constant guide;
If thou wilt daily bread supply,
And raiment wilt provide;

4 If thou wilt spread thy shield around,
Till these our wand'rings cease,
And at our Father's loved abode
Our souls arrive in peace:—

5 To thee as to our cov'nant God,
We'll our whole selves resign;
And count, that not our tenth alone,
But all we have is thine.

464 1 *Cor.* vi. 9—11.

NOT the malicious or profane,
The wanton or the proud,
Nor thieves, nor sland'rers, shall obtain
The kingdom of our God.

2 Surprising grace! and such were we,
By nature and by sin!
Heirs of immortal misery,
Unholy and unclean.

3 But we are wash'd in Jesus' blood,
We're pardon'd through his name,
And the good Spirit of our God
Has sanctified our frame.

4 O for a persevering power,
To keep thy just commands!
We would defile our hearts no more,
No more pollute our hands.

631 *"I have chosen thee in the furnace."*

THEE, Jesus, full of truth and grace,
Thee, Saviour, we adore;
Thee in affliction's furnace praise,
And magnify thy power.

2 Thy power, in human weakness shown,
Shall make us all entire;
We now thy guardian presence own,
And walk unburn'd in fire.

3 Thee, Son of man, by faith we see,
And glory in our guide;
Surrounded and upheld by thee,
The fiery test abide.

4 The fire our graces shall refine,
Till, moulded from above,
We bear the character divine,
The stamp of perfect love.

787 *Psalm* xxvi. 6—8.

I'LL wash my hands in innocence,
And round thy altar go,
Pour the glad hymn of triumph thence,
And thence thy wonders show.

2 Thy house is ever my delight,
Thy dwelling, O my God!
The place, where shrined in radiance bright,
Thy glory makes abode.

1053 *Doxology.*

NOW let the Father, and the Son,
And Spirit, be adored;
Where there are works to make Him known,
Or saints to love the Lord.

659 *Ministering spirits.*

WHICH of the petty kings of earth
  Can boast a guard like ours,
Encircled from our second birth,
  With all the heavenly powers?

2 Myriads of bright, cherubic bands,
  Sent by the King of kings,
Rejoice to bear us in their hands,
  And shade us with their wings.

3 With them we march securely on,
  Throughout Immanuel's ground;
And not an uncommission'd stone
  Our guarded feet shall wound.

4 No enemy our souls insnare,
  No casual evil grieve,
Nor can we lose a single hair
  Without our Father's leave.

661 *Ministering spirits.*

JEHOVAH'S charioteers surround;
  The ministerial choir
Encamp where'er his heirs are found,
  And form our wall of fire.

2 Ten thousand offices, unseen,
  For us they gladly do,—
Deliver in the furnace keen,
  And safe escort us through.

3 But thronging round, with busiest love,
  They guard the dying breast,
The lurking fiend far off remove,
  And sing our souls to rest:

4 And when our spirits we resign,
  On outstretch'd wings they bear,
And lodge us in the arms divine,
  And leave us ever there.

806 *New Year's day.*

REMARK, my soul, the narrow bound
  Of the revolving year;
How swift the weeks complete their round!
  How short the months appear!

2 So fast eternity comes on—
  And that important day,
When all that mortal life hath done,
  God's judgment shall survey.

3 Yet, like an idle tale, we pass
  The swift-advancing year;
And study artful ways t' increase
  The speed of its career.

4 Waken, O God, my careless heart,
  Its great concern to see;
That I may act the Christian part,
  To give the year to thee.

815 *Praying for fair weather.*

HOW hast thou, Lord, from year to year,
  Our land with plenty crown'd,
And gen'rous fruit and golden grain
  Have spread their riches round.

2 But we abuse thy mercies; we
  Thy precious gifts destroy;
And vice is fed by what was given
  T' inspire our holy joy.

3 Equal though awful is the doom,
  That fierce descending rain
Should into inundations swell,
  And crush the rising grain.

4 But, Lord, have mercy on our land,
  These floods of vengeance stay;
Dispel these glooms, and let the sun
  Shine in unclouded day.

PRIMROSE.* C. M.

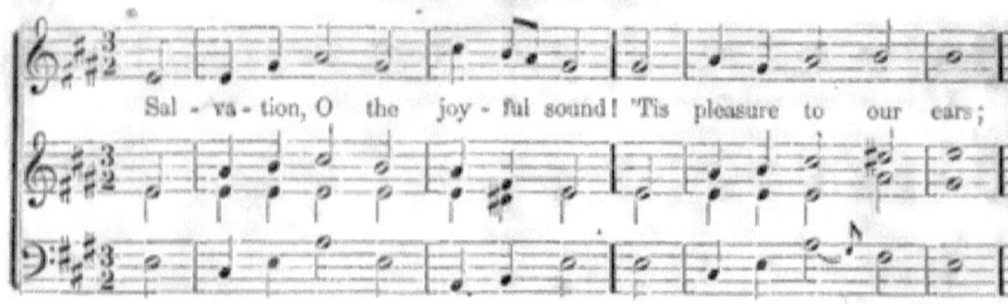

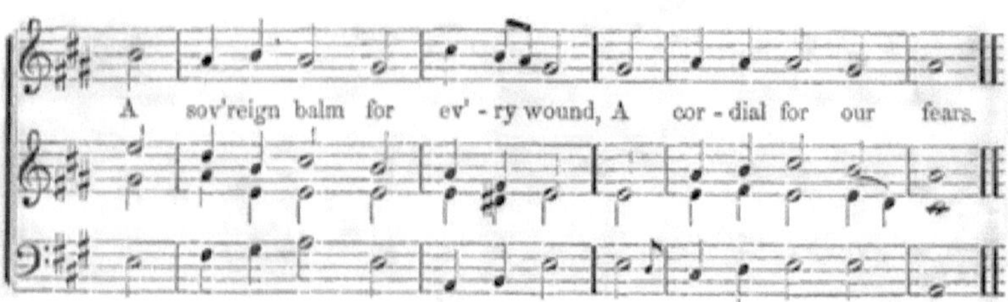

* Called, also, "MELODY," "CHELMSFORD," or "MEMPHIS."

186 *Salvation.*

SALVATION, O the joyful sound!
'Tis pleasure to our ears;
A sov'reign balm for every wound,
A cordial for our fears.

2 Buried in sorrow and in sin,
At hell's dark door we lay;
But we arise by grace divine
To see a heavenly day.

3 Salvation! let the echo fly
The spacious earth around,
While all the armies of the sky
Conspire to raise the sound.

334 *Come to Jesus.*

COME, humble sinner, in whose breast
A thousand thoughts revolve,—
Come, with your guilt and fear oppress'd,
And make this last resolve:

2 I'll go to Jesus, though my sin
Hath like a mountain rose;
I know his courts, I'll enter in,
Whatever may oppose:

3 Prostrate I'll lie before his throne,
And there my guilt confess;
I'll tell him I'm a wretch undone,
Without his sovereign grace:

4 I'll to the gracious King approach,
Whose sceptre pardon gives;
Perhaps he may command my touch,
And then the suppliant lives.

5 Perhaps he may admit my plea,
Perhaps will hear my prayer;
But if I perish, I will pray,
And perish only there.

6 I can but perish if I go,
I am resolved to try;
For if I stay away I know
I must for ever die.

7 But if I die with mercy sought,
When I the King have tried,
This were to die (delightful thought!)
As sinner never died.

209 *The Interpreter. Before sermon.*

COME, Holy Ghost, our hearts inspire,
Let us thine influence prove;
Source of the old prophetic fire,
Fountain of light and love.

2 Come, Holy Ghost—for, moved by thee,
The prophets wrote and spoke—
Unlock the truth, thyself the key;
Unseal the sacred book.

3 Expand thy wings, celestial Dove,
Brood o'er our nature's night;
On our disorder'd spirits move,
And let there now be light.

4 God, through himself we then shall know,
If thou within us shine;
And sound, with all thy saints below,
The depths of love divine.

1053 *Doxology.*

NOW let the Father, and the Son,
And Spirit be adored;
Where there are works to make Him known,
Or saints to love the Lord.

746 *Conversion of the Jews.*

DAUGHTER of Zion, from the dust
Exalt thy fallen head;
Again in thy Redeemer trust;
He calls thee from the dead.

2 Awake, awake! put on thy strength,
Thy beautiful array;
The day of freedom dawns at length,
The Lord's appointed day.

3 Rebuild thy walls, thy bounds enlarge,
And send thy heralds forth;
Say to the south, "Give up thy charge,"
And, "Keep not back, O north."

4 They come! they come!—thine exiled bands,
Where'er they rest or roam,
Have heard thy voice in distant lands,
And hasten to their home.

5 Thus, though the universe shall burn,
And God his works destroy,
With songs, thy ransom'd shall return,
And everlasting joy.

350 *Revelation iii. 20.*

COME, let us who in Christ believe,
Our common Saviour praise:
To Him, with joyful voices, give
The glory of his grace.

2 He now stands knocking at the door
Of every sinner's heart;
The worst need keep him out no more,
Or force him to depart.

3 Through grace we hearken to thy voice,
Yield to be saved from sin;
In sure and certain hope rejoice,
That thou wilt enter in.

4 Come quickly in, thou heavenly Guest,
Nor ever hence remove:
But sup with us, and let the feast
Be everlasting love.

368 *Before an awakening sermon.*

COME, O thou all-victorious Lord,
Thy power to us make known;
Strike with the hammer of thy word,
And break these hearts of stone.

2 O that we all might now begin
Our foolishness to mourn!
And turn at once from every sin,
And to the Saviour turn.

3 Give us ourselves and thee to know,
In this our gracious day;
Repentance unto life bestow,
And take our sins away.

4 Convince us first of unbelief,
And freely then release;
Fill every soul with sacred grief,
And then with sacred peace.

5 Impov'rish, Lord, and then relieve,
And then enrich the poor;
The knowledge of our sickness give,
The knowledge of our cure.

6 That blessed sense of guilt impart,
And then remove the load;
Trouble, and wash the troubled heart
In the atoning blood.

7 Our desp'rate state through sin declare,
And speak our sins forgiven:
By perfect holiness prepare,
And take us up to heaven.

SWEADNER. C. M.

E. G. E.

When I can read my ti - tle clear To man-sions in the skies,
I'll bid fare-well to ev - ery fear, And wipe my weep-ing eyes.

Coda.

O hal-le-lu-jah! O hal-le-lu-jah! Halle, hal-le-lu-jah, Praise the Lord.

655 *Inspiring hope.*

WHEN I can read my title clear
  To mansions in the skies,
I'll bid farewell to every fear,
  And wipe my weeping eyes.

2 Should earth against my soul engage,
  And fiery darts be hurl'd,
Then I can smile at Satan's rage,
  And face a frowning world.

3 Let cares, like a wild deluge, come,
  Let storms of sorrow fall;
So I but safely reach my home,
  My God, my heaven, my all.

4 There I shall bathe my weary soul
  In seas of heavenly rest,
And not a wave of trouble roll
  Across my peaceful breast.

705 *The heavenly Jerusalem.*

JERUSALEM, my happy home!
  Name ever dear to me!
When shall my labours have an end,
  In joy, and peace, and thee?

2 When shall these eyes thy heaven-built walls
  And pearly gates behold?
Thy bulwarks, with salvation strong,
  And streets of shining gold?

3 O when, thou city of my God,
  Shall I thy courts ascend,
Where congregations near break up,
  And sabbaths have no end?

4 There happier bowers than Eden's bloom,
  Nor sin nor sorrow know:
Bless'd seats! through rude and stormy scenes
  I onward press to you.

5 Why should I shrink at pain and wo?
  Or feel at death dismay?
I've Canaan's goodly land in view,
  And realms of endless day.

6 Apostles, martyrs, prophets, there,
  Around my Saviour stand;
And soon my friends in Christ below
  Will join the glorious band.

7 Jerusalem! my happy home!
My soul still pants for thee;
Then shall my labours have an end,
When I thy joys shall see.

370 *Before an inviting sermon.*

JESUS, Redeemer of mankind,
Display thy saving power;
Thy mercy let these outcasts find,
And know their gracious hour.

2 Ah! give them, Lord, a longer space,
Nor suddenly consume:
But let them take the proffer'd grace,
And flee the wrath to come.

3 O wouldst thou cast a pitying look,
All goodness as thou art,
Like that which faithless Peter's broke,
On every stony heart!

4 Who thee beneath their feet have trod,
And crucified afresh,
Touch with thine all-victorious blood,
And turn the stone to flesh.

5 Open their eyes thy cross to see,
Their ears to hear their cries:
Sinner, thy Saviour weeps for thee,
For thee he weeps and dies.

6 All the day long he meekly stands,
His rebels to receive,
And shows his wounds, and spreads his hands,
And bids you turn and live.

7 Turn, and your sins of deepest dye
He will with blood efface,
E'en now he waits the blood t' apply;
Be saved, be saved by grace!

8 Be saved from hell, from sin, and fear:
He speaks you now forgiven;
Walk with your God, be perfect here,
And then come up to heaven.

76 *Psalm cxlviii.*

PRAISE ye the Lord, ye immortal choirs
That fill the worlds above;
Praise him who form'd you of his fires,
And feeds you with his love.

2 Shine to his praise, ye crystal skies,
The floor of his abode:
Or veil in shades your thousand eyes
Before your brighter God.

3 Thou restless globe of golden light,
Whose beams create our days,
Join with the silver queen of night
To own your borrow'd rays.

4 Winds, ye shall bear his name aloud
Through the ethereal blue;
For when his chariot is a cloud,
He makes his wheels of you.

5 Thunder and hail, and fire and storms,
The troops of his command,
Appear in all your dreadful forms,
And speak his awful hand.

6 Shout to the Lord, ye surging seas,
In your eternal roar:
Let wave to wave resound his praise;
And shore reply to shore.

7 While monsters sporting on the flood,
In scaly silver shine,
Speak terribly their Maker, God,
And lash the foaming brine.

8 But gentler things shall tune his name
To softer notes than these:
Young zephyrs breathing o'er the stream,
Or whisp'ring through the trees.

9 Wave your tall heads, ye lofty pines,
To Him that bids you grow;
Sweet clusters, bend the fruitful vines
On every thankful bough.

10 Let the shrill birds his honours raise,
And climb the morning sky;
While grov'ling beasts attempt his praise,
In hoarser harmony.

11 Thus while the meaner creatures sing,
Ye mortals, take the sound;
Echo the glories of your King
Through all the nations round.

688 *The saints above.*

GIVE me the wings of faith, to rise
Within the veil, and see
The saints above, how great their joys,
How bright their glories be.

2 I ask them whence their vict'ry came:
They, with united breath,
Ascribe their conquest to the Lamb,
Their triumph to his death.

3 They mark'd the footsteps that he trod,
His zeal inspired their breast,—
And, foll'wing their incarnate God,
Possess the promised rest.

4 Our glorious Leader claims our praise
For his own pattern given;
While the long cloud of witnesses
Show the same path to heaven.

1053 *Doxology.*

NOW let the Father, and the Son,
And Spirit be adored;
Where there are works to make Him known,
Or saints to love the Lord.

706 *The heavenly Canaan.*

THERE is a land of pure delight,
Where saints immortal reign;
Infinite day excludes the night,
And pleasures banish pain.

2 There everlasting spring abides,
And never-with'ring flowers:
Death, like a narrow sea, divides
This heavenly land from ours.

3 Sweet fields beyond the swelling flood,
Stand dress'd in living green;
So to the Jews old Canaan stood,
While Jordan roll'd between.

4 Could we but climb where Moses stood,
And view the landscape o'er,
Not Jordan's stream, nor death's cold flood,
Should fright us from the shore.

707 *The heavenly Canaan.*

ON Jordan's stormy banks I stand,
And cast a wishful eye
To Canaan's fair and happy land,
Where my possessions lie.

2 O the transporting, rapt'rous scene,
That rises to my sight!
Sweet fields array'd in living green,
And rivers of delight!

3 There gen'rous fruits that never fail
On trees immortal grow:
There rocks, and hills, and brooks, and vales,
With milk and honey flow.

4 All o'er those wide-extended plains
Shines one eternal day;
There God the Son for ever reigns,
And scatters night away.

5 No chilling winds nor pois'nous breath
Can reach that healthful shore,
Sickness and sorrow, pain and death,
Are felt and fear'd no more.

6 When shall I reach that happy place,
And be for ever blest?
When shall I see my Father's face,
And in his bosom rest?

7 Fill'd with delight, my raptured soul
Would here no longer stay!
Though Jordan's waves around me roll,
Fearless I'd launch away.

559 *The pilgrimage.*

LORD! what a wretched land is this,
That yields us no supply,—
No cheering fruits, no wholesome trees,
Nor streams of living joy!

2 Our journey is a thorny maze,
But we march upward still,
Forget these troubles of the ways,
And reach at Zion's hill.

3 See the kind angels, at the gates,
Inviting us to come;
There Jesus, the Forerunner, waits
To welcome trav'lers home.

4 There, on a green and flow'ry mount,
Our weary souls shall sit,—
And, with transporting joys, recount
The labours of our feet.

5 No vain discourse shall fill our tongue,
Nor trifles vex our ear;
Infinite grace shall be our song,
And God rejoice to hear.

331 *Public supplication.*

WHEN Abrah'm, full of sacred awe,
Before Jehovah stood,
And with an humble, fervent prayer,
For guilty Sodom sued,—

2 With what success, what wondrous grace
Was his petition crown'd!
The Lord would spare, if in the place
Ten righteous men were found.

3 And could a single pious soul
So rich a boon obtain?
Great God, and shall a nation cry,
And plead with thee in vain?

4 Are not the righteous dear to thee
Now, as in ancient times?
Or does this sinful land exceed
Gomorrah in her crimes?

5 Still we are thine; we bear thy name;
Here yet is thine abode;
Long has thy presence bless'd our land:—
Forsake us not, O God.

1053 *Doxology.*

NOW let the Father, and the Son,
And Spirit, be adored,
Where there are works to make Him known,
Or saints to love the Lord.

737 *Funeral of a minister.*

WHAT though the arm of conqu'ring death
Does God's own house invade?
What though the prophet and the priest
Be number'd with the dead?—

2 Though earthly shepherds dwell in dust,
The aged and the young,
The watchful eye, in darkness closed,
And mute th' instructive tongue:

3 Th' Eternal Shepherd still survives,
New comfort to impart;
His eye still guides us, and his voice
Still animates our heart.

4 "Lo! I am with you," saith the Lord,
"My church shall safe abide:
For I will ne'er forsake my own,
Whose souls in me confide."

5 Through every scene of life and death,
This promise is our trust;
And this shall be our children's song,
When we are cold in dust.

503 *The Paradise of love.*

O JESUS! at thy feet we wait,
Till thou shalt bid us rise,
Restored to our unsinning state,
To love's sweet paradise.

2 Saviour from sin, we thee receive,
From all indwelling sin,
Thy blood, we steadfastly believe,
Shall make us throughly clean.

3 Since thou wouldst have us free from sin,
And pure as those above,
Make haste to bring thy nature in,
And perfect us in love!

4 The counsel of thy love fulfil:
Come quickly, gracious Lord!
Be it according to thy will,
According to thy word.

5 O that the perfect grace were given,
Thy love diffused abroad!
O that our hearts were all a heaven,
For ever fill'd with God!

WINTER. C. M. DANIEL READ.

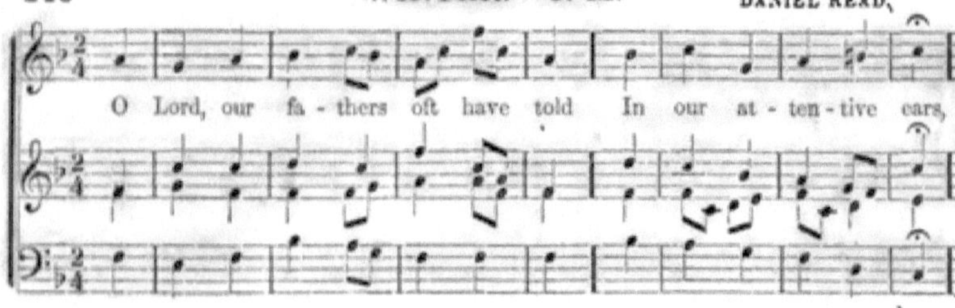

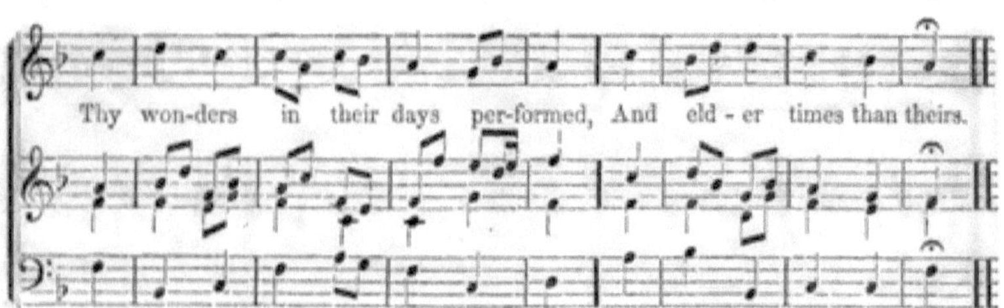

845 *For the Fourth of July.* Psalm xliv. 1—4.

O LORD, our fathers oft have told
In our attentive ears,
Thy wonders in their days perform'd,
And elder times than theirs.

2 'Twas not their courage, nor their sword,
To them salvation gave;
Nor strength, that from unequal force,
Their fainting troops could save:

3 But thy right hand and powerful arm,
Whose succour they implored;
Thy presence with the favour'd race,
Who thy great name adored.

4 As thee their God our fathers own'd,
Thou art our sovereign King;
O, therefore, as thou didst to them,
To us deliv'rance bring.

847 *For magistrates.*

ETERNAL Sovereign of the sky,
And Lord of all below,
We mortals to thy majesty,
Our first obedience owe.

2 Our souls adore thy throne supreme,
And bless thy providence
For magistrates of meaner name,
Our glory and defence.

3 The acts of pious rulers shine
With rays above the rest;
Where laws and liberties combine,
The people are made blest.

4 Nations on firm foundations stand,
While virtue finds reward;
And sinners perish from the land
By justice and the sword.

5 Let Cæsar's due be ever paid
To Cæsar and his throne,
But consciences and souls were made
To be the Lord's alone.

851 Psalm cxvi. 1—8.

O THOU, who when we did complain,
Didst all our griefs remove;
O Saviour, do not now disdain
Our humble praise and love.

2 Since thou a pitying ear didst give,
And hear us when we pray'd,
We'll call upon thee while we live,
And never doubt thy aid.

3 Pale death, with all his ghastly train,
Our souls encompass'd round;
Anguish, and fear, and dread, and pain,
On every side we found.

4 To thee, O Lord of life, we pray'd,
And did for succour flee:
O save, in our distress we said,
The souls that trust in thee.

5 How good thou art! how large thy grace!
How ready to forgive!
The helpless thou delight'st to raise,
And by thy love we live.

6 Our eyes no longer drown'd in tears,
Our feet from falling free,
Redeem'd from death and guilty fears,
O Lord! we'll live to thee!

1053 *Doxology.*

NOW let the Father, and the Son,
And Spirit, be adored;
Where there are works to make Him known,
Or saints to love the Lord.

MALAN. C. M.

L. C. E.

340 *The free invitation.*

THE Saviour calls—let every ear
  Attend the heavenly sound;
Ye doubting souls, dismiss your fear,
  Hope smiles reviving round.

2 For every thirsty, longing heart,
  Here streams of bounty flow;
And life, and health, and bliss, impart
  To banish mortal wo.

3 Here springs of sacred pleasure rise
  To ease your every pain;
(Immortal fountain! full supplies!)
  Nor shall you thirst in vain.

4 Ye sinners, come; 'tis mercy's voice,
  The gracious call obey:
Mercy invites to heavenly joys—
  And can you yet delay?

5 Dear Saviour, draw reluctant hearts!
  To thee let sinners fly,
And take the bliss thy love imparts;
  And drink, and never die.

797 *Sunday-School Celebration.*

MERCY, descending from above,
  In softest accents pleads;
O may each tender bosom move,
  When mercy intercedes!

2 Children our kind protection claim,
  And God will well approve,
When infants learn to lisp his name,
  And their Creator love.

3 Delightful work! young souls to win,
  And turn the rising race
From the deceitful paths of sin,
  To seek their Saviour's face.

4 Almighty God! thine influence shed,
  To aid this bless'd design;
The honour of thy name be spread,
  And all the glory thine.

801 *Anniversary of an orphan asylum.*

AGAIN the kind revolving year
  Has brought this happy day,
And we in God's bless'd house appear,
  Again our vows to pay.

2 Our watchful guardians, robed in light,
  Adore the heavenly King;
Ten thousand thousand seraphs bright,
  Incessant praises sing.

3 They know no want, they feel no care,
  Nor ever sigh as we;
Sorrow and sin are strangers there,
  And all is harmony.

4 If aught can there enhance their bliss,
  Or raise their raptures higher,
New joys in heaven at sights like this,
  New anthems fill the choir.

5 With what resembling care and love
  Both worlds for us appear;—
Our friendly guardians, those above,
  Our benefactors, here.

699 1 *Cor.* vi. 9, 10.

PURE are the joys above the sky,
  And all the region peace;
No wanton lip, nor envious eye
  Can see or taste the bliss.

2 Those holy gates for ever bar
  Pollution, sin, and shame:
None shall obtain admittance there,
  But foll'wers of the Lamb.

HEBER. C. M.

G. KINGSLEY.

540 *Longing to be established in love.*

MY God! I know, I feel thee mine,
And will not quit my claim,
Till all I have is lost in thine,
And all renew'd I am.

2 I hold thee with a trembling hand,
But will not let thee go,
Till steadfastly by faith I stand,
And all thy goodness know.

3 When shall I see the welcome hour
That plants my God in me!
Spirit of health, and life, and power,
And perfect liberty!

4 Jesus, thine all-victorious love
Shed in my heart abroad;
Then shall my feet no longer rove,
Rooted and fix'd in God.

544 *Seeking a perfect cure.*

DEEPEN the wound thy hands have made
In this weak, helpless soul,
Till mercy, with its balmy aid,
Descend to make me whole,

2 The sharpness of thy two-edged sword
Enable me t' endure;
Till bold to say, My hallowing Lord
Hath wrought a perfect cure.

3 I see th' exceeding broad command,
Which all contains in one;
Enlarge my heart to understand
The mystery unknown.

4 O that with all thy saints I might
By sweet experience prove
What is the length, the breadth, the height,
And depth, of perfect love!

535 *Longing to be crucified with Christ.*

JESUS, my life, thyself apply,
Thy Holy Spirit breathe;
My vile affections crucify,
Conform me to thy death.

2 More of thy life, and more, I have
As the old Adam dies:
Bury me, Saviour, in thy grave,
That I with thee may rise.

3 Reign in me, Lord, thy foes control
Who would not own thy sway;
Diffuse thine image through my soul,
Shine to the perfect day.

4 Scatter the last remains of sin,
And seal me thine abode!
O make me glorious all within,
A temple built by God!

525 *Rom. iv. 16—25.*

IN hope, against all human hope,
Self-desp'rate I believe;
Thy quick'ning word shall raise me up,
Thou shalt thy Spirit give.

2 The thing surpasses all my thought;
But faithful is my Lord;
Through unbelief I stagger not,
For God hath spoke the word.

3 Faith, mighty faith, the promise sees,
And looks to that alone;
Laughs at impossibilities,
And cries, "It shall be done!"

4 To thee the glory of thy power
And faithfulness I give!
I shall in Christ, at that glad hour,
And Christ in me shall live.

5 Obedient faith that waits on thee,
Thou never wilt reprove;
But thou wilt form thy Son in me,
And perfect me in love.

505 *A holy heart, the Saviour's home.*

WHAT is our calling's glorious hope
But inward holiness?
For this to Jesus I look up,
I calmly wait for this.

2 I wait, till he shall touch me clean,
Shall life and power impart,
Give me the faith that casts out sin,
And purifies the heart.

3 This is the dear redeeming grace,
For every sinner free;
Surely it shall on me take place,
The chief of sinners, me.

4 From all iniquity, from all,
He shall my soul redeem!
In Jesus I believe, and shall
Believe myself to him.

5 When Jesus makes my heart his home
My sin shall all depart;
And, lo! he saith, "I quickly come,
To fill and rule thy heart!"

6 Be it according to thy word,
Redeem me from all sin:
My heart would now receive thee, Lord:
Come in, my Lord, come in!

506 *"Thy will be done."*

JESUS, the life, the truth, the way,
In whom I now believe,
As taught by thee, in faith I pray,
Expecting to receive.

2 Thy will by me on earth be done,
As by the powers above,
Who always see thee on thy throne,
And glory in thy love.

3 I ask in confidence the grace,
That I may do thy will,
As angels who behold thy face,
And all thy words fulfil.

4 Surely I shall, the sinner I,
Shall serve thee without fear,
If thou my nature sanctify
In answer to my prayer.

420 *Praying for faith.*

WITH glorious clouds encompass'd round,
Whom angels dimly see;
Will the Unsearchable be found,
Or God appear to me?

2 Will he forsake his throne above,
Himself to worms impart?
Answer, thou Man of grief and love!
And speak it to my heart.

3 In manifested love explain
Thy wonderful design;
What meant the suff'ring Son of man,
The streaming blood divine?

4 Before my eyes of faith confest,
Stand forth a slaughter'd Lamb;
And wrap me in thy crimson vest,
And tell me all thy name.

5 Jehovah in thy person show,
Jehovah crucified!
And then the pard'ning God I know,
And feel the blood applied.

6 I view the Lamb in his own light,
Whom angels dimly see;
And gaze, transported at the sight,
To all eternity.

417 *Urgent pleadings.*

O THAT thou wouldst the heavens rend,
In majesty come down;
Thine arm omnipotent extend,
And seize me for thine own!

2 Descend, and let thy lightnings burn
The stubble of thy foe;
My sins o'erturn, o'erturn, o'erturn,
And make the mountains flow!

3 Thou my impetuous spirit guide,
And curb my headstrong will;
Thou only canst drive back the tide,
And bid the sun stand still.

4 What though I cannot break my chain,
Or e'er throw off my load;
The things impossible to men
Are possible to God.

5 Is there a thing too hard for thee,
Almighty Lord of all;
Whose threat'ning looks dry up the sea,
And make the mountains fall?

6 Who, who shall in thy presence stand,
And match Omnipotence?
Ungrasp the hold of thy right hand,
Or pluck the sinner thence?

7 Sworn to destroy, let earth assail
Nearer to save thou art;
Stronger than all the powers of hell,
And greater than my heart.

8 Lo! to the hills I lift mine eye;
Thy promised aid I claim:
Father of mercies, glorify
Thy fav'rite Jesus' name.

9 Salvation in that name is found,
Balm of my grief and care;
A med'cine for my every wound,
All, all I want is there.

HENRY. C. M.

S. P. POND.

893 *United in Christ.*

JESUS, united by thy grace,
And each to each endear'd,
With confidence we seek thy face,
And know our prayer is heard.

2 Still let us own our common Lord,
And bear thine easy yoke;
A band of love, a threefold cord,
Which never can be broke.

3 Make us into one spirit drink;
Baptize into thy name;
And let us always kindly think,
And sweetly speak the same.

4 Touch'd by the loadstone of thy love,
Let all our hearts agree;
And ever tow'rd each other move,
And ever move tow'rd thee.

5 To thee inseparably join'd,
Let all our spirits cleave,
O may we all the loving mind
That was in thee receive!

6 This is the bond of perfectness,
The spotless charity;
O let us (still we pray) possess
The mind that was in thee!

7 Grant this, and then from all below
Insensibly remove:
Our souls the change shall scarcely know,
Made perfect first in love!

8 With ease our souls thro' death shall glide
Into their paradise;
And thence on wings of angels ride,
Triumphant through the skies.

9 Yet when the fullest joy is given,
The same delight we prove;
In earth, in paradise, in heaven,
Our all in all is love.

900 *"See how these Christians love."*

GIVER of concord, Prince of peace,
Meek lamb-like Son of God,
Bid our unruly passions cease,
By thy atoning blood.

2 Rebuke our rage, our passions chide,
Our stubborn wills control,
Beat down our wrath, root out our pride,
And calm our troubled soul.

3 Subdue in us the carnal mind,
Its enmity destroy,
With cords of love our spirits bind,
And melt us into joy.

4 Us into closest union draw,
And in our inward parts
Let kindness sweetly write her law,
And love command our hearts.

5 Saviour, look down with pitying eyes,
Our jarring wills control,
Let cordial, kind affections rise,
And harmonize the soul.

6 O let us find the ancient way,
Our wond'ring foes to move,
And force the heathen world to say,
"See how these Christians love!"

1053 *Doxology.*

NOW let the Father, and the Son,
And Spirit be adored;
Where there are works to make Him known,
Or saints to love the Lord.

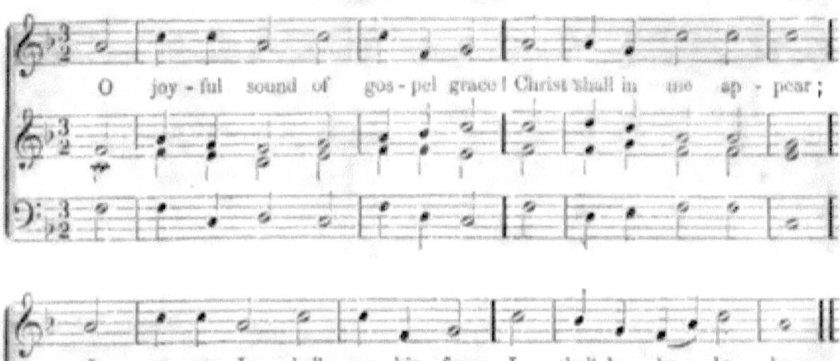

512 *Rejoicing in hope.*

O JOYFUL sound of gospel grace!
Christ shall in me appear;
I, even I, shall see his face;
I shall be holy here.

2 The glorious crown of righteousness
To me reach'd out I view;
Conqu'ror through him, I soon shall seize,
And wear it as my due.

3 The promised land from Pisgah's top
I now exult to see:
My hope is full (O glorious hope!)
Of immortality.

4 He visits now the house of clay;
He shakes his future home:
O wouldst thou, Lord, on this glad day,
Into thy temple come!

5 With me, I know, I feel, thou art;
But this cannot suffice,
Unless thou plantest in my heart
A constant paradise.

6 My earth thou water'st from on high,
But make it all a pool:
Spring up, O Well, I ever cry,
Spring up within my soul!

7 Come, O my God, thyself reveal,
Fill all this mighty void:
Thou only canst my spirit fill:
Come, O my God, my God!

574 *Living by faith.*

JESUS, to thee I now can fly,
On whom my help is laid:
Oppress'd by sins, I lift my eye,
And see the shadows fade.

2 Believing on my Lord, I find
A sure and present aid:
On thee alone my constant mind
Be every moment stay'd!

3 Whate'er in me seems wise or good,
Or strong, I here disclaim:
I wash my garments in the blood
Of the atoning Lamb.

4 Jesus, my strength, my life, my rest,
On thee will I depend,
Till summon'd to the marriage feast,
When faith in sight shall end.

295 *The invitation.*

THE King of heaven his table spreads,
And blessings crown the board;
Not paradise, with all its joys,
Could such delight afford.

2 Pardon and peace to dying men,
And endless life, are given;
Through the rich blood that Jesus shed
To raise our souls to heaven.

3 Millions of souls, in glory now,
Were fed and feasted here;
And millions more, still on the way,
Around the board appear.

4 All things are ready; come away,
Nor weak excuses frame;
Crowd to your places at the feast,
And bless the Founder's name.

1053 *Doxology.*

NOW let the Father, and the Son,
And Spirit, be adored;
Where there are works to make Him known,
Or saints to love the Lord.

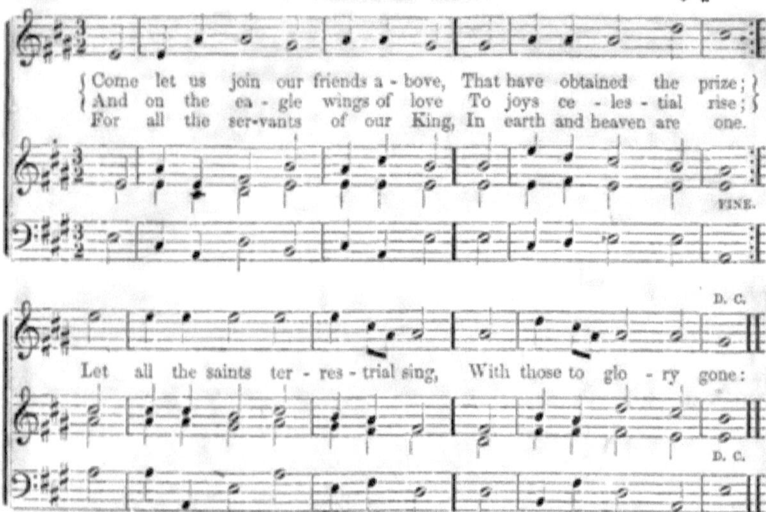

716 *The whole family in heaven and earth.*

COME, let us join our friends above,
That have obtain'd the prize;
And on the eagle wings of love
To joys celestial rise:
Let all the saints terrestrial sing,
With those to glory gone:
For all the servants of our King,
In earth and heaven, are one.

2 One family we dwell in him,
One church above, beneath,
Though now divided by the stream,
The narrow stream of death.
One army of the living God,
To his command we bow;
Part of his host have cross'd the flood,
And part are crossing now.

3 Ten thousand to their endless home
This solemn moment fly;
And we are to the margin come,
And we expect to die:
His militant embodied host,
With wishful looks we stand,
And long to see that happy coast
And reach the heavenly land.

4 Our old companions in distress
We haste again to see,
And eager long for our release,
And full felicity;
E'en now by faith we join our hands
With those that went before;
And greet the blood-besprinkled bands
On the eternal shore.

5 Our spirits too shall quickly join,
Like theirs with glory crown'd,
And shout to see our Captain's sign,
To hear his trumpet sound.
O that we now might grasp our Guide!
O that the word were given!
Come, Lord of hosts, the waves divide,
And land us all in heaven!

714 *The full assurance of hope.*

WHAT is there here to court my stay,
To hold me back from home,
While angels beckon me away,
And Jesus bids me come?
Shall I regret my parted friends
Still in the vale confined?
Nay, but whene'er my soul ascends,
They will not stay behind.

2 The race we all are running now;
And if I first attain,
They, too, their willing head shall bow,
They, too, the prize shall gain.
Now on the brink of death we stand;
And if I pass before,
They all shall soon escape to land,
And hail me on the shore.

3 Then let me suddenly remove,
That hidden life to share;
I shall not lose my friends above,
But more enjoy them there.
There we in Jesus' praise shall join,
His boundless love proclaim;
And solemnize, in songs divine,
The marriage of the Lamb.

909 *Closing the exercises.*

OUR souls, by love together knit,
Cemented, mix'd in one,
One hope, one heart, one mind, one voice,
'Tis heaven on earth begun.
Our hearts have burn'd while Jesus spoke,
And glow'd with sacred fire,
He stopp'd, and talk'd, and fed, and bless'd,
And fill'd th' enlarged desire.

2 We're soldiers fighting for our God,
Let trembling cowards fly;
We'll stand unshaken, firm, and fix'd,
With Christ to live and die.
Let devils rage, and hell assail,
We'll fight our passage through:
Let foes unite, and friends desert,
We'll seize the crown in view.

3 The little cloud increases still,
The heavens are big with rain;
We wait to catch the teeming shower,
And all its moisture drain:
A rill, a stream, a torrent, flows,
But pour the mighty flood;
O sweep the nations, shake the earth,
Till all proclaim thee God!

4 And when thou mak'st thy jewels up,
And sett'st thy starry crown,—
When all thy sparkling gems shall shine,
Proclaim'd by thee thine own,—
May we, a little band of love,
We sinners, saved by grace,
From glory into glory changed,
Behold thee face to face.

286 *Infant.*

THUS Lydia sanctified her house,
When she received the word:
Thus the believing jailor gave
His household to the Lord.
2 Thus later saints, eternal King,
Thine ancient truth embrace:
To thee their infant offspring bring,
And humbly claim the grace.

949 *The benediction. Num. vi. 24—26.*

COME, Father, Son, and Holy Ghost,
One God in persons three,
Bring back the heavenly blessing lost
By all mankind and me.
Thy favour, and thy nature too,
To me, to all, restore:
Forgive, and after God renew,
And keep us evermore.

2 Eternal Sun of righteousness,
Display thy beams divine,
And cause the glories of thy face
Upon my heart to shine.
Light, in thy light, O may I see,
Thy grace and mercy prove!
Revived, and cheer'd, and bless'd by thee,
The God of pard'ning love.

3 Lift up thy countenance serene,
And let thy happy child
Behold, without a cloud between,
The Godhead reconciled.
That all-comprising peace bestow
On me, through grace forgiven:
The joys of holiness below,
And then the joys of heaven!

406 *The prisoner of hope.*

THOU hidden God, for whom I groan,—
Till thou thyself declare,
God, inaccessible, unknown,—
Regard a sinner's prayer!
A sinner welt'ring in his blood,
Unpurged and unforgiven;
Far distant from the living God,
As far as hell from heaven.

2 An unregen'rate child of man,
To thee for faith I call;
Pity thy fallen creature's pain,
And raise me from my fall.
The darkness which through thee I feel,
Thou only canst remove;
Thy own eternal power reveal,
Thy everlasting love.

3 Thou hast in unbelief shut up,
That grace may let me go;
In hope, believing against hope,
I wait the truth to know.
Thou wilt in me reveal thy name,
Thou wilt thy light afford;
Bound and oppress'd, yet thine I am
The pris'ner of the Lord.

4 I would not to thy foe submit;
I hate the tyrant's chain:
Send forth the pris'ner from the pit,
Nor let me cry in vain.
Show me the blood that bought my peace,
The cov'nant blood apply,
And all my griefs at once shall cease,
And all my sins shall die.

5 Now, Lord, if thou art power, descend,
The mountain-sin remove;
My unbelief and troubles end,
If thou art truth and love.
Speak, Jesus, speak into my heart,
What thou for me hast done!
A ray of living faith impart,
And God is all my own.

1036 *"Our consolation aboundeth."*

WHEN languor and disease invade
This trembling house of clay,
'Tis sweet to look beyond my pains,
And long to fly away.

2 Sweet to look inward, and attend
The whispers of his love;
Sweet to look upward to the place
Where Jesus pleads above.

3 Sweet to look back, and see my name
In life's fair book set down;
Sweet to look forward, and behold
Eternal joys my own.

4 Sweet to reflect how grace divine
My sins on Jesus laid;
Sweet to remember that his blood
My debt of suff'ring paid.

5 Sweet to rejoice in lively hope,
That, when my change shall come,
Angels shall hover round my bed,
And waft my spirit home.

6 If such the sweetness of the stream,
What must the fountain be,
Where saints and angels draw their bliss
Immediately from thee?

569 *Sluggishness lamented.*

MY drowsy powers, why sleep ye so?
Awake, my sluggish soul!
Nothing hath half thy work to do,
Yet nothing's half so dull.

2 Go to the ants; for one poor grain
See how they toil and strive!
Yet we, who have a heaven t' obtain,
How negligent we live!

3 We, for whose sake all nature stands,
And stars their courses move:
We, for whose guard the angel bands
Come flying from above:

4 We, for whom God the Son came down,
And labour'd for our good:
How careless to secure that crown
He purchased with his blood!

5 Lord, shall we live so sluggish still,
And never act our parts?
Come, Holy Dove, from th' heavenly hill,
And warm our frozen hearts.

6 Give us with active warmth to move,
With vig'rous souls to rise,
With hands of faith and wings of love,
To fly and take the prize.

821 *End of the year.*

AND now, my soul, another year
Of thy short life is past;
I cannot long continue here,
And this may be my last.

2 Awake, my soul! with utmost care
Thy true condition learn
What are thy hopes? how sure? how fair?
What is thy great concern?

3 Behold, another year begins!
Set out afresh for heaven:
Seek pardon for thy former sins,
In Christ so freely given.

4 Devoutly yield thyself to God,
And on his grace depend;
With zeal pursue the heavenly road,
Nor doubt a happy end.

1053 *Doxology.*

NOW let the Father, and the Son,
And Spirit be adored;
Where there are works to make Him known,
Or saints to love the Lord.

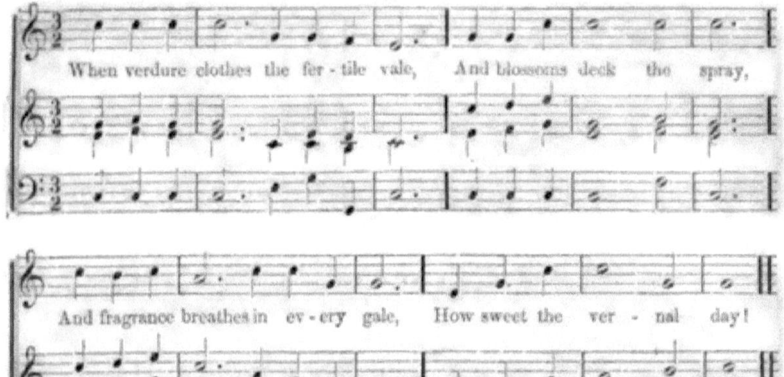

810 *Spring.*

WHEN verdure clothes the fertile vale,
And blossoms deck the spray,
And fragrance breathes in every gale,
How sweet the vernal day!

2 Hark! how the feather'd warblers sing—
'Tis nature's cheerful voice;
Soft music hails the lovely spring,
And woods and fields rejoice.

3 O God of nature and of grace,
Thy heavenly gifts impart;
Then shall my meditation trace
Spring, blooming in my heart.

4 Inspired to praise, I then shall join
Glad nature's cheerful song,
And love and gratitude divine
Attune my joyful tongue.

1043 *The farewell.*

YE golden lamps of heaven, farewell,
With all your feeble light:
Farewell, thou ever-changing moon,
Pale empress of the night.

2 And thou, refulgent orb of day,
In brighter flames array'd,
My soul, that springs beyond thy sphere,
No more demands thy aid.

3 Ye stars are but the shining dust
Of my divine abode,
The pavement of those heavenly courts,
Where I shall see my God.

4 The Father of eternal light
Shall there his beams display:
Nor shall one moment's darkness mix
With that unvaried day.

5 No more the drops of piercing grief
Shall swell into mine eyes;
Nor the meridian sun decline,
Amidst those brighter skies.

6 There all the millions of his saints
Shall in one song unite;
And each the bliss of all shall view,
With infinite delight.

899 *Psalm cxxxiii.*

LO! what an entertaining sight,
Are brethren who agree!
Brethren whose cheerful hearts unite
In bands of piety!

2 When streams of love, from Christ the [spring,
Descend to every soul,
And heavenly peace, with balmy wing,
Shades and bedews the whole:

3 'Tis like the oil, divinely sweet,
On Aaron's rev'rend head:
The trickling drops perfumed his feet,
And o'er his garments spread.

4 'Tis pleasant as the morning dews,
That fall on Zion's hill;
Where God his mildest glory shows,
And makes his grace distil.

820 *Close of the year.*

AWAKE, ye saints, and raise your eyes,
And raise your voices high;
Awake, and praise that sovereign love
That shows salvation nigh.

2 On all the wings of time it flies,
Each moment brings it near;
Then welcome, each declining day!
Welcome, each closing year!

3 Ye wheels of nature, speed your course;
Ye mortal powers, decay;
Fast as ye bring the night of death,
Ye bring eternal day.

ROCHESTER. C. M.

Now let the Fa - ther and the Son, And Spi - rit be a - dored;

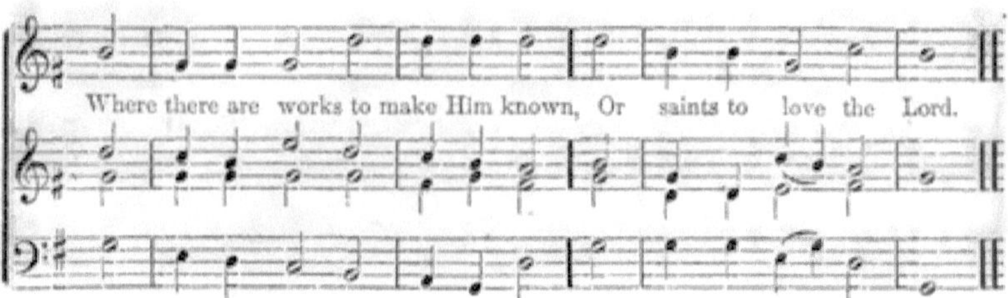
Where there are works to make Him known, Or saints to love the Lord.

849 *For a time of general sickness.*

THE Lord in judgment now appears,
And spreads his wrath abroad;
Sinners are fill'd with boding fears,
By righteous vengeance awed.

2 Seized by inveterate disease,
What crowds of victims fall;
Insatiate death relentless preys,
Nor spares the great or small.

3 Lord, we our sin and guilt confess,
Yet mercy would implore;
To mitigate our sore distress,
Display thy mighty power.

4 Say, "'Tis enough"—and give command,
Disease shall then retire,
And rosy health revive our land,
Now trembling at thine ire.

852 *Famine.*

HOW hast thou, Lord, in righteous wrath,
Blasted our promised joy
The elements obey'd thy nod,
Our prospects to destroy.

2 The sun at thy dread order now
Darts down destructive fires,
Hills, plains, and vales, are parch'd with drought,
And blooming life expires.

3 Like burnish'd brass the heaven around
In angry terrors burns,
While earth appears a joyless waste,
And into iron turns.

4 Pity us, Lord, in our distress,
Nor with our land contend;
Bid the avenging skies relent,
And showers of mercy send.

882 *Admission into the church.*

INQUIRE, ye pilgrims, for the way
That leads to Sion's hill,
And thither set your steady face,
With a determined will.

2 Invite the strangers all around
Your pious march to join;
And spread the sentiments you feel
Of faith and love divine.

3 O come, and to his temple haste,
And seek his favour there;
Before his footstool humbly bow,
And pour your fervent prayer!

4 O come and join your souls to God
In everlasting bands;
Accept the blessings he bestows,
With thankful hearts and hands.

886 *Joining the church.—The vow.*

WITNESS, ye men and angels, now,
Before the Lord we speak;
To him we make our solemn vow,
A vow we dare not break—

2 That long as life itself shall last,
Ourselves to Christ we yield;
Nor from his cause will we depart,
Or ever quit the field.

3 We trust not in our native strength,
But on his grace rely,
That, with returning wants, the Lord
Will all our need supply.

4 O guide our doubtful feet aright,
And keep us in thy ways;
And while we turn our vows to prayers,
Turn thou our prayers to praise.

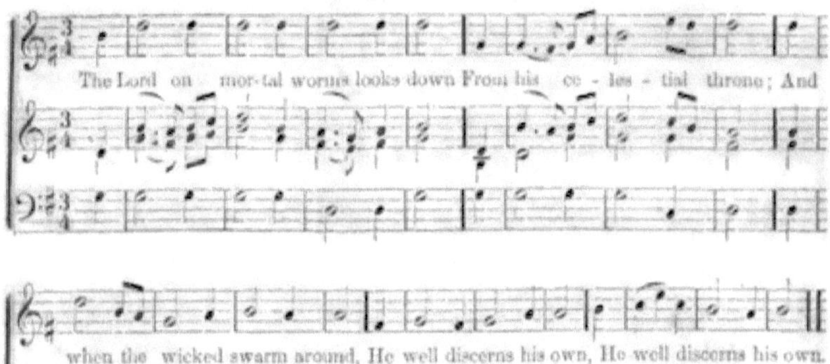

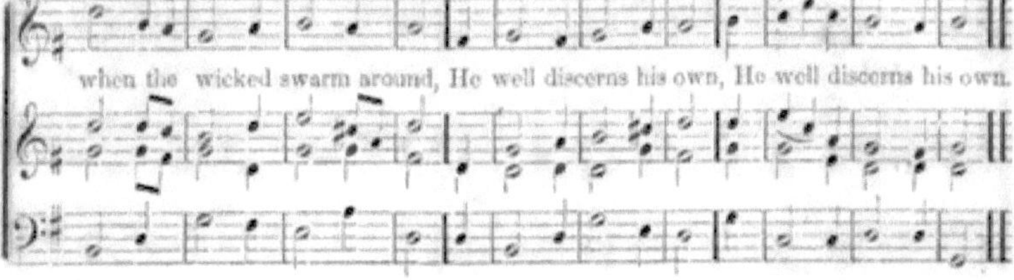

889 *Malachi iii. 16, 17.*

THE Lord on mortal worms looks down
From his celestial throne;
And when the wicked swarm around,
He well discerns his own.

2 He sees the tender hearts, that mourn
The scandals of the times;
And join their efforts to oppose
The wide-prevailing crimes.

3 Low to the social band he bows
His still attentive ear;
And, while his angels sing around,
Delights their voice to hear.

4 The chronicles of heaven shall keep
Their words in transcript fair;
In the Redeemer's book of life
Their names recorded are.

5 "Yes," saith the Lord, "the world shall know
These humble souls are mine:
These, when my jewels I produce,
Shall in full lustre shine.

6 "When deluges of fiery wrath
My foes away shall bear,
That hand which strikes the wicked through,
Shall all my children spare."

854 *After a fire.*

ETERNAL God! our humbled souls
Before thy presence bow;
With all thy magazines of wrath,
How terrible art thou!

2 Fann'd by thy breath, whole sheets of flame
Do like a deluge pour;
And all our confidence of wealth
Lies ruin'd in an hour.

3 Led on by thee in horrid pomp,
Destruction rears its head;
And blacken'd walls and smoking heaps
Through all the streets are spread.

4 Lord, in the dust we lay us down,
And mourn thy righteous ire;
Yet bless the hand of guardian love
That snatch'd us from the fire.

5 O may we view with dauntless eyes
The last tremendous day,
When earth and seas, and stars and skies,
In flames shall melt away.

975 *At table.*

ENSLAVED to sense, to pleasure prone,
Fond of created good,
Father, our helplessness we own,
And, trembling, taste our food.

2 Trembling, we taste; for ah! no more
To thee the creatures lead:
Changed, they exert a baneful power,
And poison while they feed.

3 Come, then, our heavenly Adam, come,
Thy healing influence give;
Hallow our food, reverse our doom,
And bid us eat and live.

4 Turn the full stream of nature's tide;
Let all our actions tend
To thee, their source; thy love the guide,
Thy glory be the end.

5 Earth, then, a scale to heaven shall be;
Sense shall point out the road;
The creatures all shall lead to thee,
And all we taste be God.

656 *Courage.*

AM I a soldier of the cross,—
A foll'wer of the Lamb,—
And shall I fear to own his cause,
Or blush to speak his name?

2 Must I be carried to the skies
On flowery beds of ease,
While others fought to win the prize,
And sail'd through bloody seas?

3 Are there no foes for me to face?
Must I not stem the flood?
Is this vile world a friend to grace,
To help me on to God?

4 Sure I must fight if I would reign,
Increase my courage, Lord;
I'll bear the toil, endure the pain,
Supported by thy word.

5 Thy saints, in all this glorious war,
Shall conquer, though they die;
They see the triumph from afar,
By faith they bring it nigh.

6 When that illustrious day shall rise,
And all thy armies shine,
In robes of vict'ry, through the skies,
The glory shall be thine.

377 *Praying for repentance.*

O FOR that tenderness of heart
Which bows before the Lord,
Acknowledging how just thou art,
And trembling at thy word!

O for those humble, contrite tears,
Which from repentance flow;
That consciousness of guilt which fears
The long-suspended blow!

2 Saviour, to me in pity give
The sensible distress;
The pledge thou wilt, at last, received
And bid me die in peace:

Wilt from the dreadful day remove,
Before the evil come;
My spirit hide with saints above,
My body in the tomb.

25 *Job xi. 7—9.*

SHALL foolish, weak, short-sighted man
Beyond archangels go,
The great almighty God explain,
Or to perfection know?

His attributes divinely soar
Above the creature's sight,
And prostrate seraphim adore
The glorious Infinite.

2 Jehovah's everlasting days,
They cannot number'd be;
Incomprehensible the space
Of thine immensity;

Thy wisdom's depths by reason's line
In vain we strive to sound,
Or stretch our lab'ring thought t' assign
Omnipotence a bound.

3 The brightness of thy glories leaves
Description far below;
Nor man, nor angel's heart conceives
How deep thy mercies flow:

Thy love is most unsearchable,
And dazzles all above;
They gaze, but cannot count or tell
The treasures of thy love!

805 *New-Year's day.*

LET me alone another year,
In honour of thy Son,
Who doth my Advocate appear
Before thy gracious throne.

2 Thou hast vouchsafed a longer space,
And spared the barren tree,
Because for me my Saviour prays,
And pleads his death for me.

3 Time to repent thou dost bestow,
But O the power impart!
And let my eyes with tears o'erflow,
And break my stubborn heart.

4 I'd nail my passions to the cross,
Where my Redeemer died;
And all things count but shame and loss
For Jesus crucified.

5 Giver of penitential pain,
Before that cross I lie,
In grief determined to remain
Till thou thy blood apply.

6 Forgiveness on my conscience seal;
Bestow thy promised rest;
With purest love thy servant fill,
And number with the blest.

715 *The full assurance of hope.*

O WHAT a blessed hope is ours!
While here on earth we stay,
We more than taste the heavenly powers,
And antedate that day:

We feel the resurrection near,
Our life in Christ conceal'd,
And with his glorious presence here
Our earthen vessels fill'd.

2 O would he more of heaven bestow!
And let the vessels break;
And let our ransom'd spirits go,
To grasp the God we seek;

In rapt'rous awe on him to gaze,
Who bought the sight for me,
And shout, and wonder at his grace
To all eternity.

945 *After sermon on sabbath evening.*

O BLESSED, blessed sounds of grace,
Still echoing in my ear!
Glad is the hour, and loved the place,—
But whence my sudden fear?

What if a sternly righteous doom
Have seal'd this call my last?
Before me sickness,—death,—a tomb;
Behind, th' unpardon'd past.

2 My sabbath suns may all have set,
My sabbath scenes be o'er;
The place, at least, where we are met
May know my steps no more.

The prophet of the cross may ne'er
Again preach peace to me;
The voice of interceding prayer
A farewell voice may be.

3 But, Saviour, canst thou say, Farewell?
Or, Holy Spirit, thou?
Or must I leave thy house for hell?
O save me, save me now!

While yet the life-proclaiming word
Doth through my conscience thrill,
Breathe life; and lo! divinely stirr'd,
I can repent, I will.

950 *The benediction. 2 Cor. xiii. 14.*

THE merit of Jehovah's Son
Be on his church bestow'd:
Jesus, through thy free grace alone
We have access to God·

To favour now through thee restored,
O may we still retain
The mercy of our pard'ning Lord,
And never sin again!

2 Father, thy love in Christ reveal,
Which spake us justified;
And let the gift unspeakable
In all our hearts abide:

Humbly we trust thy faithful love
Thy children to defend,
And hide our life with Christ above,
And keep us to the end.

3 Come, Holy Ghost, supply the want
Of all thy saints and me,
In all thy gifts and graces grant
Us fellowship with thee:

The Pledge, the Witness, and the Seal,
We look for thee again,
In us eternally to dwell,
Eternally to reign.

300 *The administration of the Lord's supper.*

THE flesh of our Lord Jesus Christ,
Which once was giv'n for thee,
Preserve thy body and thy soul
To immortality.

This eating—that for thee he died,
Now solemnly confess;
And feed on him within thy heart
By faith with thankfulness.

2 The blood of our Lord Jesus Christ,
Which once was shed for thee,
Preserve thy body and thy soul
To immortality.

This drinking—solemnly confess
For thee his blood was shed;
And still with new thanksgivings wreath
The Victim's hallow'd head!

DEDHAM. C. M.

916 *Opening the exercises.*

SEE, Jesus, thy disciples see,
  The promised blessing give!
Met in thy name, we look to thee,
  Expecting to receive.

2 Thee we expect, our faithful Lord,
  Who in thy name are join'd:
We wait according to thy word,
  Thee in the midst to find.

3 With us thou art assembled here,
  But O, thyself reveal!
Son of the living God, appear!
  Let us thy presence feel.

4 Breathe on us, Lord, in this our day,
  And these dry bones shall live;
Speak peace into our hearts, and say,
  "The Holy Ghost receive."

5 Whom now we seek, O may we meet!
  Jesus, the Crucified;
Show us thy bleeding hands and feet,
  Thou who for us hast died.

6 Cause us the record to receive!
  Speak, and the tokens show,
"O be not faithless, but believe
  In me, who died for you."

923 *For the water of life.*

FOUNTAIN of life, to all below
  Let thy salvation roll;
Water, replenish, and o'erflow,
  Every believing soul.

2 Into that happy number, Lord,
  Us weary sinners take:
Jesus, fulfil thy gracious word,
  For thine own mercy's sake.

3 Turn back our nature's rapid tide,
  And we shall flow to thee,
While down the stream of time we glide
  To our eternity.

4 The well of life to us thou art,
  Of joy the swelling flood;
Wafted by thee, with willing heart,
  We swift return to God.

5 We soon shall reach the boundless sea,
  Into thy fulness fall;
Be lost and swallow'd up in thee,
  Our God, our all in all.

938 *"Thy will be done."*

THY presence, Lord, the place shall fill,
  My heart shall be thy throne;
Thy holy, just, and perfect will
  Shall in my flesh be done.

2 I thank thee for thy present grace,
  And now in hope rejoice—
In confidence to see thy face,
  And always hear thy voice.

3 I have the things I ask of thee,
  What shall I more require?
That still my soul may restless be,
  And only thee desire.

4 Thy only will be done, not mine,
  But make me, Lord, thy home;
Come as thou wilt, I that resign,
  But O, my Jesus, come!

1053 *Doxology.*

NOW let the Father, and the Son,
  And Spirit, be adored;
Where there are works to make Him known,
  Or saints to love the Lord.

965 *Evening.*

NOW from the altar of our hearts
 Let warmest thanks arise;
Assist us, Lord, to offer up
 Our evening sacrifice.

2 This day God was our sun and shield,
 Our keeper and our guide;
His care was on our weakness shown,
 His mercies multiplied.

3 Minutes and mercies multiplied
 Have made up all this day;
Minutes came quick, but mercies were
 More fleet and free than they.

4 New time, new favours, and new joys,
 Do a new song require;
Till we shall praise thee as we would,
 Accept our hearts' desire.

992 *A religious household.*

HAPPY the Christian family,
 Where faith and love abound;
It rises like a lofty tree,
 With living foliage crown'd.

2 With verdant leaf, with tow'ring head,
 The parent stem shall grow,—
His branches all around him spread,
 His root deep fix'd below.

3 No blight shall hurt the tender shoot,
 Nor wasting drought destroy;
No secret worm shall nip the root,
 Or blossom of his joy.

4 From day to day, from year to year,
 The stately tree shall rise;
Till gather'd from this earthly sphere,
 And planted in the skies.

978 *At a wedding.*

SINCE Jesus freely did appear
 To grace a marriage feast,
O Lord, we ask thy presence here,
 To make a wedding guest!

2 Upon the bridal pair look down,
 Who now have plighted hands;
Their union with thy favour crown,
 And bless the nuptial bands.

3 With gifts of grace their hearts endow,
 Of all rich dowries best;
Their substance bless, and peace bestow
 To sweeten all the rest.

4 In purest love their souls unite,
 That they, with Christian care,
May make domestic burdens light,
 By taking mutual share.

984 *Praying for a sick child.*

JESUS, great healer of mankind,
 Who dost our sorrows bear;
Let an afflicted parent find
 An answer to his prayer.

2 I look for help from thee alone,
 To thee for succour fly;
My son is sick—my darling son—
 And at the point to die.

3 Surely, if thou pronounce the word,
 If thou the answer give,
My dying son shall be restored,
 And to thy glory live.

4 O save the father in the son,
 Restore him, Lord, to me;
My heart the mercy then shall own,
 And give him back to thee.

GIVE. C. M.

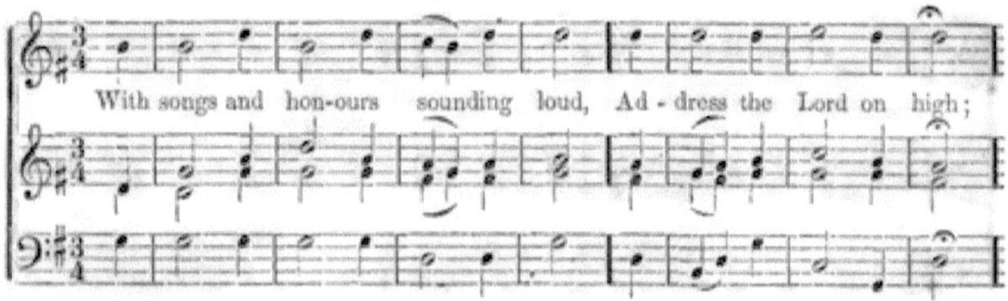

819 *Winter. Psalm cxlvii.*

WITH songs and honours sounding loud,
Address the Lord on high;
Over the heavens he spreads his cloud,
And waters veil the sky.

2 His steady counsels change the face
Of the declining year;
He bids the sun cut short his race,
And wintry days appear.

3 His hoary frost, his fleecy snow,
Descend and clothe the ground;
The liquid streams forbear to flow,
In icy fetters bound.

4 When, from his dreadful stores on high,
He pours the sounding hail,
The wretch that dares his God defy
Shall find his courage fail.

5 The changing wind, the flying cloud,
Obey his mighty word;
With songs and honours sounding loud,
Praise ye the sovereign Lord,

844 *For the Fourth of July.*

LORD, while for all mankind we pray,
Of every clime and coast,
O hear us for our native land,—
'The land we love the most!

2 O guard our shores from every foe,
With peace our borders bless,
With prosp'rous times our cities crown,
Our fields with plenteousness.

3 Here may religion shed her light
On days of rest and toil;
And piety and virtue reign,
And bless our native soil.

4 Lord of the nations, thus to thee
Our country we commend;
Be thou her refuge and her trust,
Her everlasting Friend!

866 *Thanks for preservation.*

HOW are thy servants bless'd, O Lord,
How sure is their defence!
Eternal Wisdom is their guide,
Their help, Omnipotence!

2 In foreign realms, and lands remote,
Supported by thy care,
Through burning climes they pass unhurt,
And breathe in tainted air.

3 When by the dreadful tempest borne,
High on the broken wave,—
They know thou art not slow to hear,
Nor impotent to save.

4 The storm is laid, the winds retire,
Obedient to thy will:
The sea that roars at thy command,
At thy command is still.

5 In midst of dangers, fears, and deaths,
Thy goodness we'll adore;
We'll praise thee for thy mercies past,
And humbly hope for more.

6 Our life, while thou preserv'st that life,
Thy sacrifice shall be:
And death, when death shall be our lot,
Shall join our souls to thee.

1053 *Doxology.*

NOW let the Father and the Son,
And Spirit be adored;
Where there are works to make Him known,
Or saints to love the Lord.

910 *Closing the exercises.*

GOD of all consolation, take
  The glory of thy grace!
Thy gifts to thee we render back
  In ceaseless songs of praise.

Through thee we now together came,
  In singleness of heart:
We met, O Jesus, in thy name;
  And in thy name we part.

We part in body, not in mind;
  Our minds continue one;
And each to each in Jesus join'd,
  We hand in hand go on.

Subsists as in us all one soul;
  No power can make us twain;
And mountains rise, and oceans roll,
  To sever us in vain.

Present we still in spirit are,
  And intimately nigh,
While on the wings of faith and prayer
  We each to other fly.

In Jesus Christ together we
  In heavenly places sit:
Clothed with the sun, we smile to see
  The moon beneath our feet.

Our life is hid with Christ in God!
  Our life shall soon appear,
And shed his glory all abroad
  On all his members here.

Then let us lawfully contend,
  And fight our passage through,—
Bear in our faithful minds the end,
  And keep the prize in view.

924 *For the Divine fulness.*

BEING of beings, God of love,
  To thee our hearts we raise;
Thy all-sustaining power we prove,
  And gladly sing thy praise.

2 Thine, wholly thine, we pant to be,
  Our sacrifice receive,
Made, and preserved, and saved by thee,
  To thee ourselves we give.

3 Heavenward our every wish aspires,
  For all thy mercy's store;
The sole return thy love requires
  Is, that we ask for more.

4 For more we ask; we open then
  Our hearts t' embrace thy will;
Turn, and beget us, Lord, again;
  With all thy fullness fill.

5 Come, Holy Ghost, the Saviour's love
  Shed in our hearts abroad;
So shall we ever live and move,
  And be with Christ in God.

927 *"Purge me—and I shall be clean."*

MY God, my God, to thee I cry;
  Thee only would I know:
The purifying blood apply,
  And wash me white as snow.

2 Touch me, and make the leper clean;
  Purge my iniquity:
Unless thou wash my soul from sin,
  I have no part in thee.

3 But art thou not already mine?
  Answer, if mine thou art!
Whisper within, thou Love Divine,
  And cheer my drooping heart.

4 Behold, for me the Victim bleeds,
  His wounds are open wide;
For me the blood of sprinkling pleads,
  And speaks me justified.

ASHVILLE. C. M.

FROM "NEW THES. MUS."

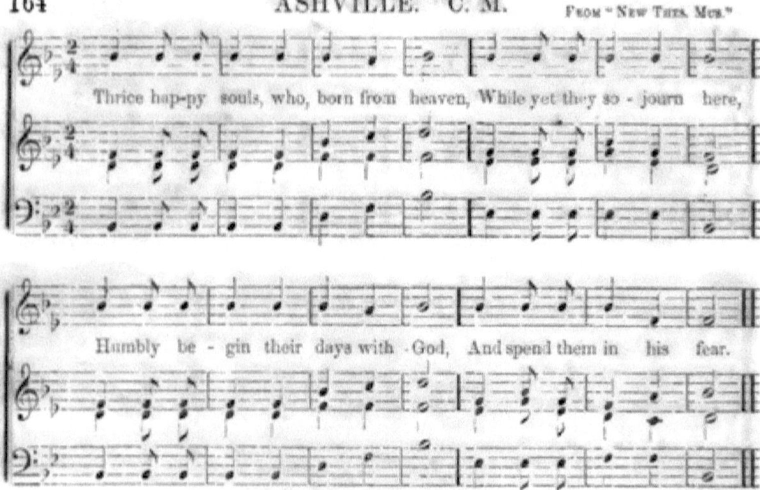

977 *"In the fear of God all the day long."*

THRICE happy souls, who, born from heav'n,
While yet they sojourn here,
Humbly begin their days with God,
And spend them in his fear.

2 So may our eyes with holy zeal
Prevent the dawning day,
And turn the sacred pages o'er,
And praise thy name, and pray.

3 Midst hourly cares, may love present
Its incense to thy throne—
And, while the world our hands employs,
Our hearts be thine alone!

4 As sanctified to noblest ends,
Be each refreshment sought:
And, by each various providence,
Some wise instruction brought!

5 When to laborious duties call'd,
Or by temptations tried,
We'll seek the shelter of thy wings,
And in thy strength confide.

6 As diff'rent scenes of life arise,
Our grateful hearts would be
With thee, amidst the social band,—
In solitude, with thee.

7 At night, we lean our weary heads
On thy paternal breast;
And, safely folded in thine arms,
Resign our powers to rest.

8 In solid, pure delights like these,
Let all my days be past;
Nor shall I then impatient wish,
Nor shall I fear, the last.

967 *Evening.*

THOU, Lord, hast bless'd my going out,
O bless my coming in!
Compass my weakness round about,
And keep me safe from sin.

2 Still hide me in thy secret place,
Thy tabernacle spread;
Shelter me with preserving grace,
And screen my naked head.

3 To THEE for refuge may I run,
From sin's alluring snare:
Ready its first approach to shun,
And watching unto prayer.

4 O that I never, never more
Might from thy ways depart;
Here let me give my wand'rings o'er,
By giving thee my heart.

983 *Parental responsibility.*

GOD, only wise, almighty, good,
Send forth thy truth and light,
To point us out the narrow road,
And guide our steps aright.

2 Made apt by thy sufficient grace
To teach as taught by thee,
We come to train in all thy ways
Our rising progeny;—

3 Their selfish will in time subdue,
And mortify their pride;
And lend their youth a sacred clue
To find the Crucified.

4 We would persuade their hearts t' obey;
With mildest zeal proceed;
And never take the harsher way,
When love will do the deed.

5 For this we ask in faith sincere,
The wisdom from above;
To touch their hearts with filial fear,
And pure ingenuous love!—

6 To watch their will, to sense inclined,
Withhold the hurtful food;
And gently bend their tender mind,
And draw their souls to God.

1026 *Consecration of property.*

FATHER, into thy hands alone
I have my all restored:
My all thy property, I own,
The steward of the Lord.

2 Confiding in thy only love,
Through Jesus strength'ning me,
I wait thy faithfulness to prove,
And give back all to thee.

3 Take when thou wilt into thy hands,
And as thou wilt require;
Resume by the Chaldean bands,
Or the devouring fire.

4 Determined all thy will t' obey,
Thy blessings I restore;
Give, Lord, or take thy gifts away,
I praise thee evermore.

713 *The full assurance of hope.*

HOW happy every child of grace,
Who knows his sins forgiven!
This earth, he cries, is not my place,
I seek my place in heaven;

A country far from mortal sight;—
Yet, O! by faith I see
The land of rest, the saints' delight,
The heaven prepared for me.

2 A stranger in the world below,
I calmly sojourn here;
Nor can its happiness or woe
Provoke my hope or fear;

Its evils in a moment end,
Its joys as soon are past;
But O! the bliss to which I tend
Eternally shall last.

3 To that Jerusalem above
With singing I repair,
While in the flesh, my hope and love,
My heart and soul, are there.

There my exalted Saviour stands,
My merciful High Priest,
And still extends his wounded hands,
To take me to his breast.

808 *New-Year's day.*

SING to the great Jehovah's praise!
All praise to him belongs,
Who kindly lengthens out our days,
Demands our choicest songs;

His providence hath brought us through
Another various year;
We all with vows and and anthems new
Before our God appear.

2 Father, thy mercies past we own,
Thy still continued care:
To thee presenting, through thy Son,
Whate'er we have or are:

Our lips and lives shall gladly show
The wonders of thy love,
While on in Jesus' steps we go,
To seek thy face above.

3 Our residue of days or hours,
Thine, wholly thine, shall be;
And all our consecrated powers
A sacrifice to thee;

Till Jesus in the clouds appear
To saints on earth forgiven,
And bring the grand sabbatic year,
The jubilee of heaven.

962 *Eternity.*

ALL praise to Him who dwells in bliss,
Who made both day and night;
Whose throne is darkness in th' abyss
Of uncreated light.

2 Each thought and deed, his piercing eyes
With strictest search survey;
The deepest shades no more disguise
Than the full blaze of day.

3 Whom thou dost guard, O King of kings,
No evil shall molest:
Under the shadow of thy wings
Shall they securely rest.

4 Thy angels shall around their beds
Their constant stations keep:
Thy faith and truth shall shield their heads,
For thou dost never sleep.

5 May we with calm and sweet repose,
And heavenly thoughts refresh'd,
Our eyelids with the morn unclose,
And bless thee, ever bless'd.

1053 *Doxology.*

NOW let the Father, and the Son,
And Spirit, be adored;
Where there are works to make Him known,
Or saints to love the Lord.

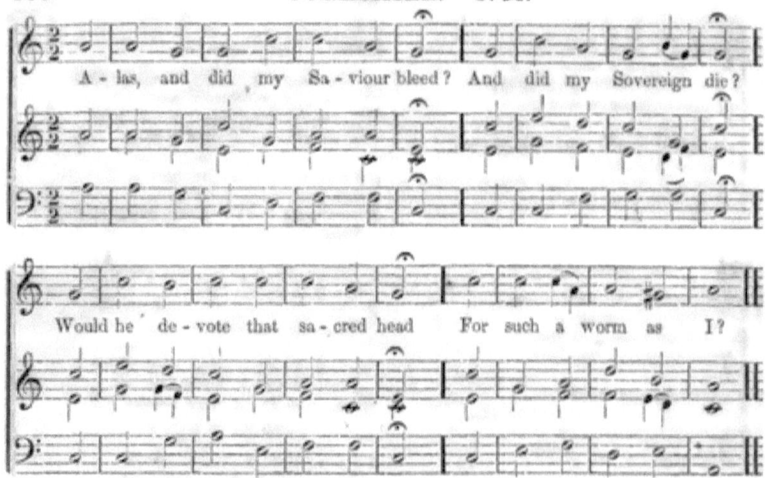

425 *Surrendering at the Cross.*

ALAS! and did my Saviour bleed?
  And did my Sovereign die?
Would he devote that sacred head
  For such a worm as I?

2 Was it for crimes that I have done
  He groan'd upon the tree?
Amazing pity! grace unknown!
  And love beyond degree!

3 Well might the sun in darkness hide,
  And shut his glories in;
When Christ, the mighty Maker, died
  For man, the creature's sin!

4 Thus might I hide my blushing face,
  While his dear cross appears;
Dissolve my heart in thankfulness,
  And melt mine eyes to tears.

5 But drops of grief can ne'er repay
  The debt of love I owe:
Here, Lord, I give myself away,
  'Tis all that I can do.

504 *Cordial obedience.*

COME, Lord, and claim me for thine own,
  Saviour, thy right assert!
Come, gracious Lord, set up thy throne,
  And reign within my heart!

2 The day of thy great power I feel,
  And pant for liberty,
I loathe myself, deny my will,
  And give up all for thee.

3 I hate my sins, no longer mine,
  For I renounce them too;
My weakness with thy strength I join,
  Thy strength shall all subdue.

4 So shall I bless thy pleasing sway
  And, sitting at thy feet,
Thy laws with all my heart obey,
  With all my soul submit.

5 Thy love the conquest more than gains,
  To all I shall proclaim,
Jesus, the King, the Conqu'ror, reigns,
  Bow down to Jesus' name.

6 To thee shall earth and hell submit,
  And every foe shall fall,
Till death expires beneath thy feet,
  And God is all in all.

776 *Before sermon.*

FATHER of all, in whom alone
  We live, and move, and breathe,
One bright, celestial ray, dart down,
  And cheer thy sons beneath.

2 While in thy word we search for thee,
  (We search with trembling awe!)
Open our eyes, and let us see
  The wonders of thy law.

3 Now let our darkness comprehend
  The light that shines so clear;
Now the revealing Spirit send,
  And give us ears to hear.

4 Before us make thy goodness pass,
  Which here by faith we know,
Let us in Jesus see thy face,
  And die to all below.

1053 *Doxology.*

NOW let the Father, and the Son,
  And Spirit, be adored;
Where there are works to make Him known,
  Or saints to love the Lord.

120 *Attraction of the cross.*

BEHOLD th' amazing sight,
The Saviour lifted high;
Behold the Son of God's delight
Expire in agony.

2 For whom, for whom, my heart,
Were all these sorrows borne?
Why did he feel that piercing smart,
And meet that various scorn?

3 For love of us he bled,
And all in torture died;
'Twas love that bow'd his fainting head,
And oped his gushing side.

4 I see, and I adore
In sympathy of love;
I feel the strong, attractive power,
To lift my soul above.

5 Drawn by such cords as these,
Let all the earth combine,
With cheerful ardour, to confess
The energy divine.

6 In thee our hearts unite,
Nor share thy griefs alone,
But from thy cross pursue their flight
To thy triumphant throne.

50 *Psalm xix. Before morning sermon.*

BEHOLD the morning sun
Begins his glorious way;
His beams through all the nations run,
And life and light convey.

2 But where the gospel comes,
It spreads diviner light;
It calls dead sinners from their tombs,
And gives the blind their sight.

3 How perfect is thy word!
And all thy judgments just;
For ever sure thy promise, Lord,
And men securely trust.

4 My gracious God, how plain
Are thy directions given?
O may I never read in vain,
But find the path to heaven!

740 *Psalm lxvii.*

TO bless thy chosen race,
In mercy, Lord, incline;
And cause the brightness of thy face
On all thy saints to shine.

2 That so thy wondrous way
May through the world be known;
While distant lands their tributes pay,
And thy salvation own.

3 Let diff'ring nations join
To celebrate thy fame;
Let all the world, O Lord, combine
To praise thy glorious name!

4 O let them shout and sing,
With joy and pious mirth!
For thou, the righteous Judge and King,
Shalt govern all the earth.

5 Let diff'ring nations join
To celebrate thy fame;
Let all the world, O Lord, combine
To praise thy glorious name!

6 Then God upon our land
Shall constant blessings shower;
And all the world in awe shall stand
Of his resistless power.

301 *At giving the bread.*

THEE, King of saints, we praise
For this our living bread;
Nourish'd by thy preserving grace,
And at thy table fed.

2 Who in these lower parts
Of thy great kingdom feast,
We feel the earnest in our hearts
Of our eternal rest.

3 Yet still a higher seat
We in thy kingdom claim,
Who here begin by faith to eat
The supper of the Lamb.

4 That glorious, heavenly prize,
We surely shall attain,
And in the palace of the skies
With thee for ever reign.

164 *Jacob's Ladder.*

LET Jacob's favoured race
The wondrous scale approve,
Through which alone we have access
To that bright throne above.

2 The foot on earth is fix'd,
He in our nature dwells,
Sinners and God he stands betwixt,
And God to man reveals.

3 The top our faith adores,
The top transcends our sight;
Above all earthly things it soars,
And all created height.

4 His glorious majesty
Our heavenly Lord maintains;
As God, he dwells above the sky,
As God for ever reigns.

299 *Approaching the table.*

JESUS, we thus obey
Thy last and kindest word;
Here in thine own appointed way
We come to meet our Lord.

2 The way thou hast enjoin'd,
Thou wilt therein appear;
We come with confidence to find
Thy special presence here.

3 Our hearts we open wide
To make the Saviour room;
And lo! the Lamb, the Crucified,
The sinner's Friend, is come.

4 His presence makes the feast;
And now our bosoms feel
The glory not to be exprest,
The joy unspeakable.

5 With pure, celestial bliss
He doth our spirits cheer;
His house of banqueting is this,
And he hath brought us here.

6 He doth his servants feed
With manna from above,
His banner over us is spread,
His everlasting love.

7 He bids us drink and eat
Imperishable food,
He gives his flesh to be our meat,
And bids us drink his blood.

8 Whate'er th' Almighty can
To pardon'd sinners give,
The fulness of our God made man,
We here with Christ receive.

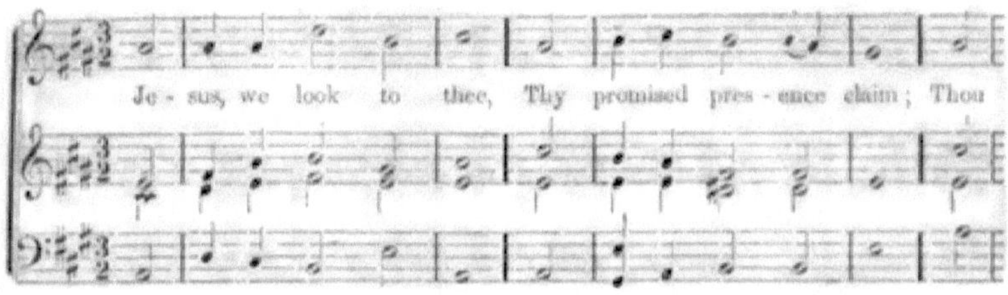

869 *Opening the exercises.*

JESUS, we look to thee,
Thy promised presence claim,
Thou in the midst of us shalt be,
Assembled in thy name:

Thy name salvation is,
Which here we come to prove;
Thy name is life, and health, and peace,
And everlasting love.

2 Not in the name of pride
Or selfishness we meet;
From nature's paths we turn aside,
And worldly thoughts forget;

We meet the grace to take,
Which thou hast freely given;
We meet on earth for thy dear sake,
That we may meet in heaven.

3 Present we know thou art,
But, O, thyself reveal!
Now, Lord, let every bounding heart
The mighty comfort feel!

O may thy quick'ning voice
The death of sin remove;
And bid our inmost souls rejoice
In hope of perfect love!

918 *Lord's Prayer.*

OUR heavenly Father, hear
The prayer we offer now;
Thy name be hallow'd far and near;
To thee all nations bow.

2 Thy kingdom come; thy will
On earth be done in love,
As saints and seraphim fulfil
Thy perfect law above.

3 Our daily bread supply
While by the word we live;
The guilt of our iniquity
Forgive, as we forgive.

4 From dark temptation's power,
From Satan's wiles, defend;
Deliver in the evil hour,
And guard us to the end.

5 Thine shall for ever be
Glory and power divine;
The sceptre, throne, and majesty,
Of heaven and earth are thine.

6 Thus humbly taught to pray
By thy beloved Son,
Through him we come to thee, and say,
"All for his sake be done."

664 *The triumph.*

"I THE good fight have fought,"
O when shall I declare!
The vict'ry by my Saviour got
I long with Paul to share.

2 O may I triumph so,
When all my warfare 's past;
And, dying, find my latest foe
Under my feet at last!

3 This blessed word be mine,
Just as the port is gain'd,
"Kept by the power of grace divine,
I have the faith maintain'd."

4 Th' apostles of my Lord,
To whom it first was given,—
They could not speak a greater word,
Nor all the saints in heaven.

GAVIN. S. M.

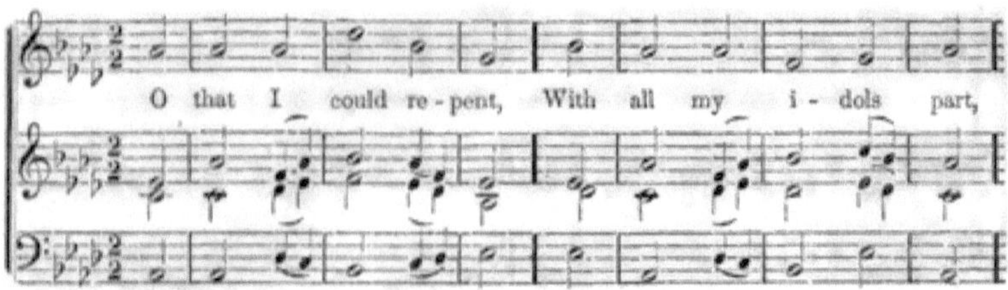

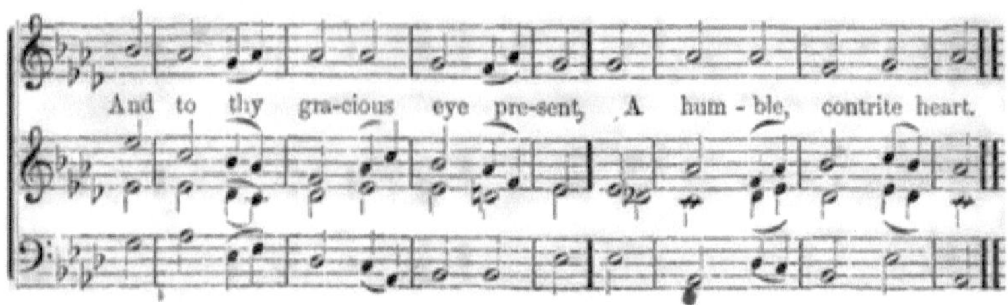

375 *Praying for repentance.*

O THAT I could repent,
With all my idols part;
And to thy gracious eye present
A humble, contrite heart:

2 A heart with grief opprest
For having grieved my God;
A troubled heart that cannot rest
Till sprinkled with thy blood.

3 Jesus, on me bestow
The penitent desire;
With true sincerity of wo
My aching breast inspire;

4 With soft'ning pity look,
And melt my hardness down:
Strike with thy love's resistless stroke,
And break this heart of stone!

395 *Surrendering the heart.*

AND can I yet delay
My little all to give?
To tear my soul from earth away
For Jesus to receive?

2 Nay, but I yield, I yield!
I can hold out no more:
I sink, by dying love compell'd,
And own thee conqueror!

3 Though late, I all forsake;
My friends, my all resign;
Gracious Redeemer, take, O take,
And seal me ever thine!

4 Come, and possess me whole,
Nor hence again remove:
Settle and fix my wav'ring soul
With all thy weight of love.

5 My one desire be this,
Thy only love to know;
To seek and taste no other bliss,
No other good below.

6 My life, my portion thou,
Thou all sufficient art;
My hope, my heavenly treasure, now
Enter and keep my heart.

577 *Depending on Christ.*

STILL stir me up to strive
With thee in strength divine,
And every moment, Lord, revive
This fainting soul of mine.

2 Persist to save my soul
Throughout the fiery hour,
Till I am every whit made whole,
And show forth all thy power.

3 Through fire and water bring
Into the wealthy place;
And teach me the new song to sing,
When perfected in grace!

4 O make me all like thee,
Before I hence remove!
Settle, confirm, and stablish me,
And build me up in love.

5 Let me thy witness live,
When sin is all destroy'd;
And then my spotless soul receive,
And take me home to God.

1052 *Doxology.*

GIVE to the Father praise,
Give glory to the Son;
And to the Spirit of his grace
Be equal honour done.

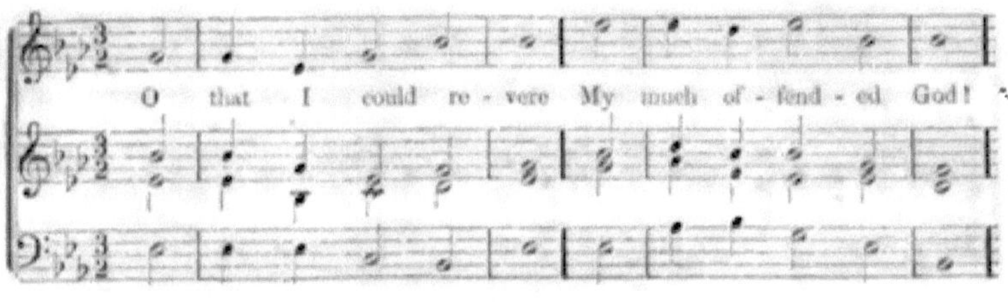

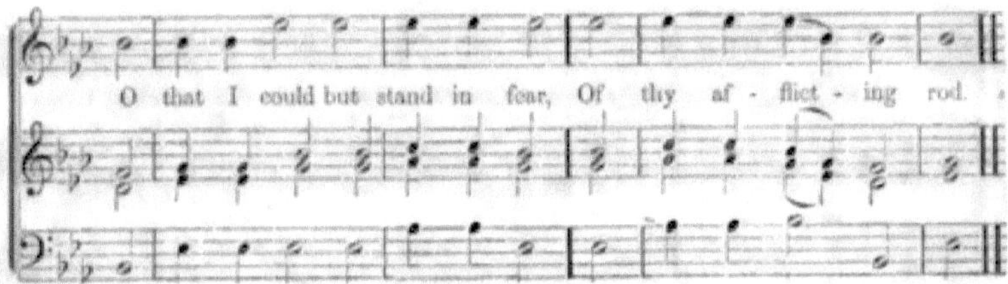

378 *Praying for repentance.*

O THAT I could revere
My much-offended God!
O that I could but stand in fear
Of thy afflicting rod!

2 If mercy cannot draw,
Thou by thy threat'ning move,
And keep an abject soul in awe,
That will not yield to love.

3 Let me with horror fly
From every sinful snare;
Nor ever in my Judge's eye
My Judge's anger dare.

4 Thou great tremendous God,
The conscious awe impart;
The grace be now on me bestow'd,
The tender fleshly heart;

5 For Jesus' sake alone,
The stony heart remove
And melt, at last, O melt me down,
Into the mould of love!

824 *Watch-night.*

THOU Judge of quick and dead,
Before whose bar severe,
With holy joy, or guilty dread,
We all shall soon appear;

Our caution'd souls prepare
For that tremendous day,
And fill us now with watchful care,
And stir us up to pray:

2 To pray, and wait the hour,
That awful hour unknown,
When, robed in majesty and power,
Thou shalt from heaven come down,

Th' immortal Son of man,
To judge the human race,
With all thy Father's dazzling train,
With all thy glorious grace.

3 To damp our earthly joys,
T' increase our gracious fears,
For ever let th' archangel's voice
Be sounding in our ears

The solemn midnight cry,
"Ye dead, the Judge is come;
Arise, and meet him in the sky,
And meet your instant doom!"

4 O may we thus be found,
Obedient to his word;
Attentive to the trumpet's sound,
And looking for our Lord!

O may we thus ensure
A lot among the blest;
And watch a moment to secure
An everlasting rest!

132 *The fountain.*

CALL'D from above, I rise,
And wash away my sin;
The stream to which my spirit flies
Can make the foulest clean.

2 It runs divinely clear,
A fountain deep and wide;
'Twas open'd by the soldier's spear
In my Redeemer's side!

1052 *Doxology.*

GIVE to the Father praise,
Give glory to the Son;
And to the Spirit of his grace
Be equal honour done.

313 *Opening morning service.*

WELCOME, sweet day of rest,
That saw the Lord arise:
Welcome to this reviving breast,
And these rejoicing eyes!

2 The King himself comes near,
And feasts his saints to-day;
Here we may sit, and see him here,
And love, and praise, and pray.

3 One day within the place
Which thou dost, Lord, frequent,
Is sweeter than ten thousand days
In sinful pleasure spent.

4 My willing soul would stay
In such a frame as this,
And sit and sing herself away
To everlasting bliss.

206 *Pentecost.*

LORD God, the Holy Ghost,
In this accepted hour,
As on the day of Pentecost,
Descend in all thy power!

2 We meet with one accord
In our appointed place,
And wait the promise of our Lord,
The Spirit of all grace.

3 Like mighty rushing wind
Upon the waves beneath,
Move with one impulse every mind,
One soul, one feeling, breathe.

4 The young, the old, inspire
With wisdom from above;
And give us hearts and tongues of fire,
To pray, and praise, and love.

5 Spirit of light, explore,
And chase our gloom away,
With lustre shining more and more
Unto the perfect day.

6 Spirit of truth, be thou
In life and death our guide;
O spirit of adoption, now
May we be sanctified!

28 *"Fearful in praises."*

STAND up, and bless the Lord,
Ye people of his choice;
Stand up, and bless the Lord your God,
With heart, and soul, and voice.

2 Though high above all praise,
Above all blessing high,
Who would not fear his holy name,
And laud, and magnify?

3 O for the living flame
From his own altar brought,
To touch our lips—our minds inspire,
And wing to heaven our thought!

4 There, with benign regard,
Our hymns he deigns to hear;
Though unreveal'd to mortal sense,
The spirit feels him near.

5 God is our strength and song,
And his salvation ours:
Then be his love in Christ proclaim'd
With all our ransom'd powers.

6 Stand up, and bless the Lord!
The Lord your God adore;
Stand up, and bless his glorious name,
Henceforth for evermore.

389 *The humbled Pharisee.*

MY gracious, loving Lord,
To thee what shall I say?
Well may I tremble at thy word,
And scarce presume to pray!

2 Yes, Lord, well might I fear,
Fear e'en to ask thy grace;
So oft have I, alas! drawn near,
And mock'd thee to thy face.

3 With all pollutions stain'd,
Thy hallow'd courts I trod;
Thy name and temple I profaned,
And dared to call thee God.

4 My nature I obey'd;
My own desires pursued;
And still a den of thieves I made
The hallow'd house of God.

5 My sin and nakedness
I studied to disguise;
Spoke to my soul a flatt'ring peace,
And put out my own eyes.

6 In fig-leaves I appear'd,
Nor with my form would part;
But still retain'd a conscience sear'd,
A hard, deceitful heart.

452 *The backslider's complaint.*

AND wilt thou yet be found?
And may I still draw near?
Then listen to the plaintive sound
Of a poor sinner's prayer.

2 Jesus, thine aid afford,
If still the same thou art;
To thee I look, to thee, my Lord!
Lift up a helpless heart.

3 Thou seest my troubled breast,
The strugglings of my will,
The foes that interrupt my rest,
The agonies I feel.

4 The daily death I prove,
Saviour, to thee is known;
'Tis worse than death my God to love,
And not my God alone.

5 O my offended Lord,
Restore my inward peace:
I know thou canst; pronounce the word,
And bid the tempest cease!

6 I long to see thy face,
Thy spirit I implore,
The living water of thy grace,
That I may thirst no more.

410 *Embracing offered mercy.*

O MY offended God,
If now at last I see,
That I have trampled on thy blood,
And done despite to thee;

2 If I begin to wake
Out of my deadly sleep;—
Into thy arms of mercy take,
And there for ever keep.

3 No other right have I
Than what the world may claim;
All, all may to their God draw nigh,
Through faith in Jesus' name.

4 Thou hast obtain'd the grace
That all may turn and live;
And lo! thy offer I embrace,
Thy mercy I receive.

463 *Psalm xxxii. 1—6.*

O BLESSED souls are they,
Whose sins are cover'd o'er!
Divinely bless'd, to whom the Lord
Imputes their guilt no more.

2 They mourn their follies past,
And keep their hearts with care,
Their lips and lives without deceit
Shall prove their faith sincere.

3 While I conceal'd my guilt,
I felt the fest'ring wound;
Till I confess'd my sins to thee,
And ready pardon found.

4 Let sinners learn to pray,
Let saints keep near the throne;
Our help in times of deep distress
Is found in God alone.

217 *Work and Witness.*

O COME, and dwell in me,
Spirit of power within:
And bring the glorious liberty
From sorrow, fear, and sin!

2 This inward, dire disease,
Spirit of health, remove;
Spirit of finish'd holiness,
Spirit of perfect love.

3 Hasten the joyful day
Which shall my sins consume,
When old things shall be done away,
And all things new become.

4 I want the witness, Lord,
That all I do is right,
According to thy will and word,
Well pleasing in thy sight.

5 I ask no higher state;
Indulge me but in this;
And soon or later then translate
To my eternal bliss.

244 *The church catholic.*

LET party names no more
The Christian world o'erspread:
Gentile and Jew, and bond and free,
Are one in Christ their Head.

2 Among the saints on earth
Let mutual love be found,
Heirs of the same inheritance,
With mutual blessings crown'd.

3 Let bitterness and wrath
Be banish'd far away.
Those should in strictest friendship dwell
Who the same Lord obey.

4 Thus will the church below
Resemble that above;
Where streams of endless pleasure flow,
And every heart is love.

278 *Closing Conference.*

AND let our bodies part,
To different climes repair:
Inseparably join'd in heart
The friends of Jesus are.

2 Jesus, the Corner-stone,
Did first our hearts unite,
And still he keeps our spirits one,
Who walk with him in white.

3 O let us still proceed
In Jesus' work below;
And, foll'wing our triumphant Head,
To further conquests go.

4 The vineyard of the Lord
Before his lab'rers lies;
And lo! we see the vast reward
Which waits us in the skies.

5 O let our heart and mind
Continually ascend,
That haven of repose to find,
Where all our labours end!

6 Where all our toils are o'er,
Our suff'ring and our pain:—
Who meet on that eternal shore,
Shall never part again.

7 O happy, happy place,
Where saints and angels meet!
There we shall see each other's face,
And all our brethren greet.

8 The church of the first-born,
We shall with them be blest,
And, crown'd with endless joy, return
To our eternal rest.

9 With joy we shall behold,
In yonder bless'd abode,
The patriarchs and prophets old,
And all the saints of God.

10 Abr'am and Isaac, there,
And Jacob shall receive
The foll'wers of their faith and prayer
Who now in bodies live.

11 We shall our time beneath
Live out in cheerful hope,
And fearless pass the vale of death,
And gain the mountain-top.

12 To gather home his own
God shall his angels send,
And bid our bliss, on earth begun,
In deathless triumph end.

297 *"Let us keep the feast."*

LET all who truly bear
The bleeding Saviour's name,
Their faithful hearts with us prepare,
And eat the paschal Lamb:

Our Passover was slain
At Salem's hallow'd place,
Yet we who in our tents remain
Shall gain his largest grace.

2 This eucharistic feast
Our every want supplies,
And still we by his death are blest,
And share his sacrifice:

By faith his flesh we eat,
Who here his passion show,
And God out of his holy seat
Shall all his gifts bestow.

3 Who thus our faith employ
His suff'rings to record,
E'en now we mournfully enjoy
Communion with our Lord;

As though we every one
Beneath his cross had stood,
And seen him heave, and heard him groan,
And felt his gushing blood.

4 O God! 'tis finish'd now!
The mortal pang is past!
By faith his head we see him bow,
And hear him breathe his last:

We too with him are dead,
And shall with him arise,
The cross on which he bows his head
Shall lift us to the skies.

355 *"Now is the day of salvation."*

TO-MORROW, Lord, is thine,
Lodged in thy sovereign hand,
And if its sun arise and shine,
It shines by thy command.

2 The present moment flies,
And bears our life away;
O! make thy servants truly wise
That they may live to-day.

3 Since on this winged hour
Eternity is hung,
Waken by thy almighty power
The aged and the young.

4 One thing demands our care;
O! be it still pursued,
Lest, slighted once, the season fair
Should never be renew'd.

5 To Jesus may we fly,
Swift as the morning light,
Lest life's young golden beam should die
In sudden, endless night.

587 *Watchfulness.*

THOU seest my feebleness,
Jesus, be thou my power,
My help and refuge in distress,
My fortress and my tower.

2 Give me to trust in thee;
Be thou my sure abode:
My horn, and rock, and buckler be,
My Saviour, and my God.

3 Myself I cannot save,
Myself I cannot keep:
But strength in thee I surely have,
Whose eyelids never sleep.

4 My soul to thee alone,
Now, therefore, I commend:
Thou, Jesus, love me as thine own,
And love me to the end.

247 *The church militant.*

HARK, how the watchmen cry!
Attend the trumpet's sound!
Stand to your arms, the foe is nigh,
The powers of hell surround.

2 Who bow to Christ's command,
Your arms and hearts prepare;
The day of battle is at hand!
Go forth to glorious war!

3 See, on the mountain top,
The standard of your God!
In Jesus' name I lift it up,
All stain'd with hallow'd blood.

4 His standard-bearer, I
To all the nations call:
Let all to Jesus' cross draw nigh;
He bore the cross for all.

5 Go up with Christ your Head;
Your Captain's footsteps see;
Follow your Captain, and be led
To certain victory.

6 All power to Him is given:
He ever reigns the same:
Salvation, happiness, and heaven,
Are all in Jesus' name.

26 *All-sufficiency.*

MY God, my life, my love,
To thee, to thee I call:
I cannot live if thou remove,
For thou art all in all.

2 Thy shining grace can cheer
This dungeon where I dwell:
'Tis paradise when thou art here,
If thou depart, 'tis hell.

3 The smilings of thy face,
How amiable they are!
'Tis heaven to rest in thine embrace,
And nowhere else but there.

4 To thee, and thee alone,
The angels owe their bliss;
They sit around thy gracious throne,
And dwell where Jesus is.

5 Not all the harps above
Can make a heavenly place,
If God his residence remove,
Or but conceal his face.

6 Nor earth, nor all the sky,
Can one delight afford;
No, not one drop of real joy,
Without thy presence, Lord.

7 Thou art the sea of love,
Where all my pleasures roll;
The circle where my passions move,
And centre of my soul.

8 To thee my spirits fly,
With infinite desire:
And yet how far from thee I lie!
O Jesus, raise me higher!

609 *Imitation of Christ.*

JESUS, I fain would find
Thy zeal for God in me,
Thy yearning pity for mankind,
Thy burning charity.

2 In me thy Spirit dwell!
In me thy bowels move!
So shall the fervour of my zeal
Be the pure flame of love.

DYER. S. M. From "New Trin. Musicus."

466 *Witness of adoption.*

HOW can a sinner know
His sins on earth forgiven?
How can my gracious Saviour show
My name inscribed in heaven?

2 What we have felt and seen
With confidence we tell;
And publish to the sons of men
The signs infallible.

3 We who in Christ believe
That he for us hath died,
We all his unknown peace receive,
And feel his blood applied.

4 Exults our rising soul,
Disburden'd of her load,
And swells unutterably full
Of glory and of God.

5 His love, surpassing far
The love of all beneath,
We find within our hearts, and dare
The pointless darts of death.

6 Stronger than death or hell
The sacred power we prove;
And conqu'rors of the world, we dwell
In heaven, who dwell in love.

447 *The backslider's return.*

O JESUS! full of grace,
To thee I make my moan;
Let me again behold thy face,
Call home thy banish'd one.

2 Again my pardon seal,
Again my soul restore,
And freely my backslidings heal,
And bid me sin no more.

3 Wilt thou not bid me rise?
Speak, and my soul shall live:
Forgive, my gasping spirit cries,
Abundantly forgive.

4 For thine own mercy's sake,
Relieve my wretchedness;
And O, my pardon give me back,
And give me back my peace!

5 Again thy love reveal,
Restore that inward heaven,
O grant me once again to feel,
Through faith, my sins forgiven!

6 Thy utmost mercy show
Say to my drooping soul,
In peace and full assurance go,
Thy faith hath made thee whole.

431 *The plea.*

JESUS, my Lord, attend
Thy feeble creature's cry;
And show thyself the sinner's Friend,
And set me up on high.

2 From hell's oppressive power
My struggling soul release,
And to thy Father's grace restore,
And to thy perfect peace.

3 Rivers of life divine
From thee, their fountain, flow;
And all who know that love of thine,
The joy of angels know.

4 That thou canst here forgive
Grant me to testify:
And justified by faith to live,
And in that faith to die.

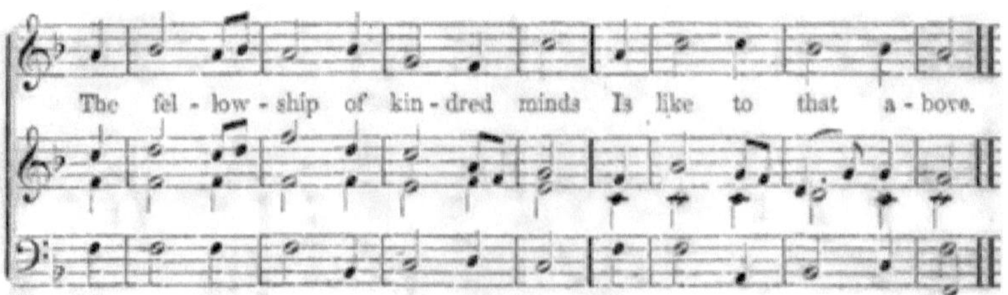

908 *Closing the exercises.*

BLESS'D be the tie that binds
Our hearts in Christian love;
The fellowship of kindred minds
Is like to that above.

2 Before our Father's throne
We pour our ardent prayers;
Our fears, our hopes, our aims, are one—
Our comforts and our cares.

3 We share our mutual woes;
Our mutual burdens bear;
And often for each other flows
The sympathizing tear.

4 When we asunder part,
It gives us inward pain;
But we shall still be join'd in heart,
And hope to meet again.

5 This glorious hope revives
Our courage by the way;
While each in expectation lives,
And longs to see the day.

6 From sorrow, toil, and pain,
And sin, we shall be free;
And perfect love and friendship reign
Through all eternity.

165 *Jacob's Ladder.*

PURSUE the mystery!
The duteous angel-train
Ascending and descending see
Upon the Son of man!

2 The ministerial host
Their heavenly Lord attend;
And us, who in his mercy trust,
He bids his guards defend.

3 Through Christ, our living Way,
Sent from above they come,
Our spirits safely to convey
To our eternal home:

4 They watch each glorious heir,
And when from flesh releast,
Up to our Father's throne they bear,
And lodge us in his breast.

685 *2 Cor. v. 1—8.*

WE know, by faith we know,
If this vile house of clay,
This tabernacle, sink below,
In ruinous decay.

We have a house above,
Not made with mortal hands;
And firm as our Redeemer's love
That heavenly fabric stands.

2 It stands securely high,
Indissolubly sure;
Our glorious mansion in the sky
Shall evermore endure:

O were we enter'd there!
To perfect heaven restored!
O were we all caught up to share
The triumph of our Lord!

3 For this in faith we call;
For this we weep and pray:
O might the tabernacle fall!
O might we 'scape away!

Full of immortal hope,
We urge the restless strife,
And hasten to be swallow'd up
Of everlasting life.

63 *Evening.*

THE day is past and gone,
The evening shades appear;
may we all remember well,
The night of death draws near.

2 We lay our garments by,
Upon our beds to rest;
o death will soon disrobe us all
Of what is here possest.

3 Lord, keep us safe this night,
Secure from all our fears;
ay angels guard us, while we sleep,
Till morning light appears.

4 And when we early rise,
And view th' unwearied sun,
ay we set out to win the prize,
And after glory run.

5 And when our days are past,
And we from time remove,
may we in thy bosom rest,
The bosom of thy love!

33 *Impending judgments.*

SINNERS, the call obey,
The latest call of grace,
he day is come, the vengeful day
Of a devoted race:

Devils and men combine
To plague the faithless seed,
nd vials full of wrath divine
Are bursting on your head.

2 Enter into the Rock,
Ye trembling slaves of sin,—
he Rock of your salvation, struck
And cleft to take you in:

To shelter the distrest
He did the cross endure;
Enter into the clefts, and rest
In Jesus' wounds secure.

812 *Praying for rain.*

O LORD, in mercy spare
The herbage of the field;
And, under thy paternal care,
May it abundance yield.

2 Restrain the burning ray,
And grant refreshing rains;
Restore the verdure from decay,
And drench the parched plains.

3 Then we our praise will show
To our preserver, God;
Our songs of melody shall flow,
And spread his name abroad.

748 *For the "dry bones of the house of Israel."*

MESSIAH, full of grace,
Redeem'd by thee, we plead
The promise made to Abrah'm's race,
To souls for ages dead.

2 Their bones, as quite dried up,
Throughout the vale appear;
Cut off and lost their last faint hope
To see thy kingdom here.

3 Open their graves, and bring
The outcasts forth, to own
Thou art their Lord, their God, their King,
Their true Anointed One.

4 To save the race forlorn,
Thy glorious arm display!
And show the world a nation born,
A nation in a day!

111 *"He beheld the city, and wept over it."*

DID Christ o'er sinners weep,
And shall our cheeks be dry?
Let floods of penitential grief
Burst forth from every eye.

2 The Son of God in tears
The wondering angels see;
Be thou astonish'd, O my soul;
He shed those tears for thee.

3 He wept that we might weep;
Each sin demands a tear:
In heaven alone no sin is found,
And there's no weeping there.

114 *"My soul is exceeding sorrowful."*

THE man of sorrow now
Thou dost indeed appear,
Beneath my guilty burden bow,
And tremble with my fear.

2 Thy pain is my relief,
And doth my load remove;
For O, if all thy soul is grief,
Yet all thy heart is love!

834 *Impending judgments.*

JESUS, to thee we fly
From the devouring sword;
Our city of defence is nigh;
Our help is in the Lord:—

Or if the scourge o'erflow,
And laugh at innocence,
Thine everlasting arms, we know,
Shall be our soul's defence.

2 We in thy word believe,
And on thy promise stay;
Our life, which still to thee we give,
Shall be to us a prey:

Our life with thee we hide
Above the furious blast,
And shelter'd in thy wounds abide
Till all the storms are past.

753 *"One fold under one Shepherd."*

FATHER of boundless grace
Thou hast in part fulfill'd
Thy promise made to Adam's race,
In God incarnate seal'd.

2 A few from every land
At first to Salem came,
And saw the wonders of thy hand,
And saw the tongues of flame.

3 Yet still we wait the end,
The coming of our Lord,—
The full accomplishment attend,
Of thy prophetic word.

4 Thy promise deeper lies
In unexhausted grace,
And new-discover'd worlds arise
To sing their Saviour's praise.

5 Beloved for Jesus' sake,
By him redeem'd of old,
All nations must come in and make
One undivided fold:

6 While gather'd in by thee,
And perfected in one,
They all at once thy glory see
In thy co-equal Son.

739 *Funeral of an aged minister.*

"SERVANT of God, well done!
Rest from thy loved employ;
The battle fought, the vict'ry won,
Enter thy Master's joy."

The voice at midnight came;
He started up to hear;
A mortal arrow pierced his frame,
He fell,—but felt no fear.

2 Tranquil amid alarms,
It found him on the field,
A vet'ran, slumb'ring on his arms,
Beneath his red-cross shield.

His sword was in his hand,
Still warm with recent fight,
Ready that moment, at command,
Through rock and steel to smite.

3 It was a two-edged blade,
Of heavenly temper keen:
And double were the wounds it made
Where'er it glanced between.

'Twas death to sin,—'twas life
To all who mourn'd for sin;
It kindled and it silenced strife,
Made war and peace within.

4 Oft with its fiery force
His arm had quell'd the foe,
And laid, resistless in his course,
The alien-armies low.

Bent on such glorious toils,
The world to him was loss,
Yet all his trophies, all his spoils,
He hung upon the cross.

5 At midnight came the cry,
"To meet thy God prepare!"
He woke,—and caught his Captain's eye,
Then, strong in faith and prayer,

His spirit, with a bound,
Left its encumb'ring clay;
His tent, at sunrise, on the ground
A darken'd ruin lay.

6 The pains of death are past,
Labour and sorrow cease;
And, life's long warfare closed at last,
His soul is found in peace.

Soldier of Christ, well done!
Praise be thy new employ;
And while eternal ages run,
Rest in thy Saviour's joy.

686 *2 Cor. v. 1—8.*

ABSENT, alas! from God,
We in the body mourn,
And pine to quit this mean abode,
And languish to return.

Jesus, regard our vows,
And change our faith to sight;
And clothe us with our nobler house
Of everlasting light!

2 O let us put on thee
In perfect holiness!
And rise prepared thy face to see,
Thy bright, unclouded face:

Thy grace with glory crown,
Who hast the earnest given;
And then triumphantly come down,
And take us up to heaven!

674 *The end of life.*

AND am I born to die?
To lay this body down?
And must my trembling spirit fly
Into a world unknown?

A land of deepest shade,
Unpierced by human thought;
The dreary regions of the dead,
Where all things are forgot!

2 Soon as from earth I go,
What will become of me?
Eternal happiness or wo
Must then my portion be!

Waked by the trumpet's sound,
I from my grave shall rise;
And see the Judge with glory crown'd,
And see the flaming skies!

3 How shall I leave my tomb—
With triumph or regret?
A fearful, or a joyful doom—
A curse, or blessing meet?

Will angel bands convey
Their brother to the bar?
Or devils drag my soul away
To meet its sentence there?

4 Who can resolve the doubt
That tears my anxious breast?
Shall I be with the damn'd cast out,
Or number'd with the blest?

I must from God be driven,
Or with my Saviour dwell;
Must come at his command to heaven,
Or else,—depart to hell.

675 *The end of life.*

O THOU that wouldst not have
One wretched sinner die;
Who diedst thyself, my soul to save
From endless misery!

Show me the way to shun
Thy dreadful wrath severe;
That when thou comest on thy throne,
I may with joy appear!

2 Thou art thyself the way,
Thyself in me reveal;
So shall I spend my life's short day
Obedient to thy will:

So shall I love my God,
Because he first loved me;
And praise thee in thy bright abode
To all eternity.

467 *Witness of Adoption.*

WE by his Spirit prove,
And know the things of God;
The things which freely of his love
He hath on us bestow'd.

2 His Spirit us he gave,
Who dwells in us, we know;
The witness in ourselves we have,
And all its fruits we show.

3 The meek and lowly heart
That in our Saviour was,
To us his Spirit does impart,
And signs us with his cross.

4 Our nature's turn'd, our mind
Transform'd in all its powers;
And both the witnesses are join'd,—
The Spirit of God with ours.

5 Whate'er our pard'ning Lord
Commands, we gladly do;
And, guided by his sacred word,
We all his steps pursue.

6 His glory our design,
We live our God to please;
And rise, with filial fear divine,
To perfect holiness.

952 *Morning.*

WE lift our hearts to thee,
O Day-Star from on high!
The sun itself is but thy shade,
Yet cheers both earth and sky.

2 O let thy orient beams
The night of sin disperse,
The mists of error and of vice
Which shade the universe!

3 How beauteous nature now!
How dark and sad before!
With joy we view the pleasing change,
And nature's God adore.

4 O may no gloomy crime
Pollute the rising day;
Or Jesus' blood, like evening dew,
Wash all its stains away!

5 May we this life improve,
To mourn for errors past,—
And live this short revolving day,
As if it were our last.

6 To God, the Father, Son,
And Spirit,—One in Three,—
Be glory, as it was, is now,
And shall for ever be.

757 *God giveth the increase.*

LORD, if at thy command
The word of life we sow,
Water'd by thy almighty hand,
The seed shall surely grow.

The virtue of thy grace
A large increase shall give,
And multiply the faithful race,
Who to thy glory live.

2 Now, then, the ceaseless shower
Of gospel blessings send,
And let the soul-converting power
Thy ministers attend.

On multitudes confer
The heart-renewing love,
And by the joy of grace prepare
For fuller joys above.

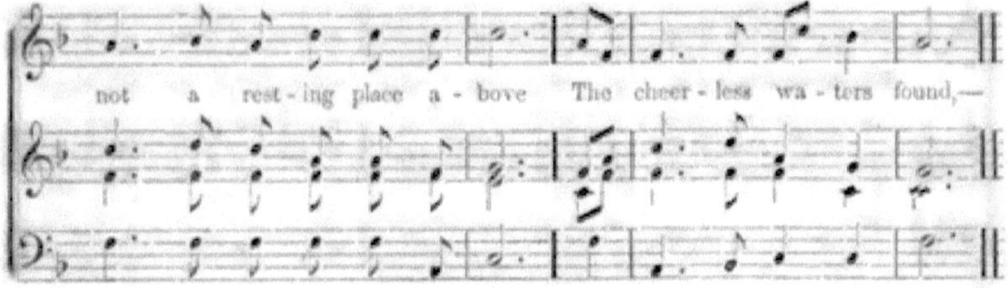

885 *Entering the Ark.*

LIKE Noah's weary dove,
That soar'd the earth around,
But not a resting-place above
The cheerless waters found,—

2 O cease, my wand'ring soul,
On restless wing to roam;
All the wide world, to either pole,
Has not for thee a home.

3 Behold the ark of God,
Behold the open door;
Hasten to gain that dear abode,
And rove, my soul, no more.

4 There, safe, thou shalt abide,
There, sweet shall be thy rest,
And every longing satisfied,
With full salvation blest.

642 *"All things work together for good—"*

AWAY! my needless fears,
And doubts no longer mine;
A ray of heavenly light appears,
A messenger divine.

2 Thrice comfortable hope,
That calms my troubled breast;
My Father's hand prepares the cup,
And what he wills is best.

3 If what I wish is good,
And suits the will divine,—
By earth and hell in vain withstood,
I know it shall be mine.

4 Still let them counsel take
To frustrate his decree;
They cannot keep a blessing back,
By Heaven design'd for me.

5 Here then I doubt no more,
But in his pleasure rest;
Whose wisdom, love, and truth, and power,
Engage to make me blest.

6 T' accomplish his design,
The creatures all agree;
And all the attributes divine
Are now at work for me.

676 *The issues of life and death.*

O WHERE shall rest be found,
Rest for the weary soul?
'Twere vain the ocean-depths to sound,
Or pierce to either pole:

The world can never give
The bliss for which we sigh;
'Tis not the whole of life to live,
Nor all of death to die.

2 Beyond this vale of tears
There is a life above,
Unmeasured by the flight of years;
And all that life is love:—

There is a death whose pang
Outlasts the fleeting breath;
O! what eternal horrors hang
Around "the second death!"

3 Lord God of truth and grace,
Teach us that death to shun,
Lest we be banish'd from thy face,
And evermore undone.

Here would we end our quest:
Alone are found in thee,
The life of perfect love,—the rest
Of immortality.

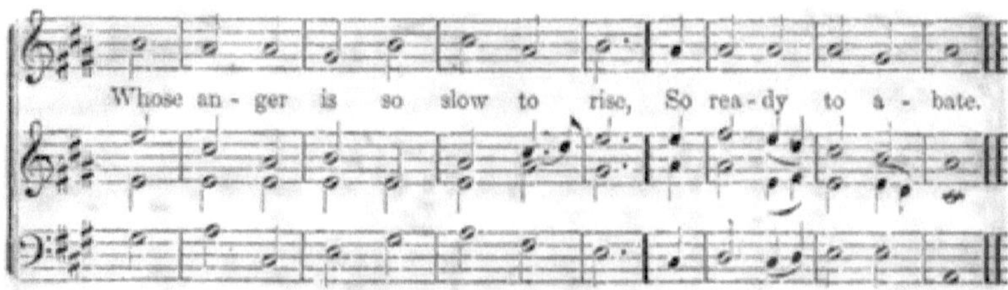

61 *Psalm ciii. 8—12.*

MY soul, repeat His praise,
Whose mercies are so great;
Whose anger is so slow to rise,
So ready to abate.

2 God will not always chide;
And when his strokes are felt,
His strokes are fewer than our crimes,
And lighter than our guilt.

3 High as the heavens are raised
Above the ground we tread,
So far the riches of his grace
Our highest thoughts exceed.

4 His power subdues our sins;
And his forgiving love,
Far as the east is from the west,
Doth all our guilt remove.

60 *Psalm ciii. 1—7.*

O BLESS the Lord, my soul;
Let all within me join,
And aid my tongue to bless his name,
Whose favours are divine.

2 O bless the Lord, my soul;
Nor let his mercies lie
Forgotten in unthankfulness,
And without praises die.

3 'Tis he forgives thy sins;
'Tis he relieves thy pain;
'Tis he who heals thy sicknesses,
And makes thee young again.

4 He crowns thy life with love,
When ransom'd from the grave;
He, who redeem'd my soul from hell,
Hath sovereign power to save.

5 He fills the poor with good;
He gives the suff'rers rest;
The Lord hath judgment for the proud,
And justice for th' oppress.

6 His wondrous works and ways
He made by Moses known;
But sent the world his truth and grace
By his beloved Son.

585 *Watchfulness.*

BID me of men beware,
And to my ways take heed,
Discern their every secret snare,
And circumspectly tread.

2 O may I calmly wait
Thy succors from above!
And stand against their open hate,
And well-dissembled love.

3 My spirit, Lord, alarm,
When men and devils join:
'Gainst all the powers of Satan arm,
In panoply divine.

4 O may I set my face,
His onsets to repel!
Quench all his fiery darts, and chase
The fiend to his own hell.

5 But above all, afraid
Of my own bosom foe,
Still let me seek to thee for aid,
To thee my weakness show;—

6 Hang on thy arm alone,
With self-distrusting care;
And deeply in the spirit groan
The never-ceasing prayer.

255 *Isaiah lii. 7—10.*

HOW beauteous are their feet
Who stand on Zion's hill;
Who bring salvation on their tongues,
And words of peace reveal!

2 How charming is their voice!
How sweet the tidings are!
"Zion, behold thy Saviour King;
He reigns and triumphs here!"

3 How happy are our ears
That hear this joyful sound,
Which kings and prophets waited for,
And sought, but never found!

4 How blessed are our eyes
That see this heavenly light!
Prophets and kings desired it long,
But died without the sight.

5 The watchmen join their voice,
And tuneful notes employ;
Jerusalem breaks forth in songs,
And deserts learn the joy.

6 The Lord makes bare his arm
Through all the earth abroad:
Let every nation now behold
Their Saviour and their God.

166 *Jacob's Ladder.*

REDEEMER of mankind,
Who on thy name rely,
A constant intercourse we find
Open'd 'twixt earth and sky.

2 Mercy, and grace, and peace,
Descend through thee alone;
And thou dost all our services
Present before the throne.

3 On us thy Father's love
Is for thy sake bestow'd;
Thou art our Advocate above,
Thou art our way to God.

4 Our way to God we trace,
And through thy name forgiven,
From step to step, from grace to grace,
On thee we climb to heaven.

555 *Strangers and pilgrims.*

IN every time and place,
Who serve the Lord most high,
Are call'd his sovereign will t' embrace,
And still their own deny,—

2 To follow his command,
On earth as pilgrims rove,
And seek an undiscover'd land,
And house, and friends above.

3 Father, the narrow path
To that far country show;
And in the steps of Abrah'm's faith
Enable me to go.

4 A cheerful sojourner
Where'er thou bidd'st me roam,
Till, guided by thy Spirit here,
I reach my heavenly home.

531 *The act of consecration.*

LORD, in the strength of grace,
With a glad heart and free,
Myself, my residue of days,
I consecrate to thee.

2 Thy ransom'd servant, I
Restore to thee thy own;
And from this moment, live or die,
To serve my God alone.

95 *"Unto us a child is born."*

FATHER, our hearts we lift
Up to thy gracious throne,
And thank thee for the precious gift
Of thine incarnate Son!

2 The gift unspeakable
We thankfully receive,
And to the world thy goodness tell,
And to thy glory live.

3 Jesus, the holy child,
Doth, by his birth, declare
That God and man are reconciled,
And one in him we are.

4 A peace on earth he brings,
Which never more shall end;
The Lord of hosts, the King of kings,
Declares himself our friend.

5 His kingdom from above
He doth to us impart,
And pure benevolence and love
O'erflow the faithful heart:

6 Changed in a moment, we
The sweet attraction find,
With open arms of charity
Embracing all mankind.

7 O might they all receive
The new-born Prince of peace!
And meekly in his Spirit live,
And in his love increase!

8 Till he convey us home,
Cry every soul aloud,
Come, thou Desire of nations, come,
And take us up to God!

32 *"And thy saints bless thee."*

ALMIGHTY Maker, God,
How glorious is thy name!
Thy wonders how diffused abroad,
Throughout creation's frame!

2 In native white and red
The rose and lily stand,
And free from pride their beauties spread
To show thy skilful hand.

3 The lark mounts up the sky,
With unambitious song;
And bears her Maker's praise on high,
Upon her artless tongue.

4 Fain would I rise and sing
To my Creator too:
Fain would my heart adore my King,
And give him praises due.

5 Descend, celestial fire,
And seize me from above!
Wrap me in flames of pure desire,
A sacrifice of love!

6 Let joy and worship spend
The remnant of my days;
And to my God my soul ascend
In sweet perfumes of praise.

976 *At table.*

THOU art that bread of life,
That meat which shall remain,
Be it our only care and strife
Thy blessed self to gain.

2 Give, Lord, and always give
Th' immortalizing food,
And strengthen us by grace to live
The glorious life of God.

622 *"Sing praises to God."*

AWAKE, and sing the song
Of Moses and the Lamb;
Tune every heart and every tongue,
To praise the Saviour's name.

2 Sing of his dying love;
Sing of his rising power;
Sing how he intercedes above
For those whose sins he bore.

3 Tell, in seraphic strains,
What he has done for you;
How he has taken off your chains,
And form'd your hearts anew.

4 His faithfulness proclaim
While life to you is given;
Join hands and hearts to praise his name,
Till we all meet in heaven.

246 *The church militant.*

URGE on your rapid course,
Ye blood-besprinkled bands;
The heavenly kingdom suffers force;
'Tis seized by violent hands.

2 See there the starry crown
That glitters through the skies!
Satan, the world, and sin, tread down,
And take the glorious prize!

3 Through much distress and pain,
Through many a conflict here,
Through blood, ye must the entrance gain,
Yet O, disdain to fear.

4 "Courage!" your Captain cries,
(Who all your toil foreknew,)
"Toil ye shall have; yet all despise,
I have o'ercome for you."

5 The world cannot withstand
Its ancient Conqueror:
The world must sink beneath the hand
Which arms us for a war.

6 This is the victory—
Before our faith they fall;
Jesus hath died for you and me;
Believe, and conquer all!

163 *Jacob's Ladder.*

WHAT doth the Ladder mean
Sent down from the Most High?
Fasten'd to earth, its foot is seen,—
Its summit to the sky.

2 Lo! up and down the scale
The angels swiftly move;
And God, the great Invisible,
Himself appears above!

3 Jesus that Ladder is,
Th' Incarnate Deity,
Partaker of celestial bliss,
And human misery.

4 Sent from his high abode,
To sleeping mortals given,
He stands, and man unites to God,
And earth connects with heaven.

20 *Glory of God.*

O ALL-CREATING God,
At whose supreme decree
Our body rose, a breathing clod,
Our souls sprang forth from thee:

2 For this thou hast design'd,
And form'd us man for this;
To know, and love thyself, and find
In thee our endless bliss.

LONGSDALE. S. M. Double. From CORRELLI.

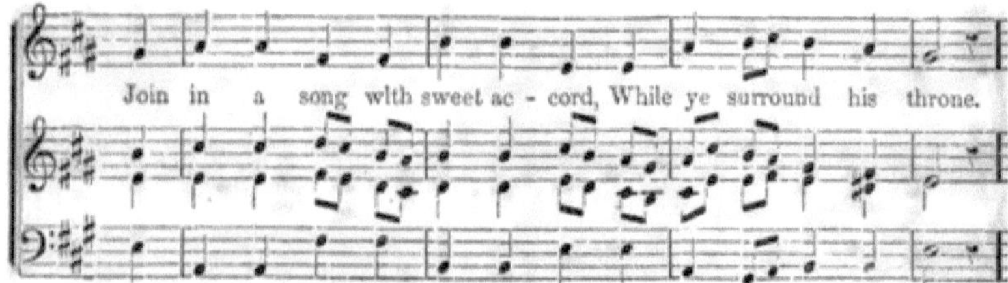

621 *Rejoicing in God.*

COME, ye that love the Lord,
And let your joys be known,
Join in a song with sweet accord,
While ye surround his throne.

2 The sorrows of the mind
Be banish'd from the place!
Religion never was design'd
To make our pleasures less.

3 Let those refuse to sing
Who never knew our God;
But servants of the heavenly King
May speak their joys abroad.

4 The God that rules on high,
That all the earth surveys,
That rides upon the stormy sky,
And calms the roaring seas;

5 This awful God is ours,
Our Father and our Love;
He will send down his heavenly powers
To carry us above.

6 There we shall see his face,
And never, never sin;
There, from the rivers of his grace,
Drink endless pleasures in:

7 Yea, and before we rise
To that immortal state,
The thoughts of such amazing bliss
Should constant joys create.

8 The men of grace have found
Glory begun below:
Celestial fruit on earthly ground
From faith and hope may grow.

9 The hill of Zion yields
A thousand sacred sweets,
Before we reach the heavenly fields,
Or walk the golden streets.

10 Then let our songs abound,
And every tear be dry;
We're marching thro' Immanuel's ground
To fairer worlds on high.

657 *Eph* vi. 10.

SOLDIERS of Christ, arise!
And put your armour on,
Strong in the strength which God supplies
Through his Eternal Son;
Strong in the Lord of hosts,
And in his mighty power,
Who in the strength of Jesus trusts
Is more than conqueror.

2 Stand, then, in his great might,
With all his strength endued;
But take, to arm you for the fight,
The panoply of God.
That having all things done,
And all your conflicts past,
Ye may o'ercome through Christ alone,
And stand entire at last.

3 From strength to strength go on,
Wrestle, and fight, and pray:
Tread all the powers of darkness down,
And win the well-fought day;
Still let the Spirit cry,
In all his soldiers, "Come,"
Till Christ the Lord descend from high,
And take the conqu'rors home.

The sorrows of the mind Be ban - ish'd from the place! Re-
li - igon nev - er was des-ign'd To make our pleasures less.

643 *Trust in Providence.*

COMMIT thou all thy griefs
And ways into His hands,
To His sure trust and tender care,
Who earth and heaven commands:
Who points the clouds their course,
Whom winds and seas obey,
He shall direct thy wandering feet,
He shall prepare thy way.

2 Thou on the Lord rely,
So safe shalt thou go on;
Fix on his work thy steadfast eye,
So shall thy work be done.
No profit canst thou gain
By self-consuming care;
To him commend thy cause, his ear
Attends the softest prayer.

3 Thine everlasting truth,—
Father, thy ceaseless love,
Sees all thy children's wants, and knows
What best for each will prove;
And whatsoe'er thou will'st,
Thou dost, O King of kings!
What's thy unerring wisdom's choice,
Thy power to being brings!

4 Thou everywhere hast sway,
And all things serve thy might;
Thine every act pure blessing is,
Thy path unsullied light.
When thou arisest Lord,
What shall thy work withstand?
When all thy children want, thou giv'st;
Who, who shall stay thy hand?

644 *Trust in Providence.*

GIVE to the winds thy fears;
Hope, and be undismay'd;
God hears thy sighs, and counts thy tears;
God shall lift up thy head:
Through waves, and clouds, and storms,
He gently clears thy way;
Wait thou his time, so shall this night
Soon end in joyous day.

2 Still heavy is thy heart?
Still sink thy spirits down?
Cast off the weight, let fear depart,
And every care be gone.
What though thou rulest not,
Yet heaven, and earth, and hell,
Proclaim, God sitteth on the throne,
And ruleth all things well.

3 Leave to his sovereign sway,
To choose and to command;
So shalt thou, wond'ring, own his way,
How wise; how strong his hand!
Far, far above thy thought
His counsel shall appear,
When fully he the work hath wrought
That caused thy needless fear.

4 Thou seest our weakness, Lord,
Our hearts are known to thee;
O lift thou up the sinking hand,
Confirm the feeble knee
Let us in life, in death,
Thy steadfast truth declare;
And publish, with our latest breath,
Thy love and guardian care.

ATHOL. S. M.

B. HARRISON.

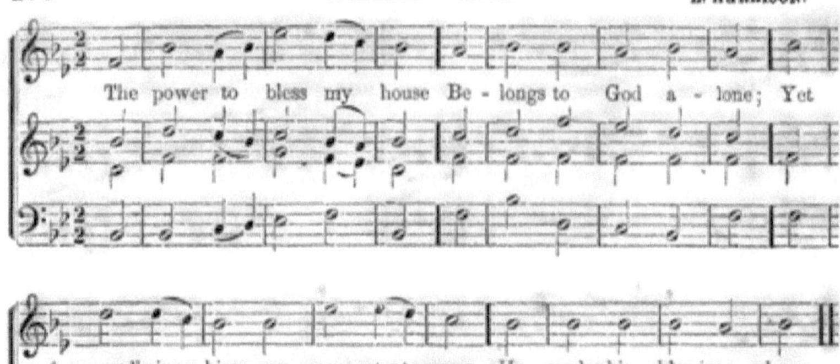

995 *Household consecrated to God.*

THE power to bless my house
  Belongs to God alone;
Yet rendering him my constant vows,
  He sends his blessings down.

2 Shall I not then engage
  My house to serve the Lord,
To search the soul-converting page,
  And feed upon his word,—

3 To ask with faith and hope
  The grace which he supplies,
In prayer and praise to offer up
  Their daily sacrifice?

4 Let each his sin eschew,
  Through thy restraining grace,
Our father Abrah'm's steps pursue,
  And walk in all thy ways.

5 Saviour of men, incline
  The hearts which thou hast made,
Which thou hast bought with blood divine,
  To ask thy promised aid.

6 Me and my house receive,
  Thy family t' increase,
And let us in thy favour live,
  And let us die in peace.

842 *Psalm lxxvi.*

GOD is in Judah known,
  Israel extols his name,
In Salem he has placed his throne,
  In Zion lives his fame.

2 There did he break the shield,
  The battle and the bow,
There to his glorious might shall yield
  The desolating foe.

3 There is the spoiler spoil'd,
  The proud have slept their sleep;
There are the men of battle foil'd,
  In one promiscuous heap.

4 When thy rebuke is heard,
  Both horse and car expire;
Thou God of Jacob shalt be fear'd,
  O who shall meet thine ire!

5 Heaven utter'd thy decree,
  Earth, trembling, paused to hear:
Soon shall the world thy judgments see,
  Thy saints no more shall fear.

6 Man's wrath shall give thee praise,
  His wrath shall be restrain'd!
A tribute to Jehovah raise,
  From all the world obtain'd!

7 Let all adore his reign,
  And own his peerless worth!
The power of chiefs he will restrain,
  And quell the kings of earth.

610 *Putting on the Lord Jesus.*

GRACIOUS Redeemer, hear!
  Into my soul come down;
Let it throughout my life appear
  That I have Christ put on.

2 O plant in me thy mind!
  O fix in me thy home!
So shall I cry to all mankind,
  Come to the waters, come!

3 Jesus is full of grace,
  To all his bowels move;
Behold in me, ye fallen race,
  That God is only love.

394 *Surrendering the heart.*

WHEN shall thy love constrain,
And force me to thy breast?
When shall my soul return again
To her eternal rest?

2 Ah! what avails my strife,
My wand'ring to and fro?
Thou hast the words of endless life:
Ah! whither should I go?

3 Thy condescending grace
To me did freely move,
It calls me still to seek thy face,
And stoops to ask my love.

4 Lord, at thy feet I fall,
I groan to be set free;
I fain would now obey the call,
And give up all for thee.

5 To rescue me from wo,
Thou didst with all things part,
Didst lead a suff'ring life below,
To gain my worthless heart.

6 My worthless heart to gain,
The God of all that breathe
Was found in fashion as a man,
And died a cursed death.

1017 *For a minister before preaching.*

EQUIP me for the war,
And teach my hands to fight;
My simple, upright heart prepare,
And guide my words aright.

2 Control my every thought;
My whole of sin remove;
Let all my works in thee be wrought—
Let all be wrought in love.

3 O arm me with the mind,
Meek Lamb, that was in thee!
And let my knowing zeal be join'd
With perfect charity.

4 With calm and temper'd zeal
Let me enforce thy call;
And vindicate thy gracious will,
Which offers life to all.

5 O may I love like thee!
In all thy footsteps tread!
Thou hatest all iniquity,
But nothing thou hast made.

6 O may I learn the art,
With meekness to reprove!
To hate the sin with all my heart,
But still the sinner love.

568 *The Christian race.*

RACERS of Christ, arise!
Stand forth, prepare to run!
Toward the goal lift up your eyes,
And manfully go on.

2 'Tis true, the race is sharp;
But, then, it is not long;
Each racer soon will take his harp,
And warble Zion's song.

3 Open the eye of faith,
And view the crown on high;
Break through the snares of sin and death,
To endless glory fly.

4 Nearer approaches make;
Run to the heavenly land;
The prize of your high calling take
In your victorious hand.

994 *Psalm* cxxxiii.

BLESS'D are the sons of peace,
Whose hearts and hopes are one;
Whose kind designs to serve and please
Through all their actions run.

2 Bless'd is the pious house
Where zeal and friendship meet,
Their songs of praise, their mingled vows
Make their communion sweet.

3 Thus on the heavenly hills
The saints are bless'd above,
Where joy, like morning dew, distils,
And all the air is love.

172 *Various offices.*

THOU very paschal Lamb,
Whose blood for us was shed,
Through whom we out of Egypt came,
Thy ransom'd people lead.

2 Angel of gospel grace!
Fulfil thy character;
To guard and feed the chosen race,
In Israel's camp appear.

3 Throughout the desert way
Conduct us by thy light;
Be thou a cooling cloud by day,
A cheering fire by night.

4 Our fainting souls sustain
With blessings from above,
And ever on thy people rain
The manna of thy love.

955 *Morning.*

SEE how the morning sun
Pursues his shining way,
And wide proclaims his Maker's praise
With every bright'ning ray

2 Thus would my rising soul
Its heavenly Parent sing;
And to its great Original
The humble tribute bring.

3 Serene I laid me down,
Beneath his guardian care;
I slept, and I awoke, and found
My kind Preserver near!

4 My life I would anew
Devote, O Lord, to thee;
And in thy service I would spend
A long eternity.

750 *Hebrew missionaries.*

ALMIGHTY God of love,
Set up th' attracting sign,
And summon whom thou dost approve
For messengers divine.

2 From favor'd Abrah'm's seed
The new apostles choose,
In isles and continents to spread
The dead-reviving news.

3 O send thy servants forth,
To call the Hebrews home!
From East, and West, and South and North,
Let all the wand'rers come

4 With Israel's myriads seal'd,
Let all the nations meet,
And show the mystery fulfill'd,
The family complete!

1052 *Doxology.*

GIVE to the Father praise,
Give glory to the Son;
And to the Spirit of his grace
Be equal honour done.

321 *Wants.*

JESUS, my strength, my hope,
On thee I cast my care,
With humble confidence look up,
And know thou hear'st my prayer.

Give me on thee to wait,
Till I can all things do,
On thee, almighty to create,
Almighty to renew.

2 I want a sober mind,
A self-renouncing will,
That tramples down, and casts behind
The baits of pleasing ill;

A soul inured to pain,
To hardship, grief, and loss,
Bold to take up, firm to sustain,
The consecrated cross.

3 I want a godly fear,
A quick-discerning eye,
That looks to thee when sin is near,
And sees the tempter fly;

A spirit still prepared,
And arm'd with jealous care,
For ever standing on its guard,
And watching unto prayer.

398 *Struggling after Christ.*

AH! whither should I go,
Burden'd, and sick, and faint!
To whom should I my troubles show,
And pour out my complaint?

My Saviour bids me come;
Ah! why do I delay?
He calls the weary sinner home,
And yet from him I stay!

13

2 What is it keeps me back,
From which I cannot part?
Which will not let the Saviour take
Possession of my heart!

Some cursed thing unknown
Must surely lurk within;
Some idol which I will not own,
Some secret bosom sin.

3 Jesus, the hind'rance show,
Which I have fear'd to see;
And let me now consent to know
What keeps me back from thee.

Searcher of hearts, in mine
Thy trying power display;
Into its darkest corners shine,
And take the veil away.

4 I now believe in thee,
Compassion reigns alone;
According to my faith, to me
O let it, Lord, be done!

In me is all the bar,
Which thou wouldst fain remove;
Remove it, and I shall declare
That God is only love.

936 *"The violent take it by force."*

O MAY thy powerful word
Inspire a feeble worm
To rush into thy kingdom, Lord,
And take it as by storm!

2 O may we all improve
The grace already given,
To seize the crown of perfect love,
And scale the mount of heaven!

876 *Opening the exercises.*

O WHAT a mighty change
Shall Jesus' suff'rers know,
While o'er the happy plains they range,
Incapable of wo!

No ill-requited love
Shall there our spirits wound:
No base ingratitude above,—
No sin in heaven is found.

2 There all our griefs are spent!
There all our sorrows end:
We cannot there the fall lament
Of a departed friend!—

A brother dead to God,
By sin, alas! undone:
No father there, in passion loud,
Cries, "O my son! my son!"

3 No slightest touch of pain,
Nor sorrow's least alloy,
Can violate our rest, or stain
Our purity of joy!

In that eternal day
No clouds or tempests rise:
There gushing tears are wiped away
For ever from our eyes.

912 *Opening the exercises.*

THE praying spirit breathe,
The watching power impart;
From all entanglements beneath
Call off my anxious heart:

My feeble mind sustain,
By worldly thoughts opprest,
Appear, and bid me turn again
To my eternal rest.

2 Swift to my rescue come,
Thine own this moment seize;
Gather my wand'ring spirit home,
And keep in perfect peace:

Suffer'd no more to rove
O'er all the earth abroad,
Arrest the pris'ner of thy love,
And shut me up in God.

359 *The warning.*

AND will the Judge descend?
And must the dead arise?
And not a single soul escape
His all-discerning eyes!—

2 And from his righteous lips
Shall this dread sentence sound,
And through the millions of the damn'd
Spread black despair around?—

3 "Depart from me, accursed,
To everlasting flame,
For rebel-angels first prepared,
Where mercy never came."

4 How will my heart endure
The terrors of that day,
When earth and heaven before his face,
Astonish'd, shrink away?

5 But ere that trumpet shakes
The mansions of the dead,
Hark, from the gospel's gentle voice
What joyful tidings spread!

6 Ye sinners, seek his grace,
Whose wrath ye cannot bear;
Fly to the shelter of his cross,
And find salvation there.

SHIPPENSBURG. S. M.

130 *Funeral of a Christian.*

AND must this body die,
This well-wrought frame decay?
And must these active limbs of mine
Lie mould'ring in the clay?

2 Corruption, earth, and worms,
Shall but refine this flesh,
Till my triumphant spirit comes
To put it on afresh.

3 God my Redeemer lives,
And ever from the skies
Looks down, and watches all my dust,
Till he shall bid it rise.

4 Array'd in glorious grace
Shall these vile bodies shine;
And every shape, and every face,
Be heavenly and divine.

5 These lively hopes we owe,
Lord, to thy dying love:
O may we bless thy grace below,
And sing thy grace above!

376 *Praying for repentance.*

O THAT I could repent!
O that I could believe!
Thou, by thy voice omnipotent,
The rock in sunder cleave!

Thou, by thy two-edged sword,
My soul and spirit part;
Strike with the hammer of thy word,
And break my stubborn heart.

2 Saviour and Prince of peace,
The double grace bestow;
Unloose the bands of wickedness,
And let the captive go:

Grant me my sins to feel,
And then the load remove;
Wound, and pour in, my wounds to he
The balm of pard'ning love.

3 This is thy will, I know,
That I should holy be;
Should let my sins this moment go,
This moment turn to thee:

O might I now embrace
Thy all-sufficient power!
And never more to sin give place,
And never grieve thee more!

339 *Invitation and warning.*

THE Lord declares his will,
And keeps the world in awe;
Amidst the smoke on Sinai's hill
Breaks out his fiery law.

2 The Lord reveals his face,
And smiling from above,
Sends down the gospel of his grace,
Th' epistles of his love.

3 These sacred words impart
Our Maker's just commands;
The pity of his melting heart,
And vengeance of his hands.

4 We read the heavenly word,
We take the offer'd grace,
Obey the statutes of the Lord,
And trust his promises.

1052 *Doxology.*

GIVE to the Father praise,
Give glory to the Son;
And to the Spirit of his grace
Be equal honour done.

DOVER. S. M.

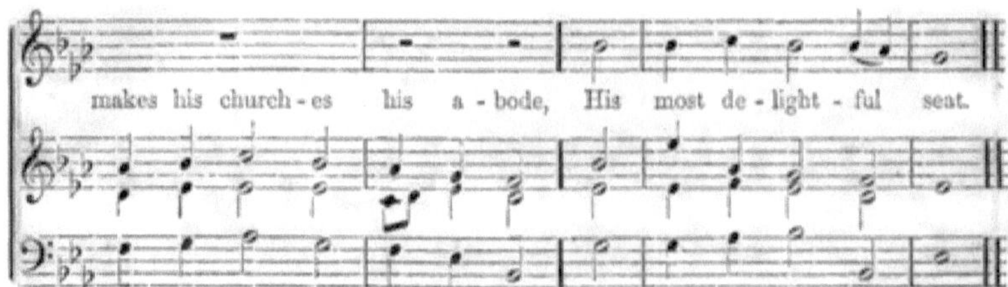

788 *Psalm* xlviii.

GREAT is the Lord our God,
And let his praise be great:
He makes his churches his abode,
His most delightful seat.

2 These temples of his grace,
How beautiful they stand!
The honours of our native place,
And bulwarks of our land.

3 In Sion God is known
A refuge in distress;
How bright has his salvation shone
Through all her palaces!

4 In every new distress
We'll to his house repair;
We'll think upon his wondrous grace,
And seek deliverance there.

607 *Eccles.* xi. 6.

SOW in the morn thy seed,
At eve hold not thy hand;
To doubt and fear give thou no heed—
Broad-cast it o'er the land.

2 Beside all waters sow,
The highway furrows stock,
Drop it where thorns and thistles grow—
Scatter it on the rock.

3 The good, the fruitful ground,
Expect not here nor there;
O'er hill, o'er dale, by plots, 'tis found:
Go forth, then, everywhere.

4 Thou know'st not which shall thrive,
The late or early sown,
Grace keeps the precious germ alive,
When and wherever strown:

5 And duly shall appear,
In verdure, beauty, strength,
The tender blade, the stalk, the ear,
And the full corn at length.

6 Thou canst not toil in vain:
Cold, heat, and moist, and dry,
Shall foster and mature the grain
For garners in the sky.

7 Thence, when the final end,
The day of God is come,
The angel reapers shall descend,
And heaven sing, "Harvest home!"

576 *Depending on Christ.*

JESUS, my truth, my way,
My sure, unerring light,
On thee my feeble steps I stay,
Which thou wilt guide aright.

2 My wisdom and my guide,
My counsellor thou art;
O never let me leave thy side,
Or from thy paths depart!

3 I lift mine eyes to thee,
Thou gracious, bleeding Lamb,
That I may now enlighten'd be,
And never put to shame.

4 Never will I remove
Out of thy hands my cause,
But rest in thy redeeming love,
And hang upon thy cross.

5 Teach me the happy art,
In all things to depend
On thee; O never, Lord, depart,
But love me to the end.

51 *Psalm xix. After sermon.*

I HEAR thy word with love,
And I would fain obey;
Lord, send thy Spirit from above
To guide me, lest I stray!

2 O who can ever find
The errors of his ways?
Yet with a bold, presumptuous mind,
I would not dare transgress.

3 Warn me of every sin,
Forgive my secret faults,
And cleanse this guilty soul of mine,
Whose crimes exceed my thoughts.

4 While with my heart and tongue
I spread thy praise abroad;
Accept the worship and the song,
My Saviour and my God.

130 *1 John v. 6.*

THIS, this is he that came,
By water and by blood!
Jesus is our atoning Lamb,
Our sanctifying God.

2 See from his wounded side
The mingled current flow,
The water and the blood applied
Shall wash us white as snow.

3 The water cannot cleanse,
Before the blood we feel,
To purge the guilt of all our sins,
And our forgiveness seal.

4 But both in Jesus join,
Who speaks our sins forgiven,
And gives the purity divine
That makes us meet for heaven.

338 *Isaiah xlv. 21–25.*

THE Lord on high proclaims
His Godhead from his throne;
"Mercy and justice are the names
By which I will be known.

2 "Ye dying souls, that sit
In darkness and distress,
Look, from the borders of the pit
To my recov'ring grace."

3 Sinners shall hear the sound,
Their thankful tongues shall own
"Our righteousness and strength are found
In thee, the Lord, alone."

4 In thee shall Israel trust,
And see their guilt forgiven,
God will pronounce the sinners just,
And take the saints to heaven.

271 *For an increase of labourers.*

LORD of the harvest, hear
Thy needy servants' cry;
Answer our faith's effectual prayer,
And all our wants supply.

2 On thee we humbly wait,
Our wants are in thy view;
The harvest truly, Lord, is great,
The labourers are few.

3 Convert, and send forth more
Into thy church abroad,
And let them speak thy word of power,
As workers with their God.

4 O let them spread thy name,
Their mission fully prove;
Thy universal grace proclaim,
Thine all-redeeming love!

Give to the Father praise, Give glo - ry to the Son; And
to the Spi - rit of his grace, Be e - qual hon - or done.

1022 *For a servant.*

JESUS, the Lord most high,
Thy poorest servant own;
And give me strength to glorify,
And serve my God alone;

Inspired with humble fear,
And principled with grace,
My earthly master to revere,
As standing in thy place.

2 Whate'er for man I do,
I do as to the Lord;
From God, the merciful and true,
Expecting my reward:

And whether bond or free,
I know thou wilt approve,
And crown our services to thee,
With thy eternal love.

875 *Opening the exercises.*

SAVIOUR of sinful men,
Thy goodness we proclaim,
Which brings us here to meet again,
And triumph in thy name:

Thy mighty name hath been
Our safeguard and our tower;
Hath saved us from the world and sin,
And all th' accuser's power.

2 Jesus, take all the praise,
That still on earth we live,
Unspotted in so foul a place,
And innocently grieve:

We shall from Sodom flee,
When perfected in love;
And haste to better company
Who wait for us above.

3 Awhile in flesh disjoin d,
Our friends that went before
We soon in paradise shall find,
And meet to part no more,

In yon thrice happy seat,
Waiting for us they are:
And thou shalt there a husband meet!
And I a parent there!

272 *Opening Conference.*

AND are we yet alive,
And see each other's face?
Glory and praise to Jesus give
For his redeeming grace!

Preserved by power divine
To full salvation here,
Again in Jesus' praise we join,
And in his sight appear.

2 What troubles have we seen,
What conflicts have we past,
Fightings without, and fears within,
Since we assembled last;

But out of all the Lord
Hath brought us by his love;
And still he doth his help afford,
And hides our life above.

3 Then let us make our boast
Of his redeeming power,
Which saves us to the uttermost,
Till we can sin no more:

Let us take up the cross,
Till we the crown obtain;
And gladly reckon all things loss,
So we may Jesus gain.

245 *The church militant.*

JESUS, the Conqu'ror, reigns,
In glorious strength array'd,
His kingdom over all maintains,
And bids the earth be glad.

2 Ye sons of men, rejoice
In Jesus' mighty love:
Lift up your heart, lift up your voice,
To him who rules above.

3 Extol his kingly power;
Kiss the exalted Son,
Who died, and lives to die no more,
High on his Father's throne.

4 Our Advocate with God,
He undertakes our cause,
And spreads through all the earth abroad
The vict'ry of his cross.

5 That bloody banner see,
And, in your Captain's sight,
Fight the good fight of faith with me,
My fellow-soldiers, fight.

6 In mighty phalanx join'd,
To battle all proceed;
Arm'd with th' unconquerable mind
Which was in Christ your head.

230 *Psalm xlviii. 10—14.*

FAR as thy name is known
The world declares thy praise;
Thy saints, O Lord, before thy throne,
Their songs of honour raise.

2 With joy let Judah stand
On Zion's chosen hill,
Proclaim the wonders of thy hand,
And counsels of thy will.

3 Let strangers walk around
The city where we dwell;
Compass and view the holy ground,
And mark the building well—

4 The order of thy house,
The worship of thy court,
The cheerful songs, the solemn vows,—
And make a fair report.

5 How decent and how wise!
How glorious to behold!
Beyond the pomp that charms the eyes,
And rites adorn'd with gold.

6 The God we worship now
Will guide us till we die:
Will be our God while here below,
And ours above the sky.

194 *Grace.*

GRACE! 'tis a charming sound!
Harmonious to my ear!
Heaven with the echo shall resound,
And all the earth shall hear.

2 Grace first contrived the way
To save rebellious man;
And all the steps *that* grace display
Which drew the wondrous plan.

3 Grace taught my wandering feet
To tread the heavenly road;
And new supplies each hour I meet,
While pressing on to God.

4 Grace all the work shall crown,
Through everlasting days;
It lays in heaven the topmost stone,
And well deserves the praise.

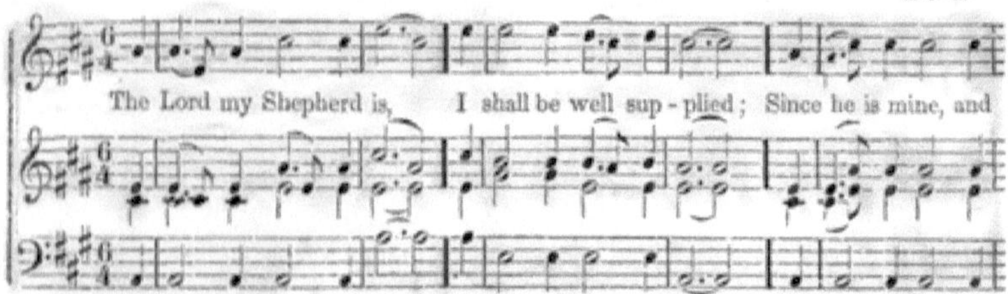

53 *Psalm xxiii.*

THE Lord my Shepherd is,
I shall be well supplied;
Since he is mine, and I am his,
What can I want beside?

2 He leads me to the place
Where heavenly pasture grows,
Where living waters gently pass,
And full salvation flows.

3 If e'er I go astray,
He doth my soul reclaim,
And guides me in his own right way,
For his most holy name.

4 While he affords his aid,
I cannot yield to fear;
Tho' I should walk thro' death's dark shade,
My Shepherd's with me there.

5 In spite of all my foes,
Thou dost my table spread;
My cup with blessings overflows,
And joy exalts my head.

6 The bounties of thy love
Shall crown my following days;
Nor from thy house will I remove,
Nor cease to speak thy praise.

180 *Psalm xlv. 1—7.*

MY Saviour and my King,
Thy beauties are divine;
Thy lips with blessings overflow,
And ev'ry grace is thine.

2 Now make thy glories known,
Gird on thy dreadful sword,
And ride in majesty, to spread
The conquests of thy word.

3 Strike through thy stubborn foes,
Or melt their hearts t' obey;
While justice, meekness, grace, and truth
Attend thy glorious way.

4 Thy laws, O God, are right,
Thy throne shall ever stand;
And thy victorious gospel proves
A sceptre in thy hand.

5 Thy Father and thy God,
Hath, without measure, shed
His Spirit, like a joyful oil,
T' anoint thy sacred head.

855 *General Thanksgiving.*

THROUGH all the lofty sky,
Through all th' inferior ground,
Th' Almighty Maker shines confess'd,
And pours his blessings round.

2 Each year the teeming earth
With flowers and fruits is crown'd;
And grass, and herbs, and harvests, grow,
And send their joys around.

3 The world of waters yields
A rich supply of food,
And distant lands their treasures send
Upon the rolling flood.

4 To serve and bless our land
The elements conspire;
And mercies mix themselves with earth,
With ocean, air, and fire.

5 O that the sons of men
To God their songs would raise,
And celebrate his power and love
In never-ceasing praise.

220 *His influences sought.*

COME, Holy Spirit, come,
With energy divine,
And on this poor, benighted soul,
With beams of mercy shine.

2 O melt this frozen heart;
This stubborn will subdue;
Each evil passion overcome,
And form me all anew!

3 The profit will be mine,
But thine shall be the praise;
And unto thee will I devote
The remnant of my days.

624 *A single eye.*

TEACH me, my God and King,
In all things thee to see;
And what I do, in anything,
To do it as for thee;—

2 To scorn the senses' sway,
While still to thee I tend:
In all I do be thou the way,
In all be thou the end.

3 All may of thee partake:
Nothing so small can be,
But draws, when acted for thy sake,
Greatness and worth from thee.

4 If done t' obey thy laws,
E'en servile labours shine:
Hallow'd is toil, if this the cause,
The meanest work divine.

5 Thee, then, my God and King,
In all things may I see;
And what I do, in anything,
May it be done for thee!

594 *Luke xii. 35—37.*

YE servants of the Lord,
Each in his office wait,
Observant of his heavenly word,
And watchful at his gate.

2 Let all your lamps be bright,
And trim the golden flame;
Gird up your loins, as in his sight,
For awful is his name.

3 Watch, 'tis your Lord's command:
And while we speak he's near;
Mark the first signal of his hand,
And ready all appear.

4 O happy servant he
In such a posture found!
He shall his Lord with rapture see,
And be with honour crown'd.

281 *Adult baptism.*

RITES change not, Lord, the heart,—
Undo the evil done,—
Or, with the utter'd name, impart
The nature of thy Son.

2 To meet our desp'rate want,
There gush'd a mystic flood;
O from His heart's o'erflowing font
Baptize this soul with blood!

3 Be grace from Christ our Lord,
And love from God supreme,
By the communing Spirit pour'd
In a perpetual stream.

1052 *Doxology.*

GIVE to the Father praise,
Give glory to the Son;
And to the Spirit of his grace
Be equal honour done.

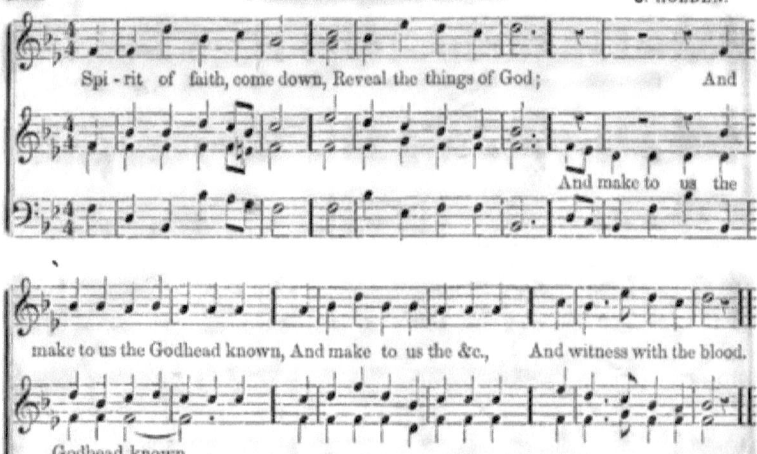

212 *Spirit of Faith.*

SPIRIT of faith, come down,
Reveal the things of God;
And make to us the Godhead known,
And witness with the blood:

'Tis thine the blood t' apply,
And give us eyes to see;
Who did for every sinner die,
Hath surely died for me.

2 No man can truly say
That Jesus is the Lord,
Unless thou take the veil away,
And breathe the living word:

Then, only then, we feel
Our int'rest in his blood;
And cry, with joy unspeakable,
"Thou art my Lord, my God!"

3 O that the world might know
The all-atoning Lamb!
Spirit of faith, descend, and show
The virtue of his name:

The grace which all may find,
The saving power, impart;
And testify to all mankind,
And speak in every heart.

4 Inspire the living faith,
Which whosoe'er receives,
The witness in himself he hath,
And consciously believes:

The faith that conquers all,
And doth the mountain move,
And saves whoe'er on Jesus call
And perfects them in love.

493 *The new creation.*

THE thing my God doth hate,
That I no more may do,
Thy creature, Lord, again create,
And all my soul renew:

My soul shall then, like thine,
Abhor the thing unclean,
And sanctified by love divine,
For ever cease from sin.

2 That blessed law of thine,
Jesus, to me impart,
The Spirit's law of life divine,
O write it in my heart!

Implant it deep within
Whence it may ne'er remove,
The law of liberty from sin,
The perfect law of love.

3 Thy nature be my law,
Thy spotless sanctity;
And sweetly every moment draw
My happy soul to thee.

Soul of my soul remain!
Who didst for all fulfil,
In me, O Lord, fulfil again
Thy heavenly Father's will!

1052 *Doxology.*

GIVE to the Father praise,
Give glory to the Son;
And to the Spirit of his grace
Be equal honour done.

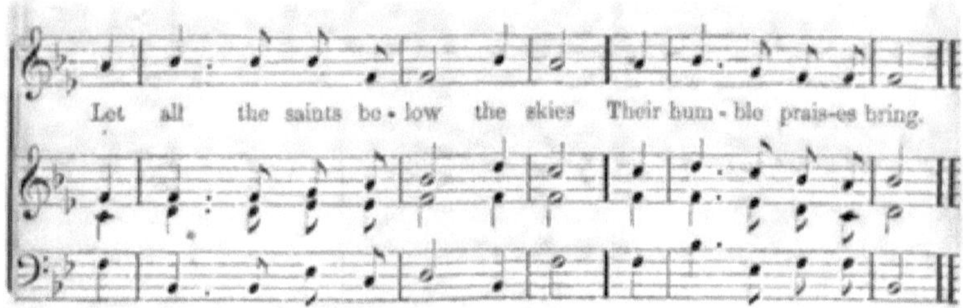

199 *Jude* 14, 25.

TO God, the only wise,
 Our Saviour and our King,
Let all the saints below the skies
 Their humble praises bring.

2 'Tis his almighty love—
 His counsel and his care—
Preserves us safe from sin and death,
 And every hurtful snare.

3 He will present our souls,
 Unblemish'd and complete,
Before the glory of his face,
 With joys divinely great.

4 Then all the chosen seed
 Shall meet around the throne;
Shall bless the conduct of his grace,
 And make his wonders known.

5 To our Redeemer, God,
 Wisdom with power belongs;
Immortal crowns of majesty,
 And everlasting songs.

47 *Psalm* viii.

O LORD, our heavenly King,
 Thy name is all divine;
Thy glories round the earth are spread,
 And o'er the heavens they shine.

2 Out of the mouths of babes
 And sucklings thou canst draw
Surprising honours to thy name;
 And strike the world with awe.

3 When to thy works on high
 I raise my wond'ring eyes,
And see the moon, complete in light
 Adorn the darksome skies;

4 When I survey the stars,
 And all their shining forms,
Lord, what is man, that worthless thing,
 Akin to dust and worms?

5 Lord, what is worthless man,
 That thou shouldst love him so?
Next to thine angels is he placed,
 And Lord of all below.

6 Thine honours crown his head,
 While beasts, like slaves, obey,
And birds that cut the air with wings,
 And fish that cleave the sea.

7 O Lord, our heavenly King,
 Thy name is all divine:
Thy glories round the earth are spread,
 And o'er the heavens they shine.

472 1 *Peter*, i. 8.

NOT with our mortal eyes
 Have we beheld the Lord;
Yet we rejoice to hear his name,
 And love him in his word.

2 On earth we want the sight
 Of our Redeemer's face;
Yet, Lord, our inmost thoughts delight
 To dwell upon thy grace.

3 And when we taste thy love,
 Our joys divinely grow
Unspeakable, like those above,
 And heaven begins below.

546 *Waiting at the Cross.*

FATHER, I dare believe
Thee merciful and true;
Thou wilt my guilty soul forgive,
My fallen soul renew

2 Come, then, for Jesus' sake,
And bid my heart be clean:
An end of all my troubles make,
An end of all my sin.

3 I cannot wash my heart,
But by believing thee,
And waiting for thy blood t' impart
The spotless purity.

4 While at the cross I lie,
Jesus, the grace bestow;
Now thy all-cleansing blood apply,
And I am white as snow.

590 *"Praying always, with all prayer."*

TO God your every want
In instant prayer display:
Pray always; pray, and never faint;
Pray, without ceasing, pray.

2 In fellowship,—alone—
To God with faith draw near:
Approach his courts, besiege his throne,
With all the power of prayer:

3 Go to his temple, go,
Nor from his altar move:
Let every house his worship know,
And every heart his love.

4 To God your spirits dart;
Your souls in words declare;
Or groan to him who reads the heart,
Th' unutterable prayer;

5 His mercy now implore,
And now show forth his praise;
In shouts, or silent awe, adore
His miracles of grace.

6 Pour out your souls to God,
And bow them with your knees;
And spread your hearts and hands abroad,
And pray for Sion's peace.

7 Your guides and brethren bear
For ever on your mind;
Extend the arms of mighty prayer,
In grasping all mankind.

922 *Wants.*

I WANT a true regard,
A single, steady aim,
Unmoved by threat'ning or reward,
To thee and thy great name;

A jealous, just concern
For thine immortal praise;
A pure desire that all may learn,
And glorify thy grace.

2 I rest upon thy word,
The promise is for me;
My succour and salvation, Lord,
Shall surely come from thee:

But let me still abide,
Nor from my hope remove,
Till thou my patient spirit guide
Into thy perfect love.

887 *Psalm cxxxvii. 5, 6.*

I LOVE thy kingdom, Lord,
The house of thine abode,
The church our bless'd Redeemer bought
With his own precious blood.

2 I love thy church, O God!
Her walls before thee stand,
Dear as the apple of thine eye,
And graven on thy hand.

3 If e'er to bless her sons
My voice or hands deny,
These hands let useful skill forsake,
This voice in silence die.

4 If e'er my heart forget
Her warfare, or her wo,
Let every joy this heart forsake,
And every grief o'erflow.

5 For her my tears shall fall,
For her my prayers ascend;
To her my cares and toils be given,
Till toils and cares shall end.

6 Beyond my highest joy
I prize her heavenly ways,
Her sweet communion, solemn vows,
Her hymns of love and praise.

309 *Closing the service.*

O WHAT a taste is this
Which now in Christ we know,
An earnest of our glorious bliss,
Our heaven begun below!

2 When he the table spreads,
How royal is the cheer!
With rapture we lift up our heads,
And own that God is here.

3 The Lamb for sinners slain,
Who died to die no more,
Let all the ransom'd sons of men,
With all his hosts adore:

4 Let earth and heaven be join'd,
His glories to display,
And hymn the Saviour of mankind
In one eternal day.

586 *Watchfulness.*

GRACIOUS Redeemer, shake
This slumber from my soul!
Say to me now, "Awake, awake!
And Christ shall make thee whole."

2 Lay to thy mighty hand;
Alarm me in this hour;
And make me fully understand
The thunder of thy power!

3 Give me on thee to call,
Always to watch and pray,
Lest I into temptation fall,
And cast my shield away.

4 For each assault prepared,
And ready may I be;
For ever standing on my guard,
And looking up to thee.

5 O do thou always warn
My soul of evil near!
When to the right or left I turn,
Thy voice still let me hear:

6 "Come back! this is thy way!
Come back! and walk herein!"
O may I hearken and obey,
And shun the paths of sin!

SILVER STREET. S. M.

I. SMITH.

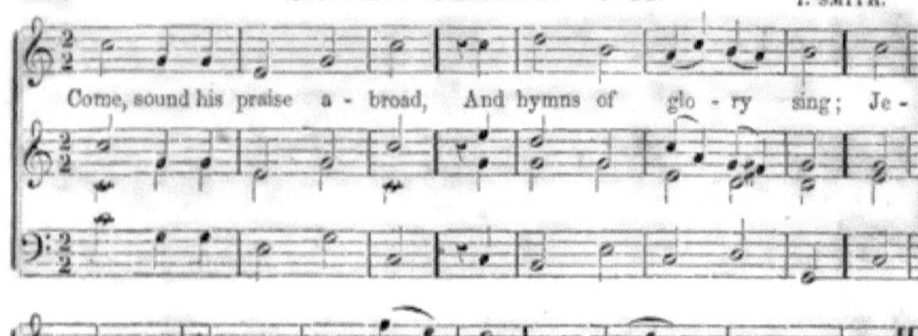

57 *Psalm xcv. Opening worship.*

COME, sound his praise abroad,
And hymns of glory sing;
Jehovah is the sovereign God,
The universal King.

2 He form'd the deep unknown;
He gave the seas their bound;
The watery worlds are all his own,
And all the solid ground.

3 Come, worship at his throne;
Come, bow before the Lord;
We are his work, and not our own,
He form'd us by his word.

4 To-day attend his voice,
Nor dare provoke his rod;
Come, like the people of his choice,
And own your gracious God.

248 *The church militant.*

ANGELS your march oppose,
Who still in strength excel,
Your secret, sworn, eternal foes,
Countless, invisible:

2 From thrones of glory driven,
By flaming vengeance hurl'd,
They throng the air, and darken heaven,
And rule this lower world.

3 But shall believers fear?
But shall believers fly?
Or see the bloody cross appear,
And all their powers defy?

4 By all hell's host withstood,
We all hell's host o'erthrow;
And conqu'ring them through Jesus' blood,
We on to conquer go.

5 Our Captain leads us on;
He beckons from the skies,
And reaches out a starry crown,
And bids us take the prize.

6 "Be faithful unto death;
Partake my victory,
And thou shalt wear this glorious wreath,
And thou shalt reign with me."

600 *Psalm cxxv.*

WHO in the Lord confide,
And feel his sprinkled blood,
In storms and hurricanes abide,
Firm as the mount of God:

Steadfast, and fix'd, and sure,
His Sion cannot move;
His faithful people stand secure,
In Jesus' guardian love.

2 As round Jerusalem
The hilly bulwarks rise,
So God protects and covers them
From all their enemies.

On every side he stands,
And for his Israel cares,
And safe in his almighty hands
Their souls for ever bears.

3 But let them still abide
In thee, all-gracious Lord,
Till every soul is sanctified,
And perfectly restored:

The men of heart sincere
Continue to defend;
And do them good, and save them here,
And love them to the end.

465 *Adoption.*

BEHOLD! what wondrous grace
The Father hath bestow'd
On sinners of a mortal race,—
To call them sons of God!

2 'Tis no surprising thing
That we should be unknown;
The Jewish world knew not their King,
God's everlasting Son.

3 Nor does it yet appear
How great we must be made;
But when we see our Saviour here,
We shall be like our Head.

4 A hope, so much divine,
May trials well endure,
May purge our souls from sense and sin,
As Christ, the Lord, is pure.

5 If in my Father's love
I share a filial part,
Send down thy Spirit, like a dove,
To rest upon my heart.

6 We would no longer lie
Like slaves beneath the throne;
My faith shall Abba, Father, cry,
And thou the kindred own.

390 *The humbled Pharisee.*

A GOODLY, formal saint,
I long appear'd in sight;
By self and Satan taught to paint
My tomb, my nature, white.

2 The Pharisee within
Still undisturb'd remain'd;
The strong man, arm'd with guilt of sin,
Safe in his palace reign'd.

3 But, O! the jealous God
In my behalf came down;
Jesus himself the stronger show'd,
And claim'd me for his own.

4 My spirit he alarm'd,
And brought into distress;
He shook and bound the strong man arm'd
In his self-righteousness.

5 Faded my virtuous show,
My form without the power;
This sin-convincing Spirit blew,
And blasted every flower.

6 My mouth was stopp'd, and shame
Cover'd my guilty face;
I fell on the atoning Lamb,
And I was saved by grace.

778 *Universal dissemination.*

JESUS, the word bestow,
The true immortal seed;
Thy gospel then shall greatly grow,
And all our land o'erspread;

Through earth extended wide
Shall mightily prevail,
Destroy the works of self and pride,
And shake the gates of hell.

2 Its energy exert
In the believing soul;
Diffuse thy grace through every part,
And sanctify the whole:

Its utmost virtue show
In pure, consummate love,
And fill with all thy life below,
And give us thrones above.

BOND. S. M. DOUBLE.

142

Resurrection.

"THE Lord is ris'n indeed;"
He lives to die no more;
He lives the sinner's cause to plead,
Whose curse and shame he bore.

2 "The Lord is ris'n indeed;"
Then hell has lost his prey;
With him is ris'n the ransom'd seed,
To reign in endless day.

3 "The Lord is ris'n indeed;"
Attending angels, hear;
Up to the courts of heaven, with speed,
The joyful tidings bear.

4 Then wake your golden lyres,
And strike each cheerful chord
Join, all ye bright, celestial choirs,
To sing our ris'n Lord.

595 *Keeping the charge of the Lord.*

A CHARGE to keep I have,
  A God to glorify;
A never-dying soul to save,
  And fit it for the sky;
To serve the present age,
  My calling to fulfil;—
O may it all my powers engage,
  To do my Master's will!

2 Arm me with jealous care,
  As in thy sight to live;
And, O thy servant, Lord, prepare,
  A strict account to give!
Help me to watch and pray,
  And on thyself rely,
Assured, if I my trust betray,
  I shall for ever die.

596 *A holy life.*

GOD of almighty love,—
  By whose sufficient grace
I lift my heart to things above,
  And humbly seek thy face,—
Through Jesus Christ, the just,
  My faint desires receive,
And let me in thy goodness trust,
  And to thy glory live.

2 Whate'er I say or do,
  Thy glory be my aim;
My off'rings all be offer'd through
  The ever blessed name.
Jesus, my single eye
  Be fix'd on thee alone:
Thy name be praised on earth, on high,
  Thy will by all be done!

3 Spirit of faith, inspire
  My consecrated heart;
Fill me with pure, celestial fire,
  With all thou hast and art.
My feeble mind transform,
  And, perfectly renew'd,
Into a saint exalt a worm—
  A worm exalt to God!

BOYLSTON. S. M.

L. MASON.

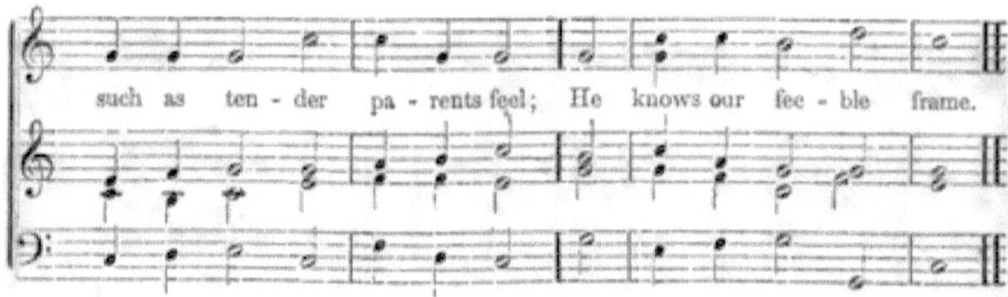

62 *Psalm ciii. 13—18.*

THE pity of the Lord,
 To those that fear his name,
Is such as tender parents feel;
 He knows our feeble frame.

2 He knows we are but dust,
 Scatter'd with ev'ry breath:
His anger, like a rising wind,
 Can send us swift to death.

3 Our days are as the grass,
 Or like the morning flower;
If one sharp blast sweep o'er the field,
 It withers in an hour.

4 But thy compassions, Lord,
 To endless years endure;
And children's children ever find
 Thy words of promise sure.

7 *The Trinity.*

FATHER, in whom we live,
 In whom we are and move,
The glory, power, and praise receive,
 Of thy creating love.

2 Let all the angel throng
 Give thanks to God on high,
While earth repeats the joyful song,
 And echoes through the sky.

3 Incarnate Deity,
 Let all the ransom'd race,
Render, in thanks, their lives to thee,
 For thy redeeming grace.

4 The grace to sinners show'd,
 Ye heavenly choirs, proclaim,
And cry, "Salvation to our God,
 Salvation to the Lamb!"

5 Spirit of holiness,
 Let all thy saints adore
Thy sacred energy, and bless
 Thy heart-renewing power.

6 Not angel tongues can tell
 Thy love's ecstatic height,
The glorious joy unspeakable,
 The beatific sight!

7 Eternal, Triune Lord,
 Let all the hosts above,
Let all the sons of men, record,
 And dwell upon thy love.

8 When heaven and earth are fled
 Before thy glorious face,
Sing, all the saints thy love hath made,
 Thine everlasting praise!

135 *The atoning sacrifice.*

NOT all the blood of beasts,
 On Jewish altars slain,
Could give the guilty conscience peace,
 Or wash away the stain.

2 But Christ, the heavenly Lamb,
 Takes all our sins away;
A sacrifice of nobler name,
 And richer blood than they.

3 My faith would lay her hand
 On that dear head of thine,—
While like a penitent I stand,
 And there confess my sin.

1052 *Doxology.*

GIVE to the Father praise,
 Give glory to the Son;
And to the Spirit of his grace,
 Be equal honour done.

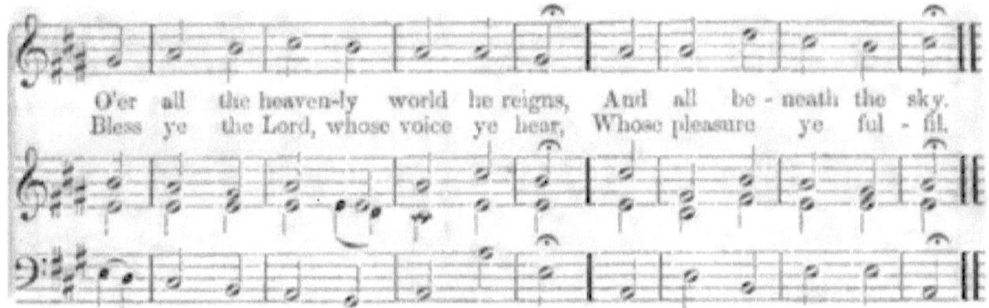
O'er all the heaven-ly world he reigns, And all be - neath the sky.
Bless ye the Lord, whose voice ye hear, Whose pleasure ye ful - fil.

Psalm ciii. 19–23.

3 Let the bright hosts who wait
The orders of their King,
And guard his churches when they pray,
Join in the praise they sing.

4 While all his wondrous works,
Through his vast kingdom, show
Their Maker's glory, thou, my soul,
Shalt sing his graces too.

BAIN. H. M. (Four 6s & Two 8s.)

Baptized into thy name, Mysterious One in Three, Our souls and bodies claim A sacri -
- fice to thee: We only live our faith to prove, The faith which works by humble love.

282

Adult.

BAPTIZED into thy name,
Mysterious One in Three,
Our souls and bodies claim
A sacrifice to thee:
We only live our faith to prove,
The faith which works by humble love.

2 O that our light may shine,
And all our lives express
The character divine,
The *real* holiness!
Then, then receive us up t' adore
The Triune God for evermore.

124 *"My Love is crucified."*

O LOVE Divine! what hast thou done!
Th' immortal God hath died for me!
The Father's co-eternal Son
Bore all my sins upon the tree!
Th' immortal God for me hath died:
My Lord, my Love, is crucified.

2 Behold him, all ye that pass by,
The bleeding Prince of life and peace!
Come, see, ye worms, your Maker die,
And say, was ever grief like his?
Come, feel with me his blood applied:
My Lord, my Love, is crucified;—

3 Is crucified for me and you,
To bring us rebels back to God:
Believe, believe the record true,
Ye all are bought with Jesus' blood;
Pardon for all flows from his side;
My Lord, my Love, is crucified.

4 Then let us sit beneath his cross,
And gladly catch the healing stream:
All things for him account but loss,
And give up all our hearts to him;
Of nothing think or speak beside,
My Lord, my Love, is crucified.

284 *Infant baptism.*

GOD of eternal truth and love,
Vouchsafe the promised aid we claim,
Thine own great ordinance approve,
The child, baptized into thy name,
Partaker of thy nature make,
And give him all thine image back.

2 Father, if such thy sovereign will,
If Jesus did the rite enjoin,
Annex thy hall'wing Spirit's seal,
And let thy grace attend the sign;
The seed of endless life impart,
Take for thine own this infant's heart.

3 Answer on him thy wisdom's end,
In present and eternal good;
Whate'er thou didst for man intend,
Whate'er thou hast on man bestow'd,
Unto this favour'd child be given,
Pardon, and holiness, and heaven.

4 In presence of thy heavenly host,
Thyself we faithfully require:
Come, Father, Son, and Holy Ghost,
By blood, by water, and by fire,
And fill up all thy human shrine,
And seal our souls for ever thine.

532 *The act of consecration.*

O GOD! what off'ring shall I give
To thee, the Lord of earth and skies?
My spirit, soul, and flesh receive,
A holy, living sacrifice;
Small as it is, 'tis all my store;
More shouldst thou have, if I had more.

2 Now, then, my God, thou hast my soul:
No longer mine, but thine I am:
Guard thou thine own, possess it whole!
Cheer it with hope, with love inflame!
Thou hast my spirit; there display
Thy glory to the perfect day.

3 Thou hast my flesh, thy hallow'd shrine,
Devoted solely to thy will
Here let thy light for ever shine:
This house still let thy presence fill:
O Source of life—live, dwell, and move
In me, till all my life be love!

608 *Sympathy.*

LET God, who comforts the distrest,
Let Israel's Consolation, hear:
Hear, Holy Ghost, our joint request,
And show thyself the Comforter;
And swell th' unutterable groan,
And breathe our wishes to the throne.

2 We weep for those that weep below,
And, burden'd for th' afflicted, sigh;
The various forms of human wo
Excite our softest sympathy,
Fill every heart with mournful care,
And draw out all our souls in prayer.

3 We wrestle for the ruin'd race,
By sin eternally undone,—
Unless thou magnify thy grace,
And make thy richest mercy known,
And make thy vanquish'd rebels find
Pardon in Christ for all mankind.

4 Father of everlasting love,
To every soul thy Son reveal,
Our guilt and suff'rings to remove,
Our deep, primeval wound to heal:
And bid the fallen race arise,
And turn our earth to paradise.

662 *The shield of faith.*

SURROUNDED by a host of foes,
Storm'd by a host of foes within;
Not swift to flee, nor strong t' oppose,
Single against hell, earth, and sin,—
Single, yet undismay'd, I am;
I dare believe in Jesus' name.

2 What though a thousand hosts engage,
A thousand worlds my soul to shake,
I have a shield shall quell their rage,
And drive the alien armies back;
Portray'd it bears a bleeding Lamb;
I dare believe in Jesus' name.

3 Salvation in his name there is;
Salvation from sin, death, and hell;
Salvation into glorious bliss;
How great salvation, who can tell?
But all he hath, for mine I claim;
I dare believe in Jesus' name.

125 *General redemption.*

WOULD Jesus have the sinner die?
Why hangs he then on yonder tree?
What means that strange expiring cry?
(Sinners, he prays for you and me:)
"Forgive them, Father, O forgive,
They know not that by me they live!"

2 Jesus, descended from above,
Our loss of Eden to retrieve,
Great God of universal love,
If all the world through thee may live,
In us a quick'ning spirit be,
And witness thou hast died for me.

3 Thou loving, all-atoning Lamb,
Thee—by thy painful agony,
Thy bloody sweat, thy grief and shame,
Thy cross and passion on the tree,
Thy precious death and life—I pray,
Take all, take all my sins away.

4 O let me kiss thy bleeding feet,
And bathe and wash them with my tears;
The story of thy love repeat
In every drooping sinner's ears;
That all may hear the quick'ning sound;
Since I, e'en I, have mercy found.

5 O let thy love my heart constrain,
Thy love for every sinner free;
That every fallen son of man
May taste the grace that found out me;
That all mankind with me may prove
Thy sovereign, everlasting love.

1027 *Trust in Providence.*

CAPTAIN of Israel's host, and Guide
Of all who seek the land above,
Beneath thy shadow we abide,
The cloud of thy protecting love:
Our strength, thy grace; our rule, thy word;
Our end, the glory of the Lord.

2 By thine unerring Spirit led,
We shall not in the desert stray;
We shall not full direction need,
Nor miss our providential way:
As far from danger as from fear,
While love, almighty love, is near.

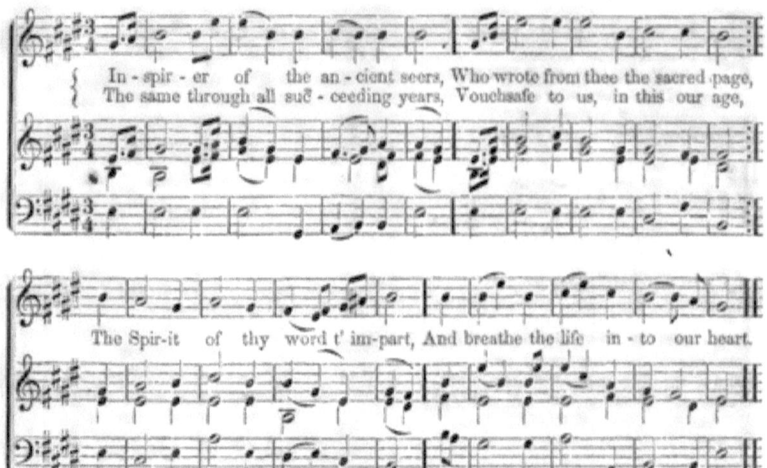

773 *Treasury of the word.*

INSPIRER of the ancient seers,
Who wrote from thee the sacred page,
The same through all succeeding years,
Vouchsafe to us, in this our age,
The Spirit of thy word t' impart,
And breathe the life into our heart.

2 Whene'er in error's paths we rove,
The living God through sin forsake,
Our conscience by thy word reprove,
Convince, and bring the wand'rers back;
Deep wounded by thy Spirit's sword,
And then by Gilead's balm restored.

3 The sacred lessons of thy grace,
Transmitted through thy word, repeat,
And train us up in all thy ways,
To make us in thy will complete:
Fulfil thy love's redeeming plan,
And bring us to a perfect man.

4 Furnish'd out of thy treasury,
O may we always ready stand
To help the souls redeem'd by thee,
In what their various states demand!
To teach, convince, correct, reprove;
And build them up in holiest love!

823 *Watch-night.*

HOW many pass the guilty night,
In revelling and frantic mirth!
The creature is their sole delight,
Their happiness the things of earth:
But O, suffice the season past!
We choose the better part at last.

2 We will not close our wakeful eyes,
We will not let our eyelids sleep,
But humbly lift them to the skies,
And all a solemn vigil keep;
So many nights on sin bestow'd,
Can we not watch one hour for God?

3 We can, O Jesus, for thy sake,
Devote our every hour to thee;
Speak but the word, our souls shall wake,
And sing with cheerful melody.
Thy praise shall our glad tongues employ,
And every heart shall dance for joy.

832 *Supplication.*

O WONDROUS power of faithful prayer!
What tongue can tell th' almighty grace?
God's hands or bound or open are,
As Moses or Elijah prays;
Let Moses in the Spirit groan,
And God cries out, "Let me alone!—

2 "Let me alone, that all my wrath
May rise, the wicked to consume!
While justice hears thy praying faith,
It cannot seal the sinner's doom:
My Son is in my servant's prayer,
And Jesus forces me to spare."

3 Father, we ask in Jesus' name;
In Jesus' power and spirit pray:
Divert thy vengeful thunder's aim!
O turn thy threat'ning wrath away!
Our guilt and punishment remove,
And magnify thy pard'ning love.

4 Father, regard thy pleading Son,
Accept his all-availing prayer;
And send a peaceful answer down,
In honour of our Spokesman there!
Whose blood proclaims our sins forgiven,
And speaks thy rebels up to heaven.

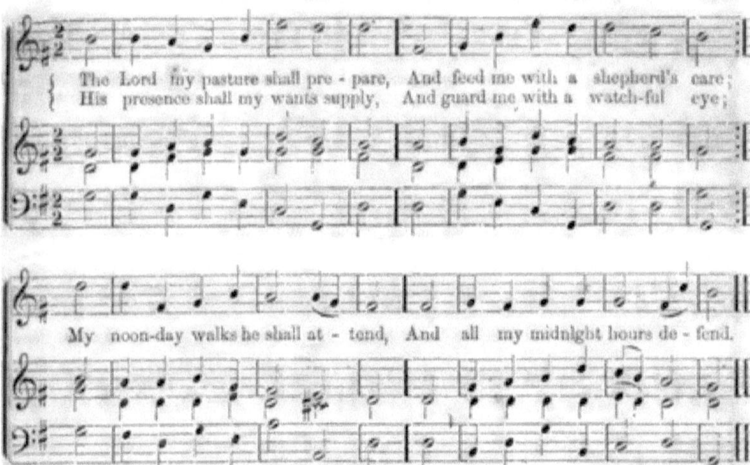

52 *Psalm* xxiii.

THE Lord my pasture shall prepare,
And feed me with a shepherd's care;
His presence shall my wants supply,
And guard me with a watchful eye:
My noon-day walks he shall attend,
And all my midnight hours defend.

2 When in the sultry glebe I faint,
Or on the thirsty mountain pant,
To fertile vales and dewy meads
My weary, wand'ring steps he leads,
Where peaceful rivers, soft and slow,
Amid the verdant landscapes flow.

3 Though in the paths of death I tread,
With gloomy horrors overspread,
My steadfast heart shall fear no ill,
For thou, O Lord, art with me still:
Thy friendly crook shall give me aid,
And guide me through the dreadful shade.

4 Though in a bare and rugged way,
Through devious, lonely wilds I stray,
Thy bounty shall my pains beguile,
The barren wilderness shall smile,
With sudden greens and herbage crown'd,
And streams shall murmur all around.

78 *Te Deum.*

INFINITE God, to thee we raise
Our hearts in solemn songs of praise;
By all thy works on earth adored,
We worship thee, the common Lord;
The everlasting Father own,
And bow ourselves before thy throne.

2 Thee all the choir of angels sings,
The Lord of hosts, the King of kings;
Cherubs proclaim thy praise aloud,
And seraphs shout the Triune God;
And "Holy, holy, holy," cry,
"Thy glory fills both earth and sky!"

3 God of the patriarchal race,
The ancient seers record thy praise;
The goodly apostolic band
In highest joy and glory stand;
And all the saints and prophets join
T' extol thy majesty divine.

4 Head of the martyrs' noble host,
Of thee they justly make their boast;
The church to earth's remotest bounds
Her heavenly Founder's praise resounds:
And strives with those around the throne
To hymn the mystic Three in One.

5 Father of endless majesty,
All might and love they render thee;
Thy true and only Son adore,
The same in dignity and power;
And God the Holy Ghost declare,
The saints' eternal Comforter.

795 *Youth devoted to God.*

CAPTAIN of our salvation, take
The souls we here present to thee,
And fit for thy great service make
These heirs of immortality:
And let them in thine image rise,
And then transplant to paradise.

2 Train up thy hardy soldiers, Lord,
In all their Captain's steps to tread!
Or send them to proclaim thy word,
Thy gospel through the world to spread;
Freely as they receive to give,
And preach the death by which we live.

LOVING KINDNESS. L. M. 6 LINES. (SIX 8s.)

470 *Glowing gratitude.*

WHAT am I, O thou glorious God!
  And what my father's house to thee?
That thou such mercies hast bestow'd
  On me, the vilest reptile, me!
I take the blessing from above,
And wonder at thy boundless love.

2 Me in my blood thy love pass'd by,
  And stopp'd, my ruin to retrieve;
Wept o'er my soul thy pitying eye;
  Thy bowels yearn'd, and sounded, "Live!"
Dying, I heard the welcome sound,
And pardon in thy mercy found.

3 Honour, and might, and thanks, and praise,
  I render to my pard'ning God!
Extol the riches of thy grace,
  And spread thy saving name abroad:
That only name to sinners given
Which lifts poor dying worms to heaven.

4 Jesus, I bless thy gracious power,
  And all within me shouts thy name!
Thy name let every soul adore,
  Thy power let every tongue proclaim;
Thy grace let every sinner know,
And find in thee his heaven below.

496 *All-absorbing love.*

JESUS, thy boundless love to me
  No thought can reach, no tongue declare;
O knit my thankful heart to thee,
  And reign without a rival there!
Thine wholly, thine alone, I am;
Be thou alone my constant flame.

2 O grant that nothing in my soul
  May dwell, but thy pure love alone!
O may thy love possess me whole,
  My joy, my treasure, and my crown!
Strange flames far from my heart remove,
My every act, word, thought, be love.

3 O love, how cheering is thy ray!
  All pain before thy presence flies;
Care, anguish, sorrow, melt away,
  Where'er thy healing beams arise;
O Jesus, nothing may I see,
Nothing desire or seek but thee!

4 Unwearied may I this pursue,
  Dauntless to the high prize aspire;

Hourly within my soul renew
  This holy flame, this heavenly fire;
And day and night be all my care
To guard the sacred treasure there.

571 *"Fervent in spirit."*

THEE will I love, my strength, my tower,
  Thee will I love, my joy, my crown,
Thee will I love with all my power,
  In all thy works, and thee alone;
Thee will I love, till the pure fire
Fills my whole soul with chaste desire.

2 Ah! why did I so late thee know,
  Thee, lovelier than the sons of men!
Ah! why did I no sooner go
  To thee, the only ease in pain!
Ashamed I sigh, and inly mourn
That I so late to thee did turn.

3 In darkness willingly I stray'd;
  I sought thee, yet from thee I roved;
Far wide my wand'ring thoughts were spread;
  Thy creatures more than thee I loved:
And now if more at length I see,
'Tis through thy light, and comes from thee.

4 I thank thee, uncreated Sun,
  That thy bright beams on me have shined,
I thank thee, who hast overthrown
  My foes, and heal'd my wounded mind;
I thank thee, whose enliv'ning voice
Bids my freed heart in thee rejoice.

5 Uphold me in the doubtful race,
  Nor suffer me again to stray;
Strengthen my feet, with steady pace
  Still to press forward in thy way;
My soul and flesh, O Lord of might,
Fill, satiate, with thy heavenly light.

6 Give to mine eyes refreshing tears;
  Give to my heart, chaste, hallow'd fires;
Give to my soul, with filial fears,
  The love that all heaven's host inspires;
That all my powers, with all their might,
In thy sole glory may unite.

7 Thee will I love, my joy, my crown,
  Thee will I love, my Lord, my God:
Thee will I love, beneath thy frown,
  Or smile,—thy sceptre or thy rod:
What though my flesh and heart decay,
Thee shall I love in endless day!

752 *For the Heathen.*

LORD over all, if thou hast made,
  Hast ransom'd every soul of man,—
Why is the grace so long delay'd?
  Why unfulfill'd the saving plan?
The bliss for Adam's race design'd,
When will it reach to all mankind?

2 Art thou the God of Jews alone,
  And not the God of Gentiles too?
To Gentiles make thy goodness known;
  Thy judgments to the nations show;
Awake them by the gospel call,
Light of the world, illumine all!

3 The servile progeny of Ham
  Seize as the purchase of thy blood,
Let all the heathen know thy name:
  From idols to the living God
The wand'ring Indian tribes convert,
And shine in every pagan heart!

4 As lightning launch'd from east to west,
  The coming of thy kingdom be;
To thee, by angel hosts confest,
  Bow every soul and every knee:
Thy glory let all flesh behold!
And then fill up thy heavenly fold.

986 *Death of a child.*

WITH all our soul, O Lord, we give
  The child thy love hath snatch'd away;
On earth we would not have him live,
  With us we would not have him stay;
The sacrifice long since was o'er,
We stand to what we gave before.

2 We *all* have left for Jesus' sake,
  And shall we grieve to part with *one!*
No, if a wish could call him back,
  We would not have our darling son
Brought from his everlasting rest,
Snatch'd from his heavenly Father's breast.

3 Pass a few fleeting days or years,
  And we shall see our child again;
When Jesus in the clouds appears,
  With him we shall in glory reign,
We and the children he hath given
Inseparably join'd in heaven.

929 *The universal Good invoked.*

COME, O thou universal Good!
  Balm of the wounded conscience, come!
The hungry, dying spirit's food,
  The weary, wand'ring pilgrim's home,—
Haven to take the shipwreck'd in,
My everlasting rest from sin!

2 Come, O my comfort and delight!
  My strength and health, my shield and sun,
My boast, and confidence, and might,
  My joy, my glory, and my crown,
My gospel hope, my calling's prize,
My tree of life, my paradise.

3 The secret of the Lord thou art,
  The mystery so long unknown,
Christ in a pure and perfect heart!
  The name inscribed in the white stone!
The life divine, the little leaven,
My precious pearl, my present heaven.

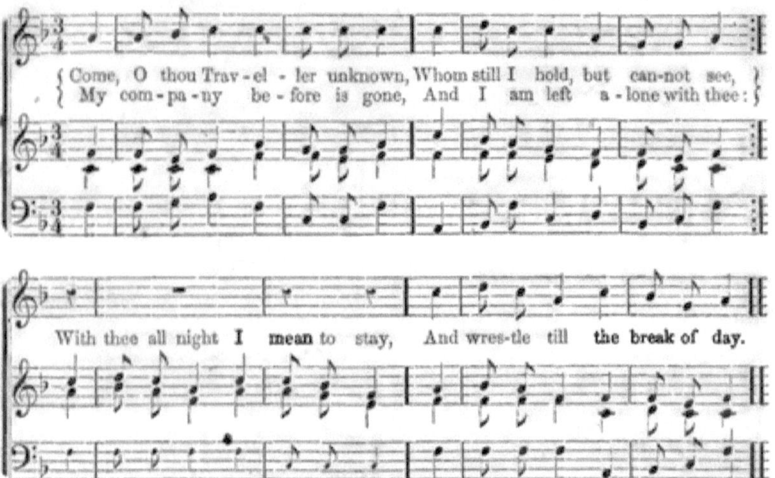

441 *Wrestling Jacob.*

COME, O thou Traveller unknown,
  Whom still I hold, but cannot see,
My company before is gone,
  And I am left alone with thee:
With thee all night I mean to stay,
And wrestle till the break of day.

2 I need not tell thee who I am;
  My sin and misery declare;
Thyself hast call'd me by my name,
  Look on thy hands and read it there;
But who, I ask thee, who art thou?
Tell me thy name, and tell me now.

3 In vain thou strugglest to get free,
  I never will unloose my hold;
Art thou the man that died for me?
  The secret of thy love unfold:
Wrestling, I will not let thee go,
Till I thy name, thy nature know.

4 Wilt thou not yet to me reveal
  Thy new, unutterable name?
Tell me, I still beseech thee, tell;
  To know it now resolved I am:
Wrestling, I will not let thee go,
Till I thy name, thy nature know.

5 What though my shrinking flesh complain,
  And murmur to contend so long?
I rise superior to my pain:
  When I am weak, then I am strong!
And when my all of strength shall fail,
I shall with the God-man prevail!

6 My strength is gone, my nature dies,
  I sink beneath thy weighty hand;
Faint, to revive—and fall, to rise;
  I fall, and yet by faith I stand;
I stand, and will not let thee go,
Till I thy name, thy nature know.

66 *Psalm cxiv.*

WHEN Israel out of Egypt came,
  And left the proud oppressor's land,
Supported by the great I AM,
  Safe in the hollow of his hand,
The Lord in Israel reign'd alone,
And Judah was his favourite throne.

2 The sea beheld his power, and fled,
  Disparted by the wondrous rod;
Jordan ran backward to its head,
  And Sinai felt th' incumbent God!
The mountains skipp'd like frighted rams,
The hills leap'd after them as lambs.

3 What ail'd thee, O thou trembling sea?
  What horror turn'd the river back?
Was nature's God displeased with thee?
  And why should hills or mountains shake?
Ye mountains huge, that skipp'd like rams?
Ye hills, that leap'd as frighted lambs?

4 Earth, tremble on, with all thy sons,
  In presence of thy awful Lord,
Whose power inverted nature owns,
  Her only law his sovereign word:
He shakes the centre with his rod,
And heaven bows down to Jacob's God.

5 Creation, varied by his hand,
  Th' omnipotent Jehovah knows!
The sea is turn'd to solid land,
  The rock into a fountain flows:
And all things, as they change, proclaim
The Lord eternally the same.

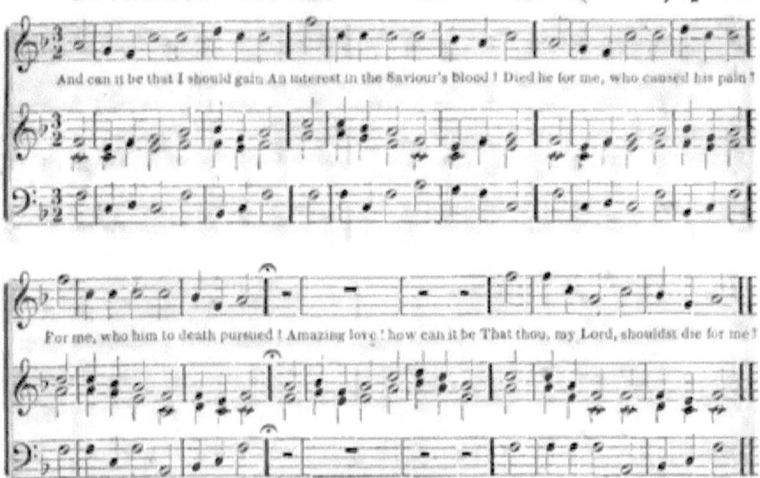

459 *An interest in Christ.*

AND can it be that I should gain
  An interest in the Saviour's blood?
Died he for me, who caused his pain?
  For me, who him to death pursued?
Amazing love! how can it be
That thou, my Lord, shouldst die for me?

2 'Tis myst'ry all! th' Immortal dies!
  Who can explore his strange design!
In vain the first-born seraph tries
  To sound the depths of love divine!
'Tis mercy all! let earth adore:
Let angel minds inquire no more.

3 He left his Father's throne above;
  (So free, so infinite his grace!)
Emptied himself of all but love,
  And bled for Adam's helpless race:
'Tis mercy all, immense and free,
For, O my God, it found out *me!*

4 Long my imprison'd spirit lay
  Fast bound in sin and nature's night:
Thine eye diffused a quick'ning ray;
  I woke; the dungeon flamed with light!
My chains fell off, my heart was free;
I rose, went forth, and follow'd thee.

5 No condemnation now I dread;
  Jesus, and all in him, is mine!
Alive in him my living Head,
  And clothed in righteousness divine,
Bold I approach th' eternal throne,
And claim the crown, through Christ, my own.

462 *Exulting in the atonement.*

NOW I have found the ground wherein
  Sure my soul's anchor may remain;
The wounds of Jesus—for my sin,
  Before the world's foundation slain,
Whose mercy shall unshaken stay,
When heaven and earth are fled away.

2 Father, thine everlasting grace
  Our scanty thought surpasses far:
Thy heart still melts with tenderness,
  Thy arms of love still open are,
Returning sinners to receive,
That mercy they may taste, and live.

3 O love, thou bottomless abyss,
  My sins are swallow'd up in thee;
Cover'd is my unrighteousness,
  Nor spot of guilt remains on me,
While Jesus' blood, through earth and skies,
Mercy, free, boundless mercy, cries!

4 By faith I plunge me in this sea,
  Here is my hope, my joy, my rest;
Hither, when hell assails, I flee;
  I look into my Saviour's breast;
Away, sad doubt and anxious fear,
Mercy is all that's written there.

5 Though waves and storms go o'er my head,
  Though strength, and health, and friends, be gone,
Though joys be wither'd all and dead,
  Though every comfort be withdrawn,—
On this my steadfast soul relies,
Father, thy mercy never dies.

6 Fix'd on this ground will I remain,
  Though my heart fail, and flesh decay;
This anchor shall my soul sustain,
  When earth's foundations melt away;
Mercy's full power I then shall prove,
Loved with an everlasting love.

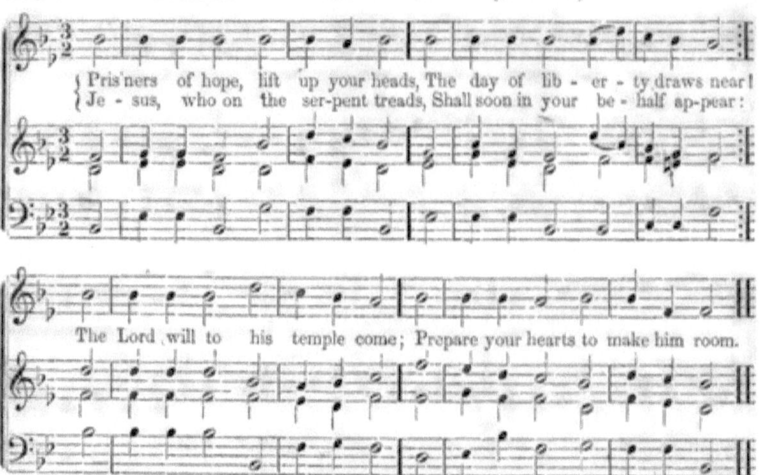

515 *Prisoners of hope.*

PRIS'NERS of hope, lift up your heads,
 The day of liberty draws near!
Jesus, who on the serpent treads,
 Shall soon in your behalf appear:
The Lord will to his temple come;
Prepare your hearts to make him room.

2 Ye all shall find whom in his word
 Himself hath caused to put your trust,
The Father of our dying Lord
 Is ever to his promise just;
Faithful, if we our sins confess,
To cleanse from all unrighteousness.

3 O ye of fearful hearts, be strong!
 Your downcast eyes and hands lift up!
Ye shall not be forgotten long
 Hope to the end, in Jesus hope!
Tell him, ye wait his grace to prove;
And cannot fail, if God is love!

4 Pris'ners of hope, be strong, be bold,
 Cast off your doubts, disdain to fear!
Dare to believe! on Christ lay hold!
 Wrestle with Christ in mighty prayer
Tell him, "We will not let thee go,
Till we thy name, thy nature know."

560 *The pilgrim's song.*

LEADER of faithful souls, and Guide
 Of all that travel to the sky,
Come, and with us, e'en us, abide,
 Who would on thee alone rely;
On thee alone our spirits stay,
While held in life's uneven way.

2 Strangers and pilgrims here below,
 The earth we know is not our place;
But hasten through the vale of wo,
 And, restless to behold thy face,
Swift to our heavenly country move,
Our everlasting home above.

3 We have no 'biding city here,
 But seek a city out of sight;
Thither our steady course we steer,
 Aspiring to the plains of light,
Jerusalem, the saints' abode,
Whose founder is the living God.

4 Patient th' appointed race to run,
 This weary world we cast behind;
From strength to strength we travel on,
 The New Jerusalem to find;
Our labour this, our only aim,
To find the New Jerusalem.

5 Through thee, who all our sins hast borne,
 Freely and graciously forgiven,
With songs to Zion we return,
 Contending for our native heaven,—
That palace of our glorious King;
We find it nearer while we sing.

6 E'en now we taste the pleasures there!
 A cloud of spicy odours comes,
Soft wafted by the balmy air,
 Sweeter than Araby's perfumes:
From Zion's top the breezes blow,
And cheer us in the vale below!

7 Raised by the breath of love divine,
 We urge our way with strength renew'd;
The church of the first-born to join,
 We travel to the mount of God;
With joy upon our heads arise,
And meet our Saviour in the skies.

287 *The institution of the Lord's supper.*

IN that sad memorable night,
When Jesus was for us betray'd,
He left his death-recording rite,
He took, and bless'd, and brake the bread,
And gave his own their last bequest,
And thus his love's intent exprest:

2 "Take, eat, this is my body, given
To purchase life and peace for you,
Pardon, and holiness, and heaven;
Do this my dying love to show:
Accept your precious legacy,
And thus, my friends, remember me."

3 He took into his hands the cup,
To crown the sacramental feast,
And full of kind concern look'd up,
And gave to them what he had blest:
"And drink ye all of this," he said,
"In solemn mem'ry of the dead.

4 "This is my blood, which seals the new
Eternal cov'nant of my grace:
My blood so freely shed for you,
For you and all the sinful race;
My blood that speaks your sins forgiven,
And justifies your claim to heaven.

5 "The grace which I to all bequeath,
In this divine memorial take,
And, mindful of your Saviour's death,
Do this, my foll'wers, for my sake,
Whose dying love hath left behind
Eternal life for all mankind."

151 *Priesthood of Christ.*

ENTER'D the holy place above,
Cover'd with meritorious scars,
The tokens of his dying love
Our great High Priest in glory bears;
He pleads his passion on the tree,
He shows himself to God for me.

2 Before the throne my Saviour stands,
My Friend and Advocate appears:
My name is graven on his hands,
And him the Father always hears;
While low at Jesus' cross I bow,
He hears the blood of sprinkling now.

3 This instant now I may receive
The answer of his powerful prayer:
This instant now by him I live,
His prevalence with God declare;
And soon my spirit, in his hands,
Shall stand where my Forerunner stands.

336 *The universal invitation.*

SEE, sinners, in the gospel glass,
The Friend and Saviour of mankind!
Not one of all th' apostate race
But may in him salvation find!
His thoughts, and words, and actions, prove,
His life and death—that God is love.

2 Behold the Lamb of God, who bears
The sins of all the world away!
A servant's form he meekly wears,
He sojourns in a house of clay,
His glory is no longer seen,
But God with God is man with men.

3 See where the God incarnate stands,
And calls his wand'ring creatures home:
He all day long spreads out his hands;
Come, weary souls, to Jesus come!
Ye all may hide you in his breast,
Believe, and he will give you rest.

4 "Ah! do not of my goodness doubt,
My saving grace for all is free;
I will in nowise cast him out
That comes a sinner unto me:
I can to none myself deny;
Why, sinners, will ye perish, why?"

1035 *"He is able to succour"*—

WHEN gath'ring clouds around I view,
And days are dark, and friends are few,
On Him I lean, who, not in vain,
Experienced every human pain,
He sees my wants, allays my fears,
And counts and treasures up my tears.

2 If aught should tempt my soul to stray
From heavenly virtue's narrow way,
To fly the good I would pursue,
Or do the sin I would not do;
Still He who felt temptation's power,
Shall guard me in that dangerous hour.

3 When vexing thoughts within me rise,
And, sore dismay'd, my spirit dies,
Yet He, who once vouchsafed to bear
The sick'ning anguish of despair,
Shall sweetly soothe, shall gently dry,
The throbbing heart, the streaming eye.

4 When, sorr'wing, o'er some stone I bend,
Which covers all that was a friend,
And from his voice, his hand, his smile,
Divides me, for a little while,
Thou, Saviour, seest the tears I shed,
For thou didst weep o'er Laz'rus dead.

5 And O! when I have safely pass'd
Through every conflict but the last,
Still, still unchanging, watch beside
My painful bed, for thou hast died;
Then point to realms of cloudless day,
And wipe the latest tear away.

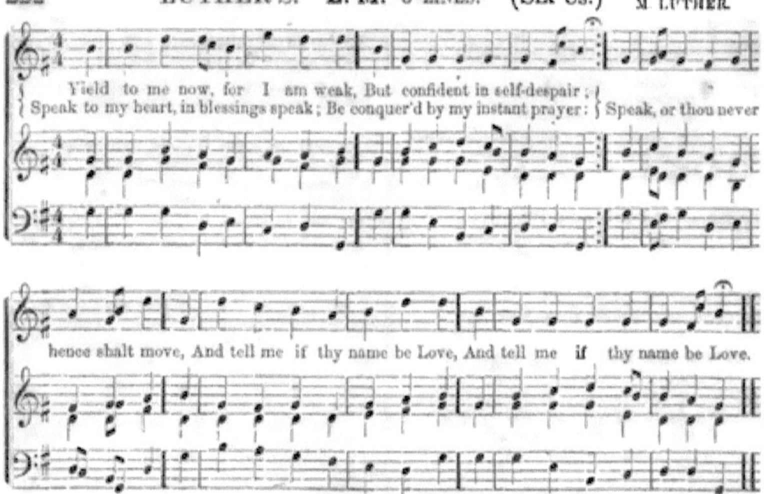

442 *Wrestling Jacob.*

YIELD to me now, for I am weak,
  But confident in self-despair;
Speak to my heart, in blessings speak;
  Be conquer'd by my instant prayer:
Speak, or thou never hence shalt move,
And tell me if thy name be Love.

2 'Tis Love! 'tis Love! thou diedst for me;
  I hear thy whisper in my heart;
The morning breaks, the shadows flee;
  Pure, universal love thou art:
To me, to all, thy bowels move,
Thy nature and thy name is Love.

3 My prayer hath power with God; the grace
  Unspeakable I now receive;
Through faith I see thee face to face;
  I see thee face to face and live!
In vain I have not wept and strove;
Thy nature and thy name is Love.

4 I know thee, Saviour, who thou art,
  Jesus, the feeble sinner's Friend:
Nor wilt thou with the night depart,
  But stay and love me to the end:
Thy mercies never shall remove;
Thy nature and thy name is Love.

5 The Sun of righteousness on me
  Hath ris'n, with healing in his wings;
Wither'd my nature's strength, from thee
  My soul its life and succour brings;
My help is all laid up above;
Thy nature and thy name is Love.

6 Lame as I am, I take the prey;
  Hell, earth, and sin, with ease o'ercome;
I leap for joy, pursue my way,
  And, as a bounding hart, fly home;
Through all eternity to prove
Thy nature and thy name is Love.

318 *Opening morning service.*

GREAT God, this hallow'd day of thine
  Demands our souls' collected powers,
May we employ in works divine
  These solemn and devoted hours:
O may our souls adoring own
The grace which calls us to thy throne.

2 Hence, ye vain cares and trifles, fly!
  Where God resides, appear no more:
Omniscient Lord, thy piercing eye
  Doth every secret thought explore;
O may thy grace our thoughts refine,
And fix our hearts on things divine!

573 *Self-renunciation.*

MASTER, I own thy lawful claim,
  Thine, wholly thine, I long to be!
Thou seest, at last, I willing am,
  Where'er thou goest to follow thee;
Myself in all things to deny;
Thine, wholly thine, to live and die.

2 Whate'er my sinful flesh requires,
  For thee I cheerfully forego;
My covetous and vain desires,
  My hopes of happiness below;
My senses' and my passions' food,
And all my thirst for creature-good.

3 Pleasure, and wealth, and praise, no more
  Shall lead my captive soul astray;
My fond pursuits I all give o'er,
  Thee, only thee, resolved t' obey:
My own in all things to resign,
And know no other will but thine.

219 *The Indwelling God.*

I WANT the spirit of power within,
 Of love, and of a healthful mind;
Of power, to conquer inbred sin;
 Of love to thee and all mankind;
Of health, that pain and death defies,
Most vig'rous when the body dies.

2 When shall I hear the inward voice,
 Which only faithful souls can hear?
Pardon, and peace, and heavenly joys,
 Attend the promised Comforter:
O come, and righteousness divine,
And Christ, and all with Christ, are mine!

3 O that the Comforter would come!
 Nor visit as a transient guest,
But fix in me his constant home,
 And keep possession of my breast:
And make my soul his loved abode,
And temple of indwelling God!

4 Come, Holy Ghost, my heart inspire!
 Attest that I am born again;
Come, and baptize me now with fire,
 Nor let thy former gifts be vain:
I cannot rest in sins forgiven;
Where is the earnest of my heaven?—

5 Where the indubitable seal,
 That ascertains the kingdom mine?
The powerful stamp I long to feel,
 The signature of love divine!
O shed within my heart abroad
Fulness of love, of heaven, of God!

46 *Opening worship.*

LO! God is here! let us adore,
 And own how dreadful is this place!
Let all within us feel his power,
 And silent bow before his face!
Who know his power, his grace who prove,
Serve him with awe, with rev'rence love.

2 Lo! God is here! him day and night
 Th' united choirs of angels sing;
To him enthroned above all height,
 Heaven's host their noblest praises bring;
Disdain not, Lord, our meaner song,
Who praise thee with a stamm'ring tongue.

3 Gladly the toys of earth we leave,
 Wealth, pleasure, fame, for thee alone:
To thee our will, soul, flesh, we give;
 O take! O seal them for thine own!
Thou art the God, thou art the Lord:
Be thou by all thy works adored!

4 Being of beings! may our praise
 Thy courts with grateful fragrance fill:
Still may we stand before thy face,
 Still hear and do thy sovereign will;
To thee may all our thoughts arise,
Ceaseless, accepted sacrifice.

5 As flowers their opening leaves display,
 And glad drink in the solar fire,
So may we catch thy every ray,
 So may thy influence us inspire;
Thou beam of the eternal beam!
Thou purging fire, thou quick'ning flame!

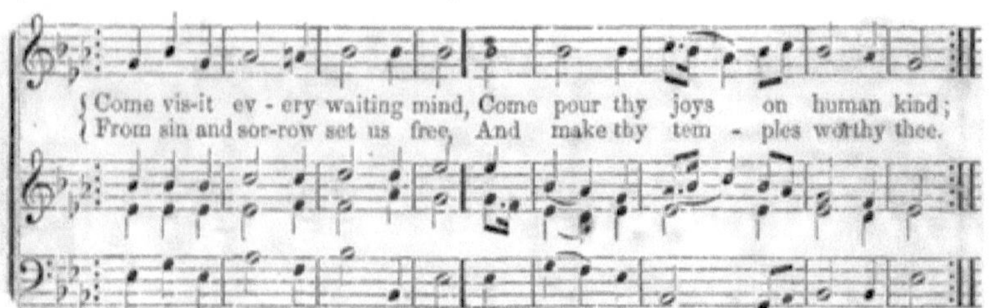

200 *Veni Creator.*

CREATOR, Spirit, by whose aid
The world's foundations first were laid,
Come visit every waiting mind,
Come pour thy joys on human kind;
From sin and sorrow set us free,
And make thy temples worthy thee.

2 O Source of uncreated heat,
The Father's promised Paraclete!
Thrice holy Fount, immortal Fire,
Our hearts with heavenly love inspire:
Come, and thy sacred unction bring,
To sanctify us while we sing.

3 Plenteous of grace, descend from high,
Rich in thy sevenfold energy!
Thou strength of His almighty hand,
Whose power does heaven and earth command,
Refine and purge our earthly parts,
And stamp thine image on our hearts.

4 Create all new; our wills control,
Subdue the rebel in our soul;
Chase from our minds th' infernal foe,
And peace, the fruit of faith, bestow:
And, lest again we go astray,
Protect and guide us in the way.

5 Immortal honour, endless fame,
Attend th' almighty Father's name;
The Saviour, Son, be glorified,
Who for lost man's redemption died:
And equal adoration be,
Eternal Comforter, to thee!

829 *Public fast.*

O GOD, thy righteousness we own:
Judgment is at thy house begun!
With humble awe thy rod we bear,
And guilty in thy sight appear:
We cannot in thy judgment stand;
But sink beneath thy mighty hand.

2 Our mouth as in the dust we lay,
And still for mercy, mercy, pray:
Unworthy to behold thy face;
Unfaithful stewards of thy grace;
Our sin and wickedness we own,
And deeply for acceptance groan.

3 Lord, do not drive us from thy face,
A stiff-neck'd and hard-hearted race,
But O! in tender mercy break
The iron sinew in our neck!
The soft'ning power of love impart,
And melt the marble of our heart!

446 *The backslider's resolve.*

YES, from this instant, now, I will
To my offended Father cry;
My base ingratitude I feel,
Vilest of all thy children, I;
Not worthy to be call'd thy son;
Yet will I thee, my Father, own.

2 Guide of my life hast thou not been,
And rescued me from passion's power?
Ten thousand times preserved from sin,
Nor let the greedy grave devour?
And wilt thou now thy wrath retain,
Nor ever love thy child again?

3 If thou hast call'd me to return,
If weeping at thy feet I fall,
The prodigal thou wilt not spurn,
But pity and forgive me all,
In answer to my Friend above,
In honour of his bleeding love.

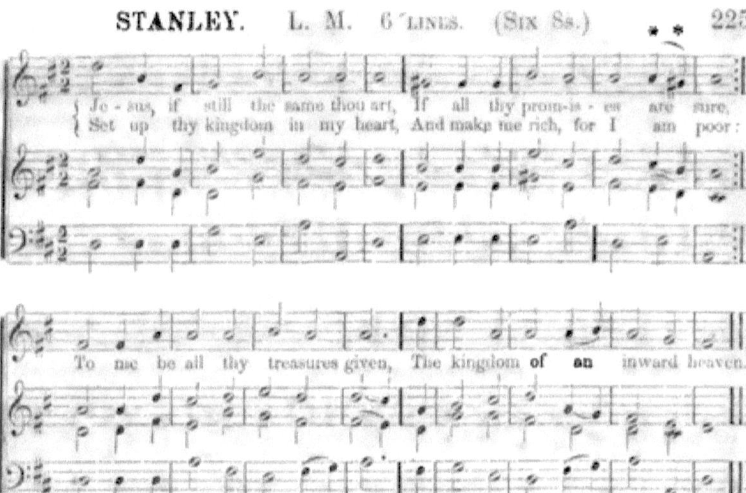

399 *The mourner.*

JESUS, if still the same thou art,
If all thy promises are sure,
Set up thy kingdom in my heart,
And make me rich, for I am poor:
To me be all thy treasures given,
The kingdom of an inward heaven.

2 Thou hast pronounced the mourners blest,
And lo! for thee I ever mourn;
I cannot, no, I will not rest,
Till thou, my only rest, return;
Till thou, the Prince of peace, appear,
And I receive the Comforter.

3 Where is the blessedness, bestow'd
On all that hunger after thee?
I hunger now, I thirst for God;
See the poor fainting sinner, see;
And satisfy with endless peace,
And fill me with thy righteousness.

4 Shine on thy work, disperse the gloom;
Light in thy light I then shall see:
Say to my soul, "Thy light is come,
Glory divine is ris'n on thee;
Thy warfare's past, thy mourning's o'er;
Look up, for thou shalt weep no more."

439 *For acceptance in the Beloved.*

FATHER of everlasting grace,
Be mindful of thy changeless word;
We worship tow'rd that holy place
In which thou dost thy name record,
Dost make thy gracious nature known,
That living temple of thy Son.

2 Thou dost with sweet complacence see
The temple fill'd with light divine;
And art thou not well pleased with me,
Who, turning to that heavenly shrine,
Through Jesus to thy throne apply,
Through Jesus for acceptance cry?

3 With all who for redemption groan,
Father, in Jesus' name I pray!
And still we cry and wrestle on
Till mercy take our sins away:
Hear from thy dwelling-place in heaven,
And now pronounce our sins forgiven.

176 *"All in all."*

THOU hidden Source of calm repose,
Thou all-sufficient Love Divine,
My help and refuge from my foes,
Secure I am if thou art mine!
And lo! from sin, and grief, and shame,
I hide me, Jesus, in thy name.

2 Thy mighty name salvation is,
And keeps my happy soul above:
Comfort it brings, and power, and peace,
And joy, and everlasting love:
To me, with thy great name, are given,
Pardon, and holiness, and heaven.

3 Jesus, my All in all thou art;
My rest in toil; my ease in pain;
The med'cine of my broken heart;
In war, my peace; in loss, my gain;
My smile beneath the tyrant's frown;
In shame, my glory and my crown;—

4 In want, my plentiful supply;
In weakness, my almighty power;
In bonds, my perfect liberty;
My light in Satan's darkest hour;
In grief, my joy unspeakable;
My life in death—my All in all.

CREATION. L. M. 6 lines. (Six 8s.) HAYDN.

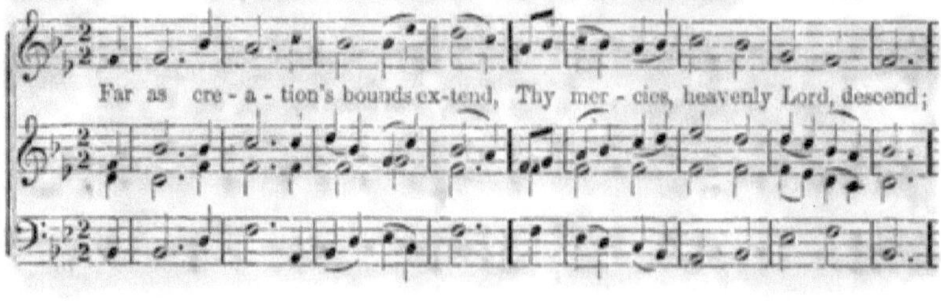

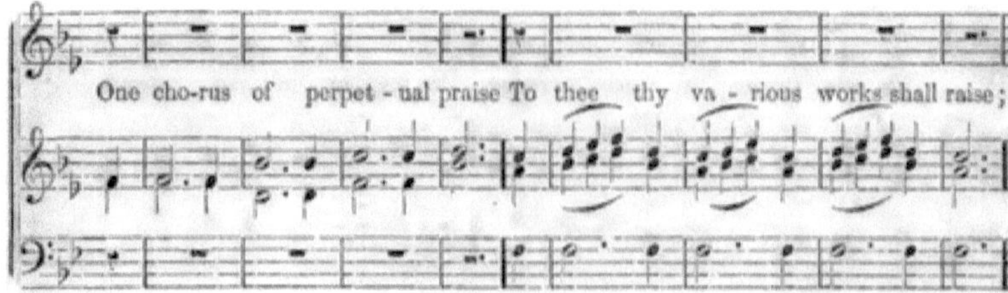

70 *Psalm cxlv.*

FAR as creation's bounds extend,
Thy mercies, heavenly Lord, descend;
One chorus of perpetual praise
To thee thy various works shall raise;
Thy saints to thee, in hymns, impart
The transports of a grateful heart.

2 They chant the splendours of thy name,
Delighted with the wondrous theme;
And bid the world's wide realms admire
The glories of th' almighty Sire,
Whose throne all nature's wreck survives,
Whose power through endless ages lives.

3 From thee, great God, while every eye
Expectant waits the wish'd supply,
Their bread, proportion'd to the day,
Thy opening hands to each convey;
In every sorrow of the heart
Eternal mercy bears a part.

4 Who ask thine aid, with heart sincere,
Shall find thy succours ever near;
To thee their prayer in each distress,
Thy suffering servants, Lord, address;
And prove thee, verging on the grave,
Nor slow to hear, nor weak to save.

4 *The Trinity.*

COME, Father, Son, and Holy Ghost,
Whom one all-perfect God we own,
Restorer of thy image lost,
Thy various offices make known:
Display, our fallen souls to raise,
Thy whole economy of grace.

2 Jehovah, in three persons, come,
And draw, and sprinkle us, and seal,
Poor, guilty, dying worms, in whom
Thou dost eternal life reveal;
The knowledge of thyself bestow,
And all thy glorious goodness show.

3 O that we now, in love renew'd,
Might blameless in thy sight appear!
Wake we in thy similitude,
Stamp'd with the triune character:
Flesh, spirit, soul, to thee resign;
And live and die entirely thine.

162 *"Seen of angels."*

ANGELS rejoice in Jesus' grace,
And vie with man's more favour'd race!
The blood that did for us atone
Conferr'd on you some gift unknown;
Your joy through Jesus's pains abounds,
Ye triumph by his glorious wounds.

2 Him ye beheld, our conqu'ring God,
Return'd with garments roll'd in blood!
Ye saw, and kindled at the sight,
And fill'd with shouts the realms of light;
With loudest hallelujahs met,
And fell, and kiss'd his bleeding feet.

3 Ye saw him in the courts above
With all his recent prints of love;
The wounds, the blood! ye heard its voice
That heighten'd all your highest joys;
Ye felt it sprinkled through the skies,
And shared that better sacrifice.

4 Not angel tongues can e'er express
Th' unutterable happiness;
Nor human hearts can e'er conceive
The bliss wherein through Christ ye live;
But all your heaven, ye glorious powers,
And all your God, is doubly ours!

529 *The act of consecration.*

BEHOLD the servant of the Lord!
I wait thy guiding eye to feel,
To hear and keep thy every word,
To prove and do thy perfect will;
Joyful from my own works to cease,
Glad to fulfil all righteousness.

2 Me if thy grace vouchsafe to use,
Meanest of all thy creatures, me,
The deed, the time, the manner, choose:
Let all my fruit be found of thee;
Let all my works in thee be wrought,
By thee to full perfection brought.

3 Here then to thee thine own I leave;
Mould as thou wilt thy passive clay;
But let me all thy stamp receive,
But let me all thy words obey;
Serve with a single heart and eye,
And to thy glory live and die.

1058 *Doxology.*

SHOUT to the great Jehovah's praise!
Ye sons of glory and of grace:
One God in persons Three adore,
The same in majesty and power;
Ye suff'ring and triumphant host,
Praise Father, Son, and Holy Ghost.

FABER. L. M. 6 LINES. (SIX 8s.)

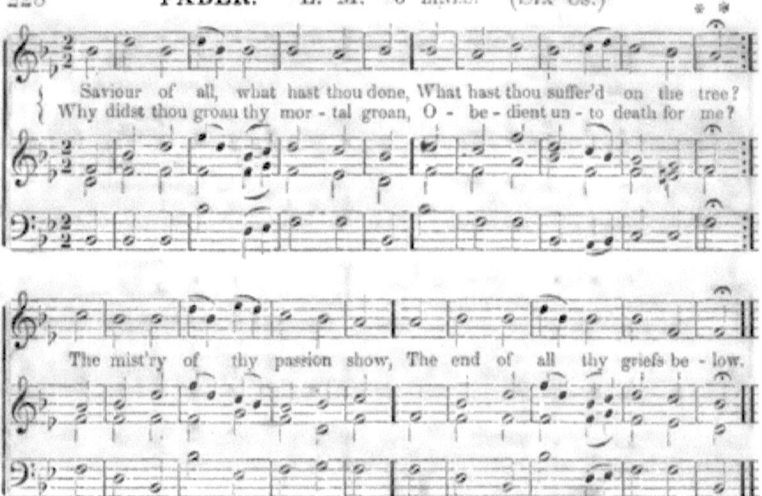

634 *"That ye should follow his steps."*

SAVIOUR of all, what hast thou done,
  What hast thou suffer'd on the tree?
Why didst thou groan thy mortal groan,
  Obedient unto death for me?
The myst'ry of thy passion show,
The end of all thy griefs below.

2 Pardon, and grace, and heaven, to buy,
  My bleeding Sacrifice expired;
But didst thou not my pattern die,
  That, by thy glorious Spirit fired,
Faithful to death I might endure,
And make the crown by suff'ring sure?

3 Thou didst the meek example leave,
  That I might in thy footsteps tread;
Might, like the Man of sorrows, grieve,
  And groan, and bow with thee my head;
Thy dying in my body bear,
And all thy state of suff'ring share.

4 Thy every suff'ring servant, Lord,
  Shall as his perfect Master be;—
To all thy inward life restored,
  And outwardly conform'd to thee,
Out of thy grave the saint shall rise,
And grasp, through death, the glorious prize.

5 This is the strait, the royal way,
  That leads us to the courts above:
Here let me ever, ever stay,
  Till, on the wings of perfect love,
I take my last triumphant flight,
From Calvary to Sion's height.

747 *For the seed of Abraham.*

FATHER of faithful Abrah'm, hear
  Our earnest suit for Abrah'm's seed;
Justly they claim the softest prayer
  From us, adopted in their stead,
Who mercy through their fall obtain,
And Christ by their rejection gain.

2 Outcast from thee, and scatter'd wide,
  Through every nation under heaven,
Blaspheming whom they crucified,
  Unsaved, unpitied, unforgiven,
Like wretched Cain, they bear their load,
Oppress'd of men, and cursed of God.

3 But hast thou finally forsook,
  For ever cast thy own away?
Wilt thou not bid the murd'rers look
  On him they pierced, and weep and pray?
Yes, gracious Lord, thy word is past,
"All Israel shall be saved at last."

4 Come, then, thou great Deliv'rer, come,
  The veil from Jacob's heart remove.
Receive thy ancient people home,
  That, quicken'd by thy dying love,
The world may their reception find,
Life from the dead for all mankind.

581 *Consistency.*

WATCH'D by the world's malignant eye,
  Who load us with reproach and shame,
As servants of the Lord most high,
  As zealous for his glorious name,
We ought in all his paths to move,
With holy fear and humble love.

2 That wisdom, Lord, on us bestow,
From every evil to depart,—
To stop the mouth of every foe,
While, upright both in life and heart,
The proofs of godly fear we give,
And show them how the Christians live.

211 *Interpreter. Before or after sermon.*

SPIRIT of truth, essential God,
Who didst thy ancient saints inspire,
Shed in their hearts thy love abroad,
And touch their hallow'd lips with fire,
Our God from all eternity,
World without end, we worship thee.

2 Still we believe, almighty Lord,
Whose presence fills both earth and heaven,
The meaning of the written word
Is by thy inspiration given;
Thou only dost thyself explain
The secret mind of God to man.

3 Come, then, divine Interpreter,
The Scriptures to our hearts apply;
And, taught by thee, we God revere,
Him in three persons magnify;
And still the Triune God adore,
Who was, and is, for evermore.

794 *"Learning and holiness combined."*

COME, Father, Son, and Holy Ghost,
To whom we for our children cry;
The good desired and wanted most,
Out of thy richest grace supply!
The sacred discipline be given
To train and bring them up for heaven.

2 Error and ignorance remove,
Their blindness both of heart and mind:
Give them the wisdom from above,
Spotless, and peaceable, and kind:
In knowledge pure their minds renew;
And store with thoughts divinely true.

3 Learning's redundant part and vain
Be here cut off, and cast aside;
But let them, Lord, the substance gain,
In every solid truth abide;
Swiftly acquire, and ne'er forego,
The knowledge fit for man to know.

4 Unite the pair so long disjoin'd,
Knowledge and vital piety;
Learning and holiness combined,
And truth and love let all men see,
In those whom up to thee we give,
Thine, wholly thine, to die and live!

913 *Opening the exercises.*

JESUS, thou sovereign Lord of all,
The same through one eternal day,
Attend thy feeblest foll'wer's call,
And O, instruct us how to pray!
Pour out the supplicating grace,
And stir us up to seek thy face.

2 We cannot think a gracious thought,
We cannot feel a good desire,
Till thou who call'dst a world from naught,
The power into our hearts inspire;
And then we in the Spirit groan,
And then we give thee back thine own.

3 To help our soul's infirmity,
To heal thy sin-sick people's care,
To urge our God-commanding plea,
And make our heart a house of prayer,
The promised Intercessor give,
And let us now thyself receive.

4 Come in thy pleading Spirit down,
To us who for thy coming stay;
Of all thy gifts we ask but one—
We ask the constant power to pray.
Indulge us, Lord, in this request,
Thou canst not then deny the rest.

1007 *Communion with God.*

TO thee, great God of love! I bow,
And prostrate in thy sight adore;
By faith I see thee passing now;
I have, but still I ask for more;
A glimpse of love cannot suffice,
My soul for all thy presence cries.

2 The fulness of my vast reward
A bless'd eternity shall be:—
But hast thou not on earth prepared
Some better thing than this for me?
What,—but one drop!—one transient sight?
I want a sun—a sea of light.

3 More favour'd than the saints of old,—
Who now by faith approach to thee,
Shall all with open face behold
In Christ the glorious Deity,—
Shall see and put salvation on,
The nature of thy sinless Son.

4 This, this is our high calling's prize!
Thine image in thy Son I claim
And still to higher glories rise,
Till, all transform'd, I know thy name,
And glide to all my heaven above,
My highest heaven in Jesus' love.

1037 *"I am old and gray-headed."*

IN age and feebleness extreme,
Who shall a helpless worm redeem?
Jesus, my only hope thou art,
Strength of my failing flesh and heart!
O, could I catch a smile from thee,
And drop into eternity!

1058 *Doxology*

SHOUT to the great Jehovah's praise!
Ye sons of glory and of grace:
One God in persons Three adore,
The same in majesty and power;
Ye suff'ring and triumphant host,
Praise Father, Son, and Holy Ghost.

641 *"Peace; be still."*

PEACE! doubting heart; my God's I am!
Who form'd me man, forbids my fear:
The Lord hath called me by my name;
The Lord protects, for ever near:
His blood for me did once atone,
And still he loves and guards his own.

2 When passing through the wat'ry deep,
I ask in faith his promised aid,
The waves an awful distance keep,
And shrink from my devoted head;
Fearless their violence I dare;
They cannot harm; for God is there!

3 To him mine eye of faith I turn,
And through the fire pursue my way;
The fire forgets its power to burn,
The lambent flames around me play,—
I own his power, accept the sign,
And shout to prove the Saviour mine.

4 Still nigh me, O my Saviour, stand!
And guard in fierce temptation's hour;
Hide in the hollow of thy hand;
Show forth in me thy saving power;
Still be thy arms my sure defence;
Nor earth nor hell shall pluck me thence.

6 Since thou hast bid me come to thee,
(God as thou art, and strong to save,)
I'll walk o'er life's tempestuous sea,
Upborne by the unyielding wave;
Dauntless, though rocks of pride be near,
And yawning whirlpools of despair.

6 When darkness intercepts the skies,
And sorrow's waves around me roll,
And high the storms of trouble rise,
And half o'erwhelm my sinking soul,—
My soul a sudden calm shall feel,
And hear a whisper, "Peace; be still!"

7 Though in affliction's furnace tried,
Unhurt on snares and death I'll tread;
Though sin assail, and hell, thrown wide,
Pour all its flames upon my head,—
Like Moses' bush, I'll mount the higher,
And flourish, unconsumed, in fire.

306

Victim divine.

VICTIM divine! thy grace we claim
While thus thy precious death we show;
Once offer'd up a spotless Lamb,
In thy great temple here below,
Thou didst for all mankind atone,
And standest now before the throne.

2 Thou standest in the holiest place,
As now for guilty sinners slain,
The blood of sprinkling speaks, and prays,
All-prevalent for helpless man;
Thy blood is still our ransom found,
And speaks salvation all around.

3 The smoke of thy atonement here
Darken'd the sun and rent the veil,
Made the new way to heaven appear,
And show'd the great Invisible;
Well pleas'd in thee our God look'd down,
And call'd his rebels to a crown.

4 He still respects thy sacrifice,
Its savour sweet doth always please;
The off'ring smokes through earth and skies
Diffusing life, and joy, and peace:
To these thy lower courts it comes,
And fills them with divine perfumes.

5 We need not now go up to heaven,
To bring the long-sought Saviour down,
Thou art to all already given,
Thou dost e'en now thy banquet crown
To every faithful soul appear,
And show thy real presence here.

79

Te Deum.

MESSIAH, joy of every heart,
Thou, thou the King of glory art;
The Father's everlasting Son,
Thee it delights thy church to own;
For all our hopes on thee depend,
Whose glorious mercies never end.

2 Bent to redeem a sinful race,
Thou, Lord, with unexampled grace
Into our lower world didst come,
And stoop to a poor virgin's womb;
Whom all the heavens cannot contain,
Our God, appear'd a child of man!

3 When thou hadst render'd up thy breath,
And, dying, drawn the sting of death,
Thou didst from earth triumphant rise,
And ope the portals of the skies,
That all who trust in thee alone
Might follow, and partake thy throne.

4 Seated at God's right hand again,
Thou dost in all his glory reign,
Thou dost, thy Father's image, shine
In all the attributes divine;
And thou with judgment clad shalt come,
To seal our everlasting doom.

5 Wherefore we now for mercy pray,
O Saviour, take our sins away!
Before thou as our Judge appear,
In dreadful majesty severe,
Appear our Advocate with God,
And save the purchase of thy blood.

6 Hallow and make thy servants meet,
And with thy saints in glory seat;
Sustain and bless us by thy sway,
And keep to that tremendous day
When all thy church shall chant above
The new, eternal song of love.

215

"The Spirit of God dwelleth in you."

COME, Holy Ghost, all-quick'ning fire,
Come, and in me delight to rest;
Drawn by the lure of strong desire,
O come and consecrate my breast!
The temple of my soul prepare,
And fix thy sacred presence there!

2 If now thy influence I feel,
If now in thee begin to live,
Still to my heart thyself reveal;
Give me thyself, for ever give:
A point my good, a drop my store,
Eager I ask, I pant for more.

3 Eager for thee I ask and pant:
So strong the principle divine
Carries me out with sweet constraint,
Till all my hallow'd soul is thine;
Plunged in the Godhead's deepest sea,
And lost in thy immensity.

4 My peace, my life, my comfort, thou
My treasure, and my all thou art!
True witness of my sonship now,
Engraving pardon on my heart,
Seal of my sins in Christ forgiven,
Earnest of love, and pledge of heaven.

5 Come, then, my God, mark out thine heir,
Of heaven a larger earnest give!
With clearer light thy witness bear;
More sensibly within me live:
Let all my powers thine entrance feel,
And deeper stamp thyself the seal!

POLK. L. M. 6 LINES. (SIX 8s.)

From "New Thes. Musicus."

266 *"The love of Christ constraineth us."*

WHERE shall my wond'ring soul begin?
  How shall I all to heaven aspire?
A slave redeem'd from death and sin;
  A brand pluck'd from eternal fire:
How shall I equal triumphs raise,
Or sing my great Deliv'rer's praise?

2 O how shall I thy goodness tell,
  Father, which thou to me hast show'd?
That I, a child of wrath and hell,
  I should be call'd a child of God!
Should know, should feel my sins forgiven,
Bless'd with this antepast of heaven!

3 And shall I slight my Father's love?
  Or basely fear his gifts to own?
Unmindful of his favours prove?
  Shall I, the hallow'd cross to shun,
Refuse his righteousness t' impart,
By hiding it within my heart?

4 No; though the ancient dragon rage,
  And call forth all his hosts to war;
Though earth's self-righteous sons engage,
  Them and their god alike I dare;
Jesus, the sinner's Friend, proclaim;
Jesus, to sinners still the same.

5 Come, O my guilty brethren, come,
  Groaning beneath your load of sin;
His bleeding heart shall make you room,
  His open side shall take you in:
He calls you now, invites you home;
Come, O my guilty brethren, come!

6 For you the purple current flow'd
  In pardons from his wounded side;
Languish'd for you the Son of God;
  For you the Prince of glory died:
Believe, and all your sin's forgiven;
Only believe, and yours is heaven!

269 *Ministerial zeal.*

GIVE me the faith which can remove,
  And sink the mountain to a plain;
Give me the child-like, praying love,
  Which longs to build thy house again:
Thy love let it my heart o'erpower,
And all my simple soul devour.

2 I want an even, strong desire,
  I want a calmly-fervent zeal,
To save poor souls out of the fire,
  To snatch them from the verge of hell,
And turn them to a pard'ning God,
And quench the brands in Jesus' blood.

3 I would the precious time redeem,
And longer live for this alone,
To spend, and to be spent for them,
Who have not yet my Saviour known;
Fully on these my mission prove,
And only breathe, to breathe thy love.

4 My talents, gifts, and graces, Lord,
Into thy blessed hands receive;
And let me live to preach thy word;
And let me to thy glory live;
My every sacred moment spend
In publishing the sinner's Friend.

5 Enlarge, inflame, and fill my heart
With boundless charity divine!
So shall I all my strength exert,
And love them with a zeal like thine;
And lead them to thy open side,
The sheep for whom their Shepherd died.

337 *The universal invitation.*

SINNERS, believe the gospel word,
Jesus is come your souls to save!
Jesus is come, your common Lord;
Pardon ye all through him may have—
May now be saved, whoever will:
This man receiveth sinners still.

2 See where the lame, the halt, the blind,
The deaf, the dumb, the sick, the poor,
Flock to the Friend of human kind,
And freely all accept their cure!
To whom did he his help deny?
Whom, in his days of flesh, pass by?

3 Did not his word the fiends expel,
The lepers cleanse, and raise the dead?
Did he not all their sickness heal,
And satisfy their every need?
Did he reject his helpless clay,
Or send them sorrowful away?

4 Nay, but his bowels yearn'd to see
The people hungry, scatter'd, faint:
Nay, but he utter'd over thee,
Jerusalem, a true complaint;
Jerusalem, who shedd'st his blood,
That, with his tears, for thee hath flow'd.

751 *For the Mohammedans.*

SUN of unclouded righteousness,
With healing in thy wings arise,
A sad benighted world to bless,
Which now in sin and error lies,
Wrapp'd in Egyptian night profound,
With chains of hellish darkness bound.

2 The smoke of the infernal cave,
Which half the Christian world o'erspread,
Disperse, thou heavenly Light, and save
The souls by that impostor led,
That Arab thief, as Satan bold,
Who quite destroy'd thy Asian fold.

3 O might the blood of sprinkling cry
For those who spurn the sprinkled blood,
Assert thy glorious deity!
Stretch out thy arm, thou Triune God,
E'en now the Moslem fiend expel,
And chase his doctrine back to hell.

4 Come, Father, Son, and Holy Ghost,
Thou Three in One, and One in Three,
Resume thy own, for ages lost,
Finish the dire apostacy;
Thy universal claim maintain,
And Lord of the creation reign!

1006 *Reading the Scriptures.*

WHEN quiet in my house I sit,
Thy book be my companion still;
My joy, thy sayings to repeat,
Talk o'er the records of thy will,
And search the oracles divine,
Till every heartfelt word be mine.

2 O may the gracious words divine
Subject of all my converse be!
So will the Lord his foll'wer join,
And walk and talk himself with me:
So shall my heart his presence prove,
And burn with everlasting love.

3 Oft as I lay me down to rest,
O may the reconciling word
Sweetly compose my weary breast,
While, on the bosom of my Lord,
I sink in blissful dreams away,
And visions of eternal day!

4 Rising to sing my Saviour's praise,
Thee may I publish all day long;
And let thy precious word of grace
Flow from my heart and fill my tongue,—
Fill all my life with purest love,
And join me to the church above.

901 *Thanks for preserving grace.*

JESUS, to thee our hearts we lift,
May all our hearts with love o'erflow!
With thanks for thy continued gift,
That still thy gracious name we know:
Retain our sense of sin forgiven,
And wait for all our inward heaven.

2 What mighty troubles hast thou shown
Thy feeble, tempted foll'wers here!
We have through fire and water gone;—
But saw thee on the floods appear,—
But felt thee present in the flame,
And shouted our Deliv'rer's name.

3 Thou who hast kept us to this hour,
O keep us faithful to the end—
When, robed in majesty and power,
Our Jesus shall from heaven descend,
His friends and witnesses to own,
And seat us on his glorious throne.

FARNSWORTH. L. M. 6 lines. (Six 8s.)

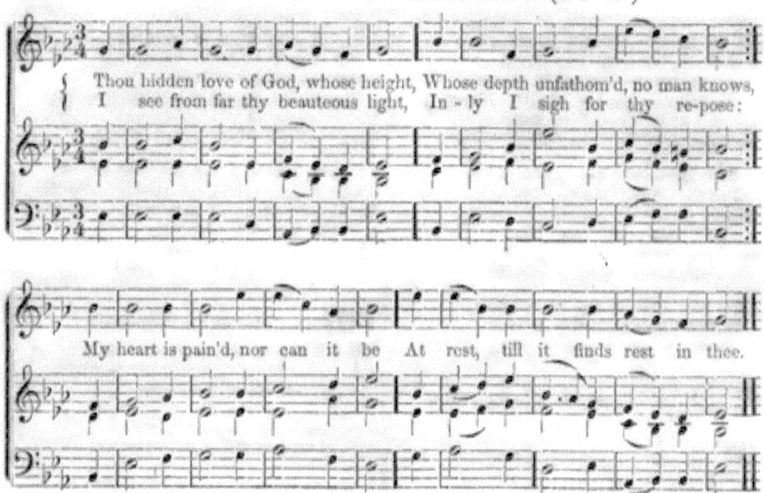

620 *Sacrificing all for Christ.*

THOU hidden love of God, whose height,
  Whose depth unfathom'd, no man knows,
I see from far thy beauteous light,
  Inly I sigh for thy repose:
My heart is pain'd, nor can it be
At rest, till it find rest in thee.

2 Thy secret voice invites me still
  The sweetness of thy yoke to prove,
And fain I would; but though my will
  Seem fix'd, yet wide my passions rove;
Yet hind'rances strew all the way;
I aim at thee, yet from thee stray.

3 'Tis mercy all that thou hast brought
  My mind to seek her peace in thee!
Yet while I seek, but find thee not,
  No peace my wand'ring soul shall see;
O when shall all my wand'rings end,
And all my steps to thee-ward tend!

4 Is there a thing beneath the sun
  That strives with thee my heart to share?
Ah, tear it thence, and reign alone,
  The lord of every motion there!
Then shall my heart from earth be free,
When it hath found repose in thee.

5 O hide this self from me, that I
  No more, but Christ in me, may live!
My vile affections crucify,
  Nor let one darling lust survive!
In all things nothing may I see,
Nothing desire or seek, but thee!

6 O Love, thy sovereign aid impart,
  To save me from low-thoughted care;
Chase this self-will through all my heart,
  Through all its latent mazes there
Make me thy duteous child, that I
Ceaseless may Abba, Father, cry.

7 Ah no! ne'er will I backward turn;
  Thine wholly, thine alone, I am!
Thrice happy he who views with scorn
  Earth's toys, for thee his constant flame
O help, that I may never move
From the bless'd footsteps of thy love!

8 Each moment draw from earth away
  My heart, that lowly waits thy call;
Speak to my inmost soul, and say,
  "I am thy Love, thy God, thy All!"
To feel thy power, to hear thy voice,
To taste thy love, be all my choice.

150 *Priesthood of Christ.*

O THOU eternal Victim, slain,
  A sacrifice for guilty man,
By the eternal Spirit made
  An off'ring in the sinner's stead;
Our everlasting Priest art thou,
  And plead'st thy death for sinners now;

2 Thy off'ring still continues new;
  Thy vesture keeps its bloody hue;
Thou stand'st the ever-slaughter'd Lamb;
  Thy priesthood still remains the same;
Thy years, O God, can never fail;
  Thy goodness is unchangeable.

3 O that our faith may never move,
  But stand unshaken as thy love:
Sure evidence of things unseen,
  Now let it pass the years between,
And view thee bleeding on the tree,
  My God, who dies for me, for me!

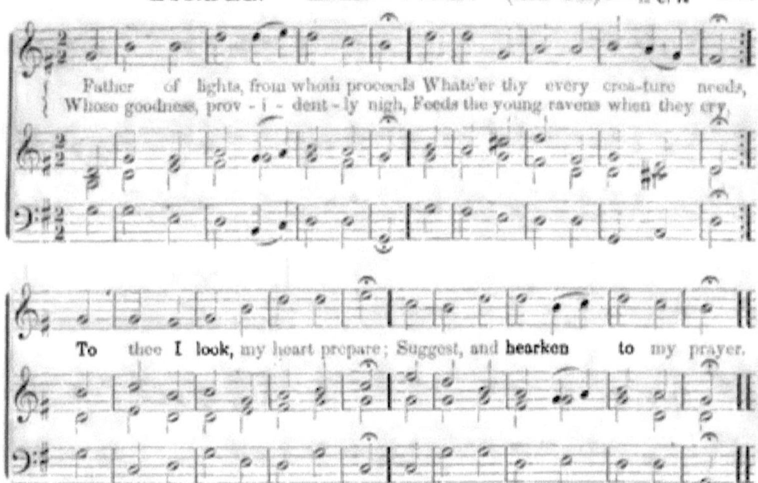

372 *Praying for repentance.*

FATHER of lights, from whom proceeds
 Whate'er thy every creature needs,—
Whose goodness, providently nigh,
Feeds the young ravens when they cry,—
To thee I look, my heart prepare;
Suggest and hearken to my prayer.

2 Since, by thy light, myself I see
Naked, and poor, and void of thee,
Thine eyes must all my thoughts survey,
Preventing what my lips would say:
Thou seest my wants, for help they call,
And ere I speak thou know'st them all.

3 Thou know'st the baseness of my mind,
Wayward, and impotent, and blind;
Thou know'st how unsubdued my will,
Averse to good, and prone to ill;
Thou know'st how wide my passions rove,
Nor check'd by fear, nor charm'd by love.

4 Fain would I know, as known by thee,
And feel the indigence I see:
Fain would I all my vileness own,
And deep beneath the burden groan!
Abhor the pride that lurks within,
Detest, and loathe myself and sin.

5 Ah! give me, Lord, myself to feel,
My total misery reveal:
Ah! give me, Lord, (I still would say,)
A heart to mourn, a heart to pray:
My business this, my only care,
My life, my every breath, be prayer.

426 *Praying for faith.*

FATHER of Jesus Christ, the just,
 My friend and advocate with thee,
Pity a soul that fain would trust
 In Him who lived and died for me!
But only thou canst make him known,
And in my heart reveal thy Son.

2 If drawn by thy alluring grace,
 My want of living faith I feel,
Show me in Christ thy smiling face;
 What flesh and blood can ne'er reveal,
The co-eternal Son display,
And speak my darkness into day.

3 The gift unspeakable impart:
 Command the light of faith to shine,
To shine in my dark, drooping heart,
 And fill me with the life divine:
Now bid the new creation be,
O God, let there be faith in me!

80 *Te Deum.*

SAVIOUR, we now rejoice in hope,
 That thou at last wilt take us up;
 With daily triumph we proclaim,
 And bless and magnify thy name;
 And wait thy greatness to adore
 When time and death shall be no more.

2 Till then with us vouchsafe to stay,
 And keep us pure from sin to-day;
 Thy great confirming grace bestow,
 And guard us all our days below;
 And ever mightily defend,
 And save thy servants to the end.

3 Still let us, Lord, by thee be blest,
 Who in thy guardian mercy rest:
 Extend thy mercy's arms to me,
 The weakest soul that trusts in thee;
 And never let me lose thy love,
 Till I, e'en I, am crown'd above.

NASHVILLE. L. P. M. (Six 8s.) ARR. BY DR. L. MASON

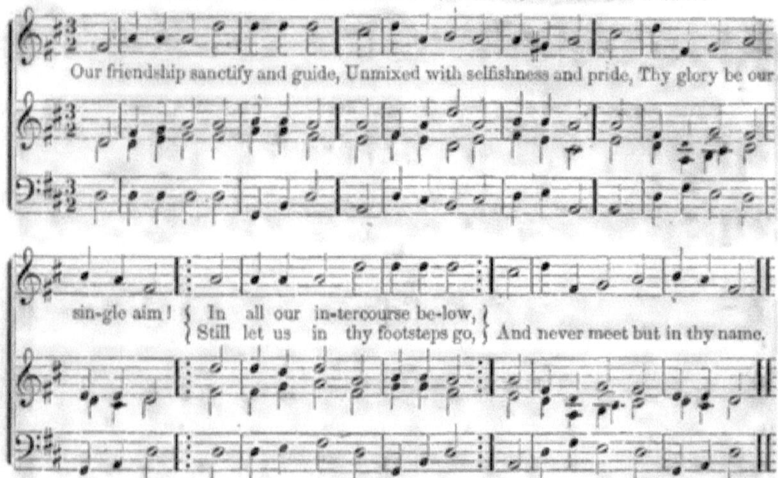

274 *Opening Conference.*

OUR friendship sanctify and guide,
  Unmix'd with selfishness and pride,
  Thy glory be our single aim!
In all our intercourse below,
Still let us in thy footsteps go,
  And never meet but in thy name.

2 Witnesses of th' all-cleansing blood,
Long may we work the works of God,
  And do thy will like those above:
Together spread the gospel sound,
And scatter peace on all around,
  And joy, and happiness, and love.

3 True yoke-fellows, by love compell'd
To labour in the gospel field,
  Our all let us delight to spend
In gath'ring in thy lambs and sheep,
Assured that thou our souls wilt keep,
  Wilt keep us faithful to the end.

23 *Majesty and mercy.*

O GOD, of good th' unfathom'd sea!
  Who would not give his heart to thee?
  Who would not love thee with his might?
O Jesus, lover of mankind!
Who would not his whole soul and mind,
  With all his strength, to thee unite?

2 Thou shin'st with everlasting rays:
Before th' insufferable blaze
  Angels with both wings veil their eyes;
Yet, free as air thy bounty streams
On all thy works; thy mercy's beams,
  Diffusive as thy sun's, arise.

3 Astonish'd at thy frowning brow,
Earth, hell, and heaven's strong pillars, bow;
  Terrible majesty is thine!
Who then can that vast love express,
Which bows thee down to me, who less
  Than nothing am, till thou art mine!

4 High throned on heaven's eternal hill,
In number, weight, and measure, still
  Thou sweetly orderest all that is:
And yet thou deign'st to come to me,
And guide my steps, that I, with thee
  Enthroned, may reign in endless bliss.

24 *Majesty and mercy.*

FOUNTAIN of good! all blessing flows
  From thee; no want thy fulness knows:
  What but thyself canst thou desire?
Yet, self-sufficient as thou art,
Thou dost desire my worthless heart;
  This, only this, dost thou require.

2 Primeval Beauty! in thy sight
The first-born, fairest sons of light
  See all their brightest glories fade:
What then to me thine eyes could turn?
In sin conceived, of woman born,
  A worm, a leaf, a blast, a shade!

3 Hell's armies tremble at thy nod,
And, trembling, own th' almighty God,
  Sovereign of earth, hell, air, and sky!
But who is this that comes from far,
Whose garments roll'd in blood appear?
  'Tis God made man, for man to die!

4 O God, of good th' unfathom'd sea!
Who would not give his heart to thee?
  Who would not love thee with his might?
O Jesus, lover of mankind!
Who would not his whole soul and mind,
  With all his strength, to thee unite?

216 *His Work.*

COME, Holy Ghost, all-quick'ning fire,
Come, and my hallow'd heart inspire,
Sprinkled with the atoning blood;
Now to my soul thyself reveal,
Thy mighty working let me feel,
And know that I am born of God.

2 When wilt thou my whole heart subdue?
Come, Lord, and form my soul anew,
Emptied of pride, and wrath, and hell;
Less than the least of all thy store
Of mercies, I myself abhor:
All, all my vileness may I feel.

3 Humble, and teachable, and mild,
O may I, as a little child,
My lowly Master's steps pursue!
Be anger to my soul unknown;
Hate, envy, jealousy, begone;
In love create thou all things new.

4 Let earth no more my heart divide;
With Christ may I be crucified;
To thee with my whole heart aspire:
Dead to the world and all its toys,
Its idle pomp, and fading joys,
Be thou alone my one desire!

5 Be thou my joy, be thou my dread;
In battle cover thou my head,
Nor earth, nor hell, I then shall fear;
I then shall turn my steady face—
Want, pain, defy—enjoy disgrace—
Glory in dissolution near

6 My will be swallow'd up in thee!
Light in thy light still may I see,
Beholding thee with open face:
Call'd the full power of faith to prove,
Let all my hallow'd heart be love,
And all my spotless life be praise.

232 *Psalm lxxxvi.*

HOW lovely are thy tents, O Lord!
Where'er thou choosest to record
Thy name, or place thy house of prayer,
My soul outflies the angel choir,
And faints, o'erpower'd with strong desire,
To meet thy special presence there.

2 Happy the men to whom 'tis given
To dwell within that gate of heaven,
And in thy house record thy praise;
Whose strength and confidence thou art,
Who feel thee, Saviour, in their heart,
The way, the truth, the life of grace.

3 Who, passing through the mournful vale,
Drink comfort from the living well,
That flows replenish'd from above;
From strength to strength advancing here,
Till all before their God appear,
And each receives the crown of love.

4 Better a day thy courts within
Than thousands in the tents of sin:
How base the noblest pleasures there!
How great the weakest child of thine!
His meanest talk is all divine,
And kings and priests thy servants are.

5 The Lord protects and cheers his own,
Their light and strength, their shield and sun,
He shall both grace and glory give;
Unlimited his bounteous grant;
No real good they e'er shall want,—
All, all is theirs, who righteous live.

6 O Lord of hosts! how bless'd is he
Who steadfastly believes in thee!
He all thy promises shall gain;
The soul that on thy love is cast,
Thy perfect love on earth shall taste,
And soon with thee in glory reign.

RINK. L. P. M. (Six 8s.)

Psalm cxlvi.

2 Happy the man whose hopes rely
On Israel's God; he made the sky,
And earth, and seas, with all their train:
His truth for ever stands secure;
He saves th' oppress'd, he feeds the poor,
And none shall find his promise vain.

3 The Lord pours eyesight on the blind;
The Lord supports the fainting mind;
He sends the lab'ring conscience peace;
He helps the stranger in distress,
The widow and the fatherless,
And grants the prisoner sweet release.

4 I'll praise him while he lends me breath,
And when my voice is lost in death,
Praise shall employ my nobler powers;
My days of praise shall ne'er be past,
While life, and thought, and being last,
Or immortality endures.

1059 *Doxology.*

PRAISE to the glorious Cause of all,
Whom one in Persons Three we call,
Be by his every creature given!
Worship divine to him be paid,
Whose hands the whole creation made,
The Triune God of earth and heaven.

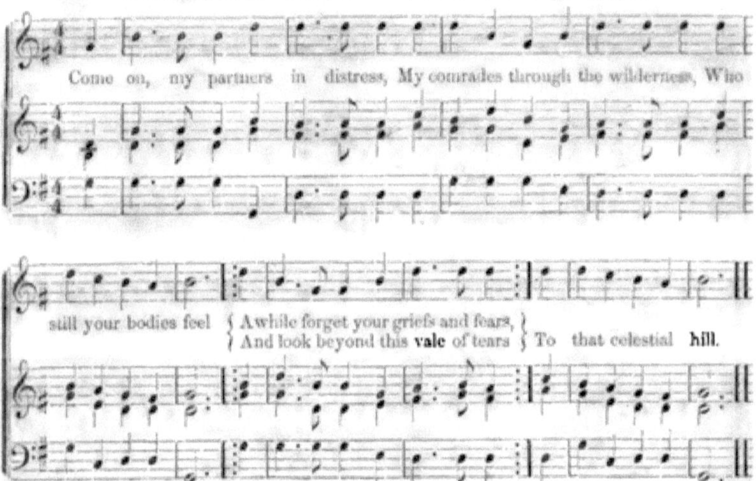

663 *Full assurance of hope.*

COME on, my partners in distress,
My comrades through the wilderness,
Who still your bodies feel:
Awhile forget your griefs and fears,
And look beyond this vale of tears
To that celestial hill.

2 Beyond the bounds of time and space
Look forward to that heavenly place,
The saints' secure abode;
On faith's strong eagle-pinions rise,
And force your passage to the skies,
And scale the mount of God.

3 Who suffer with our Master here,
We shall before his face appear,
And by his side sit down;
To patient faith the prize is sure;
And all that to the end endure
The cross, shall wear the crown.

4 Thrice blessed, bliss-inspiring hope!
It lifts the fainting spirits up,
It brings to life the dead:
Our conflicts here shall soon be past,
And you and I ascend at last,
Triumphant with our Head.

5 That great mysterious Deity
We soon with open face shall see;
The beatific sight
Shall fill the heavenly courts with praise,
And wide diffuse the golden blaze
Of everlasting light.

6 The Father, shining on his throne,
The glorious co-eternal Son,
The Spirit, one and seven,
Conspire our rapture to complete;
And lo! we fall before his feet,
And silence heightens heaven.

7 In hope of that ecstatic pause,
Jesus, we now sustain the cross,
And at thy footstool fall;
Till thou our hidden life reveal,
Till thou our ravish'd spirits fill,
And God be all in all.

826 *Watch-night.*

HOW happy, gracious Lord, are we!
Divinely drawn to follow thee,
Whose hours divided are
Betwixt the mount and multitude
Our day is spent in doing good,
Our night in praise and prayer.

2 With us no melancholy void,
No moment lingers unemploy'd,
Or unimproved below:
Our weariness of life is gone,
Who live to serve our God alone,
And only thee to know.

3 The winter's night, and summer's day
Glide imperceptibly away,
Too short to sing thy praise;
Too few we find the happy hours,
And haste to join those heavenly powers,
In everlasting lays.

4 With all who chant thy name on high,
And, Holy, holy, holy, cry—
A bright harmonious throng—
We long thy praises to repeat,
And ceaseless sing, around thy seat,
The new, eternal song.

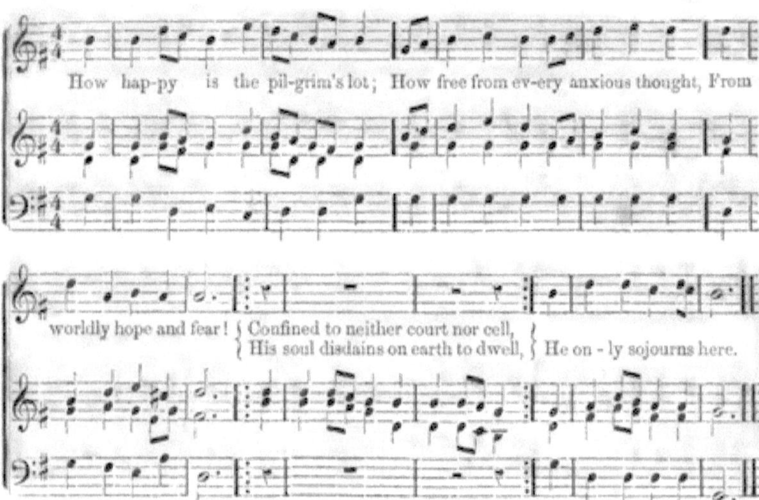

1041 *End of the journey.*

HOW happy is the pilgrim's lot;
How free from every anxious thought,
From worldly hope and fear!
Confined to neither court nor cell,
His soul disdains on earth to dwell,
He only sojourns here.

2 This happiness in part is mine,
Already saved from low design,
From every creature love!
Bless'd with the scorn of finite good,
My soul is lighten'd of its load,
And seeks the things above.

3 The things eternal I pursue;
A happiness beyond the view
Of those that basely pant
For things by nature felt and seen;
Their honours, wealth, and pleasures mean,
I neither have nor want.

4 I have no babes to hold me here,
But children more securely dear
For mine I humbly claim:
Better than daughters or than sons,
Temples divine of living stones,
Inscribed with Jesus' name.

5 No foot of land do I possess,
No cottage in this wilderness:
A poor way-faring man,
I lodge awhile in tents below;
Or gladly wander to and fro,
Till I my Canaan gain.

6 Nothing on earth I call my own,
A stranger, to the world unknown,
I all their goods despise:
I trample on their whole delight,
And seek a city out of sight,
A city in the skies.

7 There is my house and portion fair,
My treasure and my heart are there,
And my abiding home;
For me my elder brethren stay,
And angels beckon me away,
And Jesus bids me come!

8 I come,—thy servant, Lord, replies;—
I come to meet thee in the skies,
And claim my heavenly rest!
Now let the pilgrim's journey end;
Now, O my Saviour, Brother, Friend,
Receive me to thy breast!

841 *Thanksgiving for peace.*

A NATION God delights to bless,
Can all our raging foes distress,
Or hurt whom they surround?
Hid from the gen'ral scourge we are,
Nor see the bloody waste of war,
Nor hear the trumpet's sound.

2 O may we, Lord, the grace improve,
By lab'ring for the rest of love,
The soul-composing power;
Bless us with that internal peace,
And all the fruits of righteousness,
Till time shall be no more.

1057 *Doxology.*

ALL glory to th' eternal Three;
Thee, Father: thee, O Son; and thee,
The Spirit ever blest!—
That glory, which, through ages past,
Unchanged has stood, and yet shall last
When time has sunk to rest.

903 *Mutual aid.*

COME, wisdom, power, and grace divine!
Come, Jesus, in thy name to join
A happy, chosen band,
Who fain would prove thine utmost will,
And all thy righteous laws fulfil,
In love's benign command.

2 If pure essential love thou art,
Thy nature into every heart,
Thy loving self, inspire:
Bid all our simple souls be one,
United in a bond unknown,
Baptized with heavenly fire.

3 Still may we to our centre tend,
To spread thy praise our common end,
To help each other on;
Companions through the wilderness;
To share a moment's pain, and seize
An everlasting crown.

One only thing resolved to know,
And square our useful lives below
By reason and by grace.

4 Not in the tombs we pine to dwell,
Not in the dark monastic cell,
By vows and grates confined;
Freely to all ourselves we give,
Constrain'd by Jesus' love to live
The servants of mankind.

5 Now, Jesus, now thy love impart,
To govern each devoted heart,
And fit us for thy will!
Deep founded in the truth of grace,
Build up thy rising church, and place
The city on the hill.

6 O let our faith and love abound!
O let our lives to all around
With purest lustre shine!
That all around our works may see,
And give the glory, Lord, to thee,
The heavenly light divine!

273 *Opening Conference.*

EXCEPT the Lord conduct the plan,
The best-concerted schemes are vain,
And never can succeed;
We spend our wretched strength for naught,
But if our works in thee be wrought,
They shall be bless'd indeed.

2 Lord, if thou didst thyself inspire
Our souls with this intense desire,
Thy goodness to proclaim;
Thy glory if we now intend,
O let our deeds begin and end
Complete in Jesus' name!

3 In Jesus' name behold we meet,
Far from an evil world retreat,
And all its frantic ways;

580 *Circumspection.*

BE it my only wisdom here,
To serve the Lord with filial fear,
With loving gratitude;
Superior sense may I display,
By shunning every evil way,
And walking in the good.

2 O may I still from sin depart;
A wise and understanding heart,
Jesus, to me be given!
And let me through thy Spirit know
To glorify my God below,
And find my way to heaven.

MARDIE. C. P. M. (Four 8s & Two 6s.)

From "New Thes. Musicus."

522 *The beatitudes.—Matt. v. 3—8.*

SAVIOUR, on me the want bestow
Which all that feel shall surely know
Their sins on earth forgiven;
Give me to prove the kingdom mine,
And taste, in holiness divine,
The happiness of heaven.

2 Turn into flesh my heart of stone,
And, while I mourn for thee alone,
The consolation send,
O come thyself, my soul t' embrace,
And let my cheerful life of grace
In glorious comfort end!

3 Meeken my soul, thou heavenly Lamb,
That I in the new earth may claim
My hundred-fold reward,—
My rich inheritance possess,
Co-heir with the great Prince of peace,
Co-partner with my Lord.

4 Me with that restless thirst inspire,
That sacred, infinite desire,
And feast my hungry heart:
Less than thyself cannot suffice;
My soul for all thy fulness cries,
For all thou hast and art.

5 Mercy who show shall mercy find;
Thy pitiful and tender mind
Be, Lord, on me bestow'd;
So shall I still the blessing gain,
And to eternal life retain
The mercy of my God.

6 Jesus, the crowning grace impart!
Bless me with purity of heart;
That, now beholding thee,
I soon may view thy open face,
On all thy glorious beauties gaze,
And God for ever see!

928 *"Deliver us from evil."*

ARE there not in the lab'rer's day
Twelve hours, in which he safely may
His calling's work pursue?
Though sin and Satan still are near,
Nor sin nor Satan can I fear,
With Jesus in my view.

2 Light of the world, thy beams I bless,
On thee, bright Sun of righteousness,
My faith hath fix'd its eye,
Guided by thee through all I go,
Nor fear the ruin spread below,
For thou art always nigh.

3 Ten thousand snares my path beset,
Yet will I, Lord, the work complete,
Which thou to me hast given;
Regardless of the pains I feel,
Close by the gates of death and hell,
I urge my way to heaven.

4 Still will I strive, and labour still
With humble zeal to do thy will,
And trust in thy defence;
My soul into thy hands I give,
And, if he can obtain thy leave,
Let Satan pluck me thence.

Hy. 588 WILLOUGHBY. C. P. M. (Four 8s & Two 6s.)

1. Help, Lord, to whom for help I fly, And still my tempted soul stand by, Throughout the evil day; The sacred watchfulness impart, And keep the issues of my heart, And stir me up to pray.

2 My soul with thy whole armour arm,
In each approach of sin alarm,
And show the danger near:
Surround, sustain, and strengthen me,
And fill with godly jealousy
And sanctifying fear.

3 Whene'er my careless hands hang down,
O let me see thy gath'ring frown,
And feel thy warning eye;
And starting, cry from ruin's brink,
Save, Jesus, or I yield, I sink!
O save me, or I die!

4 If near the pit I rashly stray,
Before I wholly fall away,
The keen conviction dart!
Recall me by that pitying look,
That kind upbraiding glance, which broke
Unfaithful Peter's heart.

5 In me thine utmost mercy show,
And make me like thyself below,
Unblameable in grace;
Ready prepared and fitted here,
By perfect holiness, t' appear
Before thy glorious face.

1020 *For the head of a family.*

I AND my house will serve the Lord:
But first obedient to his word
I must myself appear;
By actions, words, and tempers, show
That I my heavenly Master know,
And serve with heart sincere.

2 I must the fair example set;
From those that on my pleasure wait
The stumbling-block remove;
Their duty by my life explain;
And still in all my works maintain
The dignity of love.

3 Easy to be entreated, mild,
Quickly appeased and reconciled,
A foll'wer of my God,—
A saint, indeed, I long to be,
And lead my faithful family
In the celestial road.

4 Lord, if thou didst the wish infuse,
A vessel fitted for thy use
Into thy hands receive;
Work in me both to will and do,
And show them how believers true,
And real Christians live.

5 With all-sufficient grace supply,
And, lo! I come to testify
The wonders of thy name,
Which saves from sin, the world, and hell,
Whose virtue every heart may feel,
And every tongue proclaim.

6 A sinner, saved myself from sin,
I come my family to win,
To preach their sins forgiven,
Children, and wife, and servants, seize,
And, through the paths of pleasantness,
Conduct them all to heaven.

988 *Death of a relative.*

IF death my friend and me divide,
Thou dost not, Lord, my sorrow chide,
Or frown, my tears to see;
Restrain'd from passionate excess,
Thou bidd'st me mourn in calm distress
For them that rest in thee.

2 I feel a strong, immortal hope,
Which bears my mournful spirit up
Beneath its mountain-load:
Redeem'd from death, and grief, and pain,
I soon shall find my friend again
Within the arms of God.

3 Pass a few fleeting moments more,
And death the blessing shall restore,
Which death has snatch'd away;
For me thou wilt the summons send,
And give me back my parted friend
In that eternal day,

ARIEL. C. P M. (Four 8s & Two 6s.) Dr. L. Mason.

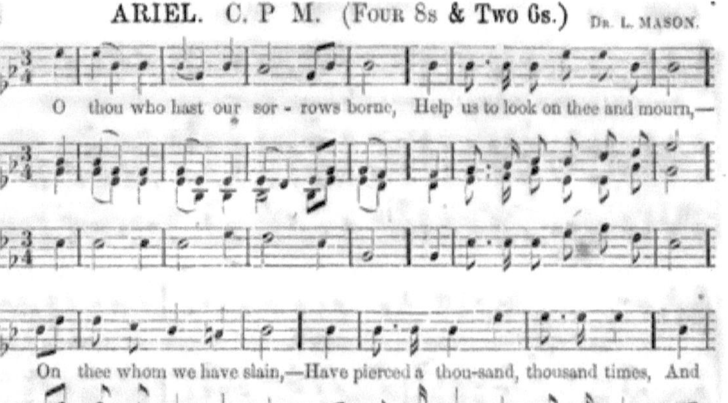

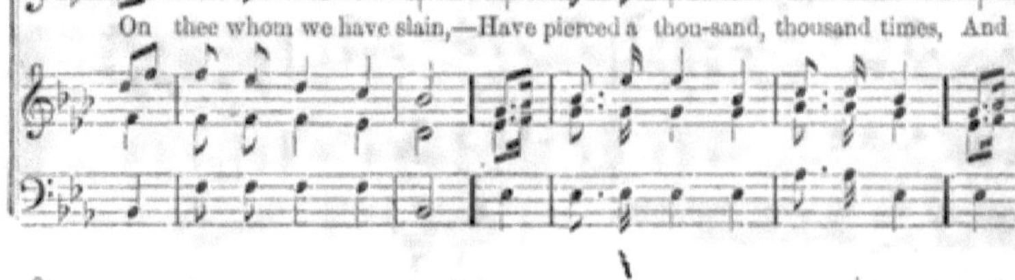

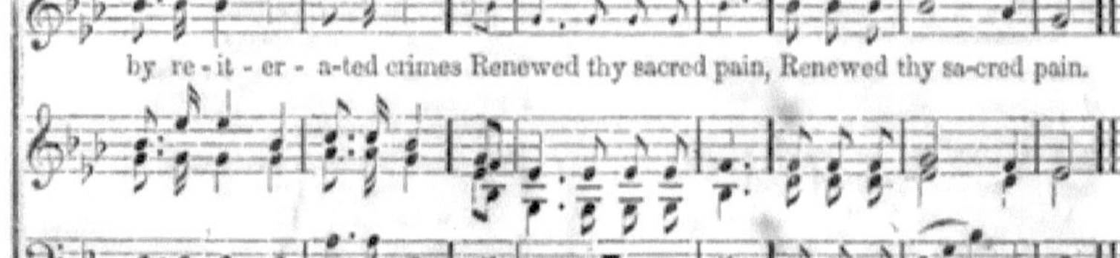

434 *Looking at the Cross.*

O THOU who hast our sorrows borne,
Help us to look on thee and mourn,—
On thee whom we have slain,—
Have pierced a thousand, thousand times,
And by reiterated crimes
Renew'd thy sacred pain.

2 Vouchsafe us eyes of faith to see
The man transfix'd on Calvary!
To know thee who thou art,
The one eternal God and true;
And let the sight affect, subdue,
And break my stubborn heart.

3 Lover of souls, to rescue mine,
Reveal the charity divine,
That suffer'd in my stead!
That made thy soul a sacrifice,
And quench'd in death those flaming eyes,
And bow'd that sacred head.

4 The veil of unbelief remove,
And by thy manifested love,
And by thy sprinkled blood,
Destroy the love of sin in me,
And get thyself the victory,
And bring me back to God.

5 Now let thy dying love constrain
My soul to love its God again,
Its God to glorify!
And lo! I come thy cross to share,
Echo thy sacrificial prayer,
And with my Saviour die!

437 *Languishing for love.*

STILL, Lord, I languish for thy grace;
Reveal the beauties of thy face,
The middle wall remove:
Appear, and banish my complaint;
Come and supply my only want,
Fill all my soul with love!

2 To thee I lift my mournful eye;
Why am I thus? O tell me why
I cannot love my God?
The hind'rance must be all in me;
It cannot in my Saviour be;
Witness that streaming blood!

3 It cost thy blood my heart to win,
To buy me from the power of sin,
And make me love again:
Come, then, my Lord, thy right assert,
Take to thyself my ransom'd heart,
Nor bleed nor die in vain.

440 *For the witness of the Spirit.*

THOU great mysterious God unknown,
Whose love hath gently led me on,
E'en from my infant days;
Mine inmost soul expose to view,
And tell me if I ever knew
Thy justifying grace.

2 If I have only known thy fear,
And follow'd, with a heart sincere,
Thy drawings from above;
Now, now the further grace bestow,
And let my sprinkled conscience know
Thy sweet forgiving love.

3 Short of thy love I would not stop,
A stranger to the gospel hope,
The sense of sin forgiven:
I would not, Lord, my soul deceive,
Without the inward Witness live,
That antepast of heaven.

4 If now the Witness were in me,
Would he not testify of thee,
In Jesus reconciled?
And should I not with faith draw nigh,
And boldly, Abba, Father, cry,
And know myself thy child?

5 Whate'er obstructs thy pard'ning love,—
Or sin, or righteousness,—remove,
Thy glory to display;
My heart of unbelief convince,
And now absolve me from my sins,
And take them all away.

6 Father, in me reveal thy Son,
And to my inmost soul make known
How merciful thou art:
The secret of thy love reveal,
And by thy hallowing Spirit dwell
For ever in my heart!

408 *The prisoner of hope.*

THEE, Jesus, thee, the sinner's Friend,
I follow on to apprehend,
Renew the glorious strife;
Divinely confident and bold,
With faith's strong arm on thee lay hold,
Thee, my eternal life.

2 Thy heart, I know, thy tender heart,
Doth in my sorrows feel its part,
And at my tears relent;
My powerful sighs thou canst not bear,
Nor stand the vi'lence of my prayer,
My prayer omnipotent.

3 Give me thy grace, the love I claim,
Thy Spirit now demands thy name!
Thou know'st the Spirit's will;
He helps my soul's infirmity,
And strongly intercedes for me
With groans unspeakable.

4 Answer, O Lord, thy Spirit's groan!
O make to me thy nature known;
Thy hidden name impart!
(Thy name and nature are the same)
Tell me thy nature and thy name,
And write it on my heart.

409 *The prisoner of hope.*

PRIS'NER of hope—to thee I turn,
And, calmly confident, I mourn,
And pray and weep for thee:
Tell me thy love, thy secret tell;
Thy mystic name in me reveal,
Reveal thyself in me.

2 Descend, pass by me, and proclaim,
O Lord of hosts, thy glorious name,—
The Lord, the gracious Lord,
Long-suffering, merciful, and kind,
The God who always bears in mind
His everlasting word.

3 Plenteous he is in truth and grace;
He wills that all the fallen race
Should turn, repent, and live;
His pard'ning grace for all is free;
Transgression, sin, iniquity,
He freely doth forgive.

4 Mercy he doth for thousands keep;
He goes and seeks the one lost sheep,
And brings his wand'rer home:
And every soul that sheep might be;
Come, then, my Lord, and gather me,
My Jesus, quickly come.

523 *The beatitudes.—Matt. v. 9—12.*

LORD, give me that pacific mind
Which spreads thy peace among mankind,
And knits them all in one:
So shall he own me for his child,
Who all, through thee, hath reconciled,
And take me to his throne.

2 Not for my fault, or folly's sake,
The name, or mode, or form I take,
But for true holiness:
Let me be wrong'd, reviled, abhorr'd,
And thee, my sanctifying Lord,
In life and death confess.

3 Call'd to sustain the hallow'd cross,
And suffer for thy righteous cause,
Pronounce me doubly blest;
And let thy glorious Spirit, Lord,
Assure me of my great reward,
In heaven's eternal feast.

SHUBERT. C. P. M. (Four 8s & Two 6s.) L. C. E.

75 *Psalm cxlviii.*

BEGIN, my soul, th' exalted lay,
Let each enraptured thought obey,
And praise th' Almighty's name:
Lo! heaven and earth, and seas and skies,
In one melodious concert rise,
To swell th' inspiring theme.

2 Ye fields of light, celestial plains,
Where gay, transporting beauty reigns,
Ye scenes divinely fair;
Your Maker's wondrous power proclaim,
Tell how he form'd your shining frame.
And breathed the fluid air

3 Ye angels catch the thrilling sound;
While all th' adoring thrones around
His boundless mercy sing,
Let every listening saint above
Wake all the tuneful soul of love,
And touch the sweetest string.

4 Join, ye loud spheres, the vocal choir:
Thou dazzling orb of liquid fire,
The mighty chorus aid:
Soon as gray evening gilds the plain,
Thou, moon, protract the melting strain,
And praise him in the shade.

5 Let every element rejoice:
Ye thunders, burst with awful voice
To him who bids you roll:
His praise in softer notes declare,
Each whispering breeze of yielding air,
And breathe it to the soul.

6 Let man, for nobler service made,
The feeling heart, the judging head,
In heavenly praise employ
Spread his tremendous name around,
Till heaven's broad arch rings back the sound,
The general burst of joy.

7 Ye, whom the charms of grandeur please,
Nursed on the downy lap of ease,
Fall prostrate at his throne;
Ye princes, rulers, all adore;
Praise him, ye kings, who makes your pow r
An image of his own.

8 Let youth its ardent passions move,
To praise th' eternal source of love,
With all its hallow'd fire·
Let age take up the tuneful lay,
Sigh his bless'd name, then soar away,
And ask an angel's lyre.

9 Let saints, redeem'd from death and hell,
In louder, loftier numbers, tell
The wonders of his grace:
Beyond creation's utmost bounds;
Above her noblest, sweetest sounds,
Declare Jehovah's praise.

436 *Panting for the love of God.*

O LOVE divine, how sweet thou art!
When shall I find my willing heart
All taken up by thee?
I thirst, I faint, I die to prove
The greatness of redeeming love,
The love of Christ to me.

2 Stronger his love than death or hell,
Its riches are unsearchable;
The first-born sons of light
Desire in vain its depths to see;
They cannot reach the mystery,
The length, the breadth, the height.

3 God only knows the love of God:
O that it now were shed abroad
In this poor stony heart!
For love I sigh, for love I pine;
This only portion, Lord, be mine!
Be mine this better part!

4 O that I could for ever sit
With Mary at the Master's feet!
Be this my happy choice:
My only care, delight, and bliss,
My joy, my heaven on earth, be this,
To hear the Bridegroom's voice!

5 O that with humbled Peter, I
Could weep, believe, and thrice reply,
My faithfulness to prove,
Thou know'st, for all to thee is known,
Thou know'st, O Lord, and thou alone,
Thou know'st that thee I love.

6 O that I could with favour'd John
Recline my weary head upon
The dear Redeemer's breast!
From care, and sin, and sorrow free,
Give me, O Lord, to find in thee
My everlasting rest!

7 Thy only love do I require,
Nothing in earth beneath desire,
Nothing in heaven above;
Let earth, and heaven, and all things go,
Give me thy only love to know,
Give me thy only love.

513 *Rejoicing in hope.*

O GLORIOUS hope of perfect love!
It lifts me up to things above!
It bears on eagles' wings;
It gives my ravish'd soul a taste,
And makes me for some moments feast
With Jesus' priests and kings.

2 Rejoicing now in earnest hope,
I stand, and, from the mountain top,
See all the land below:
Rivers of milk and honey rise,
And all the fruits of paradise,
In endless plenty grow.

3 A land of corn, and wine, and oil,
Favour'd with God's peculiar smile,
With every blessing blest;
There dwells the Lord our Righteousness,
And keeps his own in perfect peace,
And everlasting rest.

4 O that I might at once go up!
No more on this side Jordan stop,
But now the land possess!
This moment end my legal years;
Sorrows, and sins, and doubts, and fears,
A howling wilderness.

5 Now, O my Joshua, bring me in!
Cast out thy foes; the inbred sin,
The carnal mind, remove;
The purchase of thy death divide;
And, O! with all the sanctified,
Give me a lot of love!

673 *The end of life.*

AND am I only born to die?
And must I suddenly comply
With nature's stern decree?
What after death for me remains?
Celestial joys, or hellish pains,
To all eternity!

2 How then ought I on earth to live,
While God prolongs the kind reprieve,
And props the house of clay:
My sole concern, my single care,
To watch, and tremble, and prepare
Against that fatal day!

3 No room for mirth or trifling here,
For worldly hope, or worldly fear,
If life so soon is gone;
If now the Judge is at the door,
And all mankind must stand before
Th' inexorable throne!

4 No matter which my thoughts employ
A moment's misery or joy;
But O! when both shall end,
Where shall I find my destined place?
Shall I my everlasting days
With fiends or angels spend?

5 Nothing is worth a thought beneath,
But how I may escape the death,
That never, never dies!
How make mine own election sure;
And when I fail on earth, secure
A mansion in the skies.

6 Jesus, vouchsafe a pitying ray,
Be thou my guide, be thou my way,
To glorious happiness!
Ah! write the pardon on my heart!
And whensoe'er I hence depart,
Let me depart in peace!

1057 *Doxology.*

ALL glory to th' eternal Three;
Thee, Father; thee, O Son; and thee,
The Spirit ever blest!—
That glory, which, through ages past,
Unchanged has stood, and yet shall last
When time has sunk to rest.

122 *Praying for faith.*

AUTHOR of faith, to thee I cry,—
To thee, who wouldst not have me die,
But know the truth and live:
Open mine eyes to see thy face,
Work in my heart the saving grace,
The life eternal give.

2 Shut up in unbelief I groan,
And blindly serve a God unknown,
Till thou the veil remove;
The gift unspeakable impart,
And write thy name upon my heart,
And manifest thy love.

3 I know the grace is only thine,
The gift of faith is all divine;
But if on thee we call,
Thou wilt the benefit bestow,
And give us hearts to feel and know
That thou hast died for ALL.

4 Thou bidd'st us knock and enter in,
Come unto thee, and rest from sin,
The blessing seek and find:
Thou bidd'st us ask thy grace, and have;
Thou canst, thou wouldst this moment save
Both me and all mankind.

5 Be it according to thy word;
Now let me find my pard'ning Lord;
Let what I ask be given
The bar of unbelief remove,
Open the door of faith and love,
And take me into heaven!

672 *The end of life.*

THOU God of glorious majesty,
To thee, against myself, to thee,
A worm of earth, I cry!
A half-awaken'd child of man,
An heir of endless bliss or pain,
A sinner born to die!

2 Lo! on a narrow neck of land,
'Twixt two unbounded seas I stand,
Secure, insensible:
A point of time, a moment's space,
Removes me to that heavenly place,
Or shuts me up in hell.

3 O God, mine inmost soul convert,
And deeply on my thoughtful heart
Eternal things impress:
Give me to feel their solemn weight,
And tremble on the brink of fate,
And wake to righteousness!

4 Before me place in dread array
The pomp of that tremendous day,
When thou with clouds shalt come
To judge the nations at thy bar;
And tell me, Lord, shall I be there,
To meet a joyful doom?

5 Be this my one great business here,
With serious industry and fear
Eternal bliss t' ensure,
Thine utmost counsel to fulfill,
And suffer all thy righteous will,
And to the end endure.

6 Then, Saviour, then my soul receive,
Transported from this vale to live
And reign with thee above—
Where faith is sweetly lost in sight,
And hope in full supreme delight,
And everlasting love.

755 *Rapid extension.*

SAVIOUR, we know thou art
 In every age the same;
Now, Lord, in ours exert
 The virtue of thy name;
And daily, through thy word, increase
Thy blood-besprinkled witnesses.

2 Thy people, saved below
 From every sinful stain,
Shall multiply and grow,
 If thy command ordain;
And one into a thousand rise,
And spread thy praise through earth and skies.

3 In many a soul, and mine,
 Thou hast display'd thy power,
But to thy people join
 Ten thousand thousand more;
Saved from the guilt and strength of sin,
In life and heart entirely clean.

157 *Psalm xlvii. 5–9.*

GOD is gone up on high,
 With a triumphant noise,
The clarions of the sky
 Proclaim th' angelic joys!
Join all on earth, rejoice and sing,
Glory ascribe to glory's King.

2 God in the flesh below,
 For us he reigns above:
Let all the nations know
 Our Jesus' conq'ring love!
Join all on earth, rejoice and sing;
Glory ascribe to glory's King.

3 All power to our great Lord
 Is by the Father given;
By angel-hosts adored,
 He reigns supreme in heaven
Join all on earth, rejoice and sing;
Glory ascribe to glory's King.

4 Till all the earth, renew'd
 In righteousness divine,
With all the hosts of God
 In one great chorus join,
Join all on earth, rejoice and sing,
Glory ascribe to glory's King.

256 *Isaiah lv. 10–13.*

MARK the soft falling snow,
 And the diffusive rain:
To heaven from whence it fell,
 It turns not back again;
But waters earth through every pore,
And calls forth all her secret store.

2 Array'd in beauteous green
 The hills and valleys shine,
And man and beast are fed
 By providence divine:
The harvest bows its golden ears,
The copious seed of future years.

3 So, saith the God of grace,
 My gospel shall descend,
Almighty to effect
 The purpose I intend:
Millions of souls shall feel its power,
And bear it down to millions more.

4 Joy shall begin your march,
 And peace protect your ways,
While all the mountains round
 Echo melodious praise;
The vocal grove shall sing the God,
And every tree consenting nod.

158 *The Reign of Christ.*

REJOICE, the Lord is King;
Your Lord and King adore;
Mortals, give thanks, and sing,
And triumph evermore;
Lift up your hearts, lift up your voice,
Rejoice, again I say, rejoice.

2 Jesus, the Saviour, reigns,
The God of truth and love;
When he had purged our stains,
He took his seat above;
Lift up your hearts, lift up your voice,
Rejoice, again I say, rejoice.

3 His kingdom cannot fail,
He rules o'er earth and heaven,
The keys of death and hell
Are to our Jesus given;
Lift up your hearts, lift up your voice,
Rejoice, again I say, rejoice.

4 He sits at God's right hand
Till all his foes submit,
And bow to his command,
And fall beneath his feet;
Lift up your hearts, lift up your voice,
Rejoice, again I say, rejoice.

5 He all his foes shall quell,
Shall all our sins destroy:
And every bosom swell
With pure seraphic joy;
Lift up your hearts, lift up your voice,
Rejoice, again I say, rejoice.

6 Rejoice in glorious hope,
Jesus, the Judge shall come,
And take his servants up
To their eternal home;
We soon shall hear th' archangel's voice,
The trump of God shall sound, Rejoice!

74 *Psalm cxlviii.*

YE boundless realms of joy,
Exalt your Maker's fame;
His praise your song employ
Above the starry frame:
Your voices raise, Ye cherubim
And seraphim, To sing his praise.

2 Thou moon, that rul'st the night,
And sun, that guid'st the day,
Ye glitt'ring stars of light,
To him your homage pay:
His praise declare, Ye heavens above,
And clouds that move In liquid air.

3 Let them adore the Lord,
And praise his holy name,
By whose almighty word
They all from nothing came,
And all shall last, From changes free;
His firm decree Stands ever fast.

4 Let earth her tribute pay:
Praise him, ye dreadful whales,
And fish that through the sea
Glide swift, with glitt'ring scales;
Fire, hail, and snow, And misty air,
And winds that where, He bids them blow.

5 By hills and mountains, all
In grateful concert join'd;
By cedars stately tall,
And trees for fruit design'd;
By every beast, And creeping thing,
And fowl of wing, His name be blest.

6 Let all of highest birth,
With those of humbler name,
And judges of the earth,
His matchless praise proclaim:
In this design, Let youths with maids,
And hoary heads With children, join.

7 United zeal be shown
His wondrous fame to raise,
Whose glorious name alone
Deserves our endless praise:
Earth's utmost ends His power obey;
His glorious sway The sky transcends.

8 His chosen saints to grace,
He sets them up on high;
And favours Israel's race,
Who still to him are nigh:
O therefore raise Your grateful voice,
And still rejoice The Lord to praise!

161 *"Seen of angels."*

O YE immortal throng
Of angels round the throne,
Join with our feeble song,
To make the Saviour known:
On earth ye knew His wondrous grace;
His beauteous face In heaven ye view.

2 Ye saw the heaven-born child
In human flesh array'd,
Benevolent and mild,
While in the manger laid:
And praise to God, And peace on earth,
For such a birth, Proclaim'd aloud.

3 Ye, in the wilderness,
Beheld the tempter spoil'd,
Well known in every dress,
In every combat foil'd:
And joy'd to crown The Victor's head,
When Satan fled Before his frown.

4 Around the bloody tree
Ye press'd with strong desire,
That wondrous sight to see,—
The Lord of life expire;
And could your eyes Have known a tear,
Had dropp'd it there In sad surprise.

5 Around his sacred tomb
A willing watch ye keep,
Till the bless'd moment come,
To rouse him from his sleep;
Then roll'd the stone, And all adored
Your rising Lord, With joy unknown.

6 When all array'd in light,
The shining Conqu'ror rode,
Ye hail'd his rapt'rous flight
Up to the throne of God;
And waved around Your golden wings,
And struck your strings Of sweetest sound.

7 The warbling notes pursue,
And louder anthems raise;
While mortals sing with you
Their *own* Redeemer's praise;
And thou, my heart, With equal flame,
And joy the same, Perform thy part.

514 *Rejoicing in hope.*

YE ransom'd sinners, hear,
The pris'ners of the Lord,
And wait till Christ appear,
According to his word:
Rejoice in hope, rejoice with me,
We shall from all our sins be free.

2 In God we put our trust;
If we our sins confess,
Faithful is he, and just,
From all unrighteousness
To cleanse us all, both you and me:
We shall from all our sins be free.

3 The word of God is sure,
And never can remove;
We shall in heart be pure
And perfected in love:
Rejoice in hope, rejoice with me,
We shall from all our sins be free.

4 Then let us gladly bring
Our sacrifice of praise;
Let us give thanks and sing,
And glory in his grace:
Rejoice in hope, rejoice with me,
We shall from all our sins be free.

633 *"Leaving us an example."*

SEE where our great High Priest
Before the Lord appears,
And on his loving breast
The tribes of Israel bears,
Never without his people seen,
The Head of all believing men!

2 With him the corner stone
The living stones conjoin,
Christ and his church are one,
One body and one vine;
For us he uses all his powers,
And all he has, or is, is ours.

3 The motions of our Head
The members all pursue,
By his good Spirit led
To act and suffer too:
Like him, the toil, the cross sustain,
Till glorious all like him we reign.

325 *The year of Jubilee.*

BLOW ye the trumpet, blow,
The gladly solemn sound;
Let all the nations know,
To earth's remotest bound,
The year of jubilee is come;
Return, ye ransom'd sinners, home.

2 Jesus, our great High Priest,
Hath full atonement made:
Ye weary spirits, rest;
Ye mournful souls, be glad;
The year of jubilee is come;
Return, ye ransom'd sinners, home.

3 Extol the Lamb of God,
The all-atoning Lamb;
Redemption through his blood
Throughout the world proclaim!
The year of jubilee is come;
Return, ye ransom'd sinners, home.

4 Ye slaves of sin and hell,
Your liberty receive,
And safe in Jesus dwell,
And bless'd in Jesus live;
The year of jubilee is come;
Return, ye ransom'd sinners, home.

5 Ye who have sold for naught
Your heritage above,
Receive it back unbought,
The gift of Jesus' love;
The year of jubilee is come;
Return, ye ransom'd sinners, home.

6 The gospel trumpet hear,
The news of heavenly grace;
And, saved from earth, appear
Before your Saviour's face;
The year of jubilee is come;
Return, ye ransom'd sinners, home.

319 *Psalm lxxxiv.*

LORD of the worlds above,
How pleasant and how fair
The dwellings of thy love,
Thine earthly temples, are!
To thine abode My heart aspires,
With warm desires, To see my God.

2 O happy souls that pray
Where God appoints to hear!
O happy men that pay
Their constant service there!
They praise thee still; And happy they
That love the way To Zion's hill.

3 They go from strength to strength
Through this dark vale of tears,
Till each arrives at length,
Till each in heaven appears;
O glorious seat, When God our King
Shall thither bring Our willing feet!

4 To spend one sacred day
Where God and saints abide,
Affords diviner joy
Than thousand days beside:
Where God resorts, I love it more
To keep the door Than shine in courts.

1056 *Doxology.*

TO God the Father's throne
Perpetual honours raise;
Glory to God the Son,
To God the Spirit praise:
With all our powers, Eternal King,
Thy name we sing, While faith adores.

137 *The great Antitype.*

ISRAEL, in ancient days,
Not only had a view
Of Sinai in a blaze,
But learn'd the gospel too;
The types and figures were a glass
In which they saw the Saviour's face.

2 The paschal sacrifice,
And blood-besprinkled door,—
Seen with enlighten'd eyes,
And once applied with power,
Would teach the need of other blood
To reconcile the world to God.

3 The lamb, the dove, set forth
His perfect innocence,
Whose blood of matchless worth
Should be the soul's defence:
For he who can for sin atone
Must have no failings of his own.

4 The scape-goat, on his head,
The people's trespass bore;
And to the desert led,
Was to be seen no more:
In him our Surety seem'd to say,
"Behold, I bear your sins away."

5 Dipp'd in his fellow's blood,
The living bird went free:
The type, well understood,
Express'd the sinner's plea—
Described a guilty soul enlarged,
And, by a Saviour's death, discharged.

6 Jesus, I love to trace,
Throughout the sacred page,
The footsteps of thy grace,
The same in ev'ry age!
O grant that I may faithful be
To clearer light vouchsafed to me!

171 *Various offices of Christ.*

JESUS, my great *High Priest*,
Offer'd his blood and died:
My guilty conscience seeks
No sacrifice beside;
His powerful blood did once atone,
And now it pleads before the throne.

2 My *Advocate* appears
For my defence on high;
The Father bows his ear,
And lays his thunder by:
Not all that earth or hell can say
Shall turn his heart, his love away.

3 O thou almighty *Lord*,
My *Conq'rer* and my *King*,
Thy sceptre, and thy sword,
Thy reigning grace, I sing:
Thine is the power; behold I sit
In willing bonds beneath thy feet.

4 Now let my soul arise,
And tread the tempter down;
My *Captain* leads me forth
To conquest and a crown.
A feeble saint shall win the day,
Though death and hell obstruct the way.

5 Should all the hosts of death,
And powers of hell unknown,
Put their most dreadful forms
Of rage and mischief on,
I shall be safe, for *Christ* displays
Superior power, and guardian grace.

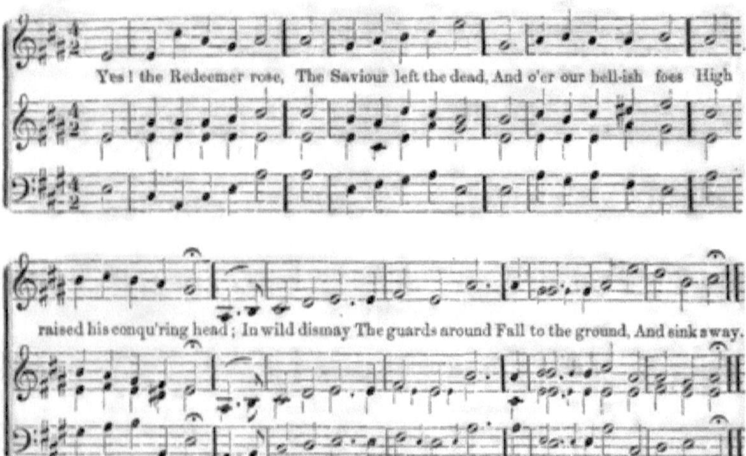

141 *Resurrection.*

YES! the Redeemer rose,
 The Saviour left the dead,
And o'er our hellish foes
 High raised his conqu'ring head:
In wild dismay, The guards around
Fall to the ground, And sink away.

2 Lo! the angelic bands
 In full assembly meet,
To wait his high commands,
 And worship at his feet;
Joyful they come, And wing their way,
From realms of day, To Jesus' tomb.

3 Then back to heaven they fly,
 The joyful news to bear:
Hark! as they soar on high,
 What music fills the air!
Their anthems say, "Jesus, who bled,
Has left the dead; He rose to-day."

4 Ye mortals, catch the sound,
 Redeem'd by Him from hell:
And send the echo round
 The globe, on which you dwell;
Transported cry, "Jesus, who bled,
Hath left the dead, No more to die."

5 All hail, triumphant Lord,
 Who sav'st us with thy blood!
Wide be thy name adored,
 Thou rising, reigning God;
With thee we rise, With thee we reign,
And empires gain, Beyond the skies.

170. *Various offices of Christ.*

JOIN all the glorious names
 Of wisdom, love, and power,
That ever mortals knew,
 That angels ever bore;
All are too mean to speak his worth,
Too mean to set my *Saviour* forth.

2 But O! what gentle terms,
 What condescending ways,
Doth our *Redeemer* use
 To teach his heavenly grace!
Mine eyes with joy and wonder see
What forms of love he bears for me.

3 Array'd in mortal flesh,
 The *Cov'nant-Angel* stands,
And holds the promises
 And pardons in his hands;
Commission'd from his Father's throne
To make his grace to mortals known.

4 Great *Prophet* of my God,
 My tongue would bless thy name;
By thee the joyful news
 Of our salvation came;
The joyful news of sins forgiven,
Of hell subdued, and peace with Heaven.

5 Be thou my *Counsellor*,
 My *Pattern* and my *Guide*;
And through this desert land
 Still keep me near thy side:
O let my feet ne'er run astray,
Nor rove, nor seek the crooked way.

6 I love my *Shepherd's* voice,
His watchful eyes shall keep
My wand'ring soul among
The thousands of his sheep:
He feeds his flock, he calls their names,
His bosom bears the tender lambs.

263 *A savour of life or death.*

PRAISE to the Lord on high,
Who spreads his triumphs wide!
While Jesus' fragrant name
Is breathed on every side:
Balmy and rich the odours rise,
And fill the earth, and reach the skies.

2 Ten thousand dying souls
Its influence feel—and live;
Sweeter than vital air
The incense they receive:
They breathe anew, and rise and sing—
Jesus, the Lord, their conqu'ring King.

3 But others scorn the grace
That brings salvation nigh:
They turn away their face,
And faint, and fall, and die.
So sad a doom, ye saints, deplore,
For O! they fall to rise no more.

4 Yet, wise and mighty God,
Shall all thy servants be,
In those who live or die,
A savour sweet to thee;
Supremely bright thy grace shall shine,
Guarded with flames of wrath divine.

804 *New-Year's day.*

THE Lord of earth and sky,
The God of ages praise!
Who reigns enthroned on high,
Ancient of endless days!
Who lengthens out our trials here,
And spares us yet another year.

2 Barren and wither'd trees,
We cumber'd long the ground!
No fruit of holiness
On our dead souls was found;
Yet doth he us in mercy spare
Another and another year.

3 When justice gave the word,
To cut the fig-tree down,
The pity of the Lord
Cried, "Let it still alone!"
The Father mild inclines his ear,
And spares us yet another year.

4 Jesus, thy speaking blood
From God obtain'd the grace;
Who therefore hath bestow'd
On us a longer space;
Thou didst in our behalf appear,
And lo! we see another year!

5 Then dig about the root,
Break up our fallow ground,
And let our gracious fruit
To thy great praise abound;
O let us all thy praise declare,
And fruit unto perfection bear!

602 *"Am I my brother's keeper?"*

MUST I my brother keep,
And share his pain and toil,
And weep with those that weep,
And smile with those that smile,
And act to each a brother's part,
And feel his sorrows in my heart?

2 Must I his burden bear,
As though it were my own,
And do as I would care
Should to myself be done?
And faithful to his interests prove,
And as myself my neighbour love?

3 Must I reprove his sin,
Must I partake his grief,
And kindly enter in,
And minister relief?
The naked clothe, the hungry feed,
And love him, not in word, but deed?

4 Then, Jesus, at thy feet
A student let me be,
And learn, as it is meet,
My duty, Lord, from thee;
For thou didst come on mercy's plan,
And all thy life was love to man.

5 O make me as thou art,
Thy Spirit, Lord, bestow;
The kind and gentle heart
That feels another's wo;
That thus I may be like my Head,
And in my Saviour's footsteps tread.

783 *Dedication.*

GOD of thine Israel true,
Their pillar, shield, and rock,
Who, all the desert through,
Didst lead them like a flock,
In this our sanctuary dwell,
Thou glorious, felt, Invisible!

2 That holy peace shed down,
The world can never give;
Thy truth with triumph crown,
Command the dead to live;
And fill this consecrated place
With living trophies of thy grace.

3 Great Shepherd of thy flock,
Our glorious leader be;
Our pillar, shield, and rock,
Till the fair land we see:
Ruler of heaven's eternal sphere,
Be thou the guardian glory here!

HADDAM. H. M. (Four 6s & Two 8s) Dr. L. Mason.

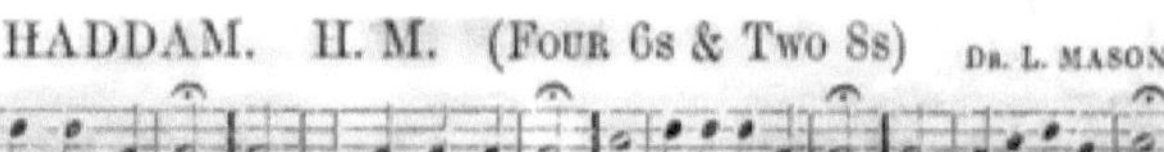

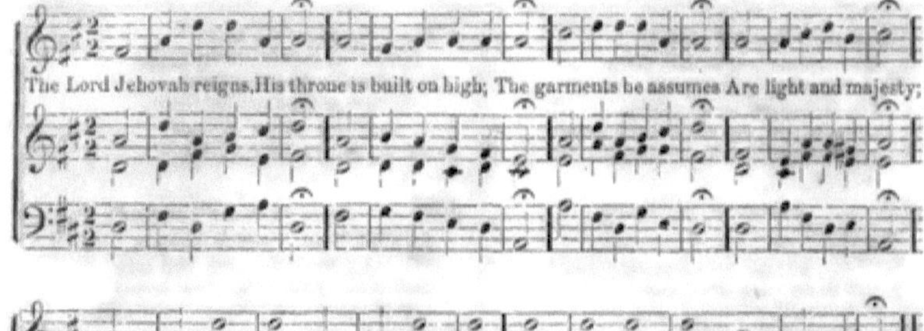

58 *Psalm xcvii.*

THE Lord Jehovah reigns,
His throne is built on high;
The garments he assumes
Are light and majesty:
His glories shine with beams so bright,
No mortal eye can bear the sight.

2 The thunders of his hand
Keep the wide world in awe;
His wrath and justice stand
To guard his holy law;
And where his love resolves to bless,
His truth confirms and seals the grace.

3 Through all his mighty works
Amazing wisdom shines,
Confounds the powers of hell,
And breaks their dark designs;
Strong is his arm, and shall fulfil
His great decrees and sovereign will.

4 And will this sovereign King
Of glory condescend?
And will he write his name,
My Father and my Friend?
I love his name, I love his word;
Join all my powers to praise the Lord!

77 *Psalm cxlviii. 12, 13.*

YOUNG men and maidens, raise
Your tuneful voices high;
Old men and children, praise
The Lord of earth and sky;
Him Three in One, and One in Three,
Extol to all eternity.

2 The universal King
Let all the world proclaim:
Let every creature sing
His attributes and name!
Him Three in One, and One in Three,
Extol to all eternity.

3 In his great name alone
All excellences meet:
Who sits upon the throne,
And shall for ever sit:
Him Three in One, and One in Three,
Extol to all eternity.

4 Glory to God belongs;
Glory to God be given;
Above the noblest songs,
Of all in earth and heaven:
Him Three in One, and One in Three,
Extol to all eternity.

177 *The Saviour's praise.*

LET earth and heaven agree,
Angels and men be join'd,
To celebrate with me
The Saviour of mankind;
T' adore the all-atoning Lamb,
And bless the sound of Jesus' name.

2 Jesus! transporting sound!
The joy of earth and heaven:
No other help is found,
No other name is given,
By which we can salvation have;
But Jesus came the world to save.

3 Jesus! harmonious name!
It charms the hosts above;
They evermore proclaim,
And wonder at his love!
'Tis all their happiness to gaze,
'Tis heaven to see our Jesus' face.

4 His name the sinner hears,
And is from sin set free;
'Tis music in his ears;
'Tis life and victory:
New songs do now his lips employ,
And dances his glad heart for joy.

5 Stung by the scorpion, sin,
My poor expiring soul
The balmy sound drinks in,
And is at once made whole:
See there my Lord upon the tree!
I hear, I feel he died for me.

6 O unexampled love!
O all-redeeming grace!
How swiftly didst thou move
To save a fallen race!
What shall I do to make it known
What thou for all mankind hast done?

7 O for a trumpet voice,
On all the world to call!
To bid their hearts rejoice
In Him who died for all!
For all my Lord was crucified;
For all, for all my Saviour died.

822 *Watch-night.*

YE virgin souls, arise,
With all the dead awake
Unto salvation wise,
Oil in your vessels take:
Upstarting at the midnight cry,
"Behold the heavenly Bridegroom nigh!"

2 He comes, he comes, to call
The nations to his bar,
And raise to glory all
Who fit for glory are
Made ready for your full reward,
Go forth with joy to meet your Lord.

3 Go meet him in the sky,
Your everlasting Friend:
Your Head to glorify,
With all his saints ascend:
Ye pure in heart, obtain the grace
To see, without a veil, his face!

4 The everlasting doors
Shall soon the saints receive,
Above yon angel powers
In glorious joy to live:
Far from a world of grief and sin,
With God eternally shut in.

17

868 *The spiritual voyage.*

JESUS! at thy command
I launch into the deep,
And leave my native land,
Where sin lulls all asleep:
For thee I would the world resign,
And sail to heaven with thee and thine.

2 Thou art my Pilot wise;
My compass is thy word:
My soul each storm defies,
While I have such a Lord!
I trust thy faithfulness and power
To save me in the trying hour.

3 Though rocks and quicksands deep
Through all my passage lie;
Yet Christ will safely keep,
And guide me with his eye:
My anchor, hope, shall firm abide,
And I each boist'rous storm outride.

4 By faith I see the land,
The port of endless rest.
My soul, thy sails expand,
And fly to Jesus' breast!
O may I reach the heavenly shore,
Where winds and waves distress no more.

5 Come, Holy Ghost, and blow
A prosp'rous gale of grace!
Waft me from all below
To heaven, my destined place.
Then, in full sail, my port I'll find,
And leave the world and sin behind.

874 *Opening the exercises.*

THOU God of truth and love,
We seek thy perfect way,
Ready thy choice t' approve,
Thy providence t' obey;
Enter into thy wise design,
And sweetly lose our will in thine.

2 Why hast thou cast our lot
In the same age and place?
And why together brought
To see each other's face?
To join with softest sympathy,
And mix our friendly souls in thee?

3 Surely thou didst unite
Our kindred spirits here,
That all hereafter might
Before thy throne appear:
Meet at the marriage of the Lamb,
And all thy gracious love proclaim.

4 Then let us ever bear
The blessed end in view,
And join with mutual care
To fight our passage through;
And kindly help each other on,
Till all receive the starry crown.

LISCHER. H. M. (Four 6s & Two 8s.) From "Carmina Sacra."

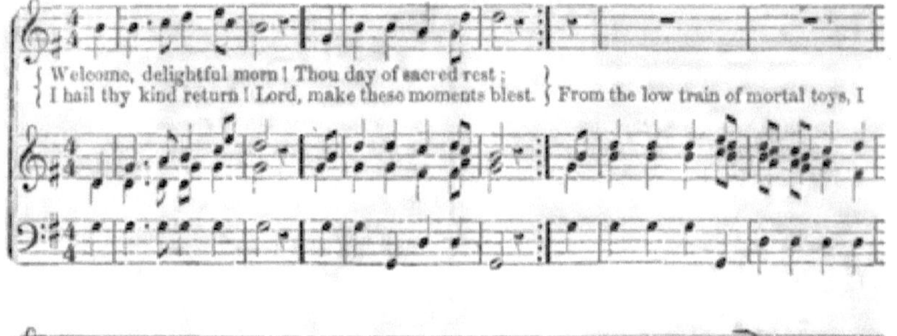

317 *Opening morning service.*

WELCOME, delightful morn,
Thou day of sacred rest;
I hail thy kind return!
Lord, make these moments blest.
From the low train of mortal toys
I soar to reach immortal joys.

2 Now may the King descend,
And fill his throne of grace;
Thy sceptre, Lord, extend,
While saints address thy face:
Let sinners feel thy quick'ning word,
And learn to know and fear the Lord.

3 Descend, celestial Dove,
With all thy quick'ning powers;
Disclose a Saviour's love,
And bless the sacred hours:
Then shall my soul new life obtain,
Nor sabbaths be indulged in vain.

276 *Closing Conference.*

JESUS, accept the praise
That to thy name belongs!
Matter of all our lays,
Subject of all our songs;
Through thee we now together came,
And part exulting in thy name.

2 In flesh we part awhile,
But still in spirit join'd,
T' embrace the happy toil,
Thou hast to each assign'd;
And while we do thy blessed will,
We bear our heaven about us still.

3 O let us thus go on
In all thy pleasant ways,
And, arm'd with patience, run
With joy th' appointed race!
Keep us and every seeking soul,
Till all attain the heavenly goal.

4 There we shall meet again,
When all our toils are o'er,
And death, and grief, and pain,
And parting, are no more:
We shall with all our brethren rise,
And grasp thee in the flaming skies.

5 O happy, happy day,
That calls thy exiles home!
The heavens shall pass away,
The earth receive its doom:
Earth we shall view, and heaven destroy'd,
And shout above the fiery void.

6 These eyes shall see them fall,
Mountains, and stars, and skies!
These eyes shall see them all
Out of their ashes rise!
These lips His praises shall rehearse,
Whose nod restores the universe.

7 According to his word,
His oath to sinners given,
We look to see restored
The ruin'd earth and heaven!
In a new world his truth to prove,
A world of righteousness and love.

6 Then let us wait the sound
That shall our souls release,
And labour to be found
Of him in spotless peace:
In perfect holiness renew'd;
Adorn'd with Christ, and meet for God!

469 *"Whereby we cry, Abba, Father."*

ARISE, my soul, arise,
Shake off thy guilty fears,
The bleeding Sacrifice
In my behalf appears;
Before the throne my Surety stands,
My name is written on his hands.

2 He ever lives above,
For me to intercede;
His all-redeeming love,
His precious blood to plead;
His blood atoned for all our race,
And sprinkles now the throne of grace.

3 Five bleeding wounds he bears,
Received on Calvary;
They pour effectual prayers,
They strongly speak for me;
"Forgive him, O forgive," they cry,
"Nor let that ransom'd sinner die!"

4 The Father hears him pray,
His dear Anointed One:
He cannot turn away
The presence of his Son:
His Spirit answers to the blood,
And tells me I am born of God.

5 My God is reconciled,
His pard'ning voice I hear:
He owns me for his child,
I can no longer fear;
With confidence I now draw nigh,
And Father, Abba, Father, cry.

897 *Psalm cxxxiii.*

BEHOLD how good a thing
It is to dwell in peace;
How pleasing to our King
This fruit of righteousness;
When brethren all in one agree,
Who knows the joys of unity!

2 Where unity is found,
The sweet anointing grace
Extends to all around,
And consecrates the place:
To every waiting soul it comes,
And fills it with divine perfumes.

3 Jesus, our great High Priest,
For us the gift received;
For us and all the rest,
Who have in him believed:
Forth from our Head the blessing goes,
And all his seamless coat o'erflows.

4 From Aaron's beard it rolls:
(Those nearest to his face;)
The humble, trembling souls,
Who feebly sue for grace—
I know the grace for all is free,
For, lo! it reaches now to me.

898 *Psalm cxxxiii.*

GRACE every morning new,
And every night, we feel,
The soft, refreshing dew,
That falls on Hermon's hill!
On Sion it doth sweetly fall;
The grace of one descends on all.

2 E'en now our Lord doth pour
The blessing from above,
A kindly, gracious shower,
Of heart-reviving love;
The former and the latter rain,
The love of God and love of man.

3 In him when brethren join,
And follow after peace,
The fellowship divine
He promises to bless,
His choicest graces to bestow,
Where two or three are met below.

4 The riches of his grace
In fellowship are given
To Sion's chosen race,
The citizens of heaven:
He fills them with the choicest store,
He gives them life for evermore.

1016 *Birth-day.*

GOD of my life, to thee
My cheerful soul I raise!
Thy goodness made me be,
And still prolongs my days;
I see my natal hour return,
And bless the day that I was born.

2 A clod of living earth,
I glorify thy name,
From whom alone my birth,
And all my blessings came;
Creating and preserving grace,
Let all that is within me praise.

3 Long as I live beneath,
To thee O let me live,
To thee my every breath
In thanks and praises give!
Whate'er I have, whate'er I am,
Shall magnify my Maker's name.

4 My soul and all its powers
Thine, wholly thine, shall be;
All, all my happy hours
I consecrate to thee;
Me to thine image now restore,
And I shall praise thee evermore.

BEALL. H. M. (Four 6s & Two 8s.)

9 *The Trinity.*

I GIVE immortal praise
  To God the Father's love,
For all my comforts here,
  And better hopes above:
He sent his own eternal Son
To die for sins that man had done.

2 To God the Son belongs
  Immortal glory too,
Who bought us with his blood
  From everlasting wo:
And now he lives, and now he reigns,
And sees the fruit of all his pains.

3 To God the Spirit's name
  Immortal worship give,
Whose new creating power
  Makes the dead sinner live
His work completes the great design,
And fills the soul with joy divine.

4 Almighty God, to thee
  Be endless honours done,
The undivided Three,
  And the mysterious One:
Where reason fails, with all her powers,
There faith prevails, and love adores.

97 *"They shall call his name Immanuel."*

LET earth and heaven combine,
  Angels and men agree,
To praise, in songs divine,
  Th' incarnate Deity;
Our God contracted to a span,
Incomprehensibly made man.

2 He laid his glory by;
  He wrapp'd him in our clay;
Unmark'd by human eye,
  The latent Godhead lay;
Infant of days he here became,
And bore the mild Immanuel's name.

3 Unsearchable the love
  That hath the Saviour brought;
The grace is far above
  Or man or angel's thought:
Suffice for us that God, we know
Our God, is manifest below.

4 He deigns in flesh t' appear,
  Widest extremes to join;
To bring our vileness near,
  And make us all divine:
And we the life of God shall know;
For God is manifest below.

5 Made perfect first in love,
  And sanctified by grace,
We shall from earth remove,
  And see his glorious face;
Then shall his love be fully show'd,
And man shall then be lost in God.

1056 *Doxology.*

TO God the Father's throne
  Perpetual honours raise;
Glory to God the Son,
  To God the Spirit praise:
With all our powers, Eternal King,
Thy name we sing, While faith adores.

473 *Love to the Saviour.*

HARK, my soul—it is the Lord!
'Tis thy Saviour, hear his word!
Jesus speaks, he speaks to thee:
"Say, poor sinner, lov'st thou me?

2 "I deliver'd thee when bound,
And, when bleeding, heal'd thy wound;
Sought thee wand'ring, set thee right,
Turn'd thy darkness into light.

3 "Can a mother's tender care
Cease toward the child she bare?
Yes, she may forgetful be,
Yet will I remember thee.

4 "Mine is an unchanging love,
Higher than the heights above,
Deeper than the depths beneath,
Free and faithful, strong as death.

5 "Thou shalt see my glory soon,
When the work of faith is done,
Partner of my throne shalt be:
Say, poor sinner, lov'st thou me?"

6 Lord, it is my chief complaint
That my love is still so faint;
Yet I love thee and adore:
O for grace to love thee more!

536 *Panting for purity.*

HOLY Lamb, who thee receive,
Who in thee begin to live,
Day and night they cry to thee,
As thou art, so let us be!

2 Jesus, see my panting breast!
See, I pant in thee to rest!
Gladly would I now be clean;
Cleanse me now from every sin.

3 Fix, O fix my wav'ring mind!
To thy cross my spirit bind:
Earthly passions far remove;
Swallow up my soul in love.

4 Dust and ashes though we be,
Full of sin and misery,
Thine we are, thou Son of God;
Take the purchase of thy blood!

5 See, ye sinners, see the flame,
Rising from the slaughter'd Lamb,
Marks the new, the living way,
Leading to eternal day.

6 Jesus, when this light we see,
All our soul's athirst for thee;
When thy quick'ning power we prove,
All our heart dissolves in love.

542 *Longing to be complete in Christ.*

SAVIOUR of the sin-sick soul,
Give me faith to make me whole;
Finish thy great work of grace;
Cut it short in righteousness.

2 Speak the second time, "Be clean!"
Take away my inbred sin:
Every stumbling-block remove;
Cast it out by perfect love.

3 Nothing less will I require,
Nothing more can I desire:
None but Christ to me be given,
None but Christ in earth or heaven.

4 O that I might now decrease!
O that all I am might cease!
Let me into nothing fall!
Let my Lord be all in all!

156 *Psalm ii.*

WHEREFORE do the nations wage
  War against the King of kings?
Whence the people's madd'ning rage,
  Fraught with vain imaginings?

2 Haughty chiefs, and rulers proud,
  Forth in banded fury run,
Braving with defiance loud
  God and his anointed Son:

3 "Let us break their bonds in twain!
  Let us cast their cords away!"—
But the Highest with disdain
  Sees and mocks their vain array.

4 "High on Zion I prepare,"
  Thus he speaks, "a regal throne:
Thou, my Prince, my chosen heir,
  Rise to claim it as thine own!"

5 "Son of God, with God the same,
  Enter thine imperial dome!
Lo! the shaking heavens proclaim,
  Mightiest Lord, thy kingdom come!

6 "Pomp or state dost thou demand?
  In thy Father's glory shine!
Dost thou ask for high command?
  Lo! the universe is thine!"

7 Ye who spurn his righteous sway,
  Yet, ah yet, he spares your breath;
Yet his hand, averse to slay,
  Balances the bolt of death.

8 Ere that dreadful bolt descends,
  Haste before his feet to fall,
Kiss the sceptre he extends,
  And adore him, Lord of all.

647 *Daily bread.*

DAY by day the manna fell:
  O, to learn this lesson well!
Still by constant mercy fed,
Give me, Lord, my daily bread.

2 "Day by day," the promise reads,
Daily strength for daily needs,
Cast foreboding fears away;
Take the manna of to-day.

3 Lord! my times are in thy hand:
All my sanguine hopes have plann'd,
To thy wisdom I resign,
And would make thy purpose mine.

4 Thou my daily task shall give:
Day by day to thee I live;
So shall added years fulfil,
Not my own, my Father's will.

572 *Persevering grace.*

SON of God, thy blessing grant;
  Still supply our every want!
Tree of life, thy influence shed!
With thy sap my spirit feed.

2 Tenderest branch, alas! am I,
Wither without thee and die;
Weak as helpless infancy;
O confirm my soul in thee!

3 Unsustain'd by thee I fall;
Send the help for which I call:
Weaker than a bruised reed,
Help I every moment need.

4 All my hopes on thee depend;
Love me, save me to the end;
Give me the continuing grace,
Take the everlasting praise.

592 *Opening worship.*

LORD, we come before thee now,
At thy feet we humbly bow;
O! do not our suit disdain;
Shall we seek thee, Lord, in vain?

2 Lord, on thee our souls depend;
In compassion now descend;
Fill our hearts with thy rich grace,
Tune our lips to sing thy praise.

3 In thine own appointed way,
Now we seek thee, here we stay;
Lord, we know not how to go
Till a blessing thou bestow.

4 Send some message from thy word,
That may joy and peace afford;
Let thy Spirit now impart
Full salvation to each heart.

5 Comfort those who weep and mourn,
Let the time of joy return;
Those that are cast down lift up,
Make them strong in faith and hope.

6 Grant that all may seek and find
Thee a gracious God, and kind;
Heal the sick, the captive free;
Let us all rejoice in thee.

453 *The backslider's plea.*

DEPTH of mercy! can there be
Mercy still reserved for me?
Can my God his wrath forbear?
Me, the chief of sinners, spare?

2 I have long withstood his grace,—
Long provoked him to his face;
Would not hearken to his calls,
Grieved him by a thousand falls.

3 Lo! I cumber still the ground:
Lo! an Advocate is found!
"Hasten not to cut him down;
Let this barren soul alone!"

4 Jesus speaks, and pleads his blood,
He disarms the wrath of God!
Now my Father's bowels move;
Justice lingers into love.

5 Kindled his relentings are;
Me he now delights to spare;
Cries, "How shall I give thee up?"
Lets the lifted thunder drop.

6 There for me the Saviour stands;
Shows his wounds, and spreads his hands:
God is love! I know, I feel,
Jesus weeps and loves me still.

7 Jesus answers from above:
Is not all thy nature love?
Wilt thou not the wrong forget?
Suffer me to kiss thy feet?

8 If I rightly read thy heart,
If thou all compassion art,
Bow thine ear, in mercy bow!
Pardon and accept me now.

9 Pity from thine eye let fall;
By a look my soul recall;
Now the stone to flesh convert,
Cast a look, and break my heart.

10 Now incline me to repent!
Let me now my fall lament!
Now my foul revolt deplore!
Weep, believe, and sin no more.

894 *United in love.*

FATHER, at thy footstool see
  Those who now are one in thee!
Draw us by thy grace alone:
Give, O give us to thy Son.

2 Jesus, Friend of human kind,
Let us in thy name be join'd;
Each to each unite and bless,
Keep us still in perfect peace.

3 Heavenly, all-alluring Dove,
Shed thy overshadowing love;
Love, the sealing grace, impart;
Dwell within our single heart.

4 Father, Son, and Holy Ghost,
Be to us what Adam lost;
Let us in thine image rise;
Give us back our paradise!

768 *Triumph.*

O WHAT blessings, lavish'd wide,
  Cover all the woes of man,—
As heaven's rainbows soft bestride
  All the gloom beneath their span.

2 Hark! what rapt'rous hymns arise
  Where the ensign-cross he rears!
Songs are tuning out of sighs,
  Smiles are wreathing out of tears!

3 All shall bless him! lift thy voice,
  Earth,—and sea,—and firmament!
Acclamation of your joys
  Peal out, in one chorus blent!

630 *Chastisement.*

'TIS my happiness below
  Not to live without the cross,
But the Saviour's power to know,
  Sanctifying every loss.

2 Trials must and will befall;
  But with humble faith to see
Love inscribed upon them all,—
  This is happiness to me.

3 Trials make the promise sweet:
  Trials give new life to prayer;
Bring me to my Saviour's feet,
  Lay me low, and keep me there.

311 *"Therefore with angels"—*

LORD and God of heavenly powers!
  Theirs—yet O! benignly ours;
Glorious King! let earth proclaim,
Worms attempt to chant thy name.

2 Thee to laud in songs divine
Angels and archangels join:
We with them our voices raise,
Echoing thy eternal praise.

3 Holy, holy, holy Lord,
Live, by heaven and earth adored!
Full of thee they ever cry,
"Glory be to God most high!"

502 *"Christ liveth in me."*

LOVING Jesus, gentle Lamb,
  In thy gracious hands I am;
Make me, Saviour, what thou art,
Live thyself within my heart.

2 I shall then show forth thy praise,
Serve thee all my happy days,
Then the world shall always see
Christ, the holy Child, in me.

1061 *Doxology.*

SING we to our God above,
  Praise eternal as his love;
Praise him, all ye heavenly host,—
Father, Son, and Holy Ghost.

360 *"Escape for thy life."*

HASTEN, sinner, to be wise;
  Stay not for the morrow's sun:
Wisdom, if thou still despise,
  Harder is she to be won.

2 Hasten, mercy to implore;
  Stay not for the morrow's sun;
Lest thy season should be o'er
  Ere this evening's stage be run.

3 Hasten, sinner, to return;
  Stay not for the morrow's sun:
Lest thy lamp should cease to burn
  Ere salvation's work is done.

4 Hasten, sinner, to be blest;
  Stay not for the morrow's sun:
Lest the curse should thee arrest
  Ere the morrow is begun.

937 *Wrestling.*

LORD, I cannot let thee go,
  Till a blessing thou bestow:
Do not turn away thy face,
Mine 's an urgent, pressing case.

2 Dost thou ask me who I am?
Ah! my Lord, thou know'st my name;
Yet the question gives a plea
To support my suit with thee.

3 Thou didst once a wretch behold,
In rebellion blindly bold,
Scorn thy grace, thy power defy:
That poor rebel, Lord, was I.

4 Once a sinner, near despair,
Sought thy mercy-seat by prayer;
Mercy heard, and set him free:
Lord, that mercy came to me.

5 Many days have pass'd since then,
Many changes I have seen;
Yet have been upheld till now:
Who could hold me up but thou?

6 Thou hast help'd in every need;
This emboldens me to plead
After so much mercy past,
Canst thou let me sink at last?

7 No; I must maintain my hold,
'Tis thy goodness makes me bold;
I can no denial take,
When I plead for Jesus' sake.

902 *Cleaving to God.*

GOD of love, that hear'st the prayer,
  Kindly for thy people care,
Who on thee alone depend;
Love us, save us to the end.

2 Save us in the prosp'rous hour,
From the flatt'ring tempter's power,
From his unsuspected wiles,
From the world's pernicious smiles.

3 Men of worldly, low design,
Let not these thy people join,
Poison our simplicity,
Drag us from our trust in thee.

4 Save us from the great and wise,
Till they sink in their own eyes,
Tamely to thy yoke submit,
Lay their honours at thy feet.

5 Never let the world break in,
Fix a mighty gulf between;
Keep us little and unknown,
Prized and loved by God alone.

6 Let us still to thee look up,
Thee, thy Israel's strength and hope:
Nothing know, or seek, beside
Jesus, and him crucified.

COOK. 7s. POPULAR OLD MELODY. ARRANGED.

561 *The pilgrim's song.*

CHILDREN of the heavenly King,
As we journey let us sing;
Sing our Saviour's worthy praise,
Glorious in his works and ways.

2 We are trav'ling home to God,
In the way our fathers trod;
They are happy now, and we
Soon their happiness shall see.

3 O ye banish'd seed, be glad!
Christ our Advocate is made:
Us to save, our flesh assumes,
Brother to our souls becomes.

4 Fear not, brethren, joyful stand
On the borders of our land;
Jesus Christ, our Father's Son,
Bids us undismay'd go on.

5 Lord! obediently we'll go,
Gladly leaving all below:
Only thou our leader be,
And we still will follow thee.

598 *Stability sought.*

JESUS, shall I never be
Firmly grounded upon thee?
Never by thy work abide?
Never in thy wounds reside?

2 O how wav'ring is my mind!
Toss'd about with every wind!
O how quickly doth my heart
From the living God depart!

3 Jesus, let my nature feel
Thou art God unchangeable:
JAH, JEHOVAH, great I AM,
Speak unto my soul thy name.

4 Grant that every moment I
May believe and feel thee nigh,
Steadfastly behold thy face,
Stablish'd with abiding grace.

763 *"Go ye therefore."*

GO, ye messengers of God!
Like the beams of morning, fly,
Take the wonder-working rod,
Wave the banner-cross on high!

2 Where th' aspirant minaret
Gleams along the morning skies,
Wave it till the crescent set,
And the "Star of Jacob" rise.

3 Go! to many a tropic isle
In the bosom of the deep,
Where the skies for ever smile,
And th' oppress'd for ever weep!

4 O'er the negro's night of care
Pour the living light of heaven,
Chase away the fiend despair,
Bid him hope to be forgiven!

5 Where the golden gates of day
Open on the palmy East,
Wide the bleeding cross display,
Spread the gospel's richest feast.

6 Circumnavigate the ball,
Visit every soil and sea;
Preach the cross of Christ to all—
Jesus' love is full and free.

1061 *Doxology.*

SING we to our God above,
Praise eternal as his love:
Praise him, all ye heavenly host,—
Father, Son, and Holy Ghost,

857 *Embarking.*

LORD, whom winds and seas obey,
Guide us through the wat'ry way;
In the hollow of thy hand
Hide, and bring us safe to land.

2 Jesus, let our faithful mind
Rest, on thee alone reclined;
Every anxious thought repress,
Keep our souls in perfect peace.

3 Keep the souls whom now we leave;
Bid them to each other cleave;
Bid them walk on life's rough sea;
Bid them come by faith to thee.

4 Save, till all these tempests end,
All who on thy love depend;
Waft our happy spirits o'er;
Land us on the heavenly shore.

993 *A religious household.*

JESUS, Lord, we look to thee,
Let us in thy name agree;
Show thyself the Prince of peace;
Bid our jars for ever cease.

2 By thy reconciling love
Every stumbling block remove;
Each to each unite, endear;
Come and spread thy banner here.

3 Make us of one heart and mind,
Courteous, pitiful, and kind;
Lowly, meek, in thought and word,
Altogether like our Lord.

4 Let us for each other care,
Each the other's burden bear;
To thy church the pattern give,
Show how true believers live.

5 Free from anger and from pride,
Let us thus in God abide;
All the depths of love express,
All the heights of holiness.

6 Let us, then, with joy remove
To the family above;
On the wings of angels fly,
Show how true believers die.

1039 *Job xvii. 13.*

READY for my earthen bed,
Let me rest my fainting head,
Welcome life's expected close,
Sink in permanent repose.

2 Jesus' blood, to which I fly,
Doth my conscience purify,
Signs my weary soul's release,
Bids me now depart in peace.

3 Thus do I my bed prepare;
O how soft when Christ is there!
Calm I lay my body down,
Rise to an immortal crown.

129 *"It is finished."*

SONS of God, triumphant rise,
Shout th' accomplish'd sacrifice!
Shout your sins in Christ forgiven,
Sons of God, and heirs of heaven!

2 Ye that round our altars throng,
Listening angels, join the song;
Sing with us, ye heavenly powers,
Pardon, grace, and glory, ours!

3 Love's mysterious work is done;
Greet we now th' atoning Son;
Heal'd and quicken'd by his blood,
Join'd to Christ, and one with God.

4 Him by faith we taste below,
Mightier joys ordain'd to know,
When his utmost grace we prove,
Rise to heaven by perfect love.

J. W. BELCHER.

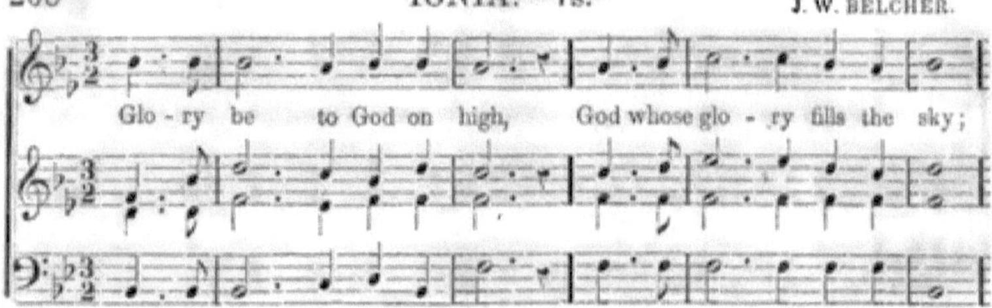

312 *Gloria in excelsis.*

GLORY be to God on high,
God whose glory fills the sky;
Peace on earth to man forgiven,
Man the well-beloved of Heaven.

2 Sovereign Father, heavenly King,
Thee we now presume to sing:
Glad thine attributes confess,
Glorious all, and numberless.

3 Hail, by all thy works adored!
Hail, the everlasting Lord!
Thee with thankful hearts we prove,
Lord of power, and God of love.

4 Christ our Lord and God we own,
Christ the Father's only Son;
Lamb of God for sinners slain,
Saviour of offending man.

5 Bow thine ear, in mercy bow,
Hear, the world's atonement, thou!
Jesus, in thy name we pray,
Take, O take our sins away!

6 Powerful Advocate with God,
Justify us by thy blood;
Bow thine ear, in mercy bow,
Hear, the world's atonement, thou.

7 Hear, for thou, O Christ, alone,
Art with thy great Father one;
One the Holy Ghost with thee;
One supreme eternal THREE.

490 *Luke* xv. 10.

SONS of God, exulting rise,
Join the triumph of the skies;
See the prodigal is come,
Shout to bear the wand'rer home!

2 Strive in joy, with angels strive,
He was dead, but now 's alive!
Loud repeat the glorious sound,
He was lost, but now is found!

3 Now the gracious Father smiles;
Now the Saviour boasts his spoils;
Now the Spirit grieves no more:
Sing, ye heavens; and earth, adore.

971 *Saturday evening.*

NOW all chafing care shall cease,
Now worn toil obtain release,
With the world we now have done,
Since "the sabbath draweth on."

2 This our "preparation" be;
Lord! our hearts we bring to thee;
May they to thyself be won
While "the sabbath draweth on."

3 At this hour, lo! from their place
Myriad households seek thy face;
We adore thee not alone
That "the sabbath draweth on."

4 When shall earth's bless'd sabbath break!
When its rest all tribes partake?
See the bright'ning signal yon,
'Tis that "sabbath draweth on."

5 And when nature sinks in death,
When heaves slow and faint our breath,
Brighter than e'er day yet shone,
Heavenly "sabbath," then draw on!

1061 *Doxology.*

SING we to our God above,
Praise eternal as his love;
Praise him, all ye heavenly host,—
Father, Son, and Holy Ghost.

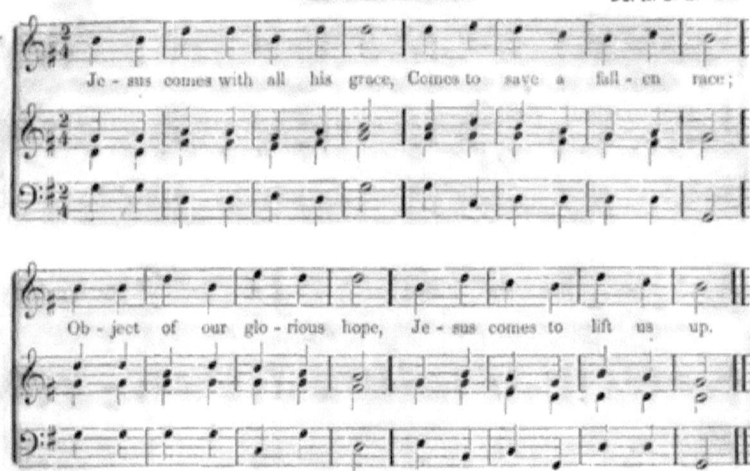

511 *Rejoicing in hope of perfect love."*

JESUS comes with all his grace,
Comes to save a fallen race;
Object of our glorious hope,
Jesus comes to lift us up!

2 Let the living stones cry out!
Let the sons of Abr'am shout:
Praise we all our lowly King,
Give him thanks, rejoice, and sing.

3 He hath our salvation wrought:
He our captive souls hath bought;
He hath reconciled to God,
He hath wash'd us in his blood.

4 We are now his lawful right,
Walk as children of the light:
We shall soon obtain the grace,
Pure in heart to see his face.

5 We shall gain our calling's prize;
After God we all shall rise,
Fill'd with joy, and love, and peace,
Perfected in holiness.

6 Let us then rejoice in hope,
Steadily to Christ look up;
Trust to be redeem'd from sin,
Wait, till he appear within.

7 Hasten, Lord, the perfect day;
Let thy every servant say,
"I have now obtain'd the power,
Born of God, to sin no more."

551 *Exulting in perfect love.*

JESUS, all-atoning Lamb,
Thine, and only thine, I am;
Take my body, spirit, soul;
Only thou possess the whole.

2 Thou my one thing needful be;
Let me ever cleave to thee;
Let me choose the better part;
Let me give thee all my heart.

3 Fairer than the sons of men;
Do not let me turn again,
Leave the fountain-head of bliss,
Stoop to creature happiness.

4 Whom have I on earth below?
Thee, and only thee, I know:
Whom have I in heaven but thee?
Thou art all in all to me.

5 All my treasure is above;
All my riches is thy love;
Who the worth of love can tell?
Infinite, unsearchable!

6 Thou, O lvoe, my portion art:
Lord, thou know'st my simple heart:
Other comforts I despise;
Love be all my paradise.

7 Nothing else can I require;
Love fills up my whole desire;
All thy other gifts remove,
Still thou giv'st me all in love!

1061 *Doxology.*

SING we to our God above,
Praise eternal as his love;
Praise him, all ye heavenly host,—
Father, Son, and Holy Ghost.

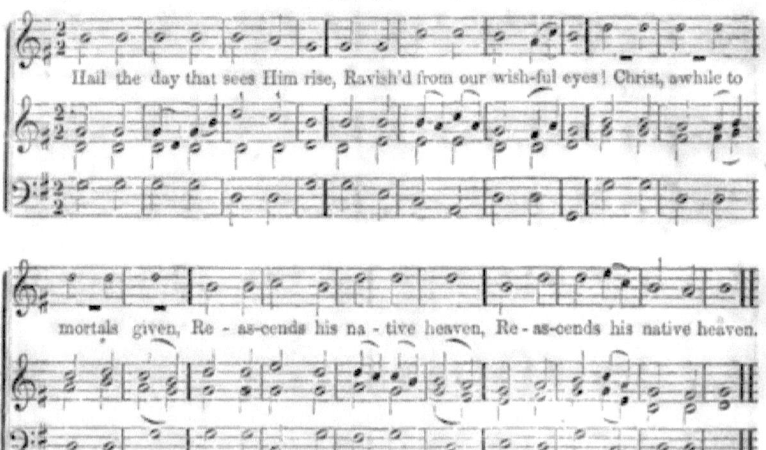

148 *The Ascension.*

HAIL, the day that sees Him rise,
Ravish'd from our wishful eyes!
Christ, awhile to mortals given,
Re-ascends his native heaven.

2 There the pompous triumph waits:
"Lift your heads, eternal gates:
Wide unfold the radiant scene;
Take the King of glory in!"

3 Circled round with angel powers,
Their triumphant Lord, and ours,
Conqu'ror over death and sin;
Take the King of glory in!

4 Him though highest heaven receives,
Still he loves the earth he leaves;
Though returning to his throne,
Still he calls mankind his own.

5 See, he lifts his hands above!
See, he shows the prints of love:
Hark, his gracious lips bestow
Blessings on his church below!

6 Ever upward let us move,
Wafted on the wings of love;
Looking when thou, Lord, shalt come,
Longing, gasping after home.

7 There we shall with thee remain,
Partners of thy endless reign;
There thy face unclouded see,
Find our heaven of heavens in thee.

68 *Psalm cxxxvi.*

LET us, with a gladsome mind,
Praise the Lord, for he is kind:
For his mercies aye endure,
Ever faithful, ever sure.

2 Let us blaze his name abroad,
For of gods he is the God;
For his mercies aye endure,
Ever faithful, ever sure.

3 All things living he doth feed;
His full hand supplies their need.
For his mercies aye endure,
Ever faithful, ever sure.

4 Let us therefore warble forth
His high majesty and worth:
For his mercies aye endure,
Ever faithful, ever sure.

146 *"Alive for evermore."*

CHRIST, the Lord, is risen to-day!
Sons of men and angels say!
Raise your joys and triumphs high!
Sing, ye heavens—thou earth, reply.

2 Love's redeeming work is done,—
Fought the fight, the battle won:
Lo! the sun's eclipse is o'er;
Lo! he sets in blood no more.

3 Vain the stone, the watch, the seal,
Christ hath burst the gates of hell;
Death in vain forbids his rise;
Christ hath open'd paradise.

4 Lives again our glorious King!
"Where, O death! is now thy sting?"
Once he died our souls to save,
"Where's thy vict'ry, boasting grave?"

5 Soar we now where Christ has led,
Foll'wing our exalted Head:
Made like him, like him we rise—
Ours the cross, the grave, the skies.

185 *Redeeming love.*

NOW begin the heavenly theme;
Sing aloud in Jesus' name:
Ye who his salvation prove,
Triumph in redeeming love.

2 Ye who see the Father's grace
Beaming on the Saviour's face,
As to Canaan on ye move,
Praise and bless redeeming love.

3 Mourning souls, dry up your tears;
Banish all your guilty fears;
See your guilt and curse remove,
Cancell'd by redeeming love.

4 Welcome all by sin oppress'd,
Welcome to his sacred rest:
Nothing brought him from above,—
Nothing but redeeming love.

5 Hither, then, your music bring;
Strike aloud each cheerful string;
Mortals, join the hosts above,—
Join to praise redeeming love.

2 *The Trinity.*

HOLY, holy, holy Lord,
God the Father, and the Word,
God the Comforter, receive
Blessings more than we can give.

2 Mix'd with those beyond the sky,
Chanters to the Lord most high,
We our hearts and voices raise,
Echoing thy eternal praise.

3 One, inexplicably three,
One, in simplest unity:
God, incline thy gracious ear,
Us thy lisping creatures hear.

4 Thee, while man, the earth-born, sings,
Angels shrink within their wings;
Prostrate seraphim above
Breathe unutterable love.

5 Happy they who never rest,
With thy heavenly presence blest!
They the heights of glory see,
Sound the depths of Deity!

6 Fain with them our souls would vie;
Sink as low, and mount as high;
Fall o'erwhelm'd with love, or soar;
Shout, or silently adore!

307 *Communion with Christ.*

JESUS, all-redeeming Lord,
Magnify thy dying word,
In thine ordinance appear,
Come and meet thy foll'wers here.

2 In the rite thou hast enjoin'd
Let us now our Saviour find;
Drink thy blood for sinners shed,
Taste thee in the broken bread.

3 Thou our faithful hearts prepare;
Thou thy pard'ning-grace declare;
Thou that hast for sinners died,
Show thyself the Crucified!

4 All the power of sin remove;
Fill us with thy perfect love;
Stamp us with the stamp divine;
Seal our souls for ever thine.

1061 *Doxology.*

SING we to our God above,
Praise eternal as his love;
Praise him, all ye heavenly host,—
Father, Son, and Holy Ghost.

134 *Rock of Ages.*

ROCK of Ages, cleft for me,
Let me hide myself in thee;
Let the water and the blood,
From thy wounded side which flow'd,
Be of sin the double cure,
Save from wrath and make me pure.

2 Could my tears for ever flow,
Could my zeal no languor know,
These for sin could not atone;
Thou must save, and thou alone:
In my hand no price I bring,
Simply to thy cross I cling.

3 While I draw this fleeting breath,
When my eyes shall close in death,
When I rise to worlds unknown,
And behold thee on thy throne,
Rock of Ages, cleft for me,
Let me hide myself in thee.

492 *"Changed—from glory to glory."*

SINCE the Son hath made me free,
Let me taste my liberty!
Thee behold with open face,
Triumph in thy saving grace!
Thy great will delight to prove,
Glory in thy perfect love!

2 Abba, Father, hear thy child,
Late in Jesus reconciled;
Hear, and all the graces shower,
All the joy, and peace, and power,
All my Saviour asks above,
All the life and heaven of love.

3 Lord, I will not let thee go
Till the blessing thou bestow:
Hear my Advocate divine!
Lo! to his my suit I join:
Join'd to his, it cannot fail:
Bless me; for I *will* prevail.

4 Heavenly Father, life divine!
Change my nature into thine!
Move, and spread throughout my soul,
Actuate, and fill the whole!
Be it I no longer now
Living in the flesh, but thou.

5 Holy Ghost, no more delay!
Come, and in thy temples stay!
Now thine inward witness bear,
Strong, and permanent, and clear:
Spring of life, thyself impart:
Rise eternal in my heart!

202 *The promise of the Father.*

FATHER, glorify thy Son,
Answ'ring his all-pow'rful prayer,
Send that Intercessor down,
Send that other Comforter,
Whom believingly we claim,
Whom we ask in Jesus' name.

2 Wilt thou not the promise seal,
Good and faithful as thou art,
Send the Comforter to dwell
Every moment in our heart?
Yes, thou must the grace bestow:
Truth hath said it shall be so.

392 *Contrition.*

HEARTS of stone, relent, relent,
Break, by Jesus' cross subdued,
See his body mangled, rent,
Cover'd with a gore of blood!
Sinful soul, what hast thou done?
Murder'd God's eternal Son.

2 Yes, your sins have done the deed,
Drove the nails that fix him here,
Crown'd with thorns his sacred head,
Pierced him with the soldier's spear,
Made his soul a sacrifice;
For a sinful world he dies.

3 Shall we let him die in vain?
Still to death pursue our God?
Open tear his wounds again?
Trample on his precious blood?
No; with all our sins we part—
Saviour, take my broken heart!

999 *Morning.*

O DISCLOSE thy lovely face;
Quicken all my drooping powers!
Gasps my fainting soul for grace,
As a thirsty land for showers:
Haste, my Lord, no more delay,
Come, my Saviour, come away!

2 Dark and cheerless is the morn
Unaccompanied by thee:
Joyless is the day's return,
Till thy mercy's beams I see,—
Till thou inward light impart,—
Glad my eyes, and warm my heart.

3 Visit, then, this soul of mine,
Pierce the gloom of sin and grief;
Fill me, Radiancy Divine;
Scatter all my unbelief:
More and more thyself display,
Shining to the perfect day.

404 *Why not now?*

WHY not now, my God, my God?
Ready if thou always art,
Make in me thy mean abode,
Take possession of my heart:
If thou canst so greatly bow,
Friend of sinners, why not now?

2 God of love, in this thy day,
For thyself to thee I cry;
Dying,—if thou still delay,
Must I not for ever die?
Enter now thy poorest home;
Now, my utmost Saviour, come!

987 *Death of a child.*

WHEREFORE should I make my moan,
Now my darling child is dead?
He to early rest is gone,
He to paradise is fled:
I shall go to him, but he
Never shall return to me.

2 God forbids his longer stay,
God recalls the precious loan,
God hath taken him away
From my bosom to his own;
Surely what he wills is best,
Happy in his will, I rest.

2 Faith cries out, It is the Lord!
Let him do as seems him good;
Be thy holy name adored,
Take the gift awhile bestow'd,
Take the child no longer mine,
Thine he is, for ever thine.

374 *Praying for repentance.*

SAVIOUR, Prince of Israel's race,
See me from thy lofty throne;
Give the sweet relenting grace,
Soften now this heart of stone!
Stone to flesh, O God, convert;
Cast a look, and break my heart!

2 By thy Spirit, Lord, reprove,
All mine inmost sins reveal;
Sins against thy light and love,
Let me see, and let me feel;
Sins that crucified my God,
Spill'd again thy precious blood.

3 Jesus, seek thy wand'ring sheep,
Make me restless to return;
Bid me look on thee, and weep,
Bitterly as Peter mourn;
Till I say, by grace restored,
"Now, thou know'st, I love thee, Lord."

4 Might I in thy sight appear,
As the publican distrest;
Stand, not daring to draw near;
Smite on my unworthy breast;
Groan the sinner's only plea,
"God be merciful to me!"

5 O remember me for good,
*Passing through the mortal vale;
Show me the atoning blood
When my strength and spirits fail;
Give my gasping soul to see
Jesus crucified for me.

530 *The act of consecration.*

FATHER, Son, and Holy Ghost,
One in Three, and Three in One,
As by the celestial host,
Let thy will on earth be done;
Praise by all to thee be given,
Glorious Lord of earth and heaven!

2 Vilest of the sinful race,
Lo! I answer to thy call,
Meanest vessel of thy grace,
Grace divinely free for all;
Lo! I come to do thy will,
All thy counsel to fulfil.

3 If so poor a worm as I
May to thy great glory live,
All my actions sanctify,
All my words and thoughts receive
Claim me for thy service, claim
All I have, and all I am.

4 Take my soul and body's powers:
Take my mem'ry, mind, and will,
All my goods, and all my hours;
All I know, and all I feel;
All I think, or speak, or do:
Take my heart;—but make it new!

5 Now, my God, thine own I am,
Now I give thee back thine own:
Freedom, friends, and health, and fame,
Consecrate to thee alone:
Thine I live, thrice happy I!
Happier still if thine I die.

6 Father, Son, and Holy Ghost,
One in Three, and Three in One,
As by thy celestial host,
Let thy will on earth be done;
Praise by all to thee be given,
Glorious Lord of earth and heaven!

981 *Birth of a child.*

GENTLE stranger, fearless come
To our quiet, happy home;
Bud of being, beauteous flower,
Sprung to birth this smiling hour,
While upon thy form we gaze,
Grateful thoughts to heaven we raise.

2 Saviour, from thy heavenly throne
Smile upon this little one;
Let thy Spirit be its guide,
Let its wants be well supplied;
Cleanse it by thy precious blood,
Fit it for thy high abode.

1032 *Psalm xlii. 1—4.*

AS the hart, with eager looks,
Panteth for the water-brooks,
So my soul, athirst for thee,
Pants the living God to see:
When, O when, with filial fear,
Lord, shall I to thee draw near?

2 Tears my food, by night, by day;
Grief consumes my strength away:
While his craft the tempter plies—
"Where is now thy God?" he cries:
This would sink me to despair,
But I pour my soul in prayer.

3 For, in happier times, I went
Where the multitude frequent:
I, with them, was wont to bring
Homage to thy courts, my King;
I, with them, was wont to raise
Festal hymns on holy days.

4 Why art thou cast down, my soul?
God, thy God, shall make thee whole;
Why art thou disquieted?
God shall lift thy fallen head;
And his countenance benign
Be the saving health of thine.

1033 *"Thy will be done."*

FATHER, if thou willing be,
Then my griefs awhile suspend,
Then remove the cup from me,
Or thy strength'ning angel send;
Wouldst thou have me suffer on?
Father, let thy will be done.

2 Let my flesh be troubled still,
Fill'd with pain or sore disease,
Let my wounded spirit feel
Strong redoubled agonies;
Meekly I my will resign,
Thine be done, and only thine.

3 Patient as my great High Priest,
In his bitterness of pain,
Most abandon'd and distrest,
Father, I the cross sustain;
All into thy hands I give,
Let me die or let me live.

1042 *Jer. xlix. 11.*

O THOU faithful God of love,
Gladly I thy promise plead,
Waiting for my last remove,
Hast'ning to the happy dead;
Lo! I cast on thee my care,
Breathe my latest breath in prayer.

2 Trusting in thy word alone,
I to thee my children leave:
Call my little ones thy own,
Give them all thy blessings, give;
Keep them while on earth they breathe,
Save their souls from endless death.

3 Whom I to thy grace commend,
Into thy embraces take;
Be her sure, immortal Friend,
Save her, for my Saviour's sake;
Free from sin, from sorrow free,
Let my widow trust in thee.

4 Father of the fatherless,
Husband of the widow, prove;
Me and mine persist to bless,
Tell me we shall meet above;
Seal the promise on my heart,
Bid me then in peace depart.

344 *Fly to Jesus.*

WEARY souls that wander wide
From the central point of bliss,
Turn to Jesus crucified,
Fly to those dear wounds of his;
Sink into the purple flood;
Rise into the life of God.

2 Find in Christ the way of peace,
Peace unspeakable, unknown!
By his pain he gives you ease,
Life by his expiring groan;
Rise exalted by his fall,
Find in Christ your all in all.

3 O believe the record true,
God to you his Son hath given;
Ye may now be happy too;
Find on earth the life of heaven:
Live the life of heaven above,
All the life of glorious love.

4 This the universal bliss,
Bliss for every soul design'd;
God's primeval promise this,
God's great gift to all mankind.
Bless'd in Christ this moment be,
Bless'd to all eternity!

SABBATH. 7s. Double. Dr. L. Mason.

315 *Opening morning service.*

SAFELY through another week
 God has brought us on our way;
Let us now a blessing seek,
 Waiting in his courts to-day:
Day of all the week the best,
Emblem of eternal rest.

2 While we seek supplies of grace,
 Through the dear Redeemer's name;
Show thy reconciling face—
 Take away our sin and shame;
From our worldly cares set free,
May we rest this day in thee.

3 Here we come thy name to praise;
 Let us feel thy presence near:
May thy glory meet our eyes,
 While we in thy house appear:
Here afford us, Lord, a taste
Of our everlasting feast.

4 May the gospel's joyful sound
 Conquer sinners, comfort saints,—
Make the fruits of grace abound,
 Bring relief from all complaints:
Thus let all our sabbaths prove,
Till we join the church above.

345 *The expostulation.*

SINNERS, turn, why will ye die?
 God, your Maker, asks you why?
God, who did your being give,
Made you with himself to live,—
He the fatal cause demands,
Asks the work of his own hands,
Why, ye thankless creatures, why
Will ye cross his love, and die?

2 Sinners, turn, why will ye die?
God, your Saviour, asks you why?
God, who did your souls retrieve,
Died himself that ye might live.
Will ye let him die in vain?
Crucify your Lord again?
Why, ye ransom'd sinners, why
Will ye slight his grace, and die?

3 Sinners, turn, why will ye die?
God, the Spirit, asks you why?
He who all your lives hath strove,
Woo'd you to embrace his love:
Will ye not his grace receive?
Will ye still refuse to live?
Why, ye long-sought sinners, why
Will ye grieve your God, and die?

346 *The expostulation.*

LET the beasts their breath resign,
Strangers to the life divine;
Who their God can never know,
Let their spirits downward go.
Ye for higher ends were born;
Ye may all to God return;
Dwell with him above the sky:
Why will ye for ever die?

2 Ye, on whom he favours showers,
Ye, possess'd of nobler powers;
Ye, of reason's powers possess'd;
Ye, with will and mem'ry bless'd;
Ye, with finer sense endued,
Creatures capable of God:
Noblest of his creatures, why,
Why will ye for ever die?

3 Ye, who own his record true;
Ye, his chosen people too;
Ye, who call the Saviour, Lord;
Ye, who read his written word;
Ye, who see the gospel light;
Claim a crown in Jesus' right:
Why will ye, ye Christians, why
Will the house of Israel die?

545 *Humble aspiration.*

WHEN, my Saviour, shall I be
Perfectly resign'd to thee?
Poor and vile in my own eyes,
Only in thy wisdom wise?
2 Only thee content to know,
Ignorant of all below?
Only guided by thy light;
Only mighty in thy might?

3 So I may thy Spirit know,
Let him as he listeth blow:
Let the manner be unknown,
So I may with thee be one.
4 Fully in my life express
All the heights of holiness,
Sweetly let my spirit prove
All the depths of humble love.

877 *Love-feast.*

COME, and let us sweetly join,
Christ to praise in hymns divine!
Give we all, with one accord,
Glory to our common Lord;
Hands, and hearts, and voices, raise;
Sing as in the ancient days;
Antedate the joys above:
Celebrate the feast of love.

2 Strive we, in affection strive
Let the purer flame revive,
Such as in the martyrs glow'd,
Dying champions for their God.
We for Christ, our Master, stand
Lights in a benighted land:
We our dying Lord confess,
We are Jesus' witnesses.

3 Witnesses that Christ hath died:
We with him are crucified:
Christ hath burst the bands of death,
We his quick'ning Spirit breathe:
Christ is now gone up on high;
Thither all our wishes fly:—
Sits at God's right hand above;
There with him we reign in love!

939 *For reviving grace.*

LIGHT of life, seraphic fire,
Love Divine, thyself impart;
Every fainting soul inspire;
Shine in every drooping heart:
Every mournful sinner cheer;
Scatter all our guilty gloom;
Son of God, appear! appear!
To thy human temples come.

2 Come in this accepted hour;
Bring thy heavenly kingdom in;
Fill us with thy glorious power,
Rooting out the seeds of sin:
Nothing more can we require,
We will covet nothing less;
Be thou all our hearts' desire,
All our joy, and all our peace.

814 *Summer.*

SEE the corn again in ear,
How the fields and valleys smile,
Harvest now is drawing near,
To repay the farmer's toil:
2 Gracious Lord, secure the crop,
Satisfy the poor with food;
In thy mercy is our hope,
We have sinn'd, but thou art good.

3 Let the praise be all the Lord's,
As the benefit is ours;
He in season still affords
Kindly heat, and gentle showers:
4 By his care the produce thrives,
Waving o'er the furrow'd lands;
And when harvest-time arrives,
Ready for the reaper stands.

769 *The song of jubilee.*

HARK! the song of jubilee,
  Loud as mighty thunders roar,
Or the fulness of the sea,
  When it breaks upon the shore:
Hallelujah! for the Lord
  God omnipotent shall reign;
Hallelujah! let the word
  Echo round the earth and main.

2 Hallelujah! hark! the sound
  From the depth unto the skies
Wakes above, beneath, around,
  All creation's harmonies:
See Jehovah's banner furl'd,
  Sheath'd his sword; he speaks: 'tis done;
And the kingdoms of this world
  Are the kingdoms of his Son.

3 He shall reign from pole to pole,
  With illimitable sway:
He shall reign, when, like a scroll,
  Yonder heavens have pass'd away!
Then the end—beneath his rod
  Man's last enemy shall fall
Hallelujah! Christ in God,
  God in Christ, is ALL IN ALL.

871 *Opening the exercises.*

GLORY be to God above,
  God from whom all blessings flow;
Make we mention of his love,
  Publish we his praise below:
Call'd together by his grace,
  We are met in Jesus' name;
See with joy each other's face,
  Foll'wers of the bleeding Lamb.

2 Let us, then, sweet counsel take,
  How to make our calling sure,—
Our election how to make,
  Past the reach of hell, secure:
Build we each the other up;
  Pray we for our faith's increase,
Solid comfort, settled hope,
  Constant joy, and lasting peace.

3 More and more let love abound,
  Let us never, never rest,
Till we are in Jesus found,
  Of our paradise possest:
He removes the flaming sword,
  Calls us back from Eden driven:
To his image here restored,
  Soon he takes us up to heaven!

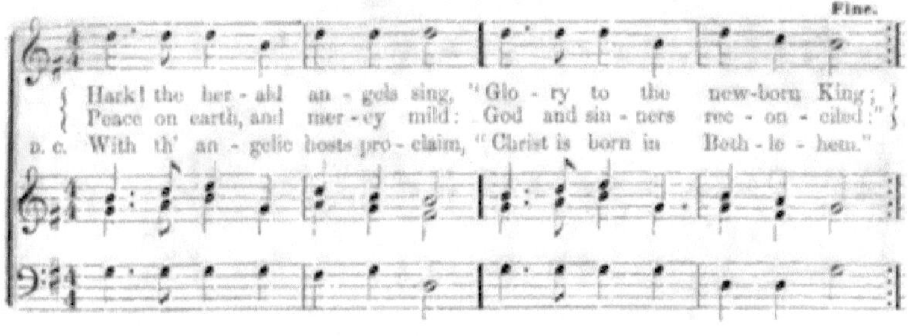

89 *The Incarnation.*

HARK! the herald angels sing,
"Glory to the new-born King;
Peace on earth, and mercy mild;
God and sinners reconciled;"
Joyful all ye nations rise,
Join the triumphs of the skies;
With th' angelic hosts proclaim,
"Christ is born in Bethlehem."

2 Christ, by highest heaven adored,
Christ, the everlasting Lord;
Late in time behold him come,
Offspring of a virgin's womb.
Veil'd in flesh, the Godhead see,
Hail th' incarnate Deity!
Pleased as man with men t' appear,
Jesus our Immanuel here.

3 Hail, the heaven-born Prince of peace!
Hail, the Sun of righteousness!
Light and life to all he brings,
Risen with healing in his wings:
Mild he lays his glory by,
Born that man no more may die;
Born to raise the sons of earth;
Born to give them second birth.

4 Come, Desire of nations, come!
Fix in us thy humble home;
Rise, the woman's conqu'ring seed,
Bruise in us the serpent's head;
Adam's likeness now efface,
Stamp thine image in its place:
Second Adam from above,
Reinstate us in thy love.

701 *Rev. vii. 9—12.*

LIFT your eyes of faith, and see
Saints and angels join'd in one:
What a countless company
Stand before yon dazzling throne!
Each before his Saviour stands;
All in whitest robes array'd,
Palms they carry in their hands,
Crowns of glory on their head.

2 Saints begin the endless song,
Cry aloud in heavenly lays,
Glory doth to God belong,—
God the glorious Saviour praise.
All salvation from him came—
Him who reigns enthroned on high:
Glory to the bleeding Lamb,
Let the morning stars reply.

3 Angel-powers the throne surround,
Next the saints in glory they;
Lull'd with the transporting sound,
They their silent homage pay:
Prostrate on their face, before
God and his Messiah fall:
Then in hymns of praise adore,
Shout the Lamb that died for all!

4 Be it so, they all reply:
Him let all our orders praise,—
Him, that did for sinners die,
Saviour of the favour'd race!
Render we our God his right,
Glory, wisdom, thanks, and power;
Honour, majesty, and might;
Praise him, praise him evermore!

ONIDO. 7s. Double. Arr. from PLEYEL.

879 *Love-feast.*

LET us join, ('tis God commands,)
 Let us join our hearts and hands;
Help to gain our calling's hope,
Build we each the other up:
Still forget the things behind,
Follow Christ in heart and mind;
Tow'rd the mark unwearied press,
Seize the crown of righteousness.

2 Plead we thus for faith alone,
Faith which by our works is shown:
God it is who justifies,
Only faith the grace applies:
Active faith that lives within;
Conquers earth, and hell, and sin;
Sanctifies, and makes us whole;
Forms the Saviour in the soul.

3 Let us for this faith contend;
Sure salvation is its end:
Heaven already is begun,
Everlasting life is won.
Only let us persevere,
Till we see our Lord appear,
Never from the Rock remove,
Saved by faith, which works by love.

878 *Love-feast.*

COME, thou high and lofty Lord!
 Lowly, meek, incarnate Word!
Humbly stoop to earth again:
Come and visit abject man!
Jesus, dear expected guest,
Thou art bidden to the feast:
For thyself our hearts prepare:
Come, and sit, and banquet there!

2 Jesus, we thy promise claim
We are met in thy great name
In the midst do thou appear,
Manifest thy presence here!
Sanctify us, Lord, and bless!
Breathe thy Spirit, give thy peace;
Thou thyself within us move:
Make our feast a feast of love.

LEBANON. 7s. DR. A. B. EVERETT.

3 Make us all in thee complete;
 Make us all for glory meet,—
 Meet t' appear before thy sight,
 Partners with the saints in light.
 Call, O call us each by name,
 To the marriage of the Lamb:
 Let us lean upon thy breast;
 Love be there our endless feast!

4 He that on the throne doth reign,
  Them the Lamb shall always feed,
 With the tree of life sustain,
  To the living fountains lead;
 He shall all their sorrows chase,
  All their wants at once remove,
 Wipe the tears from every face,
  Fill up every soul with love.

702 *Rev. vii. 13-17*

WHAT are these array'd in white,
  Brighter than the noon-day sun?
 Foremost of the sons of light,
  Nearest the eternal throne?
 These are they that bore the cross,
  Nobly for their Master stood;
 Suff'rers in his righteous cause,
  Foll'wers of the dying God.

2 Out of great distress they came,
  Wash'd their robes by faith below
 In the blood of yonder Lamb,
  Blood that washes white as snow.
 Therefore are they next the throne,
  Serve their Maker day and night:
 God resides among his own,
  God doth in his saints delight.

3 More than conquerors at last,
  Here they find their trials o'er;
 They have all their suff'rings past,
  Hunger now and thirst no more;
 No excessive heat they feel
  From the sun's directer ray;
 In a milder clime they dwell,
  Region of eternal day.

895 *"The unity of the Spirit."*

CHRIST, from whom all blessings flow,
  Perfecting the saints below,
 Hear us, who thy nature share,
 Who thy mystic body are
 Join us, in one spirit, join,
 Let us still receive of thine:
 Still for more on thee we call,
 Thou who fillest all in all!

2 Move, and actuate, and guide,
 Divers gifts to each divide:
 Placed according to thy will,
 Let us all our work fulfil:
 Never from our office move,
 Needful to each other prove;—
 Use the grace on each bestow'd,
 Temper'd by the art of God!

3 Sweetly may we all agree,
 Touch'd with softest sympathy
 Kindly for each other care;
 Every member feel its share,
 Many are we now and one,
 We who Jesus have put on:
 Names, and sects, and parties, fall:
 Thou, O Christ, art all in all.

433 *Refuge in Christ.*

JESUS, lover of my soul,
Let me to thy bosom fly,
While the nearer waters roll,
While the tempest still is high;
Hide me, O my Saviour, hide,
Till the storm of life be past;
Safe into the haven guide,
O receive my soul at last!

2 Other refuge have I none,
Hangs my helpless soul on thee;
Leave, ah! leave me not alone,
Still support and comfort me!
All my trust on thee is stay'd,
All my help from thee I bring,
Cover my defenceless head
With the shadow of thy wing.

3 Thou, O Christ, art all I want;
More than all in thee I find:
Raise the fallen, cheer the faint,
Heal the sick, and lead the blind.
Just and holy is thy name;
I am all unrighteousness;
False, and full of sin, I am,
Thou art full of truth and grace.

4 Plenteous grace with thee is found,
Grace to cover all my sin:
Let the healing streams abound,
Make and keep me pure within:
Thou of life the fountain art;
Freely let me take of thee:
Spring thou up within my heart,
Rise to all eternity!

100 *The song of Simeon.*

'TIS enough—the hour is come:
Now, within the silent tomb,
Let this mortal frame decay,
Mingled with its kindred clay;
Since thy mercies, oft of old
By thy chosen seers foretold,
Faithful now, and steadfast prove,
God of truth, and God of love!

2 Since, at length, my aged eye
Sees the day-spring from on high;
Those whom death had overspread
With his dark and dreary shade,
Lift their eyes, and, from afar,
Hail the light of Jacob's star;
Waiting till the promised ray
Turn their darkness into day.

3 Son of righteousness, to thee,
Lo! the nations bow the knee;
And the realms of distant kings
Own the healing of thy wings:
See the beams, intensely shed,
Shine on Sion's favour'd head!
Never may they hence remove,
God of truth, and God of love!

108 *"That ye should follow his steps."*

HOLY Lamb, who thee confess,
Foll'wers of thy holiness,
Thee they ever keep in view,
Ever ask, "What shall we do?"
Govern'd by thy only will,
All thy words we would fulfil,
Would in all thy footsteps go,
Walk as Jesus walk'd below.

2 While thou didst on earth appear,
Servant to thy servants here,
Mindful of thy place above,
All thy life was prayer and love:
Such our whole employment be,
Works of faith and charity;
Works of love on man bestow'd,
Secret intercourse with God.

3 Early in the temple meet,
Let us still our Saviour greet;
Nightly to the mount repair;
Join our praying Pattern there.
There by wrestling faith obtain
Power to work for God again;
Power his image to retrieve,
Power, like thee, our Lord, to live.

385 *The invitation accepted.*

COME, ye weary sinners, come,
All who groan beneath your load:
Jesus calls his wand'rers home:
Hasten to your pard'ning God.
Come, ye guilty souls opprest,
Answer to the Saviour's call,—
"Come, and I will give you rest:
Come, and I will save you all."

2 Jesus, full of truth and love,
We thy kindest word obey;
Faithful let thy mercies prove;
Take our load of guilt away:
Fain we would on thee rely,
Cast on thee our every care,
To thine arms of mercy fly,
Find our lasting quiet there.

3 Burden'd with a world of grief,
Burden'd with our sinful load,
Burden'd with this unbelief,
Burden'd with the wrath of God;
Lo! we come to thee for ease,
True and gracious as thou art;
Now our groaning souls release,
Write forgiveness on our heart.

733 *Funeral of a Christian sister.*

LO! the pris'ner is released,
Lighten'd of her fleshly load:
Where the weary are at rest,
She is gather'd into God!
Lo! the pain of life is past,
All her warfare now is o'er;
Death and hell behind are cast,
Grief and suff'ring are no more.

2 Yes, the Christian's course is run,
Ended is the glorious strife;
Fought the fight, the work is done,
Death is swallow'd up of life!
Borne by angels on their wings,
Far from earth the spirit flies:
Finds her God, and sits, and sings,
Triumphing in paradise.

3 Let the world bewail their dead,
Fondly of their loss complain:
Sister! friend! by Jesus freed,
Death, to thee, to us, is gain:
Thou art enter'd into joy:
Let the unbelievers mourn;
We in songs our lives employ
Till we all to God return.

765 *"Watchman, what of the night?"*

WATCHMAN, tell us of the night,
What its signs of promise are.
Traveller, o'er yon mountain's height,
See that glory-beaming star.
Watchman, does its beauteous ray
Aught of hope or joy foretell?
Trav'ller, yes; it brings the day,
Promis'd day of Israel.

2 Watchman, tell us of the night;
Higher yet that star ascends.
Trav'ller, blessedness and light,
Peace and truth, its course portends.
Watchman, will its beams alone
Gild the spot that gave them birth?
Trav'ller, ages are its own,
See! it bursts o'er all the earth.

3 Watchman, tell us of the night,
For the morning seems to dawn.
Trav'ller, darkness takes its flight,
Doubt and terror are withdrawn.
Watchman, let thy wand'rings cease;
Hie thee to thy quiet home.
Trav'ller, lo! the Prince of peace,
Lo! the Son of God is come.

990 *Pastor's salutation.*

PEACE be on this house bestow'd!
Peace on all that here reside!
Let the unknown peace of God
With the man of peace abide!
Let the Spirit now come down:
Let the blessing now take place:
Son of peace, receive thy crown,
Fulness of the gospel grace.

2 Christ, my Master and my Lord,
Let me thy forerunner be:
O be mindful of thy word,
Visit them, and visit me!
To this house and all herein
Now let thy salvation come:
Save our souls from inbred sin!
Make us thy eternal home!

884 *Joining the church.*

PEOPLE of the living God,
  I have sought the world around,
Paths of sin and sorrow trod,
  Peace and comfort nowhere found;
Now to you my spirit turns—
  Turns, a fugitive unblest;
Brethren, where your altar burns,
  O! receive me into rest.

2 Lonely, I no longer roam,
  Like the cloud, the wind, the wave,
Where you dwell shall be my home,
  Where you die shall be my grave;
Mine the God whom you adore,
  Your Redeemer shall be mine;
Earth can fill my soul no more,
  Every idol I resign.

3 Tell me not of gain or loss,
  Ease, enjoyment, pomp, or power;
Welcome poverty and cross,
  Shame, reproach, affliction's hour:
"Follow me;" I know thy voice;
  Jesus, Lord, thy steps I see;
Now I take thy yoke by choice;
  Light thy burden now to me.

880 *Love-feast.*

WHILE we walk with God in light,
  God our hearts doth still unite;
Dearest fellowship we prove,
Fellowship in Jesus' love
Sweetly each with each combined,
In the bonds of duty join'd,
Feels the cleansing blood applied,
Daily feels that Christ hath died.

2 Still, O Lord, our faith increase;
Cleanse from all unrighteousness:
Thee th' unholy cannot see:
Make, O make us meet for thee:
Every vile affection kill;
Root out every seed of ill;
Utterly abolish sin;
Write thy law of love within.

3 Hence may all our actions flow,
Love the proof that Christ we know:
Mutual love the token be,
Lord, that we belong to thee:
Love, thine image, love impart!
Stamp it on our face and heart!
Only love to us be given!
Lord, we ask no other heaven.

785 *Dedication.*

LORD of hosts, to thee we raise
  Here a house of prayer and praise;
Thou thy people's hearts prepare
Here to meet for praise and prayer.
2 Let the living here be fed
With thy word, the heavenly bread;
Here, in hope of glory blest,
May the dead be laid to rest;—

3 Here to thee a temple stand,
While the sea shall gird the land;
Here reveal thy mercy sure,
While the sun and moon endure,
4 Hallelujah!—earth and sky
To the joyful sound reply;
Hallelujah!—hence ascend
Prayer and praise till time shall end.

Psalm lxxiii. 25.

2 Lord of heaven, beyond our sight
Shines a world of purer light;
There, in love's unclouded reign,
Sever'd friends shall meet again:
O that world is passing fair!
Yet, if thou wert absent there,
What were all its joys to me?
Whom have I in heaven but thee?

3 Lord of earth and heaven, my breast
Seeks in thee its only rest:
I was lost; thy accents mild
Homeward lured thy wand'ring child:
O, if once thy smile divine
Ceased upon my soul to shine!
What were earth or heaven to me?
Whom have I in each but thee?

658 *"The Lord of hosts is with us."*

EARTH, rejoice, our Lord is King!
Sons of men, his praises sing;
Sing ye in triumphant strains,
Jesus our Messiah reigns!

2 Power is all to Jesus given,
Lord of hell, and earth, and heaven!
Every knee to him shall bow;
Satan, hear, and tremble now!

3 Angels and archangels join,
All triumphantly combine;
All in Jesus' praise agree,
Carrying on his victory.

4 Though the sons of night blaspheme,
More there are with us than them;
God with us, we cannot fear,—
Fear, ye fiends, for Christ is here!

5 Lo! to faith's enlighten'd sight
All the mountain flames with light;
Hell is nigh, but God is nigher,
Circling us with hosts of fire.

6 Our Messiah is come down,
Claims the nations for his own,
Bids them stand before his face,
Triumph in his saving grace.

836 *Psalm xx. 7-9.*

SOME their warrior horses boast,
Some their chariot's marshall'd host;
But our trust will we proclaim,
In our God, Jehovah's name.

2 Down they sank and fell subdued;
We arose, and upright stood.
Save, Jehovah! King of all,
Hear us when to thee we call.

807 *New-Year's day. Before Sermon.*

WHILE with ceaseless course the sun
Hasted through the former year,
Many souls their race have run,
Never more to meet us here:
Fix'd in an eternal state,
They have done with all below:
We a little longer wait,
But how little,—none can know.

2 As the winged arrow flies
Speedily the mark to find,—
As the light'ning from the skies
Darts and leaves no trace behind,—
Swiftly thus our fleeting days
Bear us down life's rapid stream;
Upward, Lord, our spirits raise,
All below is but a dream.

3 Thanks for mercies past receive;
Pardon of our sins renew;
Teach us henceforth how to live
With eternity in view;
Bless thy word to young and old,
Fill us with a Saviour's love;
And when life's short tale is told,
May we dwell with thee above.

122 *The Crucifixion.*

BOUND upon th' accursed tree,
Faint and bleeding, who is He?
By the flesh with scourges torn,
By the crown of twisted thorn,
By the side so deeply pierced,
By the baffled, burning thirst,
By the drooping, death-dew'd brow,—
Son of man! 'tis thou! 'tis thou!

2 Bound upon th' accursed tree,
Dread and awful, who is He?
By the sun at noon-day pale,
Shiv'ring rock, and rending veil,
Eden promised ere he died,
To the felon at his side,
Lord! our suppliant knees we bow,—
Son of God! 'tis thou! 'tis thou!

3 Bound upon th' accursed tree,
Sad and dying, who is He?
By the last and bitter cry,
Ghost giv'n up in agony,
By the lifeless body laid
In the chamber of the dead,
Crucified! we know thee now,
Son of man! 'tis thou! 'tis thou!

4 Bound upon th' accursed tree,
Dread and awful, who is He?
By the spoil'd and empty grave,
By the souls he died to save,
By the conquest he hath won,
By the saints before his throne,
By the rainbow round his brow,
Son of God! 'tis thou! 'tis thou!

347 *The expostulation.*

WHAT could your Redeemer do,
More than he hath done for you?
To procure your peace with God,
Could he more than shed his blood?
If your death were his delight,
Would he you to life invite?
Would he ask, beseech, and cry,
Why will ye resolve to die?

2 Sinners, turn, while God is near:
Dare not think him insincere;
Now, e'en now, your Saviour stands,
All day long he spreads his hands;
Cries, "Ye will not happy be;
No, ye will not come to me,—
Me, who life to none deny:
Why will ye resolve to die?"

3 Can ye doubt if God is love?
If to all his bowels move?
Will ye not his *word* receive?
Will ye not his OATH believe?
See, the suff'ring God appears;
Jesus weeps; believe his tears!
Mingled with his blood, they cry,
"Why will ye resolve to die?"

* Double, by repeating each strain, or 6 lines, by repeating the first strain. 8s and 7s by omitting the ties at the end of the first and third lines.

960 *Evening.*

OMNIPRESENT God! whose aid
No one ever asked in vain,
Be this night about my bed,
Every evil thought restrain:

Lay thy hand upon my soul,
God of my unguarded hours!
All my enemies control,
Hell, and earth, and nature's powers.

2 O thou jealous God! come down,
God of spotless purity;
Claim and seize me for thine own,
Consecrate my heart to thee:

Under thy protection take;
Songs in the night season give;
Let me sleep to thee, and wake;
Let me die to thee, and live.

3 Let me of thy life partake,
Thy own holiness impart;
O that I may sweetly wake,
With my Saviour in my heart!

O that I may know thee mine!
O that I may thee receive!
Only live the life divine!
Only to thy glory live.

1045 *The dying Christian to his soul.*

DEATHLESS principle, arise;
Soar, thou native of the skies,
Pearl of price by Jesus bought,
To his glorious likeness wrought,

Go to shine before his throne,
Deck his mediatorial crown:
Go, his triumphs to adorn:
Made for God, to God return.

2 Lo! he beckons from on high;
Fearless to his presence fly;
Thine, the merit of his blood;
Thine, the righteousness of God.

Angels, joyful to attend,
Hov'ring round thy pillow bend,
Wait to catch the signal given,
And escort thee quick to heaven.

3 Is thy earthly house distrest?
Willing to retain its guest?
'Tis not thou, but it must die;—
Fly, celestial tenant, fly!

Burst thy shackles! drop thy clay;
Sweetly breathe thyself away;
Singing, to thy crown remove,
Swift of wing, and fired with love.

4 Shudder not to pass the stream:
Venture all thy care on Him—
Him, whose dying love and power
Still'd its tossing, hush'd its roar.

Safe is the expanded wave,
Gentle as a summer's eve;
Not one object of his care
Ever suffer'd shipwreck there.

5 See the haven full in view;
Love divine shall bear thee through:
Trust to that propitious gale;
Weigh thy anchor, spread thy sail.

Saints in glory, perfect made,
Wait thy passage through the shade;
Ardent for thy coming o'er,
See, they throng the blissful shore.

6 Mount, their transports to improve,
Join the longing choir above;
Swiftly to their wish be given,
Kindle higher joy in heaven.—

Such the prospects that arise
To the dying Christian's eyes;
Such the glorious vista, faith
Opens through the shades of death.

767 *Success.*

SEE how great a flame aspires,
Kindled by a spark of grace!
Jesus' love the nations fires,
Sets the kingdoms on a blaze.
To bring fire on earth he came;
Kindled in some hearts it is:
O that all might catch the flame,
All partake the glorious bliss!

2 When he first the work begun,
Small and feeble was his day;
Now the word doth swiftly run,
Now it wins its widening way:
More and more it spreads and grows,
Ever mighty to prevail;
Sin's strongholds it now o'erthrows,
Shakes the trembling gates of hell.

3 Sons of God, your Saviour praise!
He the door hath open'd wide;
He hath given the word of grace,
Jesus' word is glorified;
Jesus, mighty to redeem,
He alone the work hath wrought;
Worthy is the work of Him,—
Him who spake a world from naught.

4 Saw ye not the cloud arise,
Little as a human hand?
Now it spreads along the skies,
Hangs o'er all the thirsty land;
Lo! the promise of a shower
Drops already from above;
But the Lord will shortly pour
All the Spirit of his love.

127 *Calvary.*

WHEN on Sinai's top I see
  God descend in majesty,
To proclaim his holy law,
  All my spirit sinks with awe.

2 When, in ecstasy sublime,
  Tabor's glorious height I climb,
In the too transporting light,
  Darkness rushes o'er my sight.

3 When on Calvary I rest,
  God, in flesh made manifest,
Shines in my Redeemer's face,
  Full of beauty, truth, and grace.

4 Here I would for ever stay,
  Weep and gaze my soul away:
Thou art heaven on earth to me,
  Lovely, mournful Calvary.

173 *Brazen serpent.*

O THAT I could look to thee,
  Jesus, lifted up for me,
Me, a wounded Israelite,
  Me, expiring in thy sight!

2 Guilt, the serpent's sting, I feel,
  Anguish inconceivable,
Bleeding, gasping on the ground,
  Dying of the pois'nous wound.

3 But with a believing eye,
  If I can my Lord espy,
Hanging on the sacred pole,
  I, even I, shall be made whole.

4 Give me now to find thee near,
  Now as crucified appear;
Life is through thy wounds alone,
  Mine to heal, display thy own.

727 *Funeral of a Christian. Rev. xiv. 13.*

HARK! a voice divides the sky,
  Happy are the faithful dead!
In the Lord who sweetly die,
  They from all their toils are freed.

2 Them the Spirit hath declared
  Bless'd, unutterably blest:
Jesus is their great reward,
  Jesus is their endless rest.

3 Follow'd by their works, they go
  Where their Head has gone before;
Reconciled by grace below,
  Grace had open'd Mercy's door;

4 Justified through faith alone,
  Here they knew their sins forgiven;
Here they laid their burden down,
  Hallow'd, and made meet for heaven.

486 *Bliss.*

JESUS is our common Lord,
  He our loving Saviour is;
By his death to life restored,
  Mis'ry we exchange for bliss—

2 Bliss to carnal minds unknown:
  O 'tis more than tongue can tell!
Only to believers shown,
  Glorious and unspeakable.

3 Christ, our Brother and our Friend,
  Shows us his eternal love:
Never shall our triumphs end,
  Till we take our seats above.

4 Let us walk with him in white;
  For our bridal day prepare,
For our partnership in light,
  For our glorious meeting there!

FOUNTAIN. 8s & 7s. Double. **

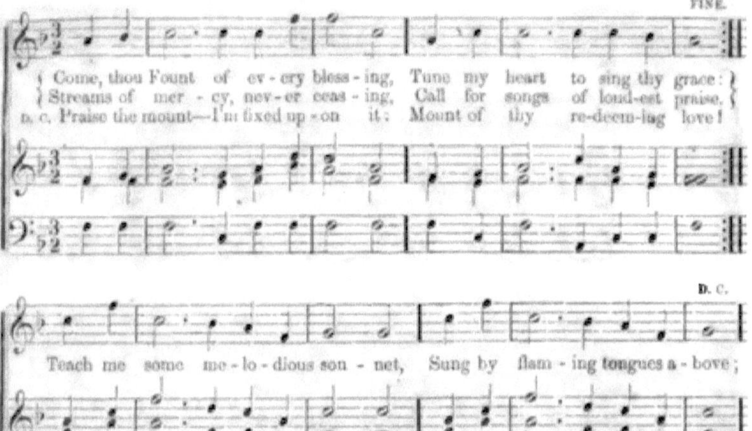

623 *Gratitude.*

COME, thou Fount of every blessing,
  Tune my heart to sing thy grace:
Streams of mercy, never ceasing,
  Call for songs of loudest praise,
Teach me some melodious sonnet,
  Sung by flaming tongues above:
Praise the mount—I'm fixed upon it;
  Mount of thy redeeming love!

2 Here I'll rise mine Ebenezer,
  Hither, by thy help, I'm come;
And I hope, by thy good pleasure,
  Safely to arrive at home.
Jesus sought me, when a stranger,
  Wand'ring from the fold of God;
He, to rescue me from danger,
  Interposed his precious blood!

3 O! to grace how great a debtor
  Daily I'm constrained to be!
Let thy goodness, like a fetter,
  Bind my wand'ring heart to thee!
Prone to wander, Lord, I feel it;
  Prone to leave the God I love—
Here's my heart, O take and seal it!
  Seal it for thy courts above!

537 *Invoking Divine Love.*

LOVE Divine, all love excelling,
  Joy of heaven, to earth come down;
Fix in us thy humble dwelling,
  All thy faithful mercies crown!
Jesus, thou art all compassion,
  Pure unbounded love thou art;
Visit us with thy salvation;
  Enter every trembling heart.

2 Breathe, O breathe thy loving Spirit
  Into every troubled breast!
Let us all in thee inherit,
  Let us find that second rest.
Take away our bent to sinning,
  Alpha and Omega be,
End of faith, as its beginning,
  Set our hearts at liberty.

3 Come, almighty to deliver,
  Let us all thy life receive,
Suddenly return, and never,
  Never more thy temples leave:
Thee we would be always blessing;
  Serve thee as thy hosts above;
Pray, and praise thee, without ceasing,
  Glory in thy perfect love.

4 Finish, then, thy new creation,
  Pure and spotless let us be;
Let us see thy great salvation
  Perfectly restored in thee:
Changed from glory into glory,
  Till in heaven we take our place,
Till we cast our crowns before thee,
  Lost in wonder, love, and praise!

1050 *Dismission.*

LORD, dismiss us with thy blessing,
  Bid us now depart in peace;
Still on heavenly manna feeding,
  Let our faith and love increase:
Fill each breast with consolation,
  Up to thee our hearts we raise;
When we reach our blissful station,
  Then we'll give thee nobler praise.

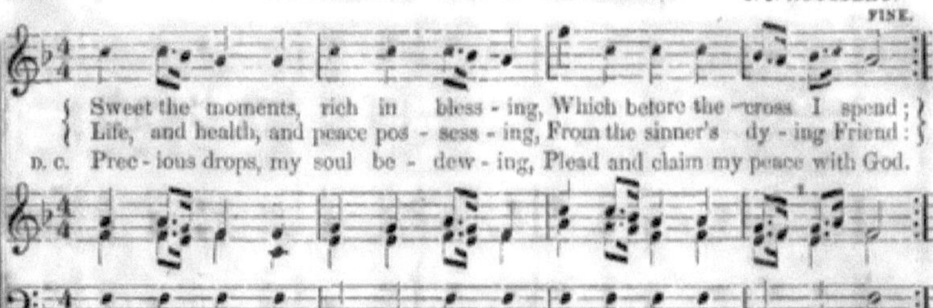

479 *Sitting at the Cross.*

SWEET the moments, rich in blessing,
Which before the cross I spend;
Life, and health, and peace possessing,
From the sinner's dying Friend:
Here I'll sit, for ever viewing
Mercy's streams in streams of blood:
Precious drops, my soul bedewing,
Plead and claim my peace with God.

2 Truly blessed is this station,
Low before his cross to lie;
While I see divine compassion
Floating in his languid eye:
Here it is I find my heaven,
While upon the Lamb I gaze:
Love I much? I've much forgiven—
I'm a miracle of grace!

3 Love and grief my heart dividing,
With my tears his feet I'll bathe;
Constant still in faith abiding,
Life deriving from his death.
May I still enjoy this feeling,
In all need to Jesus go;
Prove his wounds each day more healing,
And himself more deeply know.

941 *"Lord, revive us."*

SAVIOUR, visit thy plantation,
Grant us, Lord, a gracious rain!
All will come to desolation,
Unless thou return again.
2 Keep no longer at a distance.
Shine upon us from on high,
Lest, for want of thy assistance,
Every plant should droop and die.

3 Surely once thy garden flourish'd,
Every plant look'd gay and green;
Then thy word our spirits nourish'd—
Happy seasons we have seen.
4 But a drought has since succeeded,
And a sad decline we see;
Lord, thy help is greatly needed,
Help can only come from thee.

961 *Evening.*

SAVIOUR, breathe an evening blessing
Ere repose our spirits seal;
Sin and want we come confessing;
Thou canst save and thou canst heal.
2 Though destruction walk around us;
Though the arrow past us fly,
Angel guards from thee surround us;
We are safe, if thou art nigh.

3 Though the night be dark and dreary,
Darkness cannot hide from thee;
Thou art he, who, never weary,
Watches where thy people be.
4 Should swift death this night o'ertake us,
And our couch become our tomb
May the morn in heaven awake us,
Clad in light, and deathless bloom.

1048 2 *Cor.* xiii. 14.

MAY the grace of Christ our Saviour,
And the Father's boundless love,
With the holy Spirit's favour,
Rest upon us from above!
Thus may we abide in union
With each other in the Lord;
And possess, in sweet communion,
Joys which earth cannot afford.

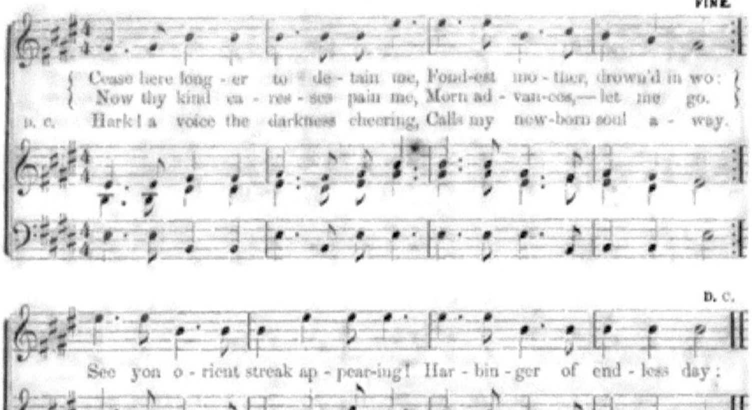

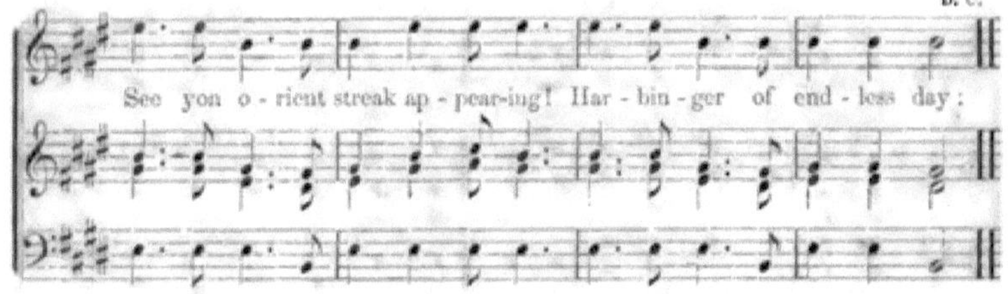

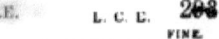

985 *Dying child to its mother.*

CEASE here longer to detain me,
  Fondest mother, drown'd in wo:
Now thy kind caresses pain me,—
  Morn advances—let me go.

2 See yon orient streak appearing!
  Harbinger of endless day:
Hark! a voice, the darkness cheering,
  Calls my new-born soul away.

3 Lately launch'd a trembling stranger,
  On the world's wide, boist'rous flood,
Pierced with sorrows, toss'd with danger,
  Gladly I return to God.

4 Now my cries shall cease to grieve thee;
  Now my trembling heart shall rest;
Kinder arms than thine receive me,—
  Softer pillow than thy breast.

5 Weep not o'er these eyes that languish,
  Upward turning to their home;
They will soon forget all anguish,
  While I wait to see thee come.

6 There, my mother, pleasures centre:
  Weeping, parting, care, or wo,
Ne'er our Father's house shall enter—
  Morn advances!—let me go!

817 *Autumn.*

SEE the leaves around us falling,
  Dry and wither'd, to the ground,
Thus to thoughtless mortals calling,
  In a sad and solemn sound,—

2 "Youth, on length of days presuming,
  Who the paths of pleasure tread,
View us, late in beauty blooming,
  Number'd now among the dead.

3 "What though yet no losses grieve you—
  Gay with health and many a grace,—
Let not cloudless skies deceive you;
  Summer gives to autumn place."

4 On the Tree of Life eternal,
  Lord, let all our hopes be stay'd!
This alone, for ever vernal,
  Bears a leaf that shall not fade.

991 *"Peace be to this house."*

PEACE be to this habitation!
  Peace to every soul herein!
Peace, the foretaste of salvation,
  Peace, the seal of cancell'd sin—
Peace that speaks its heavenly Giver,
  Peace to earthly minds unknown,
Peace divine that lasts for ever,—
  Here erect its glorious throne.

2 On the son of peace descending,
  On the daughter of thy grace,
Full of comforts never ending,
  Let the promise now take place.
Now thy love-infusing Spirit
  Shed in every heart abroad;
And, Redeemer, through thy merit,
  Make each child a child of God.

3 Claim for thine each faithful servant,
  By the reconciling word;
Pure in heart, in spirit fervent,
  Let them serve their heavenly Lord.
Visit, Lord, with thy salvation,
  Every providential guest;
Every friend and kind relation
  Take into thy people's rest!

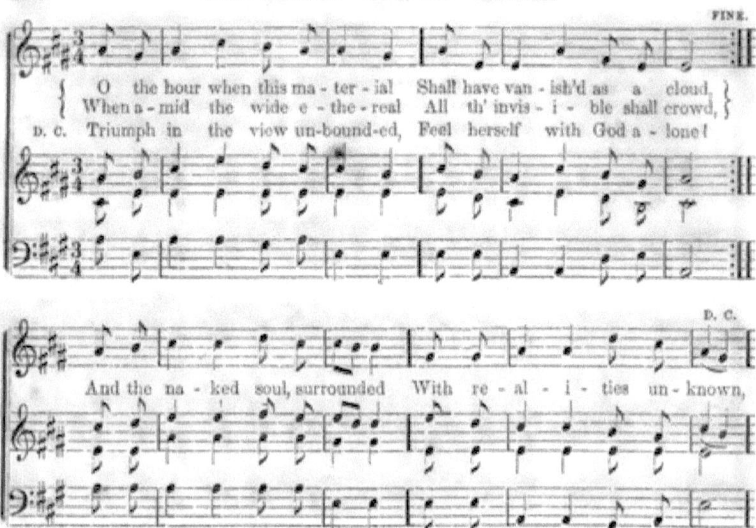

1047 *"Then cometh the end—"*

O THE hour when this material
Shall have vanish'd as a cloud;
When amid the wide ethereal
All th' invisible shall crowd,—
And the naked soul, surrounded
With realities unknown,
Triumph in the view unbounded,
Feel herself with God *alone!*

2 In that sudden, strange transition,
By what new and finer sense
Shall she grasp the mighty vision,
And receive its influence?
Angels, guard the new immortal,
Through the wonder-teeming space,
To the everlasting portal,
To the spirit's resting-place.

3 Will she, then, with fond emotion,
Aught of human love retain?
Or, absorb'd in pure devotion,
Will no earthly trace remain?
Can the grave those ties dissever,
With the very heart-strings twined?
Must she part, and part for ever,
With the friends she leaves behind?

4 No: the past she still remembers,
Faith and hope, surviving too,
Ever watch these sleeping embers,
Which must rise and live anew:
For the widow'd, lonely spirit,
Waiting to be clothed afresh,
Longs perfection to inherit,
And to triumph in the flesh.

5 Angels, let the ransom'd stranger
In your tender care be blest,
Hoping, trusting, safe from danger,
Till the trumpet end her rest—
Till the trump, which shakes creation,
Through the circling heavens shall roll,
Till the day of consummation,
Till the bridal of the soul.

6 Can I trust a fellow-being?
Can I trust an angel's care?
O thou merciful All-seeing!
Beam around my spirit there.
Jesus, blessed Mediator!
Thou the airy path hast trod:
Thou the Judge, the Consummator!
Shepherd of the fold of God!

7 Blessed fold! no foe can enter;
And no friend departeth thence;
Jesus is their sun, their centre,
And their shield, Omnipotence.
Blessed! for the Lamb shall feed them,
All their tears shall wipe away,
To the living fountains lead them,
Till fruition's perfect day.

8 Lo! it comes, that day of wonder!
Louder chorals shake the skies:
Hades' gates are burst asunder;
See! the new-clothed myriads rise.
Thought, repress thy weak endeavour:
Here must reason prostrate fall,
O th' ineffable *for ever*,
And th' eternal All in All.

154 *Priesthood of Christ.*

HAIL! thou once despised Jesus,
Hail, thou Galilean King!
Thou didst suffer to release us;
Thou didst free salvation bring:
Hail, thou agonizing Saviour,
Bearer of our sin and shame!
By thy merits we find favour;
Life is given through thy name.

2 Paschal Lamb, by God appointed,
All our sins on thee were laid;
By almighty love anointed,
Thou hast full atonement made:
All thy people are forgiven,
Through the virtue of thy blood;
Open'd is the gate of heaven;
Peace is made 'twixt man and God.

3 Jesus, hail! enthroned in glory,
There for ever to abide!
All the heavenly hosts adore thee,
Seated at thy Father's side:
There for sinners thou art pleading,
There thou dost our place prepare;
Ever for us interceding,
Till in glory we appear.

4 Worship, honour, power, and blessing,
Thou art worthy to receive;
Loudest praises, without ceasing,
Meet it is for us to give:
Help, ye bright angelic spirits,
Bring your sweetest, noblest lays;
Help to sing our Saviour's merits;
Help to chant Immanuel's praise.

239 *Supplies of the church.*

GLORIOUS things of thee are spoken,
Zion, city of our God!
He, whose word can ne'er be broken,
Form'd thee for his own abode:
On the Rock of Ages founded,
What can shake thy sure repose?
With salvation's walls surrounded,
Thou may'st smile at all thy foes.

2 See! the streams of living waters,
Springing from eternal love,
Well supply thy sons and daughters,
And all fear of want remove:
Who can faint while such a river
Ever flows their thirst t' assuage?
Grace which, like the Lord, the giver,
Never fails from age to age.

3 Round each habitation hov'ring,
See the cloud and fire appear,
For a glory and a cov'ring—
Showing that the Lord is near:
Glorious things of thee are spoken,
Zion, city of our God;
He, whose word can ne'er be broken,
Chose thee for his own abode.

1048 *2 Cor. xiii. 14.*

MAY the grace of Christ our Saviour,
And the Father's boundless love,
With the holy Spirit's favour,
Rest upon us from above!
Thus may we abide in union
With each other in the Lord;
And possess, in sweet communion,
Joys which earth cannot afford.

762 *"Freely ye have received—freely give."*

PRAISE the Saviour, all ye nations,
Praise him, all ye hosts above;
Shout, with joyful acclamations,
His divine, victorious love;
Be his kingdom now promoted,
Let the earth her monarch know,
Be my all to him devoted,
To my Lord my all I owe.

2 See how beauteous on the mountains
Are their feet, whose grand design
Is to guide us to the fountains
That o'erflow with bliss divine—
Who proclaim the joyful tidings
Of salvation all around—
Disregard the world's deridings,
And in works of love abound.

3 With my substance I will honor
My Redeemer and my Lord;
Were ten thousand worlds my manor,
All were nothing to his word;
While the heralds of salvation
His abounding grace proclaim,
Let his friends, of every station,
Gladly join to spread his fame.

764 *Missionaries charged.*

ONWARD, onward, men of heaven;
Bear the gospel banner high;
Rest not till its light is given—
Star of every pagan sky;
Send it where the pilgrim stranger
Faints beneath the torrid ray;
Bid the hardy forest ranger
Hail it, ere he fades away.

2 Where the Arctic Ocean thunders,
Where the tropics fiercely glow,
Broadly spread its page of wonders,
Brightly bid its radiance flow:
India marks its lustre stealing;
Shiv'ring Greenland loves its rays;
Afric, 'mid her deserts kneeling,
Lifts the untaught strain of praise.

3 Rude in speech, or wild in feature,
Dark in spirit, though they be,—
Show that light to every creature,—
Prince or vassal, bond or free:
Lo! they haste to every nation;
Host on host the ranks supply:
Onward! Christ is your salvation,
And your death is victory.

934 *"Come, Lord Jesus."*

COME, thou long-expected Jesus,
Born to set thy people free;
From our fears and sins release us,
Let us find our rest in thee:
Israel's Strength and Consolation,
Hope of all the earth thou art,—
Dear Desire of every nation,
Joy of every longing heart.

2 Born thy people to deliver;
Born a child, and yet a King;
Born to reign in us for ever,
Now thy gracious kingdom bring:
By thine own Eternal Spirit,
Rule in all our hearts alone;
By thine all-sufficient merit,
Raise us to thy glorious throne.

632 *Taking up the cross.*

JESUS, I my cross have taken,
All to leave, and follow thee;
Naked, poor, despised, forsaken,
Thou, from hence, my all shalt be.
Perish, every fond ambition,
All I've sought, or hoped, or known;
Yet how rich is my condition,
God and heaven are still my own!

2 Let the world despise and leave me;
They have left my Saviour too:
Human hearts and looks deceive me—
Thou art not, like them, untrue;
And while thou shalt smile upon me,
God of wisdom, love, and might,
Foes may hate, and friends disown me;
Show thy face, and all is bright.

3 Go, then, earthly fame and treasure;
Come disaster, scorn, and pain:
In thy service pain is pleasure;
With thy favour loss is gain.
I have call'd thee Abba, Father,—
I have set my heart on thee;
Storms may howl, and clouds may gather,
All must work for good to me.

4 Man may trouble and distress me,—
'Twill but drive me to thy breast;
Life with trials hard may press me,—
Heaven will bring me sweeter rest.
O! 'tis not in grief to harm me,
While thy love is left to me;
O! 'twere not in joy to charm me,
Were that joy unmix'd with thee!

5 Soul, then know thy full salvation;
Rise o'er sin, and fear, and care;
Joy to find in every station,
Something still to do or bear.
Think what spirit dwells within thee;
Think what Father's smiles are thine;
Think that Jesus died to win thee:
Child of heaven, canst thou repine?

6 Haste thee on from grace to glory,
Arm'd by faith, and wing'd by prayer;
Heaven's eternal days before thee,
God's own hand shall guide thee there.
Soon shall close thy earthly mission,
Soon shall pass thy pilgrim days;
Hope shall change to glad fruition,
Faith to sight, and prayer to praise.

933 *An Advocate with the Father.*

FATHER, hear the blood of Jesus,
Speaking in thine ears above!
From thy wrath and curse release us,
Manifest thy pard'ning love;
O receive us to thy favour,
For his only sake receive,
Give us to our bleeding Saviour,
Let us by his dying live.

2 "To thy pard'ning grace receive them,"
Once he pray'd upon the tree,
Still his blood cries out, "Forgive them,
All their sins were purged by me."
Still our Advocate in heaven
Prays the prayer on earth begun,
"Father, show their sins forgiven,
Father, glorify thy Son!"

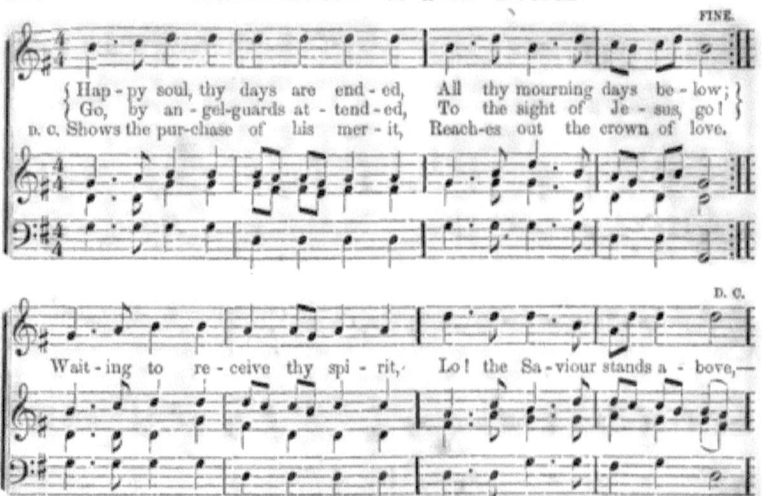

1046 *To the departing saint.*

HAPPY soul, thy days are ended,
All thy mourning days below,
Go, by angel guards attended,
To the sight of Jesus, go!
Waiting to receive thy spirit,
Lo! the Saviour stands above,—
Shows the purchase of his merit,
Reaches out the crown of love.

2 Struggle through thy latest passion,
To thy great Redeemer's breast,
To his uttermost salvation,
To his everlasting rest.
For the joy he sets before thee
Bear a momentary pain;
Die, to live a life of glory!
Suffer, with thy Lord to reign!

178 *Praise to the Redeemer.*

MIGHTY God, while angels bless thee,
May a mortal lisp thy name?
Lord of men as well as angels,
Thou art every creature's theme.

2 Lord of every land and nation,
Ancient of eternal days!
Sounded through the wide creation
Be thy just and lawful praise.

3 For the grandeur of thy nature—
Grand beyond a seraph's thought—
For created works of power,
Works with skill and kindness wrought.

4 For thy providence that governs
Through thine empire's wide domain;
Wings an angel—guides a sparrow—
Blessed be thy gentle reign.

5 But thy rich, thy free redemption,
Dark through brightness all along!
Thought is poor, and poor expression;
Who dare sing that awful song?

6 Brightness of the Father's glory,
Shall thy praise unutter'd lie?
Fly, my tongue, such guilty silence,
Sing the Lord who came to die.

7 Did archangels sing thy coming?
Did the shepherds learn their lays?
Shame would cover me, ungrateful,
Should my tongue refuse to praise.

8 From the highest throne in glory,
To the cross of deepest wo—
All to ransom guilty captives!
Flow, my praise, for ever flow.

9 Go, return, immortal Saviour;
Leave thy footstool, take thy throne;
Thence return, and reign for ever;
Be the kingdom all thine own.

304 *"It is the Spirit that quickeneth."*

COME, thou everlasting Spirit,
Bring to every thankful mind
All the Saviour's dying merit,
All his suff'rings for mankind:
True recorder of his passion,
Now the living faith impart,
Now reveal his great salvation,
Preach his gospel to our heart.

2 Come, thou witness of his dying,
Come, remembrancer divine,
Let us feel thy power applying
Christ to every soul and mine:
Let us groan thine inward groaning,
Look on him we pierced and grieve,
All receive the grace atoning,
All the sprinkled blood receive.

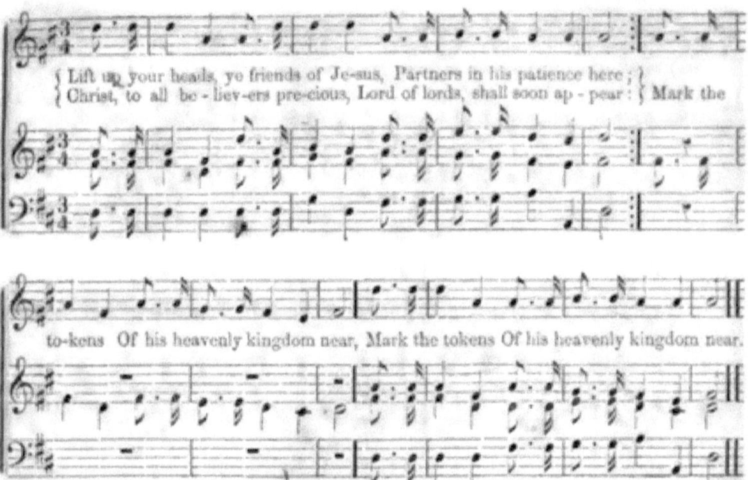

692 *The advent of the Judge.*

LIFT your heads, ye friends of Jesus,
Partners in his patience here;
Christ, to all believers precious,
Lord of lords, shall soon appear;
Mark the tokens
Of his heavenly kingdom near.

2 Close behind the tribulation
Of the last tremendous days;
See the flaming revelation!
See the universal blaze!
Earth and heaven
Melt before the Judge's face!

3 Sun and moon are both confounded,
Darken'd into endless night,
When with angel hosts surrounded,
In his Father's glory bright,
Beams the Saviour,
Shines the everlasting Light.

4 See the stars from heaven falling;
Hark, on earth the doleful cry,
Men on rocks and mountains calling,
While the frowning Judge draws nigh,
"Hide us, hide us,
Rocks and mountains, from his eye!"

5 With what different exclamation
Shall the saints his banner see!
By the tokens of his passion,
By the marks received for *me!*
All discern him,
All with shouts cry out, "'Tis He!"

6 Yes, the prize shall soon be given;
We his open face shall see:
Love, the earnest of our heaven,—
Love our full reward shall be:
Love shall crown us
Kings through all eternity.

167 *Second Advent of Christ.*

LO! He comes, with clouds descending,
Once for favour'd sinners slain!
Thousand thousand saints attending,
Swell the triumph of his train!
Hallelujah!
God appears on earth to reign.

2 Every eye shall now behold him
Robed in dreadful majesty;
Those who set at naught and sold him,
Pierced and nail'd him to the tree,
Deeply wailing,
Shall the true Messiah see.

3 The dear tokens of his passion
Still his dazzling body bears;
Cause of endless exultation
To his ransom'd worshippers;
With what rapture
Gaze we on these glorious scars!

4 Yea, Amen! let all adore thee,
High on thy eternal throne!
Saviour, take the power and glory,
Claim the kingdom for thine own!
Jah! Jehovah!
Everlasting God, come down!

1062 *Doxology.*

GREAT Jehovah! we adore thee,
God the Father, God the Son,
God the Spirit, join'd in glory
On the same eternal throne:
Endless praises
To Jehovah, Three in One.

361 *"Prepare to meet thy God."*

DAY of judgment, day of wonders!
Hark! the trumpet's awful sound,
Louder than a thousand thunders,
Shakes the vast creation round!
How the summons
Will the sinner's heart confound!

2 See the Judge our nature wearing,
Clothed in majesty divine!
You who long for his appearing
Then shall say, "This God is mine."
Gracious Saviour,
Own me in that day for thine!

3 At his call, the dead awaken,—
Rise to life from earth and sea;
All the powers of nature, shaken
By his looks, prepare to flee:
Careless sinner,
What will then become of thee?

356 *Psalm l, 16, 17, 20, 21.*

WHY, O sinner, me profaning,
Why, says God, my statutes name?
Why my cov'nant grace disdaining,
Still my cov'nant grace proclaim?
Hating counsel;
All my laws exposed to shame.

2 Long in silence I have waited,
Long thy guilt in secret grown;
Till thy heart, with pride elated,
Thought my counsels like thy own;
I'll reprove thee,
Till thy crimes exact are known.

3 Sinners, hear Jehovah speaking!
Ye who, thoughtless, God despise!
Hear, lest, in his wrath awaking,
Vengeance rend you as it flies;
None can save you,
If his arm to judgment rise.

799 *Sunday School Celebration.*

THOU, who didst with love and blessing
Gather Sion's babes to thee,
Still a Saviour's love expressing,
These, the babes of Sion, see;
Bless the labours
That would bring them up for thee.

2 Smile upon the weak endeavour,
Vain, if thou thy smile deny;
Lo! they rise,—to live for ever!
Train, O train them for the sky!
Ne'er may Satan
Plunder Sion's nursery.

3 Lord, with humble fervour bending,
We thy blessing would entreat,
On the youthful heart descending,
Make the toils of learning sweet:
Still to Sion
Guide the young disciples' feet.

4 Then, when long we both have slumber'd
Side by side in common dust,
With thy ransom'd people number'd
With th' assembly of the just,
Child and teacher,
Saviour! own our humble trust.

1062 *Doxology.*

GREAT Jehovah! we adore thee,
God the Father, God the Son,
God the Spirit, join'd in glory
On the same eternal throne:
Endless praises
To Jehovah! Three in One.

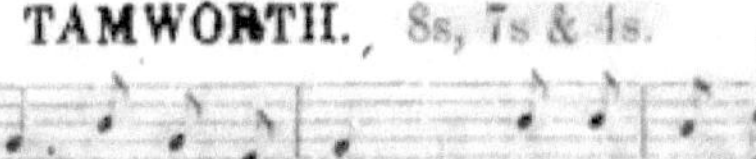

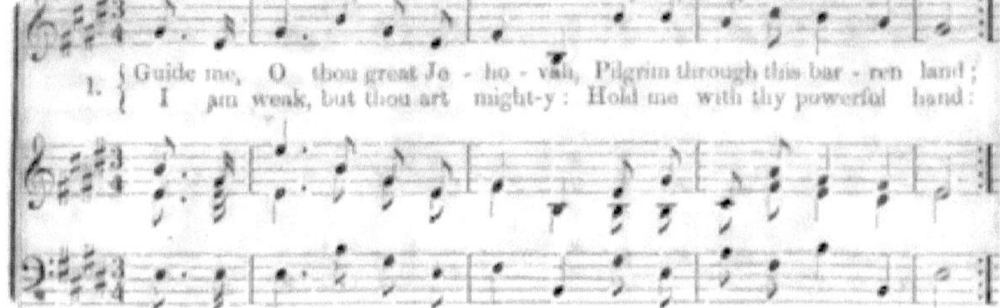

558 *The pilgrimage.*

GUIDE me, O thou great Jehovah,
Pilgrim through this barren land;
I am weak, but thou art mighty;
Hold me with thy powerful hand.
Bread of heaven,
Feed me till I want no more.

2 Open, Lord, the crystal fountain
Whence the healing waters flow;
Let the fiery, cloudy pillar,
Lead me all my journey through:
Strong Deliv'rer!
Be thou still my strength and shield.

3 When I tread the verge of Jordan,
Bid my anxious fears subside;
Death of death, and hell's destruction,
Land me safe on Canaan's side:
Songs of praises—
I will ever give to thee.

471 *"Whom not having seen, we love."*

O THOU God of my salvation,
My Redeemer from all sin,
Moved by thy divine compassion,
Who has died my heart to win,
I will praise thee;
Where will I thy praise begin?

2 Though unseen, I love the Saviour;
He hath brought salvation near,—
Manifests his pard'ning favour,
And when Jesus doth appear,
Soul and body
Shall his glorious image bear.

3 While the angel choirs are crying,
Glory to the great I AM!
I with them will still be vying,
Glory! glory to the Lamb!
O how precious
Is the sound of Jesus' name!

4 Angels now are hov'ring round us,
Unperceived they mix the throng,
Wond'ring at the love that crown'd us
Glad to join the holy song:
Hallelujah!
Love and praise to Christ belong.

5 Now I see, with joy and wonder,
Whence the gracious spring arose;
Angel minds are lost to ponder
Dying love's mysterious cause:
Yet the blessing,
Down to all, to me it flows.

6 This hath set me all on fire;
Strongly glows the flame of love;
Higher mounts my soul, and higher,
Struggles for its swift remove:
Then I'll praise Him
In a nobler strain above!

1062 *Doxology.*

GREAT Jehovah! we adore thee,
God the Father, God the Son,
God the Spirit, join'd in glory
On the same eternal throne:
Endless praises
To Jehovah, Three in One!

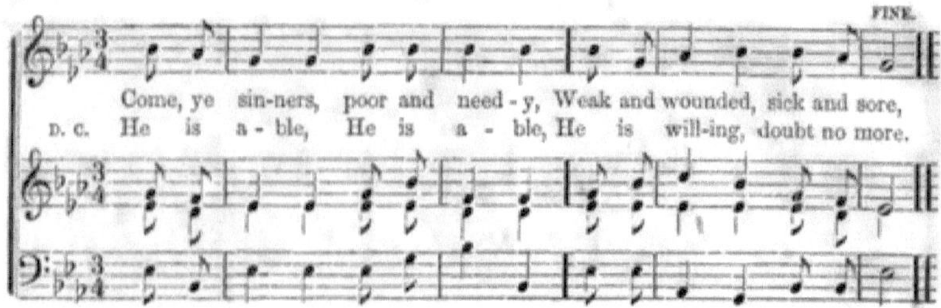

330 *The invitation.*

COME, ye sinners, poor and needy,
Weak and wounded, sick and sore,
Jesus ready stands to save you,
Full of pity, love, and power;
He is able,
He is willing, doubt no more.

2 Now ye needy, come and welcome,
God's free bounty glorify;
True belief and true repentance,
Every grace that brings you nigh,
Without money,
Come to Jesus Christ and buy.

3 Let not conscience make you linger,
Nor of fitness fondly dream:
All the fitness he requireth
Is to feel your need of him;
This he gives you,
'Tis the Spirit's glimm'ring beam.

4 Come, ye weary, heavy-laden,
Bruised and mangled by the fall,
If you tarry till you're better,
You will never come at all;
Not the righteous,
Sinners, Jesus came to call.

5 Agonizing in the garden,
Lo! your Maker prostrate lies!
On the bloody tree behold him!
Hear him cry before he dies,
"It is finish'd!"
Sinners, will not this suffice?

6 Lo! th' incarnate God ascending,
Pleads the merit of his blood;
Venture on him, venture freely;
Let no other trust intrude:
None but Jesus
Can do helpless sinners good.

7 Saints and angels, join'd in concert,
Sing the praises of the Lamb,
While the blissful seats of heaven
Sweetly echo with his name:
Hallelujah!
Sinners here may do the same.

756 *Spread of the gospel.*

O'ER the gloomy hills of darkness,
Look, my soul, be still and gaze;
All the promises do travail
With a glorious day of grace;
Blessed jub'lee,
Let thy glorious morning dawn!

2 Kingdoms wide that sit in darkness,
Grant them, Lord, the glorious light;
And from eastern coast to western,
May the morning chase the night;
And redemption,
Freely purchased, win the day.

3 Fly abroad, thou mighty gospel;
Win and conquer, never cease;
May thy lasting, wide dominions,
Multiply, and still increase;
Sway thy sceptre,
Saviour, all the world around.

1062 *Doxology.*

GREAT Jehovah! we adore thee,
God the Father, God the Son,
God the Spirit, join'd in glory
On the same eternal throne:
Endless praises
To Jehovah, Three in One.

NEWPORT. 7s & 6s.

203 *The gift of the Son.*

FATHER of our dying Lord,
  Remember us for good;
O fulfil his faithful word,
  And hear his speaking blood!
Give us that for which he prays;
  Father, glorify thy Son!
Show his truth, and power, and grace,
  And send the promise down.

2 True and faithful Witness, thou,
  O Christ, the Spirit give!
Hast thou not received him now,
  That we might now receive?
Art thou not the living Head?
  Life to all thy limbs impart;
Shed thy love, thy Spirit shed,
  In every waiting heart.

3 Holy Ghost, the Comforter,
  The gift of Jesus, come;
Glow our hearts to find thee near,
  And swell to make thee room;
Present with us thee we feel,
  Come, O come, and in us be!
With us, in us, live and dwell
  To all eternity.

754 *"Thy kingdom come."*

SAVIOUR, whom our hearts adore,
  To bless our earth again,
Now assume thy royal power,
  And o'er the nations reign:
Christ, the world's Desire and Hope,
  Power complete to thee is given:
Set the last great empire up,
  Eternal Lord of heaven.

2 Where they all thy laws have spurn'd,
  Thy holiest name profaned,
Where the ruin'd world hath mourn'd
  With blood of millions slain:
Open there th' ethereal scene,
  Claim the heathen tribes for thine;
There the endless reign begin
  With majesty divine.

3 Universal Saviour, thou
  Wilt all thy creatures bless;
Every knee to thee shall bow,
  And every tongue confess:
None shall in thy mount destroy;
  War shall then be learn'd no more:
Saints shall their great King enjoy,
  And all mankind adore.

AMSTERDAM. 7s & 6s.

556 *The pilgrimage.*

RISE, my soul, and stretch thy wings,
Thy better portion trace;
Rise from transitory things,
Tow'rd heaven, thy native place;
Sun, and moon, and stars, decay;
Time shall soon this earth remove;
Rise, my soul, and haste away
To seats prepared above.

2 Rivers to the ocean run,
Nor stay in all their course;
Fire ascending seeks the sun;
Both speed them to their source:
So a soul that's born of God
Pants to view his glorious face,
Upward tends to his abode,
To rest in his embrace.

3 Cease, ye pilgrims, cease to mourn,
Press onward to the prize;
Soon our Saviour will return,
Triumphant in the skies.
Yet a season, and you know,
Happy entrance will be given;
All our sorrows left below,
And earth exchanged for heaven.

191 *The mystery of love.*

JESUS drinks the bitter cup,
The wine-press treads alone;
Tears the graves and mountains up,
By his expiring groan:
Lo, the powers of heaven he shakes,
Nature in convulsion lies;
Earth's profoundest centre quakes;
The great Jehovah dies!

2 O my God, he dies for me,
I feel the mortal smart!
See him hanging on the tree,
A sight that breaks my heart!
O that all to thee might turn!
Sinners, ye may love him too;
Look on him, ye pierced, and mourn
For one who bled for you.

3 Weep o'er your desire and hope,
With tears of humblest love!
Sing, for Jesus is gone up,
And reigns enthroned above!
Lives our Head to die no more,
Power is all to Jesus given;
Worshipp'd as he was before,
Th' immortal King of heaven.

516 *Deut.* xxxiii. 26—29.

NONE is like Jeshurun's God,
So great, so strong, so high!
Lo! he spreads his wings abroad,
He rides upon the sky!

Sun, and moon, and stars, de - cay; Time shall soon this earth re - move;
Rise, my soul, and haste a - way To seats pre-pared a - bove.

Israel is his first-born son:
God, th' almighty God, is thine;
See him to thy help come down,
The excellence divine!

2 Thee the great Jehovah deigns
To succour and defend;
Thee th' eternal God sustains,
Thy Maker and thy Friend:
Israel, what hast thou to dread?
Safe from all impending harms,
Round thee and beneath are spread
The everlasting arms.

3 God is thine, disdain to fear
The enemy within:
God shall in thy flesh appear,
And make an end of sin;
God the man of sin shall slay,
Fill thee with triumphant joy;
God shall thrust him out, and say
"Destroy them all, destroy!"

4 All the struggle then is o'er,
And wars and fightings cease;
Israel then, shall sin no more,
But dwell in perfect peace.
All his enemies are gone;
Sin shall have in him no part:
Israel now shall dwell alone,
With Jesus in his heart.

5 In a land of corn and wine
His lot shall be below;
Comforts there, and blessings, join,
And milk and honey flow:
Jacob's well is in his soul;
Gracious dew his heavens distil,
Fill his soul, already full,
And shall for ever fill.

6 Bless'd, O Israel, art thou;
What people is like thee?
Saved from sin, by Jesus, now
Thou art, and still shalt be:
Jesus is thy sevenfold shield,
Jesus is thy flaming sword;
Earth, and hell, and sin, shall yield
To God's almighty word.

1063 *Doxology.*

FATHER, Son, and Holy Ghost,
Thy Godhead we adore,
Join with the celestial host,
Who praise thee evermore!
Live by earth and heaven adored,
The Three in One, the One in Three;
Holy, holy, holy Lord,
All glory be to thee!

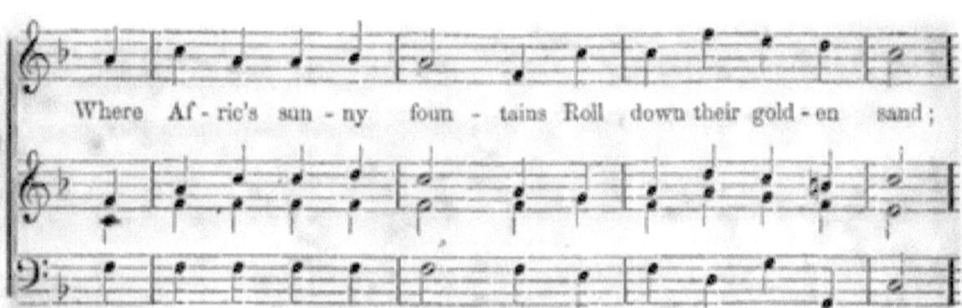

760 *"Come over—and help us!"*

FROM Greenland's icy mountains,
  From India's coral strand;
Where Afric's sunny fountains
  Roll down their golden sand;
From many an ancient river,
  From many a palmy plain,
They call us to deliver
  Their land from error's chain.

2 What though the spicy breezes
  Blow soft o'er Ceylon's isle,
Though every prospect pleases,
  And only man is vile:—
In vain with lavish kindness
  The gifts of God are strown;
The heathen in his blindness
  Bows down to wood and stone.

3 Shall we whose souls are lighted
  With wisdom from on high,
Shall we to men benighted
  The lamp of life deny?
Salvation! O salvation!
  The joyful sound proclaim,
Till earth's remotest nation
  Has learn'd Messiah's name.

4 Waft, waft, ye winds, his story,
  And you, ye waters, roll,
Till, like a sea of glory,
  It spreads from pole to pole.
Till o'er our ransomed nature,
  The Lamb for sinners slain,
Redeemer, King, Creator,
  In bliss returns to reign.

218 *"The God of all comfort."*

GOD of all consolation,
  The Holy Ghost thou art,
Thy secret inspiration
  Hath told it to my heart:
The blessing I inherit,
  Through Jesus' prayer bestow'd,
The Comforter, the Spirit,
  The true eternal God.

2 With God the Son and Saviour—
  With God the Father one,
The tokens of his favour
  Thou mak'st to sinners known:
An antepast of heaven
  Thou dost in me reveal,
Attest my sins forgiven,
  And my salvation seal.

3 Th' indubitable witness
  Of thy own Deity,
Thou giv'st my soul its fitness
  Thy glorious face to see:

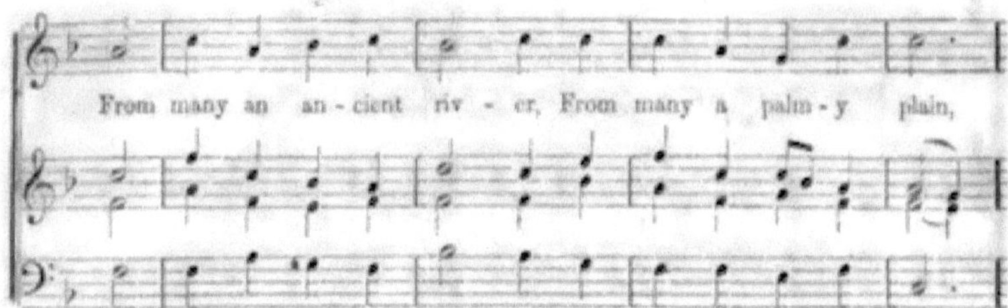
From many an an - cient riv - er, From many a palm - y plain,

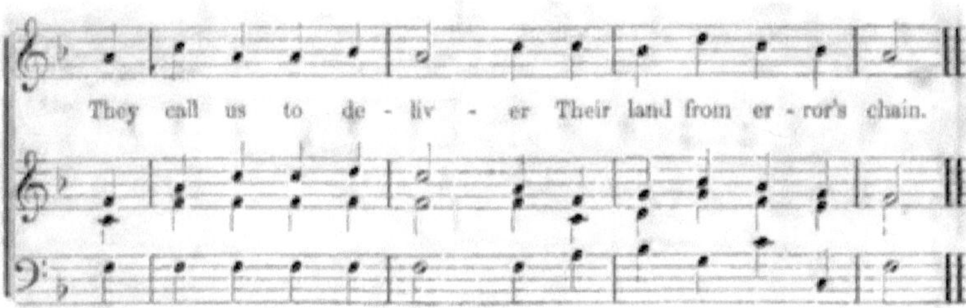
They call us to de - liv - er Their land from er - ror's chain.

Thy comforts, gifts, and graces,
  My largest thoughts transcend,
And challenge all my praises,
  When faith in sight shall end.

742 *Psalm* lxxii. 1—11.

HAIL to the Lord's Anointed,
  Great David's greater Son!
Hail, in the time appointed,
  His reign on earth begun!
He comes to break oppression,
  To let the captive free,
To take away transgression,
  And rule in equity.

2 He comes, with succour speedy,
  To those who suffer wrong;
To help the poor and needy,
  And bid the weak be strong;
To give them songs for sighing,
  Their darkness turn to light,
Whose souls, condemn'd and dying,
  Were precious in his sight.

3 He shall come down like showers,
  Upon the fruitful earth,
And love, joy, hope, like flowers,
  Spring in his path to birth:
Before him on the mountains,
  Shall peace the herald go;
And righteousness in fountains
  From hill to valley flow.

4 Arabia's desert-ranger
  To him shall bow the knee;
The Ethiopian stranger
  His glory come to see:
With off'rings of devotion,
  Ships from the isles shall meet,
To pour the wealth of ocean,
  In tribute, at his feet.

5 Kings shall fall down before him,
  And gold and incense bring;
All nations shall adore him,
  His praise all people sing:
For he shall have dominion
  O'er river, sea, and shore,
Far as the eagle's pinion,
  Or dove's light wing can soar.

979 *At a wedding.*

O God of pure affection!
  By men and saints adored,
Who gavest thy protection
  To Cana's nuptial board;
May such thy bounties ever
  To wedded love be shown,
And no rude hand dissever
  Whom thou hast link'd in one.

825

Watch-night.

HEARKEN to the solemn voice,
The awful midnight cry!
Waiting souls, rejoice, rejoice,
And see the Bridegroom nigh!
Lo! he comes to keep his word,
Light and joy his looks impart;
Go ye forth to meet your Lord,
And meet him in your heart.

2 Ye who faint beneath the load
Of sin, your heads lift up;
See your great redeeming God,
He comes, and bids you hope!
In the midnight of your grief,
Jesus doth his mourners cheer;
Lo! he brings you sure relief;
Believe, and feel him here!

3 Ye whose loins are girt, stand forth,
Whose lamps are burning bright;
Worthy in your Saviour's worth,
To walk with him in white;
Jesus bids your hearts be clean;
Bids you all his promise prove,
Jesus comes to cast out sin,
And perfect you in love.

4 Happy he whom Christ shall find
Watching to see him come;
Him the Judge of all mankind
Shall bear triumphant home!
Who can answer to his word?—
Which of you dares meet his day?—
"Rise, and come to judgment!"—Lord,
We rise and come away.

920

Psalm cxxi.

TO the hills I lift mine eyes,
The everlasting hills;
Streaming thence in fresh supplies,
My soul the Spirit feels·
Will he not his help afford?
Help, while yet I ask, is given:
God comes down—the God and Lord
That made both earth and heaven.

2 Faithful soul, pray always; pray,
And still in God confide;
He thy feeble steps shall stay,
Nor suffer thee to slide;
Lean on thy Redeemer's breast;
He thy quiet spirit keeps;
Rest in him, securely rest;
Thy Watchman never sleeps.

3 Neither sin, nor earth, nor hell,
Thy Keeper can surprise;
Careless slumbers cannot steal
On his all-seeing eyes;
He is Israel's sure defence;
Israel all his care shall prove;
Kept by watchful Providence,
And ever-waking Love.

4 See the Lord, thy Keeper, stand,
Omnipotently near
Lo! he holds thee by thy hand,
And banishes thy fear;
Shadows with his wings thy head;
Guards from all impending harms—
Round thee and beneath are spread
The everlasting arms.

5 Christ shall bless thy going out,
Shall bless thy coming in;
Kindly compass thee about,
Till thou art saved from sin;
Like thy spotless Master thou,
Fill'd with wisdom, love, and power;
Holy, pure, and perfect,—now,
Henceforth, and evermore.

499 *The work of purification.*

NOW, e'en now, I yield, I yield,
With all my sins to part;
Jesus speak my pardon seal'd,
And purify my heart?
Purge the love of sin away,
Then I into nothing fall,—
Then I see the perfect day,
And Christ is all in all.

2 Jesus, now our hearts inspire,
With that pure love of thine;
Kindle now the heavenly fire,
To brighten and refine:
Purify our faith like gold;
All the dross of sin remove;
Melt our spirits down, and mould
Into thy perfect love.

946 *"Open thy mouth wide, and I will fill it."*

GIVE me the enlarged desire,
And open, Lord, my soul,
Thy own fulness to require,
And comprehend the whole
Stretch my faith's capacity
Wider and yet wider still:
Then with all that is in thee
My soul for ever fill!

1008 *Rom. x. 6—10.*

OFT I in my heart have said,
"Who shall ascend on high,—
Mount to Christ, my glorious Head,
And bring him from the sky?
Borne on contemplation's wing,
Surely I shall find him there,
Where the angels praise their King,
And gain the Morning Star."

2 Oft I in my heart have said,
"Who to the deep shall stoop,—
Sink with Christ among the dead,
From thence to bring him up?
Could I but my heart prepare
By unfeign'd humility,
Christ would quickly enter there,
And ever dwell in me."

3 But the righteousness of faith
Hath taught me better things:
"Inward turn thine eyes," it saith,
While Christ to me it brings.
"Christ is ready to impart
Life to all, for life who sigh:
In thy mouth and in thy heart
The word is ever nigh."

169 *1 Thess. iv. 16—18.*

JESUS, faithful to his word,
Shall with a shout descend,
All heaven's host their glorious Lord
Shall pompously attend.
Christ shall come with dreadful noise,
Lightnings swift, and thunders loud;
With the great archangel's voice,
And with the trump of God.

2 First the dead in Christ shall rise;
Then we that yet remain
Shall be caught up to the skies,
And see our Lord again.
We shall meet him in the air;
All rapt up to heaven shall be;
Find, and love, and praise him there,
To all eternity.

3 Who can tell the happiness
This glorious hope affords?
Joy unutter'd we possess
In these reviving words:
Happy while on earth we breathe;
Mightier bliss ordain'd to know;
Trampling down sin, hell, and death
To the third heaven we go.

190 *The mystery of love.*

GOD of unexampled grace,
  Redeemer of mankind,
Matter of eternal praise
  We in thy passion find:
Still our choicest strains we bring,
  Still the joyful theme pursue,
Thee, the Friend of sinners, sing,
  Whose love is ever new.

2 Endless scenes of wonder rise
  With that mysterious tree,
Crucified before our eyes,
  Where we our Maker see:
Jesus, Lord, what hast thou done?
  Publish we the death divine,
Stop, and gaze, and fall, and own
  Was never love like thine!

3 Never love nor sorrow was
  Like that my Jesus show'd;
See him stretch'd on yonder cross,
  And crush'd beneath our load!
Now discern the Deity,
  Now his heavenly birth declare!
Faith cries out, "'Tis He, 'tis He,
  My God that suffers there!"

3 *The Trinity.*

MEET and right it is to sing
  In every time and place,
Glory to our heavenly King,
  The God of truth and grace.
Join we then with sweet accord,
  All in one thanksgiving join;
Holy, holy, holy Lord,
  Eternal praise be thine!

2 Thee, the first-born sons of light,
  In choral symphonies,
Praise by day, day without night,
  And never, never cease;
Angels, and archangels, all
  Praise the mystic Three in One;
Sing, and stop, and gaze, and fall,
  O'erwhelm'd before thy throne!

3 Vying with that heavenly choir
  Who chant thy praise above,
We on eagles' wings aspire—
  The wings of faith and love;
Thee, *they* sing, with glory crown'd;
  We extol the slaughter'd Lamb;
Lower if our voices sound,
  Our subject is the same.

4 Father, God, thy love we praise,
  Which gave thy Son to die;
Jesus, full of truth and grace,
  Alike we glorify;
Spirit, Comforter divine,
  Praise by all to thee be given,
Till we in full chorus join,
  And earth is turn'd to heaven.

229 *Psalm xlviii.*

GREAT is our redeeming Lord,
In power, and truth, and grace;
Him, by highest heaven adored,
His church on earth doth praise:
In the city of our God,
In his holy mount below,
Publish, spread his name abroad,
And all his greatness show.

2 For thy loving kindness, Lord,
We in thy temple stay;
Here thy faithful love record,
Thy saving power display:
With thy name thy praise is known,
Glorious thy perfections shine;
Earth's remotest bounds shall own
Thy works are all divine.

3 See the gospel church secure,
And founded on a rock;
All her promises are sure:
Her bulwarks who can shock?
Count her every precious shrine;
Tell, to after ages, tell,
Fortified by power divine,
The church can never fail.

4 Sion's God is all our own,
Who on his love rely;
We his pard'ning love have known,
And live to Christ, and die:
To the New Jerusalem
He our faithful guide shall be;
Him we claim, and rest in him,
Through all eternity.

709 *The beatific vision.*

WHERE shall true believers go,
When from the flesh they fly?
Glorious joys ordain'd to know,
They mount above the sky,
To that bright celestial place;
There they shall in raptures live,
More than tongue can e'er express,
Or heart can e'er conceive.

2 When they once are enter'd there,
Their mourning days are o'er;
Pain, and sin, and want, and care,
And sighing, are no more;
Subject then to no decay,
Heavenly bodies they put on,
Swifter than the lightning's ray,
And brighter than the sun.

3 But their greatest happiness,
Their highest joy, shall be,
God their Saviour to possess,
To know, and love, and see:
With that beatific sight
Glorious ecstasy is given:
This is their supreme delight,
And makes a heaven of heaven.

4 Him beholding face to face,
To him they glory give,
Bless his name and sing his praise,
As long as God shall live.
While eternal ages roll,
Thus employ'd in heaven they are:
Lord, receive my happy soul
With all thy servants there!

LINTON. 7s, 6s & 8s.

451 *The backslider's supplication.*

JESUS, Friend of sinners, hear,
Yet once again I pray:
From my debt of sin set clear,
For I have naught to pay:
Speak, O speak the kind release,
A poor backsliding soul restore;
Love me freely, seal my peace,
And bid me sin no more.

2 For my selfishness and pride
Thou hast withdrawn thy grace;
Left me long to wander wide,
An outcast from thy face;
But I now my sins confess,
And mercy, mercy, I implore;
Love me freely, seal my peace,
And bid me sin no more.

3 Sin's deceitfulness hath spread
A hardness o'er my heart;
But if thou thy Spirit shed,
The hardness shall depart:
Shed thy love, thy tenderness,
And let me feel thy soft'ning power;
Love me freely, seal my peace,
And bid me sin no more.

575 *Only Jesus.*

VAIN, delusive world, adieu,
With all of creature good!
Only Jesus I pursue,
Who bought me with his blood!
All thy pleasures I forego,
I trample on thy wealth and pride:
Only Jesus will I know,
And Jesus crucified.

2 Other knowledge I disdain,
'Tis all but vanity:
Christ, the Lamb of God, was slain,
He tasted death for me!
Me to save from endless wo
The sin-atoning Victim died!
Only Jesus will I know,
And Jesus crucified!

3 Here will I set up my rest;
My fluctuating heart
From the haven of his breast
Shall never more depart;
Whither should a sinner go?
His wounds for me stand open wide:
Only Jesus will I know,
And Jesus crucified!

4 Him to know is life and peace,
And pleasure without end;
This is all my happiness,
On Jesus to depend;
Daily in his grace to grow,
And ever in his faith abide:
Only Jesus will I know,
And Jesus crucified!

5 O that I could all invite,
This saving truth to prove,—
Show the length, the breadth, the height,
And depth, of Jesus' love!
Fain I would to sinners show
The blood by faith alone applied!
Only Jesus will I know,
And Jesus crucified!

308 *Calvary.*

LAMB of God, whose dying love
We now recall to mind,
Send the answer from above,
And let us mercy find;
Think on us who think on thee,
And every struggling soul release;
O remember Calvary,
And bid us go in peace!

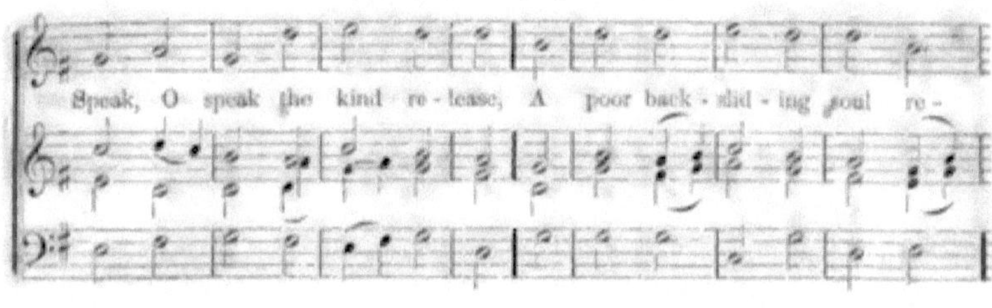

2 By thine agonizing pain,
And bloody sweat, we pray;
By thy dying love to man,—
Take all our sins away:
By thy passion on the tree,
Let all our griefs and troubles cease;
O remember Calvary,
And bid us go in peace!

3 Never will we hence depart,
Till thou our wants relieve;
Write forgiveness on our heart,
And all thine image give:
Still our souls shall cry to thee,
Till perfected in holiness
O remember Calvary,
And bid us go in peace!

423 *"Thy blood was shed for me."*

GOD of my salvation, hear,
And help me to believe;
Simply do I now draw near,
Thy blessing to receive;
Full of sin, alas! I am,
But to thy wounds for refuge flee:
Friend of sinners, spotless Lamb,
Thy blood was shed for me.

2 Standing now as newly slain,
To thee I lift mine eye,
Balm of all my grief and pain,
Thy blood is always nigh,
Now as yesterday the same
Thou art and wilt for ever be;
Friend of sinners, spotless Lamb,
Thy blood was shed for me.

3 Nothing have I, Lord, to pay,
Nor can thy grace procure;
Empty send me not away,
For I, thou know'st, am poor;
Dust and ashes is my name;
My all is sin and misery;
Friend of sinners, spotless Lamb,
Thy blood was shed for me.

4 Saviour, from thy wounded side
I never will depart;
Here will I my spirit hide,
When I am pure in heart;
Till my place above I claim,
This only shall be all my plea,
Friend of sinners, spotless Lamb,
Thy blood was shed for me.

915 *Opening the exercises.*

COME, ye foll'wers of the Lord,
In Jesus' service join:
Jesus gives the sacred word,
The ordinance divine:
Stand we in the ancient way,
And here with God ourselves acquaint,
Pray we, every moment pray,
And never, never faint.

2 Let us patiently endure,
And still our wants declare;
All the promises are sure
To persevering prayer:
Till we see the perfect day,
And each wakes up a spotless saint,
Pray we, every moment pray,
And never, never faint.

3 Pray we on when all renew'd,
And perfected in love!
Till we see our Saviour God
Descending from above,—
All his heavenly charms survey,
Beyond what angel minds can paint,
Pray we, every moment pray,
And never, never faint.

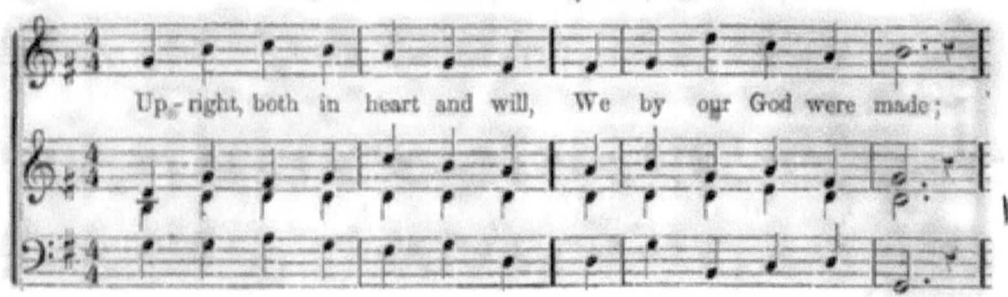

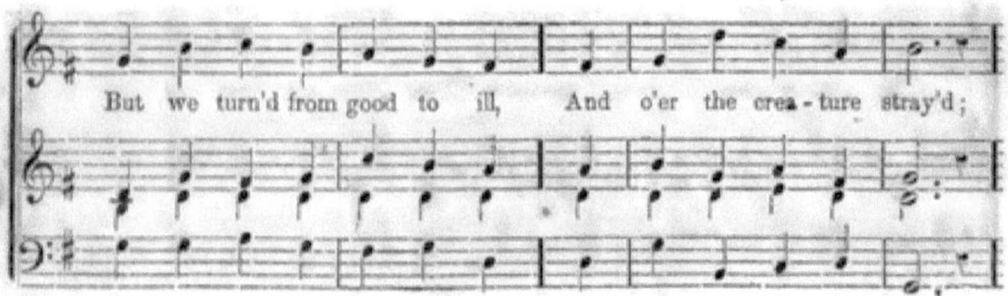

534 *Centering the soul in God.*

UPRIGHT, both in heart and will,
We by our God were made;
But we turn'd from good to ill,
And o'er the creature stray'd:
Multiplied our wand'ring thought,
Which first was fix'd on God alone;
In ten thousand objects sought
The bliss we lost in one.

2 From our own inventions vain
Of fancied happiness,
Draw us to thyself again,
And bid our wand'rings cease;
Jesus, speak our souls restored,
By love's divine simplicity;
Reunited to our Lord,
And wholly lost in thee.!

432 *The plea.*

LET the world their virtue boast,
Their works of righteousness;
I, a wretch undone and lost,
Am freely saved by grace;
Other title I disclaim;
This, only this, is all my plea,
I the chief of sinners am,
But Jesus died for me.

2 Happy they whose joys abound,
Like Jordan's swelling stream;
Who their heaven in Christ have found,
And give the praise to him;
Meanest foll'wer of the Lamb,
His steps I at a distance see:
I the chief of sinners am,
But Jesus died for me.

3 I, like Gideon's fleece, am found,
Unwater'd still and dry;
While the dew on all around
Falls plenteous from the sky;
Yet my Lord I cannot blame,
The Saviour's grace for all is free;
I the chief of sinners am,
But Jesus died for me.

4 Jesus, thou for me hast died,
And thou in me wilt live;
I shall feel thy death applied;
I shall thy life receive:
Yet when melted in the flame
Of love, this shall be all my plea,
I the chief of sinners am,
But Jesus died for me.

781 *Laying the foundation.*

THOU who hast in Zion laid
The true Foundation-stone,
And with those a cov'nant made,
Who build on that alone:
Hear us, Architect divine!
Great Builder of thy church below;
Now upon thy servants shine,
Who seek thy praise to show.

2 Earth is thine; her thousand hills
Thy mighty hand sustains;
Heaven thy awful presence fills;
O'er all thy glory reigns:
Yet the place of old prepared,
By regal David's favour'd Son,
Thy peculiar blessing shared,
And stood thy chosen throne.

Mul - ti - plied our wand'ring thought, Which first was fix'd on God a - lone;
In ten thou-sand ob - jects sought The bliss we lost in one.

3 Father, Son, and Spirit, send
The everlasting flame;
Now in majesty descend,
Inscribe the living name:
That great name by which we live
Now write on this accepted stone;
Us into thy hands receive,
Our temple make thy throne.

858 *Embarking.*

LORD of earth, and air, and sea,
Supreme in power and grace,
Under thy protection we
Our souls and bodies place.
Bold an unknown land to try,
We launch into the foaming deep;
Rocks, and storms, and deaths, defy,
With Jesus in the ship.

2 Who the calm can understand,
In a believer's breast?
In the hollow of His hand
Our souls securely rest:
Winds may rise, and seas may roar,
We on his love our spirit stay:
Him with quiet joy adore
Whom winds and seas obey.

930 *Isaiah* xxxii. 2.

TO the haven of thy breast,
O Son of man, I fly!
Be my refuge and my rest,
For O, the storm is high!
Save me from the furious blast:
A covert from the tempest be!
Hide me, Jesus, till o'erpast
The storm of sin I see.

2 Welcome as the water-spring
To a dry, barren place;
O descend on me, and bring
Thy sweet, refreshing grace!
O'er a parch'd and weary land,
As a great rock extends its shade,
Hide me, Saviour, with thy hand,
And screen my naked head.

3 In the time of my distress
Thou hast my succour been,
In my utter helplessness,
Restraining me from sin;
O how swiftly didst thou move
To save me in the trying hour!
Still protect me with thy love,
And shield me with thy power.

931 *Isaiah* xxxii. 2.

FIRST and last in me perform
The work thou hast begun:
Be my shelter from the storm,
My shadow from the sun;
Weary, parch'd with thirst, and faint,
Till thou th' abiding Spirit breathe,
Every moment, Lord, I want
The merit of thy death.

2 Never shall I want it less,
When thou the gift hast given,
Fill'd me with thy righteousness,
And seal'd the heir of heaven;
I shall hang upon my God,
Till I thy perfect glory see,—
Till the sprinkling of thy blood
Shall speak me up to thee.

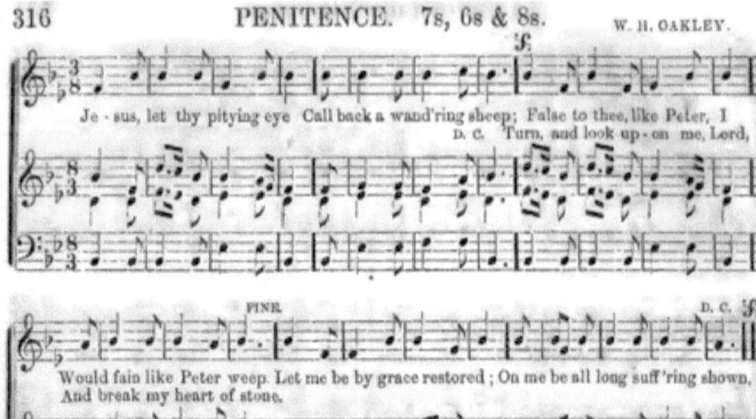

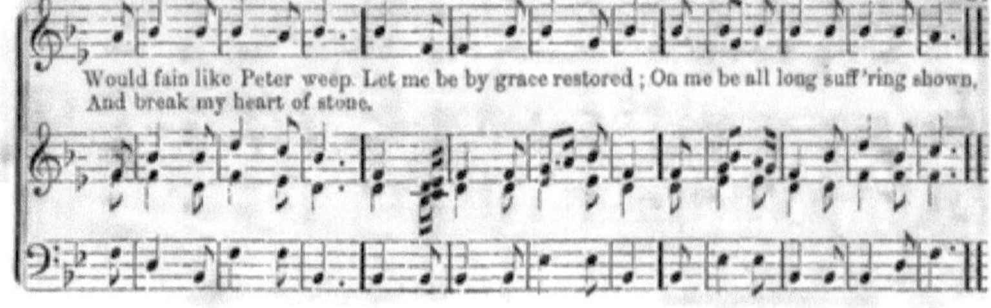

379 *Praying for repentance.*

JESUS, let thy pitying eye
  Call back a wand'ring sheep;
False to thee, like Peter, I
  Would fain like Peter weep.
Let me be by grace restored;
  On me be all long-suff'ring shown;
Turn, and look upon me, Lord,
  And break my heart of stone.

2 Saviour, Prince, enthroned above,
  Repentance to impart,
Give me, through thy dying love,
  The humble, contrite heart:
Give, what I have long implored,
  A portion of thy grief unknown;
Turn, and look upon me, Lord,
  And break my heart of stone.

3 For thine own compassion's sake,
  The gracious wonder show;
Cast my sins behind thy back,
  And wash me white as snow:
If thy bowels now are stirr'd,
  If now I do myself bemoan,
Turn, and look upon me, Lord,
  And break my heart of stone.

4 See me, Saviour, from above,
  Nor suffer me to die!
Life, and happiness, and love,
  Drop from thy gracious eye:
Speak the reconciling word,
  And let thy mercy melt me down;
Turn, and look upon me, Lord,
  And break my heart of stone.

5 Look, as when thine eye pursued
  The first apostate man;
Saw him welt'ring in his blood,
  And bade him rise again:
Speak my paradise restored;
  Redeem me by thy grace alone;
Turn, and look upon me, Lord,
  And break my heart of stone.

6 Look as when thy languid eye
  Was closed that we might live;
"Father," (at the point to die
  My Saviour gasped,) "forgive!"
Surely with that dying word
  He turns, and looks, and cries, " done!"
O my bleeding, loving Lord,
  Thou break'st my heart of stone!

455 *The backslider's pardon.*

LORD, and is thine anger gone,
  And art thou pacified?
After all that I have done,
  Dost thou no longer chide?
Let thy love my heart constrain,
  And all my restless passions sway:
Keep me, lest I turn again
  Out of the narrow way.

2 If I have begun once more
  Thy sweet return to feel,—
If e'en now I find thy power
  Present my soul to heal,—
Still and quiet may I lie,
  Nor struggle out of thine embrace;
Never more resist or fly
  From thy pursuing grace.

3 To the cross, thine altar, bind
Me with the cords of love;
Freedom never let me find
From thee, my Lord, to move;
That I never, never more
May with my much-loved Master part;
To the posts of mercy's door
O nail my willing heart!

4 See my utter helplessness,
And leave me not alone;
O preserve in perfect peace,
And seal me for thine own!
More and more thyself reveal,
Thy presence let me always find;
Comfort, and confirm, and heal
My feeble, sin-sick mind.

5 As the apple of thine eye,
Thy weakest servant keep;
Help me at thy feet to lie,
And there for ever weep:
Tears of joy mine eyes o'erflow,
That I have any hope of heaven;
Much of love I ought to know,
For I have much forgiven.

400 *Humble confession.*

WRETCHED, helpless, and distrest,
Ah! whither shall I fly?
Ever gasping after rest,
I cannot find it nigh:
Naked, sick, and poor, and blind,
Fast bound in sin and misery,
Friend of sinners, let me find
My help, my all, in thee!

2 I am all unclean, unclean,
Thy purity I want;
My whole heart is sick of sin,
And my whole head is faint:
Full of putrefying sores,
Of bruises, and of wounds, my soul
Looks to Jesus, help implores,
And gasps to be made whole.

3 In the wilderness I stray;
My foolish heart is blind;
Nothing do I know; the way
Of peace I cannot find
Jesus, Lord, restore my sight,
And take, O take the veil away!
Turn my darkness into light,
My midnight into day.

4 Naked of thy image, Lord,
Forsaken and alone;
Unrenew'd and unrestored,
I have not thee put on:
Over me thy mantle spread,
Send down thy likeness from above,
Let thy goodness be display'd,
And wrap me in thy love!

5 Poor, alas! thou know'st I am,
And would be poorer still;
See my wretchedness and shame,
And all my vileness feel.
No good thing in me resides,
My soul is all an aching void,
Till thy Spirit here abides,
And I am fill'd with God.

6 Jesus, full of truth and grace,
In thee is all I want:
Be the wand'rer's resting-place,
A cordial to the faint:
Make me rich, for I am poor:
In thee may I my Eden find,
To the dying, health restore,
And eyesight to the blind.

7 Clothe me with thy holiness,
Thy meek humility;
Put on me this glorious dress,
Endue my soul with thee:
Let thine image be restored,
Thy name and nature let me prove;
With thy fulness fill me, Lord,
And perfect me in love.

696 *The final conflagration.*

STAND th' omnipotent decree!
Jehovah's will be done!
Nature's end we wait to see,
And hear her final groan:
Let this earth dissolve and blend
In death the wicked and the just;
Let those pond'rous orbs descend,
And grind us into dust.

2 Rests secure the righteous man!
At his Redeemer's beck,
Sure t' emerge, and rise again,
And mount above the wreck
Lo! the heavenly spirit towers,
Like flame, o'er nature's funeral pyre,
Triumphs in immortal powers,
And claps his wings of fire!

3 Nothing hath the just to lose,
By worlds on worlds destroy'd;
Far beneath his feet he views,
With smiles, the flaming void;
Sees this universe renew'd,
The grand millennial reign begun;
Shouts with all the sons of God,
Around th' eternal throne!

4 Resting in this glorious hope,
To be at last restored,
Yield we now our bodies up
To earthquake, plague, or sword:
List'ning for the call divine,
The latest trumpet of the seven,
Soon our soul and dust shall join,
And both fly up to heaven.

* Sing the first note to the left of this double bar as a half note the *first* time.

1025 *Martha and Mary.* LUKE x. 38-42.

LO! I come with joy to do
  The Master's blessed will—
Him in outward works pursue,
  And serve his pleasure still.
Faithful to my Lord's commands,
  I still would choose the better part;
Serve with careful Martha's hands
  And loving Mary's heart.

2 Careful without care I am,
  Nor feel my happy toil:
Kept in peace by Jesus' name,
  Supported by his smile;
Joyful thus my faith to show,
  I find his service my reward;
Every work I do below,
  I do it to the Lord.

3 Thou, O Lord, in tender love
  Dost all my burdens bear,—
Lift my heart to things above,
  And fix it ever there!
Calm on tumult's wheel I sit,
  'Midst busy multitudes alone,
Sweetly waiting at thy feet,
  Till all thy will be done.

4 O that all the art might know
  Of living thus to thee!
Find their heaven begun below,
  And here thy glory see!
Walk in all the works prepared
  By thee to exercise their grace;
Till they gain their full reward,
  And see thy glorious face!

1030 *In affliction.*

CAST on the fidelity
  Of my redeeming Lord,
I shall his salvation see,
  According to his word;
Credence to his word I give;
  My Saviour in distresses past,
Will not now his servant leave,
  But bring me through at last.

2 Better than my boding fears
  To me thou oft hast proved;
Oft observed my silent tears,
  And challenged thy beloved
Mercy to my rescue flew,
  And death ungrasp'd his fainting prey;
Pain before thy face withdrew,
  And sorrow flew away.

3 Now as yesterday the same,
  In all my troubles nigh,
Jesus, on thy word and name
  I steadfastly rely:
Sure as now the grief I feel,
  The promised joy I soon shall have;
Saved again, to sinners tell
  Thy power and will to save.

4 To thy blessed will resign'd,
  And stay'd on that alone,
I thy perfect strength shall find,
  Thy faithful mercies own:
Compass'd round with songs of praise,
  My all to my Redeemer give;
Spread thy miracles of grace,
  And to thy glory live.

468

The Spirit of adoption.

YE simple souls that stray
 Far from the path of peace,
That unfrequented way
 To life and happiness,
How long will ye your folly love,
 And throng the downward road,
And hate the wisdom from above,
 And mock the sons of God?

2 Madness and misery,
 Ye count our life beneath,
And nothing great can see,
 Or glorious, in our death:
As born to suffer and to grieve,
 Beneath your feet we lie;
And utterly contemn'd we live,
 And unlamented die.

3 Poor pensive sojourners,
 O'erwhelm'd with grief and woes;
Perplex'd with needless fears,
 And pleasure's mortal foes,—
More irksome than a gaping tomb
 Our sight ye cannot bear,
Wrapped in the melancholy gloom
 Of fanciful despair.

4 So wretched and obscure,
 The men whom ye despise,
So foolish, weak, and poor,
 Above your scorn we rise;
Our conscience in the Holy Ghost
 Can witness better things,
For He whose blood is all our boast
 Hath made us priests and kings.

5 Riches unsearchable
 In Jesus' love we know,
And pleasures from the well
 Of life our souls o'erflow;
From him the Spirit we receive
 Of wisdom, grace, and power,
And always sorrowful we live,
 Rejoicing evermore.

6 Angels our servants are,
 And keep in all our ways,
And in their hands they bear
 The sacred sons of grace:
Our guardians to that heavenly bliss,
 They all our steps attend;
And God himself our Father is,
 And Jesus is our Friend.

7 With him we walk in white;
 We in his image shine;
Our robes are robes of light,
 Our righteousness divine:
On all the grov'ling kings of earth
 With pity we look down,
And claim, in virtue of our birth,
 A never-fading crown.

725 *Funeral of a friend.*

FRIEND after friend departs;
Who has not lost a friend?
There is no union here of hearts,
That finds not here an end.
Were this frail world our final rest,
Living or dying none were blest.

2 Beyond the flight of time,
Beyond the reign of death,
There surely is some blessed clime
Where life is not a breath,—
Nor life's affections, transient fire,
Whose sparks fly upward and expire.

3 There is a world above,
Where parting is unknown;
A long eternity of love,
Form'd for the good alone:
And faith beholds the dying here,
Translated to that glorious sphere.

4 Thus star by star declines,
Till all are pass'd away,
As morning high and higher shines
To pure and perfect day;
Nor sink those stars in empty night,
But hide themselves in heaven's own light.

734 *Funeral of a Christian sister.*

HOSANNA to Jesus on high!
Another has enter'd his rest;
Another has 'scaped to the sky,
And lodged in Immanuel's breast,
The soul of our sister is gone
To heighten the triumph above;
Exalted to Jesus's throne,
And clasp'd in the arms of his love.

2 What fulness of rapture is there,
While Jesus his glory displays,
And purples the heavenly air,
And scatters the odours of grace!
He looks—and his servants in light
The blessings ineffable meet;
He smiles—and they faint in his sight,
And fall overwhelm'd at his feet.

3 How happy the angels that fall
Transported at Jesus's name;
The saints whom he soonest shall call,
To share in the feast of the Lamb!
No longer imprison'd in clay,
Who next from his dungeon shall fly?
Who first shall be summon'd away—
My merciful Lord, is it I?

4 O Jesus, if this be thy will,
That suddenly I should depart,
Thy counsel of mercy reveal,
And whisper the call in my heart!
O give me a signal to know,
If soon thou wouldst have me remove,
And leave the dull body below,
And fly to the regions above.

704 *Rev. xxii. 17.*

THE church in her militant state
Is weary, and cannot forbear!
The saints in an agony wait,
To see Him again in the air!
The Spirit invites in the bride,
Her heavenly Lord to descend,
And place her enthroned at his side,
In glory that never shall end.

2 The news of his coming I hear,
And join in the catholic cry:
O Jesus, in triumph appear;
Appear in the clouds of the sky!
Whom only I languish to love,
In fulness of majesty come;
And give me a mansion above;
And take to thy heavenly home!

947 *Longing for Christ's appearing.*

O WHEN shall we sweetly remove,
O when shall we enter our rest!
Return to the Sion above,
The mother of spirits distrest!
That city of God the great King,
Where sorrow and death are no more;
But saints our Immanuel sing,
And cherub and seraph adore.

2 Not all the archangels can tell
The joys of that holiest place,
Where Jesus is pleased to reveal
The light of his heavenly face,—
When caught in the rapturous flame,
The sight beatific they prove,
And walk in the light of the Lamb,
Enjoying the beams of his love.

3 Thou know'st in the spirit of prayer
We long thy appearing to see,
Resign'd to the burden we bear,
But longing to triumph with thee:

The soul of our sis - ter is gone To heighten the triumph a - bove;
Ex - alt - ed to Je - sus - 's throne, And clasp'd in the arms of his love.

Tis good at thy word to be here,
Tis better in thee to be gone,
And see thee in glory appear,
And rise to a share in thy throne.

966 *Evening.*

INSPIRER and Hearer of prayer,
Thou Feeder and Guardian of thine;
My all to thy covenant care,
I, sleeping and waking, resign.
Thy minist'ring spirits descend
To watch while thy saints are asleep;
By day and by night they attend
The heirs of salvation to keep.

2 Thy worship no interval knows,—
Their fervour is still on the wing;
And while they protect my repose,
They chant to the praise of my King.
I too, at the season ordain'd,
Their chorus for ever shall join;
And live, and adore without end,
Their faithful Creator and mine.

1012 *"Thy vows are upon me."*

O HOW shall a sinner perform
The vows he hath vow'd to the Lord?
A sinful and impotent worm,
How can I be true to my word?
I tremble at what I have done:
O send me thy help from above;
The power of thy Spirit make known,
The virtue of Jesus's love!

2 My solemn engagements are vain,
My promises empty as air,—
My vows, I shall break them again,
And plunge in eternal despair,—
Unless my omnipotent God
The sense of his goodness impart,
And shed, by his Spirit, abroad
The love of himself in my heart.

3 O, Lover of sinners, extend
To me thy compassionate grace!
Appear, my affliction to end,
Afford me a glimpse of thy face!
That light shall enkindle in me
A flame of reciprocal love;
And then I shall cleave unto thee,
And then I shall never remove.

1040 *Passionate longings.*

STILL out of the deepest abyss
Of trouble, I mournfully cry,
And pine to recover my peace,
And see my Redeemer, and die.
I cannot, I cannot forbear,
These passionate longings for home:
O! when shall my spirit be there!
O! when will the messenger come!

2 Thy nature I long to put on,
Thine image on earth to regain,
And then in the grave to lay down
This burden of body and pain.
O Jesus, in pity draw near,
And lull me to sleep on thy breast,
Appear, to my rescue appear,
And gather me into thy rest!

3 To take a poor fugitive in,
The arms of thy mercy display,
And give me to rest from all sin,
And bear me triumphant away,—
Away from a world of distress,
Away to the mansions above;
The heaven of seeing thy face,
The heaven of feeling thy love.

703 *Rev. xxi.*

AWAY with our sorrow and fear!
We soon shall recover our home;
The city of saints shall appear;
The day of eternity come,
From earth we shall quickly remove,
And mount to our native abode;
The house of our Father above,
The palace of angels and God.

2 Our mourning is all at an end,
When, raised by the life-giving word,
We see the new city descend,
Adorn'd as a bride for her Lord:
The city so holy and clean,
No sorrow can breathe in the air:
No gloom of affliction or sin,
No shadow of evil is there!

3 By faith we already behold
That lovely Jerusalem here:
Her walls are of jasper and gold,
As crystal her buildings are clear;
Immovably founded in grace,
She stands as she ever hath stood,
And brightly her builder displays,
And flames with the glory of God.

4 No need of the sun in that day
Which never is follow'd by night,
Where Jesus's beauties display
A pure and a permanent light:
The Lamb is their light and their sun,
And lo! by reflection they shine;
With Jesus ineffably one,
And bright in effulgence divine!

5 The saints in his presence receive
Their great and eternal reward;
In Jesus, in heaven, they live!
They reign in the smile of their Lord·
The flame of angelical love
Is kindled at Jesus's face;
And all the enjoyment above
Consists in the rapturous gaze!

91 *"Glory to God in the highest."*

ALL glory to God in the sky,
And peace upon earth be restored!
O Jesus, exalted on high,
Appear our omnipotent Lord!
Who, meanly in Bethlehem born,
Didst stoop to redeem a lost race,
Once more to thy creatures return,
And reign in thy kingdom of grace.

2 When thou in our flesh didst appear,
All nature acknowledged thy birth;
Arose the acceptable year,
And heaven was open'd on earth:
Receiving its Lord from above,
The world was united to bless
The Giver of concord and love,
The Prince and the Author of peace.

3 O wouldst thou again be made known,
Again in thy Spirit descend,
And set up in each of thine own
A kingdom that never shall end!
Thou only art able to bless,
And make the glad nations obey,
And bid the dire enmity cease,
And bow the whole world to thy sway!

4 Come, then, to thy servants again,
Who long thy appearing to know;
Thy quiet and peaceable reign
In mercy establish below:
All sorrow before thee shall fly,
And anger and hatred be o'er;
And envy and malice shall die,
And discord afflict us no more.

5 No horrid alarum of war
Shall break our eternal repose;
No sound of the trumpet is there,
Where Jesus's Spirit o'erflows:
Appeased by the charms of thy grace,
We all shall in amity join,
And kindly each other embrace,
And love with a passion like thine.

223 *His presence earnestly desired.*

COME, holy, celestial Dove,
To visit a sorrowful breast!
My burden of guilt to remove,
And bring me assurance and rest.
Thou only hast power to relieve
A sinner o'erwhelm'd with his load,
The sense of acceptance to give,
And sprinkle his heart with the blood.

2 Thy call if I ever have known,
And sigh'd from myself to get free,
And groan'd the unspeakable groan,
And long'd to be happy in thee,—
Fulfil the imperfect desire;
Thy peace to my conscience reveal;
The sense of thy favour inspire,
And give me my pardon to feel!

3 If when I had put thee to grief,
And madly to folly return'd,
Thy pity hath been my relief,
And lifted me up as I mourn'd,—
Most pitiful Spirit of grace,
Relieve me again, and restore;
My spirit in holiness raise,
To fall and to suffer no more!

4 If now I lament after God,
And gasp for a drop of thy love,
If Jesus hath bought thee with blood,
For me to receive from above,—
Come, heavenly Comforter, come!
True Witness of mercy divine,
And make me thy permanent home,
And seal me eternally thine!

484 *Seraphic joy.*

A FOUNTAIN of life and of grace
In Christ, our Redeemer, we see:
For us, who his offers embrace,
For all, it is open and free:
Jehovah himself doth invite
To drink of his pleasures unknown;
The streams of immortal delight,
That flow from his heavenly throne.

2 As soon as in him we believe,
By faith of his Spirit we take;
And, freely forgiven, receive
The mercy for Jesus's sake!
We gain a pure drop of his love;
The life of eternity know;
Angelical happiness prove;
And witness a heaven below.

735 *Funeral of a Christian brother.*

REJOICE for a brother deceased,
Our loss is his infinite gain;
A soul out of prison released,
And freed from his bodily chain.
With songs let us follow his flight,
And mount with his spirit above;
Escaped to the mansions of light,
And lodged in the Eden of love.

2 Our brother the haven hath gain'd,
Outflying the tempest and wind;
His rest he hath sooner obtain'd,
And left his companions behind,—
Still toss'd on a sea of distress,
Hard toiling to make the bless'd shore,
Where all is assurance and peace,
And sorrow and sin are no more.

3 There all the ship's company meet,
Who sail'd with the Saviour beneath;
With shouting each other they greet,
And triumph o'er sorrow and death:
The voyage of life 's at an end,
The mortal affliction is past:
The age that in heaven they spend,
For ever and ever shall last.

GREENFIELD. 8s. Double.

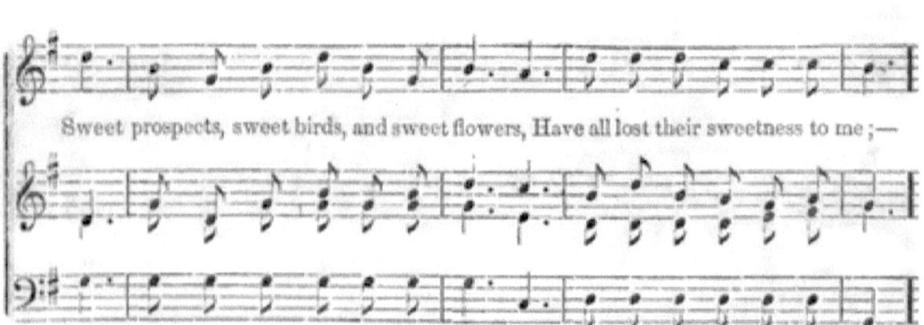

615 *Delight in Christ.*

How tedious and tasteless the hours
When Jesus no longer I see!
Sweet prospects, sweet birds, and sweet flowers,
Have all lost their sweetness to me,—
The midsummer sun shines but dim,
The fields strive in vain to look gay;
But when I am happy in him,
December 's as pleasant as May.

2 His name yields the richest perfume,
And sweeter than music his voice;
His presence disperses my gloom,
And makes all within me rejoice;
I should, were he always thus nigh,
Have nothing to wish or to fear,
No mortal so happy as I,
My summer would last all the year.

3 Content with beholding his face,
My all to his pleasure resign'd;
No changes of season or place
Would make any change in my mind
While bless'd with a sense of his love,
A palace a toy would appear;
And prisons would palaces prove,
If Jesus would dwell with me there.

4 Dear Lord, if indeed I am thine,
If thou art my sun and my song,
Say why do I languish and pine?
And why are my winters so long?
O drive these dark clouds from my sky!
Thy soul-cheering presence restore;
Or take me to thee up on high,
Where winter and clouds are no more!

445 *The Backslider's Inquiry.*

How shall a lost sinner, in pain,
Recover his forfeited peace?
When brought into bondage again,
What hope of a second release?
Will mercy itself be so kind
To spare a poor rebel like me!
And O, can I possibly find
Such plenteous redemption in thee?

2 O Jesus, of thee I inquire,
If still thou art able to save,
The brand to pluck out of the fire,
And ransom my soul from the grave:
The help of thy Spirit restore,
And show me the life-giving blood,
And pardon a sinner once more,
And bring me again unto God.

3 I sink, if thou longer delay
Thy pardoning mercy to show:
Come quickly, and kindly display
The power of thy passion below:
By all thou hast done for my sake,
One drop of thy blood I implore;
Now, now let it touch me, and make
The sinner a sinner no more.

The mid - summer sun shines but dim, The fields strive in vain to look gay;

But when I am hap-py in him, De - cember's as pleasant as May.

698 *Isaiah xxxiii. 17.*

I LONG to behold him array'd
With glory and light from above:
The King in his beauty display'd,
His beauty of holiest love.
I languish and sigh to be there,
Where Jesus hath fix'd his abode;
O when shall we meet in the air,
And fly to the mountain of God!

2 With him I on Sion shall stand,
For Jesus hath spoken the word,
The breadth of Immanuel's land,
Survey by the light of my Lord:
But when, on thy bosom reclined,
Thy face I am strengthen'd to see,
My fulness of rapture I find,
My heaven of heavens, in thee.

796 *Sunday-School Celebration.*

HOW sweet is the fragrance of flowers
That bloom at the dawning of day!
Refresh'd with heaven's kindliest showers,
How healthy and beautiful they!
Thus lovely and soothing the sight,
More lovely than nature supplies,—
Are those who at earliest light
Expand their young hearts to the skies.

2 A tribute acceptable, paid
Yet green, in the season of prime,
Ere noon hath its ravages made,
And verdure is sullied by time:
Collect for thine altars, O God,
A wreath from our garden below;
Nay, send thy refreshings abroad,
That all the plantation may grow.

3 O suffer not one to remain,
Beside living waters unfed,
But give thou the plentiful rain,
The sun of thine influence shed:
So, comely as willows that bend
Where streamlets and fountains abound,
Be these the young plants that we tend,
With blossoms and fruitfulness crown'd.

1038 *"The graves are ready for me."*

MY days are extinguish'd and gone,
My time as a shadow is fled,
And gladly I lay myself down
To rest with the peaceable dead:
The dead ever-living attend,
Whose dust is all safe in the tomb,
And many a glorified friend
Is ready to welcome me home.

2 My days are all vanish'd away,
Broke off the designs of my heart,
No longer on death I delay,
Nor linger, as loth to depart
Resolved in my Lord to abide,
This purpose I know shall remain,
And trust to be found at his side,
And Jesus eternally gain.

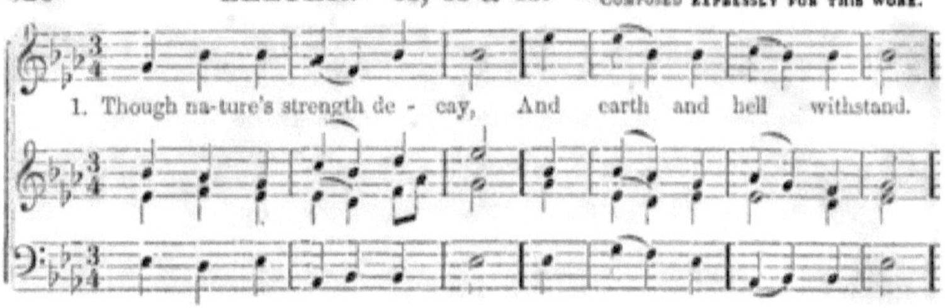

551 *The God of Abraham.*

THOUGH nature's strength decay,
And earth and hell withstand,
To Canaan's bounds I urge my way
At his command,
The wat'ry deep I pass,
With Jesus in my view;
And through the howling wilderness
My way pursue.

2 The goodly land I see,
With peace and plenty blest;
A land of sacred liberty,
And endless rest.
There milk and honey flow,
And oil and wine abound,
And trees of life for ever grow,
With mercy crown'd.

3 There dwells the Lord our King,
The Lord our Righteousness,
Triumphant o'er the world and sin,
The Prince of peace;
On Sion's sacred height
His kingdom still maintains;
And glorious with the saints in light,
For ever reigns.

4 He keeps his own secure,
He guards them by his side,
Arrays in garments white and pure
His spotless bride:
With streams of sacred bliss,
With groves of living joys,
With all the fruits of paradise,
He still supplies.

5 Before the great Three-One
They all exulting stand,
And tell the wonders he hath done
Through all their land:
The list'ning spheres attend,
And swell the growing fame,
And sing, in songs which never end,
The wondrous name.

552 *The God of Abraham.*

THE God of Abrah'm praise,
Who reigns enthroned above,—
Ancient of everlasting days,
And God of love:
JEHOVAH, GREAT I AM!
By earth and heaven confess'd;
I bow, and bless the sacred name
For ever bless'd.

2 The God of Abrah'm praise,
At whose supreme command
From earth I rise—and seek the joys
At his right hand:
I all on earth forsake,
Its wisdom, fame, and power;
And him my only portion make,
My shield and tower.

3 The God of Abrah'm praise,
Whose all-sufficient grace
Shall guide me all my happy days
In all his ways:
He calls a worm his friend!
He calls himself my God!
And he shall save me to the end,
Through Jesus' blood!

4 He by himself hath sworn;
I on his oath depend;
I shall, on eagle's wings upborne,
To heaven ascend:
I shall behold his face,
I shall his power adore,
And sing the wonders of his grace
For evermore.

554 *The God of Abraham.*

THE God who reigns on high,
The great archangels sing,
And "Holy, holy, holy," cry,
"Almighty King!
Who was and is the same,
And evermore shall be;
Jehovah, Father, great I AM,
We worship thee."

2 Before the Saviour's face
The ransom'd nations bow;
O'erwhelm'd at his almighty grace,
For ever new:
He shows his prints of love,—
They kindle to a flame!
And sound, through all the worlds above;
The slaughter'd Lamb.

3 The whole triumphant host
Give thanks to God on high,
"Hail, Father, Son, and Holy Ghost,"
They ever cry:
Hail, Abrah'm's God, and mine!
(I join the heavenly lays,)
All might and majesty are thine,
And endless praise.

870 *Opening the exercises.*

APPOINTED by thee, We meet in thy name,
And meekly agree, To follow the Lamb,
To trace thy example, The world to disdain,
And constantly trample, On pleasure and pain.

2 Rejoicing in hope, We humbly go on,
And daily take up The pledge of our crown;
In doing and bearing The will of our Lord,
We still are preparing To meet our reward.

3 O Jesus appear! No longer delay
To sanctify here, And bear us away:
The end of our meeting On earth let us see,
Triumphantly sitting In glory with thee!

302 *At giving the cup.*

IN Jesus we live, In Jesus we rest,
And thankful receive His dying bequest;
The cup of salvation His mercy bestows,
And all from his passion Our happiness flows.

2 The fruit of the vine—The joy it implies—
Again we shall join To drink in the skies,
Exult in his favour, Our triumph renew;
And I, saith the Saviour, Will drink it with you.

343 *"This man receiveth sinners."*

YE neighbors and friends, To Jesus draw near,
His love condescends, By titles so dear,
To call and invite you, His triumph to prove,
And freely delight you In Jesus's love.

2 The blind are restored Through Jesus's name;
They see their dear Lord, And follow the Lamb;
The halt—they are walking, And running their race,
The dumb—they are talking Of Jesus's grace.

3 The deaf hear his voice, And comforting word,
It bids them rejoice In Jesus their Lord:
"Thy sins are forgiven, Accepted thou art;"
They listen, and heaven Springs up in their heart.

4 The lepers from all Their spots are made clean,
The dead by his call Are raised from their sin;
In Jesus' compassion The sick find a cure,
And gospel-salvation Is preach'd to the poor.

5 O Jesus, ride on, Till all are subdued;
Thy mercy make known, And sprinkle thy blood:
Display thy salvation, And teach the new song
To every nation, And people, and tongue.

342 *Jesus recommended.*

THY faithfulness, Lord, Each moment we find,
So true to thy word, So loving and kind;
Thy mercy so tender To all the lost race,
The vilest offender May turn and find grace.

2 The mercy I feel, To others I show;
I set to my seal That Jesus is true:
Ye all may find favour, Who come at his call,
O come to my Saviour, His grace is for all.

3 To save what was lost From heaven he came;
Come, sinners, and trust In Jesus's name!
He offers you pardon; He bids you be free;
"If sin be your burden, O come unto me!"

4 O let me commend My Saviour to you;
The publican's Friend, And Advocate too:
For you he is pleading His merits and death,
With God interceding For sinners beneath.

5 Then let us submit His grace to receive;
Fall down at his feet, And gladly believe;
We all are forgiven For Jesus's sake:
Our title to heaven, His merits we take

482 *"All joy and peace in believing."*

REJOICE evermore, With angels above,
In Jesus's power, in Jesus's love:
With glad exultation Your triumph proclaim,
Ascribing salvation To God and the Lamb.

2 Thou, Lord, our relief In trouble hast been,
Hast saved us from grief, Hast saved us from sin;
The power of thy Spirit Hath set our hearts free,
And now we inherit All fulness in thee—

3 All fulness of peace, All fulness of joy,
And spiritual bliss That never shall cloy;
To us it is given In Jesus to know
A kingdom of heaven, A heaven below.

4 No longer we join, While sinners invite,
Nor envy the swine Their brutish delight;
Their joy is all sadness, Their mirth is all vain,
Their laughter is madness, Their pleasure is pain.

5 O might they at last With sorrow return,
The pleasure to taste For which they were born;
Our Jesus receiving, Our happiness prove,
The joy of believing, The heaven of love!

645 *The Lord will provide.*

THO' troubles assail, And dangers affright,
Though friends should all fail, And foes all unite,
Yet one thing secures us, Whatever betide,
The promise assures us, The Lord will provide.

2 The birds without barn, Or storehouse, are fed;
From them let us learn To trust for our bread:
His saints what is fitting Shall ne'er be denied,
So long as 'tis written, The Lord will provide.

3 We all may, like ships, By tempests be tost
On perilous deeps, But need not be lost;
Though Satan enrages The wind and the tide,
Yet Scripture engages, The Lord will provide.

4 His call we obey, like Abrah'm of old:
We know not the way, But faith makes us bold;
For tho' we are strangers, We have a sure guide,
And trust in all dangers, The Lord will provide.

5 No strength of our own, Nor goodness we claim,
Our trust is all thrown On Jesus's name;
In this our strong tower For safety we hide;
The Lord is our power, The Lord will provide.

6 When life sinks apace, And death is in view,
The word of his grace Shall comfort us through:
Not fearing or doubting, With Christ on our side,
We hope to die shouting, The Lord will provide.

732 *Funeral of a Christian.*

'TIS finish'd, 'tis done, The spirit is fled;
The pris'ner is gone, The Christian is dead;
The Christian is living, Through Jesus's love,
And gladly receiving A kingdom above.

2 Then let us record The conquering name;
Our Captain and Lord With shoutings proclaim;
Who trust in his passion, And follow our Head,
To certain salvation We all shall be led.

3 O Jesus! lead on Thy militant care;
And give us the crown Of righteousness there,
Where, dazzled with glory, The seraphim gaze,
Or prostrate adore thee, In silence of praise.

4 Come, Lord, and display Thy sign in the sky,
And bear us away To mansions on high:
The kingdom be given, The purchase divine,
And crown us in heaven Eternally thine.

FREDERICK. 11s.

G. KINGSLEY.

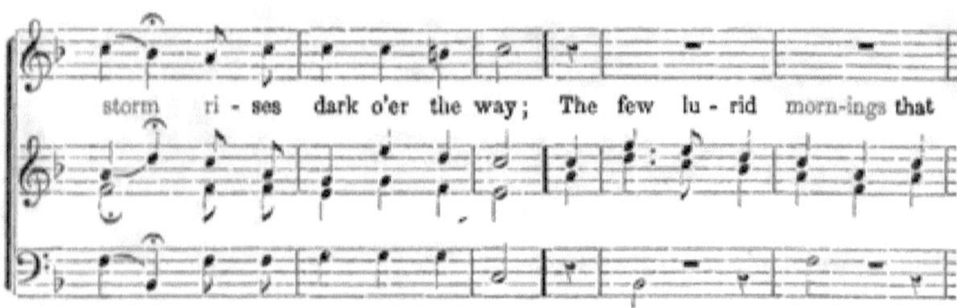

708 *"I would not live alway."*

I WOULD not live alway: I ask not to stay
Where storm after storm rises dark o'er the way;
The few lurid mornings that dawn on us here,
Are enough for life's woes, full enough for its cheer.

2 I would not live alway; no—welcome the tomb,
Since Jesus hath lain there, I dread not its gloom;
There, sweet be my rest, till He bid me arise,
To hail Him in triumph descending the skies.

3 Who who would live alway, away from his God,—
Away from yon heaven, that blissful abode,
Where the rivers of pleasure flow o'er the bright plains,
And the noontide of glory eternally reigns:

4 Where the saints of all ages in harmony meet,
Their Saviour and brethren, transported to greet;
While the anthems of rapture unceasingly roll,
And the smile of the Lord is the feast of the soul.

113 *The Garden.*

O GARDEN of Olivet, dear honour'd spot,
The fame of thy wonder shall ne'er be forgot;
The theme most transporting to seraphs above,
The triumph of sorrow, the triumph of love!

2 Come, saints, and adore him; come, bow at his feet!
O, give him the glory, the praise that is meet;
Let joyful hosannas unceasing arise,
And join the full chorus that gladdens the skies.

251 *The Song of Triumph.*

DAUGHTER of Zion, awake from thy sadness!
Awake! for thy foes shall oppress thee no more;
Bright o'er thy hills dawns the day-star of gladness,
Arise! for the night of thy sorrow is o'er

2 Strong were thy foes, but the arm that subdued them,
And scatter'd their legions, was mightier far;
They fled like chaff from the scourge that pursued them;
How vain were their steeds and their chariots of war!

3 Daughter of Zion, the power that hath saved thee,
Extoll'd with the harp and the timbrel should be;
Shout! for the foe is destroy'd that enslaved thee;
Th' oppressor is vanquish'd, and Zion is free.

864 *"Save, Lord, or we perish!"*

WHEN through the torn sail the wild tempest is streaming,
When o'er the dark wave the red lightning is gleaming,
Nor hope lends a ray the poor seaman to cherish,
We fly to our Maker—"Save, Lord, or we perish!"

2 O Jesus! once toss'd on the breast of the billow,
Aroused by the shriek of despair from thy pillow,
Now,—seated in glory,—the mariner cherish,
Who cries in his danger—"Save, Lord, or we perish!"

3 And O when the whirlwind of passion is raging,
When hell in our hearts his wild warfare is waging,
Arise in thy strength, thy redeemed to cherish,
Rebuke the destroyer—"Save, Lord, or we perish!"

CRAWFORD. 11s & 10s. L. THOMPSON.

98 *Star of the East.*

BRIGHTEST and best of the sons of the morning,
Dawn on our darkness and lend us thine aid!
Star of the East, the horizon adorning,
Guide where our infant Redeemer is laid!

2 Cold on his cradle the dew-drops are shining,
Low lies his head with the beasts of the stall,
Angels adore him in slumber reclining,
Maker, and Monarch, and Saviour of all.

3 Say, shall we yield him, in costly devotion,
Odours of Edom, and offerings divine?
Gems of the mountain, and pearls of the ocean,
Myrrh from the forest, and gold from the mine?

4 Vainly we offer each ample oblation,
Vainly with gifts would his favour secure;
Richer by far is the heart's adoration,
Dearer to God are the prayers of the poor.

5 Brightest and best of the sons of the morning,
Dawn on our darkness and lend us thine aid!
Star of the East, the horizon adorning,
Guide where our infant Redeemer is laid.

MANCHESTER. 11s & 10s. Dr. A. D. EVERETT.

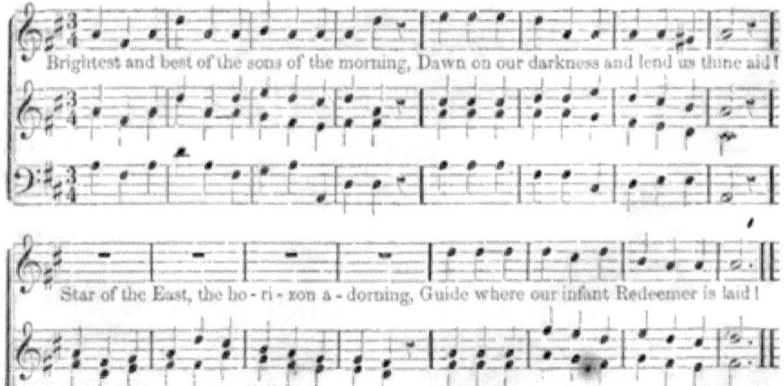

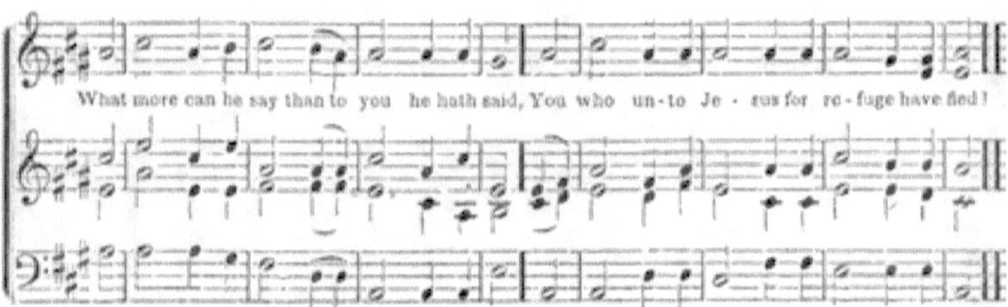

640 *Precious promises.*

HOW firm a foundation, ye saints of the Lord,
Is laid for your faith in his excellent word!
What more can he say than to you he hath said,
You who unto Jesus for refuge have fled?

2 In every condition—in sickness, in health;
In poverty's vale, or abounding in wealth;
At home and abroad; on the land, on the sea,
"As thy days may demand, shall thy strength ever be.

3 "Fear not; I am with thee; O be not dismay'd;
I, I am thy God, and will still give thee aid;
I'll strengthen thee, help thee, and cause thee to stand,
Upheld by my righteous, omnipotent hand.

4 "When through the deep waters I call thee to go,
The rivers of wo shall not thee overflow;
For I will be with thee, thy troubles to bless,
And sanctify to thee thy deepest distress.

5 "When thro' fiery trials thy pathway shall lie,
My grace, all-sufficient, shall be thy supply
The flame shall not hurt thee;—I only design
Thy dross to consume, and thy gold to refine.

6 "E'en down to old age, all my people shall prove,
My sovereign, eternal, unchangeable love;
And when hoary hairs shall their temples adorn,
Like lambs they shall still in my bosom be borne.

7 "The soul that on Jesus still leans for repose,
I *will* not, I *will* not, desert to his foes;
That soul, though all hell should endeavor to shake,
I'll never, no *never*, no *never* forsake."

487 *Heaven below.*

MY God, I am thine, What a comfort divine,
What a blessing to know that my Jesus is mine!
In th' heavenly Lamb, Thrice happy I am,—
My heart doth rejoice at the sound of his name.

2 True pleasures abound In the rapturous sound,
Whoever hath found it, hath paradise found:
My Jesus to know, And feel his blood flow,—
'Tis life everlasting, 'tis heaven below.

3 Yet onward I haste To the heavenly feast:
That, that is the fulness; but this is the taste!
And this I shall prove, Till with joy I remove
To th' heaven of heavens in Jesus's love.

738 *Funeral of a young minister.*

GO to the grave in all thy glorious prime,
In full activity of zeal and power;
A Christian cannot die before his time,—
The Lord's appointment is the servant's hour.

2 Go the grave, at noon from labour cease;
Rest on thy sheaves; thy harvest task is done;
Come from the heat of battle, and in peace,
Soldier, go home; with thee the fight is won.

3 Go to the grave; for there thy Saviour lay
In death's embrace, ere he arose on high;
And all the ransom'd, by that narrow way
Pass to eternal life beyond the sky.

4 Go to the grave:—no! take thy seat above,
Be thy pure spirit present with the Lord,
Where thou for faith and hope hast perfect love,
And open vision for the written word.

944 *A blessing invoked.*

IN boundless mercy, gracious Lord, appear,
Darkness dispel, the humble mourner cheer;
Vain thoughts remove, melt down this flinty heart,
Cause every soul to choose the better part.

2 Thy presence fills the universal space;
Thy grace appears to all the fallen race;
O visit us with light and life divine,
Fill every soul, for every soul is thine!

3 The blessed Jesus is my Lord, my Love;
He is my King, from him I would not move:
Away, then, all ye objects that divert,
Nor seek to draw from my dear Lord my heart.

4 That uncreated beauty which hath gain'd
My ravish'd heart, hath all your glory stain'd;
His loveliness my soul hath prepossess'd,
And left no room for any other guest.

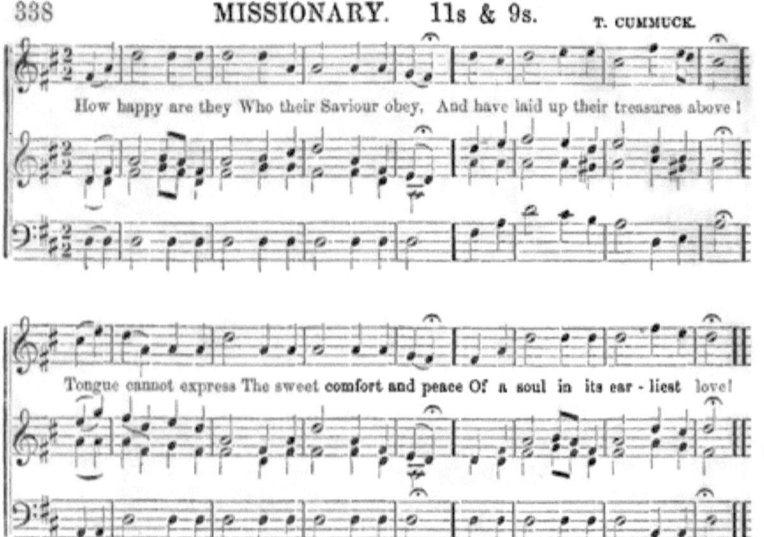

483 *Ecstasy of the new-born soul.*

HOW happy are they Who their Saviour obey,
And have laid up their treasures above!
Tongue cannot express The sweet comfort and peace
Of a soul in its earliest love!

2 That comfort was mine, When the favour divine
I first found in the blood of the Lamb;
When my heart it believed, What a joy I received,
What a heaven in Jesus's name!

3 'Twas a heaven below My Redeemer to know,
And the angels could do nothing more,
Than fall at his feet, And the story repeat,
And the Lover of sinners adore.

4 Jesus all the day long Was my joy and my song:
O that all his salvation might see!
He hath loved me, I cried, He hath suffer'd and died,
To redeem a poor rebel like me.

5 On the wings of his love I was carried above
All sin, and temptation, and pain;
I could not believe That I ever should grieve,
That I ever should suffer again.

6 I rode on the sky, Freely justified I,
Nor did envy Elijah his seat;
My soul mounted higher In a chariot of fire,
And the moon it was under my feet.

7 O the rapturous height Of that holy delight,
Which I felt in the life-giving blood:
Of my Saviour possest, I was perfectly blest,
As if fill'd with the fulness of God.

905 *The heavenly banquet.*

COME, let us ascend, My companion and friend,
To a taste of the banquet above:
If thy heart be as mine, If for Jesus it pine,
Come up into the chariot of love.

2 Who in Jesus confide, We are bold to outride
All the storms of affliction beneath;
With the prophet we soar To the heavenly shore,
And outfly all the arrows of death.

3 By faith we are come To our permanent home,
And by hope we the rapture improve:
By love we still rise, And look down on the skies,
For the heaven of heavens is love.

4 Who on earth can conceive How happy we live
In the palace of God, the great King!

What a concert of praise, When our Jesus's grace
The whole heavenly company sing!

5 Hallelujah they cry, To the King of the sky,
To the great everlasting I AM;
To the Lamb that was slain, And that liveth again,
Hallelujah to God and the Lamb!

6 The Lamb on the throne, Lo! he dwells with his own,
And to rivers of pleasure he leads;
With his mercy's full blaze, With the sight of his face,
Our beatified spirits he feeds.

7 Our foreheads proclaim His ineffable name,
And our bodies his glory display;
A day without night, We feast in his sight,
And eternity seems as a day.

980 *Birth-day of a convert.*

COME away to the skies, My beloved arise,
And rejoice in the day thou wast born:
On this festival day, Come exulting away,
And with singing to Sion return.

2 We have laid up our love And our treasure above,
Though our bodies continue below:
The redeem'd of our Lord, We remember his word,
And with singing to paradise go.

3 With singing we praise The original grace
By our heavenly Father bestow'd;
Our being receive From his bounty, and live
To the honour and glory of God.

4 For thy glory we are Created to share
Both the nature and kingdom divine:
Created again, That our souls may remain
In time and eternity thine.

5 With thanks we approve The design of thy love
Which hath join'd us in Jesus's name;
So united in heart, That we never can part,
Till we meet at the feast of the Lamb.

6 There, there at his feet, We shall suddenly meet,
And be parted in body no more!
We shall sing to our lyres, With the heavenly choirs,
And our Saviour in glory adore.

7 Hallelujah we sing, To our Father and King,
And his rapturous praises repeat:
To the Lamb that was slain, Hallelujah again,
Sing all heaven, and fall at his feet!

8 In assurance of hope, We to Jesus look up,
Till his banner unfurl'd in the air,
From our graves we shall see, And cry out, "It is he!"
And fly up to acknowledge him there.

803 *New-Year's day.*

COME, let us anew Our journey pursue,
Roll round with the year,
And never stand still till the Master appear!
His adorable will Let us gladly fulfil,
And our talents improve
By the patience of hope, and the labour of love.

2 Our life is a dream;—Our time, as a stream,
Glides swiftly away;
And the fugitive moment refuses to stay.
The arrow is flown, The moment is gone:
The millennial year
Rushes on to our view, and eternity's here.

3 O that each in the day Of his coming may say,
"I have fought my way through;
I have finish'd the work thou didst give me to do."
O that each from his Lord May receive the glad word,
"Well and faithfully done!
Enter into my joy, and sit down on my throne."

865 *Deliverance from shipwreck.*

ALL praise to the Lord, Who rules with a word
The untractable sea,
And limits its rage by his steadfast decree:
Whose providence binds Or releases the winds,
And compels them again
At his beck to put on the invisible chain.

2 E'en now he hath heard Our cry, and appear'd
On the face of the deep,
And commanded the tempest its distance to keep;
His piloting hand Hath brought us to land,
And no longer distrest,
We are joyful again in the haven to rest.

3 O that all men would raise His tribute of praise,
His goodness declare,
And thankfully sing of his fatherly care!
With rapture approve His dealings of love,
And the wonders proclaim
Perform'd by the virtue of Jesus's name.

557 *The pilgrimage.*

COME, let us anew Our journey pursue,
With vigour arise,
And press to our permanent place in the skies.
Of heavenly birth, Though wand'ring on earth,
This is not our place,
But strangers and pilgrims ourselves we confess.

2 At Jesus' call We gave up our all;
And still we forego,
For Jesus's sake, our enjoyments below.
No longing we find For the country behind;
But onward we move,
And still we are seeking a country above—

3 A country of joy, Without any alloy,
We thither repair:
Our hearts and our treasure already are there.
We march hand in hand To Immanuel's land;
No matter what cheer
We meet with on earth; for eternity's near!

4 The rougher our way, The shorter our stay;
The tempests that rise
Shall gloriously hurry our souls to the skies.
The fiercer the blast, The sooner 'tis past;
The troubles that come,
Shall come to our rescue, and hasten us home.

289 *Perpetual memorial.*

LORD, didst thou ordain Thy supper in vain,
And furnish a feast
For none but thy earliest servants to taste?
Nay, this is thy will, We know it and feel
That we should partake
The banquet for all thou so freely didst make.

2 Bring near the glad day When all shall obey
Thy dying request,
And eat of thy supper, and lean on thy breast:
Then, then let us see Thy glory, and be
Caught up in the air,
This heavenly supper in heaven to share.

736 *Funeral of a Christian brother.*

HOSANNA to God In his highest abode;
All heaven be join'd
T' extol the Redeemer and Friend of mankind!
He claims all our praise, Who in infinite grace
Again hath stoop'd down,
And caught up a worm to inherit a crown.

2 Our friend is restored to the joy of his Lord,
With triumph departs,
But speaks by his death to our echoing hearts:
Follow after, he cries, As he mounts to the skies,
Follow after your friend
To the blissful enjoyments that never shall end.

3 Through Jesus's name Our comrade o'ercame,
And Jesus is ours,
And arms us with all his invincible powers:
He looks from the skies, He shows us the prize,
And gives us a sign
That we shall o'ercome by the mercy divine.

4 For us is prepared the angelical guard
The convoy attends—
A ministering host of invisible friends—
Ready wing'd for their flight To the regions of light,
The horses are come,
The chariots of Israel to carry us home.

* This tune is inserted by the request of a friend.

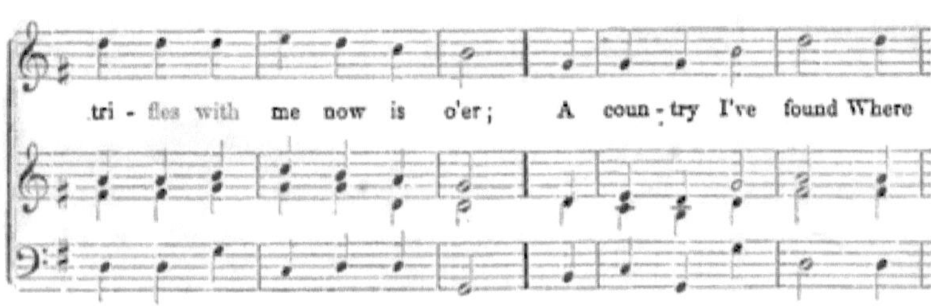

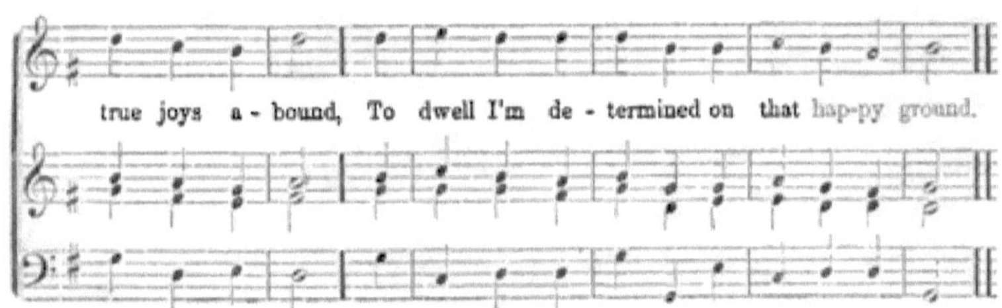

883 *"Come thou with us."—*

O TELL me no more Of this world's vain store:
The time for such trifles with me now is o'er;
A country I've found Where true joys abound,
To dwell I'm determin'd on that happy ground.

2 The souls that believe, In paradise live,
And me in that number will Jesus receive:
My soul, don't delay—He calls thee away,
Rise, follow thy Saviour, and bless the glad day.

3 No mortal doth know What he can bestow,
What light, strength, and comfort—go after him, go;
Lo, onward I move To a city above,
None guesses how wondrous my journey will prove.

4 Great spoils I shall win From death, hell, and sin,
Midst outward afflictions shall feel Christ within:
And when I'm to die, Receive me, I'll cry,
For Jesus hath loved me, I cannot tell why.

5 But this I do find, We two are so join'd,
He'll not live in glory and leave me behind:
So this is the race I'm running through grace,
Henceforth—till admitted to see my Lord's face.

6 And now I'm in care My neighbours may share
These blessings: to seek them will none of you dare?
In bondage, O why, And death will you lie,
When one here assures you free grace is so nigh?

THOU ART GONE TO THE GRAVE. Dr. CLARKE.

Thou art gone to the grave—but we will not deplore thee: Tho' sorrows and darkness en-

compass the tomb, Thy Saviour has pass'd thro' its portal before thee, And the lamp of his

love is thy guide thro' the gloom, And the lamp of his love is thy guide thro' the gloom.

731 *Funeral of a Christian.*

THOU art gone to the grave—but we will not deplore thee:
Though sorrows and darkness encompass the tomb,
Thy Saviour has pass'd through its portal before thee,
And the lamp of his love is thy guide thro' the gloom.

2 Thou art gone to the grave—we no longer behold thee,
Nor tread the rough paths of the world by thy side;
But the wide arms of mercy are spread to enfold thee,
And sinners may hope since the Sinless has died.

3 Thou art gone to the grave—and its mansion forsaking,
Perchance thy weak spirit in fear linger'd long;
But the mild rays of paradise beam'd on thy waking,
And the sound which thou heardst was the seraphim's song.

4 Thou art gone to the grave—but we will not deplore thee,
Whose God was thy ransom, thy guardian, and guide:
He gave thee; he took thee; and he will restore thee;
And death has no sting, for the Saviour has died.

8 *The Trinity.—Before sermon.*

COME, thou almighty King,
Help us thy name to sing,
Help us to praise!
Father all glorious,
O'er all victorious,
Come and reign over us,
Ancient of days.

2 Jesus, our Lord, arise,
Scatter our enemies,
And make them fall;
Let thine almighty aid
Our sure defence be made,
Our souls on thee be stay'd;
Lord, hear our call!

3 Come, thou incarnate Word,
Gird on thy mighty sword,
Our prayer attend;
Come, and thy people bless,
And give thy word success,
Spirit of holiness,
On us descend!

4 Come, holy Comforter,
Thy sacred witness bear
In this glad hour;
Thou who almighty art,
Now rule in every heart,
And ne'er from us depart,
Spirit of power!

5 To the great One and Three,
Eternal praises be
Hence—evermore!
His sovereign majesty
May we in glory see,
And to eternity
Love and adore.

352

Come, ye disconsolate.

COME, ye disconsolate, where'er ye languish,
Come, and at God's altar fervently kneel;
Here bring your wounded hearts, here tell your anguish;
Earth has no sorrow that Heaven cannot heal.

2 Joy of the desolate, Light of the straying,
Hope of the penitent, fadeless and pure;
Here speaks the Comforter, in God's name saying,
Earth has no sorrow that Heaven cannot cure.

3 Go, ask the infidel what boon he brings us,—
What charm for aching hearts he can reveal,
Sweet as the heavenly promise hope sings us,
Earth has no sorrow that God cannot heal.

64 *Psalm civ.*

O WORSHIP the King, All glorious above;
O gratefully sing His power and his love:
Our shield and Defender, The Ancient of days,
Pavilion'd in splendour, And girded with praise.

2 O tell of his might, O sing of his grace,
Whose robe is the light, Whose canopy space:
His chariots of wrath The deep thunder-clouds form,
And dark is his path On the wings of the storm.

3 This earth, with its store Of wonders untold,
Almighty! thy power Hath founded of old:
Hath stablish'd it fast, By a changeless decree,
And round it hath cast, Like a mantle, the sea.

4 Thy bountiful care, What tongue can recite
It breathes in the air, It shines in the light,
It streams from the hills, It descends to the plain,
And sweetly distils In the dew and the rain.

5 Frail children of dust, And feeble as frail,
In thee do we trust, Nor find thee to fail:
Thy mercies how tender, How firm to the end!
Our Maker, Defender, Redeemer, and Friend.

6 O measureless might, Ineffable love;
While angels delight To hymn thee above,
The humbler creation, Though feeble their lays,
With true adoration, Shall lisp to thy praise.

485 *Triumph.*

ALL praise to the Lamb! Accepted I am,
I'm bold to believe on my Jesus' name.
In him I confide, His blood is applied;
For me he has suffer'd, for me he has died.

2 Not a doubt can arise To darken the skies,
Or hide for a moment my Lord from mine eyes.
In him I am blest, I lean on his breast,
And lo! in his wounds I continually rest.

(For Sunday School Celebration.) Composed for this Work.

CHILDREN.

Children. 1. Come, let our voic - es join In one glad song of praise;
" 2. Now we are taught to read The book of life di - vine,
" 3. With - in these hal-lowed walls Our wan-d'ring feet are brought;
" 4. For bless-ings such as these Our grat - i - tude re - ceive;
Both. 5. Lord, bid this work of love Be crowned with meet suc - cess;

To God, the God of love, Our grate - ful hearts we raise:
Where our Re-deem - er's love And bright - est glo - ries shine:
Where prayer and praise as - cend, And heaven - ly truths are taught:
Lord, here ac - cept our hearts, 'Tis all that we can give:
May thou - sands yet un - born This in - sti - tu - tion bless:

CONGREGATION.

Congr. To God a - lone your praise be-longs: His love demands your ear-liest songs,
" To God a - lone the praise is due, Who sends his word to us and you,
" To God a - lone your off'rings bring; Here in his church his prais-es sing,
" Great God, ac - cept their in - fant songs; To thee alone their praise be-longs,
Both. Thus shall the praise re - sound to thee Now, and thro' all e - ter - ni - ty,

To God a-lone your praise belongs; His love de-mands your ear-liest songs.
To God a-lone the praise is due; Who sends his word to us and you.
To God a-lone your off'rings bring; Here in his church his prais-es sing.
Great God, ac-cept their in - fant songs; To thee a - lone their praise belongs.
Thus shall the praise re-sound to thee Now, and thro' all e - ter - ni - ty.

204 *Pentecost.*

LET songs of praises fill the sky!
Christ, our ascended Lord,
Sends down his Spirit from on high,
According to his word:
All hail the day of Pentecost,
The coming of the Holy Ghost!

2 The Spirit, by his heavenly breath,
New life creates within;
He quickens sinners from the death
Of trespasses and sin:
All hail the day of Pentecost,
The coming of the Holy Ghost!

3 The things of Christ the Spirit takes,
And shows them unto men;
The fallen soul his temple makes;
God's image stamps again:
All hail the day of Pentecost,
The coming of the Holy Ghost!

4 Come, Holy Spirit, from above,
With thy celestial fire;
Come, and with flames of zeal and love,
Our hearts and tongues inspire:
Be this our day of Pentecost,
The coming of the Holy Ghost!

1028 *In poverty.*

AS much have I of worldly good
As e'er my Master had;
I diet on as dainty food,
And am as richly clad,
Though plain my garb, though scant my board,
As Mary's Son and nature's Lord.

2 The manger was his infant bed,
His home the mountain-cave,
He had not where to lay his head,
He borrow'd e'en his grave;
Earth yielded him no resting spot,—
Her Maker—but she knew him not

3 As much the world's good-will I share,
Its favors and applause,
As he whose blessed name I bear,—
Hated without a cause;
Despised,—rejected,—mock'd by pride;
Betray'd,—forsaken,—crucified.

4 Why should I court my Master's foe?
Why should I fear its frown?
Why should I seek for rest below,
Or sigh for brief renown?
A pilgrim to a better land,—
An heir of joy at God's right hand.

614 *Delight in Christ.*

THOU Shepherd of Israel and mine,
  The joy and desire of my heart,
For closer communion I pine,
  I long to reside where thou art.

2 The pasture I languish to find,
  Where all, who their Shepherd obey,
Are fed, on thy bosom reclined,
  And screen'd from the heat of the day.

3 'Tis there, with the lambs of thy flock,
  There only I covet to rest;
To lie at the foot of the rock,
  Or rise to be hid in thy breast:

4 'Tis there I would always abide,
  And never a moment depart;
Conceal'd in the cleft of thy side,
  Eternally held in thy heart.

44 *"This God is our God."*

THIS, this is the God we adore,
  Our faithful, unchangeable Friend,
Whose love is as great as his power,
  And neither knows measure nor end:

2 'Tis Jesus, the first and the last,
  Whose Spirit shall guide us safe home;
We'll praise him for all that is past,
  And trust him for all that's to come.

539 *Desiring full salvation.*

WHAT now is my object and aim?
  What now is my hope and desire?
To follow the heavenly Lamb,
  And after his image aspire:

2 My hope is all centred in thee;
  I trust to recover thy love,—
On earth thy salvation to see,
  And then to enjoy it above.

948 *Isaiah xxxiii. 24.*

HOW happy the people that dwell
  Secure in the city above!
No pain the inhabitants feel,
  No sickness or sorrow shall prove.

2 Physician of souls, unto me
  Forgiveness and holiness give;
And then from the body set free,
  And then to the city receive.

Composed for this Work.

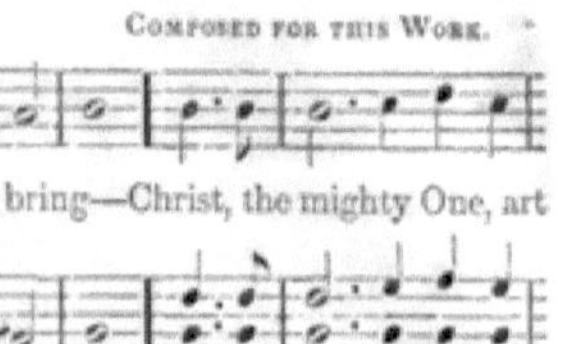

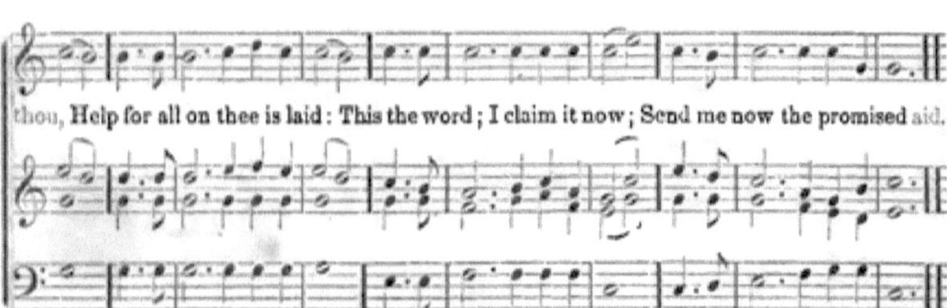

495 *The Saviour's captive.*

JESUS, thou art our King!
  To me thy succour bring—
Christ, the mighty One, art thou,
  Help for all on thee is laid:
This the word; I claim it now;
  Send me now the promised aid.

2 High on thy Father's throne,
  O look with pity down!
Help, O help, attend my call,
  Captive lead captivity:
King of glory, Lord of all,
  Christ, be Lord, be King to me!

3 I pant to feel thy sway,
  And only thee t' obey;
Thee my spirit gasps to meet:
  This my one, my ceaseless prayer,
Make, O make my heart thy seat,
  O set up thy kingdom there!

4 Triumph and reign in me,
  And spread thy victory;
Hell, and death, and sin control,
  Pride, and wrath, and every foe,—
All subdue; through all my soul,
  Conqu'ring and to conquer go.

5 *The Trinity.*

HAIL, co-essential Three,
  In mystic unity!
Father, Son, and Spirit, hail!
  God by heaven and earth adored,
God incomprehensible;
  One supreme, almighty Lord.

2 Thou sittest on the throne,
  Plurality in one:
Saints behold thine open face,
  Bright, insufferably bright;
Angels tremble as they gaze,
  Sink into a sea of light!

3 Ah! when shall we increase
  Their heavenly ectasies?
Chant, like them, the Lord most high—
  Fall, like them who dare not move—
"Holy, holy, holy," cry—
  Breathe the praise of silent love?

4 Come, Father, in the Son
  And in the Spirit, down;
Glorious Triune Majesty,
  God through endless ages blest,
Make us meet thy face to see,—
  Then receive us to thy breast.

Composed expressly for this Work.

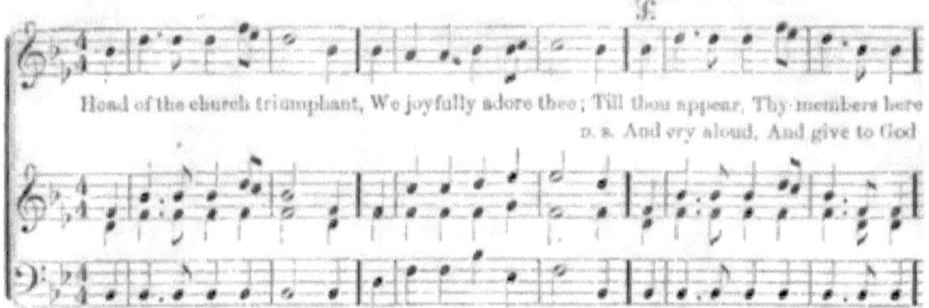
Head of the church triumphant, We joyfully adore thee; Till thou appear, Thy members here
D. S. And cry aloud, And give to God

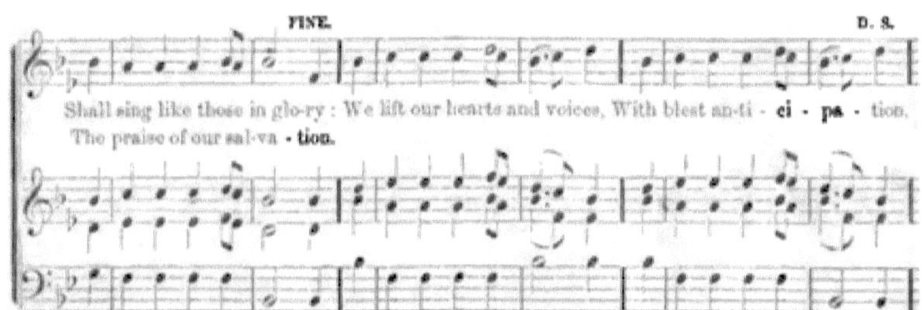
FINE.
D. S.
Shall sing like those in glo-ry: We lift our hearts and voices, With blest an-ti - ci - pa - tion.
The praise of our sal-va - tion.

665 *The triumph.*

HEAD of the church triumphant,
We joyfully adore thee;
Till thou appear, Thy members here
Shall sing like those in glory:
We lift our hearts and voices,
With blest anticipation,
And cry aloud, And give to God,
The praise of our salvation.

2 While in affliction's furnace,
And passing through the fire,
Thy love we praise, Which knows no days,
And ever brings us nigher:
We clap our hands exulting
In thine almighty favour:
Thy love divine, Which made us thine,
Can keep us thine for ever.

3 Thou dost conduct thy people
Through torrents of temptation;
Nor will we fear, While thou art near,
The fire of tribulation:
The world, with sin and Satan,
In vain our march opposes;
By thee we shall Break through them all,
And sing the song of Moses.

4 By faith we see the glory
To which thou shalt restore us,
The cross despise For that high prize
Which thou hast set before us:
And if thou count us worthy,
We each, as dying Stephen,
Shall see thee stand At God's right hand,
To take us up to heaven.

179 *Praise to Jesus.*

JESUS, take all the glory!
Thy meritorious passion
The pardon bought, Thy mercy brought
To us the great salvation.
Thee gladly we acknowledge
Our only Lord and Saviour,
Thy name confess, Thy goodness bless,
And triumph in thy favour.

2 With angels and archangels
We prostrate fall before thee:
Again we raise Our souls in praise,
And thankfully adore thee.
Honour, and power, and blessing,
To thee be ever given,
By all who know Thy love below,
And all our friends in heaven.

1060 *Doxology.*

TO Father, Son, and Spirit,
Ascribe we equal glory!
One Deity, in Persons Three,
Let all thy works adore thee.
As was from the beginning
Glory to God be given,
By all who know Thy name below,
And all thy hosts in heaven!

WINCHESTER. 8s & 6s.

1051 *Hallelujah chorus.*

SING Hallelujah! praise the Lord!
Sing with a cheerful voice;
Exalt our God with one accord,
And in his name rejoice:
Ne'er cease to sing, thou ransom'd host,
Praise Father, Son, and Holy Ghost!
Until, in realms of endless light,
Your praises shall unite.

2. There we to all eternity
Shall join the angelic lays;
And sing in perfect harmony,
To God our Saviour's praise:
"He hath redeem'd us by his blood,
And made us kings and priests to God:
For us, for us the Lamb was slain."
Praise ye the Lord! Amen.

ELIZABETHTOWN. C. M.

G. KINGSLEY

1. O God, who madest earth and sky, The dark - ness and the day,
Give ear to this thy fam - i - ly, And help us when we pray!

989

In affliction.

O GOD, who madest earth and sky,
The darkness and the day,
Give ear to this thy family,
And help us when we pray!

2 For wild the waves of bitterness
Around our vessel roar,
And heavy grows the pilot's heart,
To view the rocky shore!

3 The cross our Master bore for us,
For him we fain would bear;
But mortal strength to weakness turns,
And courage to despair.

4 Then, mercy on our failings, Lord!
Our sinking faith renew!
And when thy sorrows visit us,
O send thy patience too!

MONROE. C. M.

1. How vain are all things here be - low! How false and yet how fair!
Each pleasure hath its poi - son, too, And ev - ery sweet a snare.

619

Earthly Pleasures dangerous.

2 The brightest things below the sky
Shine with deceiving light;
We should suspect some danger nigh,
Where we possess delight.

3 Our dearest joys, our dearest friends,
The partners of our blood—
How they divide our wavering minds,
And leave but half for God!

4 The fondness of a creature's love,
How strong it strikes the sense!
Thither the warm affections move,
Nor can we call them hence.

5 Dear Saviour, let thy beauties be
My soul's eternal food;
And grace command my heart away
From all created good.

GENERAL INDEX TO TUNES.

METRICAL INDEX OF TUNES.

INDEX TO HYMNS.

(The Figures refer to the page.)

INDEX OF SUBJECTS.

(The Figures refer to the Hymns.)

NUMERICAL INDEX.

Hymn	Page	Hymn	Page	Hymn	Page	Hymn	Page	Hymn	Page	Hymn	Page	Hymn	Page	Hymn	Page	Hymn	Page
1	120	31	130	61	184	91	324	121	15	151	221	181	71	211	229	241	65
2	271	32	168	62	219	92	71	122	286	152	134	182	91	212	203	242	6
[illegible]	310	33	99	63	211	93	96	123	90	153	114	183	94	213	111	243	48
4	223	34	77	64	346	94	72	124	212	154	285	184	30	214	125	244	174
5	250	35	125	65	24	95	186	125	213	155	72	185	271	215	221	245	109
6	7	36	76	66	218	96	71	126	19	156	262	186	149	216	267	246	187
7	210	37	76	67	6	97	260	127	200	157	249	187	105	217	174	247	176
8	244	38	7	68	270	98	225	[illegible]	64	158	250	188	103	218	206	248	206
9	260	39	34	69	76	99	[illegible]	[illegible]	267	159	133	189	19	219	223	249	53
10	112	40	84	70	236	100	[illegible]	[illegible]	197	160	127	190	210	220	201	250	92
11	80	41	73	71	75	101	[illegible]	131	88	161	251	191	204	221	100	251	233
12	190	42	70	72	258	102	91	132	171	162	227	192	84	222	145	252	19
13	74	43	33	73	20	103	24	133	65	163	187	193	44	223	225	253	32
14	73	44	249	74	250	104	19	134	273	164	168	194	129	224	65	254	41
15	27	45	84	75	246	105	24	135	210	165	178	195	20	225	13	255	185
16	19	46	223	76	143	106	198	136	69	166	185	196	85	226	183	256	249
17	25	47	203	77	256	107	68	137	253	167	209	197	90	227	68	257	44
18	25	48	76	78	215	108	282	138	57	168	88	198	15	228	76	258	193
19	23	49	41	79	231	109	25	139	84	169	209	199	240	229	211	259	32
20	167	50	167	80	235	110	64	140	73	170	254	200	224	230	199	260	33
21	27	51	197	81	18	111	180	141	254	171	253	201	37	231	7	261	70
22	29	52	215	82	10	112	178	142	268	172	193	202	272	232	207	262	56
23	236	53	209	83	18	113	202	143	100	173	280	203	203	233	22	263	285
24	236	54	37	84	17	114	180	144	18	174	196	204	248	234	28	264	84
25	158	55	32	85	14	115	56	145	54	175	30	205	40	235	74	265	60
26	176	56	133	86	9	116	64	146	279	176	275	206	172	236	81	266	232
27	7	57	206	87	15	117	56	147	54	177	236	207	14	237	65	267	47
28	172	58	256	88	101	118	87	148	270	178	294	208	18	238	81	268	69
29	94	59	6	89	279	119	56	149	44	179	351	209	140	239	295	269	278
30	113	60	184	90	100	120	167	150	284	180	200	210	104	240	25	270	65

DOXOLOGIES.

www.ingramcontent.com/pod-product-compliance
Lightning Source LLC
Chambersburg PA
CBHW020318240426
43673CB00039B/849
* 9 7 8 3 3 3 7 6 4 9 3 0 2 *